A Companion to Mark Twain

Blackwell Companions to Literature and Culture

This series offers comprehensive, newly written surveys of key periods and movements, and certain major authors, in English literary culture and history. Extensive volumes provide new perspectives and positions on contexts and on canonical and post-canonical texts, orientating the beginning student in new fields of study and providing the experienced undergraduate and new graduate with current and new directions, as pioneered and developed by leading scholars in the field.

A COMPANION TO

MARK
TWAIN

EDITED BY **PETER MESSENT**
AND **LOUIS J. BUDD**

Blackwell
Publishing

© 2005 by Blackwell Publishing Ltd
except for editorial material and organization © 2005 by Peter Messent and
Louis J. Budd and chapter 17 © 2005 by Shelley Fisher Fishkin

BLACKWELL PUBLISHING
350 Main Street, Malden, MA 02148–5020, USA
9600 Garsington Road, Oxford OX4 2DQ, UK
550 Swanston Street, Carlton, Victoria 3053, Australia

First published 2005 by Blackwell Publishing Ltd

1   2005

Library of Congress Cataloging-in-Publication Data

A companion to Mark Twain / edited by Peter Messent and Louis J. Budd.
p.   cm.—(Blackwell companions to literature and culture ; 37)
Includes bibliographical references and index.
ISBN-13: 978-1-4051-2379-2 (hardcover : alk. paper)
ISBN-10: 1-4051-2379-6 (hardcover : alk. paper)
1. Twain, Mark, 1835–1910—Criticism and interpretation—Handbooks, manuals, etc.
I. Messent, Peter.   II. Budd, Louis J.   III. Series.
PS1338.C64   2005
818'.409—dc22
2005006594

A catalogue record for this title is available from the British Library.
Set in 11 on 13 pt Garamond 3
by SNP Best-set Typesetter Ltd., Hong Kong
Printed and bound in Great Britain
by TJ International Ltd, Padstow, Cornwall

The publisher's policy is to use permanent paper from mills that operate a sustainable forestry policy,
and which has been manufactured from pulp processed using acid-free and elementary chlorine-free
practices. Furthermore, the publisher ensures that the text paper and cover board used have met
acceptable environmental accreditation standards.

For further information on
Blackwell Publishing, visit our website:
www.blackwellpublishing.com

To William, Alice, Ella and Leah, with love (PM)
To Exelee, our best reader-to-be (LB)

Contents

Notes on Contributors

Lawrence I. Berkove is Professor Emeritus of English at the University of Michigan-Dearborn and President-elect of the Mark Twain Circle of America. He has published widely in his field of nineteenth- and early twentieth-century American literature, but Twain has been a special and ongoing interest of his from the beginning. His Modern Library edition of *The Best Short Stories of Mark Twain* came out in 2004. Berkove is also a leading authority on the literature of the Sagebrush School of late nineteenth-century Nevada, whose members had a formative influence on Twain. He is now working on a book-length study of Twain's religion and its influence on his literature.

John Bird is Professor of English at Winthrop University. He has published articles on Mark Twain and is the editor of the Mark Twain Circle of America's annual publication, *The Mark Twain Annual*. He is completing a book on Mark Twain and metaphor.

Louis J. Budd, James B. Duke Professor (Emeritus) of English at Duke University, has concentrated on American realism and naturalism, especially as seen in the novels of William Dean Howells. He has also published steadily on the career of Mark Twain, most often as manifested in his literary reputation, popular images, and citizenship.

Martin T. Buinicki is an Assistant Professor of English at Valparaiso University, specializing in nineteenth-century American literature and the history of the book and authorship. His work has appeared in *American Literary History*, *American Literary Realism*, and the *Walt Whitman Quarterly Review*. His book *Negotiating Copyright: Authorship and the Discourse of Literary Property Rights in Nineteenth-Century America* is forthcoming from Routledge.

Gregg Camfield is Professor of English at the University of the Pacific. He is the author of *Sentimental Twain: Mark Twain in the Maze of Moral Philosophy* (1994), *Nec-*

essary Madness: The Humor of Domesticity in Nineteenth-Century American Literature (1997), and *The Oxford Companion to Mark Twain* (2003), as well as numerous articles on American literature and culture.

Mark Dawidziak is the television critic for the *Cleveland Plain Dealer*. A theater, film, and television reviewer for 25 years, he is the author of ten books, including *Mark My Words: Mark Twain on Writing* and *Horton Foote's The Shape of the River: The Lost Teleplay about Mark Twain*. The founder and artistic director of northeast Ohio's Largely Literary Theater Company, he is the author of four produced plays, including a two-act adaptation of several Twain sketches, *The Reports of My Death Are Greatly Exaggerated*.

Andrew Dix is a Lecturer in American Literature and Film at Loughborough University. He has co-edited *Figures of Heresy: Radical Theology in English and American Writing, 1800–2000* (2005), and published journal articles and book chapters on Native American fiction, John Steinbeck, and Jonathan Raban's travel writing. He is currently writing *Beginning Film Studies* for Manchester University Press.

Victor Doyno wrote on Twain's creative processes in his *Writing Mark Twain*. When that book was at proof stage, the first half of the manuscript to *Adventures of Huckleberry Finn* (previously missing) was rediscovered. This subsequently became the subject of *Beginning to Write Mark Twain*, included on the CD-ROM *Huck Finn: The Complete Buffalo and Erie County Public Library Manuscript*. Doyno also wrote the foreword and textual addendum to the Random House *Adventures of Huckleberry Finn: A Comprehensive Edition* and the afterword to the "Oxford Mark Twain" edition of the novel. He is now working on Twain's early newspaper work, 1853–68. Vic wishes to thank the editors for help in preparing his essay for publication following his recent stroke.

Shelley Fisher Fishkin is Professor of English and Director of American Studies at Stanford University. She the author of the award-winning books *From Fact to Fiction: Journalism and Imaginative Writing in America* (1985) and *Was Huck Black? Mark Twain and African-American Voices* (1993), as well as *Lighting Out for the Territory: Reflections on Mark Twain and American Culture* (1997). She is the editor of the 29-volume "Oxford Mark Twain" (1996), the Oxford *Historical Guide to Mark Twain* (2002), and *"Is He Dead?" A New Comedy by Mark Twain* (2003), and co-editor of *Listening to Silences: New Essays in Feminist Criticism* (1994), *People of the Book: Thirty Scholars Reflect on their Jewish Identity* (1996), *The Encyclopedia of Civil Rights in America* (1997), and *Sport of the Gods and Other Essential Writings by Paul Laurence Dunbar* (2005). She is past president of the American Studies Association and of the Mark Twain Circle of America.

Christopher Gair is Senior Lecturer in American Studies at the University of Birmingham. He is the author of *Complicity and Resistance in Jack London's Novels: From*

Naturalism to Nature (1997), *The American Counterculture* (forthcoming 2006), and numerous essays on American literature and culture. He is editor of *Beyond Boundaries: C. L. R. James and Postnational Studies* (forthcoming 2006) and managing editor of *Symbiosis: A Journal of Anglo-American Literary Relations*.

Alan Gribben was one of the three founders of the Mark Twain Circle of America, and he also helped establish the American Literature Association. Since 1991 he has chaired the English and Philosophy Department at Auburn University Montgomery, where he was named a Distinguished Research Professor in 1998. Professor Gribben writes the annual "Mark Twain" essay for *American Literary Scholarship* and is currently revising and updating his *Mark Twain's Library: A Reconstruction* (1980).

Sam Halliday teaches Nineteenth-Century American Literature and Intellectual and Cultural History at Queen Mary, University of London. He is currently completing a book entitled *Thinking Electricity: Science, Technology and Culture in the Nineteenth and Early Twentieth Centuries*.

Susan K. Harris is the Hall Professor of American Literature and Culture at the University of Kansas. Her publications include *The Cultural Work of the 19th-Century Hostess: Annie Adams Fields and Mary Gladstone Drew* (2002), *The Courtship of Olivia Langdon and Mark Twain* (1996), *19th-Century American Women's Novels: Interpretive Strategies* (1990), and *Mark Twain's Escape from Time: A Study of Patterns and Images* (1982). She has edited *Mark Twain's Historical Romances* (1994) and *Adventures of Huckleberry Finn* (2000), as well as Stowe's *The Minister's Wooing* (1999), Sedgwick's *A New-England Tale* (2003), and Wiggins's *Rebecca of Sunnybrook Farm* (2005).

Gavin Jones is an Associate Professor of English at Stanford University. He is the author of *Strange Talk: The Politics of Dialect Literature in Gilded Age America* (1999), and has published articles on George W. Cable, Theodore Dreiser, W. E. B. Du Bois, Sylvester Judd, Paule Marshall, and Herman Melville, in journals such as *American Literary History*, *New England Quarterly*, and *African American Review*. He is writing a book on the representation of poverty in American literature.

Holger Kersten is Professor of American Literature and Culture at the University of Magdeburg, Germany. He has presented papers and published articles on Mark Twain, Stephen Crane, Jack London, the Lewis and Clark expedition, and humor in American literature. His research interests include the use of nonstandard language in literature, national images, and nature writing.

Randall Knoper teaches English and American Studies at the University of Massachusetts, Amherst. He is the author of *Acting Naturally: Mark Twain in the Culture of Performance* (1995) and of various essays on American literature and culture. He is working on a book about American literature and sciences of the brain and nervous system.

Leland Krauth is a Professor of English at the University of Colorado at Boulder. In addition to numerous articles on nineteenth- and twentieth-century American writers, he has published two books on Mark Twain, *Proper Mark Twain* (1999) and *Mark Twain and Company: Six Literary Relations* (2003).

James S. Leonard is Professor of English at The Citadel. He is co-editor of Prentice-Hall's two-volume *Anthology of American Literature* (8th edn., 2004), editor of *Making Mark Twain Work in the Classroom* (1999), co-editor of *Satire or Evasion? Black Perspectives on Huckleberry Finn* (1992), co-author of *The Fluent Mundo: Wallace Stevens and the Structure of Reality* (1988), editor of the *Mark Twain Circular*, and managing editor of *The Mark Twain Annual*.

Richard S. Lowry is Associate Professor of American Studies and English at the College of William and Mary. He is the author of *Littery Man: Mark Twain and Modern Authorship*, as well as essays on travel writing, photography, and the history of childhood. Currently he is working on a book project entitled *Suffer the Children: Family, Love, and the Prehistory of Welfare*.

T. J. Lustig teaches in the Department of American Studies at Keele University. He is the author of *Henry James and the Ghostly* (1994) and, more recently, of articles on Tim O'Brien and trauma theory. He is currently working on a study of nineteenth-century cultural thought in Great Britain and the United States.

Jeffrey Alan Melton is an Associate Professor of English at Auburn University, Montgomery. He is the author of *Mark Twain, Travel Books, and Tourism: The Tide of a Great Popular Movement* (2002). He has published articles on travel literature and Mark Twain in *South Atlantic Review*, *Papers on Language and Literature*, *Studies in American Humor*, *Popular Culture Review*, *Studies in American Culture*, and *Thalia: Studies in Literary Humor*.

Peter Messent is Professor of Modern American Literature at the University of Nottingham. He is the author of *New Readings of the American Novel: Narrative Theory and its Application* (1990), *Ernest Hemingway* (1992), *Mark Twain* (1997), and *The Short Works of Mark Twain: A Critical Study* (2001). He also edited *Criminal Proceedings: The Contemporary American Crime Novel* (1997). He has published in many other areas of American literature and is at present working on a study of Mark Twain and male friendship.

Scott Michaelsen is Associate Professor of English at Michigan State University. With David E. Johnson, he co-edits *CR: The New Centennial Review*, an interdisciplinary journal of theoretical inquiry into the Americas. He is the author of *The Limits of Multiculturalism: Interrogating the Origins of American Anthropology* (1999) and co-editor of *Border Theory: The Limits of Cultural Politics* (1997).

Bruce Michelson is Professor of American Literature and Director of the Campus Honors Program at the University of Illinois. His books include *Literary Wit* (2000), *Mark Twain on the Loose: A Comic Writer and the American Self* (1995), *Wilbur's Poetry: Music in a Scattering Time* (1991), and the forthcoming *Mark Twain and the Information Age*. He is a featured commentator in the "American Passages" video series produced by the Annenberg Foundation and Oregon Public Broadcasting, and he authors the "Instructor's Guide" and the website for *The Norton Anthology of American Literature*.

Linda A. Morris is Professor of English at the University of California, Davis. In addition to articles on Dorothea Lange, Mark Twain, Mary Lasswell, and American satire, she is the author of *Women Vernacular Humorists in the Nineteenth Century: Ann Stephens, Frances Whitcher, and Marietta Holley* (1988); *Women's Humor in the Age of Gentility: The Life and Work of Frances M. Whitcher* (1992); and *American Women Humorists: Critical Essays* (1994). She is currently completing a book entitled *Gender Play in Mark Twain*.

Cameron C. Nickels is Professor Emeritus of English and American Studies at James Madison University. Past president of the American Humor Studies Association and editor of its newsletter, he is currently writing a book on Civil War humor. He also plays in a bluegrass band.

Hilton Obenzinger writes fiction, poetry, history, and criticism. He is the author of *American Palestine: Melville, Twain, and the Holy Land Mania*, a literary and historical study of America's fascination with the Holy Land, as well as *A*hole*, an experimental fiction, *Running through Fire: How I Survived the Holocaust by Zosia Goldberg, as Told to Hilton Obenzinger* (an oral history of his aunt's ordeal during the war), *Cannibal Eliot and the Lost Histories of San Francisco*, a novel of invented documents that recounts the history of San Francisco to 1906, *New York on Fire*, a documentary poem of the history of New York City as seen through its fires, and *This Passover or the Next I Will Never Be in Jerusalem*, winner of the American Book Award. He teaches advanced writing and American literature at Stanford University.

Tom Quirk is Professor of English at the University of Missouri-Columbia. His publications on Mark Twain include *Mark Twain: A Study of the Short Fiction* (1997) and *Coming to Grips with "Huckleberry Finn": Essays on a Book, a Boy, and a Man* (1993). He is the editor or compiler of *Tales, Speeches, Essays, and Sketches by Mark Twain* (1994), *The Innocents Abroad* (2002), *The Penguin Portable Mark Twain* (2004), and *Dictionary of Literary Biography Documentary Series: Adventures of Huckleberry Finn* (forthcoming). He is currently writing a book with the provisional title *Mark Twain and Human Nature*.

Stephen Railton teaches American literature at the University of Virginia. His most recent book is *Mark Twain: A Short Introduction* (2003). Among his other publications are several essays on Twain, and among the online resources he has created is *Mark Twain in his Times: An Electronic Archive* (http://etext.lib.virginia.edu/ railton).

R. Kent Rasmussen holds a Ph.D. from the University of California at Los Angeles in African history, a subject on which he has published five books. His writings on Mark Twain include *Mark Twain A to Z* (1995), *Mark Twain's Book for Bad Boys and Girls* (1995), *The Quotable Mark Twain* (1997; also published as *Mark Twain: His Words, Wit and Wisdom*), and *Mark Twain for Kids* (2004). A greatly expanded edition of *Mark Twain A to Z* is scheduled for publication in fall 2005 as *Critical Companion to Mark Twain*. He is also the editor of the three-volume *Cyclopedia of Literary Places* (2003). Rasmussen is now a reference book editor in southern California. His interest in motion pictures goes back to his childhood, and he is now building a collection of 16 mm films about Mark Twain and adapted from his works for eventual donation to a library or museum.

Forrest G. Robinson is Professor of American Studies at the University of California, Santa Cruz. His writings on Mark Twain include *In Bad Faith: The Dynamics of Deception in Mark Twain's America* (1986) and three edited volumes: *Mark Twain's Pudd'nhead Wilson: Race, Conflict and Culture* (1990, with Susan Gillman), *The Cambridge Companion to Mark Twain* (1995), and a special number of *Arizona Quarterly* on "Mark Twain's Late Works," co-edited with Shelley Fisher Fishkin and forthcoming in 2005. He is presently at work on a biographical study of his favorite American humorist.

Gary Scharnhorst is Professor of English at the University of New Mexico. He is editor of *American Literary Realism*, editor in alternating years of *American Literary Scholarship*, and general editor of the "American Literary Realism and Naturalism" monograph series published by the University of Alabama Press. He is also a former president of the Western Literature Association and former chair of the American Literature Section of the Modern Language Association.

David Lionel Smith is the John W. Chandler Professor of English at Williams College, where he is also Director of the W. Ford Schumann Performing Arts Endowment. He was editor, with Jack Salzman and Cornel West, of the *Encyclopedia of African American Culture and History*, and at present he is editing with Wahneema Lubiano the *Blackwell Companion to African American Writing*.

Peter Stoneley is a Professor in the School of English and American Literature at the University of Reading. He wrote *Mark Twain and the Feminine Aesthetic* (1992), and his most recent book is *Consumerism and American Girls' Literature, 1860–1940* (2003). His current projects include *A Concise Companion to American Fiction, 1900–1950*, which he is co-editing for Blackwell with Cindy Weinstein.

Henry B. Wonham, Professor of English at the University of Oregon, is the author of several books on American literature, including *Mark Twain and the Art of the Tall Tale* (1993), *Charles W. Chesnutt: A Study of the Short Fiction* (1998), and *Playing the Races: Ethnic Caricature and American Literary Realism* (2004). He is also the editor of *Criticism and the Color Line: Desegregating American Literary Studies* (1996) and a critical edition of *Tales of Henry James* (2002).

Thomas D. Zlatic received a Ph.D. in literature from St. Louis University and has published on Mark Twain in *American Literature, Nineteenth-Century Literature, Clio,* and *Papers on Language and Literature*. His essay "Mark Twain and the Art of Memory," co-written with Thomas M. Walsh, was awarded the Foerster Prize for best article in *American Literature*.

Note on Referencing

Mark Twain's Major Works

Reference is made throughout this collection to the "Oxford Mark Twain," the set of facsimiles of the first American editions of Mark Twain's works edited by Shelley Fisher Fishkin and published by Oxford University Press, New York, in 1996. Where the texts included in the following list are used, page references immediately following quotations normally refer to these editions, which will not then be listed again in the "References and Further Reading" section of each individual essay. Where any exception is made to this convention, publication details of the edition used are given in that section, with references in the text on the usual author–date pattern.

Twain, Mark (1869). *The Innocents Abroad, or The New Pilgrims' Progress*.
Twain, Mark (1872). *Roughing It*.
Twain, Mark, and Warner, Charles Dudley (1873). *The Gilded Age: A Tale of To-Day*.
Twain, Mark (1876). *The Adventures of Tom Sawyer*.
Twain, Mark (1880). *A Tramp Abroad*.
Twain, Mark (1881). *The Prince and the Pauper: A Tale for Young People of All Ages*.
Twain, Mark (1883). *Life on the Mississippi*.
Twain, Mark (1885). *Adventures of Huckleberry Finn*.
Twain, Mark (1889). *A Connecticut Yankee in King Arthur's Court*.
Twain, Mark (1892). *The American Claimant*.
Twain, Mark (1894). *The Tragedy of Pudd'nhead Wilson and the Comedy Those Extraordinary Twins*.
Twain, Mark (1896). *Personal Recollections of Joan of Arc*.
Twain, Mark (1897). *Following the Equator*.
Twain, Mark (1906). *What Is Man?*
Twain, Mark (1907). *Christian Science*.
Twain, Mark (1909). *Extract from Captain Stormfield's Visit to Heaven*.
Twain, Mark (1910). *Mark Twain's Speeches*.

Mark Twain's Short Works

Where reference is made to Mark Twain's short works, the source is generally Louis J. Budd's two-volume Library of America edition, published in New York in 1992, details of which appear below. Again, where any exception is made, publication details for the edition used are given in the individual "References and Further Reading" section.

Twain, Mark (1992a). *Collected Tales, Sketches, Speeches, and Essays 1852–1890*.
Twain, Mark (1992b). *Collected Tales, Sketches, Speeches, and Essays 1891–1910*.

Acknowledgments

Both editors dedicate this book to Gretchen Sharlow, on behalf of the many beneficiaries of her tireless, imaginative, wise, and companionable guidance of the Elmira College Center for Mark Twain Studies.

The editors would, in addition, like to acknowledge their debt to those Twain scholars who contributed to this collection. It was a genuine pleasure to work with them. The editors also thank Gillian Somerscales for her editorial assistance at manuscript stage. Her enthusiasm for the project, the quality of her work, and the speed of her responses were all very much appreciated.

PART I
The Cultural Context

1

Mark Twain and Nation

Randall Knoper

The national consciousness so typical of the nineteenth century pervaded Mark Twain's work, from the early years, when his humor merged with the nationalist effort to define an American literature, to the later years, when his status as representative American and his anti-imperialism gave him a complicated relationship to the United States as a world power. He identified himself with American humor, and was quickly identified with it in the press, the publication of *The Innocents Abroad* (1869) conferring an international reputation for expressing an American point of view. Self-conscious Americanism, as often as not laced with irony or satire, tinged his ideas about society and culture. Intertwined as the concept of nation is with notions of race, ancestry, territory, language, modernization, politics, international relations, literature, values, and gender (among other things), it necessarily became one of Twain's topics – sometimes quite explicitly, sometimes indirectly. But Twain's own remarks about the idea of a nation, and about America, were notoriously various, changing from one occasion and audience to another. This variety has helped generate a rich range of interpretive comment about Mark Twain and the American nation. For well over a hundred years, through various moments and varieties of twentieth-century national self-definition, Twain has been used to epitomize American values and contradictions. Various critics and scholars have tracked and measured the staggering ubiquity of Mark Twain in America – from Twain T-shirts to white-suited Disney simulations – including his widely disseminated nationalist meanings.[1]

My aim here is more modest. I lay out a few of Twain's explicit comments about nation as a way of focusing some of the ideas it evoked for him and the contradictions it entailed. I also adduce examples from his fiction to show how he explored and complicated the matter – to the point, I believe, of intuiting features of national feeling and the modern nation-state as we now understand them, and of wondering how these things come into being. Then I select influential academic interpretations of Mark Twain and America that span the twentieth century and that mark the ways, both celebratory and critical, in which he has been treated as an icon of American culture and used to imagine America – in his roles as a figure of the frontier, a writer of American humor and vernacular, and a recorder of American race relations. Twain still has this function in our time, when nationalism rightly arouses suspicion in the academy and yet is experiencing an intense popular renaissance. The continued pairing of Twain and nation will undoubtedly foment more disagreement and controversy; one can hope it will also bring more insight into both.

Nation, Genealogy, and Race

A standard practice of nation-constructing is the linking of the new entity to a past, fashioning stories and elaborating genealogies that explain the nation in terms of fathers who can be celebrated, or in terms of immemorial origins, sometimes of a primordial racial sort. History is rewritten as national history; the nation is narrated in this process of self-imagining. Twain repeatedly participated in and mocked this process. For the most part, he jokes with the legends of American founding fathers and national heroes. "A New Biography of Washington" (1866), for example, berates this national patriarch for not knowing enough to tell a lie – a skill the writer claims to have learned early on – and says the chances are slim that American youth would emulate Washington's example (Twain 1992a: 205–7). "The Late Benjamin Franklin" (1870), while granting that Franklin "did a great many notable things for his country, and made her young name to be honored in many lands as the mother of such a son," aims mainly to debunk his "pretentious maxims" as ancient and "wearisome platitudes" deceptively tricked up for modern consumption (Twain 1992a: 425–7). It may be too much to credit this burlesquing Twain with sophisticated doubts about the storytelling that constitutes national identity, but his themes – casting aspersions on supposed truth-telling, humorously embracing wholesale lying, cynically discrediting the words of these fathers, doubting the likelihood that latter-day Americans could reproduce the legendary paragons – all this suggests that he has turned onto the fabrication of national myth his characteristic raillery and doubts about the possibility of truth in representation. In any case, in Twain's writing a national pantheon does *not* descend to us unbesmirched. A Fourth of July speech delivered in London in 1873 declares the United States

> A great and glorious land . . . a land which has developed a Washington, a Franklin, a William M. Tweed, a Longfellow, a Motley, a Jay Gould, a Samuel C. Pomeroy, a recent Congress which has never had its equal – (in some respects) and a United States Army which conquered sixty Indians in eight months by tiring them out – which is much better than uncivilized slaughter, God knows. (Twain 1910: 414)

If Washington and Franklin are not explicitly discredited in this passage, they are in the shady company of the corrupt boss Tweed, the rapacious capitalist Gould, the bribe-taking congressman Pomeroy, and a US Army that has "improved" upon its propensity for slaughtering Indians only through its inefficiency. Here is a mixed genealogy at best, a nation at least partly fathered by real bastards, figuratively speaking.

In this vein, Twain's most striking patricide of national fathers is "Plymouth Rock and the Pilgrims," a speech given in 1881 to the New England Society of Philadelphia (Twain 1910: 17–24). "What do you want to celebrate those people for? – those ancestors of yours, of 1620 – the *Mayflower* tribe, I mean," he asks. Those Pilgrims

> took good care of themselves, but they abolished everybody else's ancestors . . . My first American ancestor, gentlemen, was an indian – an early Indian. Your ancestors skinned him alive, and I am an orphan . . . Later ancestors of mine were the Quakers . . . Your tribe chased them out of the country for their religion's sake. (pp. 19–21)

He goes on: "All those Salem witches were ancestors of mine . . . The first slave brought into New England out of Africa by your progenitors was an ancestor of mine – for I am of a mixed breed, an infinitely shaded and exquisite Mongrel" (p. 22). In this way Twain contrasts the Pilgrim forefathers to a multiethnic and multicultural nation, embodied in a mongrelized Twain, whose ancestors – grandfathers *and* grandmothers – have been murdered, exiled, and enslaved. He beseeches his audience to disband the New England Societies and sell Plymouth Rock! And if he relents at the end – "chaff and nonsense aside, I think I honor and appreciate your Pilgrim stock as much as you do yourselves, perhaps" – this sop to his audience's dignity only briefly blunts the pointed, though humorous, denunciation that preceded it (p. 24). The English settlers themselves are given a mixed moral heritage, at the same time that a multifarious mulatto nation arises around the supposed Pilgrim origins of the American self.

True to his own sense of doubleness, and drawing perhaps inevitably on the intrinsic contradictions that lie within any conception of nation, Twain does trace national chronologies that have positive value – but these show their darker sides as we comb through them. One such narrative looks for national origins in England and the Anglo-Saxon race. In two Fourth-of-July speeches, one in 1873, the other in 1907, and both made in London, where the audience obviously affected the sentiment, Twain anchors American nationality in English soil and history. In the earlier speech he acknowledges the English "mother soil" and half-seriously asks: "With a common origin, a common literature, a common religion and common drinks, what is longer needful to the cementing of the two nations together in a permanent bond of brotherhood?" (Twain 1910: 414). His later speech, reflecting his sanguine version of American nationalism as a force for freedom, declares that the United States had five Fourths of July, in the sense of memorable moments for liberty, all of them actually bequeathed by England: the first was Magna Charta, the second the Petition of Right, the third the American colonists' principle of no taxation without representation, the fourth the Declaration of Independence, the fifth the Emancipation Proclamation. Since the first four were all made by British subjects, the only truly American one was the last, though it too followed England's abolition of slavery. Twain concludes:

Let us be able to say to Old England, this great-hearted, venerable old mother of the race, you gave us our Fourths of July that we love and that we honor and revere, you gave us the Declaration of Independence, which is the Charter of our rights, you, the venerable Mother of Liberties, the Protector of Anglo-Saxon Freedom – you gave us these things, and we do most honestly thank you for them. (p. 412)

Twain significantly invokes here a racial matrix for national origins – typical of turn-of-the-century national self-imagining – at the same time that he exalts the freeing of the slaves, making the love of liberty flow in Anglo-Saxon blood, to the benefit of African Americans. The potential miscegenation that comes with declaring emancipation a moment of national conception comes with a reassertion of white national genealogy and hierarchizing of racial difference.

Twain's most notorious treatment of this difficult muddle of nation, ancestry, and race comes in *Pudd'nhead Wilson* (1894). In that novel we learn early on that York Leicester Driscoll was "proud of his old Virginia ancestry" and that Pembroke Howard was of "proved descent from the First Families" (Twain 1894: 20–1). This went for Cecil Burleigh Essex too, "another F. F. V.," or member of a First Family of Virginia, with whom we supposedly "have no concern," though he is the father of a central character, the black slave Roxy's son (p. 22). This semi-mythical lineage and place refer to national origins, of course: the first British colony of the New World. The genealogy of these sons of the "F. F. V." is joined with the explicit declaration that they are gentlemen. In their labeling, several crucial meanings are intertwined: that these men can trace their heritage back to fathers of the nation, but also that they are slaveholders, are white, belong to a fraternity of men who stand above others, and have authority over others. That is, the crucial questions of genealogy and inheritance in this novel have implications most obviously for whiteness (does your ancestry mean you are a free white or a black slave?), but a whiteness, nonetheless, joined to pride in nation.

This genealogy of American white manhood is pointedly deranged when Roxy, perversely ratifying its importance, tells her son that, because his father was descended from the First Families of Virginia, no other "nigger [is] . . . as high-bawn as you is" (Twain 1894: 120). This is more than a moment of burlesque, more than an instance of mock-pretentious minstrelsy, more than Roxy's simply putting on airs and aping white status hierarchies. It blurts out an officially hidden, racially mixed line of descent. Roxy further disrupts the official national genealogy of the city fathers when she denounces her son Tom's manhood – because he smirched his honor by refusing to duel with Luigi after the meeting of the Sons of Liberty – and then tells him that "the nigger in him" has disgraced his birth, his Essex blood, and also the blood of John Smith, and that of Smith's "great-great-gran'mother" Pocahontas and her husband, "a nigger king outen Africa." The invocation of John Smith, of course, places this charge in the territory of national legend, and so does the invocation of Pocahontas. If Roxy avoids the Indian–white miscegenation of the marriage between Pocahontas and her actual husband John Rolfe, and instead has Pocahontas marry a

black African king, their progeny nonetheless is John Smith. Roxy's national genealogy has black roots, is miscegenated and complicated "somers along back dah" (p.
189). While her imagined heritage might be adduced for the argument that Twain
treats racial genealogies, like race itself, as a "fiction of law and custom," the lineage
she declares does more than show itself to be a fiction. It also pointedly names an
alternative national genealogy to the myth of origins that the white town fathers
embrace, remingling multiracial family-descent lines into the national narrative. In
having Roxy mime the family (and national) pride of the white males, but mime it
impurely, Twain seems quite consciously to be assaulting the constellation of whiteness, manliness, and nation. But even if he is irreverent about this configuration of
authority, his novel re-enacts Roxy's treatment of the matter, challenging the injustice but preserving a belief in character based on race and blood that underpins the
problem. He follows a pattern, as we shall see in a moment, that critics of his apotheosis as national author have traced in his treatment of race in America.

Nation and Modernization

While acknowledging the risk of seeming to retrofit Twain to our twenty-first-century
conceptions, we might nonetheless say that *A Connecticut Yankee in King Arthur's Court*
(1889), in its depiction of the (failed) transition from feudal aristocracy to Hank
Morgan's "republic," grapples with questions we still have about the emergence of a
nation and the conditions necessary for the modern nation-state. One group of historians, that is, sees nation and nationalism as products of modernization, specifically
of capitalism and industrialization, which forged the homogeneous (or standardized),
literate national populations necessary for their own development.[2] Seemingly dis-
agreeing with this idea, Hank repeatedly refers to an English "nation" (a term he uses
over 50 times – one of his favorite words), by which he means an Anglo-Saxon people
whose sense of themselves and their rights as "men" pre-existed the sixth century and
has been nearly obliterated by the church and the nobility. Nonetheless, he is quite
attuned to the importance of mass education and industry for fashioning the nation-
state he proposes (his Man-Factory combines the two), and capitalist marketing is one
of the ways he extends its influence. Notably, he says that "The first thing you want
in a new country is a patent office; then work up your school system; and after that,
out with your paper . . . You can't resurrect a dead nation without it" (Twain 1889:
109). Whether this is a new country or a resurrected nation, the connection of nation-
fashioning to newspapers suits Benedict Anderson's now ubiquitous conception of the
nation as an "imagined community" grounded in the emergence of what he calls "print
capitalism" (Anderson 1991: 37–46). This refers in part to the capitalist development
of print materials, the newspaper in particular, which enabled people to imagine themselves part of a community of individuals that included others they would never meet
– readers of the same newspaper, consumers of the same news, all privately engaging
in this same activity on the same day. The distribution of printed material and the

vernacular language of the newspaper bound people together in this new conception
of a nation – and it happened first in the Americas in the late eighteenth century.
Twain did in fact associate the birth of "the press" with the American Revolution and
the birth of the republic (Twain 1992a: 942–3). He also saw the press as a kind of
glue for the common folk. The journalistic style of Hank's able assistant Clarence is
immediately "up to the back settlement Alabama mark" – "he talked sixth century
and wrote nineteenth" (Twain 1889: 121), including disgraceful familiarities –
meaning for one thing that his backwoods language is vernacular in a very old sense:
a language that elbows out the Latin of clergy and scribes, replaces the courtly language that excludes the masses, and therefore potentially becomes a national idiom.
While it is true that, like the back-settlement Alabama paper, the *Camelot Weekly
Hosannah and Literary Volcano* is a local paper, not a national one, bits of national news
appear to foster the larger imagined community. And of course in Hank's case other
communications technologies bolster the conditions of national interconnections. His
telegraph and his "atmosphere of telephones and lightning communication with
distant regions" (p. 305) ensure this. When Morgan trounces a soothsayer's supposed
clairvoyance about the king's activities by using telegraphic information to announce
that the king is traveling and will arrive in two days – and of course is right about
this bit of national news – he exemplifies the consciousness of newspaper and nation,
of other people and events simultaneously proceeding, out of sight, within the imagined community (pp. 309–10).

Hank arguably also introduces another, related condition of the nation according
to Anderson: the dispersed "homogeneous, empty time" (Anderson 1991: 24–6), a
time measured by clock and calendar rather than by the sacred and centered time-
lessness of prefiguration and fulfillment. Hank's "miracle" of predicting the solar
eclipse puts his calendrical calculations into the place of the divine order, replacing
miracles as prefigured divine signs with the measured march of godless nature. With
this desacralized, abstractly homogeneous sense of time comes another condition for
the nation, the displacement of the king as a type of the divine by the secular admin-
istrator (or "Boss"), and the displacement of the dynasty as the principle of social organization by the state. Hank plays along with the pre-national, monarchic idea of a
chain from God to king to people: he keeps up the performance of Arthur's supposed
healing of scrofula by touch – the "king's-evil business" (p. 334) – and his other spec-
tacles seem to invoke supernatural power. But in fact all of these ostensibly sacred
symbolic moments, from going a-grailing to his staged miracle in the Valley of
Holiness, are technologically produced or at least efficiently administered. Hank's
administrative entity grows into the substratum for his nation-state, inaugurating a
system of schools, taxes, communications, American-based national currency, national
advertising and marketing, industry, and "missionary" expansion, extending his
profane influence all the way to "obscure country retreats" and the "quiet nooks and
corners" (pp. 117–18) of the nation – culminating in a network of wires and explo-
sives connecting all his innovations, ready to blow them all up. Here, with a ruthless

single-mindedness, is the nation in the sense of a geographically bounded entity, replacing a dynastically or divinely centered monarchy. Here, with wires, Hank literalizes the connections needed for national unity. Here he unashamedly establishes national unity as the grounds for capitalist investment and expansion.

Twain wrestles throughout his novel with the question of whether nation serves as a liberatory, revolutionary thing or as an excuse for exploitation and oppression. Hank senses that the creation of his nation-state has skipped the paradigmatic step of republican revolution, the event that historically provides the national political alternative to monarchy, and he declares, "The thing that would have best suited the circus-side of my nature would have been to resign the Boss-ship and get up an insurrection and turn it into a revolution." But first, as he recognizes, you have to educate your "materials up to revolution-grade" or get left (Twain 1889: 160). This of course ends up being his big problem: the Arthurians are simply not ready for a self-determined national republic. Hank's dream is a revolution without bloodshed, and then a republic with universal suffrage (p. 391). In his delusional fantasies, then, his nationalism is put in the service of freedom and liberation. But in a typical Twainian return of pessimism about the dehumanized masses, the church easily retrieves the English from the republicanism Hank tries to rouse them to (or impose on them). His republic finally unites its people only as a mass of protoplasm. With the electrified fence, gatling guns, and dynamite torpedoes in place, Clarence asks "When does the performance begin?" and Hank answers, now, by declaring a republic (p. 544). But his republic has no nation. What ensues, in a mockery of the true republican nation-state, is national solidarity through death (though Hank justifies it by saying that only the knights are dying, not the nation). Literalizing with a malapropian flourish, Hank turns *res publica*, or "public matter," into undifferentiated ooze: cohesive, perhaps, and standardized; homogeneous and interconnected. But a national subjectivity eludes his efforts to launch his new deal. Sixth-century England is not historically ready for "the nation" and "the people." And the questions arise not only whether the English nation existed before Hank's arrival, but also whether his modernization is sufficient to lure it into existence.

Nationality, Femininity, and Imperialism

In 1896, in *Personal Recollections of Joan of Arc*, Twain wrote: "With Joan of Arc love of country was more than a sentiment – it was a passion. She was the Genius of Patriotism – she was Patriotism embodied, concreted, made flesh, and palpable to the touch and visible to the eye" (Twain 1896: 461). In contrast to Hank's national republic, Joan's elicits profound emotion and loyalty. And in this case love of country undergoes no burlesque. This is patriotism revered as a holy spirit, and love of nation becomes, indeed, equivalent to a religion. Joan is the materialization of love of *patrie*, the fatherland, and the perfect such embodiment because of her pure and selfless daughter-love. In this she represents, as Twain writes, "purity from all alloy of self-seeking, self-interest, personal ambition" (p. 287); she is ready to sacrifice herself, and inspires others to make the same pure, familial self-sacrifice for the nation. While the actual Joan of Arc, and her martyrdom, may have indeed helped give form to a French nationhood that was to supersede loyalty to the monarch, Twain's Joan had benefited from nineteenth-century efforts to refabricate her as a symbol of French identity. His Joan embodies a full-fledged popular nationality. Early in the novel, after the stranger to whom she has given her food regales the folk at the local inn with a history of France and the Song of Roland, she leads the crowd as "they all flung themselves in a body at the singer, stark mad with love of him and love of France and pride in her great deeds and old renown, and smothered him with their embracings" (pp. 34–5). Here is nation-love based on the idea of a country, its history and beliefs, its anthem, its popular identity. Even if Charles VII, who finally owes his crown to Joan, fails her, the common people in Twain's novel know and love Joan as the savior of France. They live in a fifteenth-century principality and think as nineteenth-century national subjects, joined horizontally by national identity rather than vertically by authority of the crown.

Joan's Frenchness, and her France, gain such patriotic support in a way that Hank's republic could not. But even if Hank's abstract, manufactured republic could stir no patriotic emotion, could such passion for the idea of the nation as Twain's Joan inspires actually be possible before Hank's sort of mass education and print capitalism constituted the necessary imagined community? Twain's contrast between Hank and Joan resonates with a split among our current theorists of nation between those who see nationality as a modern phenomenon and those who trace it further back in history. While the former argue that nationalism as a political program is only a couple of hundred years old, and any national feeling discovered earlier than that is its own projection backward, the latter argue that the stirrings of national sentiment occurred well before the late eighteenth century, in ethnic and cultural groupings.[3] Having seen Hank's republic to its grim end, Twain seems to discount nation as it is fashioned by modernization, and instead, through Joan, to reach for older roots, for collective national feeling somehow arising from the soil, or as the realization of a national spirit. We may see in his Joan of Arc a questionable invention of full-blown nationality, but for Twain Joan represents indigenous national passion, autochthonous patriotic emotion, a mad love of nation as natural homeland. For him, she legitimately offers a national alternative to the older dynastic order, a counter-force to both nobility and clergy. The organization of principalities, indeed, is one of the villains of her story, as it arranges the marriage of Henry VI of England and Catherine of France and confers on their baby boy the throne of both countries – an unbearable outrage to Joan's Frenchness. Joan also fights the international organization of the church, the archaic institutional power that would obliterate her nationalism and her individuality. Her foes seek falsely to stifle an essential, pure, organic patriotic passion.

Joan's embodiment of nation and patriotism brings with it the equally important equation of patriotism and youthful femininity. Twain ends his novel by saying:

Love, Mercy, Charity, Fortitude, War, Peace, Poetry, Music, – these may be symbolized
as any shall prefer: by figures of either sex and of any age; but a slender girl in her first
young bloom, with the martyr's crown upon her head, and in her hand the sword that
severed her country's bonds – shall not this, and no other, stand for PATRIOTISM
through all the ages until time shall end? (Twain 1896: 461)

This comes at the end of a novel that has gloried in Joan's girlhood, feminine purity,
virginity, modesty, and chastity. The intersection of images of women and figurations
of national identity is of course immensely complex; the ways, for example, that Joan
of Arc may interweave with such American images as that of the female Columbia,
Lady Liberty, and the Republican Mother, is beyond my scope here. What becomes
obvious, however, is Twain's equation of this girlhood purity with a kind of primordial nationhood, a righteous version of nation not unlike that of American virgin land
– a nationality emergent from the soil, belonging by natural right to its true owners
and defenders. The equation enables a parallel between the melodramatically persecuted heroine, whose virtue is obscured in her sham trial and whose virginity and
feminine modesty are assaulted, and a nation violated and colonized by the predatory
English and Burgundian armies.

The melodrama of purity defiled and innocence persecuted metamorphoses into
Twain's figurative schema for understanding nationalism in the late-nineteenth-
century context of American imperialism. Never an admirer of the French nation,
Twain makes Joan an allegory of national principle that he could apply to his own
landscape of international relations. In 1901, most notably, Twain compares General
Emilio Aguinaldo to Joan of Arc, the grounds being specifically those of patriotism.
Aguinaldo had been declared the first president of the Philippine Republic in 1898,
on the assumption that the Philippines would have independence after they had joined
the United States in defeating the Spanish in Manila. The United States dashed that
aspiration, instead taking possession of the Philippines and beginning a war to maintain and extend its control over the islands. For Twain, Aguinaldo became a Joan-like
figure, a nation-lover, arising from obscure peasant origins to earn the trust of his
people, fighting against tyranny and for freedom and independence – first against
Spain and its Catholic friars, then against the United States – and finally beaten by
dishonorable subterfuge and deceitful betrayal, crushed by a more powerful force
(Zwick 1992: 99–100, 88). In these years Twain writes and speaks repeatedly about
two different kinds of patriotism: the just, nationalist, anti-colonial kind of Joan,
Aguinaldo, and George Washington, which he extols, and the newspaper-fed patriotism of conformity which he sees propelling US imperialist ventures that rob weak
nations of their freedom, which he despises (Twain 1992b: 476–8, 645; Zwick 1992,
passim). Partly gendered, the apparent weakness and natural purity of purpose of Joan
and Aguinaldo is compounded with their righteous, martial, nationalist fervor (signified in Joan, the martyr with the sword, the virgin in male armor). That contradiction is set against a domestic United States that has a weak population manipulated
into a false patriotism and an aggressively devious imperial military. Twain's contrast

may clarify meanings of nation and patriotism, but the doubled contradictions also promise intricate confusions, the kinds of inconsistencies, again, that the concept of nation seems to generate.

National Author

Twain made spirited defenses of American civilization in response to the derogatory evaluations from England by Matthew Arnold and from France by Paul Bourget. Part of his argument was that a "foreigner" can only "photograph the exteriors of a nation." To get at "its interior – its soul, its life, its speech, its thought" requires years of unconscious absorption of "its shames and prides, its joys and griefs, its loves and hates, its prosperities and reverses, its shows and shabbinesses, its deep patriotisms, its whirlwinds of political passion, its adorations – of flag, and heroic dead, and the glory of the national name." He crucially adds: "There is only one expert who is qualified to examine the souls and the life of a people and make a valuable report – the native novelist." However, Twain goes on to note, a novelist cannot "generalize the nation," but must simply capture on paper the people of "his own place." And "when a thousand able novels have been written, *there* you have the soul of the people, the life of the people, the speech of the people; and not anywhere else can these be had." Much of the rest of the piece I quote from – "What Paul Bourget Thinks of Us" (1895) – is devoted to ridiculing the very project of generalizing about national traits, characteristics, psychologies. There are basic human traits that exist across nations, Twain writes, and there is staggering variety within every nation. The only thing that seems to be peculiarly American, he facetiously adds, is the taste for ice-water – something which has "not been psychologized yet. I drop the hint and say no more" (Twain 1992b: 164–79).

Criticism of the work of Mark Twain done in a national-cultural vein has often taken up his conviction that the native novelist can capture the "soul" of a nation, but has just as often forgotten his admonition against making large cultural generalizations as it has re-imagined the nation through its accounts of Twain. This is not to say, though, that such generalizing has not been illuminating and provocative. Ten years after Twain's death, Van Wyck Brooks made the first enduringly influential and controversial sally in *The Ordeal of Mark Twain* (1920). Sometimes remembered only as a misogynistic and psycho-biographical attack on Twain's wife Livy for censoring and stunting her husband's talent, Brooks's book more largely aimed to make Twain a national type – of the artist crushed by the American environment – and to skirmish over the definition of a national literary tradition during the period of intense nationalism (and nativism) following World War I. Concerned to foster an American literature that would express the nation to itself – a notion inherited from nineteenth-century Romantic nationalism, and which for him required high literary accomplishment – Brooks offered Twain as a model to avoid, an "arch-type of the national character" only in his arrested development, his failure to know himself (Brooks 1955:

26). Tragically, Twain's genius had been starved by the cultural "desert" of the frontier (p. 40), stifled by American business-mindedness, and seduced by Victorian conventionality – much of which Brooks traced ultimately to repressive Calvinism. That last crucial point was a salvo by this aesthete-radical against the more conservative critics who had been defining an American cultural and literary tradition as rooted in New England and Puritanism; for Brooks, Puritanism was a great impediment to the national literature he sought.

Ten years later, in his *Main Currents in American Thought*, Vernon Louis Parrington similarly formulated an abidingly influential version of Twain as an embodiment of the conflict that, he argued, defined American thought – between optimistic American democratic individualism and later industrialism, with its pressure to conform and its pessimistically mechanistic science, class injustice, and capitalist exploitation. Twain was "an authentic American – a native writer" without European influences, "local and western yet continental" and "the very embodiment of the turbulent frontier that had long been shaping a native psychology." Tragically, however, Twain's "Americanism," his "embodiment of three centuries of American experience – frontier centuries, decentralized, leveling, individualistic," was too crude "to deal with the complexities of a world passing through the twin revolutions of industrialism and science"; hence, he is only "a mirror reflecting the muddy crosscurrents of American life" (Parrington 1930: 86–8). With a twist on Brooks, Parrington lays out the now-familiar picture of Twain as an intensely divided person whose tragic personal conflicts mirror national contradictions.

In a fierce defense of Twain, directed mainly against Brooks, Bernard DeVoto's *Mark Twain's America* (1932) exalted Twain as an artist of the frontier, and his work as an expression of America, by representing the frontier not as a crude, stunting desert but as the rich core of American experience. Much of DeVoto's book is a tapestry of frontier cultures, importantly including African American storytelling and music and stressing the oral tall tale as Twain's principal resource and as "sharply and autochthonously American – unique" (DeVoto 1932: 91). DeVoto attacks "literary theory," and Brooks, for making generalizations – about "The Frontier, the American, the Puritan, the Pioneer . . . [and] Industrial Philistinism" – which have little "correspondence in reality." And in his crusade against such abstractions, he criticizes the very undertaking of trying to order the chaos of "American heritage" into simplistic "categories, personifications, unities." This includes the study of "an eidolon, 'Mark Twain,' in its relation to another phantom, 'America'" (pp. 223–4). DeVoto adds, "It is unsafe to regard any artist as an embodiment of his time or its thought. An individual is not a symbol of his era" (p. 295). Nonetheless, DeVoto argues, with what he suggests is the proper and unprecedented complexity and contextual knowledge, that the frontier shaped Twain, his works express it, and, because all of America passed through the frontier stage, in Twain's works "American civilization sums up its experience; they are the climax of a literary tradition" (p. 241). For DeVoto, *Adventures of Huckleberry Finn*, in its account of frontier variety, "comes nearer than any other [book] to identify itself with the national life. The gigantic amorphousness of our past makes impossible, or merely idle, any attempt to fix in the form of idea the meaning of nationality. But more truly with 'Huckleberry Finn' than with any other book, inquiry may satisfy itself: here is America" (p. 314). DeVoto ends his book by declaring that Twain himself, through his multiple occupations and by living through multiple eras, "more completely than any other writer, took part in the American experience. There is, remember, such an entity." Twain "wrote books that have in them something eternally true to the core of his nation's life. They are at the center; all other books whatsoever are farther away" (DeVoto 1932: 320). Loath to schematize Twain as the embodiment of a national contradiction, DeVoto is nonetheless ready to extol Twain as the distillation of a peculiarly American cultural variety.

DeVoto had drawn on the work of Constance Rourke and showed deep affinities with her in his high valuation of folklore as the source of Twain's art. But Rourke, drawing on Herderian ideas of national identity as emerging from folk culture, more explicitly tried to identify a populist and democratic "American character." In *American Humor: A Study of the National Character* (1931), Rourke described an American character expressed in lore, and she limned three complex figures who rose from regional folk origins to the level of national myth: the rural deadpan Yankee, the tall-tale-telling backwoodsman, and the black-faced minstrel. Mark Twain became an important national figure himself "because of the regional elements which he freely mixed, the Yankee with the Californian, the backwoodsman with both of these" (Rourke 1931: 219–20). Notably, she did not include in Twain's personal mix her third important component of American humor – the minstrel tradition and the authentic African American culture from which she thought it grew. Also drawing on Rourke, Walter Blair's *Native American Humor (1800–1900)* (1937) defined a national tradition that began to emerge around 1830, when American humorists finally recognized funny things in American characters and scenes and developed techniques to exploit this humor, thereby fashioning a comic tradition imbued, he declared, with the customs and convictions of the nation. Twain, in Blair's estimation, was the climax in the development of this tradition, because he brought together the strands Blair's research tracked – Down East Yankee humor, Southwest frontier oral storytelling, literary comedy, and local color writing (Blair 1966: 147). Significantly, Blair dropped Rourke's tradition of minstrelsy altogether, and he more fully exalted Twain's contribution to the creation of a national humor, with *Huckleberry Finn* as the culmination.

Jonathan Arac has recently argued, nonetheless, that it was not really until the years from 1948 to 1964 that *Huckleberry Finn* was plucked from Twain's œuvre and idolized as the ultimate expression of American national culture. This arguably was accomplished especially in essays on the novel in the 1940s by Lionel Trilling, and in the work of Leo Marx and Henry Nash Smith in the 1950s and 1960s. Trilling called the novel "one of the central documents of American culture" (Trilling 1950: 101). By this he meant that the book expressed a post-Civil War change in what was "accepted and made respectable in the national ideal"; Twain's novel was a "hymn to an older America" that, despite its faults and violence and cruelty (slavery was not specified), "still maintained its sense of reality, for it was not yet enthralled by money, the father of ultimate illusion and lies" (p. 110). Its rural, frontier "river-god" stood against the newer, urban, machine-culture, capitalist "money-god." The book, like Mark Twain himself, embodied this conflict. Though Trilling criticized Parrington for characterizing American culture as a stream rather than a conflict – that is, for not being dialectical enough in his conception of American culture – he plainly borrowed from Parrington in making Twain's book epitomize this national contradiction.

The writing of Smith and Marx on Twain was intertwined with their postwar effort to establish American Studies as a project devoted to defining the broader contours of national culture and identity. Smith's 1957 essay on method in American Studies broached the topic of Twain and nation by arguing that Twain's style and characters had to be explained in relation to American culture (that is, they were not amenable to New Critical literary analysis), and that Twain's complex art explains much more about American culture than pop-art stereotypes do. This suggestion got fuller treatment in *Mark Twain: The Development of a Writer* (1962), where Smith argued that Twain's difficult task was "to deal with the conflict of values in American culture" (Smith 1962: 21), namely a conflict between the dominant culture's conventional ideality, quite divorced from reality, and the vernacular mentality's rejection of this. Twain's "development" was toward seeing ideal values in the commonplace, bringing the serious into the vernacular style, giving the everyday the dignity of art, and criticizing genteel ideality from this standpoint. This was the revolutionary accomplishment of *Huckleberry Finn*, which "approaches perfection as an embodiment of American experience in a radically new and appropriate literary mode" (p. 137). Leo Marx's *The Machine in the Garden: Technology and the Pastoral Ideal in America* (1964) built on Smith's work, seeing, too, "a conflict at the center of American experience" (Marx 1964: 320) – this time a conflict precipitated by the rapid industrialization of the nineteenth century, a conflict perceived and symbolized by America's most perceptive artists as a pastoral ideal shattered by the machine. *Huckleberry Finn*, Marx argued, brilliantly turns Huck and Jim's raft into an Arcadia of fraternity and freedom, the very image of American promise, and then has the raft smashed by the steamboat, and the American ideal figuratively smashed by history. "No book," Marx writes, "confirms the relevance of the pastoral design to American experience as vividly as the *Adventures of Huckleberry Finn*" (p. 319). Twain's literary crystallization of the tragic version of Arcadia fixes the conflict at the heart of America and makes him an exemplary national artist.

From the 1960s on, as notions of national character or American collective consciousness were increasingly criticized for supposing a holistic consensus that disguised dominant culture and ideology, academic criticism about Mark Twain that made claims about his exceptional "Americanness" grew rarer. But gradually through the 1970s and 1980s national-cultural studies of Twain returned, partly as pointed critiques of his writings that saw them as embodiments of dominant ideologies. As an example, I would suggest Forrest G. Robinson's *In Bad Faith: The Dynamics of Deception in Mark Twain's America* (1986), which takes Twain's popularity in America, rather than any peculiarly perceptive artistry, as grounds for learning about national culture through his texts ("enduringly popular works are full and clear windows" [Robinson 1986: 10]). Drawing on a model oriented by Marxist and New Historicist theory, Robinson sees Twain's work as representing, but then also repeating, both the tissue of lies that holds national culture together and the general denial of this social deceit. Although much of Robinson's analysis is devoted to Twain's representation in *Tom Sawyer* of the mechanisms of this denial – a national addiction to entertaining distraction, to evasion from acknowledging the deceptions that socially construct US culture – the paradigmatic example is still *Huckleberry Finn*. The explicit tissue of lies there, of course, enables race slavery. And the performances in the novel are distractions from it, including, especially, Tom's showmanlike "evasion" at the end, which is also an evasion on the part of Twain, enacted for an American audience inclined to disavow its racism and history of slavery and to embrace principles of liberty and equality while shirking the recognition of their betrayal. "Mark Twain's enormous American audience has assented to his authority with them as the interpreter and guardian of their deepest cultural selves," Robinson writes (p. 108). By this he means that Twain does crystallize the lies and self-deceptions of American cultural selves, but then repeats the act of bad faith, skirts the matter, wishes them away, contains his threat to them. *Huckleberry Finn* remains a favorite, despite raising the issue of race slavery, "because it seems to invite the dismissal or disavowal of as much of its darkness as we cannot bear to own" (p. 215). For Robinson, Twain's relation to America is that of a pre-eminent national myth-sustainer, in the sense of myth as something that shapes, invokes, and sustains the historical experience, memory, and collective psychology of a "people" – and operates, too, to forget and deny anything that rends the precarious stability of the intersubjective national-cultural fabric.

National literary tradition, and Twain's place in it, was similarly revisited for criticism by Toni Morrison in *Playing in the Dark: Whiteness and the Literary Imagination* (1992). For Morrison there is indeed a "national literature," but it is "the preserve of white male views, genius, and power." And its very "sense of Americanness," as well as its defining values – including freedom, individualism, masculinity, and innocence – is actually a response to "a real or fabricated Africanist presence" (Morrison 1992: 4–6). To a great extent, this response involves projecting a black presence constructed of white fears and desires, which is then often silenced or evaded but persistently erupts into or infuses the psychology and literature of white America. Black slaves became "a playground for the imagination" of white authors, who cooked up "a fabricated brew of darkness, otherness, alarm, and desire that is uniquely American" (p. 38). No exception to this, Twain's *Huckleberry Finn* fashions Jim into a figure whose enslavement is necessary both for Huck's freedom and for his moral maturation. Twain once again is an exemplary national author, this time in the way his book embodies "the parasitical nature of white freedom." And if the novel does criticize antebellum America and its formations of race and class, it also participates in the national evasion of injustice by doing so through humor that allows its contestatory sallies to be dis-

missed (pp. 54–7). Like Robinson's Mark Twain, Morrison's enacts a national subterfuge on behalf of a white "we the people."

The frank celebration of Twain as a national author was resurrected by Shelley
Fisher Fishkin in *Was Huck Black? Mark Twain and African-American Voices* (1993).
But, for Fishkin, the nation Mark Twain expresses and interprets is a nation of dif-
ferences. We might say that Fishkin retrieves DeVoto's stress on the influence of
African American storytelling in Twain's work and combines it with the insistence of
Morrison and Ralph Ellison that there is a complicated black presence throughout
American literature. The result is an argument that "the mainstream American literary tradition" so profoundly shaped by Twain's vernacular style is actually constituted
by a "multicultural polyphony" that includes black voices (Fishkin 1993: 4–5) and
which therefore requires us to rethink "how African-American voices have shaped our
sense of what is distinctively 'American' about American literature" (p. 9). Fishkin
concretizes the idea by declaring that she has discovered the source of Huck's voice
in the language of a black character in an earlier Twain sketch, and therefore "the
voice of Huck Finn, the beloved national symbol and cultural icon, was part black"
(p. 144) – hence her sensational book title and the flurry of national media attention
surrounding the publication of her study. Whatever one may think about this "discovery," Fishkin's work influentially reframed our understanding of what she characterizes as "the novel that we have embraced as most expressive of who we really are"
(p. 144). It also rehabilitated Twain as a national author, and rescued and reconceived
the nationalist literary tradition he heads, this time for the era and purposes of
multiculturalism.

Fishkin's kind of nationalist "idolization" of *Huckleberry Finn* comes in for sharp
criticism in Jonathan Arac's Huckleberry Finn *as Idol and Target: The Functions of Criticism in our Time* (1997). But Fishkin is simply the latest example of the "hypercan-
onization" of the novel that began during the Civil Rights era, Arac argues, when the
novel did something for its white readers similar to what it had done for their fore-
runners in the 1880s. When it was first published, that is, white readers in a culture
that had repudiated slavery could self-approvingly identify with Huck's decision to
help Jim to freedom – and therefore watch him become as good as them. In the 1960s
(and ever since), liberal white readers in a culture in which white supremacy was being
challenged could similarly, and again self-approvingly, identify with Huck, feeling
that their hearts were right even if their society was still racist. Indeed, "Northern
liberal smugness" embraced the book as enlightened while assuming that the bigots
of Little Rock were too racist to appreciate it (Arac 1997: 65). Liberal intellectuals,
similarly, could get "moral self-satisfaction in articulating the values Huck couldn't,"
and therefore the book was hypercanonized as "a talisman of self-flattering American
virtue" (p. 62). African Americans who attacked the book, and Huck's use of "nigger,"
therefore managed to "challenge 'us' just where 'we' feel ourselves most intimately
virtuous" (p. 13), and liberal literary experts accordingly lined up to defend the book's
anti-racism. In a manner similar to Forrest Robinson's, Arac sees the novel as helping

its readers evade problems of race relations by making them feel warm about their own anti-racist feelings; and he further sees the alignment of Twain and his book with the nation as intimately wedded to this complacency-breeding process. Even if Fishkin's nationalism is put in the service of "interracially progressive purposes," turning this national icon into a positive version of "hybridized antiracism," Arac suggests, is complicit with a process which, by hypercanonizing the novel as an American document, wrongly validates the nation's claim to moral goodness (pp. 184–5). He contrasts Fishkin's nationalist framework with Edward Said's critique of such celebratory nationalism and his effort to bring colonialism, imperialism, and international relations into our critical picture. We ought to put "less weight on the exceptionalist, nationalist project" (p. 209), Arac finally asserts, and think more of the United States as a nation among others – and also think of Mark Twain in an international frame. This might begin a cure, Arac suggests, to a self-congratulatory nationalist myopia in the American literary and cultural criticism represented by the idolization of *Huckleberry Finn*.

Indeed, in our period of globalization and nationalist ethnic cleansing, when "post-nationalism" runs up against post-9/11 patriotism, critical attention to Mark Twain directly engages the question of nation and Twain's place in the international arena. Amy Kaplan's *The Anarchy of Empire in the Making of US Culture* (2002) is perhaps the foremost example of such engagement. Paradigms for the study of US culture have had a national focus, Kaplan notes, which she aims to question and disrupt by opening the international context. She undertakes to show that Mark Twain in particular, whose name "has long been synonymous with American culture," looks different when recontextualized: "his international travels in the routes of empire profoundly shaped both the iconic stature of Twain as an American writer and his complex representation of race" (Kaplan 2002: 19). Observing that Twain has often been characterized as embodying divisions that symbolize contradictions in national culture, Kaplan aims to correct this through triangulation, by opening up the imperial sphere: "Twain's career, writing, and reception as a national author were shaped by a third realm beyond national boundaries: the routes of transnational travel, enabling and enabled by the changing borders of imperial expansion." In short, "the national identity of Mark Twain, his 'Americanness'," was created in this international context (p. 52). Kaplan's readings of Twain's early writings about Hawaii, especially, and her analysis of the complex relations between his exoticization of Hawaiians and his memories of slavery, work to situate Twain in her larger argument that the intricacies and contradictions of American imperial relations, and depictions of the foreign and the alien, helped shape "representations of American identity at home" (p. 1). Twain's ambiguous treatments of Hawaiians call up and mingle with his contradictory boyhood memories of slaves, generating the writing most embraced as "American." Twain's writing career, as well as the icon of Mark Twain as American, is shown to be suffused with the same sort of anarchy and ambiguity that characterized images of the world abroad. They deeply involved "both remembering and forgetting the inextricable connections between national identity and imperial expansion" (p. 22).

Despite the current surge of popular US patriotism, the literary-critical landscape for the study of Twain and nation seems to have been decisively reoriented by work that has put into question the construction of nation and national literature and urged new models of understanding that connect these constructions to global contexts. If today's intense nationalisms remind us that we hardly live in a "post-national" world, we nonetheless have rightly lost the unexamined platform from which commentators talked about "American literature" as a self-evident or transcendent national entity, an a priori source of coherence, or a teleological goal. Projects pursuing Twain as exemplary American, or otherwise connecting Twain and nation, will have to scrutinize their scaffolding before going further, or make the scaffolding, and its foundations, their object of study. But this is inspiriting, as new horizons for understanding open up, as seemingly self-evident assumptions about the importance of *American* literature are questioned, and as the implications and effects of joining Mark Twain and nation are thoughtfully exposed. At the same time, our new questions about nation and nationalism enable us to ask different things of Twain's writing and to subtilize our sense of the relation between his work and the phenomenon of nationality.

NOTES

1   The work of Louis J. Budd is the fullest and shrewdest on this topic. See *Our Mark Twain* (1983) for the popular meanings of Twain, mainly during his lifetime, along with Twain's self-conscious cultivation of them; "Mark Twain as an American Icon" (1995), which more fully surveys the multiple national meanings of Twain in the twentieth century; and "Mark Twain Sounds Off on the Fourth of July" (2002), which goes well beyond its title as it addresses Mark Twain and America. Budd's *Mark Twain: Social Philosopher* (1962) also gives a full account of Twain's patriotism

and Americanism from the political side. See also Fishkin (1997).

2   See Gellner (1983); Hobsbawm (1990); Anderson (1991).

3   Among those who allow for earlier national formations are Anthony D. Smith (1986), who sees national identities emerging in reconstructions of ethnic symbolism prior to the era of nationalism, and Adrian Hastings (1997), who locates nationhood, evidenced and partly fashioned in the vernacular literature of ethnic groups, in the Middle Ages, notably in England.

REFERENCES AND FURTHER READING

Anderson, Benedict (1991). *Imagined Communities: Reflections on the Origin and Spread of Nationalism*, rev. edn. London: Verso.

Arac, Jonathan (1997). Huckleberry Finn *as Idol and Target: The Functions of Criticism in our Time.* Madison: University of Wisconsin Press.

Blair, Walter (1960). *Native American Humor (1800–1900)*. San Francisco: Chandler. (First publ. 1937.)

Brooks, Van Wyck (1955). *The Ordeal of Mark Twain*. New York: Meridian. (First publ. 1920.)

Budd, Louis J. (1962). *Mark Twain: Social Philosopher*. Bloomington: Indiana University Press.

Budd, Louis J. (1983). *Our Mark Twain: The Making of his Public Personality.* Philadelphia: University of Pennsylvania Press.

Budd, Louis J. (1995). "Mark Twain as an American Icon." In Forrest G. Robinson, ed., *The Cambridge Companion to Mark Twain*, 1–26. New York: Cambridge University Press.

Budd, Louis J. (2002). "Mark Twain Sounds Off on the Fourth of July." *American Literary Realism* 34: 3 (Spring), 265–80.

DeVoto, Bernard (1932). *Mark Twain's America.* Boston: Little, Brown.

Fishkin, Shelley Fisher (1993). *Was Huck Black? Mark Twain and African-American Voices.* New York: Oxford University Press.

Fishkin, Shelley Fisher (1997). *Lighting Out for the Territory: Reflections on Mark Twain and American Culture.* New York: Oxford University Press.

Gellner, Ernest (1983). *Nations and Nationalism.* Oxford: Blackwell.

Hastings, Adrian (1997). *The Construction of Nationhood: Ethnicity, Religion and Nationalism.* New York: Cambridge University Press.

Hobsbawm, E. J. (1990). *Nations and Nationalism since 1780: Programme, Myth, Reality.* New York: Cambridge University Press.

Kaplan, Amy (2002). *The Anarchy of Empire in the Making of US Culture.* Cambridge, Mass.: Harvard University Press.

Marx, Leo (1964). *The Machine in the Garden: Technology and the Pastoral Ideal in America.* New York: Oxford University Press.

Morrison, Toni (1992). *Playing in the Dark: Whiteness and the Literary Imagination.* Cambridge, Mass.: Harvard University Press.

Parrington, Vernon Louis (1930). *Main Currents in American Thought: An Interpretation of American Literature from the Beginnings to 1920*, vol. 3: *The Beginnings of Critical Realism in America 1860–1920.* New York: Harcourt, Brace.

Robinson, Forrest G. (1986). *In Bad Faith: The Dynamics of Deception in Mark Twain's America.* Cambridge, Mass.: Harvard University Press.

Rourke, Constance (1931). *American Humor: A Study of the National Character.* New York: Harcourt, Brace.

Smith, Anthony D. (1986). *The Ethnic Origins of Nations.* Oxford: Blackwell.

Smith, Henry Nash (1957). "Can American Studies Develop a Method?" *American Quarterly* 9, 197–208.

Smith, Henry Nash (1962). *Mark Twain: The Development of a Writer.* Cambridge, Mass.: Belknap/Harvard University Press.

Trilling, Lionel (1950). *The Liberal Imagination: Essays on Literature and Society.* New York: Anchor/Doubleday.

Zwick, Jim, ed. (1992). *Mark Twain's Weapons of Satire: Anti-Imperialist Writings on the Philippine–American War.* Syracuse, NY: Syracuse University Press.

2
Mark Twain and Human Nature
Tom Quirk

When Mark Twain died in 1910, newspapers and magazines throughout the country printed obituaries that attempted to sum up the man and the significance of his writings. "He was a humanist," and his writings were illuminated by "the keenest insight into human nature" (April 22, 1910, *Kansas City Star*). "How keen he was in his knowledge of human nature" (April 22, 1910, *Hartford Courant*). He had "a deep knowledge of human nature, which made every character that he described live and breathe. He knew men, through and through" (April 22, 1910, [Richmond] *Times Dispatch*). His writings "go to the very heart of human nature and sound the depths of its aspirations, aims, and hopes" (April 22, 1910, *Los Angeles Times*). I could multiply instances of this sort of encomium, but what is interesting here is not so much the notes of appreciation articulated along similar lines as the fact that, in 1910, "human nature" was a vexed concept, as it had been for a hundred years.

This is an inquiry into a central feature of Mark Twain's thinking – his long-standing fascination with human nature – but I am not concerned with deciding whether human beings are socially constructed, culturally conditioned, genetically programmed, divinely sanctioned, or satanically hatched. In one sense, the "truth" of the concept of human nature lies entirely outside the scope of this essay. Nevertheless, if, as William James said, "Truth is what happens to an idea," one can say that Mark Twain profoundly "happened" to the idea of human nature. And he happened to it so variously, even recklessly, so antically and, at times, so irreverently, that it is more than a bit surprising he should have come to be regarded as its great interpreter. Throughout his career, Twain spoke confidently of human nature, in America and abroad, in his own day and, in wholly imaginative terms, in the days of prelapsarian Eden, King's Arthur's Camelot, and the imagined future kingdom of "Eddypus." He inflicted his insights indifferently upon animate and inanimate nature, upon the heavens and the microbe, upon angels and devils, and nearly always with a comic flair that limbered up any rigid conception of the human.

The phrase "human nature" itself is impossibly vague and full of contradictions; in our own day it is immediately suspect. Broadly speaking, human nature is that impulse, condition, or force that somehow explains physical and mental activity, moral or immoral inclination, god-like aspirations or pitiful mortal shortcomings. It is grounded in the assumption that there is a fundamental disposition of character that permits one to speak meaningfully of humanity, or humanness, as an intelligible and universal possession. As such, any notion of human nature is a theory of the human. Merle Curti has identified four fundamental theories of human nature:

1   Human nature is innately constituted apart from experience.
2   Human nature has alleged psychological powers or faculties – perception, memory, judgment, desire.
3   Human nature is essentially empty or formless.
4   Human nature can be identified only through its institutions or products – language, religion, government, etc. (Curti 1980: 4–7)

Revolutionary scientific advances in the twentieth and twenty-first centuries – in genetics, biology, physiology, and psychology – have considerably modified our notion of the human. But for a profile of nineteenth-century attitudes, Curti's description is sufficient, and I would add to his list only the concrete yet indefinite theory of the human that I will call "vernacular." This is the arena of commonsense realism. It tends to elude system and often to express itself in anecdote or familiar observation.

Stray comments on the oddities of human conduct are convincing to the degree that they conform to familiar experience. Mark Twain pondered in imaginative terms competing theories of human nature, but he had a special genius for expressing or dramatizing the vernacular point of view, as in his maxim, "Nothing so needs reforming as other people's habits" (Twain 1894: 197). Wry remarks on human foibles (direct or oblique) do not, and probably cannot, add up to a theory of human nature as such, but they may, as in the case of Mark Twain, reflect a sensibility that was always interested in and often exasperated by his fellow creatures. The following pages attempt to chart in chronological but rather piecemeal fashion Twain's path of curious inquiry into, and his developing views of, human nature.

Twain's Developing Ideas about Human Nature

In the early decades of the nineteenth century, America was heir to an Enlightenment notion of human nature, though by 1835, the year of Samuel Clemens's birth, the inheritance of the eighteenth century was being reshaped by the enthusiasms of men as different from one another as Ralph Waldo Emerson and Andrew Jackson. For the man or woman of the Enlightenment, knowledge and conduct were ultimately referable to right reason; for the Romantic, to subjective intuition. Both notions are detectable in Twain's writings. Furthermore, whatever understanding of human nature the young Sam Clemens may have had, it would almost certainly have been colored in some measure by those surviving ingredients of Calvinism in his own religious training. At length, Clemens was to make his own departure from the religious orthodoxy of his upbringing, but all his life he suffered from an overly tender conscience he would have happily throttled could he but have got his hands on it. In imaginative terms, he did precisely that in "The Facts Concerning the Recent Carnival of Crime in Connecticut" (1876).

Clemens was probably helped along in his thinking by a thorough and impressionable reading of Thomas Paine's *The Age of Reason* while he was a riverboat pilot. That book cultivated in Clemens a fundamentally secular outlook. Sherwood Cummings may well be right in maintaining that it is "nearly impossible to exaggerate the impact of *The Age of Reason* on the mind of Samuel Clemens" (Cummings 1988: 20). Still, one needs to be cautious in assigning too much influence to a single book. Paine may have liberated Twain's thinking, but he did not necessarily revise ingrained attitudes. In his early years, Clemens freely confessed to anti-Catholic and anti-Jewish sentiments, and he frequently demonstrated little understanding or sympathy for people of color. In his "Letters from the Sandwich Islands" (1866), Twain could describe the native Hawaiians and their customs with genuine liking, and he characterized Protestant missionaries as having many good qualities but also as being "bigoted; puritanical; slow; ignorant of all white human nature and natural ways of men" (Twain 1966: 129). He could say these things and still wind up concluding, in light of the earlier native license and feudalism, that "the missionaries have made a better people of this race than they formerly were" (p. 131). Paine may have inspired Mark Twain to think more freely, but he did not prevent Twain from thinking some pretty dumb things at times.

There were, of course, many other influences upon Twain's thinking. Walter Blair and Howard Baetzhold have charted Clemens's ambivalent reactions to W. E. H. Lecky's *History of European Morals* (1869). Gregg Camfield has traced the influence upon the writer of the Scottish Common Sense philosophers. Leland Krauth has convincingly shown just how much Twain wanted to be a card-carrying member of his own Victorian culture. Jason Horn has explored the friendship and the affinities Twain had with William James and with pragmatism. Others have detected more general formative influences in region and characterize Twain as a quintessentially Southern, Western, or Midwestern writer. Any conception of human nature in the nineteenth century was tested by the revolutionary science of the time, a subject Sherwood Cummings has thoroughly explored. Twain read Charles Darwin and Herbert Spencer, and the magazines that dealt with scientific subjects. All in all, he seems to have accepted with relative calm the Darwinian revolution that so disturbed many of his contemporaries.

In short, several competing or contradictory explanations of human nature (what the human creature is and how it came to be that way) coexisted, somewhat uneasily, in the nineteenth-century mind. If Twain's thinking on the matter eventually became more deliberate and acute than that of his contemporaries, it was no less stratified.

Understood as political and social animals, human beings, Twain came to believe, were shaped by training and motivated by the desire for self-approval – the self-esteem achievable only through others' approbation. From a strictly scientific point of view, human nature was a collection of ancient impulses and chemical properties. As the "damned" creation of an all-powerful God, human beings were plagued with a painful moral sense but without the wherewithal to lead the sort of life that would appease it. From the vernacular perspective, human beings had always shared certain foibles, yielded to common temptations, and demonstrated common sympathies.

Nevertheless, Twain was ever alert to alternate frames of reference he could bring into comic conjunction, as, for example, in this 1878 journal entry: "The bronze man on the clock tower once killed a workman with his hammer. It is said he was tried – & acquitted because he did it without premeditation. Not so – he had been getting ready an hour" (Twain 1975: 196). The comedy of this remark consists in the rapid succession of three conceptions of human conduct applied to a distinctly nonhuman event. The bronze man is, of course, a mere mechanism. However, the scientific mate-rialism of the day argued for just such a notion applied broadly to human conduct. All life could be explained in terms of mechanical transformations, with even the mind considered the insignificant motor accompaniment to the operations of the brain. When the bronze man is subjected to judicial review, however, his peers acquit him on the grounds that his act was the result of a sudden upwelling of powerful feel-ings. In other words, his reason was momentarily dethroned, and he was prey to tem-porary insanity. Twain will have none of it. The circumstantial evidence demonstrates that the bronze man took a full hour to prepare himself for the act; the murder was the result of clear-eyed volition. What is remarkable here is how, in a mere squib written for his own amusement, Twain could so easily move between and among these competing frames of reference, and to such diverse comic effect.

Twain was aware that human nature was modified and shaped by all manner of things – race, gender, class, health, climate, superstition, geography, creed, history, economics, opportunity, accident, and the like. He was equally aware that real dif-ferences existed between and among individuals – differences in intelligence, ability, ambition, and temperament, but also in opportunity and circumstance. Nevertheless, variable as human creatures are, there was for him something that was pretty much the same in all of us. That was not necessarily a heartening conviction. In response to the news of President McKinley's assassination, Clemens wrote Joseph Twichell in 1901: "Why, no one is sane, straight along, year in and year out, and we all know it . . . [A]n immense upheaval of feeling can at any time topple us distinctly over the sanity-line for a little while; and then if our form happens to be of the murderous kind we must look out – and so must the spectator" (Twain 1917: vol. 2, 713).

Every person is subject to a certain mental and emotional weather that may well bring out violent feelings. But for Twain there was also something else in humankind, a quality precious and distinctive, decent and forbearing, at times heroic. That common something might be past knowing, but without it the democratic vision that was so obviously a part of Clemens's own nature was not much more than a curious astigmatism. In "The Curious Republic of Gondour" (1875), he argued in favor of women's suffrage and for a genuine meritocracy in which power and influence were distributed according to education and achievement. Later, he felt compelled to move his utopia to heaven. In *Extract from Captain Stormfield's Visit to Heaven* (1909), Twain imagined a true meritocracy, where a man or woman was rewarded not according to firm belief or good deeds, but according to an innate quality that might have come to fruition if the conditions had been right. Behind this late piece of fantasy is the conviction that there is a quality or force that makes us human and implicates us, for good or ill, in a common destiny. Even so, there are no final statements or pat answers about Twain's view of human nature. His humor was so habitual and expansive that it tended to nullify or confound plain statement or philosophical system.

Even in clear-cut instances of intellectual transformation, one must be careful. The way of Twain's thinking was not straight, and it sometimes doubled back on itself. This is probably true for most people, but in a man with the powerful imaginative resources of memory, at times capable of vividly displacing present realities, the situation may be extremely complex. In 1902, Joseph Twichell loaned Twain a copy of Jonathan Edwards's *Freedom of the Will*. At a time in his life when theology, particularly of the Calvinist sort, had ceased to disturb him, he showed an excitable anger towards Edwards. The book left him with a "strange and haunting sensation of having been on a three days' tear with a drunken lunatic. It is years since I have known these sensations" (Twain 1917: vol. 2, 719). We have no reason to doubt that the remembered "sensations" Edwards awakened in him were real enough. The variegated thoughts and feelings of Samuel Clemens concerning human nature, over the course of his 75 years, spread out in space easily enough, but they move forward in time by fits and starts. And always his constitutional temptation to be humorous tends to undercut any clear demarcation of his intellectual development. There is, though, a discernible trend in Clemens's philosophical thinking.

In *Mark Twain and Science*, Sherwood Cummings describes four stages or intellectual "strata" in Clemens's life. His youth until the age of around 17 was markedly Calvinistic. Inspired in part by his reading in Thomas Paine when he was an apprentice riverboat pilot, Clemens became something of a deist. From 1868 to 1870 (the period, not so coincidentally, when he was courting Olivia Langdon) Clemens was a believing Christian – espousing not the severe Christianity of his youth, but a liberal kind expressed by Horace Bushnell and others. The final stratum began shortly after reading Darwin's *Descent of Man* in 1871. During the 1880s Clemens was content to reaffirm, in a quasi-scientific way, his earlier deism and to assume that God, if there is one, has a rational plan for human beings. After 1891 and until his death in 1910, however, there is no trace of belief in a teleological plan for the universe. Occasionally, however, eruptions of earlier feelings break through the strata of settled conviction – sometimes in volcanic seizures (as in his reaction to Jonathan Edwards); as often in bubbling reminiscences of youth.

Twain took on board new ways of thinking, and jettisoned old ones. His peripatetic readings and global travels broadened his vision of human nature. Still, he insisted in his notebook that "Human nature cannot be studied in cities except at a disadvantage – a village is the place. There you can know your man inside & out – in a city you but know his crust; & his crust is usually a lie" (Twain 1975: 503). But the village was by no means a fixed, laboratory environment. Twain's renderings of the village of his youth, Hannibal, Missouri (the St. Petersburg of *Tom Sawyer* and *Huckleberry Finn* and the Dawson's Landing of *Pudd'nhead Wilson*) are different enough from one another to signal real changes in attitude. More important, though, is the apparent fact that he took human nature as a thing worthy of study and understanding.

In his youth, Sam Clemens received religious instruction, sometimes in the Presbyterian church, sometimes in the Methodist. In either he would have experienced the lingering aftertaste of a Puritan dispensation – that God is an all-powerful and jealous presence in everyday life and that boys are pitiful sinners absolutely dependent on his mercy. This passage from Isaac Watts's *Divine Songs Attempted in Easy Language for the Use of Children* (1785) is suggestive:

> Have we not heard what dreadful plagues
>   Are threatened by the Lord,
> To him who breaks his father's law,
>   Or mocks his mother's word?
> What heavy guilt upon him lies!
>   How cursed is his name.
> The raven shall pick out his eyes,
>   And eagles eat the same.

That such fear and self-loathing were an intimate part of Clemens's childhood is evident in chapter 54 of *Life on the Mississippi* ("Past and Present"), when he describes revisiting Hannibal in 1882:

> I presently recognized the house of the father of Lem Hackett (fictitious name). It carried me back more than a generation in a moment, and landed me in the midst of a time when the happenings of life were not the natural and logical results of general laws, but of special orders, and were freighted with very precise and distinct purposes – partly punitive in intent, partly admonitory; and usually local in application.

This Wordsworthian "spot of time" is accompanied by the recollection that Lem Hackett had drowned. That was to be expected, of course. "Being loaded with sin he went to the bottom like an anvil"; it was a clear case of "special judgment" (Twain 1883: 530).

Not very long before Clemens revisited the river for the purposes of gathering material for his Mississippi book, he wrote in his notebook: "Geology. Paleontology.[*sic*] destroyed Genesis" (Twain 1975: 417). By the 1880s, and actually long before, Clemens had come to believe that natural law trumped any special providence from on high. Fear of God's wrath was a survival from his youth. Nevertheless, all his life Clemens contemplated the effects of a guilty conscience, and he tended, if only for the comedy it produced, to measure an infinitely vast cosmos against the more comprehensibly human picture of Adam and Eve in the Garden. In sum, the picture of human nature Clemens eventually articulated was an amalgam of inherited belief, intellectual conviction, and the accumulated insights into human conduct he gleaned from observation and introspection. His confidence about and authority over this subject were acquired by degrees and elaborated, refined, and modified over several decades.

Twain as Humorist, Moralist, and Sage

In order to see more precisely how Twain's thinking about human nature evolved, we might begin by characterizing the conclusions he eventually reached in *What Is Man?* (1906). In that work, an Old Man and a Young Man debate the human condition. The Old Man casually sets forth his major premises – that thought is merely the mechanical assembly of sense impressions and human reason differs from a like process in animals only in degree, not in kind; that we are ruled by an interior master, or conscience, which commands us to gratify its dictates; that all our ideas are attributable to heredity and temperament, or environment and training, and are in no way original with us; and finally, that instinct is merely petrified thought passed on from one generation to the next as inherited habit. Clemens himself thought his philosophy was scandalous. The philosopher Paul Carus found it something of a commonplace and observed that Twain's thinking accorded well enough with the facts of science and psychology. Nonetheless, Carus was puzzled by a peculiarity: Clemens's evident belief that the mind (or "me") was separable from the mechanical operations of thought. A related peculiarity has to do with his insistence on individual "temperament" as part of human nature. It is probably too much to say that his system attained to the rank of philosophy. It is really a piece of social psychology that helped the writer explain to himself and others why human beings act as they do.

In any event, we should not hold Twain too severely to account on the grounds of logical consistency. Neither by training nor inclination was he a full-fledged philosopher. It is probably better to regard him, as Leland Krauth does, as a "Victorian sage" – a public figure who put on display "an interest of a general or speculative kind in what the world is like, where man stands in it, and how he should live" (Krauth 2003: 134). Twain was always something of a moralist, but he was also a humorist – rambunctious, mischievous, and antic. Both those tendencies were suggested in the preface to *The Innocents Abroad* (1869). His purpose in writing the book was "to suggest to the reader how he would likely see Europe and the East if he looked at them with his own eyes instead of the eyes of those who traveled in those countries before him." Contrary to the determinism of his later years, here he purports to elude the burden of history and custom and to see the Old World afresh.

For the sophisticate on the Grand Tour he substitutes the new American abroad, whose Anglo-American biases precondition the way he will see and judge the Old

World. But if he is irritated by guides, sales clerks, and beggars, he is also aggravated by those self-righteous, pretentious fellow travelers he called "pilgrims." Nor does he exempt himself from satire. Twain ridicules the American vandals who chip away at holy monuments for keepsakes, but when he meets the Czar of Russia, he wants to steal his coat. The narrator claims he deplores the poverty of several native peoples and curses their lack of energy and enterprise, but he also commends Europe for its sense of comfort and wishes he could export some of it "to our restless, driving, vitality-consuming marts at home" (Twain 1869: 186). At times, he gives in to profane annoyance with those who would instruct him: " 'Don't – now don't inflict that most in-FERNAL old legend on me anymore today!' There –; I had used strong language after promising I would never do so again; but the provocation was more than human nature could bear. If you had been bored so, . . . you might have even burst into stronger language than I did" (p. 67).

Time and again, Twain recurs to his confident sense of human nature as the basis of his judgment, the warrant of his excessive indignation, and the excuse for his social transgressions. In a review of *The Innocents Abroad*, Howells discerned a quality that set him apart from other humorists: "There is an amount of pure human nature in the book that rarely gets into literature; the depths of our poor unregeneracy – dubious even of the blissfulness of bliss – are sounded by such a simple confession as Mr. Clements [*sic*] makes in telling of his visit to the Emperor of Russia" (Budd 1999: 73). For whatever reasons, Twain believed in a common human nature, and from time to time he announces that belief: "Human nature is *very* much the same all over the world," he says in chapter 23 (Twain 1869: 231). The Israelites "were not always virtuous enough to withstand the seductions of a golden calf," he observes in chapter 46, but then, "Human nature has not changed much since then" (p. 480). Elsewhere, he notes that guides took a special pleasure in showing admiring travelers strange sights: "It is human nature to take delight in exciting admiration. It is what prompts children to . . . 'show off' when company is present" (p. 290). Human nature is an explanatory principle for Twain: it accounts for human vanity, cowardice, pettiness, and irritability; it excuses the narrator's occasional outbursts of profanity and his more than occasional lapses in decorum and judgment. The operant notion of a shared humanity is the basis for the reader's identification with the Twain persona – not a condescending guide on this pilgrimage, but a companionable presence whose peculiar way of seeing the world combines with a sense of humor that never seems forced or artificial.

In an 1870 letter to Will Bowen, Clemens wrote: "I am too old & have moved about too much, & rubbed against too many people not to know human beings as well as we used to know 'boils' from 'breaks' " (Twain 1995: 52).[1] This boast was underwritten by his diverse experience and not by any theory. In 1871, however, he read Charles Darwin's *Descent of Man* and may have recognized that there were still other ways to understand human behavior. In any event, in his next travel book, *Roughing It* (1872), he sometimes plays the role of a homespun naturalist cataloguing the wonders west of the Rockies, and freely mingling tall-tale humor and amusing endorsements of the ways of Providence with documentary fact. It is too much to say that Twain meant to play his own version of Darwin beyond the Great Divide. He was content to dismiss the Goshoot Indians on those grounds, however: "The Bushmen and our Goshoots are manifestly descended from the self-same gorilla, or kangaroo, or Norway rat, whichever animal-Adam the Darwinians trace them to" (Twain 1872: 147). On the other hand, something more interesting (and personal) than his predictable rant about the Noble Red Man may have been at work in the book as well.

In the margin of his copy of *The Descent of Man*, where Darwin discusses the intellectual faculties of animals, Clemens wrote, "War horses learn the bugle notes. Fire horses rush at the fire alarm" (quoted in Cummings 1988: 33). Similarly, in *Roughing It*, Twain interpolates an apparently invented recollection of hiring a horse recently retired from pulling a milk wagon in order to take a young lady for a drive. To impress her, he pretended that he owned the horse, but the ingrained behavior of the animal gave him away. It "delivered imaginary milk at a hundred and sixty-two different domiciles . . . and finally brought up at a dairy depot and refused to budge" (1872: 545). Twain also describes horses that have been raised above the range of running water and satisfied their thirst by eating dewy leaves and grasses. When they were removed to lower elevations and presented with a pail of water, they tried to "take a bite out of the fluid, as if it were a solid" (p. 546). Such is the force of training and habit.

It was instinct that permitted the three miners' horses to discover shelter in a snow-storm, while Twain, Ballou, and Ollendorff, sensing the "battle of life was done," rededicate what remains of their sad lives to reforming their characters, and swear off their bad habits. They awake the next morning to discover they are not 15 steps from a stage station, but are now saddled with their resolve to lead better lives. Within a couple of hours each man has guiltily resumed his wicked ways. Here Twain is the simpleton, but just as often he plays the role of a droll and peripatetic cultural anthropologist with saddle sores. In Utah he discovers a patriarchal, polygamous society in the Mormons; in Hawaii there are remnants of a matrilineal, polyandrous society among the Kanakas. The Mormons are guided by the ungrammatical and infelicitous but otherwise essentially Christian teachings of the *Book of Mormon*; the Kanakas are ruled by superstition and a feudal aristocracy. The Chinese are ancestor worshippers and for that reason resist progress, but they are also efficient, industrious, literate, kind, and well-meaning, and he objects to their ill-treatment by the "worst class of white men." But the Native American, and particularly the Goshoot, is Twain's own scapegoat. He describes the nature of Mormons, Hawaiians, and the Chinese as shaped by creed and custom, but not so the Goshoots. They are innately timid beggars: "wherever one finds an Indian tribe he has only found Goshoots more or less modified by circumstances and surroundings – but Goshoots after all" (Twain 1872: 149). As Twain contemplated the motive springs of human conduct, however, he became less and less satisfied with racial explanations. A case in point is his treatment of Injun Joe in *The Adventures of Tom Sawyer* (1876).

Tom and Huck both believe Joe to be the consort of Satan himself. For others, Joe's particular brand of cruelty is attributable to the Indian side of his character. The Welshman says of Joe's plan to slit the widow's nostrils and notch her ears, "white men don't take that sort of revenge. But an Injun! That's a different matter altogether" (Twain 1876: 230). Even Joe says of his desire for revenge upon Dr. Robinson, "The Injun blood ain't in me for nothing" (p. 90). Though Twain was originally content to explain Joe's evil character as a product of race, he apparently emphatically rejected that explanation in revision. Most of Joe's motivation for revenge has to do with his sense of wounded pride. The Widow Douglas's husband once had Joe arrested for vagrancy, but Joe adds, "And that ain't all! It ain't all! It ain't a millionth part of it! He had me *horsewhipped*! – horsewhipped in front of the jail, like a nigger! – with all the town looking on! HORSEWHIPPED! – do you understand?" (p. 223). Twain inserted this passage in the manuscript, and the punctuation alone (seven exclamation points) signals the emphasis he wanted to give it.[2]

Twain had moved beyond the facile racial explanations concerning Native Americans he revealed in *Roughing It*. Joe's motives are different in degree but not in kind from Tom Sawyer's own desire to be the hero of his own life. Tom is not by temperament violent, but when he feels that he is not appreciated, he wants to make people sorry that they treated him so meanly by running away, getting in trouble, or even dying (so long as he can attend the funeral). For all that, the reader is never tempted to believe Tom will not turn out well. Despite Aunt Polly's fretting, not for a moment does she actually believe that Tom's immortal soul is in peril or that she has been morally lax in her guardianship. She may assent to notions of innate depravity and eternal damnation when they issue from the pulpit on Sunday, but better instincts prevail in the household.

What keeps Tom in the reader's affections and establishes his good nature is the boy's emotional and intellectual involvement in social relations. Unlike Injun Joe, who is proud but essentially anti-social, Tom desires the approbation of the world. The village of St. Petersburg, despite the failure of its institutions (from Sunday school to the Cadets of Temperance) to inculcate right feelings in the boy, has its claims upon him. Tom "acts up," but he also feels the pangs of a guilty conscience when he causes worry or distress. Twain's interest in the subject of conscience became deeper and more thoughtful soon after *Tom Sawyer* was published, but even here it is apparent that he understood the origins of conscience to be rooted in the social.

As Howells said in his review of the novel, "The story is a wonderful study of the boy-mind . . . and in this lies its great charm and its universality, for boy-nature, however human nature varies, is the same everywhere" (Budd 1999: 157–8). Twain makes it clear that Tom Sawyer is ever mindful of the sort of self-respect that can only be conferred (or withheld) by others. The boy is shaped by the common, and rather adult, desire to be thought well of, and in this sense conforms to the analysis of human nature Twain articulated in later years. In some measure, the works of the 1880s and 1890s at once advance and dramatize his thinking on this subject. Or, to put the point another way, many of his narratives were conceived as pragmatic tests in which he might explore how certain characters would act under given circumstances; how they *did* act, in turn, confirmed his views of the human condition.

Twain as Determinist

During the 1880s and perhaps before, Twain was inching his way toward Hank Morgan's bold pronouncement in *A Connecticut Yankee* that "Training is everything." But this conclusion was reached by degrees, and his reasoning in that direction was more nuanced than has sometimes been supposed. If, as he said in "Corn-Pone Opinions" (c.1901), the chief desire of men and women was self-approval, but that approval would be attained only through the approval of others, then the human animal was enmeshed in a social order that was in many ways unnatural. In *A Tramp Abroad*, contrary to a natural animal instinct, the German student duelists do not quail before the imminent blow of a sword, nor do they wince when attended to by the surgeon. These are clear instances of the force of usage and custom, eventuating, through training, in habit. Habit is stronger than impulse, reason, or law. What is more, as a part of human nature, it is an ally to social stability but an enemy to democratic reform. Habit alone, wrote William James, "is what keeps us all within the bounds of ordinance, and saves the children of fortune from the envious uprisings of the poor. It alone prevents the hardest and most repulsive walks of life from being deserted by those brought up to tread therein" (James 1890: vol. 1, 121). It was not the church or Merlin but ingrained habit that Hank Morgan was really fighting when he tried to reform sixth-century England overnight. Hank's failure was due to his eagerness to transform a nation, and his failure taught him a lesson previously announced by Herbert Spencer: "the difficulty of understanding that human nature, though indefinitely modifiable, can be modified but very slowly; and that all laws and institutions and appliances which count on getting from it, within a short time, much better results than present ones, will inevitably fail" (Spencer 1972: 110).

On the other hand, raw instincts and swarming impulses, unchecked and disorganized, make individual and collective life chaotic. Habits may come in conflict with one another and limit one's possibilities, but they also permit intelligent choice. More to the point, habit is formed along the lines of action in the world, though it may persist as blind custom that is deleterious, not to say absurd. The Shepherdsons and Grangerfords indulge in a feud long after the original reason for it has been forgotten. In *Life on the Mississippi* Twain is fascinated by the effects of progress after the war, but he is also disturbed by the continuance of noxious customs, such as the burial practices in and around New Orleans. On the other hand, extraordinary experiences quickly become familiar, even routine, and he is intrigued to find that during the war the citizens of Vicksburg quickly adapted to the constant shelling as a "commonplace." Similarly, in *The Prince and the Pauper*, Tom Canty soon quits being uneasy about the attendants who dress and feed him; and in *A Connecticut Yankee* Hank Morgan, the principled republican, detests all manner of aristocratic pretense but nonetheless warms to his reputation as "The Boss" and insists on his privileges.

If, as Twain had been stressing from the early 1880s, man is merely a machine automatically functioning in response to outside influences, then a change in "habitat" (Twain 1906: 60) will result in a change in the sort of life one may lead. For that reason, perhaps, Twain was fond of contriving plots around dramatically altered circumstances. The adventitious exchange of social station between Tom Canty and Edward Tudor allowed him to reveal commonalties in the boys that in themselves argued against aristocratic privilege, but it also permitted him to install in Edward the realization that "the world is made wrong, kings should go to school to their own laws, at times, and so learn mercy" (Twain 1881: 330). The exchange of identities in *Pudd'nhead Wilson* is more deliberate. Roxana, by swapping the infants Chambers and Tom Driscoll, hoped to cheat fate, and indeed the altered circumstances and their training fashion the boys' characters along predictable lines. Of greater interest, though, is Roxy's disclosure to the haughty and conniving Tom Driscoll that he is her son:

> For days he [Tom] wandered in lonely places, thinking, thinking, thinking – trying to get his bearings. It was new work. If he met a friend, he found that the habit of a lifetime had in some mysterious way vanished – his arm hung limp, instead of involuntarily extending the hand for a shake. It was the "nigger" in him asserting its humility. (Twain 1894: 123)

Tom, and Roxana too, may explain human nature according to the inheritance of "blood," but Twain never does. From the beginning, he has made it clear that race is a legal fiction, though slavery and racism are surely "habitats" to be reckoned with. The narrator notes that Tom imagines his fundamental character has changed with the news of his racial identity, but he adds, "the main structure of his character was not changed and could not be changed. One or two very important features of it were altered, and in time effects would result from this, if opportunity offered – effects of a quite serious nature, too" (p. 125). One of those effects is that Tom is eventually sold down the river as a slave; but Twain would have us understand that Tom (a.k.a. Chambers) was "black" because he was sold and not the other way round. In the published text, Tom docilely accepts this judgment, but in excised portions of the manuscript the author gave Tom's conflicted sense of himself an edge and a purpose:

> Whence came that in him which was high, and whence that which was base? That which was high came from either blood, and was the monopoly of neither color; but that which was base was the *white* blood in him debased by the brutalizing effects of a long-drawn heredity of slave-owning, with the habit of abuse which the possession of irresponsible power always creates and perpetuates, by a law of human nature. So he argued. (See Twain 1980: 191)

Had Twain retained this passage, it would have nicely illustrated his conviction that instinct is merely *"petrified thought*; solidified and made inanimate by habit" (Twain 1906: 101).

In the case of *Huckleberry Finn*, Twain committed himself to a different sort of inquiry into the sources of human nature. Because Huck was not formed by the improving influences of school, family, or church, and had at best an uneven involvement in the society inhabited by Tom and his comrades, his character was not the product of any systematic moral training. Even the widow and Miss Watson's efforts are largely devoted to housetraining the boy. In the eyes of the "sivilized" community, he is a social pariah – ignorant, idle and shiftless, immoral and corrupting – but that was not what Twain had in mind when he described Huck in *Tom Sawyer* as "conscience-free" (Twain 1876: 120). Instead, the author found in Huck's point of view an original way to satirize the absurdity and cruelty of established institutions and behavior, whether they come in the form of funerals, prayers, feuds, churchgoing, popular entertainment, domestic manners, or lynchings. In Huck's eyes, the very authority of civilization is evidence of its social and ethical correctness. By the same token, his usually failed attempts to understand, admire, or emulate the world that had for some time excluded him, serve for the reader as a stinging rebuke of that world. Huck's persistent questioning of Buck Grangerford about the nature and origin of the feud underscores the futility of clannish pride. When Huck "sours" on Miss Emmeline, he tries to atone by "sweating" out a verse or two as his tribute to her departed soul; he is disappointed, but we as readers are gratified that he can't "make it go" (Twain 1885: 141).

In *Huckleberry Finn*, Twain gave Huck certain moral sympathies (a "sound heart" he once called it) and a tender but confused conscience, but they are far from trustworthy. Huck trembles more over the fate of the supposed drunk at the circus than he worries about Boggs. On the *Walter Scott* he is eager to save Jim Turner's life, though it is not clear that this scoundrel deserves such anxious care. When Huck sees the duke and king tarred and feathered, he feels kind of "ornery," though they had only recently betrayed him by selling Jim. He is grateful for the "good turn" the doctor does Jim by advising the mob not to be any rougher on him than they have to. His conscience bothers him when he thinks he is causing Tom to become a low-down abolitionist. In chapters 16 and 31, Huck resolves to turn Jim in, and he feels light as a "feather." He attributes his failure to act on those resolutions as the result of cowardice and insufficient Sunday-school instruction; instead, Huck commits himself to a life of "wickedness" and decides to "go to hell" by stealing Jim out of slavery. That damning transgression is just for starters: "if I could think up anything worse, I would do that, too; because as long as I was in, and in for good, I might as well go whole hog" (Twain 1885: 272). Far from becoming the moral hero of the book at this point, Huck has quelled his moral sense for the moment and, in a manner reminiscent of the narrator of "Facts Concerning the Recent Carnival of Crime in Connecticut" who kills his conscience and goes on a crime spree, looks forward to outdoing the freeing of Jim by committing unspeakable acts in the future. These are the thoughts of a

13-year-old boy and should not be given much credence. On the other hand, neither should one think of Huck as a Rousseau-like noble savage or necessarily credit him with making a moral decision that somehow speaks powerfully on the possibilities of national life.

Twain's Final Thoughts on the Damned Human Race

Part of the genius of *Huckleberry Finn* is that Twain could simultaneously satirize the mores of life along the river through the untutored reactions of his title character and provide a glimpse into the nature of a boy largely uncontaminated by outside influences. At the same time, though the very concept of human nature is a large and unwieldy abstraction, Twain was able to dramatize a palpable sense of life as lived at that time and in that place. The author anchored his narrative in the boy's idiom, supplied telling descriptions of weather, scenery, and various types of Southerners in Huck's voice, and adjusted his own adult convictions to fit a child's understanding. Sometimes, however, Twain's desire to characterize human nature in this novel introduces certain improbabilities. In chapter 26, for example, when the Wilks girls serve supper, they keep apologizing for it. Huck comments on "all that kind of humbug talky-talk, just the way people always does at supper, you know" (Twain 1885: 221). This remark amusingly illustrates Twain's principle that all people desire self-approval but must rely on the approval of others to obtain it, for the girls' apologies are transparent bids for compliments. The problem is that nothing in Huck's background would permit him to make this sort of generalization; certainly the Widow Douglas did not apologize for anything she fed to Huck nor, we assume, did Pap. The point to be made here, though, is that Twain's desire to inspect and comment on the human race also pushed him toward generalized, which is to say less particularized, dramatic fictions. His situations, themes, and characters tended to become deracinated conceptions. Many of his stories became fables, fantasies, science fictions, all describing a wider and wider arc of human experience, but unmoored to plausible human occasions.

"The Man That Corrupted Hadleyburg" is a case in point. This familiar tale of a mysterious stranger tempting and corrupting an American village is a fable of human greed and hypocrisy. It focuses on Mary and Edward Richards, but their experience is a "plagiarism" of the 18 other families who see the opportunity to claim unearned riches. Twain was explicit on this common human desire in his essay on Paul Bourget's *Outre-Mer: Impressions of America*, a book highly critical of American materialism: "The world seems to think that the love of money is 'American'; and that the mad desire to get suddenly rich is 'American.' I believe that both of these things are merely and broadly human, not American monopolies at all" (Twain 1992b: 173). Hadleyburg could be almost any American village, and its citizens are representative of the world at large. The town, like the individuals within it, is vain and self-satisfied, but it relies on the envy of neighboring towns to corroborate its inflated sense of self-regard. The intellectual firmness of the story gives it the feel of moral parable, but it is saturated with unanswered questions and narrative improbabilities. We do not know how the injured stranger could have been insulted by an entire town, and even the stranger's calculated revenge is a disappointment to him because, to the end, he believes that the Richardses are blameless. Edward Richards's deathbed confession is a sincere act of atonement, but it is prompted by a mistaken note of sarcasm he discerned in Reverend Burgess's note to him. Even the local cynic, Halliday, who delights in the town's come-uppance, does not suspect the true depth of Hadleyburg's corruption. The announced moral of the tale is "Lead Us Into Temptation," and indeed the story is an indictment of self-righteousness, unearned because untested by experience. On the other hand, if Twain meant to impart a moral lesson that had application in the actual lives of men and women, it is difficult to discover in the example of Hadleyburg how effective that lesson might be. Amid the jeering, sardonic taunts, and self-recrimination of the townsfolk and the tangle of misunderstandings that seem to multiply rather than diminish, the possibilities of coherent moral conduct seem obscure at best. If, on the other hand, Twain meant to study the human animal under controlled, albeit imagined, laboratory conditions, he succeeded in masterly fashion.

Mark Twain had entered his so-called dark period, but his way was lighted by a perpetual fascination with human nature. In *My Mark Twain*, William Dean Howells noted that, even after he had experienced personal losses, Clemens remained a curious observer of his kind: "Life had always amused him, and in the resurgence of its interests after his sorrow had ebbed away he was again deeply interested in the world and in the human race, which, though damned, abounded in subjects of curious inquiry" (Howells 1910: 91). In several of the writings of his last years, Twain continued to speculate on the workings of human nature, but under more and more fantastic circumstances – in bits of future history ("The Secret History of Eddypus"), dream visions ("Captain Stormfield's Visit to Heaven"), dialogues (*What Is Man?* and "Little Bessie"), unlikely encounters (the *Mysterious Stranger* manuscripts), science fictions ("The Great Dark" and "Three Thousand Years Among the Microbes"), epistles from Satan ("Letters from the Earth") and diaries (of Adam and Eve, but also of Methuselah). He continued to preach his "gospel" of human nature, but in important ways he pressed beyond it as well. Because all perceptions are new to Adam and Eve, there is no question of inherited habit or prior training, and they discover – one might almost say they stumble on – their own humanity by trial and error. When Captain Stormfield enters heaven (at the wrong port, it must be added), all the expectations about the hereafter that had been trained into him from an early age prove comically irrelevant. He finds himself in the company of one-legged blue people, discovers that the planet Earth is so insignificant that it is referred to as "the Wart," and – perhaps most surprisingly – learns that heaven is a true meritocracy, where a man is judged by the greatness he had in him, even though circumstances did not contrive to allow that greatness to flourish. To the last, Twain continued to scold a God he did not believe in and to populate a Heaven that did not exist. Although, in its baseness and profligacy, the human race was undoubtedly "damned" and vastly lower than the lowest animals, he extenuated his kind from absolute contempt, even against the abuse he himself heaped on it. For all that, part of Mark Twain's legacy has to do with what he taught his fellow creatures about themselves and the exasperated but still congenial way he had of doing it. William Lyon Phelps, writing shortly after the author's death, in *The American Review of Reviews* (June 1910), thought those lessons would last a very long time: "The humor of Mark Twain is American in its point of view, . . . but it is universal in that it deals not with passing phenomena, or with matters of temporary interest, but with essential and permanent aspects of human nature."

NOTES

1 Twain refers here to his and Bowen's knowledge of the river. A "boil" is an eddy, and a "break" is a streak on the water that may indicate a snag or some other submerged danger.

2 See Twain 1982, MS p. 713.

REFERENCES AND FURTHER READING

Baender, Paul (1973). "Introduction." In Mark Twain, *What Is Man? and Other Philosophical Writings*, 1–34. Berkeley: University of California Press.

Baetzhold, Howard G. (1970). *Mark Twain and John Bull: The British Connection*. Bloomington: Indiana University Press.

Blair, Walter (1960). *Mark Twain and "Huck Finn."* Berkeley: University of California Press.

Budd, Louis J., ed. (1999). *Mark Twain: The Contemporary Reviews*. Cambridge, UK: Cambridge University Press.

Camfield, Gregg (1994). *Sentimental Twain: Samuel Clemens in the Maze of Moral Philosophy*. Philadelphia: University of Pennsylvania Press.

Carus, Paul (1913). "Mark Twain's Philosophy." *Monist* 23, 181–223.

Cummings, Sherwood (1988). *Mark Twain and Science: Adventures of a Mind*. Baton Rouge: Louisiana State University Press.

Curti, Merle (1980). *Human Nature in American Thought*. Madison: University of Wisconsin Press.

Dewey, John (1922). *Human Nature and Conduct: An Introduction to Social Psychology*. New York: H. Holt and Co.

Gribben, Alan (1972). "Mark Twain, Phrenology and the 'Temperaments': A Study of Pseudo-Scientific Influence." *American Quarterly* 24, 45–68.

Horn, Jason Gary (1996). *Mark Twain and William James: Crafting a Free Self*. Columbia: University of Missouri Press.

Howells, William Dean (1910). *My Mark Twain: Reminiscences and Criticisms*. New York: Harper & Bros.

James, William (1890). *Principles of Psychology*, 2 vols. New York: Henry Holt & Co.

Krauth, Leland (2003). *Mark Twain and Company: Six Literary Relations*. Athens: University of Georgia Press.

Spencer, Herbert (1972). *Herbert Spencer on Social Evolution*, ed. J. D. Y. Peel. Chicago: University of Chicago Press.

Tuckey, John (1972). "Introduction." In *Mark Twain's Fables of Man*, 1–29. Berkeley: University of California Press.

Twain, Mark (1917). *Mark Twain's Letters*, 2 vols., ed. Albert Bigelow Paine. New York: Harper and Bros.

Twain, Mark (1966). *Mark Twain's Letters from Hawaii*, ed. A. Grove Day. New York: Appleton-Century.

Twain, Mark (1975). *Mark Twain's Notebooks and Journals*, vol. 2: *1877–1883*, ed. Frederick Anderson, Lin Salamo, and Bernard L. Stein. Berkeley: University of California Press.

Twain Mark (1980). *Pudd'nhead Wilson and Those Extraordinary Twins*. New York: Norton.

Twain, Mark (1982). *The Adventures of Tom Sawyer, a Facsimile of the Author's Holograph Manuscript*, 2 vols., intr. Paul Baender. Frederick, Md., and Washington DC: University Publications of America.

Twain, Mark (1995). *Mark Twain's Letters*, vol. 4: *1870–1871*, ed. Victor Fischer and Michael Frank. Berkeley: University of California Press.

Wagner-Martin, Linda (1993). *"What Is Man?"* In J. R. LeMaster and James D. Wilson, eds., *The Mark Twain Encyclopedia*, 73–5. New York: Garland.

3

Mark Twain and America's Christian Mission Abroad

Susan K. Harris

"To the Person Sitting in Darkness," which Mark Twain published in the *North American Review* in 1901, attacks Western imperialism as it was manifesting itself in South Africa, China, Cuba, and the Philippines. It names its villains – McKinley, Joseph Chamberlain, the Kaiser, the Czar – and their instruments, especially the Reverend William Ament, a Congregationalist minister who was affiliated with the American Board of Commissioners for Foreign Missions. Although the essay encountered hostility from a number of pro-imperialist groups, the most outraged were the missionaries, who took it as a direct attack on their program to bring Christianity to the heathen abroad. And even though subsequent readers have suggested that Twain was using the missionary enterprise as an example of an imperialist project rather than as the core of his attack, their perception may have been the right one. By the start of the twentieth century, Twain, whose feelings about religion generally and about missionaries specifically had always been ambivalent, may have felt that "imperialist" and "Christian" had come to mean the same thing.

This essay will examine the intersection of American Christianity and imperialism in Mark Twain's writings of the late nineteenth and early twentieth centuries. I am particularly interested in the ways that Twain perceived the confluence of two hitherto separate strains of American life: Protestant Christian identity and capitalist identity. I argue that the US entry into the global economy by way of imperialist expansion had a profound effect on Twain's understanding of the underlying agenda of American Christianity, especially as manifested by the missionary movement. As with so many of his ideas, Twain projected this understanding in terms of an inside/outside paradigm. Inside US borders, the American Christian had a limited usefulness; but outside US borders, American Christianity revealed itself as the core of what later generations would call the "ugly American."

The American Christian

The national Christian is, of course, a legacy from the New England settlers, the Calvinists whom later generations saw as the national progenitors and to whose religious ideology we are indebted for the idea of American exceptionalism. In this redaction of white settlement the nation is descended from Protestant radicals who fled England in order to practice religious freedom and who subsequently saw themselves as an exemplar to other, still-benighted, nations. Iconized in the nineteenth century, when US writers and historians, largely from New England, were creating founding narratives, this became the dominant story of American settlement, the one which Samuel Clemens imbibed as he grew up – despite the fact that the Mississippi River valley in which he was reared had been settled as much by French Catholics as by British Protestants.

One of the legacies of this theocentric imaginary has been a national obsession with the idea of Christian communal perfectionism and, as a corollary, a national debate over ways and means of achieving that state. From a local perspective, confined to national borders and, largely, to Protestant sects, this has often taken the form of a debate over the moral character of the national subject in relation to current events. Although the debate's specifically literary manifestation begins with early Republican writers such as Catharine Sedgwick, it is probably best known through the slavery issue, for instance through Stowe's *Uncle Tom's Cabin* or Douglass's *The Heroic Slave*, which focused on the values marking the exemplary Christian as they were manifested in furious arguments over the moral legitimacy of slavery. Framed, generally, in terms of binary opposites, the arguments tended to pit "good" Christians against "bad" ones, each side attempting to expose the opposition as inherently un-Christian. At the heart of the debate was the question of how Christian identity mapped onto American identity and how the rhetoric of American Christianity figured a generic "American Christian." For the citizens of the nineteenth century, especially the legatees of the New England founding narrative, the national Christian became the figure representing the virtues of rationalist democracy fused with the moral zeal of the Protestant believer.[1] After the Civil War, when the explicit need for moral heroism should have faded, xenophobic responses among white American Protestants to new influxes of immigrants and to the appeal to Catholic voters of an increasingly corrupt Tammany Hall revitalized the figure. By the turn into the twentieth century, that population saw the figure of the national Christian as a representative of political, economic, social, and religious order.

The US as an Imperial Power

Just as this figure stabilized within national borders, however, the United States emerged onto the world stage as an economic and military power. The twentieth century brought with it not only US expansion beyond national borders during the

Spanish–American War, but also widely reported news about the complicity of missionaries in the mayhem following the Boxer Rebellion in China, events that introduced a new element into the debate about the national Christian. Two men in particular came to represent these issues: the Reverend William Ament, who demanded that the Chinese pay reparations for damages to property belonging to Christians of 13 times the property's worth, and General Frederick Funston, who masterminded the capture of Emilio Aguinaldo and countenanced American military torture of Filipino insurgents. In both cases, press coverage highlighted the suffering inflicted on noncombatants, especially the impoverishment of Chinese peasants forced to pay Ament's fines and the torture of civilians and priests in the Philippines (which included the "water cure," in which the victim was forced to swallow gallons of water, after which a soldier jumped on his stomach until he either confessed or died). Although the official line was, in President McKinley's words, that Americans had a duty "to educate the Filipinos, and uplift and civilize and Christianize them, and by God's grace do the very best we could by them" (Millis 1931: 383–4), the brutality the United States exhibited in these initial forays onto the world stage shook many citizens' faith in the nature of American exceptionalism and the moral standing of the American Christian. Removed from local contexts – issues specific to internal US concerns – the American Christian looked very different when he appeared on foreign soil. As they absorbed the information that their military practiced torture and that their elected representatives approved it, Americans were forced to confront the possibility that the American Christian might be a force for evil rather than for good. Revelations of complicity between the missionaries, the military, and capitalist interests further suggested the difficulty of distinguishing between the national Christian and the national corporation. Many Americans suddenly woke up to the fact that the national narrative about saving souls and bringing the blessings of democracy to oppressed peoples was a way of announcing readiness to compete with the colonial powers for economic dominance of resource-rich and/or strategically located third world countries.

Mark Twain and Missionaries

In 1901, in the wake of public protests over "To the Person Sitting in Darkness," Mark Twain told the German writer Rudolph Lindau that

> I have been criticizing the American missionaries in China . . . and have gotten myself into hot water with the clergy and the other goody-goody people, but I am enjoying it more than I have ever enjoyed hot water before. Indeed I think I am having a very good time. I detest a missionary and his trade, and in writing about those missionaries in China I have not been able altogether to conceal this feeling, and perhaps I have not tried very hard. (To Rudolph Lindau, April 24, 1901, Mark Twain Papers [henceforth MTP])

Jim Zwick, the pre-eminent investigator concerning Mark Twain's relationship to anti-imperialism, has demonstrated the plenitude of writings, both published and unpublished, public and private, in which Twain expressed his anti-imperialist sentiments. However, a missing piece of the picture, it seems to me, is where Twain weighed in on America's Christian mission. At the beginning of the Spanish–American War, in the face of his family's opposition, Clemens himself supported US intervention in Cuba, writing to his publishers, "From the beginning the family have been rabid opponents of this war & I've been just the other way," and complaining that "I come across no end of people who simply can *not* see the Cuban situation as America sees it – people who cannot believe that *any* conduct can justify one nation in interfering with the domestic affairs of another" (to Chatto & Windus, May 13, 1898, MTP). By 1900, however, he had made a 180-degree turn, recognizing that the rhetoric of democratic solidarity with aspiring third world democracies actually announced America's intention to make their economies work to its benefit. Recognizing too that the national citizen was by this time inextricable from the national Christian, he bitterly excoriated his countrymen for violent exploitation in the name of benevolent Christianity. Consequently, even though Twain's attack on missionaries began in explicit reference to Ament's exploitation of the Chinese, it did not stop there. Rather, the events of 1898–1905 convinced him that Ament was merely representative. The historical binary between "good" and "bad" Christians within the nation's borders made no sense once American Christians left their home shores. By the middle of the twentieth century's first decade, when Twain said "missionary" he was referring not to a particular profession, but rather to the generic American Christian as he existed abroad.

Despite his pronouncement to Lindau that he detested missionaries, Twain's treatment of them in his writing wobbles, often depending on whether he is figuring their activities within or beyond US borders. For example, in "The United States of Lyncherdom," also written in 1901 (although not published until 1923), one of Twain's solutions to the epidemic of lynchings in the United States is to bring missionaries home from China to deal with the American roughs. He argues that the missionaries' experience facing mobs overseas has equipped them for the task of facing homegrown terrorists, and, most importantly, he judges that the Americans need to be converted far more than do the Chinese. Although the suggestion that experiences in foreign fields have equipped missionaries to confront their compatriots has ironic undertones, these are balanced by a tone of equal earnestness. Twain argues that the Chinese are generally considered "excellent people, honest, honorable, industrious, trustworthy, kind-hearted, and all that" (Twain 1992b: 484), and concludes that they do not need the "benefits" of Western civilization, whereas our compatriots do. This vision of Chinese character not only directly contradicts the understanding of Chinese culture prevalent among Americans at the beginning of the twentieth century, it illustrates Twain's own perception of what, exactly, missionaries do when they operate in countries where neither Christianity nor Western sensibilities prevail. Here, "missionizing" is not limited to the theological; it is not simply a question of convincing pagans that Jesus is their savior. Rather, here "Christianizing" really means "Westernizing," changing converts' entire value systems and, as a consequence, their way of life. In "The United States of Lyncherdom" Twain suggests that missionaries might be useful at home, where their work would consist of convincing the already Westernized and putatively Christianized that they were doing wrong within their own cultural values, but he sees that they are not needed in China, where a different set of values undergirds a wholly viable culture.

One important point here is that Twain sees Chinese culture positively even though it is not Western – that he has come far enough from American ethno-/Christocentrism to value the cultural "Other." Most importantly for our purposes, however, is that we see here the beginnings of Twain's revised understanding of the role of American Christians both "inside" and "outside" the United States. In a paradigm where geopolitical borders also come to represent cultural borders, Twain sees that the missionaries, repatriated (brought back "inside"), would fall into the historical pattern of representing the "good" Christian to the lynchers' "bad" one. Outside US borders, however, conversion ceases to be the relatively simple matter of a change of heart and becomes the far more complex matter of destroying another people's culture.

Twain had been wobbling about missionary complicity in American-initiated cultural shifts at least since the writing of his 1866 letters from the Sandwich Islands for the Sacramento *Union*, later to be revised and incorporated into *Roughing It*. In the letters he contains his ambivalence within the humorous, his contrasting of pre- and post-contact native life underwritten by his conviction that this Hawaiian Eden had been excessively bloodthirsty and that missionizing was therefore a good thing. His rhythmic, lyrical comparisons and contrasts present the old religion humorously and the missionaries ambivalently, but in the end the missionaries win out. In a set sketch describing the ruin of a "heathen temple," Twain first evokes "those old bygone days when the simple child of nature, yielding momentarily to sin when sorely tempted, acknowledged his error . . . and came forward with noble frankness and offered up his grandmother as an atoning sacrifice." He then continues evoking the days

> long, long before the missionaries braved a thousand privations to come and make [the natives] permanently miserable by telling them how beautiful and how blissful a place heaven is, and how nearly impossible it is to get there . . . [the days when the missionary] showed [the native] what rapture it is to work all day long for fifty cents to buy food for next day with, as compared with fishing for pastime and lolling in the shade through eternal Summer, and eating of the bounty that nobody labored to provide but Nature. (Twain 1972: 41)

Later in this passage, however, Twain segues into describing how, "if these mute stones could speak, what tales they would tell, what pictures they could describe, of fettered victims writhing under the knife; of dense masses of dusky forms straining forward out of the gloom, with eager and ferocious faces lit up by the weird light of sacrificial fires." Moreover in other, less formulaic, passages, he celebrates the literacy levels among natives that are also the results of missionary labor and defends American missionaries against a British prelate's accusation that contact with them had caused a decline in the moral and religious condition of the native islanders (p. 102).

At the same time, however, Twain's own listing of the missionaries' attributes ranges from "pious," "hard-working," "self-sacrificing," and "devoted to the well-being of this people and the interests of Protestantism" to "bigoted," "puritanical," "uncharitable," and "ignorant" (Twain 1972: 101–2). He also recognizes that "the great bulk of the wealth, the commerce, the enterprise and the spirit of progress in the Sandwich Islands centers in the Americans" (p. 104). In the end – for all his ambivalence – Twain endorses the missionaries because they have inculcated Western values, figured here as clothing, literacy, and a Protestant work ethic. In a concise summary of the effects of American missionaries on the Sandwich Islands, Twain argues that in contrast to the British prelate's efforts to import a "Reformed Catholic [i.e. Anglican] Church" into the islands, "the moneyed strength of these islands – their agriculture, their commerce, their mercantile affairs – is in the hands of Americans – republicans; the religious power of the country is wielded by Americans – republicans; the whole people are saturated with the spirit of democratic Puritanism, and they are – republicans" (p. 118).

Despite his dislike for the missionaries' narrow self-righteousness – and his wistful evocations of a carefree paradise lost – for Twain the American missionaries have been the harbingers of American capitalism, a development of which, in 1866 (and especially given his California readership) he heartily approves. The fact that they have substituted a benevolent Christianity for a paganism that he understood as based in warlike and bloodthirsty values made it all the better.

More than 30 years intervene between Twain's Sandwich Islands letters and "To the Person Sitting in Darkness," decades in which Samuel Clemens evolved from a fugitive from the Midwest into an international cosmopolitan, and Mark Twain evolved from a fledgling literary humorist into an internationally celebrated novelist, travel writer, essayist, and lecturer. What happened between those letters and "To the Person Sitting in Darkness" was Twain's life – a life passed richly imbricated with the events and people of the second half of the nineteenth century. Three personal developments (and of course a host of historical events) are especially relevant here. The first personal development concerns Twain's progressive loss of belief in Christian revelation or any other metaphysical system. The second is his fumbling appreciation for the racial Other, his struggle to surmount his gut assumption that racial differences denote a cultural and mental hierarchy. The third has to do with the evolution of Twain's own spatial imagination, with the paradigm, so evident in his late unfinished writings, of "inside/outside." The confluence of these developments within the context of America's sudden manifestation as a world power accounts for the seemingly contradictory writings that alternately celebrate the ideal national Christian and denounce Christian missionaries abroad.

Twain had never been an exemplary Christian – a fact that he used in his autobiographical construction and a position in which he reveled increasingly as the years passed. The middle-class, Midwestern Presbyterian environment in which he was reared bored him when he was young and repelled him when he matured. Like many of his contemporaries, he would have liked to have had a faith to cling to, but both his personal experiences of unexpected and unjustifiable death (such as his young brother Henry being blown up in a steamboat explosion, or his talented daughter Susy's sudden death from meningitis) convinced him that if a Deity existed, it could only be malevolent. Despite his facility with the stories and language of the King James Bible, he put no stock in revelation. For him Jesus represented the very best of human possibilities, but he was still only a historical figure. Twain admired Jesus for his moral courage. But he was far more interested in Satan, whom he regarded as the ultimate trickster.

Twain's personal inability to believe made him both wary of, and curious about, those who could. He was wary because he hated to be preached at, and to be forced to observe religious strictures such as keeping the Sabbath (a source of friction with George Washington Cable during their joint lecture tour in 1884–5). His own observation that the world, both natural and manmade, operated on amoral principles made him curious about – and often impatient with – the mental and emotional faculties that enabled other people to read divine benevolence into apparently random events. Eventually, this fed his misanthropy: he concluded that most people were too cowardly to face a world where they had to take moral responsibility for themselves. Although he continued to respect Christian moral teachings, he was convinced that most professing Christians never practiced them, instead substituting rote rules for original, and courageous, moral action. Late in his life he became convinced that human moral agency did not exist – rather, that man is "moved, directed, COMMANDED, by *exterior* influences – *solely*" (Twain 1906: 7). In an almost Althusserian move, Twain understood that those outside forces were socially constructed. In "As Regards Patriotism," unpublished in his lifetime, he describes the process through which the media, working with jingoistic politicians, construct the national citizen, a "newspaper-and-politician-manufactured Patriot" who "knows that the maker of his Patriotism, the windy and incoherent six-dollar sub-editor of his village newspaper – would bray out in print and call him a Traitor" if he tried to "revolt" against "an insane and shabby political upheaval" (Twain 1992b: 476). In "Corn-Pone Opinions," he claims that "hardly a man in the world has an opinion upon morals, politics, or religion which he got otherwise than through his associations and sympathies" (Twain 1992b: 510).

By the early twentieth century, Twain's determinism processed both religion and patriotism (itself "merely a religion" [Twain 1992b: 476]) as both socially constructed and self-interested. Most people who think they are obeying religious rules are merely hypocrites, even when they are well-intentioned. In "Was It Heaven? Or Hell?" a doctor, known alternately as "The Christian" and "The Only Christian," seems to speak for Twain when he berates two pious women who believe that lying is the worst of sins. "Like all the rest of the moral moles," the doctor tells them:

you lie from morning till night, but because you don't do it with your mouths, but only with your lying eyes, your lying inflections, your deceptively misplaced emphasis, and your misleading gestures, you turn up your complacent noses and parade before God and the world as saintly and unsmirched Truth-Speakers, in whose cold-storage souls a lie would freeze to death if it got there! (Twain 1992b: 535)

All of these observations boded ill for Mark Twain's evaluation of missionaries and America's Christian mission abroad. In "The Dervish and the Offensive Stranger," one of his platonic dialogues, Twain makes his position clear when his Stranger gives "yet one more instance" (of good intentions bringing as much evil as good): "With the best intentions the missionary has been laboring in China for eighty years." The evil result of this is "that nearly a hundred thousand Chinamen have acquired our Civilization," and the good result is "that by the compassion of God four hundred millions have escaped it" (Twain 1992b: 549).

Mark Twain and the Racial Other

At the same time that he was losing faith in both Christian revelation and the national Christian, Twain was also learning how to experience racial and ethnic differences in new, and enlightening, ways. This was a long journey for him, never easy, and – from our vantage-point – only partly successful. But even partial success meant that he had done better than most of his contemporaries. At the turn into the twentieth century, the fact that many white Americans felt solidarity with the Cubans and the Filipinos in their battle for independence from Spain did not mitigate the fact that these same Americans held these same Cubans and Filipinos to be racially inferior. Businessman Horace Davis, President of the Sperry Flour Company in San Francisco, writing to Edward Ordway, the secretary of the Anti-Imperialist League of New York, probably expressed the majority opinion when he rejected Ordway's invitation to join the League, saying that although he was opposed to "any further annexation of inferior races," he also held that it was our duty to see that the Filipinos are "fit for self-government before we thrust it upon them." For Davis, the Filipinos were the equivalent of the "uneducated negroes" of the South. His argument against annexation was based on the belief that "We have too much load of that kind to carry now" (February 5, 1904, Ordway Papers). Davis expressed his racism more openly than most of the men Ordway solicited, but most of them nevertheless held similar sentiments. For instance, Felix Adler, educator and founder the of the New York Ethical Culture Society, also declined to join the League, noting that although "I am thoroughly anti-imperialist myself . . . at the same time I am persuaded that the civilized races have certain duties toward the backward races" (January 2, 1900, Ordway Papers). And Samuel Gompers, President of the American Federation of Labor, framed his anti-imperialism as the fear that "If the Philippines are annexed, what is to prevent the

Chinese, the Negritos and the Malays coming to our country? . . . Can we hope to close the flood-gates of immigration from the hordes of Chinese and the semi-savage races coming from what will then be part of our own country?" (December 1898).

Samuel Clemens shared many of these assumptions. However, between his trip to the Sandwich Islands in 1866 and his writing of "To the Person Sitting in Darkness" in 1901 he also had had much contact with alien cultures. Most pertinent, of course, was his lecture tour around the world, completed in 1896, which had exposed him to people – including people of color – in Australia, New Zealand, India, and South Africa. Although it did not alter his emotional understanding of racial difference – *Following the Equator* displays ample evidence that Samuel Clemens still saw people of color as culturally exotic and intellectually less complex than whites – by 1900 he had a rational understanding that colonialism had been a major cause of economic and cultural degradation. The change, in other words, was in his assessment of white people's relationship to brown people, his understanding of the ironies underlying whites' proclamations that they had a responsibility for carrying the "white man's burden." This had as much to do with his developing misanthropy as with his racial consciousness. The point was not that black and brown people were as smart as white people, but that white people were a lot less civilized than they thought they were. "There are many humorous things in the world," he would note bitterly in a chapter concerning European exploitation of native peoples generally, "among them the white man's notion that he is less savage than the other savages" (Twain 1897: 213). As impressed by the ancient civilizations of India and Ceylon as by white methods of undermining native cultures, Twain became increasingly dubious about the benefits of white "civilization." Subsequent events in South Africa, China, the Philippines, the Congo, and other "hot spots" contributed to his disillusionment with European and American motives for intervening in other countries' affairs. At some level, he recognized that cultures that had had the least contact with Christianity might be the healthiest. In a copy of Darwin's *Voyage of the Beagle*, acquired in 1890 but annotated nearly 20 years later, he wrote "Pagan civilization" above a description of the ruins of an "ancient Indian village," about which Darwin remarks that "it is impossible not to respect the considerable advance made by them in the arts of civilization." On the previous page, next to Darwin's description of the modern city of Callao as "a filthy, ill-built, small sea-port" rife with government corruption, Twain wrote "Christian civilization."[2]

Mark Twain's Spatial Aesthetic

The other significant event in Twain's thinking at this time was the development of his "inside/outside" aesthetic. Although Twain had always tended to think in binary opposites (especially when he was impassioned), had always been fascinated by the idea of time travel and time-lapses, and was a master of the literary form that positions readers both inside and outside dialect environments, the last two decades of his life saw a conceptual development in which he compared points of view from inside and outside a given spatial locale. This spatial formation is most evident in late, generally unfinished works such as "The Great Dark" or "Three Thousand Years Among the Microbes." In "The Great Dark," for instance, a man looking at a drop of water through a microscope suddenly finds himself inside it; in "Three Thousand Years," the narrator is a microbe traveling through the veins of a tramp, able, as he reports, "to observe the germs from their own point of view," but also "from a human being's point of view" (Twain 1968: 435). This "inside/outside" paradigm became one of the means by which Twain transcended a simple view of the generic American Christian. As he watched his compatriots abroad, especially in traditionally non-Christian or predominantly Catholic countries, he began to see how the American Christian's beliefs, values, and lifestyles became tools for oppression when they were exported. In "The Great Dark," the narrator of the tale is a happy and virtuous man, living contentedly with his family, until he goes "inside" the drop of water and discovers a nightmare world. In Mark Twain's thinking about Americans abroad, the virtuous and contented American on the home front becomes a ruthless aggressor when he goes "outside." This is nowhere more evident than in the religious arena, where the missionary, as representative of the best of American culture, ends up delivering cultural genocide rather than the "blessings" of Christian benevolence. The evaluation, as Mark Twain the writer well knew, is all in the observer's point of view.

Mark Twain and America's Christian Mission Abroad

In 1900 Twain wrote a letter to the London *Times* entitled "The Missionary in World-Politics."[3] The letter begins by claiming that "the source of religion & of patriotism is one & the same – the heart, not the head." He then proceeds to argue that the only reason we respect missionaries is because missionaries from non-Christian countries (from "Turkey or China or Polynesia") have not intruded into our lives and won away our children. Warming to his subject, he focuses on the imperialist agenda behind the proselytizing, and the force necessary to convert most populations: "there is no capable missionary except fire & sword or the command of a King whose subjects have no voice in the government." He discusses the reprisals England and Germany demanded for the murder of missionaries in China, and concludes with a jeremiad that, while it holds forth hope that China may yet survive the European onslaught, also implies that the whole Christian enterprise is an imperialist front:

> [The missionary] has surpassed all his former mischiefs this time. He has loaded vast China onto the Concert of Christian Vultures;[4] & they were glad, smelling carrion; but they have lit & are astonished, finding the carcase alive. And it may remain alive – Europe cannot tell, yet. . . . The China war may turn out a European war, & China go free & save herself alive. Then, when the world settles down again, let us hope that the missionary's industries will be restricted to his native land for all time to come. Is the

man in the street concerned? I think he is. The time is grave. The future is blacker than has been any future which any person now living has tried to peer into. (Clemens to C. F. Moberly Bell, July 9, 1900, MTP)

At first sight it is easy to assume that, in accusing the missionaries of fomenting war with China, Twain was following in the "good/bad" tradition of Stowe, Douglass, and others. An argument can be made for this if we look at his essay on "Christian Citizenship," which he published anonymously in *Collier's* magazine in 1905. In this essay Twain calls for Christians to "vote their duty to God at the polls," holding that "if the Christians of America could be persuaded to vote God and a clean ticket, it would bring about a moral revolution that would be incalculably beneficent. It would save the country – a country whose Christians have betrayed it and are destroying it." Written more in reference to Tammany Hall than to America's policies overseas, this essay fits into the traditional framework. It is a specifically Protestant text, assuming that "Christian" means "Protestant" and addressing Protestant anxieties about the spectre of Irish Catholic political influence. It also assumes a positive identity between "Christian" and "moral," and predicates "manhood" on the ability to activate "Christian" voting patterns. Even a clergyman, Twain claims, has a right to confront his congregation's demand that he reveal his vote by standing "upon his manhood and answer[ing] that they [have] no Christian right (which is the same as saying no moral right, and, of course, no legal right) to ask the question" (Twain 1992b: 658–60). Here the "Christian" is also manly, bravely standing up for principles – but his very courage makes him a lone figure when set against his putatively Christian congregation. Most importantly, the whole point of the essay "Christian Citizenship" is that Twain assumes that the Protestant passion for moral order is an appropriate ideology for regulating politics. Moral order here becomes a political agenda. But it is an agenda useful only when applied within US borders.

I think we can see the direction in which Twain's thought about the American Christian was evolving if we look at other pieces Twain wrote during the same period in which he composed "Christian Citizenship." The chronological ordering of the Library of America's edition of the *Collected Tales, Sketches, Speeches, and Essays* (Twain 1992b) shows "Christian Citizenship" preceded by "The War Prayer" and "A Humane Word from Satan" and followed by "King Leopold's Soliloquy." In "The War Prayer," of course, Twain points out that a prayer for victory in battle means a prayer not only that the enemy's soldiers will be killed but that their families will be destroyed and their children starved, while "King Leopold" exposes the Belgian ruler's blood-thirstiness through his meditations on his strategies in the Congo. "A Humane Word from Satan" is an intervention in a dispute, widely reported in the press, over whether the American Board of Commissioners for Foreign Missions should be allowed to take contributions from John D. Rockefeller, given his unfair business practices. Here Satan argues that the Board should have no such scruples, since they take money from him, Satan, on a regular basis.

All of these contextualizing essays move beyond national borders in some way. "Christian Citizenship" stands out as the only essay to situate the ideal American

Christian exclusively within the United States, even highlighting recent state and city elections rather than federal ones. Its Christian citizen operates locally, and he is never imagined beyond national borders. Sandwiched as the essay is between articles that unfailingly reference the global, it is the anomaly in Mark Twain's late political writings; and as such, it may provide the standard against which Twain sees the *global* Christian failing so badly. For we can see that when Twain restricts his idea of "the public Christian" to issues that are local – on the "inside" – he sees Christianity as nineteenth-century political Protestantism had always seen it: as a vehicle for cleaning up corruption, for setting the nation back on a moral track. As soon as he looks at Christianity operating beyond national borders – on the "outside" – however, it takes on an entirely different cast. Evidence of American Christians' activities in China and the Philippines shows that abroad, rather than bringing order, American Christianity takes advantage of local disruptions to increase disorder – the most glaring instances being the Reverend Ament's activities in China and General Funston's in the Philippines. Here the missionaries – whom, in "The US of Lyncherdom," Twain had summoned home to convert the "un-Christian" lynchers of America – have themselves become the equivalent of lynchers in China and the Philippines, both through wanton killing of the civilian population and through calculated torture of insurgents. For Twain, whose entire being revolted from the specter of pain, this was the ultimate in moral corruption. The Christian mission that the young Mark Twain had seen rescuing Hawaiians from a bloodthirsty religion has, in its latest imperial push, revealed its own penchant for murder and torture.

Mark Twain was not alone in his disillusionment. Much has been written about the engagement of Twain's contemporaries – especially fellow writers such as Howells and William James – with the anti-imperialist leagues, and I will not rehearse this material here. Suffice it to say that writings by James such as his "Moral Equivalent of War," or his letter to the *Boston Evening Transcript* on "The Philippine Tangle," excoriates Americans for embracing

> a national destiny which must be "big" at any cost, and which for some inscrutable reason it has become infamous for us to disbelieve in or refuse. We are to be missionaries of civilization, and to bear the white man's burden, painful as it often is. We must sow our ideals, plant our order, impose our God. The individual lives are nothing. Our duty and our destiny call, and civilization must go on. Could there be a more damning indictment of the whole bloated idol termed "modern civilization" than this amounts to? (James 1899)

Minor writers also contributed to the cause. Twain's own revisionary "Battle-Hymn of the Republic" takes its place with poems such as David B. Page's "War Is Hell," which features stanzas such as the following:

> *"War is hell."*
> Ah well!
> *Peace on Earth*

> The angels sang.
> Ah Christ, we worship thee
> Mid clang of arms
> And battle's roar,
> Where hate and wrath
> Shed human gore.
> And think we serve Thee well
> With cruel shot and deadly shell
> *In making hell.*
> (Page 1899: 146)

And in *Captain Jinks, Hero*, Ernest Crosby brilliantly satirizes American policy through the "adventures" of a gullible young patriot who, entering China in the wake of the international effort to subdue the Boxer Rebellion, watches the "bodies drifting past, brainless skulls, eyeless sockets" on the river, and agrees with his companion's opinion that the sight of murdered civilians "is really a fine example of the power of civilization." When the United States, with Japan, is criticized for not having been tough enough with the Chinese insurgents, the protagonist, Jinks, defends his country by noting that "We are only just starting out on our career as a military nation . . . We'll soon get our hand in. As for the Japs, why they're heathen. They can hardly be expected to behave like Christians. But we were afraid that the war was over and that we should find nothing to do" (Crosby 1968: 260).

In this writerly environment, Twain's own notes for a sketch about China show him joining a conversation that openly recognizes Christian complicity in mass destruction:

> Second Advent. Begins triumphal march around the globe at Tien Tsin preceded by Generals, Warships, cavalry, infantry, artillery, who clear the road & pile the dead & the loot for "propagation of the Gospel," . . . singing "where every prospect pleases & only man is vile." Christ arrives in a vast war-fleet furnished by the Great Powers. (Twain 1901)

To sum up: over time, not only did Twain's assessment of the US justification for involvement overseas shift, but because that justification was framed in explicitly Christian benevolent terms, so did his assessment of American Christianity. Current events, especially as concerned American interventions abroad, combined with Twain's longstanding doubts about missionaries and his growing conviction that human moral agency was impossible, led him to conclude that the generic American Christian did not and could not play the same role beyond US borders as he had traditionally played within them. I suggest that for Twain, the American Missionary Board's collaboration with military and commercial interests in China and the Philippines highlighted the inherent contradiction of proselytizing the Gospel in a world where "foreign fields" increasingly referred to market factors and a capitalist determination to use any means, religious or military, to secure them. Rather than continuing the nineteenth-century conversation that first mapped "Christian" onto "American," and then divided Christians into the good and the bad, the early twentieth-century conversation mapped "American Christian" onto "imperialist," feeding Twain's cynicism about the "damned human race" generally and confirming his suspicions that the United States in particular had set a course destined to bring economic domination at the price of moral damnation.

NOTES

1   In *Race, Religion, and the Continuing American Dilemma*, C. Eric Lincoln reviews the history of this phenomenon, which (following Elwyn W. Smith in *The Religion of the Republic* [1968]), he labels "Americanity." "Americanity," Lincoln argues, "is the semi-secular, unofficial, but characteristic religion to which most Americans appeal when an appeal to religion is indicated. It is the religion most Americans feel when they feel any religion at all. It transcends the classical sectarian delineations and joins Protestant, Catholic, and Jew . . . [T]hose who think well of America's culture religion [*sic*] see it as 'a creative, dynamic, and self-critical national religion that gives transcendent meaning and a high set of moral values to individual Americans, and produces just, humane goals for the nation.' Others see it as a 'third force . . . [one] that is capable of significantly altering a culture, or that is symptomatic of a significant new shift in the dynamics of a culture' " (Lincoln 1984: 131–2). The paradigm I see differs from Professor Lincoln's national religion in that it does not transcend sectarian borders. On the contrary, the national Christian is a particularly Protestant figure, to whom Catholics, Jews, and aberrant sects such

as Mormons are suspect even when they are tolerated.

2   Charles Darwin, *Journal of Researches into the Natural History and Geology of the Countries Visited during the Voyage of the H.M.S. Beagle Round the World Under the Command of Captain Fitz Roy, R.N.* (London: T. Nelson & Sons, 1890). Property of the Mark Twain House, Hartford, Connecticut. The opening page is inscribed "SL Clemens, Hartford, Oct. 28 / 90." Nasty marginal references to Ralph Ashcroft and Isabel Lyon, however, suggest that he was reading (or perhaps re-reading) it in 1909 or 1910.

3   The manuscript of this essay, plus the cover letter and envelope addressed to C. F. Moberly Bell, are held by the Mark Twain Papers. The envelope is marked, in Clemens's handwriting, "Not sent." The essay is published in vol. 23 of the microfilm edition of Mark Twain's literary manuscripts available in the Mark Twain Papers, ed. Anh Quynh Bui, Victor Fischer, Michael B. Frank, Robert H. Hirst, Lin Salamo, and Harriet Elinor Smith, 42 vols. (Berkeley: Bancroft Library, 2001).

4   In the manuscript, "Christian vultures" is crossed out, and "Birds of Prey" substituted.

REFERENCES AND FURTHER READING

Crosby, Ernest (1968). *Captain Jinks, Hero.* Upper Saddle River, NJ: Gregg Press. (First publ. 1902.)

James, William (1899). "The Philippine Tangle." *Boston Evening Transcript*, March 1. Repr. on the internet at www.boondocksnet.com/ai/ailtexts/tangle.html.

Kaplan, Amy (1997). "Imperial Triangles: Mark Twain's Foreign Affairs." *Modern Fiction Studies* 43: 1, 237–48.

Kaplan, Amy (2002). *The Anarchy of Empire in the Making of US Culture.* Cambridge, Mass.: Harvard University Press.

Kaplan, Fred (2003). *The Singular Mark Twain*. New York: Doubleday.

Lincoln, E. Eric (1999). *Race, Religion, and the Continuing American Dilemma*. New York: Hill & Wang. (First publ. 1984.)

Millis, Walter (1931). *The Martial Spirit*. Cambridge, Mass.: Riverside.

Page, David B. (1899). "War is Hell." In *Our Dumb Animals*. 31: 12 (May), 146.

Putz, Manfred (1990). "Mark Twain and the Idea of American Superiority at the End of the Nineteenth Century." In Serge Ricard (ed.), *An American Empire: Expansionist Cultures and Policies, 1881–1917*, 215–36. Aix-en-Provence: Université de Provence.

Santiago-Valles, Kelvin (1999). "'Still Longing for de Old Plantation': The Visual Parodies and Racial National Imaginary of US Overseas Expansionism, 1898–1903." *American Studies International* 37: 3, 18–42.

Twain, Mark (1901). Notebook 44. Mark Twain Papers, Bancroft Library, University of California, Berkeley.

Twain, Mark (1968). *Mark Twain's Which Was the Dream? And Other Symbolic Writings of the Later Years*, ed. John S. Tuckey. Berkeley: University of California Press.

Twain, Mark (1972). *Letters from the Sandwich Islands, Written for the Sacramento Union*, ed. G. Ezra Dane. New York: Haskell House.

Zwick, Jim, ed. (1992). *Mark Twain's Weapons of Satire: Anti-Imperialist Writings on the Philippine–American War*. Syracuse, NY: Syracuse University Press.

Collections Cited

Edward Warren Ordway Papers, 1893–1914. Rare Books and Manuscripts Division, New York Public Library, Astor, Lenox, and Tilden Foundations.

Mark Twain Papers, Bancroft Library, University of California, Berkeley.

4

Mark Twain and Whiteness

Richard S. Lowry

Over the past half-century there has emerged a critical consensus that the matter of race in America lies uneasily at the heart of Mark Twain's art. Stimulated in part by the seismically restless controversies over the racial politics of *Adventures of Huckleberry Finn*, readers have sought to come to terms not only with Twain's engagement with slavery, but with an imagination rooted firmly in the dynamics of race relations. The "half-breed" Injun Joe in *Tom Sawyer*, the slave-like serfs of *Connecticut Yankee*, even the grotesque appearance of No. 44 in a late fifteenth-century castle as Mr. Bones, "Cunnel Bludso's nigger fum Souf C'yarlina," in *The Mysterious Stranger* (Twain 1969: 137): all of these – not to mention such biting commentaries as "The United States of Lyncherdom" – attest to the breadth of this vision. To some extent, of course, it would be difficult to expect anything else from a writer who crafted virtually all of his writing out of a "personal experience" which included growing up in a slave-holding state with a father who sold slaves and prosecuted abolitionists, and living through the most racially unsettling decades in US history.[1] Less predictable is the ability of his writings to continue to provoke readers anew to confront issues that remain painful and volatile in the United States today.

Controversies around Twain and race can be loosely grouped around two opposing interpretations of *Huckleberry Finn*.[2] Is this novel, told in the voice of a racist white-trash boy, shaped deeply by its author's knowledge of and love for blackface minstrelsy, and ending with its disheartening burlesque abuse of the escaped slave Jim, an example of, as one black educator has put it, "white men blacking up to entertain other whites at the expense of black people's humanity" (Fishkin 1997: 81)? Or is it, as many have insisted, a novel that exposes exactly that kind of cruelty, and in doing so stands, in the words of Shelley Fisher Fishkin, perhaps its most eloquent defender, as "one of the most scathing critiques of racism by an American" (Fishkin 1997: 74)? There is evidence in Twain's writing to support both sides of this debate. On one hand, his free use of the word "nigger," and the ways he employs the casual racism of many of his characters for humorous effect (consider Aunt Polly, whose tender heart

makes it impossible for her to discipline her adopted charge, Tom Sawyer, yet who
turns out to watch Injun Joe get horsewhipped), suggest a writer at ease with white
supremacy. On the other, Huck's struggle to overcome a conscience that insists that
Jim is only property, and the harsh irony concluding *Pudd'nhead Wilson*, point insistently to a writer alive to the absurd and heartbreaking violence of slavery and racism.

Twain's biography only complicates these issues. Early in his life, he seems to have
shared the same racial intolerance as his friends and family in Missouri, and he never
gave up a lifelong delight in the racial mimicry of blackface minstrelsy. However,
after marrying into a family with abolitionist antecedents and, most particularly, after
discovering "the Matter of Hannibal" as the source of his writerly inspiration, Twain's
attitudes towards African Americans clearly underwent a change. By the 1880s he
was speaking at blacks-only gatherings, and in that same period he paid the board
for the final years of the first African American to graduate from Yale Law School.
Accompanying these liberal politics was a deep personal investment in African American culture that was evident in his relish for African American gospel music and in
his use of black voices to animate the "low-down and ornery" voice of Huck. Twain
was explicit about his debts to African America: he identified both the signifying
brilliance of the Hannibal slave Jerry, and the delicate artistry of the spoken
ghost tale "The Golden Arm," which he heard as a boy performed by the slave "Uncle
Dan'l," as vital to his own aesthetic.[3]

As scholars and readers have come to understand the profundity of Twain's lifelong
engagement with race, they have come in turn to see his writings as a particularly
rich site of racial hybridity, where African and Anglo America meet in a heady stew
of discomfiting humor. It has also become clear that his work will not yield readily
to the kinds of resolution for which debates like those over *Huckleberry Finn* often
strive. To a large extent, this is because, quite simply, Twain wrote to stir up such
controversy; he wrote, in Tom Sawyer's words, to "make talk." At its best, Twain's
was an art of parody. It unfolded as a performance of wily mimicry – whether of the
mincing cadences of Sunday-school discipline, the lachrymose elegies of sentimental
grief, the reverence of cultural dilettantism, the double-edged subtleties of African
American signifying, or the howls of racist brutishness. Racism, violence, and imperial exploitation served as much to provide material for his writings and performances
as they did to provide targets for his impatience, even outrage, at the hypocrisies and
bad faith that made such things possible. In short, Twain's was a complex morality
that strove in the end to make his readers and audiences uncomfortable – even if only
for a moment in a burst of laughter or applause.[4]

More importantly, the hybrid nature of Twain's writing suggests that it is not
enough to focus on his representation of, and borrowing from, other races and their
cultures if we are to understand the power of his work to stir controversy about race.
Sensitive as Twain was to racial and cultural difference, he was equally attentive to
what scholars have recently come to call "whiteness."[5] At the very least, his discovery of African America as an imaginative resource for his writing coincided with an
equally energizing discovery of white racial identity as both a category of experience

and a mode of domination with its own languages and strategies. And it could be that his well-known pessimism late in life about the "The Damned Human Race" (to quote the title to one of his essays) stemmed from his suspicions of the racist origins of rhetoric celebrating manifest destiny, US nationalism, and civilization. Thus, to look at whiteness in Twain is not to ignore his important engagement with African American culture and his critiques of racism, but to integrate his work in a broader historical continuum of race relations. It is to see Jim, and Tom Driscoll, and his other black characters as the unruly, even disruptive progeny of a national culture that has made racial Others the objects of fantasy, fear, and desire.[6] Such a perspective also asks us to look anew at Twain's "white" characters. After all, Huck's voice, even his point of view, may well be "black" (see Fishkin 1997); but what makes him, and Tom Sawyer, and Hank Morgan, and David Wilson, so disturbing is how they, and so much of the world they inhabit, act so "white." Finally, it compels us to weigh the import and significance of Ralph Ellison's insistence on "the true interrelatedness of blackness and whiteness" (Ellison 1953: 85).

White of a Different Color

"I reckon I had better black my face, for in these Eastern States niggers are considerably better than white people."[7]

Seventeen-year-old Mark Twain wrote these words to his mother in 1853 from New York City, where he had journeyed from St. Louis in search of work as a printer. On his way there he had visited the courthouse in Syracuse, which had become nationally famous when some "infernal abolitionists" had prevented a slave arrested under the Fugitive Slave Act from being returned to his Southern master. Twain's response here voices the unreflective racism of a Southern youth far away from home. In fact, his brother Orion would publish the letter in his newspaper as a bit of travel correspondence, much more interesting for what it says about a pair of Borneo freaks than for its reflections on abolition. More importantly, the letter offers insight into Twain's understanding of his, and his society's, culture of whiteness.

Both Twain's dismissal of the abolitionists' aims, and his wide-eyed fascination with the half-white half-apes from Borneo, express a popular comfort with a white supremacy justified by God (as was often argued from Southern pulpits) and, later in the century, legitimated by evolution and certified by "blood." He also echoes, maybe consciously, the racial intolerance that he would have shared with his fellow printers and other working- and lower-class whites. After all, he too was confronting threatening changes, not just in his working conditions but in his social prospects, that made any group seemingly willing to work cheaply an object of suspicion. Twain's journey east was the impulsive effort of a skilled worker ambitious to ply his trade and realize the republican ideal of individual independence. Instead, he encountered a labor market organized around depressed wages and increasingly rationalized industrial work routines, and would return home in less than a year. In short, Twain was facing the prospect of working as a "wage slave," instead of realizing the manly independence, status, and good income traditionally offered by the printing profession. In this context, his dismissal of "niggers" and abolitionists expresses his anxiety over not receiving his "wages of whiteness," the privileged access to autonomy due to his race.[8]

There is, however, another dimension to Twain's racial awareness in the letter. As Eric Lott has pointed out, the young printer's joke about blacking his face expresses a "subterranean" fantasy: "the lure to *be* black" that was expressed most popularly in minstrel shows, where white men literally did blacken their skin, and sing, dance, and joke as "authentic" darkies from the plantation and the urban street (Lott 1995a: 130; see also Lott 1995b). Delighted white audiences, including Twain, found such entertainment a powerful vehicle for fantasies of identification with pre-industrial frivolity, leisure, sexuality, and playfulness, all of which they both longed for and feared. At the same time, the accompanying caricature and ridicule of black lives so crucial to minstrelsy made such feelings safe by creating a wall of racial difference, and a distinct hierarchy which allowed audiences to accrue an ancillary wage of whiteness by virtue of their distance "above" the antics they saw on stage. Out of this dynamic of anxiety and ambition, lure and loathing, emerged another increment of the wage of whiteness: the distinct awareness of "whiteness" as a dominant, and dominating, racial category.

The logic for such racial formation would change over the course of Twain's lifetime as popular versions of Darwinian evolutionary theory came to characterize race as a biological essence and a historical destiny for both groups and individuals. Twain, too, would change his views on race, but it is clear that the working-class whiteness he experienced as a youth served as the basis for his earliest forays into the painful humor of race relations. In 1870 he published "Disgraceful Persecution of a Boy," a short satirical commentary on a newspaper report of a "well-dressed boy, on his way to Sunday School," arrested in San Francisco "for stoning Chinamen." Twain asks: Why the arrest? "How should [the boy] suppose it was wrong to stone a Chinaman?" After all, California mandates a tax on all foreigners for prospecting, but only levies it (sometimes twice) on the Chinese. The boy would also have known "that when a white man robs a sluice-box (by the term white man is meant Spaniards, Mexicans, Portuguese, Irish, Hondurans, Peruvians, Chileans, etc., etc.), they make him leave the camp; and when a Chinaman does that thing, they hang him." A Chinaman has no rights, is due no pity: "neither his life nor his liberty [is] worth the purchase of a penny when a white man need[s] a scapegoat." Given this state of affairs, of course a white boy would throw rocks; he would only be fulfilling his duty by doing so (Twain 1992a: 379–82).

The article's ironic voice repeats the rhetorical strategy Twain had deployed in an earlier, vitriolic attack on the gentlemanliness of Southern lynching entitled "Only a Nigger": "mistakes will happen . . . surely there is no good reason why Southern gentlemen should worry themselves with useless regrets, so long as only an innocent 'nigger' is hanged."[9] His skill at mimicking, and thus holding up for ridicule, languages of intolerance would serve him repeatedly as a rhetorical frame that allowed him to speak as an insider to insiders, or, as he makes explicit in "Disgraceful Persecution of a Boy," as one white to another. "We," writer and audience, are white; and whites are made, not born – made by a popular, arbitrary racism (Peruvians are white; Chinese are not) that not only persecutes others but animates a structural social whiteness that reaches from the state legislature into the heart of a "well-dressed boy." As such, these early pieces by Twain seek to make visible, and to hold up for ridicule, what George Lipsitz has called "the possessive investment in whiteness": the ways in which, culturally, economically, and socially, Americans have come to install and maintain whiteness as an invisible condition of normalcy.[10] They also suggest that early in his career, the well-known intolerance of, and fascination with, hypocrisy, lying, and "bad faith" that marked so much of his writing may well have had its roots in his recognition of the culture of white racial supremacy.[11]

Over the course of his career, Twain would adapt three characteristic strategies for writing about whiteness. First – as he did in his early articles – he would make whiteness visible, exposing, as it were, the naked emperor beneath his gaudy clothes to the laughter and derision of his subjects. Second, he would deflate the pretensions to purity and reverence that underlay white supremacy by deconstructing the categories of race on which it relied to maintain itself. And finally, he would trace the conversion of explicit racial ideologies into a transparent hegemony, a whites-cycle laundering of intolerance that would displace whiteness with nationality and, finally, civilization. What follows will examine only the most obvious manifestations of each of the strategies that together nourished Twain's fiction at its deepest roots.

Visible Whiteness

"There warn't no color in his face where his face showed; it was white; not like another man's white, but a white to make a body sick, a white to make a body's flesh crawl – a tree-toad white, a fish-belly white." (Twain 1885: 39)

When, early in *Adventures of Huckleberry Finn*, Huck returns to his now tolerably comfortable room at the Widow Douglas's after an evening with Jim and Tom, he meets his father – the very embodiment of amphibian horror. Simmering with sullen anger at Huck's pretensions to a better life – what he calls Huck's "frills" and "airs" – Pap threatens violence: "You think you're better'n your father, now, don't you . . . I'll take it out of you . . . I'll lay for you my smarty . . . I'll give you a cowhide" (p. 40). Comically, Pap acts the part of the unappreciated parent, abandoned by his ungrateful son. More disturbingly, however, he sets the tone for Twain's most compelling exploration of whiteness, particularly as it formed around a core of male anger.

Fueling Pap's pain is the rage of a man dispossessed of his privileges. Pap is, in effect, "stiffed," as he makes clear in a subsequent drunken rant.[12] "The law takes a man worth six thousand dollars and up'ards, and jams him into an old trap of a cabin like this, and lets him go round in clothes that ain't fitten for a hog. They call that a govment! A man can't git his rights in a govment like this" (Twain 1885: 49). For Pap, though, it is not just a matter of manhood; his rights are due to his whiteness as well. Hence his outrage at a "mulatter" professor who is free to travel the state for six months until he can be returned to slavery. Pap shoves the man off the road as his right; but what kind of government, he wants to know, allows "a prowling, thieving, infernal, white-shirted free nigger" to go free, and treats a *real* white man so shabbily?

Pap gets no answers, and so lives a life fumed by a toxic cocktail of failure, disillusion, and whiskey, gripped by an equal-opportunity violence that will take as its object anything at hand – an old barrel, a black professor, his son, himself. Within the world of *Huckleberry Finn* this irrational explosiveness, despite Huck's insistence to the contrary, makes Pap's whiteness *just* "like another man's white." His fulminations make no more sense than does the bloody Grangerford–Shepherdson feud; the bogus tales of the Duke and the Dauphin comically echo Pap's sense of dispossession; and Pap's need to "boss" anticipates both the haughty challenge of Colonel Sherburn to the lynching mob and the self-serving machinations of Tom Sawyer. Most suggestive is Pap's ghostlike ability to appear when he is least expected – an attribute he shares with Tom, but more strikingly with the stock figure of abolitionist literature: the evil slave-owner or overseer. Frederick Douglass's Covey, Harriet Beecher Stowe's Simon Legree, and Harriet Jacobs' Dr. Flint are each obsessed in their own way with "bossing"; and each terrorizes his charge with his mysterious unpredictability. In short, Pap's fish-belly white colors the entire novel, transforming Huck's escape into a journey to the heart of whiteness.

One other of Pap's attributes typifies the novel's engagement with whiteness: his self-absorption. In a world inhabited by blacks and whites, the white characters have eyes only for each other. Indeed, what is so disturbing about the race relations in the text, and so unsettling about Huck's own racial identity, is how simply casual is the racism, and how irrelevant blacks are to the affective world of whites. Aunt Sally asks if anyone died in the steamboat explosion. "No'm. Killed a nigger," answers the boy who has decided to go to hell to rescue Jim (Twain 1885: 280). Tom may endanger Jim's life and freedom, may subject him to a host of arbitrary humiliations in the name of helping "a prisoner of style escape," but really it is all in fun, and certainly worth the 40 dollars he gives Jim "for being prisoner for us so patient, and doing it up so good" (p. 365). Tom's attention, like Pap's, and like that of everyone else, is turned to white society. Only other whites will grant them the "rights" or, in Tom's case, the recognition they so crave. Jim and the other slaves are allowed to participate in this economy of honor only as props and opportunities. Their role is to wait in the rushes, watch and listen, and above all avoid attracting the barbaric attentions of whites, who are liable to suddenly see them as a source of wealth. As one country boy tells Huck, finding Jim is "like picking up money out'n the road" (p. 268).

The distance between white and black makes the alliance between Huck and Jim all the more significant. Like a slave, Huck, too, can only watch and wait. He "never let on," he tells us, that he knew the Duke and Dauphin were frauds: "it's the best way; then you don't have no quarrels, and don't get into no trouble" (Twain 1885: 166). Perhaps Twain drew on more than black speech in crafting Huck; perhaps he crafted a point of view, a strategy for living, from his knowledge of slave life.[13] Certainly the similarity of their condition accounts for Huck's being able to overcome his slave-holding conscience and link his fate with Jim's. But Huck's affection for the word "nigger" suggests this bond is never more than conditional. Caught in the outrageous con game of the Duke and Dauphin as they exploit the grief of the Wilkses, Huck fumes, "Well, if ever I struck anything like it, I'm a nigger" (p. 210) – which means, of course, he hasn't, because of course he's not. *Jim* is a "nigger," as Huck repeatedly reminds both of them whenever they grow too close. When Jim calls Huck "trash" after being made a fool of by one of Huck's jokes, Huck does not argue because, as he had discovered earlier, "you can't learn a nigger to argue" (p. 114). In this sense, Huck is no more than his father's son. And in fact, as he is careful to tell us, it was Pap, not Jim, who taught him to lie low and get along.

Pap haunts Huck's story like a madman in the attic, compromising – or coloring – his every effort to find his heart in a world of deformed conscience. In this context, momentous as it is, Huck's decision to go to hell in the name of friendship represents as much a fantasy of escape from the painful ambivalences of race as it does a liberal commitment to equality. From a broader perspective, the way Pap's intolerance drunkenly echoes the working-class anger Twain knew only too well suggests that Twain included his voice both as a kind of exorcism of voices from his own life and as a provocation to his readers. On one hand, Pap's hyperbolic anger makes his racism easy to dismiss as an individual pathology. On the other, the way he saturates the novel as its racial unconscious makes it very difficult to respond to Huck's sheer likeability without discomfort. The rhetorical bond of whiteness, the intimate "we" Huck's voice solicits, sits – as the novel's popular history attests – very uneasily.

At the novel's conclusion, Huck – unlike Jim – can plan to escape into anonymous whiteness, vanishing like a ghost in the "Territory." Twain, however, considered the opposite direction for his own career, making himself and, at times, whiteness – his own and that of his characters and his audience – more visible, even the object of parody. This impulse may help account for his insisting at the last minute on adding a profile photograph of a white bust of himself as "famous author" opposite the title-page of *Huckleberry Finn*. And a parodic exposure of racial whiteness may have prompted, at some deep level, his decision to testify on copyright reform to a US congressional committee in December 1906 dressed in a spectacularly out-of-season all-white suit – a style of dress he took up from time to time until his death. "Nothing," wrote his friend William Dean Howells, "could have been more dramatic" than his standing "forth in white from his feet to the crown of his silvery head" (Howells 1910: 80). Jim may be, as Huck admiringly tells us, "white inside" (Twain 1885: 341), but on such occasions Twain was white from top to toe, a performance perhaps designed to show the world its own true colors.

Invisible Blackness

"The 'nigger' in him went shrinking and skulking here and there and yonder, and fancying it saw suspicion and maybe detection in all faces, tones, and gestures." (Twain 1894: 123)

If Jim is white inside, Tom Driscoll, a.k.a. Chambers, in *The Tragedy of Pudd'nhead Wilson*, is black inside, as he apparently discovers after learning he was born a slave and switched at birth with his master's son by his mother, Roxy. Within days of the revelation, Tom's inner "nigger" threatens to transform him into a limp-armed Sambo, "involuntarily giving the road" to a "white rowdy and loafer," and fearful about visiting his sweetheart and sitting "with the dread white folks on equal terms" (Twain 1894: 123). Pushed to this shock of tragic recognition, he laments, "why is this awful difference made between white and black?" (p. 122). The answer, Twain's text suggests, is because whites need blacks to affirm their supremacy. To be white in Dawson's Landing, to paraphrase Robert Farris Thompson, is to be very black.[14] The inverse, it seems, is equally true in the novel. Roxy is three generations removed from her single black ancestor, "as white as anybody," but "by a fiction of law and custom" a slave and black (pp. 32–3). Or, as her son (and the ostensible "Tom") tells her, he may be, as she has put it, an "imitation nigger," but really they are both "imitation *white*" (p. 99). However, as they both know, the law brooks no imitations, and so they are legally black and rightfully slaves – which makes black ancestry at least 31 times more powerful than white. Roxy herself believes this. When her son "Tom" refuses a duel of honor, she explodes, "It's de nigger in you," that makes him such a coward. "Thirty-one parts o' you is white, en on'y one part nigger, en dat po' little one part is yo' *soul*" (p. 188).

Caught in the energies of post-Reconstruction racial politics, on the cusp of the Supreme Court decision in *Plessy* v. *Ferguson* that would legalize American apartheid under the rubric "separate but equal," Twain's last major novel searchingly explores what W. E. B. Du Bois would call "the problem of the color-line" (Du Bois 1996: 13). Set in the same antebellum world as *Huckleberry Finn*, *Pudd'nhead Wilson* explores the twisted ironies, hypocrisies, and violence of legal efforts to segregate the races, and undo the horrible intimacy of generations of slavery. Who, asks the novel, in a world that whites and slaves had forged together, is racially pure? And why, and to whom, does it matter?

Twain had already raised these questions in 1881, when he delivered a speech at the New England Society of Philadelphia, celebrating their pilgrim ancestors' arrival at Plymouth Rock. Seizing on the occasion's pretenses to genealogical purity, Twain chose to offer up his own lineage as comic leavening. After all, he chided, "the Pilgrims were a hard lot. They took good care of themselves, but they abolished everybody else's ancestors," including his own: "My first American ancestor, gentleman, was an Indian," who was skinned alive. They treated his other forebears similarly, including the Quakers, the Salem witches, and the first slave in New England. For Twain represents himself, too, as "of mixed breed, an infinitely shaded and exquisite mongrel" whose "complexion is the patient art of eight generations" of slavery. But those ancestors, as well, were lost with the Civil War, which leaves him "bereft": "no drop of my blood flows in the veins of any living being who is marketable" (Twain 1992a: 782–4). The humor here is complex and ultimately accommodating. As a mongrel he is the product of centuries of racial exploitation and sexual contact – the survivor of a forgotten violence of which he reminds his audience. By the same token, as a white man he has the privilege to shake the surety of racial purity from the by and large safe standpoint of a member of the club. Nonetheless, the question stands: who in the audience has not some "mongrel" part?

The humor in *Pudd'nhead Wilson* is less gentle, more despairing. Tom, like Twain's earlier persona, is a "mongrel." But the fact of his mixed ancestry is caught up in the novel's relentless discourse of differentiation and racial purity that underwrites the project of white supremacy. The effort to rationally legitimate these distinctions is, as Twain makes apparent, doomed from the beginning. Pudd'nhead Wilson's finger-printing of course identifies Tom as Roxy's son, and thus legally a slave. But finding the "nigger" in him is a lot more difficult, simply because that "nigger" – that alternately compulsively deferential and raging kernel of subjectivity – is in fact an essential component of the whiteness he has been trained to inhabit. For what appears momentarily in Tom, what in him feels so fundamental that he will not question Roxy's revelation, is the fantastic counterpart to his easy assumption of racial privilege, the psychic imprint of his relationship with his personal slave, Chambers. As boys, both Chambers and Tom were each taught their places with the whip and the cudgel. Like the Italian brothers, they are in effect twins: neither can be himself without the inner, often unquestioned, presence of the other.

Twain would explore his own "inner black" throughout his career most productively in his enthusiasm for African American oral and performance cultures. At the same time, he would have difficulty making explicit how this cross-cultural embrace shaped the white world he inhabited. His methods of fictional composition may have had something to do with this. While his penchant for parody, and his ability to bring languages into comic collision, produced the kinds of surprising conjunctions that animate such passages as those in *Pudd'nhead Wilson*, they also left him unable, or unwilling, to resolve the contradictions thereby produced. However, it could also be that for Twain the issue of racial codependency itself was particularly intractable, which could account for the particular difficulties he had writing this novel. That the topic was nonetheless compelling is suggested by his continuing to explore racial reversals in such stories as "Which Was It?," as well as in his fascination with twins and twinning. By the same token, most such projects remained incomplete.

White Hegemony

"My idea of our civilization is that it is a shabby poor thing full of cruelties, vanities, arrogancies, meannesses, and hypocrisies."[15]

In the Dawson's Landing of *Pudd'nhead Wilson* (as in the late nineteenth-century United States of Mark Twain) heredity, or "blood," legitimates one's claims to the social and economic privileges which accrue to whiteness. But this does not tell the whole story of race in the novel. David Wilson and many of the town's inhabitants qualify as white, but only the sons of Virginia who can document their lineage can enjoy "a recognized superiority," even a "supremacy," over everyone else. And Roxy carries at least as illustrious a heritage as Judge Driscoll, but of course her lineage is not pure, and so she is not white. Whiteness comes in gradations, which is why it must be cultivated and preserved. A man may be "born a gentleman," but to qualify for such status he must "watch over that inheritance and keep it unsmirched. He must keep his honor spotless" (Twain 1894: 156), or risk falling from the ranks. With its duels and its elaborate codes of honor and humiliation, *Pudd'nhead Wilson* represents one of Twain's most searching explorations of how questions of "blood" became practices of culture, and how society worked to consolidate and reproduce its collective investment in whiteness. Equally importantly, the novel points to how we might begin to understand Twain's later occasional and uncompleted writings as at least partially extending his exploration of the fictions of whiteness.

In a world of impure lineages, honor both supports and displaces the regulation of blood: only the unsmirched may make a claim to honor, but only the honorable may make a claim to pure blood. Gentlemen must live their lives above the petty disputes of the law, which functions only to resolve questions of property, including wills and slave ownership. For issues of personal truthfulness and integrity, they are required to resort to the duel, a mechanism that efficiently calibrates character as courage. Tom violates this code when he takes Luigi to court for kicking him in public. When his uncle discovers that "blood of my race has suffered a blow and crawled to a court of law about it," he insists on Tom's challenging the Italian to a duel. When Tom blanches in fear at the prospect, Judge Driscoll does what every gentleman must do: he purifies his line by disinheriting the "cur" and himself issuing a challenge (Twain 1894: 161). In doing so, he acts in accordance with what Twain had described in *Life on the Mississippi* as the "Sir Walter disease," named after the writer whose romances of medieval fantasy had endowed "rank and caste" with an alluring aura, and inspired "the duel, the inflated speech, and the jejune romanticism of an absurd past that is dead" (Twain 1883: 469, 468). In describing the cult of honor as a disease of the imagination, Twain here stresses the sheer irrationality of Southern ways, a perspective that frames the bloody feud in *Huckleberry Finn*. In *Pudd'nhead Wilson*, though, the logic of honor is as rigorous as it is appalling. The novel's "one spot rule" of honor echoes nothing other than the notorious "one drop rule" at the heart of racial segregation in the post-Reconstruction United States, which decreed that anyone with *any* African ancestry, no matter how distant, was black. The rituals of honor obfuscate that connection, imbuing whiteness with an aura of individual integrity and fortitude, qualities that are embodied in the tight fraternity of men who are allowed to indulge in such symbolic cleansing.

David Wilson's identification of Tom as a murderer and a slave, and Tom's subsequent selling down the river, emphasizes with violent irony the absurdity of such
attempts at racial classification. But the extent to which this law is broadly upheld,
and the extent to which Wilson and Roxy in particular relish the duel, and invest
their interests in the code of heredity, honor, and whiteness, point to how racial superiority can function as a form of hegemony, a discourse of difference that both shapes
norms for those who benefit from it, and compels the consent of those who suffer from
it. In this, Twain's novel is situated firmly in its time, when not just racial ideologies,
but national representations, equated Anglo-Saxon manhood with Civilization, and
mapped all the other of the world's "races" (a term that could be fluid) on a geography of relative savagery. Nowhere was this blend of millennial Darwinism, scientific
knowledge, and national imperialism made more explicit than at the 1893 Chicago
Columbian World's Exposition, where the faux-classical architecture of the White
City rose above anthropologies and amusements of those races and cultures the United
States was destined to civilize. And in few places were these pretensions as clearly
exposed as in Twain's novel.[16]

Later in his life, Twain would match the globalizing scope of American aspirations
by shifting his critique of whiteness to the imperial ambitions of civilization, an imaginative direction he had discovered in *Connecticut Yankee*, his fantasy of the origins of
Anglo-Saxonism. Yet even such essays as "To the Person Sitting in Darkness," "As
Regards Patriotism," and his last great attack on American racism, "The United States
of Lyncherdom," are grounded in his growing sense that the mass of people, like the
serfs of medieval England, are passive victims to training and demagoguery. But, on
the whole, the character of Western society Twain invokes in his critiques, and targets
in the nihilistic weariness that saturates such late texts as *The Mysterious Stranger*, recalls
the same self-righteous fury, the same "fish-belly" bad faith, that shaped his representation of domestic whiteness. Civilization, like whiteness, and *as* whiteness, was indeed
"a shabby poor thing." Twain, like Huck, couldn't stand it; he'd been there before.

NOTES

1 In an 1891 letter to an unidentified recipient,
Twain wrote: "the most valuable capital or
culture or education usable in the building of
novels is personal experience" (Twain 1917:
541).

2 On the controversies surrounding *Huckleberry
Finn*, see Leonard et al. (1992).

3 The tale is included in "How To Tell A Story"
(1895). See Twain (1992b: 201–6). Twain
reminisces about hearing it in his *Autobiography*. Jerry is recalled in "Corn-Pone Opinions"
(1901). See Twain (1992b: 507–11).

4 I discuss Twain's parodic imagination in
Lowry (1996).

5 The literature on whiteness is broad. hooks
(1995) and Dyer (1997) developed key early
discussions. Morrison's book (1992) brought
the issue of whiteness specifically to American literature. Frankenberg (1997), Hill
(1997), Lipsitz (1998), Rasmussen (2001),
Roediger (1991), and Wexler (2000) offer
extremely useful cultural analyses of the issue.

6 As Ruth Frankenberg reminds us, we can
"learn much about whiteness from asking

how white people depict people of color" (Frankenberg 2001: 79).

7 Letter to Jane Lampton Clemens, 24 August 1853 (Twain 1988: 4).

8 The phrase forms the title of David Roediger's book (1991).

9 Mark Twain, "Only a Nigger," *Buffalo Express*, 26 August 1869, p. 2. Quoted in Fishkin (1997: 82).

10 The phrase forms the title of George Lipsitz's book (1998).

11 See Robinson (1986) for discussion of these issues.

12 Susan Faludi (1999) explores contemporary expressions of this feeling of dispossession.

13 I allude, of course, to Fishkin's rhetorical question, *Was Huck Black?* (1993).

14 Thompson's famous pronouncement is: "To be white in America is to be very black. If you don't know how black you are, you don't know how American you are." It was made in a 1992 lecture entitled "The Kongo Atlantic Tradition," cited in Fishkin (1993: 132).

15 "Civilization and War: Letter to Joseph H. Twichell," *Mark Twain's Letters* (New York: Harper & Bros., 1917). See http://www.boondocksnet.com/ai/twain/letter000127.html in Jim Zwick, ed., *Anti-Imperialism in the United States, 1898–1935*. http://www.boondocksnet.com/ai/ (accessed Sept. 30, 2004).

16 Another place to find such critique would be in the work of the African American writer Charles Chesnutt, who kept a bust of Twain on his mantel. On ideologies of race and civilization, with attention to the Columbian Exposition, see Bederman (1995)

References and Further Reading

Bederman, Gail (1995). *Manliness and Civilization: A Cultural History of Gender and Race in the United States, 1880–1917*. Chicago: University of Chicago Press.

Du Bois, W. E. B. (1996). *The Souls of Black Folk*. New York: Penguin. (First publ. 1903.)

Dyer, Richard (1997). *White*. New York: Routledge.

Ellison, Ralph (1953). "Change the Joke and Slip the Yoke." In *Shadow and Act*, 45–59. New York: Random House.

Faludi, Susan (1999). *Stiffed: The Betrayal of the American Man*. New York: Morrow.

Fishkin, Shelley Fisher (1993). *Was Huck Black? Mark Twain and African American Voices*. New York: Oxford University Press.

Fishkin, Shelley Fisher (1997). *Lighting Out for the Territory: Reflections on Mark Twain and American Culture*. New York: Oxford University Press.

Frankenberg, Ruth (2001). "The Mirage of an Unmarked Whiteness." In Rasmussen et al., eds., *The Making and Unmaking of Whiteness*, 72–96. Durham, NC: Duke University Press.

Frankenberg, Ruth, ed. (1997). *Displacing Whiteness: Essays in Social and Cultural Criticism*. Durham, NC: Duke University Press.

Gillman, Susan (1989). *Dark Twins: Imposture and Identity in Mark Twain's America*. Chicago: University of Chicago Press.

Gillman, Susan, and Robinson, Forrest G., eds. (1990). *Mark Twain's Pudd'nhead Wilson: Race, Conflict, and Culture*. Durham, NC: Duke University Press.

Hill, Mike, ed. (1997). *Whiteness: A Critical Reader*. New York: New York University Press.

hooks, bell (1995). "Representations of Whiteness in the Black Imagination." In *Killing Rage, Ending Racism*, 31–50. New York: Holt.

Howells, William Dean (1910). *My Mark Twain: Reminiscences and Criticisms*. New York: Harper & Bros.

Leonard, James S., Tenney, Thomas A., and Davis, Thadious M., eds. (1992). *Satire or Evasion? Black Perspectives on Huckleberry Finn*. Durham, NC: Duke University Press.

Lipsitz, George (1998). *The Possessive Investment in Whiteness: How White People Profit from Identity Politics*. Philadelphia: Temple University Press.

Lott, Eric (1995a). "Mr. Clemens and Jim Crow: Twain, Race, and Blackface." In Forrest G. Robinson (ed.), *The Cambridge Companion to*

Mark Twain, 129–52. Cambridge: Cambridge University Press.

Lott, Eric (1995b). *Love and Theft: Blackface Minstrelsy and the American Working Class*. New York: Oxford University Press.

Lowry, Richard S. (1996). *"Littery Man": Mark Twain and Modern Authorship*. New York: Oxford University Press.

Morrison, Toni (1992). *Playing in the Dark: Whiteness and the Literary Imagination*. Cambridge, Mass.: Harvard University Press.

Rasmussen, Birgit Brander; Klinenberg, Eric; Nexica, Irene J.; and Wray, Matt, eds. (2001). *The Making and Unmaking of Whiteness*. Durham, NC: Duke University Press.

Robinson, Forrest G. (1986). *In Bad Faith: The Dynamics of Deception in Mark Twain's America*. Cambridge, Mass.: Harvard University Press.

Roediger, David R. (1991). *The Wages of Whiteness: Race and the Making of the American Working Class*. London: Verso.

Sundquist, Eric (1993). *To Wake the Nations: Race in the Making of American Literature*. Cambridge, Mass.: Harvard University Press.

Twain, Mark (1917). *Mark Twain's Letters*, 2 vols., ed. Albert Bigelow Paine. New York: Harper & Bros.

Twain, Mark (1969). *Mark Twain's Mysterious Stranger Manuscripts*, ed. William M. Gibson. Berkeley: University of California Press.

Twain, Mark (1988). *Mark Twain's Letters*, vol. 1: *1853–1866*, ed. Edgar Marquess Branch, Michael B. Frank, and Kenneth M. Sanderson. Berkeley: University of California Press.

Wexler, Laura (2000). *Tender Violence: Domestic Visions in an Age of US Imperialism*. Chapel Hill: University of North Carolina Press.

5

Mark Twain and Gender

Peter Stoneley

Such was Twain's fame that, when he died in 1910, numerous cartoons were published in newspapers and journals to mark his passing. The artists offered sketches of his best-known characters and personae – Tom Sawyer, the steamboat pilot, Colonel Sellers, the innocent abroad. Others showed a tearful Uncle Sam, his hat off and his head bowed. The most popular figure with the cartoonists was Huckleberry Finn, a boy in rags who, in one drawing, ushers Twain into the Hall of Fame.[1] Huck seems to invoke the most cherished aspects of Twain's reputation: the democrat who was from and who remained close to ordinary people; a man who took an interest in the friendless and outcast, and who paid no attention to pernicious social distinctions. Perhaps Huck also suggests the typically American youthfulness of the Twain image. In spite of the man's well-publicized bankruptcy and domestic tragedies, the prevailing idea of him is that of good-natured hopefulness.

There were some quite murky and complicated truths behind this image, and later generations have been told at length of Twain's rages, his bitterness, and his social vanity. One other thing that might now make us pause is that, in every cartoon, Twain is pictured in the company of men and boys. Given some historical understanding, this should not come as a surprise. In Twain's day the sexes were usually considered to belong within different domains. At the level of the middle class, in particular, men were preoccupied by their public, professional lives, while women supposedly found fulfillment in the home. It was characteristic of the age that Twain should automatically be identified with other men. But there is also the more particular sense that Twain was a "man's man," and even, at his most characteristic, a man's writer. He tended to present himself as uncomfortable in a genteel, feminine environment, and in spite of a few aberrant texts such as *Joan of Arc* (1896), his work – and especially his best work – was very much concerned with the interactions, codes, and pursuits of men and boys.

At various points in the nine decades since his death, Twain's gendered allegiances have not been accepted in the apparently unpremeditated way of the cartoonists of

1910, but have become the grounds of fierce debate. In *The Ordeal of Mark Twain* (1920), Van Wyck Brooks presented Twain as an agonized and oppressed figure. Brooks argued that Twain was a great writer when he functioned as his natural self, but that his genius was smothered by the women in his life and by a domineeringly feminine culture, his bold and bawdy democratic vision tamed and diminished. If only he had been able to withstand the pious and narrow-minded cabal of feminine interests, Brooks suggests, we would have had more novels of the stature of *Adventures of Huckleberry Finn*, and fewer insipidly polite works like *The Prince and the Pauper* (1881). In Leslie Fiedler's impassioned and influential study, *Love and Death in the American Novel* (1960), Twain was less obviously a victim. Fiedler observed a more widespread failure to write about adult, heterosexual relationships. He noted the relatively infantile, or naïvely homosexual, aspect of American literary culture. In *Moby-Dick* (1851), Melville takes us to the all-male world of the whaling-ship, and his narrator finds safety in the noble, nonsexual embrace of a new friend. The events of Hawthorne's *The Scarlet Letter* (1852) turn on an adulterous liaison, but this has more or less run its course in the novel's prehistory. In turn, Huck runs from the fussy women who would "sivilise" him, and joins Jim on the raft. Fiedler's Twain is typical of a culture that was limited and evasive when it came to describing the relations between the sexes.

Many scholars and critics have followed Fiedler's lead, and argued that Twain's female characters belong within a narrow range of stereotypes: the charmingly innocent girl; the dull, fussy, maternal figure; the dangerously wild "mulatta." Other critics have occasionally found that Twain's more feminine works were of interest, and that they confirmed important aspects of his imagination, as, for instance, in Susan K. Harris's discussion of *Joan of Arc* in relation to Twain's search for a transcendent "escape from time." The whole field of nineteenth-century literary studies, though, took on a new aspect with the rise of feminist scholarship. Ann Douglas's *The Feminization of American Culture* (1977) seemed a final flowering of the Brooksian thesis, in that she argued that male writers and clerics had been undermined by a self-indulgent female culture. Jane P. Tompkins opposed Douglas's arguments in *Sensational Designs* (1985), pointing to the complexities and strengths of feminine, domestic culture.

Within Twain studies in particular, it was soon recognized that Twain was no helpless victim of feminized gentility. He came to be seen as a keen enforcer of a culture in which, after all, men had power and control over women's lives. Twain had not been dominated by his wife, it was argued. He had made her his "censor" because he thrived on the idea of rebellion against – and surrender to – the polite reader. My own *Mark Twain and the Feminine Aesthetic* (1992) explored Twain's strong interest in women's culture. I assessed the ways in which Twain was complicit with and exploited the values of a genteel and allegedly feminized culture. Laura Skandera-Trombley's *Mark Twain in the Company of Women* (1993) offered a more specifically biographical approach, arguing the positive benefits of some of the female environments through which Twain moved. In *Mark Twain, Culture and Gender: Envisioning America through*

Europe (1994), John D. Stahl presented a subtle critique of the way in which Twain constructs gender and nation in relation to each other. In Twain's writing on Europe and on the female Other, Stahl argued, there is a coalescence of sexual and cultural anxiety. This treatment of gender in a more complex cultural context is also a feature of books by Susan Gillman (1989) and Randall Knoper (1995), both of whom locate gender in relation to theatricality. These critics take on such topics as Twain's interest in transvestism as it relates to the uncertainty of identity, and the way in which Twain's writing and persona emerged out of a male subculture of music halls and burlesque shows. In a recent essay that gives a usefully synoptic view of the field, Susan K. Harris also discusses transvestism, suggesting that Twain's cross-dressing narratives show him questioning "social categories that most people took for granted" (Harris 2002: 166). But Harris concludes that Twain does not escape from such categories. Rather, she reminds us of his sexual conservatism. She suggests that we see this in relation to the economic exchange of women in the nineteenth century. Harris cites a late essay on the age of consent, in which Twain writes that there is *"no* age at which the good name of a member of a family ceases to be a part of the *property* of that family – an asset, and worth more than all its bonds and moneys" (p. 170). Twain returns to us as that typically bourgeois figure, the anxiously assertive paterfamilias.

Following on from quite intense phases of feminist and gender analysis, race has emerged as currently the most intensely and extensively debated topic in Twain studies. Gender, though, continues to be a critical focus within the field, as earlier work is refined and supplemented by later scholars, and also as men and masculinity have come under scrutiny.[2] It is this latter aspect – the characteristically masculine figure, as sketched by the cartoonists – that I want to consider in more detail here. Perhaps it has been inevitable that "Mark Twain and women" should have been the focus for so much work. As several of the abovementioned studies suggest, Twain often defined himself – his literary identity – in oppositional terms. His masculinity was constructed in relation to a feminine other. For all the instances of diverse and particular men, the notion of manhood is implicitly offered as a naturalized and universalized phenomenon. Like the cartoon figures, who are all from different walks of life, but who all relate comfortably to Twain, manhood is easily assumed to be a taken-for-granted *ground*. Individual men may fascinate Twain, but manhood barely exists as a subject. When he does address himself to the idea of manliness, his writing becomes formulaic, grand, and empty. Similarly, friendship in the writing is often assumed so quickly that it cannot constitute a topic as such. In focusing on some aspects of manliness and friendship in Twain's life and work, I want to try to take a more conscious look at the values that are otherwise both so obvious and so elusive.

In his teens, Clemens contributed numerous sketches to small-town newspapers, but he sprang to prominence in the 1860s as the rough and ready humorist of the mining communities of Nevada and California. He became Mark Twain in 1863, when writing for the Virginia City *Territorial Enterprise*, and he subsequently acquired the sobriquet "The Wild Humorist of the Pacific Slope." His sketches gave some sense of the disreputable lives of the miners, and made play of Twain's own supposed laziness, and his fondness for drinking and for bar-room society. This improper, unrefined, and very masculine world was the source of some of the liveliest of Twain's early humor. Yet there is a self-consciousness in much of this early work that reveals that the writer was still the cautious, conscientious son of a decent family. He flirted with the off-color anecdotes and language that made his writing, at times, inappropriate for a mixed readership. But he was ambivalent about this emphatically masculine identification. He felt miscast and confined as a crude jester, and came to resent the way in which audiences and readers seemed to have such low expectations of him. That ambivalence is already implicit in some of his earliest "bar-room" stories.

In the sketch that brought him to national attention, "Jim Smiley and His Jumping Frog," we get a sense of some of the tensions within Twain's manly world. The narrator addresses a formal letter to fellow humorist Artemus Ward, in which he allows that he has probably been the victim of one of Ward's pranks. Ward has supposedly sent Twain to call on one Simon Wheeler to inquire after the Reverend Leonidas W. Smiley, a "cherished companion of [Ward's] boyhood" (Twain 1992a: 171).[3] In itself, this presents Ward in an unlikely, nostalgic, and religiose guise, and Twain offers himself as the fool who fell for Ward's fake sentimentality. In making the call, the narrator becomes the victim of the "garrulous" Wheeler's endless, rambling anecdotes of mining men he has known. Twain recounts how Wheeler "backed me into a corner and blockaded me there with his chair" (p. 171). Wheeler then tells him at some length not of the Reverend Smiley but of the gambler Jim Smiley, who had been around back in the spring of '49 or '50. So strong was Smiley's compulsion to gamble, Wheeler recounts, that "if there was a dog-fight, he'd bet on it; if there was a cat-fight, he'd bet on it; if there was a chicken-fight, he'd bet on it; why if there was two birds setting on a fence, he would bet you which one would fly first" (p. 172). When, one morning, the Parson said that his wife was recovering from her serious illness, Smiley burst out, "Well, I'll resk two-and-a-half that she don't, anyway" (p. 173).

Wheeler's longest anecdote concerns Smiley's jumping frog, Dan'l Webster, which Smiley had trained to jump (in itself a seemingly odd and unnecessary process). Smiley bets a stranger that his frog can out-jump any other. The stranger replies he would accept the bet, only he "ain't got no frog." Smiley offers to find him one, and while he is gone, the stranger fills Dan'l Webster with a teaspoon of quailshot. Inevitably, Smiley loses the bet. When the moment comes for Dan'l to jump, he shrugs his shoulders up "like a Frenchman," but does not get off the ground (Twain 1992a: 175–6). Wheeler is only too ready to carry on with tales of Smiley, but when he launches into events concerning Smiley's "yaller one-eyed cow that didn't have no tail only just a short stump like a bannanner," the narrator curses Smiley and "his afflicted cow" (p. 177) and walks out.

The story seems simple, and yet there are nuances, both in the story itself and in the relation of the story to the Twain persona. First, there is an ironic relation between the story and its fabled context. Twain would become one of the great celebrants of Gold and Silver Rush culture in *Roughing It* (1872), and he would extol the manly vigor of the young men who went in search of a fortune. He was aware of the widespread violence of the mining camps but, like many others, he preferred to praise the energy, enterprise, and good nature of the latter-day "Argonauts." Here, though, he offers neither the virility of the gold-seekers, nor the brutality. Instead, he presents the inconsequential memories of a harmless old-timer, a man who seems never to have been young or vigorous, and who clearly failed to make his mark during or after the heyday of the Gold Rush. The violence and sharp practice of the mines comes to us in a delicately attenuated form. The narrator has been duped by Ward's sharp practice, and he is then bested by Wheeler, who finds it only too easy to back the narrator into a corner and to "blockade" him. The moral laxity of the camps – with their bars and brothels – here appears in the boyishly "wicked" form of small, opportunistic bets and a joke at the expense of a parson's wife. The heroic enterprise of the Gold Rush is, in Wheeler's version, an account of small victories, and equally small defeats. Wheeler's narrative is full of the pathos that Twain thought was definitive of humor. Alongside the jokes, there is a gentle sadness to Smiley's and Wheeler's enthusiasms. The fun is at their expense, but this is not satire. Twain does not invite us to judge them so much as to spend time with them and to appreciate their maddening charms. The position of the author-as-narrator is complex, though, and it lends the sketch a certain tension. Twain does not give this narrator any of the easy-going charm that he uses elsewhere. This narrator is telling the story at his own expense, but not exactly with a good grace. While Twain liked, in his early career, to make great play of his own laziness and his pleasure in hanging around bars, this narrator exhibits more of the ambition of the times. He has been "victimized" in the sense that his time has been wasted, and with his primly mild cursing of Smiley and his "afflicted cow," he reveals himself as someone who is as keen to get on as the next man.

Twain sets up a contrast between himself and Wheeler. For all the smallness of his existence, it is Wheeler's vernacular energy that gives the sketch its life. And while we may be glad that it was the narrator and not ourselves who was "blockaded" by Wheeler, we might also find ourselves warming to Wheeler and his lore rather than to the punctilious man who cuts him short. Twain ingratiates himself with his readership at the start by claiming friendship with the much-loved Artemus Ward. Further, he offers us a sketch that is in the tradition of Ward. But he also complicates and enriches the humor by inter-cutting it with a slightly unsympathetic narrator. Already, shortly after the invention of "Mark Twain," Clemens is slightly impatient with the identity he is fashioning for himself. But this gives the sketch a dynamic that takes it well beyond simple literary buffoonery. It might be tempting to see the narrator here as the "real" author, Clemens as opposed to Twain. He complained in a letter to his mother and sister that he was being acclaimed as the writer of "a villainous backwoods sketch," a sketch that he claimed he had only written "but to please Artemus Ward" (Twain 1988: 327), as though, like the narrator, he is in part contemptuous of his material. But surely the letter is another instance of posturing. He is preparing the way for his success with his pious and censorious female relations by affecting disdain. There may be some genuine measure of shame there, in that Twain's upbringing, if not "villainous," was not far from "backwoods." Throughout his life, he would try to escape the taint of the provincial, even though it fascinated him and inspired his finest work.

In "Jim Smiley and His Jumping Frog," a rough-hewn masculinity is set beside the clean-cut and supercilious manliness that has superseded it. There is a strong tradition of such comic contrasts in American vernacular humor, as Kenneth Lynn and others have shown, and this basic scenario certainly recurs throughout Twain's work. His earliest known publication, "The Dandy Frightening the Squatter" (1852), turns on a similar confrontation between types of masculinity, and his first full-length book, *The Innocents Abroad* (1869), presents the same idea with extensive variations.[4] In *The Innocents Abroad* Twain again seems to hesitate between various personae: he is by turns romantic and moralistic, but the definitive self to which he returns is that of the humorous, incorrect, but good-natured man's man, who makes light of some of the most revered images of European culture.

Although this is to simplify, there is a gendered thematics at work in most of Twain's key books. *Roughing It* recounts Twain's experience of going West. In this process, the "tenderfoot" narrator is initiated in the practices and styles of a rougher, more spontaneous masculinity. The sense is that, in the West and far from feminine influence, men have either regressed or recovered themselves. In *Life on the Mississippi* (1883), too, the narrator undergoes a similar virilizing process, as his romantic notions of the river are stripped away by the foul-mouthed but admirable pilots and engineers that he encounters. Both before and after Huck ran away from the women who would civilize him, Twain's guiding inclination was to immerse himself in the worlds of men. This is a questioning experience, though, in that there is a critical awareness of the values and possibilities of the manliness he describes. For all his occasional backwoods posturing and his mischievous "bad boy" comments, Twain must be assumed to be quite a progressive, urbane figure, in that he can mediate between a polite, narrow, and even prissy manhood, and its rough-and-ready counterpart.

The centrality of this theme, and the subtlety with which he handles it, is perhaps best indicated in the so-called "boy books." Huckleberry Finn, the son of the town drunkard and a virtually unmentioned and perhaps unmentionable mother, was for his time a scandalously impolite boy. He is an extravagant example of "bad influence," and anxious mothers try to keep their sons from mixing with him. Huck chews tobacco and spits; he uses incorrect and blasphemous language; his ragged and dirty clothes are an affront to decency. He has a tendency to squirm and yawn, and his unacceptable bodiliness, implied by his inadequate clothing, is further suggested by his habit of scratching himself. Other boys see in him a freedom from constraint, and in spite of, or because of, their mothers' prohibitions, they find the idea of him beguiling.

In *The Adventures of Tom Sawyer* (1876), Tom himself is Twain's main focus. Tom is an interesting hero because he is adventurous, and Twain makes gentle fun of his immature, vainglorious notions. But Tom often casts remorseful backward glances to the aunt who adopted him on his mother's death. She remains his point of reference, and even when, in *Adventures of Huckleberry Finn* (1885), he journeys a vast distance downriver, it is to stay with another aunt and to resume his infantile games. Tom is ultimately tiresome because, like any boy who is, at heart, a "good boy," he requires his every experience to fit in some way with the values and opinions he has acquired from home, school, and books. Huck is more free and genuine in his responses to his experiences, and it is his story rather than Tom's that is Twain's finest achievement.

This is not to say that Twain grants an easy contrast between a tamed and implicitly feminized masculinity on the one hand, and a stronger, less socialized masculinity on the other. Huck is certainly wary of the various middle-aged women who wish to adopt him. He finds the new clothes that the Widow Douglas makes him wear stiflingly uncomfortable, and he quietly rejects her endless criticism of his tobacco-chewing, and his yawning, and his scratching. However, he gets used to the Widow's ways, and even starts to enjoy going to school. By the time his father reappears, Huck has a different perspective on his old, rough, hand-to-mouth life. In his father, Huck sees a scary and dangerous side to freedom from genteel strictures:

> He was most fifty, and he looked it. His hair was long and tangled and greasy, and hung down, and you could see his eyes shining through like he was behind vines. It was all black, no gray; so was his long, mixed-up whiskers. There warn't no color in his face, where his face showed; it was white; not like another man's white, but a white to make a body sick, a white to make a body's flesh crawl – a tree-toad white, a fish-belly white. (Twain 1885: 39)

In his father, Huck sees a simplicity that amounts to subhuman ignorance. Huck is no unreflecting exemplar and promoter of a "natural" masculinity, even if he likes to get away from the fussing of women. He moves among the various possibilities of fastidiousness and negligence, care and freedom, and never finds himself entirely at home.

What, though, about the nature of chosen relations between men? For all that Twain was celebrated as an author for boys and men, and above all as an author of friendship between boys, criticism – even that which has paid attention to gendered behavior – has seldom focused on friendship. We tend, perhaps, to assume that the nature of friendship is automatic and unchanging, or that it is too casual and happenstance to bear much analysis. This relative neglect is as true of Twain's life as of his work. We may know that Twain was great friends with William Dean Howells or Henry Huttleston Rogers, and we may have read the published correspondence. But these relationships have, perhaps understandably, not attracted the same attention as Twain's intense and difficult relationships with his wife and daughters.[5] Friendship was much less important to Twain. As Howells commented, his love for his wife was "a greater part of him than the love of most men for their wives" (Howells 1910: 10). But friendship is of interest, both in the life and in the work. I do not want to collapse the two, and see the work as a sort of oblique autobiography. The writing is subject to other impulses and requirements, and there is no actual, close, and consistent similarity between the Huck–Jim, or Huck–Tom friendship, and the Twain–Howells or Twain–Twichell friendship.

What we can seek to delineate in moving between the life and the work, though, is a more generalized sense of the value and function of friendships between men. To persevere for a moment with the boy-books, Huck and Tom are the same age, and we might assume that they have a strong bond based simply in that recognition of sameness, of common interest. Yet each is clearly attracted by the other's difference. Tom, a clean boy from a proper home, has a classy glamor for Huck. Huck assumes a high and worthy moral standard in Tom, and is shocked when Tom suggests they set free somebody else's slave. Tom sees a corresponding glamor in Huck, in that Huck seems to be entirely free of all the protocols and constraints of life with women. Huck and Tom's friendship is focused around society and how to deal with it. Huck venerates the idea of proper society, but his own outcast status means that he does not think that the rules fail in any important way when he breaks them. He can take up friendship where he finds it, with a runaway slave, and he can, to some extent, form a sense of Jim that is to one side of the latter's social and legal status as a slave. The two develop a relationship that has a kind of improvisatory aspect. Their friendship incorporates the qualities of other types of relationship: Jim worries about Huck and, as it were, "mothers" him, while, from time to time, Huck takes Jim for granted and acts, as it were, like an erring husband. But they also develop a routine that has its own logic and its own pleasures. They travel at night so as to avoid problems, and during the heat of the day they hide their raft and sit about naked in the coolness of the river-mud. Their friendship is endangered whenever Huck falls back into the regular, shore-dwelling, proper way of thinking. Once Huck allows normal social obligations to re-enter his thoughts, he remembers that Jim is somebody else's property, and that he ought to return him to his legal owner.

The friendship, then, depends upon alienation from normal life. It depends upon the suspension of the normal rules of manhood and race. It is a common paradox that manhood is often sustained by the moments at which it forgets itself. Male social relations are, in this Mississippi world, ordinarily constituted in terms of recognizing other people's property rights, but a truer friendship requires a dereliction of normal duties. There is, then, an infantile quality or even an infantile requirement. Friendship is the safe microsphere in which Huck and Jim can relax and, after the manner of infants, play about in the mud. What this means, though, is that friendship, while it is special and protected, is to one side of life; it is not, as it were, binding in the real world. While critics have waxed loquacious on the friendship between Huck and Jim, its value seems to fall into question the moment they return to shore life. Huck and Jim's friendship is dangerous, and it is as well for Huck that he seems to place more value in his friendships with fellow white boys, Buck Grangerford and Tom Sawyer. Tom breaks the rules and, in a sense, friendship is again represented in the willingness to forge a personal bond at the expense of a wider social bond. But the social bond is ultimately geared toward the will and needs of white manhood, and so the alliance between Huck and Tom might be assumed to be the moment of contained or futile subversion that, over the longer term, will affirm the status quo.

I have argued that friendship is constituted by regressive moments, as though, by passing through such infantile pleasures together, men or boys then seem to share a longer and naturalized history: they create a sense that they were children together. An alternative suggestion here might be that the infantile aspect again raises the racial issue. Huck is a boy, and Jim seems boyish because Twain espoused a benevolent but racist understanding of African Americans as innocent and simple. While Twain did at times envisage African American men as harmless and sweet, this is also a reflection of Twain's most deeply held ideal of masculinity and of friendship, and this becomes apparent when we look at his relationship with one of his own closest friends.

Twain knew the novelist and editor William Dean Howells for over 40 years. While Howells was embraced by a New England literary establishment that never quite took to Twain, both had started out as Westerners of modest origins, and both broke into social elites. They could share the serious adventures of professional life, but when Howells remembers the friendship, he often remembers it as an escape from responsibility. Of their first lunch in Boston in the company of other writers, Howells recollected nothing "but a sense of idle and aimless and joyful talk-play, beginning and ending nowhere" (Howells 1910: 6). Howells also makes clear the impolite aspects of Twain, aspects that Howells found appalling and beguiling in equal measure. He mentions Twain's "breadth of parlance, which I suppose one ought not to call coarse without calling one's self prudish," and he recounts how, on receiving letters from Twain in which Twain "loosed his bold fancy to stoop on rank suggestion," he would hide such letters away "in discreet holes and corners" (pp. 3–4). There is an echo of the fiction here, as the constrained "good boy" guards from wives or mothers the talismans of masculine defiance – not pilfered tobacco or alcohol in this case, but letters with bad language and off-color anecdotes.

But this remains a very cautious and partial defiance on the parts of both men. In noting that Twain had "the heart of a good boy, or a bad boy, but always a wilful boy" (Howells 1910: 5), Howells implies that Twain was ultimately submissive to "adult" or established authority. For the brief periods that they spent together, Twain pushed Howells into a raft-like, vagabond existence. They sat up late into the night and "talked and talked and talked." They became excitable in each other's company, even within the prosaic scenes and situations of adult life. Howells commented on their sharing hotel rooms in New York: "We wished to be asleep, but we could not stop, and he lounged through the rooms in the long nightgown which he always wore in preference to the pajamas which he despised" (pp. 9–10). Twain overturned Howells's orderly and hard-working life to the extent that Howells would be left feeling "hollow" and "realizing myself best in the image of one of those locust-shells which you find sticking to the bark of trees at the end of the summer" (p. 9). Even on Howells's last visit with Twain when both were in their seventies, Howells recalled:

> Every morning before I dressed I heard him sounding my name through the house for the fun of it and I knew for the fondness; and if I looked out of my door, there he was in his long nightgown swaying up and down the corridor, and wagging his great white

head like a boy that leaves his bed and comes out in the hope of frolic with some one. (p. 99)

Both men were married and, as writers, were engaged in a competitive activity that depended on discipline and native wit. They discussed serious matters in those endless late-night talks: politics, religion, morality, death, their past lives and losses. In letters, they acknowledged each other's personal tragedies with fondness and tact. Each placed great trust in the other, whether in private nightgowned discussions or in public statements on each other's value. The relationship may have had a boyish element, but it was also a first and last testing-ground for their most keenly held ideas and beliefs. And yet, here as elsewhere, there was something slightly stagy and less than close in all this. Howells knew Twain well enough to know the limits of Twain's temperament, and he was careful to stay on the right side of those limits. And while Howells wrote a book on Twain, Twain expatiated rather less on Howells. Twain was more of the moment, and became more completely embroiled in his various enthusiasms and rages. Perhaps he was insufficiently introspective to speculate or theorize at length on Howells (Howells described Twain as "essentially histrionic" [1910: 52]). Perhaps, also, Twain was too much of an egotist. When, in later years, Twain was engaged in his autobiography, Howells joked with him as to how he himself would appear in the work. Twain gave him "some sort of joking reassurance" (p. 94). The curious fact is that Howells barely appears at all in the autobiographical writings. Even when Twain set himself the task of writing an essay entitled "William Dean Howells," while his praise is fervent, it is pitifully limited. He writes at some length and repetitiously on Howells's "verbal exactness." It is interesting that Twain values so highly the clear and precise quality of Howells's prose, but his critique is a cautious and dutiful assessment that never engages with the themes and values of his friend's work.[6]

Twain's friendships left no monuments of themselves, except where they went wrong and were recorded in testaments of towering bitterness. The nature of the friendship between Twain and Howells, and its implicit preconditions, indicate much concerning masculinity and men's lives in the nineteenth century and beyond. Twain's and Howells's association was enabled by the fact that they had such different literary identities; they were not in competition with each other. The friendship's charm, duration, and effectiveness lay in part in the fact that it was slightly out of the way of adult life. Unlike his marriage or his business relations, it had (for Twain) no substantial legal or financial features. Its precondition was that of "boyish innocence," and it was more Twainian travelogue than structured Howellsian novel. It was a discourse or a practice rather than a determining act; it was vitally inconsequential.

We might wish to avoid the topic of friendship, then, because it is curiously delicate and paradoxical. But perhaps we should not accept too readily the informal and self-consciously juvenile aspects of Twain's friendships. In another sense, he was following the advice that Anson Burlingame had given him in 1866: that he be aspirational in such relationships. When Twain and Howells met, Howells was an increasingly influential figure who had just given Twain a good review. When Twain and Twichell met, Twichell was the Yale-educated pastor who could ensure Twain's acceptance into the more exclusive circles of Hartford. When Twain and Rogers met, Twain was bankrupt and Rogers was a millionaire. I do not think there was a cynical motive on Twain's part in any of these relationships, but, as with Huck and Tom, the unexpected and playful aspects were underpinned by a more mundane social logic.[7]

More generally, one might argue that Twain's understanding of gender was too simplistic, too naïvely subject to the middle-class conventions of his day, for him to serve as the grounds of sustained study. His female characters are often one-dimensional, and are determined in relation to clumsy and troubling categories: the pure, girlish woman; the fussy, interfering woman; the hungry, dangerous woman. Even his male characters might seem to lack subtlety. But, as critics such as Stahl and Knoper remind us, gender manifests itself in all kinds of subtle and important ways. Perhaps Twain's genius is most apparent in his vivid sketches of people and scenes, and not in his more analytical phases. He creates the experience of the encounter with a liveliness and an ironic depth that have seldom been matched. Twain and his characters are of interest not so much for any quality of interiority, but rather as personae through whom we get telling glimpses, through whom we seem to gain an intense and immediate sense of "the times." But Twain is still interesting in relation to gender *per se*. With regard to women, certain conventions and tendencies emerge in particularly clear and dramatic form. With regard to masculinity, boyishness, and friendship, he wrote about these themes with such detail and brilliance that his version of boyhood has come to be accepted as an unchanging and essential phase. His powers as a writer have caused one of his main topics to be seen as beyond comment, as something that can only be agreed to and enjoyed. All the more reason, perhaps, to think through the contexts and functions of Twain's versions of femininity and masculinity.

NOTES

1 Louis J. Budd (1983) reprints and discusses a selection of these cartoons; see pp. 2–3, 5, 232.

2 For recent work on the domestic contexts of Twain's life, see e.g. Harris (1996); Lystra (2004).

3 The sketch was first published as "Jim Smiley and His Jumping Frog" in the *Saturday Press* (November 18, 1865). For a reprint and textual history, see Twain (1981). The story was retitled and altered in the book version, in which the reference to Ward is removed.

4 For studies of Twain and of the tradition of American humor, see especially Lynn (1959), and the relevant essays in this volume. Twain's first book was a short collection of sketches,

The Celebrated Jumping Frog of Calaveras County (1867).

5 This area has received some attention in the past, for example from Duckett (1964), Lowry (1996), Hoffman (1995), and Stoneley (1996), and is gaining renewed attention in the present: see e.g. Messent (2003 and forthcoming).

6 This essay was first published in *Harper's Monthly Magazine* (July 1906), and is reprinted in Twain (1992b: 722–30).

7 Harris notes that Twain's relationships with men such as Howells, Twichell, and Rogers were "sentimental" or "affective," rather than legal or contractual. She also suggests that this is a sign of Twain's "generation's search for

alternatives to existing male power relations" (Harris 2002: 179). The implication of my argument is rather that such friendships functioned as an approved alternative sociality that re-enabled men to take up their usual rights and obligations. One also thinks here of Knoper, and his comment that nineteenth-century male performances of identity "aimed to occupy margins *and* to marginalize" (Knoper 1995: 23).

REFERENCES AND FURTHER READING

Brooks, Van Wyck (1920). *The Ordeal of Mark Twain*. New York: Dutton.

Budd, Louis J. (1983). *Our Mark Twain: The Making of his Public Personality*. Philadelphia: University of Philadelphia Press.

Douglas, Ann (1977). *The Feminization of American Culture*. New York: Knopf.

Duckett, Margaret (1964). *Mark Twain and Bret Harte*. Norman: University of Oklahoma Press.

Fiedler, Leslie (1960). *Love and Death in the American Novel*. New York: Criterion.

Gillman, Susan (1989). *Dark Twins: Imposture and Identity in Mark Twain's America*. Chicago: University of Chicago Press.

Harris, Susan K. (1982). *Mark Twain's Escape from Time: A Study of Patterns and Images*. Columbia: University of Missouri Press.

Harris, Susan K. (1996). *The Courtship of Olivia Langdon and Mark Twain*. Cambridge, UK: Cambridge University Press.

Harris, Susan K. (2002). "Mark Twain and Gender." In Shelley Fisher Fishkin (ed.), *The Oxford Historical Guide to Mark Twain*, 163–97. Oxford: Oxford University Press.

Hoffman, Andrew Jay (1995). "Mark Twain and Homosexuality." *American Literature* 67: 1, 23–49.

Howells, William Dean (1910). *My Mark Twain*: Reminiscences and Criticisms. New York: Harper & Bros.

Knoper, Randall (1995). *Acting Naturally: Mark Twain and the Culture of Performance*. Berkeley: University of California Press.

Lowry, Richard S. (1996). *"Littery Man": Mark Twain and Modern Authorship*. New York: Oxford University Press.

Lynn, Kenneth S. (1959). *Mark Twain and Southwestern Humor*. Boston: Little, Brown.

Lystra, Karen (2004). *Dangerous Intimacy: The Untold Story of Mark Twain's Final Years*. Berkeley: University of California Press.

Messent, Peter (2003)."Mark Twain, Joseph Twichell, and Religion." *Nineteenth-Century Literature* 58: 3, 368–402.

Messent, Peter (forthcoming). "Mark Twain, Manhood, the Henry H. Rogers Friendship, and 'Which Was the Dream?'" *Arizona Quarterly*.

Skandera-Trombley, Laura (1993). *Mark Twain in the Company of Women*. Philadelphia: University of Philadelphia Press.

Stahl, John D. (1994). *Mark Twain, Culture and Gender: Envisioning America through Europe*. Athens: University of Georgia Press.

Stoneley, Peter (1992). *Mark Twain and the Feminine Aesthetic*. Cambridge, UK: Cambridge University Press.

Stoneley, Peter (1996). "Rewriting the Gold Rush: Twain, Harte, and Homosociality." *Journal of American Studies* 30: 2, 189–211.

Tompkins, Jane (1985). *Sensational Designs: The Cultural Work of American Fiction, 1790–1860*. New York: Oxford University Press.

Twain, Mark (1981). *Early Tales and Sketches*, vol. 2: *1864–1865*, ed. Edgar Marquess Branch and Robert H. Hirst. Berkeley: University of California Press.

Twain, Mark (1988). *Mark Twain's Letters*, vol. 1: *1853–1866*, ed. Edgar Marquess Branch, Michael B. Frank, and Kenneth M. Sanderson. Berkeley: University of California Press.

6

Twain and Modernity

T. J. Lustig

"All modern American literature," Ernest Hemingway once famously observed, "comes from one book by Mark Twain called *Huckleberry Finn*" (1965: 29). Twain's ending was "cheating." Even so, "all American writing comes from that. There was nothing before. There has been nothing as good since" (p. 29). For Jonathan Arac, Hemingway's remark calls attention to the "dialectic terms" of literary history: "tradition and innovation" (1992: 24–5). It is Twain's role as innovator, his status as "iconoclastic idol," that Arac wants to question, arguing that *Huckleberry Finn* has (alongside *The Scarlet Letter* and *Moby-Dick*) come to "monopolize . . . critical attention" in a major instance of "hypercanonization" (p. 14). In what follows, though, I will be concerned less with "American literature" than with Hemingway's initial specification, "modern". Just what exactly is "modern" about Mark Twain?

Shortly after meeting Hank Morgan in *A Connecticut Yankee in King Arthur's Court*, the narrator of the introductory chapter sits by the fire in his hotel, dreaming of "the olden time" and dipping into "old Sir Thomas Malory's enchanting book":

HOW SIR LAUNCELOT SLEW TWO GIANTS, AND MADE A CASTLE FREE

Anon withal came there upon him two great giants . . . with two horrible clubs in their hands. Sir Launcelot put his shield afore him, and put the stroke away of the one giant, and with his sword he clave his head asunder. When his fellow saw that, he ran away . . . and Launcelot after him with all his might, and smote him on the shoulder, and clave him to the middle. (Twain 1889: 18–19)

The narrator is enchanted by Malory's "feast of prodigies" and, at least according to his first biographer, Twain himself "loved Sir Thomas Malory to the end of his days" (Paine 1912: vol. 2, 891). Although the foregoing passage (from book 6, chapter 11 of *Le Morte d'Arthur*) seems designed to set the ground-note for Twain's burlesque, this dream of the "olden time" is far from dead. Indeed, the patterns of Malory's narrative – two giants, two clubs, and two cleavings – look uncannily like the dualistic

structures of Twain's own work. Mapping these oppositions has been a major preoccupation for Twain's critics, and Twain himself was perfectly aware of his doublings
and divisions. "Humor should take its outings in grave company," he told the publisher S. S. McClure some ten years after the publication of *A Connecticut Yankee*.
Turning down an offer to edit a comic magazine, Twain reminded his correspondent
that "of the twenty-three books which I have written eighteen do not deal in humor
as their chiefest feature, but are half & half admixtures of fun & seriousness" (see Paine
1912: vol. 2, 1100). Twain would surely have included *A Connecticut Yankee* as one of
those "admixtures." Yet the book was a matter of multiplication as well as division,
of omission as well as mixture. When Twain finished *Yankee*, he wrote on September
22, 1889 to William Dean Howells, telling him that the things he had left out "burn
in me; & they keep multiplying & multiplying; but now they can't ever be said. And
besides, they would require a . . . pen warmed-up in hell" (Twain and Howells 1960:
vol. 2, 613). Journeying through the duplicating and duplicitous spaces of Arthurian
England, Malory's knights split the heads and bodies of their opponents. With his
burning apprehension of a virtually satanic multitudinousness, Twain had a more
complex sense of a more pervasive duality than is to be found in the world of *Le Morte
d'Arthur*. And his awareness of the mixture of "fun & seriousness" bears an intriguing, potentially significant relation to Marshall Berman's description of modernity:

> To be modern is to find ourselves in an environment that promises us adventure, power,
> joy, growth, transformation of ourselves and the world – and, at the same time, that
> threatens to destroy everything we have, everything we know, everything we are . . . [I]t
> is a paradoxical unity, a unity of disunity: it pours us all into a maelstrom of perpetual
> disintegration and renewal, of struggle and contradiction, of ambiguity and anguish.
> (1982: 15)

It might be said that all criticism of Mark Twain comes from one book by Van
Wyck Brooks called *The Ordeal of Mark Twain* (1920). Brooks's case – that "the making
of the humorist was the undoing of the artist" – is certainly one of the most influential statements of the dualities in Twain (Brooks 1922: 26). Subsequent scholars have
played numberless variations on this founding opposition, exploring Twain's commitments to the West and to the East, to North and to South, to idealism and realism,
fact and fantasy, tragedy and melodrama, satire and sentimentalism. We have had
Twain the hack and Twain the genius, Twain smooth and Twain rough, old Twain and
young Twain, light Twain and dark Twain, Twain the rogue and Twain the sage, Mark
philanthropic and Mark misanthropic. From its title onwards, Justin Kaplan's 1966
biography may well be the most comprehensive portrait of the "half & half" author
whose divisions and ambivalences kept "multiplying & multiplying." *Mr. Clemens and
Mark Twain* presents us with the "Hartford literary gentleman" and the "sagebrush
bohemian," the "confederate irregular" and friend of Ulysses S. Grant, the "theoretical socialist" and the "practical aristocrat" (Kaplan 1966: 25, 421, 440). "A double
creature" from the outset, Twain even rerouted a chimney in his Hartford mansion so
he could watch "snowflakes and flames at the same time" (pp. 25, 278).

With the generative grammar of Twain's life and work so fully construed, the need to contextualize – to do more than point to Twain's twainings – became increasingly apparent. It was increasingly difficult to maintain a master binary: Twain's divided halves could never be lined up column left and column right. And it was no longer clear that Brooks was right – that the battle between artist and businessman had been resolved by the victory of the latter. For a critic like Henry Nash Smith, Twain's multifold personae and the shifting ironies of his work were positive aesthetic values in themselves. Even those who remained committed to formal unity could argue that, in *Huckleberry Finn*, Twain succeeded in overcoming the rifts and tensions that elsewhere marred his work. Leo Marx spoke of the novel's "convincing sense of life, the fresh lyricism, the wholeness of point of view" (Smith 1963: 47).[1] For Tony Tanner, similarly, the "oscillation of attitude" that marked Twain's earlier work was suddenly resolved in favor of "concrete local particulars" rather than abstraction and generality (1965: 110, 121). Breaking with "respect and reverence" by adopting the viewpoint of Huck, Twain overcame the antinomies of American democracy as set out by Alexis de Tocqueville: for a moment, wonder won through (p. 110).

In the 1980s Brooks's insights remained influential, though Twain's polarities – or, to echo Berman's account of modernity, the maelstrom of contradiction and ambiguity that one finds in his work – became the object of the analysis rather than a mere symptom of Twain's artistic difficulties. For George E. Toles, Twain's "intensely divided consciousness" was an attempt to "stave off . . . absolute scepticism" (1982: 56). In *Pudd'nhead Wilson* (1894) it was as if Twain managed to create "a succession of 'reality' chambers" (Toles 1982: 66): "situated in one room, his vision successfully accommodates itself to its dimensions, however limited. For the time being, no other room exists. After an indefinite period has elapsed, he awakens, as it were, in another room, and the process repeats itself" (p. 65). For Forrest G. Robinson, similarly, opposition itself was the subject. Where Toles had written of the "bifocal perspective" in *Pudd'nhead* (1982: 62), Robinson identified a "biformal pattern" in *The Innocents Abroad* and noted "the dizzying pace" of Twain's "mental movement between extremes" (p. 46). Offering a 15-point itemization of Twain's "emphatically binary sensibility," Robinson concluded that Twain's inability to achieve "equipoise" pointed to his "complex consciousness" rather than to his failure as a writer (pp. 47, 51).

In the last decade or so, although they have largely avoided modernity as a framing concept, Twain's critics have been increasingly attentive to historical explanations for the dualities of his work. Noting the "doubleness, duplicity, and division" in *Pudd'nhead Wilson*, Catharine O'Connell has argued that the novel's formal disjunctions match "the social irregularity that it figures and critiques" (2002: 100). Wilson's identification of Tom Driscoll as Roxy's son represents the failure of the "ironic distance" he had previously maintained, his conscription by Dawson's Landing and slaveholding at large (p. 114). For Stephen Railton, the key opposition in *Pudd'nhead Wilson* is that between the insider and the outsider. At first, Wilson "describes what is really there," seeing no difference between Roxy's "black" and Percy Driscoll's "white" baby. As we reach the courtroom scene, however, Wilson sees only "what is not there, except ideologically" and "the former outsider becomes the definitive insider" (2002: 526). This crucial shift of loyalties extends to Twain, who recognizes the violence of the racial binary but falls victim to a "re-vision" which re-establishes that division and presents Twain's contemporary white readers with "the Other that they are looking for" (p. 535). Despite his contemporary terminology, Railton's conclusions are not dissimilar to those of Brooks: by "repressing the truth that his novel had earlier tried to tell," Twain sold out (p. 532).[2]

Although modernity has rarely been invoked as a paradigm for Twain's work, the larger significance of his dualism has become increasingly clear. This is most notably the case with the issue of race in *Pudd'nhead Wilson* and still more so in *Huckleberry Finn*, whose paired scenes, as Peter Schmidt observes, generate similar "patterns of paired opposition in its interpreters." For Schmidt the dilemma facing critics of *Huckleberry Finn* is nothing less than "the central difficulty facing all cultural analysis: how to strike the proper balance between free will and determinism" (2002: 452). Was Twain a racist? To say he was seems inevitably to rest one's claim on determinism: novelists reproduce the social relations of production in the "political unconscious" of their works. To say he was not seems ultimately to depend on the argument from free will: authors are not bound by their time, and texts contrive to establish areas of resistance within the hegemonic order. It clearly matters whether or not one reads *Huckleberry Finn* as a racist novel (though each alternative lacks fineness of grain). But Twain's dualities cannot be reduced to formal, ahistorical patterns. Nor can they be understood simply as instances of his extraordinarily quixotic responses to the world around him. For the very terms in which the critical analysis of Twain has been couched are themselves historically conditioned. To talk about Huck as a "vehicle for the new point of view" as Tanner does is inevitably to raise questions about newness (1965: 105). To suggest that literary history is defined by the "dialectic" of innovation and tradition is similarly to imply a broader context. "*Modern* American literature": Hemingway got the point. So too did Leo Marx when he described the tension between "two modes of perception, one analytic and instrumental, the other emotive and aesthetic" in *Life on the Mississippi* as a "familiar modern conflict" (Smith 1963: 51). Twain's binaries and our own belong to a common history.

Derek Parker Royal's discussion of "the tensions inherent in Twain's discordant roles as democrat and capitalist" has been one of the more historically attuned recent reformulations of Brooks (2003: 13). Royal's work is also relevant to any discussion of Twain and modernity. In *Culture and Society*, Raymond Williams influentially positioned "democracy" and "industry" as two of the "key points . . . in our modern structure of meanings" (1993: xiii). Another of these key words was "culture," which became what Williams called the "watchword" for a tradition of social thought in Matthew Arnold's *Culture and Anarchy* (p. 114). The preface to *Culture and Anarchy* memorably defined culture as "a pursuit of our total perfection by means of getting to know . . . the best which has been thought and said in the world; and through this knowledge, turning a stream of fresh and free thought upon our stock notions and habits, which we now follow staunchly but mechanically" (Arnold 1868: 233–4).

In what follows I will attempt to account for Twain's complex response to modernity by tracing his engagement with Arnold and, more broadly, with a transatlantic
debate about culture and civilization. From Williams on, the "culture and society"
tradition has almost always been seen in an exclusively British context. But if British
cultural thought was a response to modernity – to democracy and to industrialization
– it was by the same token simultaneously and inevitably a response to the United
States. America played an important role in the development of the idea of culture
and was for Arnold in particular, as Lionel Trilling was the first to point out, "a symbol
and at times an obsession" (1963: 392).[3] In *Culture and Anarchy*, Arnold implied that
he shared Ernest Renan's views on the *"vulgarity of manners"* in America and explicitly argued that "in culture and totality, America, instead of surpassing us all, falls
short" (Arnold 1868: 241–2). His position had changed little since "The Popular
Education of France," in which he had claimed that democracy posed a threat to "fine
culture" and suggested that America was "limited in its culture, and . . . unconscious
of its limitation" (Arnold 1861: 17, 161). A similar judgment was repeated in
Arnold's last work, "Civilisation in the United States," which argued that Americans
had not yet solved the "human problem" and concluded that "a great void exists in
the civilisation over there" (Arnold 1888: 363).

    "All sorts of objections," as Arnold himself noted in *Culture and Anarchy*, were
raised against his idea of culture, both in England and in America (Arnold 1868:
115). As early as 1867, "A Plea for the Uncultivated" had appeared in the *Nation*.
The author ("A Philistine") put forward what Arnold described as a "specious" proposal to "call industrialism culture, and the industrialists the men of culture"
(1868: 129, 430n). Twain's "objections" came later and in response to Arnold's essay
on General Grant, whose *Personal Memoirs* had been published in 1885–6 by Charles
L. Webster, the company Twain had set up to market *Huckleberry Finn*. Arnold snob-
bishly criticized Grant's English on the grounds that it lacked "high breeding"
(Arnold 1887: 146). In a speech given in Hartford on April 27, 1887, Twain retali-
ated by contending that Arnold's English was "slovenly." Read four times, the ambiguities in one passage of "General Grant" were enough to "make a man . . . drunk"
(Twain 1976: 226). Twain instinctively knew that Arnold's criticism extended to
himself. Indeed, the attack had been quite open in "A Word About America," in
which Arnold described Twain's humor (after the manager of the wine company in
Dickens's *David Copperfield*) as "Quinionian," and went on to cite Twain as an example
of the "rowdy Philistine" (Arnold 1882: 14, 18). In "Civilisation in the United States,"
Arnold would later (though without mentioning Twain) describe the American
"addiction to 'the funny man'" as "a national misfortune," thus setting the terms for
Brooks's later critique (one instance of the way in which Twain's critical reception
belongs to a wider cultural history) (1888: 360–1).

    Somewhat surprisingly, it was "Civilisation in the United States" rather than
"A Word About America" that moved Twain to take up a public stance on Arnold
and civilization. On June 29, 1888, he wrote to Timothy Dwight, President of Yale.
Although Arnold had "rebuked the guild of American 'funny men'," Twain felt that
his own honorary master's degree would "remind the world that ours is a . . . worthy

calling" (Twain 1976: 237). Some weeks earlier, William Dean Howells had encouraged Twain to "listen, and seriously" to a request from Lorettus Metcalf, editor of the *Forum*, for a rejoinder to "Civilisation in the United States." For months Twain collected in his notebook a series of squibs intended, as Howells hoped, to "hurt awfully" (Twain and Howells 1960: vol. 2, 600). Arnold's civilization was *"superficial polish"* (Twain 1979: 383). It was "worm-eaten," fit only for "slave-making ants" (pp. 406, 398). The memory of a dream suggested to Twain a still more promising tactic: he was going to "refer to M the A simply as 'Mike'" (p. 384).

Metcalf never got his article, though the campaign against Arnold rumbled on in Twain's speeches and there was for a while a plan to collect the material into a book of letters to a fictional correspondent in England. Instead, Twain channeled his energies into *A Connecticut Yankee*, his most sustained engagement with the discourse of "civilization." John B. Hoben has argued that the "central factor" in Twain's escalating Anglophobia during the 1880s was the encounter with Arnold, who was indirectly responsible for transforming "an unpromising sentimental romance into a promising satire" and for dispelling the "lethargy" that had beset Twain since *Huckleberry Finn* (1946: 205, 211). If "Civilisation in the United States" was the main impetus behind Twain's decision to mount a "defense of American civilization" (p. 210), it was only the latest in a series of provocations which had begun with "A Word About America" and very likely continued when "Mike" ran into the "rowdy Philistine" at a reception in Hartford on November 14, 1883. The pair met again after Arnold's lecture the following evening and, according to Howells, "were not parted for long." Disappointingly, Howells could not "say . . . what they made of each other," though he suspected that Arnold had been impressed by Twain's "glamour" (1910: 28). Relying on *My Mark Twain*, Paine also suggests that Twain "dazed" Arnold (1912: vol. 2, 759). Yet Arnold said nothing either during or after his American tour to modify the "incredulous sniff" he had initially emitted when he was told that Howells was visiting Twain: " 'he doesn't like *that* sort of thing, does he?' " (Howells 1910: 28).

Evidence that the meeting between Twain and Arnold was a major event for either writer is thin. Arnold didn't change his views on "*that* sort of thing" between 1882 and 1888, and Twain made no public response to Arnold until the Grant episode.[4] Yet Twain's silence was surprising, for Arnold's Hartford lecture ("Numbers") anticipated the attack on the "funny man" with the provocative assertion that the popularity of humorous writing in America (Bret Harte was the example on this occasion) recalled the "craving for amusement" that had accompanied the collapse of Athenian democracy (Arnold 1883: 146). That Twain was not pricked by these remarks may have been because he found it as difficult as Grant to hear what Arnold was saying.[5] Even when moved to comment, he seemed at any rate not to have been listening with much care:

Must all the advice be emptied upon us? And all the criticism? May we not respond? May we not turn – like other worms? Or is Europe perfect that she has no discoverable flaw, & hence no need of advice & no tainted matter for criticism to smell at & forage upon?

> To judge by the air of the visiting critic, Europe *is* perfect, at any rate England – to
> him. (quoted in Hoben 1946: 206)

Twain's comments on the "visiting critic" were as ill-informed as those he later
made on the "foreign critic" who "won't concede that we have a . . . 'real' civilization"
(Twain 1976: 257).[6] Arnold was being somewhat disingenuous when, in "A Word
About America," he claimed that he was only entering into "friendly conversation";
his remarks on Grant's lack of "breeding" (Arnold 1882: 15) were insufferable. But
he was in no way claiming that England was "perfect." In "A Word About America,"
he said at the outset that the British social system was "far from perfect" (p. 4). He
began the "Numbers" lecture by pointing out that he could not be accused "of having
flattered the patriotism of that great country of English people on the other side of
the Atlantic, amongst whom I was born" (1883: 143). Nor was America simply a
target for Arnold, as Twain seemed to think. In an essay on Theodore Parker, Arnold
had hailed Whitman as "a genuine American voice"; in "Numbers," he asserted that
Emerson's *Essays* were, "in our language, during the present century . . . the most
important work done in prose" (Arnold 1867a: 81; 1883: 182). And though he had
reservations about the auxiliaries and participles, Arnold recognized that Grant said
"in the fewest possible words what had to be said . . . with shrewd and unexpected
turns of expression" (1887: 146). The distinction that Twain seemed unable to grasp
was not between perfect and imperfect, between Britain and the United States, but
between a material and a human civilization.

"What is civilisation?" Arnold put the question in "Civilisation in the United
States." It was, he thought, "the humanisation of man in society, the satisfaction for
him, in society, of the true law of human nature." Civilization was a matter of conduct,
of intellect and knowledge, of beauty, social life, and manners. We were "perfectly
civilised only when all these instincts in our nature" were "recognised and satisfied"
(1888: 352). "What is a 'real' civilization?" Twain posed his version of Arnold's question in the speech "On Foreign Critics." His initial answer was negative: "any system
which has in it . . . human slavery, despotic government, inequality, numerous and
brutal punishments for crimes, superstition almost universal, ignorance almost universal, and dirt and poverty almost universal – is not a real civilization." As Arnold
knew perfectly well, most Americans had "liberty, equality, plenty to eat, plenty to
wear, comfortable shelter, high pay, abundance of churches, newspapers, libraries,
charities, and a good education." Since it was clear that "we furnish the greatest good
to the greatest number," it could only be "ingratitude" that had led "the foreign critic"
to deny America's status as a "real" civilization (Twain 1976: 258–9).

Yet the more he said about American civilization, the more Twain made it obvious
that he was approaching the issue from the perspective of what, for Arnold, was mere
materialism and utilitarian liberalism. As early as "A French Eton," Arnold had
refused to follow Richard Cobden and John Bright in lamenting the break-up of the
Union. The Civil War corrected America's satisfaction in its "unchecked triumph,"
offering the nation the chance "to become something higher, ampler, more gracious"

(Arnold 1864: 319). When Arnold wrote that America fell short "in culture and total-ity" he was already suggesting that the nation had not embraced its opportunity (1868: 242). Arnold's respect for American institutions markedly increased following his visit to the United States in 1883. As he reminded his readers in "A Word More," however, institutions were only *"machinery"* (1885: 196). America had solved "the political and social problem," but the "human problem" remained (p. 202). Although America was the civilization of the future, its successes were as yet those of "Philistines," creators of what Arnold had described in "On the Study of Celtic Literature" as "the comforts and conveniences of life," among which were "doors that open, windows that shut, locks that turn, razors that shave, coats that wear" and "watches that go" (Arnold 1867b: 348).

Having become "the second personage in the Kingdom," Hank Morgan is given "the choicest suite of apartments in the castle, after the King's." As for "conveniences," however, "there weren't any":

> There was no soap, no matches, no looking-glass – except a metal one, about as pow-erful as a pail of water. And not a chromo . . . There wasn't even a bell or a speaking-tube . . . There was no gas, there were no candles . . . no books, pens, paper, or ink, and no glass in the openings they believed to be windows . . . But perhaps the worst of all was, that there wasn't any sugar, coffee, tea, or tobacco. (Twain 1889: 83–5)

In Morgan's view, the patent office and Persimmons' soap (*"All the Prime-Donne Use It"*) are major steps toward "civilising . . . this nation" (Twain 1889: 190). Putting his faith in "machinery," Morgan establishes "nuclei of future vast factories, the iron and steel missionaries of my future civilisation" (p. 117). As *A Connecticut Yankee* reaches its climactic moment and, dressed only in "the simplest and comfortablest of gymnast costumes," Morgan prepares to face Sir Sagramour in single combat, he sees himself as the representative of "hard unsentimental common sense" (pp. 499, 498). Although this scene belongs to a complex series in Twain's work,[7] it also echoes the Carlylean image that Arnold found for American institutions in "A Word More" and elaborated in "Civilisation in the United States" – that of "a man in a suit of clothes which fits him to perfection, leaving all his movements unimpeded and easy; a suit of clothes loose where it ought to be loose, and sitting close where its sitting close is an advan-tage" (1888: 351).

It would be easy to position Twain and Arnold at opposite ends of the debate about civilization, to align Arnold's emphasis on the state and social hierarchy with Edmund Burke, and Twain's concern for the people with Thomas Paine. Morgan is certainly a devotee of *Common Sense*, since in his view "reverence for rank and title" obscures the "legitimate source" of sovereignty, which comes "from the nation itself" (Twain 1889: 101–2). Following Arthur's death and the church's interdict, Morgan proclaims that "political power has reverted to its original source, the people of the nation" (p. 544). Yet, as Leland Krauth rightly points out, Twain could also quote Burke with "delight and confidence" (2003: 141). To what extent, then, was Twain as much a supporter as an opponent of "culture and society" thought? It is worth recalling the full title of the lecture Arnold gave at Hartford that evening in 1883: "Numbers; Or, The Majority and the Remnant." For Arnold, the problem of "numbers" had always related to "the dangers of America" and "the dangers which come from the multitude being in power" (Arnold 1861: 18). But the question of the "remnant" became increasingly important in Arnold's later work. In "A Word About America," he argued that the scattered "lovers of perfection" in America needed to organize themselves more effectively (1882: 9). Reformed secondary schools ought to "form . . . the youth of America" and yearly "throw a supply of them . . . into circulation" (p. 23). Arnold restated the case in "Numbers" (and Twain surely pricked up his ears at this point): "to reform the State in order to save it . . . a body of workers is needed as well as a leader; – a considerable body of workers, placed at many points, and operating in many directions" (1883: 149).

It was surely a "body of workers" as well as a "leader" – a *Philistine* remnant, so to speak – that Twain set out to imagine in *A Connecticut Yankee*. For Morgan, "civilisation" involves "training a crowd of ignorant folks into experts" (Twain 1889: 117–18). This is "machinery" of a kind that Arnold himself supported. "Numbers" contained a back-of-the-envelope calculation that would have appealed to Twain. If the remnant was "a tenth of the whole," then in Athens and Judah, with populations of 350,000 and 1,250,000 respectively, there were not enough people "to give us a remnant capable of saving . . . the community" (Arnold 1883: 147, 149). That was why, with its 50 millions, America promised a remnant of "irresistible efficacy" – although, as Arnold cautioned, "mere multitude will not give us a saving remnant with certainty" (p. 163). The problem of numbers seems more practicable, by contrast, in Arthurian Britain. In the Battle of the Sand-Belt, Morgan, Clarence, and "fifty-two . . . young British boys" annihilate a feudal order consisting of some 25,000 knights (Twain 1889: 549). What brings down Morgan's civilization is not the small size of the remnant. It is not the state and it is not the church. Nor (though he sends Morgan into a 13-centuries' sleep in "a delirium of silly laughter") is it Merlin (p. 570). In the end it was Twain's recognition that the majority – the people – presented the most insuperable obstacle to civilization. And it is this that turned the encounter with Arnold into a convergence rather than a collision. In "Numbers," Arnold insisted on "the hard doctrine of the unsoundness of the majority" (1883: 159). Morgan must also confront the "large and disenchanting fact" that "the mass of the nation had . . . shouted for the republic for about one day, and there an end!" (Twain 1889: 551).

For Twain as for Arnold, it is easier to mend leaky wells than to turn "a stream of fresh and free thought upon our stock notions and habits" (Arnold 1868: 233–4). If anything, Morgan's restoration of the fountain confirms "stock notions": he becomes another enchanter rather than ending enchantment, a fact which suggests that Twain's "hard doctrine" applies to the leader of the remnant as well as the majority. In one sense, Morgan obviously embodies the "superior liveliness and naturalness" which Arnold in "A Word More" had found in the "American Philistine" (1885: 203). He represents "the American people" as Arnold described them in "The Popular Education of France": "an energetic people, a powerful people, a highly-taught people." But Twain also gives Morgan the "overweening" and "self-conceited" tendencies which for Arnold left a void in American civilization (Arnold 1861: 160). Morgan is, in Arnold's phrasing, limited, and unconscious of his limitation. He *is* the "human problem" (Arnold 1888: 363). Morgan's limited rationalist insistence that "there is no such thing as nature," that "training is everything," is undercut when his "base hankering" to be president convinces him that "there was more or less human nature in me" (Twain 1889: 217, 514). When it is not simply "base," however, Morgan's "nature" seems disturbingly compartmentalized. Morgan introduces himself as a "Yankee of the Yankees," saying that he is "nearly barren of sentiment . . . or poetry" (p. 20). John Stuart Mill's criticism of Jeremy Bentham and Mill's own crisis spring to mind. Yet Morgan's problem is not that he *can't* feel poetry but that he doesn't know he *can* feel it. He misses Puss Flanagan but, as he sternly reminds himself, "there was no sense in sighing, for she wasn't born yet." "We don't reason, where we feel," he tells himself: "we just feel" (p. 134). The pat opposition of "reason" and "feeling" is telling enough, but the "we just feel" is pure fatalism – it treats emotions as if they were weather. When Morgan later adopts a similar tone ("You can't reason with your heart; it . . . thumps about things which the intellect scorns") he attributes his "thumps" to the anxiety produced by having reached an "ogre's castle." Given the remarks on Puss Flanagan, however, it seems more likely that Morgan is – entirely unwittingly – falling in love with Sandy (pp. 242–3). Lacking insight into the difference between fear and desire, he cannot see his own responses as pathological. So deeply alienated is Morgan from himself that the part of him which "is truly *me*" seems to him the size only of "one microscopic atom" (p. 217).

In a planned speech on the American press that was later incorporated into *The American Claimant*, Twain objected to Arnold's remarks in "Civilisation in the United States" on the "discipline in which the Americans are wanting" ("awe and respect") (Arnold 1888: 360), arguing instead that "discriminating irreverence" was the "protector of human liberty" (Twain 1892: 99). Acting on similar beliefs, Morgan is quick to start up a weekly newspaper for his "civilisation-nurseries" (Twain 1889: 121). Yet the first headlines ("HIGH TIMES IN THE VALLEY OF HOLINESS!") produce "a quivery little cold wave": even Morgan finds the "pert little irreverences" disconcerting. And this "quiver" has wider ramifications. While Morgan's selfhood shrinks to an atom, Arthur seems increasingly to stand for a human order. The king, as Morgan acknowledges, "was a good deal more than a king – he was a man" (p. 458). The established church is undoubtedly a "political machine," but "the great majority" of its priests are "devoted to the alleviation of human troubles" (pp. 215–16). And where Morgan feels only "drunk with enjoyment" when the monks pore over his newspaper "as cautiously and devoutly as if it had . . . come from some supernatural region," the text leaves us in little doubt that their gentle piety represents something of real value (p. 344). Twain's joke is at the expense less of medieval credulity than of modern cynicism: for him if not for Morgan, wonder is going out of the world. In *A Connecticut Yankee*, Twain was not simply offering a counterweight to Arnold or to Thomas Carlyle, who in *Past and Present* (1843) had described medieval England as a "green solid place" in which "men then had a *soul*" (Tennyson 1984: 412, 415). For Williams, Carlyle's portrait of "medieval community" was a sign of his "essential quality": a "*reverence*" which was evident in his "governing seriousness" (1993: 82, 86). Alongside Burke, Carlyle, and Arnold – three of the central figures in Williams's "culture and society" tradition – Twain, too, possessed both "seriousness" and "reverence."

By the time of *The American Claimant*, Twain was indeed "jousting with a dead man" (Krauth 2003: 164). Krauth argues that Twain was never able to organize a "full-scale" riposte to Arnold (p. 156). Yet, as I have shown, *A Connecticut Yankee* needs to be read as a sophisticated response to Arnold, to the civilization debate and, more generally, to modernity. One might argue that the rediscovery of reverence in *A Connecticut Yankee* forms part of an "oscillation of attitude" in Twain's work (Tanner 1965: 110). Before and after *Yankee* he was an enthusiastic Anglophile.[8] In *Life on the Mississippi*, he had maintained (in a passage tactfully cut from the first edition) that Americans were "ludicrously sensitive to foreign criticism" (Twain 1984: 295). So the irritation with the "foreign critic" was a temporary stance rather than a final position. But the successive "'reality' chambers" imagined by Toles cannot explain Twain's views on democracy, one of the "key points" in Williams's "modern structure of meanings." *A Connecticut Yankee* seems simultaneously Jeffersonian, Jacksonian, Hamiltonian, and plain Machiavellian (Toles 1982: 66). This is no pendulum swing: Twain was, as Kaplan writes, "capable of sustaining two moods of belief at the same time" (1966: 432). Even as he dismissed Arnold's civilization as "worm-eaten," Twain was deploring Arnold's treatment by the American press (see Krauth 2003: 165). A similar contradiction-in-simultaneity affects *A Connecticut Yankee*, which, as I have argued, was by no means consistently anti-Arnoldian. Twain obviously invested in his "rowdy Philistine," but Morgan was by no means simply his delegated "glorying" self (Twain 1889: 295). According to Paine, Twain told his illustrator, Dan Beard, that "this Yankee of mine is a perfect ignoramus; he is a boss of a machine shop; he can build a locomotive or a Colt's revolver . . . but he's an ignoramus, nevertheless" (Paine 1912: vol. 2, 887–8). Twain did not necessarily share Morgan's conception of civilization and clearly felt that a world inhabited by people who make trains and guns would be insufficient. On occasions, he was as keen on the "soap and civilization" formula as his protagonist (1889: 191). But for him, as for Tom Sawyer, the conveniences of "modern civilization" did not make up for the loss of "outlaws" like Robin Hood (1876: 84). One side of Twain no more wanted to be "sivilized" than Huck Finn. By the time of *Life on the Mississippi*, moreover, Twain had come to feel that civilization was founded on something other than soap: "the earliest pioneer of civilization . . . is never the steamboat, never the railroad, never the newspaper, never the Sabbath-school, never the missionary – but always whiskey! Such is the case. Look history over; you will see" (1984: 586). The comforts associated with civilization are surfaces or shams, mere limits on older, more unruly impulses. Seen like this, Hank

Morgan and the Widow Douglas are only missionaries. Civilization's true pioneer is Pap Finn.

I have traced Twain's engagement with Arnold and with "culture and society" thought. But my framing concept – modernity – is not without its problems. From one point of view, it would be possible to describe anybody who lived through what Twain called "the raging, tearing, booming nineteenth century" as "modern," though to do so would be essentially uninteresting (Kaplan 1966: 391). To see Twain through the lens of modernity might also involve presenting him as a simple, unmediated effect of his context, the representative embodiment of his age. Thus for Vernon Louis Parrington, Twain was an "American document." To know him was to know "the muddy cross-currents of . . . the frontier spirit," the "puzzling contradictions of the Gilded Age" (1930: 88). But Twain did not shade off into his own materials in the way Parrington suggests. He was not simply an incarnation of America, and his engagement with the discourse of civilization, though complex and at times contradictory, was in fact carefully calibrated, thoroughly mediated. To the extent that *A Connecticut Yankee* argued that the United States and not Britain had a "real" civilization, Twain's contribution was admittedly limited. As he worked with the concept, however, Twain came to see that American "civilization" was at best a "mixed good," achieving a level of insight that for Williams characterizes the recognition of "a whole modern social process" (1988: 59).

Finally, though, Twain's ability to maintain a dialectical balance gave way: it seemed to him that civilizations were always based on or bound up with violence. If the "march of civilisation" is to begin, Morgan must put on his costume and Sir Sagramour must be killed (Twain 1889: 507). Civilization is not "conveniences"; it is the trail of the serpent. This is why Twain's position is in the end unlike Arnold's. He veered between conservatism (human nature is wicked and society exists to control it) and radicalism (society is exploitative and its assault on human nature is structural). But nowhere did Twain set out a positive definition of civilization, as Arnold had done. Howard G. Baetzhold rightly suggests (1970: 161) that, for both writers, the world was a place in which ignorant armies clashed by night. Yet although he shared the momentous loss of faith recorded in "Dover Beach," Twain rarely displayed Arnold's confidence in the "human," and his more thoroughgoing skepticism inevitably manifested itself in the "epistemological uncertainty" that, as Peter Messent argues, "shadows Twain's writing" (1998: 219). This uncertainty is "modern" in exactly Berman's sense, and Twain can indeed be seen as a notable instance of the decline of liberalism, rationalism, and materialism in the final quarter of the nineteenth century.

In the final part of this essay, I want to suggest that the "maelstrom of perpetual disintegration and renewal" into which Twain's work plunges us can be given still greater specificity. Alongside "industry" and "democracy," Twain was also concerned with the "social divisions" that form yet another "key point" in modernity (Williams 1993: xiii). In England, these divisions were a matter of class. In Twain's America, from the Civil War to *Plessy* v. *Ferguson*, the primary fissure was that of race. As Eric

J. Sundquist and others have shown, this is clearly the immediate historical context for *Pudd'nhead Wilson*. But more recent work by, for example, Paul Gilroy, points to the centrality of black experience in the diasporic identity formations commonly associated with modernity. In *Seeing Things Hidden*, Malcolm Bull builds on the work of Gilroy by arguing that "the coming into hiding of unknowable true contradictions is a characteristic feature . . . of late modernity" (1999: 31–2). For Bull, one of modernity's most typical experiences is "realising that you are committed to inconsistent beliefs" (p. 34). The "multiple selves of nineteenth- and twentieth-century literature" provide particularly important testimony in that they "reflect the multiple social emancipations that . . . occurred in the same period" (p. 262). "Unknowable true contradictions" only "come into hiding" (Bull wants to underline the known existence of the unknowable as a distinctively modern epistemological preoccupation) with these multiple and uneven emancipations, first and foremost of which was the abolition of slavery in America. Bull therefore follows Gilroy in seeing W. E. B. Du Bois' account of "double consciousness" (Du Bois 1999: 11) in *The Souls of Black Folk* as a central statement of modernity. Indeed, it is for Bull the most distinctive instance of "the limit condition of modernity," in which "the contradictory multiple selves of emancipation have come fully into hiding." In this state – Bull calls it "living in hiding" in order to suggest that the predicament is more persistent than the relatively fleeting paradoxes experienced as coming into hiding – the subject lives in "a continuous state of frustrated knowledge" (1999: 288). At the same time and more happily, though, the dialectic of modernity produces a "recognition of self in other" and therefore ultimately promises "de-alienation" (p. 207). I lack space for a fuller exegesis, but would suggest that Bull's work provides a useful frame in which to set Twain's persistent and agonized sense of division, his awareness of the "tearing" nineteenth century. In *Pudd'nhead Wilson*, for example, Tom Driscoll, Valet de Chambre, and the Capello twins seem in various ways to rehearse Bull's "coming into hiding of unknowable true contradictions." One might even argue that Twain himself, committed here and elsewhere to inconsistent beliefs, can be seen as an instance of living in hiding and thus of what Bull describes as modernity's "limit condition." For the inhabitants of Dawson's Landing there is, of course, no recognition of "self in other." Even Wilson's insight into the implications of "killing half" (both dog and man) is temporary. Yet the joke that sets the novel going affirms the necessity of the dialectic and therefore points toward some ultimate if as yet unrecognized totality.

In *Pudd'nhead Wilson*, Twain's sense of the social divisions constructed around race constitutes a very particular and historically attuned response to the experience of modernity in nineteenth-century America. *A Connecticut Yankee* seems by contrast more of a transatlantic text, and its preoccupation with democracy and industrialism sounds very similar notes to those in the British "culture and society" tradition. Yet even here, Twain was concerned to make connections between medieval serfdom, antebellum slavery, and structures of exploitation in the Gilded Age. And his rejection of the liberal narrative of progress helps to explain why the opening quotation from

Malory needs to be seen in contexts other than those of Arthurian England. The impulse to short-circuit a teleological historicism might usefully be applied to Twain's own literary career. Hoben (1946: 198–200) and Kaplan (1966: 407) repeat Paine's account (1912: vol. 2, 790–1) of George Washington Cable introducing Twain to Malory in 1884. Yet it is worth remembering that Twain had already made extensive use of historical parody in *A Tramp Abroad* (1880) and, still earlier, in *The Innocents Abroad*. What I am suggesting is that Twain did not arrive at his images of halved dogs and cloven giants as the result of later disillusionment. As with his skepticism about civilization, Twain's sense of division was present from the start. The man who immersed himself in "Malory's enchanting book" was not just the future author of *A Connecticut Yankee*: he was also the passenger on the *Quaker City*, imagining himself watching gladiators in the Coliseum: "the audience gave way to uncontrollable bursts of laughter; but when the back of his weapon broke the skull of one . . . and clove the other's body in twain, the howl of enthusiastic applause . . . was the acknowledgment . . . that he was a master" (1869: 282). Twain here signs himself in modernity's sunderings. But this foreshadowing of *A Connecticut Yankee* is no more startling than Twain's anticipation of the contradictions of post-Reconstruction America in a subsequent skit on the Crusades, where the sword of Godfrey of Bouillon is described in the following terms: "It was with just such blades as these that these splendid heroes of romance used to segregate a man, so to speak, and leave the half of him to fall one way and the other half the other" (p. 563).

NOTES

1 Marx modified his position in *The Machine in the Garden* (1964: 319–41).

2 For the claim that recent criticism of *The Prince and the Pauper* has been "a sophisticated version" of Brooks, see Stahl (1986: 203).

3 On Arnold and America, see Raleigh (1961) and Lustig (2000).

4 Fatout (in Twain 1976: 229–30) suggests that Twain might not have read Arnold's article on Grant. Twain seems not to have owned much Arnold, though apparently he had the 1888 book version of "Civilisation in the United States" (see Gribben 1980: 28). According to Krauth (2003: 160), Arnold had not read Twain when he cited him in "A Word About America."

5 Arnold's first lecture on his American tour (also "Numbers") was inaudible. Grant, who was in the audience, said to his wife: "we have

paid to see the British lion; we cannot hear him roar, so we had better go home" (Arnold 1887: 429n).

6 Hoben believes that the unpublished article on the "visiting critic" was written before Arnold completed his 1883 lecture tour. Fatout dates the "foreign critic" speech to 1890 (1976: 257).

7 Morgan's costume recalls that of the athlete who sheds 17 suits in the circus episode of *Huckleberry Finn*, who himself recalls the lecturer Henry Clay Dean, described as a "stranger" and "an escaped archangel" in *Life on the Mississippi* (Twain 1883: 558, 561). Running through Morgan, the sequence terminates with the shape-shifting figure of Satan in the "Mysterious Stranger" manuscripts.

8 See Kaplan (1966: 232–58) and Twain (1976: 305, 322–4).

REFERENCES AND FURTHER READING

Arac, Jonathan (1992). "Nationalism, Hypercan-onization, and *Huckleberry Finn.*" *boundary 2*, 19: 1, 14–33.

Arnold, Matthew (1960–77). *The Complete Prose Works of Matthew Arnold*, 11 vols., ed. R. H. Super. Ann Arbor: University of Michigan Press. Individual citations as follows:

(1861). "The Popular Education of France." vol. 2 (1962), 1–211.

(1864). "A French Eton." Vol. 2 (1962), 262–325.

(1867a). "Theodore Parker." Vol. 5 (1965), 78–84.

(1867b). "On the Study of Celtic Literature." Vol. 3 (1962), 291–386.

(1868). *Culture and Anarchy.* Vol. 5 (1965), 85–256.

(1882). "A Word About America." Vol. 10 (1974), 1–23.

(1883). "Numbers; Or, The Majority and the Remnant." Vol. 10 (1974), 143–64.

(1885). "A Word More About America." Vol. 10 (1974), 194–217.

(1887). "General Grant." Vol. 11 (1977), 144–79.

(1888). "Civilization in the United States." Vol. 11 (1977), 350–69.

Baetzhold, Howard G. (1970). *Mark Twain and John Bull: The British Connection.* Bloomington: Indiana University Press.

Berman, Marshall (1982). *All That Is Solid Melts into Air: The Experience of Modernity.* London: Verso.

Brooks, Van Wyck (1922). *The Ordeal of Mark Twain.* London: Heinemann. (First publ. 1920.)

Brown, Bill (2002). "The Tyranny of Things (Trivia in Karl Marx and Mark Twain)." *Critical Inquiry* 28: 1, 442–69.

Bull, Malcolm (1999). *Seeing Things Hidden: Apocalypse, Vision and Totality.* London: Verso.

Du Bois, W. E. B. (1999). *The Souls of Black Folk*, ed. Henry Louis Gates, Jr. and Terri Hume Oliver. New York: Norton. (First publ. 1903.)

Gilroy, Paul (1993). *The Black Atlantic: Modernity and Double Consciousness.* London: Verso.

Gribben, Alan (1980). *Mark Twain's Library: A Reconstruction*, vol. 1. Boston: G. K. Hall.

Hemingway, Ernest (1965). *Green Hills of Africa.* London: Cape. (First publ. 1935.)

Hoben, John B. (1946). "Mark Twain's *A Connecticut Yankee*: A Genetic Study." *American Literature* 18: 3, 197–218.

Howells, William Dean (1910). *My Mark Twain: Reminiscences and Criticisms.* New York and London: Harper & Bros.

Kaplan, Justin (1966). *Mr. Clemens and Mark Twain: A Biography.* Harmondsworth: Penguin.

Krauth, Leland (1999). *Proper Mark Twain.* Athens: University of Georgia Press.

Krauth, Leland (2003). *Mark Twain and Company: Six Literary Relations.* Athens: University of Georgia Press.

Lustig, T. J. (2000). "'Seeing the Elephant': Constructing Culture in Britain and the United States after Jumbo." *Symbiosis: A Journal of Anglo-American Literary Relations* 4: 2, 111–32.

Marx, Leo (1964). *The Machine in the Garden: Technology and the Pastoral Idea in America.* London: Oxford University Press.

Messent, Peter (1998). "Carnival in Mark Twain's 'Stirring Times in Austria' and 'The Man That Corrupted Hadleyburg'." *Studies in Short Fiction* 35, 217–32.

O'Connell, Catharine (2002). "Respecting *Those Extraordinary Twins*: *Pudd'nhead Wilson* and the Costs of 'Killing Half'." *Nineteenth-Century Literature* 57: 1, 100–24.

Paine, Albert Bigelow (1912). *Mark Twain: A Biography. The Personal and Literary Life of Samuel Langhorne Clemens*, 3 vols. New York and London: Harper & Bros.

Parrington, Vernon Louis (1930). *Main Currents in American Thought: An Interpretation of American Literature from the Beginnings to 1920.* New York: Harcourt, Brace.

Railton, Stephen (2002). "The Tragedy of Mark Twain, by Pudd'nhead Wilson." *Nineteenth-Century Literature* 56: 4, 518–44.

Raleigh, John Henry (1961). *Matthew Arnold and American Culture.* Berkeley: University of California Press.

Robinson, Forrest G. (1986). "Patterns of Consciousness in *The Innocents Abroad.*" *American Literature* 58: 1, 46–63.

Royal, Derek Parker (2003). "Eruptions of Performance: Hank Morgan and the Business of Politics." *Midwest Quarterly* 45: 1, 11–30.

Schmidt, Peter (2002). "Seven Recent Commentaries on Mark Twain." *Studies in the Novel* 34: 4, 448–64.

Smith, Henry Nash, ed. (1963). *Mark Twain: A Collection of Critical Essays*. Englewood Cliffs, NJ: Prentice-Hall.

Stahl, John Daniel (1986). "American Myth in European Disguise: Fathers and Sons in *The Prince and the Pauper*." *American Literature* 58: 2, 203–16.

Sundquist, Eric J. (1990). "Mark Twain and Homer Plessy." In Susan Gillman and Forrest G. Robinson (eds.), *Mark Twain's 'Pudd'nhead Wilson': Race, Conflict, and Culture*, 46–72. Durham: Duke University Press.

Tanner, Tony (1965). *The Reign of Wonder: Naivety and Reality in American Literature*. Cambridge, UK: Cambridge University Press.

Tennyson, G. B., ed. (1984). *A Carlyle Reader: Selections from the Writings of Thomas Carlyle*. Cambridge, UK: Cambridge University Press.

Toles, George E. (1982). "Mark Twain and *Pudd'nhead Wilson*: A House Divided." *Novel* 16: 1, 55–75.

Trilling, Lionel (1963). *Matthew Arnold*. London: Unwin. (First publ. 1939.)

Twain, Mark (1976). *Mark Twain Speaking*, ed. Paul Fatout. Iowa City: University of Iowa Press.

Twain, Mark (1984). *Life on the Mississippi*, ed. James M. Cox. New York: Penguin.

Twain, Mark (1979). *Mark Twain's Notebooks and Journals*, vol. 3: *1883–1891*, ed. Robert Pack Browning, Michael B. Frank, and Lin Salamo, 297–393. Berkeley: University of California Press.

Twain, Mark, and Howells, William Dean (1960). *Mark Twain–Howells Letters: The Correspondence of Samuel L. Clemens and William D. Howells, 1872–1910*, 2 vols., ed. Henry Nash Smith and William M. Gibson. Cambridge, Mass.: Belknap.

Williams, Raymond (1988). *Keywords: A Vocabulary of Culture and Society*. London: Fontana. (First publ. 1976.)

Williams, Raymond (1993). *Culture and Society: Coleridge to Orwell*. London: Hogarth. (First publ. 1958.)

7

Mark Twain and Politics

James S. Leonard

Mark Twain once remarked (in "From The 'London Times' of 1904") that "in America politics has a hand in everything" (Twain 1992b: 270). Certainly it played a major role in Twain's own life. He had a consuming interest in politics and believed in its value in that he thought political struggle was necessary for the health of a society. Politics was a game for him – a wholesome one when played well, but prone to being subverted by the corruption of those who did not adequately respect its role or by the ignorance and general worthlessness of an electorate not up to the task of government "by the people." He was involved in politics as a commentator from the time he was a young contributor to his brother Orion's newspaper to the much later period when he became a venerable sage whose every utterance, it seemed, was news. But at the same time that he participated, sometimes enthusiastically, in politics, he also had a tendency, particularly in his later years, to draw back from the political contest at hand and think about politics in general – how it functioned and what that functioning revealed about the foibles and possibilities of humankind.

Twain's standing as spokesman for democracy is an important element of his lasting image. He is the outspoken cultural ambassador who, in *The Innocents Abroad*, *A Tramp Abroad*, and elsewhere, debunks the myths of superiority of Europe's monarchical and aristocratic traditions. Among his major works of fiction, *Adventures of Huckleberry Finn* and *Pudd'nhead Wilson* contain satire of aristocracy and monarchy, and *The Prince and the Pauper* and *A Connecticut Yankee in King Arthur's Court* directly confront questions of monarchy versus democracy. In his *Autobiography*, Twain remembers the composition of *A Connecticut Yankee* as

> an attempt to imagine, and after a fashion set forth, the hard conditions of life for the laboring and defenseless poor in bygone times in England, and incidentally contrast these conditions with those under which the civil and ecclesiastical pets of privilege and high fortune lived in those times. I think I was purposing to contrast that English life . . . with the life of modern Christendom and modern civilization – to the advantage of the latter, of course. (Twain 1959: 271)

But, of course, the king and duke in *Huckleberry Finn* are imposters, the aristocrats in *Pudd'nhead Wilson* are caricatures, and the relative virtues of the nobility and the common people in *A Connecticut Yankee* and *The Prince and the Pauper* are problematic. For that matter, Twain in *The Innocents Abroad*, for all his satire of European traditions, seems in awe of Emperor Napoleon III, praising all he has done for France and calling him "the representative of the highest modern civilization, progress, and refinement" (Twain 1869: 126); and he seems equally enchanted by the personal qualities of Czar Alexander II of Russia and his family. Further, in the late nineteenth-century United States, or Great Britain for that matter, the triumph of the middle class had made monarchy and aristocracy, in almost everyone's view, not very viable entities anyway. So, in a sense, these are all straw-man comparisons. And yet there is a serious side to them in the issue of the proper composition of the electorate, and thereby of the nature of those chosen to rule – questions in which Twain maintained a lifelong interest.

Mark Twain, Political Reporter

Samuel Clemens's parents were Jane Lampton Clemens, who believed herself descended from British aristocracy (a situation that Twain later used as a plotline in *The American Claimant*), and John Marshall Clemens – a small-time Whig politician, sometime slave-owner, and big-time believer in the importance of his Virginia ancestry. Consequently, young Sam fell quite naturally into the Whig tradition of faith in limited democracy, advocating rule by the qualified few rather than the promiscuous many. The belief in dominance of the superior over the inferior also fitted easily with an acceptance of slavery – a connection Twain made himself in his *Autobiography*. In the Hannibal of his childhood, he said, "nobody put on any visible airs; yet the class lines were quite clearly drawn and the familiar social life of each class was restricted to that class" (Twain 1924: vol. 1, 120). He reasoned that the "aristocratic taint" in the situation must have been closely related to slavery – though when it was happening, of course, it was seen not as "taint" so much as, like slavery itself, the natural order of things.

In his later recollection of the politics of his youth, however, Twain thought of himself not as a Whig but as an "Anti-Doughnut." As he told the story in a speech entitled "Municipal Corruption" (given at a dinner of The City Club on January 4, 1901), the Anti-Doughnut party arose within a local society ("patterned after the Freemasons") of which he was a member. A major problem of the society, in his view, was that when elections were held, some of the society's members were willing to sell their votes for bribes, payable in doughnuts. When some of the other members, including 14-year-old Sam, united against such corrupt practices, they were labeled (by their adversaries) the Anti-Doughnut party. "I suppose we would have had our price," says Twain in recounting the incident, "but our opponents weren't offering anything but doughnuts, and those we spurned" (Twain 1910: 121). In the next election the Anti-Doughnuts put up a candidate, but he was soundly defeated. According to Twain's account:

> That taught us a lesson. Then and there we decided never again to nominate anybody for anything. We decided simply to force the other two parties in the society to nominate their very best men . . . The next time we had an election we told both the other parties that we'd beat any candidates put up by any one of them of whom we didn't approve. In that election we did business. We got the man we wanted. (Twain 1910: 121)

Although this may at first seem like an innocuous anecdote detailing an anomalous (and perhaps entirely fictitious) incident, it in fact lays out a political plan of action that Twain followed in much of his later relation to party politics.

The main feature of that plan was a rejection of political principles – the basis for a political party's identity – in favor of a focus on personal integrity. Thus, the vote was to be always for the *best* man – i.e., the most honest, conscientious, and capable – rather than awarded by judging the candidates on their approaches to particular political issues. As Twain says in "Municipal Corruption," "Principles aren't of much account anyway, except at election-time" (Twain 1910: 121). The truly defensible object was not to promote one's own party but to disinterestedly work for the ethical and efficient functioning of the whole. It might also be reasonable to speculate that even at an early age Twain tended toward the sort of disinterestedness appropriate to a future novelist – that of the amused commentator more concerned with fathoming and describing the truth of the situation than with actively participating in it.

Meanwhile, Sam's elder brother Orion, who had in effect assumed the role of head of the Clemens family after John Marshall Clemens died in 1847, had also inherited his father's adherence to Whig politics. Sam, who worked for his brother for a time in the newspaper business, followed suit, writing articles for Orion's newspaper that sometimes satirized politicians with whom they disagreed. In addition to their affiliation with the Whigs, both Sam and Orion were drawn to the exclusionist politics (especially aimed at Roman Catholics and the Irish) of the Know-Nothings, a party that thrived in the 1850s. Both backed the Know-Nothings' candidate, former President Millard Fillmore, in the election of 1856. However, Sam and Orion's views evidently diverged to some extent on the question of slavery. Orion tended toward the abolitionist view and, in fact, moved north from the slave-holding state of Missouri to Iowa, a free state where he could be more vocal in his anti-slavery views. Sam, on the other hand, remained mildly supportive (or at least tolerant) of slavery and went south as a river pilot on boats serving mainly the slave-holding states. Although he evidently felt sympathy for African Americans and other oppressed groups, that sympathy was based on a paternalistic outlook assuming the superiority of European Americans – especially those, like the Clemenses and Lamptons, of supposedly aristocratic origins. Sam, sounding a bit like Pap Finn, refers in a letter to his mother from New York (dated August 24, 1853, and subsequently published by Orion in his

Hannibal *Journal*) to the "infernal abolitionists," and remarks, "I reckon I had better black my face, for in these Eastern States niggers are considerably better than white people" (Twain 1988: 4).

In the pivotal election of 1860, Sam sided with neither the pro-slavery Democrats, whose candidate was Stephen Douglas, nor the anti-slavery Republicans, whose candidate was Abraham Lincoln. Instead he supported the Constitutional Union Party in its attempt to preserve the Union through a compromise position, and he evidently voted for its presidential candidate, John Bell. When the Civil War began, Sam briefly embraced the secessionist cause by joining a volunteer militia in Hannibal (as recounted in "The Private History of a Campaign That Failed" [1885]), but soon thought better of it and deserted. He then joined Orion (who had sufficiently ingratiated himself with the victorious Republicans to be appointed Secretary to the Governor of the Territory of Nevada) in a cross-country trip away from the anguish of war and into a politically charged atmosphere of a different sort. In Nevada, while Orion worked seriously and often effectively in prosecuting the duties of his position (including a substantial period as acting Governor), Sam assisted him in political matters, prospected for silver, and wrote for the Virginia City *Territorial Enterprise* and other newspapers. As a frontier journalist he honed his satirical powers, using them frequently on the politicians of Nevada. Later, as a newspaperman in San Francisco, he continued the political satire, here focusing on Democrats, Irishmen, corrupt police, and political corruption in general. By his own account (which is, of course, not always reliable), his departures first from Nevada in 1864 and then from San Francisco in 1865 were both hastened by his confrontational, intentionally controversial style of political reporting. Twain's sketches during this period include "The Story of the Bad Little Boy That Bore a Charmed Life," whose protagonist, contrary to the stories in the Sunday-school books, does not find that his misdeeds lead to disaster. At the end of the story, the bad little boy, now an adult, is "the infernalest wickedest scoundrel in his native village, and is universally respected, and belongs to the Legislature" (Twain 1992a: 194).

By the time Sam Clemens, now professionally established under the pseudonym Mark Twain, journeyed from the West Coast to New York City in 1866–7, the Whigs, the Know-Nothings, and the Constitutional Union Party – the three political entities to which he had given some measure of allegiance in the past – had all faded into irrelevance or nonexistence. But the Mark Twain persona that emerged from the Western sojourn was that of a fearlessly pugnacious reporter with enough satirical irreverence to go around for whatever political entities he might encounter. He maintained that image throughout the tour of the *Quaker City* (June–November, 1867), in the resulting letters published in the *Alta California* and other newspapers, and in his largely satirical travel book *The Innocents Abroad* (1869). He apparently was much more interested in finding political actions and situations to ridicule than in identifying the party that should be supported. Twain also spent two months in Washington DC in 1867 as secretary to Senator William M. Stewart of Nevada, who had been a target of Twain's satire when he was a lawyer and local politician (and Twain was writing for the *Territorial Enterprise*). Now, though, and perhaps in view of Twain's growing celebrity, Stewart was willing to consign that skirmish to the past. However, the *rapprochement* was brief, and Twain returned to satire, both of Stewart (now a Republican with Radical Reconstructionist views) and of Washington politics in general, in such sketches as "My Late Senatorial Secretaryship" (*Galaxy*, 1868). "Cannibalism in the Cars" (*Broadway*, 1868), one of Twain's better-known pieces from this period, satirizes Congress by superimposing parliamentary procedures – nominations, amendments, committees, etc. – onto a situation in which a group of travelers is starving and some members of the group must cannibalize others in order to survive. In the heated debates that ensue over who is to be eaten, a suitable decorum is maintained, but the quality of the individual as food substitutes for personal qualities that might elevate one to a high political position. Besides the burlesque aspect, there is also the suggestion that politics may be a sort of cannibalism.

Party Politics

Twain's political homelessness ended, for the moment, as he made new acquaintances in the late 1860s and early 1870s: Olivia Langdon, whom he met in 1867 and married in 1870; Olivia's abolitionist father Jervis Langdon and her brother Charles (who, as a member of the *Quaker City* expedition, was actually the first Langdon Twain encountered); William Dean Howells, whom Twain met in 1869 when Howells was assistant editor of the *Atlantic Monthly* and had just written a favorable review of *The Innocents Abroad*; and his neighbors in Nook Farm in Hartford, where Twain and Olivia made their home beginning in 1871. If none of these new friends could rightly be called "Radical Republicans," they were at least clear in their allegiance to the party and its political agenda of, among other things, a Southern Reconstruction that made adequate provision for the rights and needs of the freed slaves. Twain had been opposed to the strongly abolitionist Republican position that had helped precipitate the Civil War, and it was only many years later that he showed evidence of having warmed appreciably to Abraham Lincoln, when, in his speech to the American Society in London on July 4, 1907, he cited "Lincoln's proclamation, which not only set the black slaves free, but set the white man free also" (Twain 1910: 411). In spite of the tardiness of his conversion, the transition to Republicanism probably was not a difficult one for Twain since the Republican party was the heir of the Whigs and Know-Nothings as the party of limited democracy. Republicans believed, as Twain clearly did, in rule by the privileged – those it considered capable of ruling well – as opposed to indiscriminate democracy. His conversion was no doubt also helped considerably by his having met, and apparently liked and admired from the beginning, Ulysses S. Grant. Grant, as the Republican presidential candidate in both 1868 and 1872, must have been much easier for Twain to take than Lincoln had been in 1860 and 1864.

In the 1872 election Grant defeated Horace Greeley, a former Republican who had left the party over his disagreements with Grant and been adopted by the Democrats.

Twain had earlier written a satirical article ("Private Habits of Horace Greeley" [*Spirit of the Times*, 1868]) in which he complained about Greeley's supposedly illegible hand-writing and proposed that whenever his proofreaders could not decipher a word, they simply inserted "reconstruction" or "universal suffrage" (Twain 1992a: 280). In the midst of the 1872 campaign he published (under the pseudonym Ujijiji Unyembe-mbe) "The Secret of Dr. Livingstone's Continued Voluntary Exile" in the Hartford *Courant* (July 20, 1872) – the secret being that when Livingstone heard that "Horace Greeley is become a democrat and the ku-klux swing their hats and whoop for him" (Twain 1992a: 542), he decided to remain in Africa. After the election of November 1872, Twain wrote to Thomas Nast, whose cartoons lampooning Greeley were per-ceived to have had an important impact in the campaign: "Nast you, more than any other man, have won a prodigious victory for Grant – I mean, rather, for Civilization and progress . . . We all do sincerely honor you & are proud of you" (Twain 1997: 249).

But Twain could also see the other side of making the political candidate fair game for any attacker, as his sketch "Running for Governor" (*Galaxy*, 1870) illustrates. Here he presents himself as a conscientious citizen, with a clean record of conduct, who enters the race for Governor of New York because, having read the newspaper accounts of his opponents, he sees that, "if ever they had known what it was to bear a good name, that time had gone by. It was plain that in these latter years they had become familiar with all manner of shameful crimes" (Twain 1992a: 490). But as soon as he enters the race, he finds that he, too, is accused of hideous crimes and moral lapses – deeds that he could not possibly have committed. And, no matter how outrageous the accusations are, they stick to him and become part of his reputation; no one pays attention to his explanations to the contrary. The piece concludes, "I was not equal to the requirements of a Gubernatorial campaign in the State of New York, and so I sent in my withdrawal from the candidacy, and in bitterness of spirit signed it, 'Truly yours, once a decent man, but now . . . MARK TWAIN'" (Twain 1992a: 494).

Twain collaborated with fellow Republican and Nook Farm neighbor Charles Dudley Warner on *The Gilded Age* (1873), his first novel and his most extended effort at political satire. The novel's title plays ironically on "Golden Age" – in Greek mythology, the time of innocence equivalent to the time of Adam and Eve in Par-adise, and in the histories of both Greece and Rome the name given to the eras of those civilizations' highest achievements. In the conversion to "gilded age," the shift is from substance to surface, and from innocence to a sham virtue. The name thus signifies the authors' estimation of the shallowness and falseness prevalent in the political and social climate of the post-Civil War United States. The book features politicians like Patrick O'Riley, who makes a fortune through political corruption, and his friend Wm. M. Weed (obviously modeled on Tammany Hall political boss William Marcy Tweed), whose political shenanigans net him $20 million through graft of various sorts. The result (reminiscent of the ending of "The Bad Little Boy That Led a Charmed Life") is that "the people rose as one man (voting repeatedly) and elected the two gentlemen to their proper theatre of action, the New York legislature" (Twain and Warner 1996: 303) – which then declines to expel them when their misconduct is exposed.

As for Washington DC, where much of the action takes place, the novel portrays it as the locus of sordid intrigues and scandals – a place where influence is everything, actual merit means little, and nothing happens without resort to the pulling of political strings. Overall, politics is seen in the novel as a disreputable profession. Philip Sterling, a non-politician, and one of the novel's most admirable characters, remarks, "the chances are that a man cannot get into congress now without resorting to arts and means that should render him unfit to go there" (Twain and Warner 1996: 457–8). The news that a man intends to enter politics, according to Philip, is a matter to make one suspicious of him: "Why, it is telegraphed all over the country and commented on as something wonderful if a congressman votes honestly and unselfishly and refuses to take advantage of his position to steal from the government" (p. 458). The novel also complains, in good Republican fashion, about the perils of universal suffrage, which in Twain's view leaves the political process vulnerable to being hijacked by zealous malcontents from society's lower reaches. With respect to a shocking revelation of bribery, the novel's third-person narrator speculates:

> Perhaps it did not occur to the nation of good and worthy people that while they continued to sit comfortably at home and leave the true source of our political power (the "primaries,") in the hands of saloon-keepers, dog-fanciers, and hod-carriers, they could go on expecting "another" case of this kind, and even dozens and hundreds of them, and never be disappointed. (pp. 530–1)

During this period Twain also published "The Curious Republic of Gondour" (perhaps a melding of the French "gondoler," meaning "to warp," with the English – or French – "grandeur") in the *Atlantic Monthly* (1875). In Twain's imagined republic, universal suffrage is at first the rule – one man, one vote. However, this method of conducting elections "seemed to deliver all power into the hands of the ignorant and non-tax-paying classes; and of a necessity the responsible offices were filled from these classes also" (Twain 1992a: 634). Rule, at this stage, is – in effect – by the "hod-carriers" and others of the poor and ignorant working (or nonworking) class. The Gondourians, however, solve this problem, and establish what turns out to be a utopian state, by what Twain calls an "enlargement" of suffrage: that is, by giving additional votes to the educated and the wealthy. The result is that, "for once, – and for the first time in the history of the republic, – property, character, and intellect were able to wield a political influence; for once, money, virtue, and intelligence took a vital and a united interest in a political question . . .; for once the best men in the nation were put forward as candidates" (p. 634). The cure adopted by Gondour for its political ills fits the elitist, paternalistic agenda of the Republican party of Twain's time, showing that agenda in its most optimistic light, and suggests Twain's readiness to back Republican principles and candidates in the practical politics of the day.

By the time of the hotly contested presidential election of 1876, Twain was entirely ready to give enthusiastic support to the Republican candidate Rutherford B. Hayes.

Howells, a long-time Republican (who had, in fact, been appointed Consul to Venice during the Civil War on the strength of his campaign biography of Lincoln), encouraged Twain to come out publicly for Hayes, suggesting he could have an important influence in the candidate's favor. Twain responded, in a letter of August 23, 1876, "I am glad you think I could do Hayes any good, for I have been wanting to write a letter or make a speech to that end" (Twain and Howells 1960: 146). In another letter to Howells, on September 14, 1876, he reiterated his enthusiasm: "I will not & do not believe that there is a possibility of Hayes's defeat, but I want the victory to be sweeping . . . It seems odd to find myself interested in an election. I never was before" (p. 151). In the same election year, Twain also took an interest in a gubernatorial race, telling Howells in a letter of October 11, "I came near agreeing to make political speeches with our candidate for Governor . . . but I had to give up the idea, for [Bret] Harte and I will be here [in Hartford] at work then" (p. 159). Twain did give a planned interview favorable to Hayes in the New York *Herald* on August 28, 1876, but otherwise did no campaigning for either the presidential or the gubernatorial candidate – demonstrating, despite his expressions of enthusiasm, the continuing ambivalence about party politics articulated in his September 14 letter to Howells: "I can't seem to get over my repugnance to reading or thinking about politics, yet. But in truth I care little about any party's politics – the man behind it is the important thing" (p. 151).

Hayes was elected, as Twain had hoped, but the victory was far from sweeping. In fact, the race was so tight that, in the post-election wrangling, Hayes traded away all the important features of the Republican Reconstruction in order to gain the crucial support of three swing states in the South. Thus, the election of the Republicans' own candidate brought an end to the Reconstruction program they had fostered, enabling the resubjugation of the South's black population under Jim Crow laws. When Twain realized what had happened, his distrust of party politics must have been magnified, along with his belief that honesty and resistance to corrupt practices were more important matters than the political and socioeconomic principles that political parties represented. Thus, when the 1880 presidential election came around, he seemed less concerned with the campaign than the fact that it was drawing interest away from his pet concern of the moment: the copyright issue. Albert Bigelow Paine, in his edition of *Mark Twain's Letters*, indicates that Twain did support the campaign of the Republican candidate, James A. Garfield. However, while Twain in his *Autobiography* praises Grant's energetic campaigning for Garfield, he has nothing to say about his own opinion of Garfield's candidacy. After the election, nonetheless, he wrote to Garfield (then president-elect) on January 12, 1881, on behalf of Frederick Douglass, asking Garfield to "retain Mr. Douglass in his present office of Marshall of the District of Columbia, if such a course will not clash with your own preferences or with the expediencies and interest of your administration." Identifying Douglass, who had escaped from slavery and become one of the most effective spokesmen for abolition, as "a personal friend of mine," and demonstrating how far he had come from the thoughtless racial prejudice of his youth, Twain told Garfield that he made the request "with peculiar pleasure and strong desire, because I so honor this man's high and blemishless character and so admire his brave, long crusade for the liberties and elevation of his race" (Twain 1917: vol. 1, 294).

Twain's support for Douglass, who continued to be one of the great advocates of the rights of African Americans, also suggests the degree to which he had come by this time to support what we would today call "liberal causes." His publication of "A True Story, Repeated Word for Word as I Heard It" (*Atlantic Monthly*, 1874), had poignantly and sympathetically told the story of the sufferings of Susan and Theodore Crane's housekeeper Mary Ann Cord, a former slave (fictionalized in Twain's story as Aunt Rachel), and such pieces as the satirical "Disgraceful Persecution of a Boy" and the more sober "John Chinaman in New York" (both published in *Galaxy* in 1870) extended the sympathy for non-European racial groups in America to the Chinese immigrants whose mistreatment he had witnessed during his time in San Francisco. In "Disgraceful Persecution of a Boy," Twain describes how a boy who has been abusing the Chinese has been taught to do so (much as Huck Finn has been taught to behave toward African Americans):

> the boy found out that a Chinaman had no rights that any man was bound to respect; that he had no sorrows that any man was bound to pity; that neither his life nor his liberty was worth the purchase of a penny when a white man needed a scapegoat . . . Everything conspired to teach him that it was a high and holy thing to stone a Chinaman. (Twain 1992a: 380–1)

In his essay "The Temperance Insurrection" (London *Standard*, 1874), and in "The Curious Republic of Gondour," Twain also moved definitively in the direction of an advocacy of women's suffrage – contrary to the attitude of his earlier pieces "Female Suffrage" (*Sunday Mercury*, April 7, 1867) and "Female Suffrage: Views of Mark Twain" (*Missouri Democrat*, March 12, 1867), which had given light and not particularly sensitive treatment to the subject. In "The Temperance Insurrection," Twain sees the fervor of the women's temperance movement as resulting partly from the frustration that "They find themselves voiceless in the making of laws and the election of officers to execute them." This concern for women's political impotence dovetails with his expression of contempt for the great mass of those who do have the franchise: "They see their fathers, husbands, and brothers sit inanely at home and allow the scum of the country to assemble at the 'primaries,' name the candidates for office from their own vile ranks, and, unrebuked, elect them." However he may feel about the temperance movement in general, he clearly states, "I cannot help glorying in the pluck of these women" (Twain 1992a: 565), and ironically comments, "I dearly want the women to be raised to the altitude of the Negro, the imported savage, and the pardoned thief, and allowed to vote" (pp. 565–6). On the other hand, in the enlightened Republic of Gondour, women have been granted the right not only to vote but to hold office. The head of state in Gondour is the "Grand Caliph," a position which "had twice been ably filled by women . . . Members of the cabinet, under many administrations, had been women" (pp. 638).

Mark Twain, Mugwump

It was the 1884 presidential election that prompted Twain's farewell to Republican party allegiance. Although he had backed Garfield, however tepidly, in spite of the candidate's having been implicated in the Crédit Mobilier scandal (which occurred during Grant's Republican administration), he was less forgiving toward James G. Blaine, the 1884 Republican presidential nominee. Blaine had likewise been soiled by the Crédit Mobilier scandal, and in addition had been accused both of involvement in a railroad-financing scandal in Arkansas and of a subsequent cover-up of that involvement. Grover Cleveland, the Democratic candidate, had his own scandal to cope with, acknowledging that he had fathered an illegitimate child more than a decade earlier; but despite this private indiscretion he had a reputation as an honest politician strongly opposed to tolerance of political corruption. Twain, like many other Republicans, denounced the Republican candidate and declared himself a Mugwump (from an Algonquin word meaning "big chief") – that is, a free agent willing to support the best candidate regardless of his party. Cleveland's motto, "a public office is a public trust," perfectly suited Twain and other Mugwumps, with their emphasis on truth-telling and resistance to corruption. As Twain described the movement in his *Autobiography*:

> We, the mugwumps, a little company made up of the unenslaved of both parties, the very best men to be found in the two great parties – that was our idea of it – voted sixty thousand strong for Mr. Cleveland in New York and elected him. Our principles were high and very definite. We were not a party; we had no candidates; we had no axes to grind . . . When voting, it was our duty to vote for the best man, regardless of his party name. We had no other creed. (Twain 1924: vol. 2, 160–1)

This was a crucial moment in Twain's relation to politics: the moment in which he apparently rejected party politics permanently. The Mugwumps, as Twain suggested, were not so much a party as an anti-party. They were, in fact, a sort of real-life incarnation of the Anti-Doughnut party, saying to both the Democrats and the Republicans, "give us the superior candidate, and especially the most honest one, and we will vote for him." Twain wrote to Howells, who still remained loyal to Republicanism, on September 17, 1884:

> My Dear Howells:
>   Somehow I can't seem to rest quiet under the idea of your voting for Blaine. I believe you said something about the country and the party. Certainly allegiance to these is well; but as certainly a man's *first* duty is to his own conscience & honor – the party & the country come second to that, & never first. I don't ask you to vote *at all* – I only urge you to not soil yourself by voting for Blaine. (Twain and Howells 1960: 508)

This was to become his personal standard for political involvement: that integrity was more important than political efficacy, and that, rather than support corruption, it is better to withhold one's vote altogether.

In his autobiographical dictations Twain recalled, many years after the event, what he saw as the significance of his stand in the election of 1884 against the Republican candidate and against the pressure brought to bear on him by his Republican friends in Hartford:

> I said that no party held the privilege of dictating to me how I should vote. That if party loyalty was a form of patriotism, I was no patriot, and that I didn't think I was much of a patriot, anyway, for oftener than otherwise what the general body of Americans regarded as the patriotic course was not in accordance with my views; that if there was any valuable difference between being an American and a monarchist it lay in the theory that the American could decide for himself what is patriotic and what isn't; whereas the king could dictate the monarchist's patriotism for him. (Twain 1924: vol. 2, 17)

The problem with this formulation is that his principal reason for becoming a Republican in the first place (other than the social pressure he felt from his Republican acquaintances) was that the party purported to stand against the sort of "lowest common denominator" rule that he believed to result from universal suffrage. So he was left with two incompatible propositions: that, on the one hand, each person should be afforded the opportunity to form, express, and make known his or her own opinion, and that, on the other hand, it was necessary to keep political life out of the hands of the "hod-carriers" – his favorite term for the ignorant rabble to whom, he believed, too many politicians made their appeals.

In 1884, the same year as the Cleveland–Blaine face-off, Twain completed *Adventures of Huckleberry Finn*, which includes, in Pap Finn's tirade against the "govment," a parody meditation on the individual's responsibilities as member of the electorate. Pap chooses to go his own way, but not because he disagrees with candidates on political issues or because he is concerned about the integrity of the candidates or the political process. He chooses to withdraw because in voting he would put himself into the same category with a "white-shirted free nigger" (Twain 1885: 50) who, though superior to Pap in both education and economic condition (and no doubt morally and in many other ways), is nonetheless a member of a group that Pap enjoys a social sanction to discriminate against. Huck, on the other hand, is confused about political principles but (like Twain-as-Mugwump) is willing to follow his own conscience even when those around him disagree. Society has caught Huck in a tug-of-war between competing principles: those of the abolitionists, whose desire to dismantle the Southern social and economic system must seem unthinkably destructive to him, and those of the defenders of slavery, whose insensitivity to the plight of African Americans violates his sense of common humanity. His choice is to withhold support from either "party" pending the emergence of some approach that fits his own idea of right and wrong. He decides to help Jim in spite of the risk of being branded a "low down Ablitionist" (p. 69); wants to help the men on the wrecked *Walter Scott* in defiance of the conventional conception of the deserts of murderers (p. 103); and decides to "go to hell" when his own moral judgment about the right treatment of Jim runs counter to his society's strictures

(p. 272). Huck-as-Mugwump votes his own conscience, and Jim is the good man of his choosing. In "The Private History of a Campaign That Failed," published in that same year (1885), Twain arrives at a view of war as a kind of extreme version of party politics: "all war must be just that . . . the killing of strangers against whom you feel no personal animosity; strangers whom, in other circumstances, you would help if you found them in trouble, and who would help you if you needed it" (Twain 1992a: 880). Its protagonist, like Huck Finn, takes the Mugwump route; he declines to participate in what seems, finally, a conflict destructive to all concerned.

Although Twain did not himself become a Democrat after the 1884 election, he continued to be an admirer of Grover Cleveland, who ran unsuccessfully for a second term as President in 1888, but then returned for a successful campaign in 1892. Cleveland seems to have served as a sort of model of political virtue for Twain. Twain, true to his Mugwump creed, regarded Cleveland's forthright approach to political questions as more important than agreement or disagreement with the political principles he advocated. In his *Autobiography* he recalls writing to Cleveland after his retirement from political life, saying:

> HONORED SIR: – Your patriotic virtues have won for you the homage of half the nation and the enmity of the other half. This places your character as a citizen upon a summit as high as Washington's . . . Where the votes are all in a man's favor the verdict is against him. It is sand, and history will wash it away. But the verdict for you is rock, and will stand. (Twain 1924: vol. 2, 164)

The implication seems to be that a politician with whom everyone agrees cannot be taking legitimate stands on tough issues; to be a true leader, one must be willing to incur the anger of the electorate. As for the majority of politicians, though, Twain's *The American Claimant* offers a suggestion for much-needed reform in Colonel Sellers' visionary plan for the "materialization of departed spirits" (Twain 1892: 43):

> I will dig up the trained statesmen of all ages and all climes, and furnish this country with a Congress that knows enough to come in out of the rain – a thing that's never happened yet, since the Declaration of Independence, and never will happen till these practically dead people are replaced with the genuine article (p. 46).

In 1889 Twain published *A Connecticut Yankee in King Arthur's Court*, which could reasonably be called his most political book other than *The Gilded Age*. Hank Morgan, the novel's narrator and protagonist, in his better moments seems a political agent after Twain's own heart, believing that a sincere interest in the country's welfare can transcend political differences: "You see my kind of loyalty was loyalty to one's country, not to its institutions or its officeholders. The country is the real thing, the substantial thing, the eternal thing; it is the thing to watch over, and care for, and be loyal to" (Twain 1889: 158). However, Hank (no doubt a relative of financier J. P. Morgan, a late nineteenth-century "robber baron" and, like Hank, a "Connecticut Yankee" from Hartford) is also the man who vows that "if . . . it was really the sixth century . . . I would boss the whole country inside of three months" (p. 36). And when he has succeeded in gaining effective control of the government of Arthur's kingdom, he disdains other titles in favor of "The Boss," a title surely drawn from Boss Tweed and Richard Croker, the principal "bosses" of New York City's corrupt Tammany Society. Hank, it seems, is corrupted in his own way by the power he gains. He is like Butterworth Stavely in Twain's "The Great Revolution in Pitcairn" (1882). Stavely is the only American in the idyllic realm of Pitcairn's Island, where he manages to foment a revolution, declares himself Butterworth I, and immediately introduces the corrupting influences of party politics, militarism, and social rank. Hank, in *A Connecticut Yankee*, abolishes the nobility, declaring that "all men are become exactly equal," yet his proclamation of this fact is prefaced with the assertion that "it becomes my duty to continue the executive authority vested in me, until a government shall have been created and set in motion" (Twain 1889: 544), and he signs the proclamation "The Boss," leaving the reader to wonder whether such a republic is really any advance over the monarchy that preceded it.

In both 1896 and 1900 the presidential candidates were William McKinley for the Republicans and William Jennings Bryan for the Democrats. Although the 1896 election was one of the most emotional and bitterly fought of the era, Twain was out of the country throughout the election year (on his *Following the Equator* tour), and his daughter Susy died on August 18, 1896, extinguishing any chance that he would take an interest in the election. As for the 1900 election, Twain's attitude toward both candidates was at best indifference, at worst active hostility. In his "Municipal Corruption" speech to the City Club, given soon after the election (January 4, 1901), he told those present:

> I had a vote this fall, and I began to make some inquiries as to what I had better do with it. . . . I know some pretty shrewd financiers, and they told me that Mr. Bryan wasn't safe on any financial question . . . and I rather thought – I know now – that McKinley wasn't just right on this Philippine question, and so I just didn't vote for anybody. I've got that vote yet, and I've kept it clean, ready to deposit at some other election. It wasn't cast for any wildcat financial theories, and it wasn't cast to support the man who sends our boys as volunteers out into the Philippines to get shot down under a polluted flag. (Twain 1910: 122)

Here he reiterates the Mugwump principle (and the advice he gave to Howells with respect to the 1884 election) that if there is no candidate worthy of one's vote, then one should not vote at all. He also alludes to his distaste for Bryan's populist "free silver" campaign and to McKinley's military adventures in the Philippines and elsewhere – which Twain, like Howells and many other Americans, regarded as imperialism. With respect to Bryan's unsoundness on financial questions, Twain's reliance on "shrewd financiers" who favored the gold standard, the choice of big business, is revealing of the degree to which he still identified more with privilege than with the common people to whom Bryan appealed.

However, Twain had already begun to put aside his old opposition to political power for "hod-carriers" and the like – as suggested by Hank's flirtation with endorsement of rule by the masses in *A Connecticut Yankee* and, still more strongly, by his own praise of the Knights of Labor in his speech "The New Dynasty," given to the Monday Evening Club on March 22, 1886 (see Twain 1992b: 883–90). He had come to think that labor unions were perhaps a necessity for coping with the power of the big-time financiers and industrialists, and that political combinations were a viable mechanism for improving the plight of oppressed groups. In "Concerning the Jews" (1899), for instance, he praises the capabilities of the Jews but blames many of their troubles on their failure to undertake concerted action. The remedy, he says, is to organize:

> In our days we have learned the value of combination. We apply it everywhere – in railway systems, in trusts, in trade unions, in Salvation Armies, in minor politics, in major politics, in European Concerts. Whatever our strength may be, big or little, we *organize* it. We have found out that that is the only way to get the most out of it that is in it. We know the weakness of individual sticks, and the strength of the concentrated faggot. (Twain 1996: 275)

Nonetheless, his distrust of political organizations remained. In a speech of May 1900 at the Royal Literary Fund Banquet in London, he reiterated his dissatisfaction with parties based on pre-established principles, telling his audience that he was planning to enter the 1900 presidential race (which he was not, of course) because the other candidates were "too much hampered by their own principles, which are prejudices." He urged Twichell (letter of November 4, 1904), "get out of that sewer – party politics – dear Joe" (Twain 1917: vol. 2, 761). And in *Following the Equator* (1897) he offered the proposition that "there is no distinctly native American criminal class except Congress" (Twain 1897: 99). As he summed up the matter in "Concerning the Jews," we should have more respect than we do for Satan since, after all, he has "for untold centuries maintained the imposing position of . . . political head of [the human race]" (Twain 1992b: 355).

Theodore Roosevelt, who became President after McKinley's assassination in 1901 and then was re-elected in his own right in 1904, was something of an enigma to Twain – an enigma who fitted nicely into his preoccupation with the question of personal responsibility. Twain viewed Roosevelt as the antithesis of Cleveland, whose personal life included scandal but whose public life was marked by unimpeachable integrity. He testified in a letter (February 16, 1905) to Twichell:

> Every time, in 25 years, that I have met Roosevelt the man, a wave of welcome has streaked through me with the hand-grip; but whenever (as a rule) I meet Roosevelt the statesman and politician, I find him destitute of morals and not respectworthy. It is plain that where his political self and his party self are concerned he has nothing resembling a conscience. (Twain 1917: vol. 2, 766)

This formulation – recalling Twain's 1876 "The Facts Concerning the Recent Carnival of Crime in Connecticut," in which a man murders his conscience and then is free to do whatever he wants – gives a simple explanation of the Roosevelt

phenomenon: "Theodore the man is sane; in fairness we ought to keep in mind that
Theodore, as statesman and politician, is insane and irresponsible" (Twain 1917: vol.
2, 766). But then, in Twain's opinion, the whole practice of politics is insane in the
way one political party unwaveringly advocates its own idea as undeniable truth,
in opposition to the other party's contrary idea which it just as fervently holds as
incontrovertible. We are all insane, each in his or her own way, and with insanity goes
irresponsibility. And this is, one might say, his final word on party politics. As he
articulates the matter in *Christian Science*:

> All Democrats are insane, but not one of them knows it; none but the Republicans and
> Mugwumps know it. All the Republicans are insane, but only the Democrats and Mug-
> wumps can perceive it. The rule is perfect: *in all matters of opinion our adversaries are insane*
> . . . [T]here's no end to the list [of insane groups of zealots]; there are millions of them!
> And all insane; each in his own way; insane as to his pet fad or opinion, but otherwise
> sane and rational. (Twain 1907: 41–2)

For Twain only the Mugwumps, the anti-party offering no candidates and standing
for no principles other than the election of the best man, are sane.

References and Further Reading

Andrews, Kenneth R. (1950). *Nook Farm: Mark
    Twain's Hartford Circle*. Cambridge, Mass.:
    Harvard University Press.
Budd, Louis J. (1962). *Mark Twain: Social Philoso-
    pher*. Bloomington: Indiana University Press.
Emerson, Everett (2000). *Mark Twain: A Literary
    Life*. Philadelphia: University of Pennsylvania
    Press.
Fanning, Philip Ashley (2003). *Mark Twain and
    Orion Clemens: Brothers, Partners, Strangers*.
    Tuscaloosa: University of Alabama Press.
Fishkin, Shelley Fisher (1993). *Was Huck Black?
    Mark Twain and African American Voices*. New
    York: Oxford University Press.
Fishkin, Shelley Fisher, ed. (2002). *A Historical
    Guide to Mark Twain*. New York: Oxford Uni-
    versity Press.
Foner, Philip S. (1958). *Mark Twain: Social Critic*.
    New York: International.
Twain, Mark (1917). *Mark Twain's Letters*, 2 vols.,
    ed. Albert Bigelow Paine. New York: Harper &
    Bros.
Twain, Mark (1924). *Mark Twain's Autobiography*,
    2 vols., ed. Albert Bigelow Paine. New York:
    Harper & Bros.

Twain, Mark (1959). *The Autobiography of Mark
    Twain*, ed. Charles Neider. New York: Harper &
    Bros.
Twain, Mark (1988). *Mark Twain's Letters*, vol. 1:
    1853–1866, ed. Edgar Marquess Branch,
    Michael B. Frank, and Kenneth M. Sanderson.
    Berkeley: University of California Press.
Twain, Mark (1996). *The Man That Corrupted
    Hadleyburg and Other Stories and Essays*. New
    York: Oxford University Press. (First publ.
    1900.)
Twain, Mark (1997). *Mark Twain's Letters*, vol. 5:
    1872–1873, ed. Lin Salamo and Harriet
    Elinor Smith. Berkeley: University of California
    Press.
Twain, Mark, and Howells, William Dean
    (1960). *Mark Twain–Howells Letters: The
    Correspondence of Samuel L. Clemens and William
    D. Howells, 1872–1910*, 2 vols., ed. Henry
    Nash Smith and William M. Gibson.
    Cambridge, Mass.: Belknap/Harvard University
    Press.
Twain, Mark, and Warner, Charles Dudley (1996).
    The Gilded Age. New York: Oxford University
    Press (First publ. 1873).

8

"The State, it is I": Mark Twain, Imperialism, and the New Americanists

Scott Michaelsen

[A nation is] a group of people united by a mistaken view about the past and a hatred of their neighbors. Ernest Renan (quoted in Bronner 2004)

What, if anything, does Mark Twain have to say to us, today, about imperialism? Twain's writings on imperialism are multitudinous and varied. These late, and often short and fragmentary texts encompass particular published statements on imperial theaters (Cuba, the Philippines, the Congo, and the like) as well as broad remarks on imperialism in general. They include well-known full-length works (*A Connecticut Yankee* and *Following the Equator*, pre-eminently), complex fragments of science fictions and metafictions which remained unpublished in Twain's lifetime (the *Nightmare of History* materials and "Three Thousand Years Among the Microbes," for example), and a multitude of shorter statements, a good many of which were suppressed by Twain or his publishers, or simply remained in manuscript at the time of his death (see Twain 1973; Twain 1992c). In the last decade of his life Twain devoted himself to a series of experiments in both content and form as he attempted to write a text sufficient to the problem of imperialism. These assembled writings appear to us today as a kind of toolbox of options, which a new generation of scholars now needs to carefully investigate and evaluate. It is no exaggeration to suggest that Twain's many statements on imperialism encompass most of the major theories and sub-theories of imperialism which have arisen in the last 100 years, focusing causally on such matters as capitalism, race, militarism and arms, nationalism, the state-form, and all manner of moralisms and anti-moralisms concerning wealth and human being.[1] And the sheer number of such works, and their many forms, should give one pause before making all-encompassing judgments of them.[2]

These works do indeed have something to offer our ongoing and important conversations regarding the problem of imperialism, its presuppositions and its limits. It is very difficult, however, to read Twain with clarity or accuracy in this context given the current constraints of that very discussion. At present, the set of critics informally grouped together as "New Americanists" have emphatically taken up the burden of reading anti-imperialism, including Twain's texts. But this essay will argue that, if we are to begin to comprehend Twain, it will be necessary to read him *against* the grain of "New Americanism."

The New Americanist readings of the anti-imperialist record, following the lead of Edward W. Said, seek generally to score variants of a particular point: that imperialism can and should be confronted and combated on neo-Gramscian "cultural" grounds. This means, first, that a variety of ways of thinking about imperialism are disposed of, relegated to secondary position, or, at the very least, de-emphasized (for instance, "the economic, social, and political realms," according to Said) in relation to a something called "culture," which rhymes with "history" (Said 1993: xii). This division between culture and its others is not only wholly artificial, but premised on a false understanding of culture and history as realms of agency (agential to their core), and its others (such as the economic) as systemic. Given the presumed relative auton- omy of the cultural realm in Antonio Gramsci's work, it becomes quite unimportant to these New Americanists to concern themselves with structural limits – either the structural limits of the very idea of culture (see Michaelsen 1999), or structural limits imposed on cultural agency through its relationship with other domains. For the most part, too, this body of work has cut itself off from the celebrated theorists of imperi- alism and the traditions of critical thought they have established. One searches in vain through the nearly 700 pages of Amy Kaplan and Donald E. Pease's collection *Cul- tures of United States Imperialism* (1993) for even a single, passing reference to the classic statements of J. A. Hobson, Thorstein Veblen, Rosa Luxemburg, Joseph Schumpeter, V. I. Lenin, and the like. A trawl through the nearly 400 pages of John Carlos Rowe's *Literary Culture and US Imperialism* (2000) is just as dispiriting: nothing but two brief references to Lenin (and Lenin only), but no actual discussion of his theory of imperialism.[3] Kaplan, for instance, encapsulates twentieth-century debates over imperialism through reference only to the thinking of George F. Kennan and William Appleman Williams, which means that her analysis of imperialism comes down to a showdown between historically based "realists" (Kennan) and the "economic approach" (Williams); and she sides with the former because of Kennan's contingent, and therefore potentially agential, view of the problem (Kaplan 1993: 13, 14).[4] It should, moreover, cause some disquiet that Kaplan's avatar for a properly oriented anti-imperialist criticism (the figure capable of displacing Marxism, for example), is Kennan, the architect of Cold War containment, and the crucial cheer- leader for modern CIA interventions and atrocities around the globe. (With Kennan, "realism" as a worldview corresponds to Machiavellian "realpolitik," and it is not so certain that this pairing can be disentangled.)

The full implications of this New Americanist amnesia are well worth contemp- lating. Kaplan, for example, is quite explicit in rejecting a focus "primarily on the economic sources of imperial expansion" at the expense of "the role of culture in the unfolding of imperial politics": "If economics is privileged as the site of the 'real,' then cultural phenomena such as the belief in markets, or racialist discourse, or the ideology of 'benevolent assimilation,' can only be viewed as 'illusions' that have little impact on a separate and narrowly defined political sphere" (Kaplan 1993: 13–14). Here, Kaplan writes against any model for imperialism which begins from a Marxian economic "base" at the expense of the significance of "superstructural" beliefs. But in order to accomplish this, she positions herself against structural determination itself, as she moves onto a ground where imperialism is merely a matter of that which is "enacted" and "contested" – where imperialist beliefs "abet the subjugation of others," while countercultural tendencies "foster their resistance" (Kaplan 1993: 14). Though at times she seems interested merely in redressing a certain balance, her aim ulti-mately is to "foreground culture" at the expense of other methods of description.

Rowe's full-length account of *Literary Culture and US Imperialism* functions in much the same way. He outlines a kind of table or grid of classic American authors on the basis of their attitudes toward imperialism. One third of the writers "contribute directly, if not always self-consciously, to . . . imperial ambitions"; another third "aggressively criticize the United States for its imperialist policies and their impact on subjugated people and individual lives"; and a final group "find themselves deeply divided between obligations to a certain national consensus and their outrage at spe-cific failures of US democracy" (Rowe 2000: x). Rowe worries that "these judgments may sound reductive and categorical," but they also are agential formulations limited only by "concrete historical circumstances." (Kaplan might well agree regarding this limitation, since her method involves limiting Twain's thinking through her choice to base her account of his position on his earlier, concrete experiences, such as his trip to Hawaii.) Again, nowhere does imperialism need to confront embedded structural limitations. "History," understood as nothing but *"contingencies"* – a network of "chances and weird determinisms" – finally does not limit thought, but instead lib-erates it (Rowe 2000: 137). The "future" cannot be predicted if history is nothing but "weird," and therefore the future is absolutely open to each and all of our agencies.

To be as clear as possible here: philosophically, one cannot and therefore should not *choose* between questions of agency and structure. Agency conditions structure, just as structure conditions agency. They are in what deconstruction would call "strange rela-tion" with each other, and constitute in their relationship what Jacques Derrida calls a *"différance."* That is, each agential decision takes place only in the context of struc-tural determination (just as each appearance of structure is conditioned by various agencies). Kaplan and Rowe imagine, then, that which is strictly unimaginable: either a moment or a space outside of structure. One need not insist that the economy is the *only* or even the *most important* determinant (Twain will posit something else entirely, for example) to conclude that "beliefs" cannot exist entirely separately and apart from structural contexts. There is no first instance, in other words, in which "beliefs" simply subjugate or liberate, or in which attitudes toward imperialism simply "contribute" or "criticize." But the New Americanists agree that there really are only two points needed to map imperialism – culture-as-agency, which is both separate from, and capable of trumping, everything else in this world; and the everything else. One is tempted to reiterate Mommsen's remark about Mao in order to grasp the New Americanists' limitations and goals: "What the Maoist doctrine lacks in theoretical precision is made up for by its enthusiastic fighting spirit. Sober analysis is replaced by voluntaristic readiness for action at any cost" (Mommsen 1980: 62). Mark Twain, in reverse, will suggest that a certain form of agency remains the unthought problem which vexes and undermines anti-imperialist discourse.

The New Americanist approach, when applied to Twain, results in readings which privilege Twain's decisions and choices relative to historical embeddedness, but which make nearly invisible his *actual interventions into political or legal theory*. Rowe notes, for instance, that Twain himself is a theorist of agency: "Twain teaches us that there are possibilities for resisting, even occasionally overturning" historical situations (Rowe 2000: 137). But both Kaplan and Rowe criticize Twain for not being quite historically perspicacious enough. Kaplan argues, for instance, that Twain never really overcame the early determinations of his visit to Hawaii in 1866, as evidenced in the anthologized *Mark Twain's Letters from Hawaii*. She draws a direct line between Twain's racism and his attitude of imperial "rescue" toward Cuba and the Philippines, for instance (Kaplan 2002: 52, 92).[5] And Rowe believes – through reference to *A Connecticut Yankee in King Arthur's Court* (1889) – that Twain's anti-imperialism is all bound up in a sentimental idea of writing and narrating our way out of it (Rowe 2000: 138).[6] Twain was anti-imperial, but in such a way as to miscomprehend the neo-imperialism all around him, which already had captured communications technologies (p. 139). In both Kaplan's and Rowe's readings, a later historical situating, or a clearer view of the totality of history, might have resulted in "purer theories" of imperialism, and more concerted interventions (p. 139). It is historical knowledge, finally, which permits such unencumbered and free interventions. Their own volumes, perhaps, are perfected examples of this.[7]

Neither Rowe nor Kaplan shows a great deal of interest in the huge number of anti-imperial statements written by Twain in the last years of his life. Kaplan apparently premises her entire understanding of Twain's anti-imperialism on "To the Person Sitting in Darkness" (1901).[8] Rowe, if anything, has even less interest in these writings. He declares them "powerful" to read, but notes only that they "require little interpretation" (Rowe 2000: 122, 138). To the list of things overlooked, then, by New Americanists in their rush to recast imperialist criticism, one will have to add nearly the whole of Twain's own work in this area.

It is certainly true that Twain's original position on imperialism mutated from a Mugwump-inflected isolationism to (in his early understanding of the matters of the Spanish–American and Philippine–American wars) a brief championship of the view that the United States should serve as a benevolent "protector" of helpless and backward portions of the globe. But, *contra* Kaplan's implications, it is equally true that Twain, by 1900, had converted once again, and this time to become a ceaseless and probing critic of imperial tendencies.[9] One might focus for a moment on one of the earliest of Twain's published texts that reflect this sea-change, which just happens to be Kaplan's text of choice: "To The Person Sitting in Darkness" (1901). Kaplan cites the following passage in order to show that Twain could not comprehend the link between a "national commitment" to freedom and "foreign" imperial intervention: "There must be two Americas: one that sets the captive free, and one that takes a once-captive's new freedom away from him, and picks a quarrel with him with nothing to found it on; then kills him to get his land." Yet this is *not* Mark Twain's claim, but instead is voiced through "the person" in "darkness" of the title. For Twain continues ironically: "The truth is, . . . [he] is saying things like that, and for the sake of the Business we must persuade him to look at the Philippine matter in another and healthier way" (Twain 1973: 14). Twain, *contra* Kaplan, suggests that America *seems* as if it is cut in two to those who have heard its global ideological messages and experienced its imperial power. The goal of "Business" is to propose and successfully transmit a more holistic counter-message which will reconcile the Filipinos to the imperialist practices of which they are the victims. Twain's own goal, on the other hand, is to seek an alternative account which might allow us to comprehend the two-sided quality of US discourse. In "To the Person Sitting in Darkness," his primary suggestion, for example, is that the logic and language of "Civilization" form the pretext for such a double standard (p. 10). Here, Twain rapidly suggests that only an anti-sociology or anti-anthropology that is focused on the exposure of a key category of racial formation, and refuses to categorize groups in terms of a logic of progressive development, might suffice (p. 8). And he toys with this view as early as January 1901, when he contrasts the Boers' idea of civilization to that of the United States, and personally criticizes the latter: "My idea of our civilization is that it is a shabby poor thing and full of cruelties, vanities, arrogances, meannesses, and hypocrisies" (p. 184). In short, civilization, at one and the same time, encompasses the justification for one person's freedom *and* for another's imperial oppression, both at once – and so provides cover for a generalized, global white supremacy (Twain 1992c: 56).

   Elsewhere, and even within "To the Person Sitting in Darkness," Twain tries out a number of ideas regarding the right way to think and theorize imperialism. Does imperialism all come down to money lust (Twain 1973: 32)? Or is it, perhaps, merely an imported and therefore foreign, European idea (Foner 1958: 304)? Perhaps, if properly disentangled, European and other "false" patriotisms could be surgically removed from the "golden" patriotisms of the Founding Fathers (p. 303). Perhaps, then, republics have nothing to do with monarchies or dictatorships, once they are purified (Zwick 1992: xxxi). But perhaps, in line with the *Nightmare of History* materials, and certain moments in *Connecticut Yankee*, the whole of history is nothing but an endless circle of theft and occupation: "No tribe, however insignificant, and no nation, howsoever mighty, occupies a foot of land that was not stolen" (Twain 1973: 172). Here, Twain prefigures a relatively aberrant moment in Lenin: "Colonial policy and imperialism existed before this latest stage of capitalism, and even before capitalism. Rome, founded on slavery, pursued a colonial policy and achieved imperialism" (Lenin 1996: 83). Along with other late Twain remarks, this might lead one toward a conclusion regarding an inescapable and ineradicable "human nature" (Twain 1992c: 85). Or perhaps, again prefiguring a central tenet of Leninism, this is merely a matter of the improper "training" of all men to date (p. 118).

It is possible, however, that the most intriguing and original line of inquiry on which Twain embarks is focused on the form of the state and the question of law; and the rest of this essay will attempt to sketch out the contours and implications of this pathway of his thought. As a first, non-textual intervention, in December 1900 Twain sought out the expertise of Grover Cleveland in order to ascertain whether the Treaty of Paris (1898), signed at the end of the Spanish–American War, might be judged unconstitutional by the US Supreme Court. While it is not clear precisely how Twain might have formulated his nascent legal critique of the treaty, what is interesting here is that he believed that the US Constitution, in general, might provide a framework which ruled out colonial/imperial occupation, and the transfer of sovereignty from Spain to the United States (for a lump sum payment of $20 million, Puerto Rico and Guam were tossed in too, as part of the package).

One might productively contrast this Twain with the one in evidence in "The Stupendous Procession" of early 1901, which recognized that the Constitution was really "a ragged blanket full of holes," and therefore incapable of walling off liberal constitutionalism from imperialism (Twain 1992c: 50). To put this in different words, following the logic of legal theorist Carl Schmitt: any state sovereignty is dependent on "exceptionalism" (gaps or holes in its holistic logic, points at which the governing principles of its polity are suspended in radically exceptional ways) as its founding and ultimate gesture (Schmitt 1985: 5–15). Furthermore, following Giorgio Agamben, the first implication of sovereignty is the division of the world into citizens and "bare life," or those "who *may be killed and yet not sacrificed.*" Bare life is "included solely through its exclusion" in relation to a particular polity, and thus enters a kind of legal "black hole," without rights or traditional legal recourse (Agamben 1998: 8, 18). Twain's "The Stupendous Procession" glimmers with anticipation of this argument, as a "Band of Filipinos" pass by during the Pageant, bearing a sign reading "Unclassifiable," and the ghost of George Washington converses with a Stranger from the sidelines:

> *Shade of Washington.* To the Frivolous Stranger. "Why are those brown people marked 'Unclassifiable?'"
>
> *The Stranger.* "They do not resist our Government, therefore they are not rebels; they do not acknowledge the authority of our Government, therefore in a sense they are not subjects; they are not saleable, therefore in a sense they are not slaves; they are a part of the population of the United States, but they are not citizens; they belong to America, but are not Americans. Politically, they are mongrels – the only ones on the planet, Sir."
> (Twain 1992c: 52)

Not this, not that; inside, relentlessly, but somehow outside as well – Filipinos, therefore, are a form of bare life conjured forth by sovereignty itself. And Twain registers elsewhere, as already suggested, that the Filipinos are "sitting in darkness" – which metaphorically, and rather smartly, captures their legal positioning.

A good deal of Twain's late writing examines the other side of the same problem of radical political exclusion: the character and power of sovereignty itself. In "On the Russian Revolution: The Czar's Soliloquy" (1905), Twain carefully outlines the strange position of sovereignty. In the first place, the founding of sovereignty – the establishment of the "kingly office" – is always itself a type of crime, and the king remains (always) "but the symbol of a crime" (Twain 1973: 181). The king is nothing but a "highwayman" or a "pirate" in his position as keeper of the law, but beyond the reach of it: "Our family is above all law; there is no law that can reach us, restrain us, protect the people from us. Therefore, we are outlaws" (p. 162). Twain makes the same points, in more detail, in the opening to one of the most well-known of the anti-imperialist pieces, "King Leopold's Soliloquy on the Belgian Congo" (1905). Intriguingly, this piece of writing is sometimes published without its illustrations (which are rich with implication), and also sometimes without its actual head-notes, entitled "It Is I."[10] The first head-note argues, through quotation:

> "Leopold II is the absolute Master of the whole of the internal and external activity of the Independent State of the Congo. The organization of justice, the army, the industrial and commercial regimes are established freely by himself. He would say, and with greater accuracy than did Louis XIV., 'The State, it is I.'" *Prof. F. Cattier, Brussels University* (Twain 1905)

Numerous features need to be remarked here, in line with the legal theory of the state. First, the king is commensurate with the state, which means that the figure in which sovereignty resides is equivalent to sovereignty itself. In this way, the state has become oddly like an "I" – a Cartesian identity which is, as Schmitt and others following him have argued, one of the fundamental features of the state (Schmitt 2003: 141ff.; see also Ashley 1989). Indeed, the state founds itself on a moment of agential identity (perhaps "I found, therefore I am"), and then reserves to itself, even as it creates a constitution and body of law, the right to abrogate such law through yet additional acts of exceptional agency. All of this explains why Twain would choose the form of the soliloquy to make his observations about King Leopold (and Czar Nicholas II as well). The soliloquy (Hamlet's being perhaps the most famous example) is a form for self-contemplation and the construction of self-identity, separate and apart from all others.

The sovereign and her/his relationship to the territory's own polity is one of agency in relationship to system. An act of sovereign force or agency brings polity into being (though, of course, only in relation to already existing bodies of law and sovereignties), and polity finds itself subject to yet other acts of sovereign agency, and so forth. In this way, as Hobbes relentlessly argues in *Leviathan*, sovereigns have "absolute" sovereignty over both their home territory and territories of either "*Paternall* and *Despoticall* Dominion . . . alike; or else there is no Sovereignty at all" (Hobbes 1996: 142). And the sovereign, as Twain worried, is figured "outside" the law: "he that is bound to himself only, is not bound" (p. 184). Twain notes that the sovereign is not a "trustee," and is, instead, "sovereign absolute, irresponsible, above the law" (Twain 1973: 42). He is "*sole* master" – "*one man alone*; one solitary man" (p. 60).

Twain in these ways puts his finger on the crucial problem for legal analysis relative to imperialism. As Hegel rightly reminds us, the state "is most supremely its own" when it exercises its sovereignty through war against other states, and through military or police actions directed against "barbarians . . . who lag behind them in institutions which are the essential moments of the state" (Hegel 1967: paras. 323, 351). With regard to such unrecognized, non-stated or de-stated peoples, the state "treats their autonomy as only a formality" (para. 351). In other words, both war as such and imperialism find their common origin in states which approach the "completion" of their identity. Neither war nor imperialism necessarily follows statehood, but the creation of the state is a mode of weaponizing. There are good arguments as to why individuals should not wander the streets with loaded and cocked guns. In the same manner, Twain's musings suggest that states are not fit figures for cosmopolitan companionship. States are arbiters over life and death – whether within the state or without. The decision to kill and subjugate others is the apex of sovereign power.

This explains Twain's proposed monument to Leopold, illustrated at the beginning of Twain's original pamphlet, and described in some detail by "Leopold" himself:

> Another madman wants to construct a memorial for the perpetuation of my name, out of my 15,000,000 skulls and skeletons, and is full of vindictive enthusiasm over his strange project. He has it all ciphered and drawn to scale. Out of the skulls he will build a combined monument and mausoleum to me which shall exactly duplicate the Great Pyramid of Cheops, whose base covers thirteen acres, and whose apex is 451 feet above ground. He desires to stuff me and stand me up in the sky on that apex, robed and crowned, with my "pirate flag" in one hand and a butcher-knife and pendant handcuffs in the other . . . Radiating from the pyramid, like the spokes of a wheel, there are to be forty grand avenues of approach, each thirty-five miles long, and each fenced on both sides by skulless skeletons standing a yard and a half apart and festooned together in line by short chains stretching from wrist to wrist and attached to tried and true old handcuffs stamped with my private trade-mark, a crucifix and a butcher-knife crossed, with motto, "By this sign we prosper." (Twain 1973: 54–5)

Twain uses the pyramid as a succinct visual symbol of sovereignty, with power collected in a single, skyward point, as if Leopold held, in life, the power of the gods. But this god, of course, is the god of death. And just in case it was unclear how this related to US matters, Twain imagines Leopold, at the end of this passage, dreaming of the possibilities should Twain decide to craft a monument to Andrew Carnegie, who had authorized the Pinkerton massacre of the Homestead Works' unionized steel workers at Pittsburgh in July 1892: "*If he should think of Carnegie* – but I must banish that thought out of my mind!" (Twain 1973: 55). Twain, as always, is trying to thread together domestic and international concerns, seeking out the domestic analogue to King Leopold's Congo. As in those moments of *Connecticut Yankee* where slavery, serfdom, and capitalist wage labor are all thought as one and the same, Twain in his anti-imperialist writings connects Russian serfdom, Congo imperialism, Philippines "rescue," and US corporate control of worker populations, as relative equivalents.

By pinpointing the problem of sovereignty, Twain undoubtedly achieved an intellectual breakthrough which was rare among men of letters of his time. Coupling his remarks on sovereignty with his recognition that all states have behaved this way throughout history leads one toward an idea that even he was only barely able to acknowledge, here and there. The United States, no matter how much one might wish to assert that sovereignty had been tamed in this republican form of government, remained fundamentally (and perhaps necessarily) tainted by sovereignty and its exceptional powers.

From a certain doctrinaire Marxist perspective, Twain indeed seems like an odd old man, babbling about kings and czars all the time and charging that European remnants of sovereign exceptionalism had infected the US polity. From a certain (perhaps overly careful) historical perspective, intent on laying out precise boundary markers (temporally and conceptually) for nineteenth- and twentieth-century colonialism, imperialism, and neo-colonialism, Twain might be understood as unforgivably sloppy and imprecise.[11] He sometimes seems, in short, like a man out of time, focused on everything but the particularities of late nineteenth-century imperialism. Seen from another angle, however, from a time when it can be ventured that it is "untenable to describe imperialism as a direct consequence of growth crises of the capitalist system" (Mommsen 1980: 147), and when the question of what endures across centuries in imperialism is definitely on the agenda, then Twain's focus on the state and sovereignty begins to seem prescient.

Indeed, if one were to locate Twain in the great twentieth-century debates on imperialism, he most closely matches the thought of Hannah Arendt. Arendt, for example, devotes two-fifths of her study to white supremacy and "race"-thinking. A crucial section of her text focuses on the Hobbesian state, and in particular Hobbes's elaboration of sovereignty as a form of "tyranny" which necessarily follows its "own inherent law" outward; and on imperial bureaucracy, which governs by sovereign "decree" rather than defined law in order to produce, endlessly, the figure of the "refugee" or stateless person (Arendt 1968: 19–27, 123–9, 147ff.). Twain and Arendt find much common ground, then, on the question of sovereignty as the fundamental problem of imperialism.

One might, as an important aside, further compare Twain with the most famous theorist of imperialism in the first decade of the twentieth century, J. A. Hobson, a figure with whom Twain met and dined during 1902 (Zwick 1992: xxiii). Hobson wrote on imperialism for more than 30 years, but most directly in *The Psychology of Jingoism* (1901), *Imperialism: A Study* (1902, rev. 1905), and his one explicitly literary work, *The Recording Angel: A Report from Earth* (1932).[12] Hobson undoubtedly accomplishes many things, but most certainly fails to reach Twain's far-reaching conclusions regarding the state-form.[13] Kaplan's criticism of Twain, for example, would better have been addressed to Hobson, who concluded, regarding the difference between nationality and nationalism, that "Nationalism, as witnessed to-day in competing armaments, hostile frontiers, exclusive tariffs, restrictions upon emigration, struggles for gold, has converted Nationality from an internal bond of union into an external policy of exclusion based on fear, suspicion, jealousy, and hate" (Hobson 1932: 32).

Hobson therefore upholds as fundamental the division between the interior of the nation (and its handmaiden, the state) and its outward mobilizations. This is an untenable position, as Kaplan argued. But Hobson held to this sort of hardened distinction between the inside and outside of the polis throughout his writings on imperialism. The nation-state is a fundamental and necessary unit of thought for Hobson. It is the necessary incubator for "individualism," for example, which is the only hope for "internationalism" as opposed to imperialism (Hobson 1965: 362–3). The possibility of preventing nationality from turning into a pathological nationalism, and thereby of opening the door to internationalism rather than imperialism, depends upon democratic rather than class-based rule (for example, business rule) of the state (p. 171). "Imperialism and popular government have nothing in common," he asserts (p. 150). Perhaps unsurprisingly, Hobson's insistence on the theoretical separation between the interior and the exterior of the nation-state leads to a certain political slippage. A democratically led quasi-imperialism might be of benefit to non-democratic, "backward peoples" around the globe, assuming that "due regard . . . be paid to the welfare of the inhabitants, who should be the gainers, not losers, by the development of the country" (Hobson 1932: 78). For Hobson, this would fulfill the mandates of internationalist thought and be, then, an imperialism which is non-imperial in content. The relationship to twenty-first-century "humanitarian" neo-imperialism could not be closer.

Twain's logic, when it conceptualizes sovereignty itself as the problem, turns away from Hobson. Yet Twain runs into his own difficulties when he tries to argue, in the text on the Russian Czar, that "In civilized countries they [laws] restrain all persons, and restrain them alike, which is fair and righteous" (Twain 1973: 162). Here, a certain privileging of democratic form as the imperial antidote brings Twain and Hobson into rough alignment. And while the attempt to use law to limit sovereignty – because of the latter's relationship to exceptionalisms which suspend constitutionalisms, which place "other" beings beyond constitutional polity – appears to make good common sense, the knot that ties sovereignty to constitutionalism (agency to system) can never be cut or permanently undone. As another contemporary of Twain's, the legal theorist Francis Lieber, understood, popular-based government can always take up sovereignty power, "whether there be a Caesar or not" (Lieber 1877: 388). Constitutionalism itself demands sovereignty, just as system demands agency.[14] This is not to suggest that Twain's view is problematic because of its general commitment to democratization, and to a democratization in relation to sovereignty (all of this is to the good), but only that it is problematic because of its misunderstanding of the philosophical problem of an intractable sovereignty. In other words, Twain, like Hobson, is in danger of leaving the state in its central place in international relations (unlike, say, Karl Marx, who famously forecast the necessity of its "withering away"), and therefore leaving in place the state's inherent "political behavior" with regard to enemies in war and in war's many analogues.

What Twain does manage to achieve on the terrain of sovereignty, however, brings him into a rather strange relationship with New Americanism. While the new Americanists search for an agency which cannot be reduced or limited by system, Twain seeks to end one particular form of agency which he finds fundamental to imperial structure. How, finally, can this impasse be resolved? As a third New Americanist position, perhaps Donald Pease's attempt to provide some form of complexity to the problem of agency will help. While Pease too seeks to newly elevate a cultural and agential agenda within the conversation about imperialism, he does at least acknowledge a form of criticism that attempts to articulate the limits of such agency, which he calls "global-localism." In this alternative critical practice, each instance of anti-imperialism is read as coopted by a recapitulation of imperialism in various ways, such as leaving "nation-states" in place, or endorsing a dominating "process of globalization" (Pease 1993: 26). Global-localists would insist, therefore, that each anti-imperial act typically reinforces retrogressive elements which actually bolster imperialism or neo-imperialism.

Pease's answer to this dilemma is worth considering: "To begin to keep track of the terms missing from each discourse [both anti-imperialism and global-localism], they would be taken together as equivalently important modes for understanding cultures of US imperialism" (Pease 1993: 26–7). But agency (in the form of anti-imperialism) and structure (in the form of global-localism's insistence on certain discursive limits and recapturings) cannot be "taken together" and cast in Hegelian "dialectical relations" – they are, instead, separate-and-related as an irreducible agon (p. 27). To state the obvious, relative to the themes of the present essay: the problem of the form of state is not effectively challenged in Pease's overly optimistic scheme. It is, instead, sublated into a higher level of governance, such as the globe and the problem of world government. But even the most inclusive form of global governance will necessarily have its "enemies," ripe for imperial and neo-imperial domination, both external and internal to it (for example, those deemed "animal" or "alien," and in general all those deemed "bare life"). Such is the permanent lesson of the problem of state-form, which haunts the period of decolonization.

It is true, however, that both poles of Pease's "opposition" must be thought of in relation to each other, and in relation to the infinite possibilities of democractization and justice. Perhaps one can sharpen the idea of a (coming) "global-local" form of critique, in line with Jacques Derrida's work on justice, and suggest that such critique should assess each instance of anti-imperialism both in relation to structural recapturings and recapitulations, and in relation to the "possibility of justice" in general (see Derrida 1992). As Twain would suggest, anti-imperialism which stops short of, or indeed recapitulates, the logic of the state has not yet risen to the challenge. Only those forms of anti-imperialism which work toward the deconstruction and the unworking of the state, then, will be "important," in Pease's sense, for the purposes of producing a future different from the past.

Agency, moreover, must be understood not only as the possibility of anti-imperialism, but also, as housed in the state-form, as its greatest challenge or dilemma. Returning to Twain one last time: if sovereignty is one of the core problems in the imperial matrix, then his only proposed solution – law without sovereignty; legal code or structure without sovereign agency – must be judged intellectually impossible and politically wrongheaded. Instead, an irreducible sovereignty must be rethought in terms of its possibilities, and brought to bear on the inequitable structure of every polity and on constitutionalism in general, in the name of an always incomplete justice. Being and acting "against" imperialism, then, is never enough, so long as post-colonial state sovereignty – or, finally, global sovereignty – is anti-imperialism's only thinkable alternative. Only an endless movement and praxis of *sovereignty against sovereignty* can begin both to face the problem which Twain so clearly marked out and to recast the matter of New Americanist agency in line with a recognition of structural or systemic constraint.

NOTES

1   See Mommsen (1980) for a useful round-up of theoretical opinion on imperialism.

2   Along with Philip Foner, perhaps the most important of scholars on Twain's relationship to social life in general is Louis J. Budd. I fully accept Budd's assessment that Twain's anti-imperial commitments were not Leninist (Budd 1962: 177–8), but do not accept that this therefore disqualifies Twain as a "man of the left," as the following remarks will demonstrate.

3   None of these writers and their texts are difficult to locate, and at least two books in recent years attempt to survey all of these figures, and more, in general fashion. See Mommsen (1980) and Semmel (1993).

4   It should be noted that Kaplan's later, book-length treatment of imperialism and American literature, *The Anarchy of Empire in the Making of US Culture* (2002), does go a bit further. Hobson shows up, for example, but only in relation to his remarks on "jingoism," spectatorship, and desire (Kaplan 2002: 113–14, 149), and her fleeting remark on Veblen folds into this same argument (p. 112). Kaplan finally shows no interest in the debates over imperialism, and, like her many peers in this regard, is simply in a hurry to advance toward a culturalist reading.

5   The first principle of the group which Twain joins in 1901, The Anti-Imperialist League, was: "self-government is fundamental, good government is incidental" (Zwick 1992: xxxii). So while Kaplan's remarks on Twain make sense, perhaps, for the Twain of 1898, they in no way represent the position to which he was soon thereafter to shift.

6   As an aside: This reading is not without its difficulties. Once one accepts that the thematically overdetermined *Connecticut Yankee* has something to say about imperialism, a view that Twain himself was retrospectively eager to endorse (Michaelsen 1992: 268–9), one must confront the fact that history is nothing but endless repetition in the novel (serfdom = slavery = modern wage labor), and that therefore Twain's ending, which magically narrates him out of Arthurian England, only opens, rather than closes, the question of present-day, equivalent dominations. As I have argued elsewhere at some length (Michaelsen 1992: 261–335), *Yankee* is an account of the limits of colonial or occupational logic, with Hank Morgan positioned both as "foreign" and class-distanced from the possibility of representing anti-imperialism (or, indeed, liberation in any form, or from any

sovereign/subject condition which appears in the novel).

7　Though precisely how Kaplan and Rowe, from and in their own time, manage to escape the problem of historical boundedness remains unanswered.

8　Or, at least, this is the only one of the late anti-imperialist texts she manages to cite in her very brief remarks on them (Kaplan 2002: 92).

9　See e.g. Foner (1958: 254–6, 260–1); Zwick (1992: xix–xx).

10　This preface is missing from, for example, Twain (1973: 41).

11　As an example of such an attempt, see Young (2001: 15–56).

12　Twain, of course, wrote a "Letter from the Recording Angel" in 1887, as a part of his Captain Stormfield text.

13　Hobson, however, taught Lenin much about the linked crises of overproduction and low wages in England in the late nineteenth century; and he surely would be a fellow traveler of the New Americanists, in the way that he reads this crisis as necessitating a culture campaign of "jingoism" ("a most serious factor in Imperialism" [Hobson 1965: 215]), which masks business interests. Read this way, in other words, Hobson can be interpreted as suggesting that the battle over imperialism must be fought on the terrain of national culture, focused on "the party, the press, the church, the school" (Hobson 1965: 221).

14　See also Schmitt (1985: 12). The impossible dream of permanently taming sovereignty links Twain to Arendt, and both of them to a long tradition of what Schmitt identifies as "romantic" thought (see e.g. Schmitt 1986: 124).

References and Further Reading

Agamben, Giorgio (1998). *Homo Sacer: Sovereign Power and Bare Life*, trans. Daniel Heller-Roazen. Stanford: Stanford University Press.

Arendt, Hannah (1968). *Imperialism* (part two of *The Origins of Totalitarianism*). New York: Harcourt, Brace & World.

Ashley, Robert K. (1989). "Living on Border Lines: Man, Poststructuralism, and War." In James Der Derian and Michael J. Shapiro (eds.), *International/Intertextual Relations*. Lexington: Lexington/D. C. Heath.

Bronner, Ethan (2004). "Who is To Blame for the Creation of Palestinian Refugees?" *New York Times*, 20 Feb. Repr. on the internet at http://www.nytimes.com/2004/02/20/opinion/20FRI3.html.

Budd, Louis J. (1962). *Mark Twain: Social Philosopher*. Bloomington: Indiana University Press.

Derrida, Jacques (1992). "Force of Law: The 'Mystical Foundations of Authority'." In Drucilla Cornell, Michael Rosenfeld, and David Gray Carlson (eds.), *Deconstruction and the Possibility of Justice*, 3–67. New York: Routledge.

Foner, Philip S. (1958). *Mark Twain: Social Critic*. New York: International.

Hegel, G. W. F. (1967). *Hegel's Philosophy of Right*, trans. T. M. Knox. London: Oxford University Press.

Hobbes, Thomas (1996). *Leviathan*, ed. Richard Tuck. Cambridge, UK: Cambridge University Press.

Hobson, J. A. (1932). *The Recording Angel: A Report from Earth*. London: Allen & Unwin.

Hobson, J. A. (1965). *Imperialism: A Study*. Ann Arbor: University of Michigan Press. (First publ. 1902.)

Kaplan, Amy (1993). "'Left Along With America': The Absence of Empire in the Study of American Culture." In Amy Kaplan and Donald E. Pease (eds.), *Cultures of United States Imperialism*, 3–21. Durham, NC: Duke University Press.

Kaplan, Amy (2002). *The Anarchy of Empire in the Making of US Culture*. Cambridge, Mass.: Harvard University Press.

Lenin, V. I. (1996). *Imperialism: The Highest Stage of Capitalism*. London: Pluto. (First publ. 1916.)

Lieber, Francis (1877). *On Civil Liberty and Self-Government*. Philadelphia: Lippincott.

Michaelsen, Scott (1992). "Mark Twain's Capitalism: Gilded Age Capitalists and Aspirants, 1862–1909." Ph.D. diss., State University of New York at Buffalo.

Michaelsen, Scott (1999). *The Limits of Multiculturalism: Interrogating the Origins of American Anthropology*. Minneapolis: University of Minnesota Press.

Mommsen, Wolfgang J. (1980). *Theories of Imperialism*, trans. P. S. Falla. Chicago: University of Chicago Press.

Pease, Donald E. (1993). "New Perspectives on US Culture and Imperialism." In Amy Kaplan and Donald E. Pease (eds.), *Cultures of United States Imperialism*, 22–37. Durham, NC: Duke University Press.

Rowe, John Carlos (2000). *Literary Culture and US Imperialism: From the Revolution to World War II*. Oxford: Oxford University Press.

Said, Edward W. (1993). *Culture and Imperialism*. New York: Knopf.

Schmitt, Carl (1985). *Political Theology: Four Chapters on the Concept of Sovereignty*, trans. George Schwab. Cambridge, Mass.: MIT Press.

Schmitt, Carl (1986). *Political Romanticism*, trans. Guy Oakes. Cambridge, Mass.: MIT Press.

Schmitt, Carl (2003). *The* Nomos *of the Earth in the International Law of the* Jus Publicum Europaeum, trans. G. L. Ulmen. New York: Telos.

Semmel, Bernard (1993). *The Liberal Ideal and the Demons of Empire: Theories of Imperialism from Adam Smith to Lenin*. Baltimore: Johns Hopkins University Press.

Twain, Mark (1905). *King Leopold's Soliloquy*. Repr. on the internet at http://www.boondocksnet.com/congo/kls/congo_kls_01.html.

Twain, Mark (1972). *Mark Twain's Fables of Man*, ed. John S. Tuckey. Berkeley: University of California Press.

Twain, Mark (1973). *Mark Twain and the Three Rs: Race, Religion, Revolution and Related Matters*, ed. Maxwell Geismar. Indianapolis: Bobbs-Merrill.

Twain, Mark (1992c). *Mark Twain's Weapons of Satire: Anti-Imperialist Writings on the Philippine–American War*, ed. Jim Zwick. Syracuse, NY: Syracuse University Press.

Young, Robert J. C. (2001). *Postcolonialism: An Historical Introduction*. Oxford: Blackwell.

Zwick, Jim (1992). "Introduction." In *Mark Twain's Weapons of Satire: Anti-Imperialist Writings on the Philippine–American War*, ed. Jim Zwick, xvii–xlii. Syracuse, NY: Syracuse University Press.

PART II
Mark Twain and Others

9
Twain, Language, and the Southern Humorists
Gavin Jones

Mark Twain's plan to include in *A Tramp Abroad* (1880) a burlesque correspondence with the era's most prominent philologists stands as a humorous equivalent to a complex and, at times, deeply serious correspondence between Mark Twain, the most public of authors, and a field of language study that burgeoned in the last decades of the nineteenth century. The burlesque correspondence was to concern Twain's theories of German grammar (which did appear in Appendix D of *A Tramp Abroad*), theories to which the philologists were to reply with abuse or silence (Twain 1975: 266). The real correspondence between Twain and his era's philologists and lexicographers was marked by something verging on scholarly respect. William Dwight Whitney, Professor of Sanskrit and Comparative Philology at Yale, cited Twain's *Roughing It* (1872) in his landmark study, *The Life and Growth of Language* (1875), as textual evidence of the laws of human language creation. Rather than being abused or ignored, Twain's books were mined for new locutions and distinctively American usages (Lerer 2003), even as they practiced forms of self-ironizing humor that always threatened to undermine philological seriousness. This coincidence of the "instructive" and the "amusing" – to use Whitney's terms (Whitney 1979: 114) – is nowhere clearer than in Twain's most concise and explicit contemplation of language politics, his sketch "Concerning the American Language" (1882). On one level an astute challenge to the hegemony of Noah Webster's *Dictionary* in its call for attention to the speech of the "vast uneducated multitude" (Twain 1992a: 831), Twain's sketch inevitably turns the spotlight of irony on his own "education": by the end, Twain has become incomprehensible to his English interlocutor not because of his American pronunciation but because of his exaggeration, absurd contradictions, and general lack of rationality. The sketch is a study in class ambivalence, a celebration of the vernacular that expresses skepticism about democratic values – after all, to say that a language must remain sensitive to the usages of a "vast uneducated multitude" demeans the masses educationally even as it respects them democratically.

The following essay represents an overview of Twain's career-long interest in the subject of language, an interest that engaged with the topics of race and nation but always centered on issues of social class, just as the comedy that accompanied Twain's amateur philology so frequently involved an insecure vacillation between social registers. My main aim is thus to highlight the "vertical" structures of social hierarchy that dominate Twain's language consciousness, in an effort to supplement a recent emphasis on "horizontal" conflicts and interactions between different cultural identities and speech communities.[1] But I want to revisit, as well, the relationship between Mark Twain and the tradition of Southern humor, a relationship highlighted by earlier scholars such as Kenneth Lynn and Walter Blair but more recently de-emphasized, particularly in analyses of Twain and race. Running throughout this genre's humorous interest in vernacular expression, I suggest, Twain would have found ample speculation on the links between language and social class, together with a remarkably self-conscious consideration of linguistic representation.

The Language of Southern Humor

The tradition of Southern (or "Southwestern") humor, which includes the works of writers such as Augustus B. Longstreet and Thomas B. Thorpe from the 1830s and 1840s, together with a second wave of more narrowly political writing that intensified around the Civil War, cannot be viewed separately from a broader field of American humorous–political writing that included many regions and diverse political viewpoints. From Maine's "Jack Downing" to Tennessee's "Sut Lovingood," the humor of this regional writing emerged from the contrast between standard and vernacular voices, the latter providing channels of communication through which those divorced from centers of power could express political resistance to authority, and even offer advice to specific politicians. Whatever its political ideology, this literature highlighted forms of lower-class speech that represented limited literacy and education, whether to imply a "native shrewdness [that] beats book learning" (Blair and Hill 1978: 181) or else to satirize opposing political and regional factions by constructing linguistically their foolish ignorance and provinciality. The tradition of Southern humor was just one part of a complex network of regional writing, but it demands special attention for the tremendous stress it placed on dialect as a consequence of political democracy (Cmiel 1992: 919–20), and on language as a tool of representational and social power. This was especially true in the works of the first generation of nationally popular writers who were particularly aware of the vernacular traditions of "tall talk" that gave Southern humor its uniqueness, and that fascinated Twain throughout his career.

Longstreet's "Georgia Theatrics" (1835) – to offer one of two brief examples – deals explicitly with the emergence of a lower-class way of talking that is violent, densely figurative, and oath-ridden, a dialect that contrasts orthographically with the standard language of the genteel narrator. The two linguistic registers of the sketch embody sharp distinctions in class culture and, moreover, an instability in the class relations of power, as the elitist narrator is both fascinated with, and ill-equipped to appreciate, the vernacular language he encounters (Longstreet 1937b: 288). The narrator has failed entirely to realize that what he hears is not the language of a violent fight between two farmhands, but the purely rhetorical performance of such a conflict by a young man who "was jist seein' how I could 'a' fout" (p. 289). Rather than describing the violence of the frontier, or offering a lesson in the linguistic contours of class, the overheard discourse emphasizes instead the signifying system itself, a system that has sprung free from the world it purports to represent. Longstreet makes a similar point in "The Fight," a tale in which the horrendous physical reality of injury comes to obey, "as if by supernatural power" (Longstreet 1937a: 296), rules that seem possible only in the realm of figurative expression.

The phenomenon of tall talk to which Longstreet introduces us – the vernacular style of hyperbolic, undisciplined, densely figurative expression, which marks an entry into linguistic exuberance that creates the world rather than merely representing it – has traditionally been interpreted as a psychological response to frontier experience (Lynn 1959: 27–8). In his reading of Joseph Baldwin's "Ovid Bolus, Esquire" (1853), Neil Schmitz argues that tall talking had both political and theoretical functions as well: that Baldwin was linking its exaggeration to the socio-economic phenomenon of Jacksonian inflation, while exploring the elastic nature of the relationship between words and things (Schmitz 1992: 195–9). Bolus manipulates language to secure social power and to ensure his economic rise above the condition of a "common man" by selling fake land titles to gullible citizens (Baldwin 1937: 358). He is a type of confidence trickster and is eventually discovered by the community in which he operates. An individual can only go so far in transgressing a society's contracts of meaning and economics. Yet the sketch demonstrates, too, how easily unpolished backwoods communities fall prey to an eloquence that depends fundamentally on at least the appearance of superior education and cultural literacy.

Arguments for the influence of Southern humorists like Longstreet and Baldwin on Twain have received recent, and necessary, re-evaluation (Sloane 1979). But to dismiss this tradition altogether, or to reduce it solely to a vestigial influence on Huck Finn's vernacular or on the development of Twain's comic persona, is to miss its intense linguistic self-consciousness – its complex discourses on the relationships between language and reality, language and mind, language and socio-economics. Schmitz has likewise argued for the complex ways in which the tall talk of Southern humor can "speak about language," though he does so in order to sever the link between Twain and his alleged precursors (1992: 208–9). In fact, Twain would revisit the language politics of Southern humor throughout his career, I argue, in a number of broad thematic concerns that help us sharpen the tool of social class as a means to dissect Twain's work – a tool that inevitably opens our realm of inquiry far beyond the tall talk of backwoodsmen.

In his history of popular speech in America, Kenneth Cmiel has criticized the tendency to describe the nineteenth century as a period when folk speech became the prevailing patois; he argues instead that Americans were always being pulled in contradictory directions, simultaneously toward the lowly and the refined (Cmiel 1990: 90, 56). In the influential analyses of H. L. Mencken and Richard Bridgman, Twain likewise becomes the exponent of a colloquial prose that successfully digests the class antagonisms of the Southern humorists. Close attention to Twain's linguistic interests, however, reveals a writer who, like Longstreet and Baldwin before him, saw language as a fund of humor that was nevertheless a sign of socio-cultural division, a realm of class anxiety, and an agent of social power.

Social Philology in *Roughing It* and *A Connecticut Yankee*

Twain's engagement with the world of Southern humor informs the famous dialogue in *Roughing It* between the Virginia "rough," Scotty Briggs, and the parson from an eastern theological seminary: a dialogue that stages in extreme form a humorous polarization of class languages, as the parson's hyper-genteel "trade" language of theology contrasts with Scotty's low-status discourse of the card table. William Dwight Whitney's interest in this dialogue marks the way that *Roughing It* lifts ideas incipient in the Southern humorist tradition into something like a philological debate over the nature and uses of language itself. The narrator's friend Mr. Ballou's "fashion of loving and using big words *for their own sakes*, and independent of any bearing they might have upon the thought he was purposing to convey" (Twain 1872: 200) is on one level the epitome of tall talk. But it also bears an uncanny resemblance to the assumptions of mid-nineteenth-century linguistic science: what Linda Dowling describes as the new emphasis on language as an autonomous realm determined by phonetic roots and laws that exist independently of human thought and meaning (Dowling 1986: 62). Beginning with the preface, language seems to control Twain according to an internal phonetic patterning rather than a representational function – a point that relates to the structuring of the narrative, as digressions emerge from homophonic puns and word associations rather than from physical events. Just as Twain's desires are kindled by the sounds of words alone, his descriptions at times avalanche out of control as he gets seduced along chains of signifiers with less and less representational relevance.

Roughing It is a remarkable document of philological self-consciousness that enacts, rather than merely refers to, the linguistic debates of Twain's era. At times, Twain seems close to the ideas of Max Müller, the hugely popular Romantic philologist who argued that language is a natural force that embodies thought in its phonetic roots. Language is described repeatedly in *Roughing It* as a liquid that literally gushes out of individuals and remains beyond their control, a force that possesses the speaker and that threatens life itself if suppressed. But the spark of Twain's text emerges by striking this idea against the views associated with Twain's compatriot and Müller's nemesis, William Dwight Whitney – that language is a social institution, a tool of communication whose signs are entirely arbitrary and conventional expressions of thought. Much of *Roughing It* can be read as a test of Whitney's belief that "The speakers of a language . . . constitute a republic, or rather, a democracy, in which authority is conferred only by general suffrage" (quoted in Dowling 1986: 92). Mr. Arkansas's attempt to assert his social power by bending others' words to mean what he wants ends with a tongue-lashing defeat as the community re-establishes the contract of meaning (Twain 1872: 221–6). But of course, any democratic theory of language presupposes the functionality of democracy itself; *Roughing It* is punctuated by incidents in which the individual's participation in the community of language begins to overpower the consensus of the many. Stage-drivers, desperados, and Mormons, according to Twain, are all able to bend language to command belief, establish credibility, and claim social authority in a Western territory that lacks the counterweight of pre-established civic control.

At key moments in *Roughing It*, Twain shows that he is less interested in making moral criticism of linguistic corruption than he is in the ways that language is so inevitably embroiled in the world of social class, material possession, and economic power. This interrelation is evident from the discovery of a "salted" silver mine, in which the native ore has been mixed with melted half-dollars – a discovery made when the minted legend "TED STATES OF" appears in the alleged ore (1872: 319). On the one hand, this discovery demonstrates succinctly a predominant characteristic of Western culture: the attempt to create social and economic power by manipulating its symbolic representation (or at least, in this case, by reducing the symbolic aspect of the coin to its constitutive metal). There is, within this process, all the danger of exaggeration, inflation, tall talk, and anarchy that we glimpse repeatedly in *Roughing It*. But the persistence of language in this particular instance – the persistence of the fragmented "TED STATES OF" – demonstrates equally how written texts can work to maintain social order by exposing the fraudulent attempt to fictionalize value. This discovery of federal coinage suggests how such texts establish the conventions of economic exchange upon which the national infrastructure depends. Just as in Baldwin's "Ovid Bolus, Esquire," the moments of linguistic self-consciousness in *Roughing It* perform a social and economic critique. Twain's concern with "claiming," to offer another example, unites the assertive latitude of the West with the socioeconomic sphere of silver mining – the fact that land potentially rich in silver is captured and controlled by written assertions of ownership.

The coincidence of humor and a kind of social philology in *Roughing It* recurs in *A Connecticut Yankee in King Arthur's Court* (1889): another tall tale, this time of temporal collapse between nineteenth-century America and sixth-century England. The theme of language bears the burden of this collapse: sixth-century verbal culture, for example, shows remarkable affinities with the frontier world of Southern humor, especially its linguistic inflation and profanity (Twain 1889: 54–7). Echoing the concerns of writers like Longstreet and Baldwin, the novel combines contemplations of political democracy and considerations of language on a theoretical level, particularly with regard to the question of word origins and histories. This becomes clear from the moment that Hank Morgan receives his title of "the Boss" from the people of sixth-century England: "This title fell casually from the lips of a blacksmith, one day, in a village, was caught up as a happy thought and tossed from mouth to mouth with a laugh and an affirmative vote; in ten days it had swept the Kingdom, and was become as familiar as the King's name" (pp. 102–3). The irony of this moment of coinage lies in the fact that, in the decades after the American Civil War, the term *boss* also signified the corrupt leaders of urban political machines, figures like New York's Boss Tweed who were widely perceived as antithetical to the democratic principles that, in Twain's description of a vocal and affirmative vote, bring the word into existence. Flipping on its head the idea that Hank is building the civilization of the nineteenth century beneath that of the sixth, the sixth century exists in the nineteenth like a geological stratum (the book, like Victorian philology, is full of geological metaphor): a stratum, though, that contains not the natural fusion of language and reason, or a purer spiritual essence – the ideology of Max Müller's Romantic theory of phonetic roots or "cells" – but a kind of moral insanity. In an era when American philologists, particularly those in the postwar South, were revitalizing regional identity by claiming linguistic and cultural affinity with pre-Norman Britain (Lerer 2002: 203–5), Twain implies that the linguistic roots of a Saxon and implicitly racial past merely suggest the transhistorical continuation of class, caste, slavery, and political thuggery, which makes the late nineteenth century just as irrational, anti-democratic, and brutal as the sixth century that Hank tries to reform but ends up destroying.

The Innocents Abroad and *A Tramp Abroad*: Language and National Difference

Roughing It and *Connecticut Yankee* are perhaps the most philologically self-conscious of Twain's works, though this coincidence of social critique and linguistic examination continues throughout his major writings. If *Roughing It* is centrally concerned with the socio-economics of "inflated" American English, then *The Innocents Abroad* (1869) is no less embroiled in a global tourist economy that necessitates the Americans' efforts to make themselves understood in foreign tongues, and brings into being new forms of "tourist guide English" (Twain 1869: 183) – trade languages that generate humor by their faultiness while drawing attention to the new economic contexts in which they grow.[2] Far from the backwoods of the Southern humorists, questions of humor, language, and social class are again intertwined, as is clearly the case with the Oracle, the tall-talking character who accompanies the narrator on his European pilgrimage, and who "never uses a one-syllable word when he can think of a longer one, and never by any possible chance knows the meaning of any long word he uses, or ever gets it in the right place" (p. 69). Unlike the sincere young poet aboard the ship, the Oracle's tall talking proves entertaining to his audience, in large part because he translates humorously the class anxieties of his fellow passengers. Twain described the American art of the humorous story as dependent upon the performance of a lower-class simplicity and ignorance, illustrated by James Whitcomb Riley's telling of a story "in the character of a dull-witted old farmer" (Twain 1992b: 203–4). The direction of the Oracle's performance is, counterwise, from low to high – his highfalutin discourse is founded on an ungrammatical vernacular – but the dynamic of incongruity is the same, an incongruity of class and cultivation in which ignorance collides with the impersonation of elite cultural and technical knowledge.[3] Unlike Mr. Ballou in *Roughing It*, the Oracle practices not a love of the autonomous sounds of language but rather a subversive satire of elitist discourse that represents, in its very grammar, a kind of mobility (the Oracle thus "slides" between opposing points, and refuses to allow words to sit in their proper positions) as well as a freedom to generate language on an individual authority that refuses to recognize decorum and appropriateness. The Oracle thus offers comic relief from the tourists' own "innocence," represented most pervasively by their nervousness handling European cultural artifacts – a nervousness built on their anxious status as middle-class Americans pulled simultaneously toward "higher" and "lower" forms of cultural knowledge and linguistic registers.

What the Oracle represents in terms of class – a refusal to respect an intellectual hierarchy in language – is applied in *Innocents* to much deeper cultural and national differences, as the tourists constantly run up against, and frequently refuse to recognize, the limitations imposed on them by their own incomplete educations in non-English languages and cultures. At the most basic level, the language prejudice of *Innocents* registers the ebb and flow of the tourists' economic power and vulnerability. The moments when foreign languages seem noisy, for example, involve feelings of economic exploitation and cultural alienation, while the book's episodes of aggressive monolingualism reflect the frustrations of limited fluency (Twain 1869: 381). Much of the book's humor is directed ironically back at the tourists themselves, particularly in situations of "middling" linguistic competence, such as when the command of at least some French makes its final evasion more enraging still.

The Innocents Abroad establishes Twain's interest in language as an index of social class broadly construed – class defined less by its economic roots than by the individual's potential access to the tools of literate knowledge (see Guillory 1993 for this understanding of class). Twain shared in his era's tremendous valuing of literacy as a prerequisite of a community's civilization and cultural health, and of an individual's social power and worth (Cmiel 1990: 121; Whitney 1979: 285). His emphasis on the power of education fuels, at times, an anti-racist belief in egalitarian linguistic capacities – witness the multilingual ability of Twain's European-educated guide, born in South Carolina of slave parents (Twain 1869: 241) – but most often this power works to limit individuals to levels and types of literacy within which they are trained and from which they cannot easily escape. This point remains true for entire nations. The United States is valued as the land of pervasive literacy among "common country people," the land of mechanized printing (pp. 267, 269), whereas the relative economic poverty of other nations relates to the educational level of their populations (p. 57). Twain's comment that "[t]he Moors, like other savages, learn by what they see; not what they hear or read" (p. 86) stands free, to an important extent, from the self-ironizing humor of the book, while the joke that Tahoe "means grasshopper soup" in

"Indian" links the alleged cultural degradation of native peoples to their material poverty (they are forced to subsist on such fare) and to their linguistic poverty, the lack of poetry in their tongues (p. 205). With increasing frequency, the linguistic frustrations and repulsions of the American tourists register their reactions to an alleged want of civilization in the foreign cultures they visit, particularly as they descend into southern Europe and the Muslim countries of the Middle East.

Twain's self-ironizing humor occasionally deflates the seriousness and derails the consistency of ethical viewpoint in *Innocents*, though the predominant direction is one in which the humor and the language politics emerge simultaneously and thus work to reinforce what verges on an equation of linguistic quality, civilized traits, and intellectual sophistication. The same is true in *A Tramp Abroad* (1880), a work that again fuses moments of humor and linguistic self-consciousness – centered on the topic of translation – to debate the relationship between social and national difference. The anecdote involving Jim Baker, the Western miner who claims the capacity to translate the language of animals, is a tall tale of outrageous incident, told with the kind of credulity-testing simple-hearted sincerity that Twain observed elsewhere as a characteristic of Western vernacular culture. The anecdote emerges from a moment that combines Twain's feelings of alienation abroad and his anxiety that his middle-class status is being threatened by those farther down the social scale – lost in a German wood, he encounters a group of vociferous ravens who force his retreat, which they enjoy "as much as any low white people could have done" (Twain 1880: 35). Baker's anecdote is itself concerned with the links between language and social hierarchy: his claim that the blue-jay is the best talker is founded on a belief in class difference between animals, as defined by their access to educational culture. Blue-jays have more and different kinds of feelings than other creatures, argues Baker, while possessing the power to describe these feelings in "out-and-out book-talk" too (p. 36). Baker's ability to translate animal language seems a consequence of his own class status – his fall into backwoods primitivism – though this incident of collapsed linguistic difference (between humans and animals) reinscribes a hierarchical understanding of the links between educational class, intellectual strength, and emotional capacity.

This trend in Twain's thinking continues in *A Tramp Abroad*'s other explicit contemplation of translation, the appendix "The Awful German Language." Despite its occasional light fun and self-ironizing critique of Twain's own ignorance and arrogance, the appendix is remarkable for the seriousness with which it deals with the apparent peculiarities of German: its long sentences and long compound words, its piling up of parentheses within parentheses, its tendency to put the verb toward the end of the sentence, and so on. Twain translates his own non-native confusion with the language into an implication that confusion is inherent in the discourse itself; its "Parenthesis disease," for example, signaling "that sort of luminous intellectual fog which stands for clearness among these people" (Twain 1880: 604). Echoing Twain's criticisms of the social diseases of language, revealed in extreme mobility (Twain repeatedly uses a liquid imagery to describe his confusion) and "ragged poverty" (p. 605), the German language sets a limit on intellectual coherence and sophistication.

In this sense, German behaves like one of Twain's many class dialects: it reveals and contains the intellectual culture of its speaker. If Twain seems close to Romantic philologists like Müller in his stated belief that certain sounds naturally capture emotional meanings "with truth and with exactness" (p. 616), then he shares too in the widely held Victorian, and implicitly post-Romantic belief that words are less arbitrary conventions than they are natural and organic expressions of thought, and, at times, indices of the moral character and intellectual substance of their speakers. Even those late nineteenth-century scholarly philologists who rejected the earlier view that language embodied or even created the moral spirit of human communities found it difficult to maintain a sense of language disconnected from cultivation, intellectual development, and social power (see Lounsbury 1901: 188).

Race and Class: *Pudd'nhead Wilson* and *Life on the Mississippi*

To stress this side of Twain is to conflict with a common view of him as a writer who tends to expose and undermine society's tendency to take arbitrary conventions as natural facts, especially where racial difference is concerned. In *Pudd'nhead Wilson* (1894), for example, the act of child-swapping central to the book's plot undoes the absolutism of "one drop" racial logic, as the legally black Chambers comes to talk and act white, while the white Tom comes to talk and act black. Attention to the links between speech and identity, however, illustrates how the disruption of racialized boundaries only leaves in its place a version of upbringing that can seem every bit as absolute and "natural" as the biological determinism it trumps. Thus, when "Tom" first discovers that he is really black, his white behavior collapses momentarily, but he inevitably drops back into his old "conditions of feeling and manner of speech" (Twain 1894: 126). And when the real heir suddenly finds himself rich and free, he nevertheless remains in a most embarrassing situation: "He could neither read nor write, and his speech was the basest dialect of the negro quarter" (pp. 301–2). Culturally at least, identity remains solid when racialized patterns of speech and behavior are trained into individuals over an extended and formative period of time. There is a point at which words stop being conventions and become natural, with language coming to "speak" people into being – it is not Roxy's appearance but her speech, and the assumptions of social power it encodes, that make her black. The novel may disrupt racialized thinking but it leaves in place the virtual absoluteness of class as a process of acculturation. Though not born into people in the same way as the fingerprints that Dave Wilson uses to such effect at the end of the novel, speech types do function as autographs of self that cannot be counterfeited, disguised, or hidden away – autographs that tie individuals to social groups with differing levels of literacy and cultivation.

This situation may register racially in *Pudd'nhead Wilson*, but it remains most significant and consistent in Twain's consideration of individuals who, having either changed their social status or attempted to convince others that they hail from a higher social class, are haunted – or humorously exposed – by the accents and speech patterns they can never fully shake. *Life on the Mississippi* (1883) is one of Twain's most expansive considerations of how the power dynamics of society are determined by the language politics of education and literacy. Twain's complex attitude toward the language of the working classes, for example, emerges from his reaction to the night-watchman aboard the *Paul Jones*, who deceives Twain with his sentimental, romantic tales of personal adventure: "What was it to me that his grammar was bad, his construction worse, and his profanity so void of art that it was an element of weakness rather than strength in his conversation? . . . It was a sore blight to find out afterwards that he was a low, vulgar, ignorant, sentimental, half-witted humbug, an untravelled native of the wilds of Illinois" (Twain 1883: 76, 78). The natural direction of profanity is toward conversational strength, Twain implies – a point corroborated by the admiration expressed throughout the book for those whose brutal language represents genuine social power and improvisational ability. An energetic exuberance resides in aspects of vernacular expression, with even the most outrageously tall talk possessing a positive social value when it is delivered to the right kind of audience that self-consciously realizes, regulates, and enjoys its tall performance (pp. 373–4). The night-watchman's tall tales, however, represent an effort not to compete with an audience in outrageous banter but to impose on a naïve audience a high-prestige discourse of aristocratic origins and heroic importance. His rhetorical attempt at class "passing" provokes intense narrative outrage that translates into a significant failure to sympathize with the environmental forces that may have limited the watchman's access to the educational and cultural resources that Twain seems to value. The watchman is not *illiterate* (Twain implies elsewhere that a basic level of literacy runs throughout river society) – in fact, his outrageous narrative derives from the "wildcat literature" he reads (p. 78). The real danger emerges when literate skills are possessed without the education necessary to control them.

Twain's socio-linguistic critique echoes that within Richard Grant White's *Words and their Uses* (1870), one of many books of "verbal criticism" that blamed the linguistic problems of the Gilded Age – an alleged collapse of meaning and rise of bombastic expression, for example – on the rise to public prominence of "half educated" individuals lacking "inborn cultivation" (White 1870: 32, 42). Twain's assault on the tyrannical steamboat pilot Mr. Brown targets his poor grammar, the result of an upbringing that seems debased, linguistically and culturally, because of its poverty, or at least its low class status – Twain calls Brown's attention "to the advantage of pure English over the bastard dialect of the Pennsylvania collieries whence he was extracted" (Twain 1883: 231).[4] Of course, Twain's "classist" outburst is motivated by a justifiable protest at Brown's behavior, yet it only reinforces a pattern that runs throughout the book: a suspicion of attempts to change social class, which echoes the verbal critic's anxiety that social deference was collapsing before social mobility. Matching the satire of parvenus that David Sewell describes in *The Gilded Age* (1873) – where characters who pretend to linguistic elegance are exposed by the lowness of their original vernacular (Sewell 1987: 41) – Brown's discourse reveals the degree to which he lacks the requisite equation of good character and good education associated with this new middle-class status of steamboat pilot.

Twain's verbal criticism of uneducated figures such as Mr. Brown is matched by similar criticism of the genteel classes of the Mississippi Valley. If lower-class characters are reprimanded for attempting to leap up a linguistic register, then upper-class characters are equally targeted for their downward slips. Twain thus echoes another dominant theme in American speculation on its spoken idiom: the fear that the prestige speech itself is impregnated by grammatical infelicities commonly associated with individuals lacking formal education. Twain's criticism is on occasion harshly prescriptive, holding the spoken language to the same standards as the written, but his main point is that "blasphemous grammar" (Twain 1883: 288) is acceptable provided it is the unconscious and widely accepted usage of the entire community. Specific languages are natural to specific communities; change within that community is the inevitable product of its social evolution. The trouble begins when a community attempts to impose a class structure by adopting a language from beyond its natural borders – a point Twain takes to its extreme by implying that the retrogressive sociopolitical structure of the South, its unhealthy concern with rank and caste, emerged from its obsession with the inflated, sentimental, and obsolete literary language of Sir Walter Scott (pp. 468–70).

If *Life on the Mississippi* pays close attention to the linguistic environments of the lower and the upper social orders, then the same is true for the book's analysis of its professional, middle-class steamboat pilots whose technical expertise secures them rank and dignity as "the only unfettered and entirely independent human being[s] that lived in the earth" (Twain 1883: 166). The social power of these pilots derives from their knowledge of the Mississippi River, which Twain describes as a "wonderful book" that he learns to read during his pilot education (pp. 118–19). Despite its capacity to secure professional status for its "scholars," though, river literacy is unable to provide a true alternative to the conventional book literacy it opposes. The specialized training in the shifting signifiers of the natural world inevitably deflates the professional status of the pilot because it prevents vision of and adaptation to changes within the commercial economy – that is, the growth of the railroad, which forces the steam-boatman to become part of the "common herd" (pp. 254–5). The use of textual metaphors to describe the river does not finally imply parity between river- and book-literacy, but rather the priority of the latter; just as Twain *needs* the textual metaphor in the first place to explain the virtually obsolete science of river piloting to the general reader.

Conclusion: Sut and Huck

Twain's diverse interest in the politics of language boils down to a central concern with *cultural literacy*, which he implicitly understands not just as the basic quantity of information needed to communicate and thrive in a mainstream world of shared assumptions (the way that E. D. Hirsch has recently defined the term), but as the technique and skill to interpret and apply this information successfully. I have argued that these links between literacy, class, and social power were laid out for Twain in the tradition of Southern humor he admired – as becomes especially clear in the relationship between *Adventures of Huckleberry Finn* (1885) and George Washington Harris's "Sut Lovingood" tales, which Twain reread during the composition of his novel (Rickels 1965: 112). In his 1867 review of *Sut Lovingood's Yarns* (1867), Twain praised Sut's dialect for seeming regionally accurate (Rickels 1965: 109), though the most striking characteristic of Sut's speech is not its Tennessean inflection but its representation of illiteracy and, by implication, of poverty (the first tale in the *Yarns*, one that stuck in Twain's mind, tells of a poverty so extreme that Sut's father has to "play horse" by hitching himself to his plough). Harris's dense, at times impenetrable misspelling was on one level part of the wider craze for ungrammatical, misspelled "dialects" that offered relief from – and seemed funny only in relation to – an intense educational pressure toward "correct" spelling (Blair and Hill 1978: 276). But Sut's illiterate lingo, as transcribed by the literate listener, George, also represents a sectarian narrowness that is at once socio-economic, political, and educational. Sut is less illiterate than *anti*-literate: Harris's preface to the *Yarns* records not just Sut's occasional wish that he "cud read an' write, jis' a littil" but his belief that "ove all the fools the world hest tu contend wif, the edicated wuns am the worst" (p. 25). Sut's attacks are directed not at the over-educated or the pompous but, much more desperately, at the agents of education and civilization itself.

Harris's influence on Twain has been downgraded by recent critics – not surprisingly, for Sut represents social and political values that diverge enormously from the relatively progressive version of Twain implied by his interest in racial questions and in black vernacular expression (Fishkin 1993: 39–40). To recognize something of the figurative energy and violence of Sut's language in Huck's vernacular athleticism is to approach tainting Huck with a character who, according to Edmund Wilson, is "a peasant squatting in his own filth," a sadistic figure whose cruel vengeance is a confession of his own irredeemable inferiority (Wilson 1994: 510). But to oust Sut from *Huckleberry Finn* altogether may tend to obscure the novel's complex dealings with questions of class as well as race. Twain may or may not have been thinking specifically of Sut in his reference to "the extremest form of the backwoods South-Western dialect" in his explanatory note to *Huckleberry Finn* (Twain 1885: 7); certainly there is no speech-type in the novel as orthographically extreme as Sut's, though at least one critic has tried to pin this dialect on a single community of speakers (Carkeet 1979: 322–3). The shadow of Sut's language is thrown across the entire novel, not in a regionally specific sense but in a broader thematic concern with the links between social class and literacy, between educational level and ethical outlook.

The character in *Huckleberry Finn* who comes closest to Sut's virtually nihilistic railing against the assumptions of educational hierarchy and "civilization" is Huck's father, an archetypal poor white who is intensely jealous that Huck has escaped the generational illiteracy on both sides of his family. Pap's mindset is clearly revealed in his famous "call this a govment" speech, in which literacy – represented by a free black professor's multilingual ability and accumulation of knowledge – implies not just material wealth but a capacity for citizenship that transgresses even racial boundaries. The power of literacy is implicitly admired (Pap dwells in detail on the professor's material possessions and social poise) while simultaneously being rejected in a manner reminiscent of Sut at his worst. Pap cusses the free man of color with a rage that expresses his intense hatred and jealousy, reveals his own comic powerlessness and inferiority, and most importantly establishes his further retreat from the realms of educated thought and from the responsibilities of his own citizenship. Pap's vow to "never vote again as long as I live" (Twain 1885: 50) predicts Hirsch's argument that illiterate and semiliterate Americans are condemned not just to poverty but to an ignorance and distrust of the system which results in their effective disenfranchisement (Hirsch 1988: 12). Pap's poverty is so irredeemable, Twain implies, because it rests on an internal linguistic and educational deficiency, a lack of cultural literacy that condemns him to backwoods isolation and his "white trash" status.

Pap's "call this a govment" speech is mirrored in the "can't learn a nigger to argue" scene between Huck and Jim at the end of chapter 14: both feature the question of multilingualism, which highlights complex interactions between cultural literacy, class, and race. If the earlier scene emphasizes educational class differences that can, in limited circumstances, cut across a racial divide, then the later scene illustrates some degree of class parity between races – that is, if we continue to define class in terms of access to the cultural capital of literate knowledge. In one sense, the scene demonstrates Huck's educational rise to a level beyond what would have been possible for a slave. Yet Huck's rhetorical inability to convince Jim that nations speak different languages – he chooses the inappropriate example of differences between the "talk" of different animal species – implies some overlap in the cultural literacy of poor white and black, as does their mutual adherence to a folk-transmitted culture of natural signs. Whether or not we agree with Fishkin's compelling argument that Huck's language is mixed racially, there is little doubt that it remains mixed in terms of social class, as it lies somewhere between an educated standard and a less formally educated vernacular – a point emphasized most strongly by Twain's insertion of misspellings and eye dialect, designed to evoke semi-literacy rather than regional inflection. Carkeet argues that the novel's variety of white Southern speech that shares most with the speech of blacks is that of "lower-class rural whites" (1979: 331–2). In this sense, at least, the complex racial interaction between Huck and Jim should not be seen outside the bounds of the class background that makes it possible.

David Sewell writes that "Mark Twain's central linguistic insight in *Huckleberry Finn* is that the heterogeneity of language goes beyond surface features like pronunciation and morphology" to include a moral variety (1987: 108–9). On one level this seems right. Huck's speech and the speech of his father look similar on the page, thus underlining a common class horizon, yet their moral values are very different. Huck's language is orthographically different from Jim's, yet they share many ethical values. The king and the duke speak in different registers of formal correctness, yet their confidence trickery is identical. But to argue that varieties of language are moral rather than formal is in essence to argue that the moralities of characters exist independently of the discourses that speak them. People are good or bad independently of their levels of education or cultural literacy: this seems to be the central insight of *Huckleberry Finn*. If the linguistic and the moral realms are disconnected in Twain's novel, however, the same cannot be said for the links between cultural literacy and social power. The murderous Colonel Sherburn may be no better, morally speaking, than the loafers who confront him, yet his educated discourse marks his domination of the mob. The schemes of the king and the duke are always eventually discovered, but only after they successfully abuse the communities they target. Following in the footsteps of Baldwin's Ovid Bolus, the king and the duke succeed in their confidence trickery by faking, often through the medium of print, a level of cultural literacy that depends on isolated rural communities lacking the kind of world knowledge necessary to blow their cover. The controversial "Phelps Farm" ending of the novel can be interpreted as a final, sustained contemplation of this link between cultural literacy and social persuasion, as Tom Sawyer's education in the literary "authorities" of adventure fiction gains total control over the less literate Huck and the illiterate Jim. The emphasis in this final section on acts of writing, focused most cruelly on Tom's insistence that the imprisoned Jim write mysterious messages in blood, and keep a journal of his captivity, underscores how Tom's power is less racial than educational and class-based, thus ensuring his control over a black slave *and* a white boy whose subservience is linked earlier in the novel to his impoverished upbringing (Twain 1885: 166).

By distinguishing between discourse as morality and discourse as power, Twain seems finally to be saying that the realm of cultural literacy – what Hirsch describes as the mastery of a language's cultural content, which enables social success – is not ideologically neutral: a critique that can easily be made of Hirsch's argument too. Mainstream cultural literacy in the South undoubtedly contained racist ideologies that perpetuated slavery in the period when *Huckleberry Finn* is set, and justified the increasing disenfranchisement of free blacks during the time it was written. This is how the moral irony of the novel works. By helping a slave to escape, thus doing what he feels is right, Huck is forced to contravene the dominant moral codes in which he is educated as a child (Twain 1885: 128). His celebrated crisis of conscience culminates in Huck's tearing up his letter to Miss Watson – a written document, perfectly spelled, and with only a few grammatical errors, that represents the school-transmitted, racist cultural literacy of the mainstream South (pp. 271–2). We are hardly back in the world of Sut Lovingood, where education itself becomes the object of backwoods envy and hatred. But there is something in Huck's distrust of civilization that echoes Sut's distrust of propriety and authority, just as Huck's misspelling of "sivilize" echoes the illiteracy of the extremest form of the backwoods Southwestern dialect. The focus of the final sections on a child's understanding of adventure fiction is a deadly serious business: it represents Twain's growing understanding that the training of childhood inculcates levels of cultural literacy that determine an individual's social power, and styles of thinking that shape the moral contours of the adult world.

NOTES

1 I am thinking of the most extensive consideration of Twain's interest in language (Sewell 1987) and the most influential (Fishkin 1993). Although Sewell emphasizes, at times, the hierarchical nature of Twain's thought – adherence, for example, to the doctrines of prescriptive grammarians (p. 16) – his main emphases are on Twain's Bakhtinian identification of linguistic diversity as a sign of human heterogeneity, and his later, pessimistic belief in the inevitability of cacophonous miscommunication. Fishkin analyzes the linguistic structures of *Adventures of Huckleberry Finn* to stress the interaction between black and white racial cultures.

2 The strong interrelation, in Twain's early work, between *Roughing It* and *The Innocents Abroad* suggests another crucial trend in Twain's linguistic speculation: the simultaneity of his interest in intra-national issues – the different and often conflicting varieties of American English – and international linguistic issues: the conflict between American English and other national tongues.

3 In this regard, the Oracle provides a moment of self-analysis, a distillation of Twain's self-ironizing, comic persona at large, described by Kenneth Lynn as the fusion of "the Gentleman and the Clown of the Southwestern tradition into a single character" (Lynn 1959: 148) – a technique shared by stage personas such as Artemus Ward.

4 Verbal critics were by no means alone in their class consciousness. Whitney's relativistic belief that all languages are dialects still presupposed that there was a "cultivated language," defined by the social class of those who speak it – a language largely free of the "ungrammatical forms, mispronunciations, blunders of application, slang words, [and] vulgarities" of the uncultivated (Whitney 1979: 155).

REFERENCES AND FURTHER READING

Baldwin, Joseph G. (1937). "Ovid Bolus, Esquire" (first publ. 1835). In Walter Blair (ed.), *Native American Humor (1800–1900)*, 356–67. New York: American Book Co.

Blair, Walter, and Hill, Hamlin (1978). *America's Humor: From Poor Richard to Doonesbury*. New York: Oxford University Press.

Carkeet, David (1979). "The Dialects in *Huckleberry Finn*." *American Literature* 51: 3, 315–32.

Cmiel, Kenneth (1990). *Democratic Eloquence: The Fight over Popular Speech in Nineteenth-Century America*. New York: Morrow.

Cmiel, Kenneth (1992). "'A Broad Fluid Language of Democracy': Discovering the American Idiom." *Journal of American History* 79: 3, 913–36.

Dowling, Linda (1986). *Language and Decadence in the Victorian Fin de Siècle*. Princeton: Princeton University Press.

Fishkin, Shelley Fisher (1993). *Was Huck Black? Mark Twain and African-American Voices*. Oxford: Oxford University Press.

Guillory, John (1993). *Cultural Capital: The Problem of Literary Canon Formation*. Chicago: University of Chicago Press.

Harris, George Washington (1966). *Sut Lovingood's Yarns*. New Haven: College & University Press. (First publ. 1867.)

Hirsch, E. D., Jr. (1988). *Cultural Literacy: What Every American Needs to Know*. New York: Vintage.

Jones, Gavin (1999). *Strange Talk: The Politics of Dialect Literature in Gilded Age America*. Berkeley: University of California Press.

Lerer, Seth (2002). *Error and the Academic Self: The Scholarly Imagination, from Medieval to Modern*. New York: Columbia University Press.

Lerer, Seth (2003). "Hello, Dude: Philology, Performance, and Technology in Mark Twain's *Connecticut Yankee*." *American Literary History* 15: 3, 471–503.

Longstreet, Augustus Baldwin (1937a). "The Fight." In Walter Blair (ed.), *Native American Humor (1800–1900)*, 289–98. New York: American Book Co. (First publ. 1835.)

Longstreet, Augustus Baldwin (1937b). "Georgia Theatrics." In Walter Blair (ed.), *Native American Humor (1800–1900)*, 287–89. New York: American Book Co. (First publ. 1835.)

Lounsbury, Thomas (1901). *History of the English Language*. New York: Holt.

Lynn, Kenneth S. (1959). *Mark Twain and Southwestern Humor*. Boston: Little, Brown.

Mitchell, Lee Clark (1989). "Verbally *Roughing It*: The West of Words." *Nineteenth-Century Literature* 44, 67–92.

Rickels, Milton (1965). *George Washington Harris*. New York: Twayne.

Schmitz, Neil (1992). "Tall Tale, Tall Talk: Pursuing the Lie in Jacksonian Literature." In Louis J. Budd and Edwin H. Cady (eds.), *On Humor: The Best from "American Literature,"* 190–210. Durham, NC: Duke University Press.

Sewell, David R. (1987). *Mark Twain's Languages: Discourse, Dialogue, and Linguistic Variety*. Berkeley: University of California Press.

Sloane, David E. E. (1979). *Mark Twain as a Literary Comedian*. Baton Rouge: Louisiana State University Press.

Twain, Mark (1975). *Mark Twain's Notebooks and Journals*, vol. 2: *1877–83*, ed. Frederic Anderson, Lin Salamo, and Bernard L. Stein. Berkeley: University of California Press.

White, Richard Grant (1870). *Words and their Uses*. New York: Sheldon.

Whitney, William Dwight (1979). *The Life and Growth of Language: An Outline of Linguistic Science*. New York: Dover. (First publ. 1875.)

Wilson, Edmund (1994). *Patriotic Gore: Studies in the Literature of the American Civil War*. New York: Norton. (First publ. 1962.)

10

The "American Dickens": Mark Twain and Charles Dickens

Christopher Gair

Promptly at 8 P.M., unannounced, and without waiting for any stamping or clapping of hands to call him out, a tall, "spry," (if I may say it,) thin-legged old gentleman, gotten up regardless of expense, especially as to shirt-front and diamonds, with a bright red flower in his button-hole, gay beard and moustache, bald head, and with side hair brushed fiercely and tempestuously forward, as if its owner were sweeping down before a gale of wind, the very Dickens came! He did not emerge upon the stage – that is rather too deliberate a word – he strode. He strode – in the most English way and exhibiting the most English style and appearance – straight across the broad stage, heedless of everything, unconscious of everybody, turning neither to the right nor the left – but striding eagerly straight ahead, as if he had seen a girl he knew turn the next corner. . . . But that queer old head took on a sort of beauty, bye and bye, and a fascinating interest, as I thought of the wonderful mechanism within it, the complex but exquisitely adjusted machinery that could create men and women, and put the breath of life into them and alter all their ways and actions, elevate them, degrade them, murder them, marry them, conduct them through good and evil, through joy and sorrow, on their long march from the cradle to the grave, and never lose its godship over them, never make a mistake! I almost imagined that I could see the wheels and pulleys work. This was Dickens – Dickens. (Twain 1868)

An evening in late December 1867 was to prove particularly significant in Mark Twain's private life and professional career. Not long returned to New York from his *Quaker City* excursion to Europe and the Holy Land, during which he had been writing the articles later collected as *Innocents Abroad*, Twain reported in the San Francisco *Alta California* that he was accompanied by "a highly respectable young white woman" (Olivia Langdon, on their first date) to hear Charles Dickens perform at the city's Steinway Hall. Dickens was on his second visit to the United States, having conducted an earlier reading tour in 1842, and was attracting full houses wherever he played, one result being that Twain and his partner were seated "rather further away from the speaker than was pleasant or profitable." Even so, Twain was close enough to note that

Dickens was "a little Englishy in his speech" and to applaud aspects of his portrayal of Pegotty as "excellent acting – full of spirit" and of Mrs. Micawber as "good" (Twain 1868).

Despite finding such moments to admire, Twain was not altogether enthusiastic about the performance, writing that Dickens was a "bad reader . . . because he does not enunciate his words sharply and distinctly . . . and therefore many and many of them fell dead before they reached our part of the house." But this does not mean that Twain underestimated either the impact made by Dickens on American culture or the significance of the reading to his own subsequent career. Thus, in a piece titled "The Approaching Epidemic" published in the *Galaxy* (September 1870), Twain warned that Dickens's recent demise would result in the United States being "lectured to death and read to death all next winter, by Tom, Dick, and Harry, with poor lamented Dickens for a pretext." Twain's own personal and professional response was slightly more subtle, but no less significant, in that his observation of the popularity of Dickens's performances (and the phenomenal income that they generated) led him greatly to refine his own lecturing career, and to model subsequent public readings on what he had witnessed at the Steinway Hall. Justin Kaplan reiterates Twain's own belief that Dickens's second visit to America effected a change in "public platform entertainment," with the author's dramatic "reading" of his work replacing the humorous lecture (see Everdell 1992: 182). There is no doubt that Twain himself benefited from this change. He believed that his own public performances in New York gave him access to the East Coast publishing world, as well as an income that outstripped what he could earn from most of his novels. Most famously, of course, he was able to pay off his debts after the bankruptcy of 1894 by conducting what he described as a "lecturing raid around the world" (Everdell 1992: 183).[1]

Of even more significance, at least in terms of Twain's continuing canonical status in the twenty-first century, the *Alta California* report indicates the impact that Dickens's fiction had made on him well before he saw the stage show. The satirical description of the Englishman's physical appearance – itself doubly Dickensian in its attention to the comic possibilities inherent in physical quirkiness, since Dickens is described as if he is one of his own creations – does not conceal the reverence with which Twain esteems Dickens's fiction. Although the old man on stage is faintly ridiculous in appearance, in Twain's report this serves only to emphasize the American's sense of awe that "this puissant god seemed to be only a man, after all." The disappointment he feels is with the performance, never – most certainly – with the work itself, and he leaves the hall as impressed by the fiction as when he entered. Further, it is easy to speculate that this recognition spurred on Twain in his own writing – his well-known anxieties about his own merits as a "serious" writer are likely to have been soothed somewhat by the thought that the "exquisitely adjusted machinery" of Dickens's creative mind (itself, a quintessential example of Twain's search for the ideal combination of body and machine) was stored within a rather ordinary head.

If Twain felt anxieties when judging himself alongside the master of the Victorian tragicomic novel, there is no doubt that the American public was willing to see links between the two writers. From early in his career, Twain was regularly labeled the "American Dickens" (Bradbury 1995: 169) by reviewers who admired the ability of his vernacular irony to undercut social and religious pretension. In some ways, the analogy seems obvious, not least because scenes and characters from Dickens's novels are echoed in Twain's. Thus, the grave-robbing episode from *A Tale of Two Cities* reappears in *Tom Sawyer*, and the Eden sub-plot of *Martin Chuzzlewit* anticipates the Stone's Landing/Napoleon scam in *The Gilded Age*. Likewise, Louis J. Budd has pointed out that *The Gilded Age*'s Colonel Beriah Sellers is closely related to Mr. Micawber, and that Sellers's famous feast of turnips and water is "Micawberish" (Budd 2001: xix). But, in what follows, I would like to suggest that to become the "American Dickens" was a far from straightforward operation, and that Dickens's own attempts to write about the United States were, at best, only moderately successful. To be the "American Dickens" entailed redirecting both the formal and the thematic approaches to representations of English culture in (for the purposes of this essay) Dickens's early novels, written in the 1830s and early 1840s, and making them relevant to the very different conditions of the United States of the late nineteenth century.[2]

Dickens in America

To begin to understand these transformations, I will offer a brief reading of Dickens's representation of the old and new worlds in *American Notes* (1842) and, at greater length, *Martin Chuzzlewit* (1844), in order to suggest the obstacles that prevented the Englishman becoming an "American Dickens" himself. When Twain heard Dickens perform in 1867, the Englishman was full of praise for what he witnessed in America. In a postscript appended to subsequent (post-1868) editions of both *American Notes* and *Martin Chuzzlewit* – the two works in which he represents American life most directly and extensively – he declares himself

> astounded . . . by the amazing changes I have seen around me on every side, – changes moral, changes physical, changes in the amount of land subdued and peopled, changes in the rise of vast new cities, changes in the growth of older cities almost out of recognition, changes in the graces and amenities of life, changes in the Press, without whose advancement no advancement can take place anywhere. (Dickens 1996: 253)

These remarks are in sharp contrast to the observations reported in *American Notes*, published soon after Dickens's return to England from his first visit, and they were made long after he had written and published his major works. Following his 1842 trip, Dickens's writings express a combination of disappointment at the degree to which the realities of American daily life failed to live up to the ideals that he had long imagined, and a frustration at the lack of privacy afforded to the celebrity novelist. Even in 1842, however, Dickens's *first* impressions of America were also largely favorable: although Boston has the appearance of a "pantomime," with the suburbs "even more unsubstantial-looking than the city" (Dickens 1996: 26), he is impressed by the "humanising tastes and desires" (p. 27) engendered by the university, and by the "nearly perfect" (p. 28) public institutions and charities that he inspects in Massachusetts. Although he is characteristically playful in his account of Transcendentalism – "whatever was unintelligible", "much that is dreamy and fanciful" – Dickens also applauds the "true and manly, honest and bold" substance of Emerson's essays and concludes that, "if I were a Bostonian, I think I would be a Transcendentalist" (p. 57).

The remainder of *American Notes for General Circulation* is a narrative of almost constant decline. The full title puns on Dickens's increasing disgust at the extent to which (often corrupt) commerce overshadows all other aspects of everyday life; he is appalled by the snobbery and parochialism of most of the people he encounters, almost all of whom profess to celebrate democracy but adopt either a military, religious, or academic title, and whose ignorance of Old World customs and cultures is almost as great as their disdain for them. And the further south and west he travels, the baser American life seems to become. He is shocked by the pigs in New York, and by the degrading conditions he witnesses in the city's Five Points slums, where the "coarse and bloated faces at the doors, have counterparts at home, and all the wide world over" (1996: 89). Unlike in England, where Dickens is able to intersperse his social comments on the effects of poverty with moments of sentimental reassurance or with comic characters like *Martin Chuzzlewit*'s Mrs. Sairey Gamp or Bailey Junior, there is no relief. Dickens finds nothing comic about the spitting that maintains an "incessant shower of expectoration" (p. 97) in every public and domestic space that he visits, and he suggests that a "considerable amount of illness is referable" to the fact that "the American customs, with reference to the means of personal cleanliness and wholesome ablution are extremely negligent and filthy" (p. 157). By the time that he takes a steamboat westward, Dickens is in despair at the discrepancy between his earlier lofty visions of American life and the reality of what he witnesses. On board *The Messenger*, there is "no conversation, no laughter, no cheerfulness, no sociability, except in spitting; and that is done in silent fellowship round the stove, when the meal is over" (p. 158).

Unquestionably, however, Dickens's greatest disgust with the United States stems from his reactions to slavery, and to the hypocrisy that it bred. Unlike Twain, whose general opposition to race slavery did not prevent him deploying its victims to comic effect – for example, through the terror expressed by Uncle Dan'l when he believes that an approaching steamboat is "de Almighty" in *The Gilded Age* (Twain and Warner 1873: 37), or through the tortures undergone by the superstitious, "chuckle-headed" slave who guards Jim in the final section of *Huckleberry Finn* (Twain 1885: 297) – Dickens can find no humor in slavery. On the one hand, he is outraged by the degradation experienced by the slaves themselves, chronicled through a lengthy list of advertisements in the public papers seeking information on runaways, all wearing irons or dog collars, and many marked with the effects of lashing or branded with hot iron on their face. Many of the runaways are identifiable through physical deformities caused during their captivity, or in previous attempts to escape (Dickens 1996: 232–5). On the other, he is scathing of the double standards that he observes in Washington, where he notes that it is the "Inalienable Right of some among them [the politicians], to take the field after *their* happiness equipped with cat and cartwhip, stocks, and iron collar, and to shout their view halloa! (always in praise of Liberty) to the music of clanking chains and bloody stripes" (p. 120). Dickens had traveled to America expecting "an assemblage of men [in the House of Representatives], bound together in the sacred names of Liberty and Freedom . . . as to exalt at once the Eternal Principles to which their names are given . . . in the admiring eyes of the whole world." By the time he leaves Washington, however, he sees in the politicians, "the wheels that move the meanest perversion of virtuous Political Machinery that the worst tools ever wrought" (pp. 119, 120).

Old and New Worlds in *The Life and Adventures of Martin Chuzzlewit*

Dickens's general sense of despair about what he found in America clearly has ramifications for his relationship with Twain. Given that the latter's best-known fictions are largely (though by no means exclusively) set in or allegorize the United States, and that much of their popularity at and since the time of publication depends upon their humorous representation of the same serious cultural and political problems that Dickens identified, it should already be clear that transplanting Dickensian structures of representation across the Atlantic involves major ideological shifts. Before proceeding to fuller analysis of what these shifts entail, however, it is also necessary to examine the effects of Dickens's responses to America in his own fiction. What I want to suggest, through a brief comparison of the English and American sections of *The Life and Adventures of Martin Chuzzlewit*, is that Dickens's understanding of the United States was incompatible with the prose styles that he had deployed with such critical and commercial success in his novels of British life published before his first Atlantic crossing.

In *Imagining America*, Peter Conrad has argued that the "equality which is the [United States'] social and economic glory is, for Dickens, its imaginative affliction: in making men equal it makes them all alike" (Conrad 1980: 55). In the American sections of *Martin Chuzzlewit*, the result is that Martin and his companion, Mark Tapley, encounter a series of national types, "without exception," as Conrad continues, "listless, hollow-cheeked, tedious, and portentously verbose" (p. 57). Each character is introduced as "one of the most remarkable men in our country" and each is interchangeable with the last. Dickens, of course, was not the only writer to think this way at the time, nor was his opinion expressed solely by non-Americans: most famously, Nathaniel Hawthorne justifies his decision to set *The Scarlet Letter* in the past through the extended meditation on the tarnished homogeneity of contemporary American life that he represents in "The Custom House." Unlike Hawthorne, of course, Dickens does set his novel in the present, and his hostility toward American customs caused great offence when the novel was published in the United States. Conrad suggests that the difference between the English and American sections of the book is "deliberate, for it is intended to denote an imaginative difference between England and America" (p. 53). But I will demonstrate that, although such a contrast does emerge, it is the result of Dickens's inability to reshape his prose to the demands of a different culture rather than an intentional stylistic deviation.

During *American Notes*, Dickens makes what could be mistaken for an insignificant aside about the design of Philadelphia:

> It is a handsome city, but distractingly regular. After walking about it for an hour or two, I felt I would have given the world for a crooked street. The collar of my coat appeared to stiffen, and the brim of my hat to expand, beneath its quakery influence. My hair shrank into a sleek short crop, my hands folded themselves upon my breast of their own calm accord, and thoughts of taking lodgings in Mark Lane over and against the Market Place, and of making a large fortune by speculations in corn, came over me voluntarily. (1996: 98)

In one sense, the passage does manage to capture the best-known aspects of Philadelphia. With echoes of Benjamin Franklin's famous first walk around the city, more than a century earlier, Dickens conveys the general air of calm prosperity generated by the Quakers' version of the American speculative economy. But while his fantasy about making a fortune in corn-trading echoes the suggestion of what could be a disturbingly amorphous selfhood already hinted at in his earlier musings on Transcendentalism, Dickens's desire for a "crooked street" is based upon considerably more than simple nostalgia for home and the confirmation of personal identity that this would bring. His public, professional status as a particular kind of writer is threatened by what he sees, and his longing for the "crooked street" is grounded in the search for something distinctively eccentric to represent in his own fashion. In the description of Philadelphia, all that Dickens can imagine is something already familiar – a series of clichés about the people's appearance and behavior, with none of the imaginative idiosyncrasy that marks his writing about England.

The point becomes clear when the above passage is contrasted with a characteristic description of London from *Martin Chuzzlewit*:

> You couldn't walk about in Todgers's neighbourhood, as you could in any other neighbourhood. You groped your way for an hour through lanes and bye-ways, and court-yards, and passages; and you never once emerged upon anything that might be reasonably called a street. A kind of resigned distraction came over the stranger as he trod these devious mazes, and giving himself up for lost, went in and out and round about and quietly turned back again when he came to a dead wall or was stopped by an iron railing, and felt that the means of escape might possibly present themselves in their own good time, but that to anticipate them was hopeless. . . . Cautious emigrants from Scotland or the North of England had been known to reach it safely, by impressing a

charity-boy, town-bred, and bringing him along with them; or by clinging tenaciously to the postman; but these were rare exceptions, and only went to prove the rule that Todgers's was in a labyrinth, whereof the mystery was known but to a chosen few. (Dickens 1968: 185)

The "mazes" of Todgers's neighbourhood generate authorial power and control for Dickens in a number of ways. First, there is the conventional realist manner in which the knowing narrator is able to act as guide to readers presumed ignorant of the geographical intricacies of the district, piloting them through the area and (subsequently) hinting at the moral labyrinth allegorized through urban space. In contrast, the visitor to straight-streeted Philadelphia requires no guide, and the author's supremacy is lost. The way that Dickens's language appears to mimic the landscape reinforces his power: the convoluted sentences, packed with semi-colons and subordinate clauses, compel careful attention from readers, while reminding them that the narrator is familiar with his surroundings and has the time to mock strangers. As such, Dickens is able to bridge the gap between two very different worlds. On the one hand, he can identify with the charity-boys and postmen with whom he shares intimate knowledge of Todgers's neighbourhood; on the other, he possesses the linguistic skills that mark him as a member of a class that would normally visit such a landscape only at second hand, when reading fiction, religious tracts, or journalism.

Dickens's fiction is peppered with such descriptions of the poorer, or seedier, areas of London (and, compared to many, Todgers's neighborhood is relatively prosperous), but these are, of course, just one aspect of his representation of Englishness. *Martin Chuzzlewit* is typical of his work in its exploration of urban and rural society, new and old money, wealth and poverty, the ongoing impact of the past on the present, the illustration of the iniquities and hypocrisies of nineteenth-century culture, and (for Dickens) the ability of the honest middle-class family unit to triumph over adversity, and to assist the "deserving" poor. Although Dickens is never afraid to shock his readers with descriptions of the most impoverished regions of the country, or with representations of the most villainous activities of rich and poor alike, his novels invariably have (in terms of early Victorian culture) morally satisfying endings. Thus *Martin Chuzzlewit* concludes with the death of the murderous Jonas Chuzzlewit, the exposure and ruin of the sanctimonious hypocrite Seth Pecksniff, and the transformation of the younger Martin from selfish adolescent into a man worthy of inheriting his grandfather's fortune and marrying his sweetheart. Dickens's fiction is characterized not only by its dependence on the seemingly infinite possibilities of region, class, and individual behavior, but also by its ability to show the interconnections and mobility that exist between them.

The shadow cast over Todgers's neighbourhood by the Monument provides symbolic verification of the extent to which Dickens's fiction depends for its success upon many aspects of English history, culture, and character. Martin's trip to America is the catalyst for his transformation from selfish snob into considerate "gentleman"; yet the absence of these familiar landmarks in America results in a failure of narrative representation during the American sections of the novel. Thus, while the Anglo-Bengalee Disinterested Life and Loan Assurance Company scam concocted by Tigg Montague, Esquire (formerly the down-at-heel "needy sharper," Montague Tigg [Dickens 1968: 50]), is ideally suited to Dickens's style, since it enables him to illustrate both the workings of the English class structure and also the (generally invisible) instability of that structure, no such opportunities arise from its American counterpart, the Eden scam that entraps Martin. Instead of the dual identity possessed by Montague, who is able to charm his victims out of a few coppers or a fortune according to his circumstances, but is also portrayed sympathetically in his concern when Bailey Junior is thrown from the carriage and expected to die, the American fraudster, Scadder, who sells Martin his disease-infested plot in Eden, has no redeeming qualities. Although he also embodies a kind of doubleness, with one side of his face paralyzed and in the "coldest state of watchfulness" (p. 418), Scadder is represented as physically repugnant and morally bankrupt. The only American character not to represent such depravity is a Massachusetts physician, Mr. Bevan, whose chief defining feature is his disgust with the behavior of his countrymen, and who lends Martin the money to return to England.

Although the purpose of this essay is to suggest the ways in which Twain was indebted to Dickens, and also to indicate the degree to which he had to modify the Englishman's narrative strategies in order to accommodate an American culture very different from Dickens's world, it is worth qualifying my comments on Dickens and America in one respect. So far, the model that I have constructed offers little sense of transatlantic exchange in Dickens's work: I have argued that the American section of *Martin Chuzzlewit* is an artistic failure, marred by the author's inability to develop a representational style apposite to American life. Even Martin's redemption and reformation as a result of his serious illness in Eden are made possible only by the overwhelmingly negative quality of all aspects of the United States in the novel. Oddly, however, there appears to be one instance where Dickens does appropriate that culture, and integrates it into the English portions of the book. In the character of Bailey Junior, initially "boots" at Todgers's, and later "tiger" to Tigg Montague,[3] Dickens imports an oblique version of blackface that anticipates Twain's work.

Bailey Junior is an adept mimic (both verbally and physically), with an eye for bright clothes, and his efforts at smoking cigars and being shaved, despite having a chin "as smooth as a new-laid egg or a scraped Dutch cheese" (Dickens 1968: 530), serve to undercut the pretensions of the surrounding adults, who are invariably pompous and vain. There is no doubt that Bailey Junior is white, and the racism inherent in blackface is sublimated into class parody, enabling Dickens to appropriate a racist aspect of American culture without appearing to express any racism himself. But the representation of Bailey Junior is unlike that of any of Dickens's characters prior to his American tour. It imitates precisely the kind of blackface that was so popular in the United States in the 1840s, and suggests that, whatever the strength of his opposition to slavery, Dickens was not averse to adopting comic stereotypes based upon imagined racial difference to suit the needs of his own fiction.

In some ways, this parody of upper-class manners anticipates scenes in Twain's work, most notably Tom Driscoll's return from Yale wearing fashionable Eastern clothes in *Pudd'nhead Wilson*. Yet there are also significant differences: apart from very brief moments such as the description of an (apparently free) coach driver in *American Notes* (Dickens 1996: 131), Dickens is unable to see any humor in the treatment of the African American in the United States, making use of the blackface tradition only when it is transplanted to England and stripped of its obvious racial connotations. In contrast, the comedy elicited from Driscoll's behavior has a more obvious and disturbing racial dimension, since it is an apparent parody of the contemporary image of the black dandy. Although the "young fellows" of Dawson's Landing who dress the "deformed negro bell-ringer . . . in a flamboyant curtain-calico exaggeration of [Tom's] finery" (Twain 1894: 69) are unaware of the full extent of their joke (since they share Tom's belief that he is white), the reader already knows Tom's origins and is likely to read Twain's representation accordingly. Ultimately, however, the depictions of Bailey Junior and Tom Driscoll point to ambivalence on the part of both Dickens and Twain about racism in the United States. Although both are professedly opposed to slavery and tend also to be anti-racist, residual traces of a contrary position emerge in Dickens's adaptation of blackface and Twain's construction of an unknowingly "black" character that *does* manifest many racial stereotypes.

The "American Dickens": *The Gilded Age* and *Huckleberry Finn*

In *The Gilded Age*, Twain and Charles Dudley Warner managed to evade the question of race in America by virtually writing African Americans out of the novel.[4] Following the sale of Uncle Dan'l and his family during an early instance of one of the Hawkins family's regular financial crises, slaves and the race question play only a peripheral role in the book. Instead, the novel focuses on a combination of the romance plot, a narrative of thwarted inheritance, and legal and political corruption. The synopsis sounds like the basis for a Dickens novel and there are obvious similarities. In its concluding chapters, in particular, *The Gilded Age* is closer to Dickens's tales than are Twain's best-known later works since, as Louis J. Budd has noted, the novel manifests the "underlying consensus of middle-class certainties about how society and its morals should work" (Budd 2001: xiii). Philip Sterling is doubly rewarded for his dedication to the work ethic rather than reliance on speculation, since he will earn a fortune from his rich seam of coal (uncovered through his own toil) and achieve happiness in his marriage to Ruth Bolton, in a reassuringly Dickensian resolution of domesticity and the estranged hero. A similar model is promised for Washington Hawkins, who abandons the "curse" of the Tennessee Land and vows to return home to marry and "begin my life over again, and begin it and end it with good solid work!" (Twain and Warner 1873: 556–7). Although Colonel Sellers is portrayed much more sympathetically than Dickens's American speculators, and the corrupt Washington politicians are not exactly punished within the novel – even Senator Dilworthy's "ruin" is trivial compared with Pecksniff's in *Martin Chuzzlewit*, and he is welcomed back to his home state – the narrative voice is as severe as Dickens's in *American Notes* in its condemnation of the political betrayal of national ideals. Laura Hawkins is less of a Dickensian character than the others, more closely resembling Thackeray's Becky Sharp than any other English model, but, unlike Becky, she is not allowed to profit from her machinations, and her public disgrace and humiliation are swiftly followed by a death laden with moral overtones. Ultimately, for both Dickens and Twain, the fear that speculation has replaced endeavor, and personality superseded character, is counterbalanced by an insistence on the continuing currency of traditional moral values and actions.

Perhaps in acknowledgement of the limitations implicit in setting a "Dickensian" novel like *The Gilded Age* in America (and a marker too of Twain's artistic development in the 12 years that followed the latter's appearance), there are major formal and thematic differences between Dickens's American writings and Twain's representations of landscape and character in *Adventures of Huckleberry Finn*. In *American Notes*, Dickens is scathing in his accounts of the Ohio and Mississippi rivers and their surrounds. Where the rare signs of human life appear, the Ohio is banked by poor fields of wheat, "full of great unsightly stumps, like earthy butchers'-blocks"; and, apparently yearning for more marks of human history to describe, Dickens imagines that the river "shared one's feelings of compassion for the extinct tribes who lived so pleasantly here, in their blessed ignorance of white existence" (1996: 159, 160). The Mississippi is even worse, an "enormous ditch . . . running liquid mud." Everything about the river signifies corruption, decay, and death, from the huge logs "rolling past like monstrous bodies, their tangled roots showing like matted hair," to the "dwarfish" trees, the "marshes swarming with frogs, the wretched cabins . . . their inmates hollow-cheeked and pale," and the "mosquitoes penetrating into every crack and crevice of the boat." Dickens finds "nothing pleasant" about "this foul stream" (pp. 171–2), and is delighted when his two-day journey comes to an end.

The same tone characterizes the descriptions of the river and of Eden (based on Cairo) in *Martin Chuzzlewit*, where the disparity between the "flourishing city" (Dickens 1968: 419) described to Martin by Scadder and the "hideous swamp" where he almost dies of fever allegorizes the difference between rhetoric and reality in Dickens's America. Although virtually every aspect of American life that he has encountered has disappointed Martin, this is undoubtedly the nadir of his experience. For Martin, the frontier promises the possibility of self-making but brings only sickness, disillusionment, and the desire for a swift and penitent return to England. Although, as a consequence of his own illness and, even more, of his belated recognition of the worth of Mark Tapley, Martin is transformed by his Edenic ordeal, the change occurs only as a result of an ironic undercutting of his American dream.

Of course, this is also the landscape of *Huckleberry Finn*, a novel set at around the time of Dickens's visit, but one that balances episodic instances of extreme cruelty with nostalgic visions of mid-nineteenth-century life along the Mississippi. Thus, although passages such as the description of Pap Finn echo Dickens's portrayal of frontier life, there are also moments where accounts of the river's power and beauty offer a restorative counterpart to the violence that Huck and Jim encounter during their journey. The power of Twain's descriptions of the river and its surrounds has been described many times and there is no need for a detailed reiteration of the point here. Of more direct significance is the very different relationship that exists between community and landscape in *Martin Chuzzlewit* and *Huckleberry Finn*. For Dickens, as I have suggested above, there is a direct analogy between the "foul stream" and the people who live alongside it, with Eden representing the failure of the relationship between the American people and their promised land. Twain rejects such a view, turning instead to a Transcendental model in which that landscape offers therapeutic compensation for the corruption of American life. Thus, it is notable that the most idyllic description of the "monstrous big river" where Huck and Jim spend their days swimming, fishing, and reflecting on a life that is "quiet and smooth and lovely" (Twain 1885: 157) comes immediately after the Grangerford–Shepherdson massacre. Huck elides the events that take place there, saying "I don't want to talk much about the next day" (p. 152), and "I ain't agoing to tell *all* that happened" (p. 154), and focuses instead on a world where the only human intrusion is faraway "jumbled up voices" and trading scows (p. 158). Where Dickens is unable or unwilling to separate the people from the land, Twain insists upon the need for such a separation if Huck is to be able to sustain any kind of distance from the dominant culture's corruption. Ultimately, however, such moments are not enough, since even the relatively private space of the raft is invaded by the king and duke and, by the end of the novel, Huck is as desperate to abandon the region as is Martin Chuzzlewit.

For Dickens (and for Martin), the trouble with the United States is its lack of culture, and the consequent sense that there is nothing significant to describe. In contrast, Huck feels stifled by a dominant culture and language that place severe limits on individual freedom, but is able to counter these forces through flight and through his vernacular representation. In my discussion of the relationship between landscape and language in *Martin Chuzzlewit*, I have pointed out how Dickens's descriptions of the maze around Todgers's are shaped within lengthy, complex sentences containing numerous subordinate clauses and phrases. In contrast, the language used to describe the United States is more straightforward, contributing to the more general "flatness" of the American sections. Unsurprisingly, given that Huck is an adolescent with limited education, his sentences also tend to be fairly simple, but this does not mean either that they are particularly short or that they are "flat." As Janet Holmgren McKay has pointed out, Huck's language is marked by a "lack of overt indications of subordination between clauses and phrases," so that he "characteristically uses the conjunction *and* to link any number of subordinate and coordinate ideas" (McKay 1985: 69). McKay cites several examples to illustrate her argument, but I will focus on one extraordinary sentence from Twain's novel in order to summarize her key points and then suggest the more specific cultural and historical necessity for this move away from Dickensian style.

When the king and the duke impersonate the brothers of Peter Wilks, Huck – who has "never seen anything so disgusting" – records:

> Well, by-and-by the king he gets up and comes forward a little, and works himself up and slobbers out a speech, all full of tears and flapdoodle about its being a sore trial for him and his poor brother to lose the diseased, and to miss seeing diseased alive, after the long journey of four thousand mile, but it's a trial that's sweetened and sanctified to us by this dear sympathy and these holy tears, and so he thanks them out of his heart and out of his brother's heart, because out of their mouths they can't, words being too weak and cold, and all that kind of rot and slush, till it was just sickening; and then he blubbers out a pious goody-goody Amen, and turns himself loose and goes crying fit to burst. (Twain 1885: 212–13)

In some ways, Huck's vernacular idiosyncrasies gain their power through Twain's refusal to replicate the language of the middle-class elite, whose expressions of speech and grammatical competence often serve as markers of their users' complicity in structures of violent oppression. For example, much of Colonel Grangerford's ability to impress Huck (and command respect in the community) stems from the linguistic authority implied by the prominent display of Henry Clay's speeches in his parlor (Twain 1885: 137). Whereas Bailey Junior's power (as a vehicle for Dickens's social critique) comes from his ability to mimic dominant discourse, Huck's reliance on distinctively American idioms acts as a marker not only of his democratic spirit, but also of Twain's need to find American expressions to represent American life.

The king's performance resembles the kind of play-acting that pervades *Martin Chuzzlewit*, where a string of questionable (as opposed to completely bogus) claimants attempt to charm old Martin into leaving them his fortune. In particular, the combination of sham piety, sentimentality, tears and "flapdoodle" echoes Seth Pecksniff's hypocritical obsequiousness toward old Martin Chuzzlewit throughout the novel, such as when he professes to act as a "shield" against young Martin's attempts at reconciliation with his grandfather (Dickens 1968: 741). Indeed, the narrator's observation that "the more [Pecksniff] was found out the more hypocrisy he practised" (p. 753) is equally applicable to the king, in his increasingly desperate attempts to bluster his way around detection. But Huck's language hints at the differences between the two books and also their respective cultures. The fact that the king is here trying (with some success, when Pecksniff is taken as a model) "to talk like an Englishman" (p. 209) suggests that Twain is rejecting a particular kind of old-world discourse of obfuscation, and advocating American plain-talking in its place. Although Huck regularly deploys his own tall tales, they tend to be used to deflect suspicion away from Jim's and his own flight rather than to defraud unsuspecting victims. They are sharply different from the king's cynical narratives, or from the potentially deadly fantasies that Tom Sawyer conjures from his readings of British and European literature, and it is only when Huck remembers Tom's ideas that he puts himself in danger. Thus, in general, Huck's spur-of-the-moment improvisations tend (as McKay suggests of his language more generally) to be "colloquial and seemingly unaffected and unrehearsed"

(McKay 1985: 70), whereas the king and Tom repeat overused and melodramatic clichés that appear to be out of place and destructive in Huck's America.

Ultimately, this points to a key difference between *Huckleberry Finn* and Dickens's narratives of inheritance. Dickens's youthful protagonists – such as Martin Chuzzlewit and Oliver Twist – inherit money and an accompanying social status. They are happy to do so because, as Martin's case makes clear, even when they are near destitution they believe themselves to be "gentlemen" by virtue of their bloodline, and accept the values of *their* class when properly applied. In contrast, Huck (who has no such hereditary ties) abandons first his money and later Aunt Sally's promise to "sivilize" him (Twain 1885: 366) because he discovers that, unlike in Dickens's English society, where wealth and manners equal power and freedom, in America they bring danger (the threat from Pap) and constriction.[5]

Huck's decision to "light out for the Territory ahead of the rest" (Twain 1885: 366) is an obvious rejection of what Huck (and Twain) sees as the stifling mores of an American respectability that is profoundly un-American in its adoption of Old World values. Throughout *Huckleberry Finn*, Twain stresses the links between middle-class models of education, religion, and economic activity, and the patterns of violence and exploitation that characterize his South. Although there is a difference between the kind of life promised by Aunt Sally and an implicitly *genuine* moral culture shared by Twain and his readers, this culture is absent from the novel itself (as it is not, for example, from *Martin Chuzzlewit* or *The Gilded Age*), and its certainties are destabilized by Huck's vernacular challenge to what Alan Trachtenberg has usefully labeled the "discourse of respectability" (Trachtenberg 1982: 189). Although Dickens presents many protagonists whose vernacular voice imparts important moral lessons to grammatically "correct" characters – for example, Mark Tapley in *Martin Chuzzlewit* – these voices are always framed within the authoritative standard English of the narrator, and are more than counterbalanced by the deployment of vernacular for comic effect, as with the much longer speeches of Mrs. Gamp. Thus, both Huck's refusal to live with Aunt Sally and Twain's rejection of the discourse of respectability renounce the comfortable resolutions of Dickens's novels, and invite both character and reader to look elsewhere for moral instruction.

Conclusion: The "American Dickens" and Beyond

Critics such as David Miller and Robert Weisbuch have argued that Dickens's sentimental resolutions participate in the very social values that generate the disturbing conditions represented in his novels, and undermine the books' value as social critiques. Weisbuch suggests that Herman Melville's "Bartleby, the Scrivener" (1853) responds to this failing by attacking "a kind of cowardly refusal on Dickens's part to dig for disturbing, obscure truth" (1986: 41).[6] But, if *The Gilded Age* is guilty of a similar kind of complicity in its nostalgia for value-systems that were becoming increasingly anachronistic in the age to which the novel lent its name, Twain's later novels' disturbingly *un*resolved structures suggest one way in which he is able to move beyond Dickens and Melville, uniting the former's popularity with the latter's desire to expose unpleasant truths in his critique of institutional and authorial practice.

In contrast to *The Gilded Age*, the conclusions to *A Connecticut Yankee in King Arthur's Court* and *Pudd'nhead Wilson* are as uncomfortable as *Huckleberry Finn* in their challenges to both middle-class customs and generic norms. Much of *Connecticut Yankee* appears to condone (albeit somewhat hyperbolically) the patterns of application and reward that appear in Dickens and in *The Gilded Age*, with Hank Morgan's industriousness recompensed by power and a fulfilling marriage. Unlike his counterparts in these novels, it takes Morgan some time to realize that he loves Sandy, but once he does so, he is swift to resort to the sentimental celebration of a Victorian womanhood earlier represented in Mary Graham, Ruth Pinch, and Ruth Bolton. But Morgan, of course, has little time to enjoy these pleasures, and by the end of the book his world has been destroyed. In a novel that encourages a multiplicity of dystopian allegorical readings – for example, of the South, the West, the Gilded Age, American colonialism and imperialism – the representation of worthy women as trophies for successful men is no longer enough. While Dickens could incorporate the effects of the first wave of the industrial revolution within a structure that implies continuity within an organic national whole, Twain's response to the twin threats of electricity and the Gatling gun is, unsurprisingly, more pessimistic. In the face of these resources, Morgan's attempt to recreate a reassuringly familiar world through a combination of old and new in medieval England serves only to demonstrate the incompatibility of traditional values and contemporary technologies, and the irrevocable fragmentation of the modern United States.

Pudd'nhead Wilson is equally pessimistic in its conclusions, and Twain's frustrated extraction of the *Extraordinary Twins* narrative serves, at least in part, as further demonstration of his inability to bring together the romance plot and effective social comment. Where Melville could condemn Dickens's refusal to dig for uncomfortable truths, Twain is unrelenting in his exposé of the cynicism, hypocrisy, and self-contradiction at the heart of American ideology. The book's conclusion is a savage parody of the norms of the Victorian novel, with every character's life – bar that of Wilson himself – destroyed by his or her inability to escape the consequences of the "fiction[s] of law and custom" (Twain 1894: 33) that determine not only racial but all forms of identity in the modern world. Whereas *Huckleberry Finn* implies – albeit problematically – a space outside the South of the novel's staging from which judgments can be made with integrity, and *Connecticut Yankee* suggests the irreconcilability of old and new social orders, the friendship between Judge Driscoll and Wilson seems to signify a new alliance between traditional white Southern codes and new legal and scientific Northern ones that reimposes old constraints on the African American and excludes the immigrant from integration into the Southern or national "family."

The ideological discontinuities within and across what are generally considered to be Twain's three most important novels contrast with a more settled pattern in at least those of Dickens's books published across a similar time-span in the 1830s and early 1840s. To a great extent, this is the result of Twain's efforts to represent a nation made even more complex than Dickens's England of the 1840s by accelerated industrial-ization and urbanization, by the re-emergence of race as an topic of intense national debate after Reconstruction, by immigration, and by American imperialist ideology at the end of the nineteenth century. Each of these issues undermined the kind of middle-class securities imagined in the conclusions to Dickens's novels and meant that, after *The Gilded Age*, such resolutions were impossible for Twain. By looking backward, Dickens was still able to imagine an organically united England; Twain's own glimpses into the past – in *Huckleberry Finn, Connecticut Yankee*, and *Pudd'nhead Wilson* – merely illustrate the contradictions at the heart of hegemonic American ide-ology and the apparent impossibility of representing the nation as the kind of whole depicted in Dickens's England. While Twain could continue to make use of the form of public performance he had learned from Dickens in 1867, his fictions of the 1880s and 1890s move increasingly further away from the forms that had seen him labeled the "American Dickens."

NOTES

1   See Everdell (1992) for a more detailed treat-ment of Twain's career as public speaker.

2   Dickens was astonishingly productive during this period, publishing *Sketches by Boz* (1836), *Pickwick Papers* (1836–7), *Oliver Twist* (1838), *Nicholas Nickleby* (1838–9), *The Old Curiosity Shop* (1840–1), and *Barnaby Rudge* (1841), all before his thirtieth birthday. His work was as popular in the United States as in Britain, although it was a source of constant frustration to Dickens that most of the American market consisted of pirated copies for which he received no royalties. Several critics have sug-gested that this was one of the factors behind his hostile response in *American Notes* (see Bradbury 1995: 95–104).

3   These are the terms that Dickens uses to describe Bailey Junior's roles in the list of char-acters at the start of the novel.

4   For the purposes of this essay, I am uncon-cerned with the debate over which sections of the novel were written by Twain, and which by Warner. Louis J. Budd provides a useful and concise summary in his introduction to the Penguin Classics edition.

5   In "Huck and Oliver," W. H. Auden makes a similar point about the relationship among money, freedom, and power in Europe, and how this shapes the conclusion to *Oliver Twist*. His views on money in America – that it "rep-resents a proof of your manhood" and that "once you have made it you can perfectly well give it all away" (Hutchinson 1993: 316) – are less convincing, and seem irrelevant to Huck, who did not make his money in the first place and appears to be little concerned with proving this kind of "manhood."

6   Also see Miller (1989: 58–106).

REFERENCES AND FURTHER READING

Bradbury, Malcolm (1995). *Dangerous Pilgrimages: Trans-Atlantic Mythologies and the Novel*. London: Secker & Warburg.

Budd, Louis J. (2001). "Introduction." In Mark Twain and Charles Dudley Warner, *The Gilded Age: A Tale of Today*. New York: Penguin.

Conrad, Peter (1980). *Imagining America*. London: Routledge & Kegan Paul.

Dickens, Charles (1968). *The Life and Adventures of Martin Chuzzlewit*, ed. P. N. Furbank. Harmondsworth: Penguin. (First publ. 1844.)

Dickens, Charles (1996). *American Notes*. Oxford: Oxford University Press. (First publ. 1842.)

Everdell, William R. (1992). "Monologues of the Mad: Paris Cabaret and Modernist Narrative from Twain to Eliot." *Studies in American Fiction* 20: 2, 177–96.

Hutchinson, Stuart, ed. (1993). *Mark Twain: Critical Assessments*, vol. 2. Mountfield, E. Sussex: Helm Information.

McKay, Janet Holmgren (1985). "'An Art So High': Style in *Adventures of Huckleberry Finn*." In Louis J. Budd (ed.), *New Essays on Huckleberry Finn*, 61–81. Cambridge, UK: Cambridge University Press.

Miller, D. A. (1989). *The Novel and the Police*. Berkeley: University of California Press.

Trachtenberg, Alan (1982). *The Incorporation of America: Culture and Society in the Gilded Age*. New York: Hill & Wang.

Twain, Mark (1868). "The Great Dickens." San Francisco *Alta California*, Feb. 5. Repr. on the internet at http://twainquotes.com/18680205.html.

Twain, Mark (1870). "The Approaching Epidemic." *Galaxy*, Sept. Repr. on the internet at http://twainquotes.com/Galaxy/187009e.html.

Weisbuch, Robert (1986). *Atlantic Double-Cross: American Literature and British Influence in the Age of Emerson*. Chicago: University of Chicago Press.

11

Nevada Influences on Mark Twain

Lawrence I. Berkove

The Matter of the West constitutes, after the Matter of Hannibal and the Matter of
the River, the third major formative period of Mark Twain's career. It began in 1861,
when he and his brother Orion left Missouri for Nevada Territory. Over the next three
years, in that rapidly developing but as yet sparsely settled region, he would encounter
writers and humorists who would both shape and put the finishing touches on his literary art. It is, admittedly, difficult to absolutely separate Nevada from California
influences in this period, mainly because writers, like the rest of the mining population of both states, were highly transient and moved back and forth between Nevada
and California, sometimes writing for periodicals located in one state while residing
in the other. Nevertheless, Nevada can be given primary weight because it is where
Twain first encountered the West and acquired his Western character. California was
also important to him, but in terms of a continuation of techniques and values already
assimilated. Retrospectively estimating the weight of the lessons, personal contacts,
and experiences Twain had in Nevada, it is hard to conceive how he could have evolved
as we have come to know him had this stage in his development been omitted.

The writers of Nevada and the eastern slope of the Sierras were informally known
as "the Sagebrush School," after the hardy bushes that grew in the dry country of the
high desert region east of the Sierras. Almost all of these writers were journalists who
were attached to the newspapers of the mining communities that sprang up overnight
around the mines of the Nevada Territory after 1859. It was in that year that the
Comstock Lode, the most important by far of the Nevada mineral deposits, was discovered – an astonishingly rich concentration of silver and gold ores in a belt approximately 4 miles long and 200–1,000 feet wide. Virginia City and Gold Hill were the
two main towns of the Comstock, situated near the opposite ends of the Lode. In just
a few years, despite the Comstock's location in a remote area, difficult of access and
distant from water, a major industrial enterprise – the most technologically advanced
mining complex in the world – was established there. Roads and a railroad were built,
pipelines were laid to bring water from miles away, and forests on the eastern slopes

of the Sierras were cut down and transported to supply timber and fuel for the mining and refining operations and the towns. At each mine deep shafts were sunk, from which horizontal tunnels stretched out to reach the ore; some eventually connecting to tunnels from other mines, making it possible to travel entirely underground between Virginia City and Gold Hill. Ultimately, one historian has estimated (probably conservatively), the mineral riches extracted from the Comstock between 1859 and 1885 totaled over 300 million nineteenth-century dollars – approximately four billion early twenty-first-century dollars (Smith 1943: 292–3).

Once word of the Comstock's riches got out, just as California's gold-mining operations slowed down and many smallholdings there were consolidated under the control of a few large corporations, immigrants began to flood into Nevada. From only a few hundred in 1859, the settled population of the Comstock shot up to between 20,000 and 25,000 by the mid-1870s, with a floating population of thousands more. Other mines were discovered in Nevada and eastern California away from the Comstock Lode, at Esmeralda, Lundy, Bodie, Austin, Lincoln County, and other locations, and thousands of miners were attracted to those sites as well. Most of those mining sites – certainly all the substantial ones – had at least one newspaper apiece, and sometimes several. Since Nevada was a thinly populated state, the writers cohered into a close-knit fraternity within the larger society, sharing experiences, subject matter, techniques, and attitudes. Because most of the mining communities were short-lived and their populations transient, an ongoing tradition of literature was not established in Nevada, but that which did emerge lasted long enough to have a definite and in some cases determinative impact on contemporary authors – of whom Mark Twain is the most important – and it has been possible to recover much Sagebrush literature out of newspaper files and archives and, from that, to reconstruct connections and influences.

Unlike most of the other migrations in previous American history, the main population flow to Nevada consisted not of farmers and cattlemen who intended to claim land and settle down, but largely of industrial workers and skilled technicians who were attracted by the money to be made. A common miner's wages on the Comstock began at 4 dollars a day, so far above the prevailing salaries elsewhere that immigrants were drawn to Nevada from all over the world as well as the rest of the United States. So great were the profits to be made that not only prospectors and workers came to Nevada but also financiers, engineers, geologists, lawyers, doctors – and journalists. In short, the lure of wealth attracted men who were ambitious and unusually talented. As a consequence, any tendency to regard Nevada journalism as being low-level, practiced by rough and semi-skilled writers, would be wrong. On the contrary, Nevada had more than its fair share of the best journalistic and literary talent in America.

The story of why Mark Twain came to Nevada at all and began his writing career there has applications to other Sagebrush authors as well. To put it plainly, Twain was probably fleeing the Civil War. When the war began, it was widely believed in both North and South that hostilities would be over in three months' time, and in chapter 1 of *Roughing It* Twain makes reference to this expectation. At the time he left

Missouri, young men inspired by patriotism were beginning to volunteer for either the Union or Confederate forces; and, although the draft had not yet started, remaining a civilian was not exactly an honorable course of action for an unemployed – the onset of hostilities closed the Mississippi River to steamboat traffic and thus ended Twain's occupation as a pilot – unmarried, and able-bodied young man. The pressure to enlist was much lower, however, in the West, especially in Nevada. The reason for this was that by 1861 the Comstock had already begun to pour much-needed money into the Union treasury. Nevada needed men to operate its mines, and the Lincoln administration in effect treated mining as an essential occupation. The Union also needed another state to strengthen its majority in Congress, so it did not push recruitment efforts in Nevada Territory but rather allowed the population to build up so that Nevada could be quickly admitted to the Union, as it was in 1864.

When his brother Orion was appointed Secretary of Nevada Territory, therefore, an ideal opportunity presented itself for Twain to leave the established part of the United States in a socially acceptable way and distance himself from the war. Working for his brother assured him of an occupation and an income. But after a few months the temptation to become rich by discovering a silver or gold mine persuaded him to cease being the secretary to the Secretary and to strike out on his own as a prospector.

The early chapters of *Roughing It* tell of Twain's activities while intoxicated by silver fever: the excited rush from place to place in the naïve belief that gold or silver was practically lying on the surface of the ground ready to be claimed and gathered. He soon learned that prospecting and mining were hard work – very hard work. When his hopes of becoming wealthy from prospecting did not materialize, he subsequently tried work in a stamping mill, only to find out that that also was hard work. Although he did not succeed as a prospector, miner, or mill employee, Twain did meet with some success in placing humorous articles that he wrote in Nevada's Virginia City *Territorial Enterprise*; and in 1862, when the *Enterprise* offered him a job, he gave up mining and walked 130 miles from his cabin in Aurora, Nevada Territory, to Virginia City, and began full-time employment as a journalist.

If Twain's experiences were not exactly duplicated by other Sagebrush journalists, they nevertheless conformed to a discernible pattern. Almost all of them came to the West from the eastern part of the country between the late 1850s and late 1860s. Most tried their luck at mining, but none succeeded. Most remained in the West because they could earn high wages at whatever other jobs they did, and drifted into journalism because they found they had a talent and a taste for it, and because it was not as physically draining as mining. Whether their practical exemption from military service was an added inducement is something that cannot be presently ascertained. But, although all of them were strong Union supporters, none of them who were in Nevada during the war years gave up their careers in journalism to return to the States and serve in the army.

Roughing It is an indispensable source of information about the Sagebrush School, but the information is so thoroughly subordinated to the narrative that unless one comes to the book with prompts from other sources, it is easy to miss its importance as a record of Sagebrush personalities, and what Twain learned from them. When Twain joined the *Enterprise* in September 1862, it had been under the ownership of Joseph T. Goodman and Denis McCarthy for little more than a year. These two men had bought the paper when it was a weekly with money they had saved from jobs as typesetters, and converted it to a daily. Under their direction, but especially that of Goodman, who – three years younger than Twain, but much more mature and self-confident – soon bought out McCarthy, the paper quickly became unique: the best paper on the Comstock and on the West Coast, and certainly one of the most remarkable in the country. Twain was fortunate in taking employment on it. It is impossible to imagine any newspaper in the country more (and almost providentially) constituted to bring him out and shape him than the *Enterprise*. It had quickly become the most reliable source of information about the Comstock mines and acquired a readership far beyond Nevada. Because investment in the mines was of international interest, the *Enterprise* was read in the major financial centers of New York, Boston, London, Paris, and Berlin, and it exchanged subscriptions with many eminent newspapers back in the States. Goodman and McCarthy hired the best staff members they could find, paying top wages and giving their reporters great latitude, only provided that they earned their wages by good work and stood behind what they wrote. Within a year or two, the paper had the most talented staff on the West Coast, many of whom went on, in time, to distinguished careers (Berkove 1991).

Joe Goodman (1838–1917) was undoubtedly the most important of these men in terms of his impact on Twain. An early biographer, Eva Adams, considered him "the man who made Mark Twain" (Adams 1936). The claim is not as extravagant as it might appear. Goodman started off as Twain's employer, but soon became his friend and confidant. In a 1910 newspaper memoir, Goodman recounted how the two men frequently stayed at the office after everyone else had left and discussed serious ideas.[1] This is important testimony to the fact that there was an intellectual, reflective, even philosophical Twain unsuspectedly deeper than the public man that almost all of his other friends knew. The two men remained close friends for the rest of Twain's life. Almost from the beginning, Twain looked to Goodman as a model of integrity and self-confidence and frequently sought, and took, advice from him. Repeated visits by Goodman to Twain after the latter moved East reinforced his lifelong influence on Twain's style and character.

It was Goodman, more than anyone else, who established the principled character of the newspaper, which remained for Twain one of the most lasting of his formative impressions. The *Enterprise* was strongly pro-Union and anti-slavery in a place where there were many Confederate sympathizers and at a time when Nevada's alignment was not a foregone conclusion. Inasmuch as Twain himself came from a community that was pro-Southern and a family that had owned slaves, the *Enterprise* experience was likely influential in his conversion to Union and anti-slavery convictions. Additionally, although pro-Lincoln, the paper under Goodman's editorship opposed corrupt and inept political appointments. Chapter 34 of *Roughing It* delightfully narrates how one such appointee, the "Gen. Buncombe" of "The Great Land-Slide Case," is persuaded to leave office through an elaborate hoax which everyone knew about but he.[2] The account slightly fictionalizes a real event, but beneath the humor is a revelation of how pro-Union Nevadans refused to allow the territory to be the dumping ground of inept political appointees. In that same spirit, early in his editorship of the *Enterprise*, Goodman exposed the corruption of the territorial Supreme Court bench and forced the resignation of its members (Berkove 2001a: 18). Goodman was no saint, and sometimes used his influence to further his own agendas; but he strongly supported honest government and was fearlessly outspoken and relentless on the attack, even against his own party, when it came to standing up for basic principles. Although it cannot be definitively proven that Goodman incarnated ideals that Twain wished to emulate, it is nevertheless a likely hypothesis.

Because of the excellence and reliability of its reporting, the high quality of its writing staff, and its large and extensive readership, the *Enterprise* was able to be one of those rare newspapers that were truly independent. It was free of the patronage either of the government, through the assignment of official notices, or of the powerful mining interests. Under Goodman's editorship the *Enterprise* strove for a high ideal of accuracy. In chapter 42 of *Roughing It*, Twain recollected the standard Goodman advocated:

> Never say "We learn" so-and-so, or "It is reported," or "It is rumored," or "We understand" so-and-so, but go to headquarters and get the absolute facts, and then speak out and say "It is so-and-so." Otherwise, people will not put confidence in your news. Unassailable certainty is the thing that gives a newspaper the firmest and most valuable reputation.

For much of his career, Twain did not have the moral judgment or strength to quite come up to Goodman's standards by himself. In 1863, when one of the first manifestations of his literary genius, the sly hoax "A Bloody Massacre Near Carson," was received on the Comstock with outrage (because most readers fell for it), Twain was shaken by the denunciations. It was a critical moment in his career; but Goodman's steady support helped pull him through. Later, when a foreman on the paper warned Goodman of possible repercussions from Twain's exposé of corruption in the San Francisco police department, Goodman again backed Twain: "Let it go in, every word. If Mark can stand it, I can," he said. Where Goodman led, the other *Enterprise* staffers followed, and the solid support Twain received from them reinforced his moral inclination and contributed to its eventually establishing a characteristic presence in his works (Berkove 1994).

Nevertheless, where Goodman was direct and courageous in his moral stands, Twain was insecure and felt himself vulnerable to disapproval during the lengthy period when he was establishing his reputation, and he consequently cultivated circumspection. In 1871, for example, Twain wrote an effusively complimentary piece on Conrad Wiegand, a Comstock assayer who was scrupulously honest in a place and at a time where such honesty was exceedingly rare. Twain probably intended to

incorporate this into *Roughing It*, which he was then completing. Wiegand also established a newspaper in which he exposed the almost ubiquitous corruption on the Comstock. Unbeknown to Twain at the time he wrote the piece, Wiegand had been
manhandled and his life threatened by thugs hired by one of his targets. Instead of
arming himself and fighting them physically, Wiegand asked for police protection
and complained about his situation in another newspaper. It was a rational, moral,
and even brave thing to do, especially considering that he would have had no chance
against the thugs and might have bought his safety by silence; but the Comstock did
not see it that way. Journalists were expected personally to back up what they wrote
with fists or even weapons, and if they did not, they lost respect (Drury 1984: 169).
That is what happened to Wiegand. Goodman was in Europe while this event
occurred, but when he learned of it he was convinced that while Wiegand had been
right about his charges, he had also acted in such a way as to discredit himself
(Goodman 1997: 10). After Goodman returned to America, he visited Twain in
Elmira, where Twain was writing *Roughing It*, and possibly left the impression that
any praise of Wiegand would open the book to criticism on the Comstock. Twain
acted shamefully. It would have been bad enough if he had merely withdrawn his
praise from the book, but in the interest of ensuring good sales he completely reversed
what he had written just several months before, and wrote a scathing denunciation of
Wiegand as a coward and included it as Appendix C of the book. Twain also largely
suppressed his own criticisms of working conditions in the mines and the fact that
he himself had not been very popular on the Comstock (for a fuller treatment of this
episode, see Berkove 1995). Much later in his career, Twain would be more like
Goodman – fearlessly outspoken in defense of his principles – but while he was establishing his career he admired Goodman but still lacked his strength of character.

William Wright (1829–98), better known by his pen name of Dan De Quille, was
an easier mentor. De Quille, hired by Goodman and McCarthy in 1861, was one of
the original *Enterprise* staffers. Today, we can look back on his life and recognize that
not only was De Quille the most respected and beloved writer on the Comstock, he
was one of the most accomplished authors of the Old West (Berkove 1990b: xiii–xxiii;
1994), ranking just behind Twain, Ambrose Bierce, and Bret Harte. In personality,
however, De Quille was a mild-mannered and diffident individual. On the *Enterprise*,
he had the main responsibility for reporting on the mines and also was in charge of
local news. He quickly established a reputation for accuracy and probity in his mine
reports, and for interesting and even creative local reporting. One day, for instance,
when little was happening in Virginia City, he interviewed a farmer who had brought
a load of hay into town, and magnified that normally inconsequential event into a
major story by expanding into such related but tangential topics as the weather, the
state of the crops, and prospects for agricultural income. The story occasioned much
good-natured but respectful ribbing of De Quille, and it also demonstrated how good
a reporter he was. De Quille took Twain under his wing and gently taught him the
tricks of the trade, as Twain graciously acknowledged in chapter 42 of *Roughing It*.
Although De Quille was six years older than Twain, the two men were kindred spirits.
They shared a sense of humor and literary ability, and later became room-mates.

Few records survive of what they discussed nights after the paper was put to bed, but De Quille undoubtedly made available to Twain the saved clippings of his publications, and ample evidence exists that demonstrates that the two men shared ideas and plots, both then and later, and that Twain's indebtednesses to De Quille were many, substantial, and sometimes surprising. For example, a series of highly entertaining travel letters De Quille wrote for Iowa's *Cedar Falls Gazette* in 1861 mix fact and fiction, and utilize a mildly self-deprecating and naïve narrator who confesses to participating in, and succumbing to, hoaxes. This series deserves inclusion in the short list of possible models for *Innocents Abroad* and, especially, *Roughing It*.[3] That Twain almost certainly read this series has been persuasively argued by Edgar Branch, who identified incidents in it which Twain later adapted for use in *Adventures of Huckleberry Finn* and other books (Branch 1966: 105). I have shown that yet other narratives and passages from De Quille's writings were incorporated by Twain into *Roughing It* and *Life on the Mississippi*, and probably also into *Huckleberry Finn*.[4]

In moments of playful creativity, De Quille concocted for the *Enterprise* and other publications very convincing short hoaxes he termed "quaints" which, although tongue-in-cheek, were disguised as plausible news stories. In this limited genre De Quille has no peer, including Twain. This may be seen by studying the artistry of his classic two-part scientific quaint, "Solar Armor" (1874), and by comparing his "A Silver Man" (1865) to Twain's celebrated hoax "The Petrified Man" (1862), which inspired it. In the comparison, Twain deserves credit for his originality and genius, but his humor is short and sharp with a satiric edge, whereas De Quille's sketch is very graceful, skillfully expansive, detailed, and persuasive, and his humor is gentle, with no after-bite. De Quille's literary hoaxes were models for Twain to follow, and set the bar for Twain for subtlety of style.

These limited examples of literary hoaxes are, however, but obvious instances of the larger technique of the hoax, which was developed into a high art form by Sagebrush authors, and which Twain learned not only from De Quille and other Sagebrushers, but from real life – from what he and all Comstockers saw going on around them (Berkove 1998).[5] The Comstock artistic hoax's origin in, and close connection to, the real world is an important, perhaps essential feature that distinguishes it from tall tales or the obvious exaggerations that the later Sagebrusher Fred H. Hart included in his very popular book *The Sazerac Lying Club* (1878). Indeed, Hart himself points out in his introduction that there is a major difference between the innocent and amusing fibs included in his book and the lies of politicians, stockbrokers, newspaper men, and others "who lie for money." Tall tales and mere "stretchers" are intended to amuse and are usually so obvious that no particular skill or information is necessary to detect them. Indeed, the pleasure in them comes from knowing upfront that we are being lied to, so that we can enjoy the way the anecdote invents something fantastic, or delightfully distorts or exaggerates an incident.

The Comstock artistic hoax, on the other hand, is intended to deceive. It begins with something impossible or highly improbable that the narrator undertakes to make plausible with convincing but specious details. As soon as an audience concedes that there might be some validity to what is in essence an outrageous claim, its gullibility makes it vulnerable, and the narrator can set the hook and reel it in. Sometimes, the hoax is perpetrated on an individual or a small group – newcomers, for example – in which case the joke is enjoyed by an in-group. But sometimes the entire audience is taken in, and then the narrator can enjoy the deferred or private satisfaction of having outwitted it. The Comstock artistic hoax differs from an outright lie in three respects, however. One is that it aims to entertain, and often to inform as well. The second is that it does not result in harm. And the third is that there is some clue, however subtle, in the hoax that, once detected, can lead to its exposure. It therefore places a premium on close and thoughtful attention.

The main reason for the development of the hoax in Nevada can be found in the battle of wits that passed for daily business practice there and made *caveat emptor* the rule for any and all large financial transactions. The early mining industry in Nevada, and especially on the Comstock, was close to being unregulated by the legal system – indeed, it was perhaps unregulatable. The financial stakes were so high, the laws governing mining and promoting were so complicated and inadequate to the situation, corruption was so rife, and the population so transient, that swindles and frauds were everyday occurrences. Chapter 44 of *Roughing It* reports the wild and unrestricted speculation that dominated the prospecting phase of Nevada mining, with hopes, expectations, and promises represented largely as illusions, and the atmosphere of "silver fever" treated by Twain as a literal malady characterized by madness. He also describes gambling fever in reference not only to the ubiquitous games of chance, in which fortunes could be made or lost on the turn of a card, but also to the enterprises of prospecting and mining, in which an unforeseeable quirk of geology made the difference between fortune and failure. It was Nevada that made Twain see that Nature was deeply deceptive, and that human nature had both a fatal fondness for deception and a fatal susceptibility to it. It was as if Nature had conspired with human nature to tempt men to gamble beyond their capacity to resist; and as if, while gambling, they acted as if the cold laws of cause and effect were suspended. *Roughing It* abounds in hoaxes, both little and big, both obvious and extremely subtle.

The Sagebrush authors observed the signs of hoaxes on every hand, and naturally incorporated hoaxing into their writing as both technique and subject matter. The best writers, however, of whom De Quille was the prime example, were reflective and went beyond mere hoaxing to supply their readers with material for practical and moral instruction. Having learned from the best, Twain eventually bettered his instructors. Every substantial work of fiction that he wrote for the rest of his life has hoaxes at its core – some of them extremely subtle and sophisticated and very serious. This was the principal Nevada legacy to his writing. It was one of two distinguishing constituents of his style. The other was theological: his growing conviction that God was malevolent.

The deep thoughts that Twain and Goodman discussed after hours at the *Enterprise* office must have included the doubts Twain had about religion. From his youth, but especially after he encountered the writings of Tom Paine,[6] Twain had been attempting to free himself of his Calvinist indoctrination, and the struggle to do so would last his whole life. Intellectually, he detested Calvinism; but not only did he never break free of it, it actually grew in strength, albeit in a somewhat heretical form, and went deeper the more he attempted to extirpate it. *Roughing It* is the first of Twain's major works that show it to be the most characteristic element of his thought, and the book also illuminates how the Nevada legacy helped make it so. Briefly stated, the ubiquity of hoaxes Twain saw in Nature and the fatal affinity for hoaxes he saw in human nature merged with his belief in a vindictive Deity: Who created a flawed human race; who presented it with an original temptation that it could not resist, and that so corrupted itself by its disobedience that all human beings after Adam and Eve would be born with an original sin so heinous that they deserved damnation; Who promised freedom but predestined every action, word, and thought of every human creature, requiring them nonetheless to choose (futilely) between good and evil; and Who preached love but practiced capricious malice throughout history. Twain came to see a grand pattern of hoaxing throughout all creation. *Roughing It*, for all its surface humor, is organized around its revelation of a trickster Deity, a deceptive Nature, and a deceived humanity (Berkove 2001b). The Nevada hoax and Twain's heterodox Calvinism were congenial to each other in his mind, and thereafter typically, melded and manifested as an ideological unit, featured as the major theme in his creative works. Although he explores it variously and from different perspectives, the common, unifying motif of his best art is always the same: freedom is a delusion, and all hopes of it are hoaxes.

There were, of course, other Nevada authors who left less central imprints on Twain. Two minor ones were Rollin Mallory Daggett (1831–1901) and James William Emery Townsend (1838–1900). Daggett was a talented and versatile individual who, while an editor on the *Enterprise*, was noted for his strong views and forceful style. The parodic portrait of the editor in "Journalism in Tennessee" (1869) bears some exaggerated resemblance to him, and in real life, especially as he grew older, Twain too was often forceful when expressing his views in non-fictional form (Berkove 1993a; 1999a). Townsend, better known as "Lying Jim" and ironically called "Truthful James," was an itinerant journalist celebrated for being able to concoct gorgeous lies on the spur of the moment, and even as he was setting type. In chapter 35 of *Roughing It*, Twain mentions him in reference to a mining company's audacious assessment on shareholders to pay for a proposed 250-foot tunnel through what turned out to be a "hill" only 25 feet wide. Townsend points out to a couple of the putative tunnelers that 225 feet of the tunnel would have to be "on trestle-work!" For Comstockers who knew Townsend, the incident was doubly humorous, first because it was true, and second because Townsend was at last involved in a real-life lie that rivaled some of the ones he concocted. While it is unlikely that Townsend made any deep impression on Twain, he typified the Sagebrush admiration of a well-told "stretcher," a talent Twain quickly learned and used for the rest of his life (Berkove 1993b).

Even after Twain left the West, he maintained contacts with some of his Comstock friends – in particular Goodman and, to a lesser extent, De Quille, Daggett, and the very talented Samuel Post Davis, who arrived on the Comstock after Twain left but who became a friend nevertheless – and there are some indications that he continued to occasionally read the *Territorial Enterprise* and the publications of his friends. In short, Twain did not make a clean break with his Nevada background. He looked back frequently, and always drew inspiration and renewed strength from the friendships and lessons of the Sagebrush School.

One more major impact on Twain in Nevada was made, not by a Westerner, but by the humorist Artemus Ward, an Easterner from Maine who spent a memorable week on the Comstock in late December 1863. Ward, the pseudonym of Charles Farrar Browne (1834–67), was on a lecture tour of the West, and was extremely popular. Because his writings are the most easily accessible part of his legacy, the tendency has been to regard Ward as one of the "Phunny Phellows," the literary humorists whose forte was erratic spelling and vernacular idiom. While his writings certainly did contribute to his popularity, the most important influence – and it can justly be regarded as a major influence – he had on Twain came from his lectures and his distinctive style of oral presentation.[7]

Ward caught Twain's attention at a dinner by a spontaneous *tour de force* of double-talk that left the latter befuddled and wondering how he had missed the point of what seemed to be a straightforward question. Twain recorded this in "A Reminiscence of Artemus Ward" (1867), and similar extended recollections were later published by Dan De Quille and Joe Goodman.[8] Although Twain seldom if ever used that particular technique, he was deeply impressed during that memorable week by both Ward's brilliant and versatile wit and his artistry, and Twain stuck close to him for most of that time, paying close attention to everything he said and did. Twain was a quick learner, and he not only appreciated Ward's techniques, he absorbed them and assimilated them so completely that he was soon able to develop his own extensions of them.

By all accounts (and there are many of them), Ward had developed a distinctive if not unique style of humorous lecture, one that had something in common with theatrical performance. He chose topics which he then never addressed directly, just making occasional brief allusions to them. He spoke without notes, rambled entertainingly over many subjects, maintained a grave demeanor even when his audience roared with laughter, and made comical errors as he appeared to fumble for the right word. Much of what Twain describes in "How to Tell a Story" (1895) is his internalization of techniques he learned from Ward, a point he readily admits. It is worth quoting his acknowledgment from that essay:

> Very often, of course, the rambling and disjointed humorous story finishes with a nub, point, snapper, or whatever you like to call it. Then the listener must be alert, for in many cases the teller will divert attention from that nub by dropping it in a carefully casual and indifferent way, with the pretence that he does not know it is a nub.
>
> Artemus Ward used that trick a good deal, then when the audience presently caught the joke he would look up with innocent surprise, as if wondering what they had found to laugh at. Dan Setchell used it before him, [Edgar Wilson, aka "Bill"] Nye and [James Whitcomb] Riley and others use it to-day. (Twain 1996: 3–4)

Ward's famous "The Babes in the Wood" lecture was recreated by Edgar Branch from abridged contemporary reviews and stenographic records. But it is obvious that a mere record of the words of a lecture cannot capture many of the characteristic features that transform a flat text into a charming live performance: the speaker's appearance, timbre of voice, tone, pronunciation, pauses, inflections, emphases, and gestures, to say nothing of the extemporaneous asides or additions he may introduce for particular audiences. Thanks to Hal Holbrook, whose dramatic renditions of Twain's lectures have restored to life many of his lecture routines, we are now able to approximate the totality of a Twain performance. That is not yet possible for Ward, and parenthetical records by reporters of pauses, laughter, applause, and even overheard conversations from members of the audience still fall short of a rendition which enables us to hear, let alone see, the kind of performance which evoked such praise in America and England, and which persuaded Twain to imitate him. Even so, a close reading of the re-created text suggests something that Twain certainly picked up and perfected. Ward did not just ramble arbitrarily from anecdote to anecdote. He recurred almost subliminally to certain themes (such as patriotism and tradition, in the published version of the lecture "The Babes in the Wood" Branch reconstructed in 1978). In other words, although Ward studiously avoided addressing the announced topic, there was nevertheless an underlying order to his lecture. An audience would have enjoyed the apparently rambling discourse, but at the end it would have been left with some carefully implanted ideas. The greatest art is that which disguises itself. Ward demonstrated to Twain how this could be done entertainingly in oral performances, and Twain immediately began adapting the new knowledge to his writings.

According to Branch, it is possible to see the Setchell–Ward lesson in operation in "Jim Smiley and His Jumping Frog" (1865), that early and undoubted manifestation of Twain's literary genius which, significantly, begins with an address to Ward (Branch 1967). The story depends heavily on the oral style of Simon Wheeler, with vernacular narratives which appear to be linked, if at all, by a loose chain of association. Scholarship, however, has established that, contrary to appearances, the story is tightly structured.[9] Within seven years of its appearance, Twain had perfected Ward's technique to the point where he could use it as the organizing principle of *Roughing It*, also heavily dependent on conversational tone, conversations, anecdote, and seemingly rambling and digressive incidents (Berkove 2001b).

Ordered and purposeful structure in the book can be inferred from a letter Twain wrote to Dan De Quille in 1875, inviting him to come to Hartford and stay while he worked on the manuscript of the book that became *The Big Bonanza*:

> Dan, there is more than one way of writing a book, & your way is *not* the right one. You see, the winning card is to nail a man's interest with *Chapter I*, & not let up on him till you get him to the word "finis." That can't be done with detached sketches, but I'll show you how to make a man read every one of those sketches, under the stupid impression that they are mere accidental incidents that have dropped in on you unawares in the course of your *narrative*. (quoted in Berkove 1999b: 32)

Presumably, the model for De Quille's book would have been *Roughing It*. Twain's book deals largely with Nevada, and De Quille's book is totally devoted to it. Both books share anecdote; a mixture of humor, fact, and fiction; and character sketches. Insofar as De Quille's *Washoe Rambles* is one of the precursors of *Roughing It*, this letter is testimony to how far Twain advanced in a little over ten years, from De Quille's apprentice to his mentor. The difference was Artemus Ward. De Quille as well as Twain was in Virginia City when Ward visited it, but De Quille found Ward to be only entertaining, whereas Twain found him to be instructive as well.

It is a strange fact that while Twain is considered to be one of America's greatest authors, at the same time conventional wisdom has maintained that his main books – *Roughing It* (1872), *Huckleberry Finn* (1885), and *Connecticut Yankee* (1889) – all suffer from weak organization. *Roughing It* is thought too anecdotal, with the majority of the book on the West divided from its final section on Hawaii. *Huckleberry Finn* is usually criticized for being thematically disappointing in its final section, the "evasion" chapters. *Connecticut Yankee* has been generally censured for being torn between humor and tragedy, and fiction and autobiography. But a main distinguishing characteristic of great books is that they are well written. If these books all suffer from weak organization, on what ground can Twain be called a great author? The reply to this question is that the books are indeed well organized, using the principle of disguised organization which he learned from Ward. Twain refined Ward's technique far beyond the original, strictly oral, example of "The Babes in the Wood" and far beyond the adaptation of oral narrative to writing in "Jim Smiley and His Jumping Frog," and extended it from humor to tragedy. Thematic structure that is disguised by hoax and irony is at the heart of all of his major books, and some of the others as well. As Twain warned in "How to Tell a Story," readers must be alert, for in many cases the author will divert attention from the story's nub by dropping it in a casual and indifferent way, with the pretence that he does not know it is the nub. Twain is a sophisticated master of subtlety, indirection, and circumvention; but for all their disguise, powerful central themes hold his works together.[10]

Twain arrived in Nevada in August 1861 and left it in May 1864. In the intervening period – somewhat less than three years – he was transformed from a former steamboat pilot into a masterly writer. In the hothouse atmosphere of the *Territorial Enterprise*, mentored by Joe Goodman, Dan De Quille, Rollin Mallory Daggett, Jim Townsend, and other accomplished members of the remarkable fraternity of the Sagebrush School, and exposed to the art of Artemus Ward, he was introduced to ideas and standards that shaped his personality, and to advanced techniques that, once assimilated, would enable him to become one of the greatest authors of world literature.

Nevada was just a phase of his education. Much had preceded it and much was to follow it. In the final analysis, it is no more accurate to describe him as a Nevada author, or a Sagebrush author, than it is to call him a Missouri or New York or Connecticut or Hawaii author. He was an original thinker, and what he did with what he learned qualifies as original artistry. He transcends all local identities and labels, for he made of himself something unique and rare, something that blended and incorporated all that he learned with all that he thought. But not all of his experiences were of equal importance. It is impossible to imagine Mark Twain without his boyhood experiences in Hannibal, or his early manhood experiences on the Mississippi River. By the same token, Nevada was essential to his development.

NOTES

1   In a surviving fragment of a column that Goodman wrote for the *Nevada Mining News* in 1910 on the occasion of Twain's death, Goodman recollected that: "He was of a profoundly philosophical turn of mind, with a rare capacity for original thought. I discovered this as long ago as when he first came on the Enterprise. Frequently, when our work for the night was over and the other editors had gone, he would cast off the sportive guise he wore in the presence of the crowd, and of most men, and he and I would sit quietly by ourselves for hours, discussing literary, scientific or philosophical questions in an entirely abstract and impersonal way. His talk on such occasions was not only interesting; it was fascinating. He would sometimes flush a new or strange idea, so to speak, and pursue it till he had thought it out in all its bearings. He liked to get at the real core or significance of things." (Personal collection of author.)

2   The full story of this remarkable hoax can be found in Twain (1972).

3   Another set of travel letters that De Quille wrote that may have served as a model for *Roughing It* has been collected by Richard E. Lingenfelter. Entitled *Washoe Rambles*, the collection consists of letters first published in the *Golden Era* in 1861, reporting a prospecting trip that De Quille and some companions took. Although the letters are mostly factual, there is some fictionalizing in them.

4   The fullest account, at present, of the two men's influence on each other's writings can be found in Berkove (1999b: 31–9).

5   Edgar Branch (1966) devotes a section of chapter 3 to an informative discussion of what Twain learned about hoaxes while in Nevada. I hold that the technique of the hoax penetrated more deeply into Twain's artistic psyche than Branch recognizes and is far more extensive and important in Twain's literature than he suggests.

6   "It is nearly impossible to exaggerate the impact of *The Age of Reason* on the mind of Samuel Clemens. . . . The book converted him. Paine's equating traditional religions with superstition helped Clemens submerge his dreadful Calvinism" (Cummings 1988: 20–1).

7   One of the better essays enumerating specific instances of specific or probable borrowings from Ward by Twain is by Robert Rowlette (1973). While not discounting this sort of scholarship, I am proposing that Ward's influence on Twain is deeper and more subtle.

8   In addition to Twain's own 1867 reminiscence and the previously known accounts by Goodman (1892) and De Quille (1893), there is also an 1888 newspaper memoir by De Quille which is similar but not identical to his 1893 essay. There are substantial differences of detail among all accounts of the event, but all agree on their recognition of Ward as being verbally brilliantly adroit.

9   The story has evoked a good deal of scholarly interpretation, including notable discussions by Branch, Krause, and Messent. My own position is that it is an intricate nest of hoaxes, one inside the other.

10 My discussions of these unifying themes at work in each of his three major books (essentially the same ones, in my opinion, and all involving hoaxes) can be found in Berkove 1968, 1984, 1990a, 2001b, and 2003.

References and Further Reading

Adams, Eva B. (1936). "Joseph T. Goodman: The Man Who Made Mark Twain." M.A. thesis, Columbia University.

Bellamy, Gladys Carmen (1941). "Mark Twain's Indebtedness to John Phoenix." *American Literature* 13, 29–43.

Berkove, Lawrence I. (1968). "The 'Poor Players' of *Huckleberry Finn*." *Papers of the Michigan Academy* 51, 291–310. Repr. in *Mark Twain Journal* 41: 2 (Fall 2003).

Berkove, Lawrence I. (1984). "The Reality of the Dream: Structural and Thematic Unity in *A Connecticut Yankee*." *Mark Twain Journal* 22: 1, 8–14.

Berkove, Lawrence I. (1990a). "*A Connecticut Yankee*: A Serious Hoax." *Essays in Arts and Sciences* 19, 28–44.

Berkove, Lawrence I. (1990b). "Introduction." In *The Fighting Horse of the Stanislaus: Stories and Essays by Dan De Quille*. Iowa City: University of Iowa Press.

Berkove, Lawrence I. (1991). "Life after Twain: The Later Careers of the *Enterprise* Staff." *Mark Twain Journal*, 29: 1, 22–8.

Berkove, Lawrence I. (1993a). "Daggett, Rollin Mallory." In J. R. LeMaster and James D. Wilson (eds.), *The Mark Twain Encyclopedia*, 201. New York: Garland.

Berkove, Lawrence I. (1993b). "Townsend, James William Emery." In J. R. LeMaster and James D. Wilson (eds.), *The Mark Twain Encyclopedia*, 742. New York: Garland.

Berkove, Lawrence I. (1994). *Ethical Records of Twain and his Circle of Sagebrush Journalists*. Elmira, NY: Elmira College Center for Mark Twain Studies.

Berkove, Lawrence I. (1995). "'Assaying in Nevada': Twain's Wrong Turn in the Right Direction." *American Literary Realism* 27: 3, 64–79.

Berkove, Lawrence I. (1998). "The Comstock Matrix of Mark Twain's Humor." In David E. E. Sloane (ed.), *New Directions in American Humor*, 160–70. Tuscaloosa: University of Alabama Press.

Berkove, Lawrence I. (1999a). "Daggett, Rollin Mallory." In *American National Biography*, vol. 6, 3–4. New York: Oxford University Press.

Berkove, Lawrence I. (1999b). *Dan De Quille*. Boise, Idaho: Boise State University Press.

Berkove, Lawrence I. (2001a). "Joe Goodman, in his own Write." *Nevada Magazine* 61: 1, 16–19.

Berkove, Lawrence I. (2001b). "The Trickster God of *Roughing It*." In Jeanne Campbell Reesman (ed.), *Trickster Lives: Culture and Myth in American Fiction*, 84–96. Athens: University of Georgia Press.

Berkove, Lawrence I. (2003). "No 'Mere Accidental Incidents': *Roughing It* as a Novel." *Mark Twain Annual*, 7–17.

Branch, Edgar M. (1966). *The Literary Apprenticeship of Mark Twain, with Selections from his Apprentice Writings*. New York: Russell & Russell. (First publ. 1950.)

Branch, Edgar M. (1967). "'My Voice Is Still for Setchell': A Background Study of 'Jim Smiley and His Jumping Frog'." *PMLA* 82: 7 (Dec.), 591–601.

Branch, Edgar M. (1978). "'The Babes in the Wood': Artemus Ward's 'Double Health' to Mark Twain." *PMLA* 93 (Oct.), 955–72.

Cummings, Sherwood (1988). *Mark Twain and Science: Adventures of a Mind*. Baton Rouge: Louisiana State University Press.

De Quille, Dan [William Wright] (1888). "Artemus Ward: His Great Definition of Genius, as Confided to Mark Twain." *San Francisco Examiner*, Feb. 26, 11: 4.

De Quille, Dan [William Wright] (1947). *The Big Bonanza*, intr. Oscar Lewis. New York: Thomas Y. Crowell. (First publ. 1876.)

De Quille, Dan [William Wright] (1963). *Washoe Rambles*, intr. Richard E. Lingenfelter. Los Angeles: Westernlore. (First publ. 1861.)

De Quille, Dan [William Wright] (1990). "Artemus Ward in Nevada" (first publ. 1893). In Richard A. Dwyer and Richard E. Lingenfelter (eds.), *Dan De Quille, The Washoe Giant*, 219–24. Reno: University of Nevada Press.

Drury, Wells (1984). *An Editor on the Comstock Lode*. Reno: University of Nevada Press. (First publ. 1936.)

Dwyer, Richard A., and Lingenfelter, Richard E., eds. (1984). *Lying on the Eastern Slope: James Townsend's Comic Journalism on the Mining Frontier*. Miami: Florida International University Press.

Goodman, Joseph T. (1997). "An Irregular Correspondent: *The European Travel Letters of Mark*

Twain's Editor and Friend Joe Goodman," ed. and intr. Lawrence I. Berkove. *Mark Twain Journal* 35: 2 (Fall), 1–44. [was dated 1870.]

Goodman, Joseph T. (1977). "Artemus Ward on the Comstock Lode" (first publ. 1892). In Phillip I. Earl (ed.), *Heroes, Badmen and Honest Miners: Joe Goodman's Tales of the Comstock Lode*. Reno: Great Basin Press.

Hart, Fred H. (1878). *The Sazerac Lying Club*. San Francisco: Samuel Carson.

Krause, Sidney J. (1964). "The Art and Satire of Twain's 'Jumping Frog' Story." *American Quarterly* 16: 4, 562–76.

Messent, Peter (1995). "Caught on the Hop: Interpretive Dislocation in 'The Notorious Jumping Frog of Calaveras County'." *Thalia* 15: 1–2, 33–49.

Rowlette, Robert (1973). "'Mark Ward on Artemus Twain': Twain's Literary Debt to Ward." *American Literary Realism* 6 (Winter), 13–25.

Smith, Grant H. (1943). *The History of the Comstock Lode: 1850–1920*. *University of Nevada Bulletin* 37: 3. Reno: University of Nevada Press.

Twain, Mark (1972). *The Great Landslide Case*, with editorial comment by Frederick Anderson and Edgar M. Branch. [San Francisco:] Friends of the Bancroft Library, University of California Press.

Twain, Mark (1996). *How to Tell a Story and Other Essays*. New York: Oxford University Press. (First publ. 1897.)

12

The Twain–Cable Combination

Stephen Railton

On Saturday, December 6, 1884, about a month into their "Twins of Genius" reading tour, Mark Twain and George Washington Cable were walking in Rochester, New York, when a sudden rain drove them to take shelter in a bookstore. Cable was a strict Sabbatarian who refused to travel on Sundays, so while on tour Twain usually spent that day in his hotel room resting up, and he needed something to read in Rochester. On Cable's recommendation he left the bookstore with a copy of *Le Morte D'Arthur*, Thomas Malory's tales about the Round Table. The rest, as they say, is Mark Twain's version of medieval history – *A Connecticut Yankee in King Arthur's Court*. Cable proudly claimed the "godfathership of that book,"[1] but that title only begins to indicate his role in the novel Twain wrote, and the influence that the reading tour had on its genesis and development. The novel, in turn, can help us appreciate the complex relationship between these "Twins."

The two men first met in 1881, in Twain's hometown of Hartford, when Cable visited in-laws there. They became friends in 1882, in Cable's hometown of New Orleans, when Twain spent a week there gathering material for the travel book *Life on the Mississippi*. In that book he refers to Cable as "the South's finest literary genius," a "master" in the writing of French dialects who also "reads them in perfection" (Twain 1883: 442, 472). Though at this time Cable had not yet given a public lecture, he was interested in professional speaking as a means of supplementing his modest royalties from the three books he had published; Twain, a seasoned veteran of the platform, urged him to try it. In early April 1883, after Cable had lectured successfully at the University of Mississippi and Johns Hopkins, Twain helped him arrange a public reading in Hartford. Even before that exhibition took place, Twain began thinking about some kind of collaboration. On March 17 he wrote Cable to discuss his upcoming lecture, and to throw out this suggestive hint:

> Now to *other* business. This morning, while I was getting out of bed, an idea struck me;
> & when I had finished putting on my socks it was already in a state of completion, & I

said "Now I'll write to Cable & say, *don't make any more lecture engagements till we've had a talk*." That is what I *do* say. What you *have* made, *fill*, but don't make any more till you've seen me. (Cardwell 1953: 91)

This sort of jumping into a speculation with both feet was entirely characteristic of Twain, though it wasn't until just over a year later that he engaged Cable, at a salary of $450 a week and expenses, to share the stage with him on the "Twins of Genius" reading tour: four months, over one hundred performances, eighty stops throughout the Northeastern and Midwestern United States, with a ten-day break at Christmas and about a week in Canada.

The "Twins" had different reasons for undertaking the tour. A dozen years earlier Twain had come off the road after three consecutive campaigns on the lyceum circuit. At first he was glad to be done with its rigors, but just as "store clothes" and "an audience" were "always nuts for Tom Sawyer" (Twain 1885: 286), so Twain loved center stage, and in 1881 began talking about going on the road again (see Fatout 1969: 204). In 1884 there were immediate material incentives to do so. His new publishing company was about to bring out its first book, *Adventures of Huckleberry Finn*. Lecture receipts would furnish ready cash to help capitalize that venture. And while book tours were not yet part of the publishing industry's standard practice, Twain had learned that the free publicity that accompanied a traveling lecturer helped promote book sales. He even advertised himself this time as a "reader" rather than a lecturer, and "selections from his forthcoming novel" made up part of every evening's performance. The tour's swing through Canada was timed to secure a copyright that would prevent pirated Canadian editions eating into American sales, as had happened with his previous books.

Cable also was promoting a new novel, *Dr. Sevier*, excerpts from which formed the heart of his part of every Twins performance. He was coming off a profitable 1883–4 reading tour, and the weekly salary Twain agreed to pay him was about what he could make going out again on his own. J. B. Pond, Cable's manager and the man whom Twain hired to manage the Twins tour, tactfully warned Cable to "Think and be wise" about whether the "double team" with Twain was in his best interests (Cardwell 1953: 8). But Cable not only liked Twain personally; he saw him as a writer who had already triumphantly established himself with the two constituencies that he was courting: the national reading public and New England's community of letters. Cable was nine years younger than Twain; his first story had been published ten years after Twain's "Jumping Frog" had launched the older man's career; his first lecture tour came 14 years after Twain's. At the time he got that letter from Mark Twain hinting at a big new idea, Cable was the author of three books that had enjoyed great critical and good popular success, but he was nonetheless flattered and excited by the favor the famous man was showing him. From a train leaving Hartford after his public reading there in April 1883, Cable wrote his mother that a "new future appears to be opening before me" (Turner 1960: 21). By the following summer he had moved his family from New Orleans to Connecticut, and was making plans to share the limelight with Mark

Twain. He was by no means blinded by that light – he negotiated for $100 more per week than Twain initially offered – but he was happy to bask in its glow.

It is easier to see what Cable could get from teaming up with Twain than it is to understand why Twain wanted a partner. Almost as much as he loved the attention of an audience, he hated the long, lonely hours of travel between performances: as he told a reporter in Iowa, "I wanted good company on the road and at the hotels" (Bikle 1928: xx). Pond could just as appropriately have warned Twain to think and be wise about whether Cable would meet his criteria for "good company": not only did he refuse to travel on Sundays, he neither smoked nor swore, he didn't play billiards, and he seldom drank. But Twain's affection for his friend had survived both the time Cable fell sick while on a visit and apparently spread the mumps to members of the Clemens family, and the April Fool's Day joke Cable played on him in 1884 by getting 150 acquaintances to send him requests for his autograph. Twain could tell the two men's performance styles would complement each other very well on stage. Although he would have to share that stage, by hiring Cable he could expect to maintain control over the venture and his own place as its star. As far as performing was concerned, Cable was in a sense his apprentice. At barely five feet tall, he was physically much smaller too. When in September the two men began planning the show, it was decided that they would each take several turns before the audience. In every variant program Twain considered, he gave himself top billing and the last word. Although in their temperamental differences they might resemble Luigi and Angelo, those "Extraordinary Twins" who have so much difficulty living together, Twain clearly intended to dominate all aspects of what Pond's promotional material called the Twain–Cable combination.

The tour began in New Haven on November 6, 1884. From the first Cable was delighted. Almost daily he sent his wife Louise reports from backstage, written while Twain was out in front of the audience, and in these letters we can hear how much those audiences and Cable were enjoying themselves. "Mark is on the platform; there goes a roar of applause!" he writes from Philadelphia, "Mark says, as he passes me on the retiring room steps, 'Old boy, you're doing nobly'" (Bikle 1928: 133). "Mark is on stage reading (reciting) his 'Desperate Encounter with an Interviewer'," he writes a week later, "and the roars of laughter fall as regularly as surf. I think it's a great thing to be able to hold my own with so wonderful a platform figure" (p. 134). Newspaper reviews confirm the audiences' enthusiasm, and praise the work of both performers equally. But Twain himself was unhappy. In an autobiographical dictation 20 years later he remembers the beginning of the tour as "ghastly" (Twain 1966: 176). Houses were smaller than he had anticipated, but the main cause of his dissatisfaction was his own performance. According to his 1907 autobiographical account, the problem lay in the distinction Cable implies above between "reading" and "reciting." By the end of the first week on tour Twain realized he would have to leave his books offstage, recast the sections he "read" into "the common forms of unpremeditated talk," and commit the revised passages to memory so he could maintain eye contact with the audience while delivering them. Even after making this adjustment, however, he was still dissatisfied. When he and Cable separated after their December 17 performance in Cleveland to spend Christmas with their families, Twain determined to spend the 12-day break revamping the show. In his notebook from this period are about a dozen possible programs, with the length of each of his and Cable's selections carefully measured in minutes. Writing to Pond on December 22, Twain revealed that the deepest source of his frustration with the way the tour had gone was, as Lorch puts it, his "feeling of jealousy" (Lorch 1968: 173):

> If any programs have been printed for the rest of our season, it will be necessary to destroy them; for I *must* invent some way to curtail Cable. His name draws a sixteenth part of the house, & he invariably does two-thirds of the reading. I cannot stand that any longer. He may have 35 or 38 minutes on the platform, & no more. (Twain 1979: 84)

Pond tried tactfully to point out how valuable Cable's contribution was, but Twain remained adamant that (as he wrote his wife on January 18) "there has been a thundering sight too much" Cable in the show (Twain 1979: 85). By then they had been back on the road for two weeks. The program had been changed, especially Twain's selections, although despite all his calculations Cable still split the two hours evenly with him. He now required Cable, however, to begin each night promptly at 8 p.m., and so, as Twain gloated to Livy, he "talks 15 minutes to an *assembling* house," which means half the audience never hears his first piece, "so there isn't too much of C any more."

Even as Twain wrote this, however, Cable was stealing the show everywhere but onstage. The January issue of *Century* magazine (which also contained a pre-publication extract from *Huckleberry Finn*) featured "The Freedman's Case in Equity," Cable's carefully written but deeply felt protest against the emerging system of racial segregation in the South. As Cable wrote Louise from Milwaukee on January 29, the article had made "a profound impression" (Turner 1960: 92). Newspapers across the South condemned him as a traitor to the region and the white race, big-city papers around the nation covered the controversy, and at stops along the tour Cable not only was interviewed by local reporters seeking his views on "the Southern problem" but also was often visited by groups of people – "yellow, black, brown," as he told his wife; "white men & black men" (pp. 85, 89) – who came to thank him for his courageous (and almost solitary) stand against the rise of Jim Crow. The evidence of the media coverage makes it clear that for the tour's final six or eight weeks Cable's notoriety eclipsed his partner's. Twain himself remained curiously silent about all of this in his letters from the road, and it probably surprises modern readers of *Huck Finn* that no interviewer thought of asking him if there was anything he wanted to say about American race relations. But it was in the middle of the commotion aroused by Cable's essay that Twain wrote Livy calling Cable "one of the most spoiled men, by success in life, you ever saw" (Wecter 1947: 237). Cable would have agreed at least about the success: writing Louise from the hotel he shared with Twain in Chicago, he told her "I wish you could see my table – covered with letters full of tender expressions of gratitude and admiration . . . That paper is turning out to be the greatest thing I've ever done" (Turner 1960: 89).

The tour was enjoying success too. Yet while reviews and audiences remained almost unanimously enthusiastic, and Cable's reports from backstage continued to radiate the warmth of that reception, behind Cable's back Twain grew increasingly bitter toward his "Twin." His letters to Livy grew more and more abusive, calling Cable a "pious ass" on February 10 and "the pitifulest human louse I have ever known" a week later (Wecter 1947: 236, 237). In that second letter Twain gives vent to the most sustained of his grievances about the selection from *Dr. Sevier* that Cable used to bring his part of the show to a climax: "Cover the C H I L D! Do you know, that infernal Night Ride of Mary's has grown from 6 minutes (in New Haven) to *fifteen*! And it is in *every* program." In his notebook he wrote that "Cable costs me $550 to $600 a week – that is, $450 a week & expenses. He is not worth the half of it" (Twain 1979: 88). Cable's expenses, and what Twain called his "closeness" with money, were part of the problem. Twain even complained that he saved his dirty clothes from the Christmas break to have them laundered at the tour's expense (Wecter 1947: 234). Cable's piety grew more aggravating, too: writing Howells two days from the end of the tour, Twain said that the four months on the road had "taught me that Cable's gifts of mind are greater & higher than I had suspected. But –":

> That "but" is pointing toward his religion. You will never never know, never divine, guess, imagine, how loathsome a thing the Christian religion can be made until you come to know & study Cable daily & hourly. Mind you, I like him; he is pleasant company; I rage & swear at him sometimes, but we do not quarrel; we get along mighty happily together; but in him & his person I have learned to hate all religions. He has taught me to abhor & detest the Sabbath-day & hunt up new & troublesome ways to dishonor it. (Twain and Howells 1968: 246)

Howells knew how to adjust for Mark Twain's hyperbole, as did Pond, and Livy Clemens was if anything too well acquainted with her husband's habitual exasperations and exaggerations. But after the tour ended Twain unfortunately allowed his emotional dirty laundry to get an airing in public when he spoke too freely to "the New York Correspondent" for the Boston *Herald*, which printed a pair of stories claiming to expose the "Personal Peculiarities of a Well Known Author." In what Cable labeled, in his protest to the *Herald*, "the first careful [i.e. deliberate] slander upon my private character I have ever known," the reporter used details about Cable's behavior while sick in the Clemens house and on the tour, details that could only have come from Twain, to belittle him as "A Small Man," miserly and self-righteous.[2] Shocked and hurt, Cable telegraphed Twain on May 15 asking him to deny these allegations, and when nothing was heard from Hartford, wrote a letter the next day. After telling Twain that "I esteem you more highly since our winter's experience than I ever did before," he again implicitly asked him to give the lie to the *Herald*'s representations (Cardwell 1953: 108). On May 18 Twain wrote Cable a short letter assuring him that the newspaper stories "did not distress me," not even for "one single half of a half of a hundredth part of a second" (p. 109). Let's hope Twain is oblivious here to the way this measurement recalls his compulsion to time Cable's share of their joint performances; but could he possibly have been as unaware as this reply seems to indicate that the issue was Cable's distress, not his? Yet even after the *Herald*'s Cable-bashing was reprinted in other papers, Twain never offered any public defense of his former partner. To Cable, after all the happy sounds of the tour, Twain's silence must have been a strange note on which to end their "twinship." They remained formally friends, but there was little contact between them for the remainder of Twain's life.

For students of that life, the pattern of Twain's relationship with Cable – affection, collaboration, suspicion and rage – is a familiar one. The Twain–Cable combination has additional significance for students of Twain's art, because of the way it helps illuminate *A Connecticut Yankee in King Arthur's Court*. Malory's *Morte D'Arthur*, the book Cable advised him to buy on December 6, 1884, quickly became one of the Twins' few dependable sources of pleasure. On December 14 Twain wrote Charles Webster, his nephew by marriage and head of his publishing company, asking him to send a copy of Malory to Ozias Pond, J. B. Pond's brother who was traveling with the team (Webster 1946: 283). As Twain wrote Livy, he and Cable had dubbed Ozias "Sir Sagramore le Desirous," adding that "We have all used the quaint language of [Malory's] book in talk in the [railroad] cars & hotels" (Smith 1979: 2). It was probably only a week or two after the purchase in Rochester that Twain entered into his notebook the inspired idea from which *Connecticut Yankee* grew: "Dream of being a knight errant in armor in the middle ages. Have the notions & habits of thought of the present day mixed with the necessities of that. No pockets in the armor. No way to manage certain requirements of nature. Can't scratch . . ." (Twain 1979: 79). Although he didn't start writing the novel until the next winter, the marginal comment Twain put next to this notebook entry five years later, just as *Connecticut Yankee* was about to be published, makes explicit the ligature by which the tour and the novel were bound together. It was, he notes, "while Cable & I were giving readings" that "I began to make notes in my head for a book" (p. 80).

The evidence of the novel confirms the significance of this relationship. On the one hand, it's easy to see why the *Morte D'Arthur* would have struck Twain immediately as raw material for his kind of art. Comically toppling the high cultural icon of the knight in shining armor by giving him itches and the other "requirements of [common human] nature" is the type of irreverent and liberating imaginative work that endeared Twain to his reading public. Just as Huck Finn allowed Twain to take a matter of fact look at "Tom Sawyer's lies" (Twain 1885: 33), so the first-person narrator he created for his next novel, Hank Morgan, Yankee, "practical" and "barren of sentiment . . . or poetry," gives Twain a perspective from which to re-view and un-write the accounts of medieval romancers like Malory and Walter Scott by depicting the poverty, ignorance, and injustice that their stories leave out (Twain 1889: 20). On the other hand, as Twain composed it, Hank's story rewrites *itself* in ways its author never seems to be fully conscious of, along lines that lead directly back to the Twins of Genius tour. Hank has only been in the sixth century a few hours before he steps out of his character as a factory foreman to reveal himself as a well-rehearsed public performer. With that change, *Connecticut Yankee* becomes less dramatically about what Hank can show his readers about the Dark Ages than about the shows he puts on for the people of the time, thus giving Twain a story in which he can explore his own ambitions and anxieties as a performer. One indication of how completely Twain erases the distinction between himself and Hank as a created persona is the joke Hank says "I had heard oftenest and had most hated and most loathed all my life." It's the one about "a humorous lecturer who flooded an ignorant audience with the killingest jokes for an hour and never got a laugh," because his talk was booked into a church and his listeners were afraid to "laug[h] right out in meetin'" (pp. 111–12). This is not a joke men in factories would ever be likely to tell or hear. It was Twain himself, the humorous lecturer, for whom this parable about getting an audience to respond hit too close to home. In fact, he ordered his managers never to book him into a church, though because churches often contained the biggest halls in town, they were the sites of many of his performances, including at least a dozen on the tour with Cable.

That tour isn't just where *Connecticut Yankee* began; in many ways it defined the issues that usurp the novel's storyline. The tour as subtext to the novel, for instance, makes explicable Hank's otherwise mystifying rivalry with Merlin. Throughout the story Hank refers to "The Church" as the most dangerous of the medieval forces he has to contend with, but the antagonist the narrative gives him in its most dramatic scenes is almost always Merlin. It is Merlin who has him stripped naked in his first appearance at the Round Table, who "spoil[s] all" by doubting Hank's claims to be a magician (Twain 1889: 67), who orders the monk to "Apply the torch!" to Hank at the stake (p. 75). When Hank decides to perform another "miracle," it is Merlin's Tower he destroys; he restores the fountain in the Valley of Holiness only after making sure Merlin fails; he defines even his joust against Sir Sagramore as a "duel between two mighty magicians" – himself and Merlin (p. 497). Before most of this has even happened, Hank tells Clarence that his quarrel with Merlin pre-dates the story: "I've known Merlin seven hundred years . . . he is always blethering around in my way, everywhere I go; he makes me tired." As he goes on to dismiss Merlin's credentials as a magician, he sounds more and more like Mark Twain fulminating against the "Twin" with whom he and Sir Sagramore Pond had traveled: "He is well enough for the provinces – one-night stands and that sort of thing, you know – but dear me, *he* oughtn't to set up for an expert – anyway not where there's a real artist" (p. 64).

Another echo of the tour can be heard when Clarence's complaint about the tale Merlin tells in the opening scene at Camelot recalls Twain's grievance against Cable's nightly rendition of "Mary's Night Ride" – "that same old weary tale that he hath told a thousand times in the same words, and that he *will* tell till he dieth . . . Would

God I had died or I saw this day!" (Twain 1889: 46). Like Cable, Merlin is the figure with whom center stage has to be shared. The rivalry in *Connecticut Yankee*, then, follows the pattern of the Twins tour. The dynamic is fully established in chapter 7. After striking a pose as a mighty wizard at "The Eclipse" and being promoted to the King's minister, Hank finds himself the "centre of all the nation's wonder and reverence" (p. 72). His celebrity status turns "Brer Merlin green with envy and spite" (p. 86), but soon "old Merlin was making himself busy on the sly among those people . . . spreading a report that I was a humbug" (p. 87). In response, Hank advertises and arranges an elaborate show. The program for this evening's performance brings Merlin onstage first, to show what he can do to cast a spell to protect his tower. But after he begins to "mutter and make passes in the air with his hands," Hank displaces him: telling Merlin that "You have had time enough" – a line that recalls all those notebook attempts to shorten Cable's share of the Twins show – Hank makes "about three passes in the air," then exults as Merlin's tower goes up with a bang and "Merlin's stock" as a performer gets knocked "flat" (pp. 89–91). Twain and Cable took the stage together over a hundred times. Hank and Merlin re-enact this scene just twice – at "The Restoration of the Fountain" and again at "The Yankee's Fight with the Knights" – but these staged triumphs over another performer are among the most elaborate and dramatic scenes in the novel.

In keeping with the book Twain set out to write, Hank defines his rivalry with Merlin as ideological, pitting the "magic of fol-de-rol," of medieval superstition, against the "magic of science," the enlightened truths that Hank brings with him from the nineteenth century (Twain 1889: 507). But as written, Twain's narrative stages this conflict as a battle of showmen, not of ideas; what they are competing for are the various live audiences, the Arthurian crowds, in front of whom the struggle essentially takes place. Behind the scenes of the novel, Hank tells us, he puts in place the Man Factories and other forms of a modern, industrialized, capitalist democracy that will, eventually, enable him to bring the light of progress to the Dark Ages. But this part of the story takes place almost entirely off the book's narrative stage. The events he describes for us are almost all public displays, in which Hank tries to keep himself in the spotlight. The schedule of these performances gives him little respite. Right after sending "Merlin home on a shutter" (p. 294) in the Valley of Holiness, for example, he is confronted by another "Rival Magician," and again faces the threat of losing his "supremacy": "this fellow would capture my following, I should be left out in the cold" (p. 307). This rival too must be upstaged, for it is only when "his reputation [is] in the mud" that Hank's can be "in the sky again" (p. 311). Such scenes help us appreciate the difference between a European fairy-tale, like one of those collected by the Brothers Grimm, and Twain's American fantasy. The fairy-tale would end when Hank saves the sun, receiving the reward Arthur offers him at that time, "the halving of my kingdom" (p. 76); but since in a democracy identity and social rank are determined by status, Hank lives anxiously ever after. When a man's place depends on creating an image, on what Hank calls "keep[ing] his trade-mark current," he has "got to be on deck and attending to business, right along" (p. 311). Hank could just as well have said "on stage," where the business is show business. In the fairy-tale you get to marry the King's daughter, but in Hank's story the love he competes for is found in the eyes of an audience.

In *Connecticut Yankee* Twain set out to reveal the evils of the *ancien régime*: what Hank calls the "older and real [reign of] Terror" (Twain 1889: 157). But seen from the vantage-point provided by the tour with Cable, what the book he wrote betrays most vividly are the anxieties of Sam Clemens's performance as Mark Twain, particularly his dependence on his audience's attention and approval. That is why the novel's deepest conflict, though neither Hank nor his creator seems to recognize it, is not ideological but psychological, or psychosocial: the almost schizophrenic split between Hank Morgan and his public alter ego Sir Boss – between who Hank is, to himself and (in the privacy of his narrative) to us, and his image, the somebody else he becomes in order to succeed with the audience of the period in which he finds himself. As we know him through his written narrative, Hank hates slavery, established religion, and the aristocracy, and is the sworn enemy of magic and superstition who watches Merlin weave his spells with pure contempt. But Hank's contempt is well disguised. The people of the sixth century know him as Sir Boss, the mighty wizard who performs "miracles" for the Church and the King by weaving spells himself.

Hank does resolve one time to speak publicly against slavery. It's a telling moment: traveling incognito with Arthur, he sees a gang of chained slaves only a few feet away from an orator making a speech about "our glorious British liberties!" (Twain 1889: 448). This "hideous contrast" is too much for Hank, who decides to displace the speaker and take his turn at center stage: "Cost what it might, I would mount that rostrum and . . ." On this one occasion when Hank is not in character as Sir Boss, the script changes drastically: before he can even finish this thought, he and the King are handcuffed to be sold as slaves themselves. The cause-and-effect relationship between challenging an audience's prejudices by speaking your own mind and losing all status is not spelled out, but this scene of Hank's abasement recalls the beginning of his adventures among the Arthurians, when he is stripped naked, thrown into prison, and condemned to die at the stake before another crowd of spectators. He saves himself in chapter 6 by striking the pose of Sir Boss – clothing his nakedness with his audience's preconceptions, putting on an act as an even mightier wizard than Merlin. If giving an audience what it wants makes Hank great, the scene of his enslavement in chapter 34 suggests how fast and far he can fall if he steps outside the popular image he has created.

Another way to express the conflict here is through the distinction between reforming and entertaining a public. Hank sees himself as a reformer, working behind the scenes to free the people from the false ideas that enslave their minds. But he enacts himself as Sir Boss, who puts on spectacular shows that rely entirely on flattering and manipulating that public's beliefs. This is another issue that the tour with Cable would have forced so close to the surface of Twain's consciousness that it is no wonder it haunts the imagination at work in *Connecticut Yankee*. As noted above, after the Christmas break Twain went back on the road determined to reclaim the show from the partner whom his need for attention had turned into his rival. The tour resumed in Pittsburgh on December 29, where he premiered the centerpiece of his redesigned program: a 45-minute reading from *Huck Finn* that he performed in two parts, allowing Cable to "sing a couple of songs in the middle" (Wecter 1947: 223). Back in his hotel room after the show Twain shared his sense of triumph with Livy: "I read the new piece . . . and it's the biggest card I've got in my whole repertoire . . . It went a-booming." The new piece, he explains to Livy, is "the episode where Tom & Huck stock Jim's cabin with reptiles, & then set him free." Since the 1920s this slapstick ending of *Huck Finn* has made commentators and readers uncomfortable, but reviews of Twain's performance in places like Cincinnati, Indianapolis, and Baltimore all mention how much the audience loved that episode, and Twain continued to exult in its effectiveness in letters home. "Tom & Huck setting Jim free from prison," he wrote Livy from Chicago, "just went with a long roll of artillery-laughter all down the line" (Wecter 1947: 230–1). Thus, by a contrast that might seem nearly as "hideous" as the medieval orator lauding British liberty in the presence of chained slaves, Twain was onstage entertaining America with his burlesque version of "the freed man's case" at the same time that around the Twins' performances eddied the controversy aroused by Cable's attack on America's failure to take "The Freedman's Case in Equity" seriously.

Twain's notebooks indicate that in the months before the tour started he considered over a dozen different episodes from *Huck Finn* for use in the program. He also asked both Cable and Pond to read proof sheets and give him their ideas about which scenes might work best. Cable's first choice was "the runaway Jim's account of his investments" (Cardwell 1953: 104) – Jim's conversation with Huck in chapter 8 about "specalat'n" in stock (livestock). Twain did use that piece in the shows, although not as often as the two runaways' conversation about "King Sollermun" and the French language, which was part of almost every performance before the break. Like the "evasion" Tom stages to "free" Jim from the Phelpses, these dialogues licence white audiences to laugh as much as they want at Jim's ignorance and haplessness from a position of racial privilege. Other passages Twain thought of using, however, included "Jim's little girl – dumb," "Huck – Ch. 33 – 'All right, I'll *go* to hell,'" and "waking Jim" (Twain 1979: 60–1; also see pp. 69, 71). Each of these scenes would have pushed white audiences outside the comfortable zone of minstrel entertainment, toward less stereotypical ways of looking at blacks. "Waking Jim" – assuming that refers to the scene in chapter 15 in which Jim eloquently upbraids Huck for trying to play a joke on him – might even have prodded contemporary audiences to re-examine the very terms by which racial difference was used *as* entertainment. These are the parts of *Huck Finn* that modern readers tend to admire the most, but Twain chose not to include any of them on the tour.

Cable's onstage performances went along with the minstrel emphasis of Twain's selections from *Huck*. If Huck and Jim's dialogues about "busted banks" and "Sollermun's harem" imitate Mr. Interlocutor questioning Tambo or Bones, several of Cable's selections from *Dr. Sevier* derive their fun from dialect routines involving Irish brogues and Creole French accents. Those songs Cable sang have a still more direct affinity with blackface minstrelsy: he introduced them as slave songs from antebellum New Orleans and sang them in black dialect. "Nigger from the ground up" is how one admirer described them (Turner 1966: 184). Yet as Twain watched Cable being interviewed about his ideas on racism and injustice, he witnessed a very different mode of public performance. From the start, Cable's career on American stages embodied the possibility of forcing an audience to confront its own preconceptions. It was in 1882 that, with the encouragement of his new friend Mark Twain, he decided to test his promise as a speaker by giving a speech at the University of Mississippi. In that speech, as Arlin Turner puts it, "Cable had gone to the platform as one with a mission" (Turner 1955b: 6), and although he had compelling reasons to seek simply to please his listeners, on this occasion his mission involved trying to change their minds. With the prospects of Southern literature as his topic, he argued that the South must abandon its sectional prejudices. The very next day he wrote Twain to say his maiden performance had been "a decided success" (Cardwell 1953: 83). Two years later Cable showed even more rhetorical courage when he gave the first version of "The Freedman's Case" in a speech to another Southern audience at the University of Alabama. Publicly this was a decided failure, condemned by all the local newspapers; that abuse, however, did not prevent Cable from revising it for publication six months later in the *Century*, an act that led to his ostracism by the white South.

    Although Southern audiences gave him no further chance to speak to them at all, Cable was popular throughout the rest of the country for many years as a reader of his fiction and a singer of slave songs. His income from these performances was crucial to him, but he never was entirely comfortable with the act itself. "I don't fancy this reading business overmuch. It looks too much like working merely to get money," he wrote his wife from the road in the fall of 1883. His popularity as a performer was most acceptable to him as a means: pleasing live audiences would "increase the sale of my books, & I do think my books ought to do good" (Cardwell 1953: 118). Twain also lectured in part to increase the sale of his books, and he too sometimes felt very ambivalent about going onstage – about what his familiar advertising slogan called "The Trouble" that began "At Eight." One night on the Twins tour, according to an anecdote in Paine's authorized biography, on the way back to the hotel after making a crowd laugh for his hour, Twain turned to his partner and said, "Oh, Cable, I am demeaning myself. I am allowing myself to be a mere buffoon" (Paine 1912: 785–6). Some scholars doubt this scene ever occurred. Paine's source for it could only have been Cable, who perhaps wanted to air some dirty laundry himself to get even with Twain for talking to that *Herald* correspondent. But Cable told the first version of this story in Twain's own presence, at his former partner's seventieth birthday party in 1905. There he identifies the scene of Twain's discomfiture as "a certain Canadian City" (Turner 1960: 127). The tour went into Canada twice, before and after the Christmas break, so we cannot say which passage from *Huck Finn* was on the program that evening – "King Sollermun" or the "evasion" section. Either way, though, the performance featured an excerpt from the novel that pandered to the racial superstitions of his audience, demeaning the book's achievement and depicting Jim as a buffoon, all in the name of entertainment. Yet despite such fits of misgiving, Twain remained dependent on the favor of his audiences. Almost 20 years after the tour with Cable, for example, he thought about publishing his own exposé of the treatment of African Americans, whose case in equity was still viciously unresolved. He even wrote a preface for this book, called "The United States of Lyncherdom." But he never published it. Perhaps he was thinking of how Cable had been ostracized when he told his publisher in 1901 that such a book would kill his sales in the South: "I shouldn't have even half a friend down there after it issued from the press" (Kaplan 1966: 365). This risk of rupture with an audience was too high a price to pay.

Ozias Pond, the "Sir Sagramore" who traveled with the Twins, kept a diary of his experiences on the tour, at the end of which he offers this valedictory appraisal of each half of the double team: Cable "has the courage of his convictions, and will make his influence felt in this land if his health is spared"; "[I] shall always love [Twain] as one most desiring *the love of his friends*" (Cardwell 1953: 54). Pond, who sincerely liked both, meant nothing invidious by this comparison. It does give us, though, one good way to tell these Twins apart.

When he totaled up the returns from the tour, Mark Twain decided that he would have done better to stay home and write another book (Webster 1946: 297). He didn't think to factor in the book for which he was already making mental notes, a book he never would have imagined if he hadn't gone on the road with Cable – *Connecticut Yankee*, the story of a traveler in time who gets trapped inside the persona he creates to impress his audience. The ending of that story brings Hank and Merlin together again one last time. Surprisingly, this time the spell Merlin casts works, giving him the last word and, literally, the last laugh at Sir Boss. It's not easy to know how to read this ending, or what it might indicate about Twain's final verdict on his competitive relationship with Cable. Ten years after the Twins of Genius had separated, Cable wrote to compliment Twain on *Joan of Arc*, and in his reply Twain let his former partner know that (in his mind at least, if not in the pages of the Boston *Herald*) he had always admired and (on the road at least, if not onstage) enjoyed his friend: "Yes *sir*! I liked you in spite of your religion; & always said to myself that a man that could be good & kindly with that kind of a load on him was entitled to homage – & I *paid* it. And I have always said, & still maintain, that as a railroad-comrade you were perfect" (Cardwell 1953: 111).

For his part, Cable came away from the tour with "a lifetime's affection for Mark Twain," telling the crowd at Twain's seventieth birthday dinner that he always "count[ed] that experience in the years 1884 and 1885 as one of the most notable in my life" (Turner 1960: 126). In many respects that winter traveling the nation with a new novel, a famous partner, and the fame and sense of moral purpose provided by his "Freeman's" essay was the high point of Cable's career. For the next five years he continued courageously to address the country's failure to do the right thing in the case of its African American citizens, in occasional speeches and in essays collected in *The Silent South* (1885) and *The Negro Question* (1890). But as Cable's biographers are forced to note, after 1885 Cable was slowly defeated by mounting resistance and then indifference to this cause. The admirers and letters that came to the hotels he stayed in while traveling with Twain gave him a false sense of what it would require to make his influence felt on the country's discriminatory policies. It was not health that Cable lacked, but *support*. During the decade that led up to the Supreme Court's decision in *Plessy* v. *Ferguson* legitimizing the Jim Crow system, Cable's was just about the only white voice raised in protest. As Edmund Wilson puts it, "the slow strangulation of Cable as an artist and a serious writer is surely one of the most gruesome episodes in American literary history" (Wilson 1966: 579). Cable continued publishing books until 1918, but after 1892 he abandoned the quest for black rights, and his fiction became increasingly mannered. Wilson correctly lays most of the blame for the erosion of Cable's powers at the feet of the Southern newspapers, which were anything but silent in their unanimous rejection of his ideas, and the Northern publishers who too often rejected Cable's fiction when it tried to treat contemporary social problems. But it wouldn't be amiss to include Mark Twain among the culprits, for his failure to speak out on Cable's behalf, even to defend Cable against the *Herald*'s malicious attacks, although Cable asked him to, and although Southern papers, happy to use anything that would discredit the renegade who had dared to question Southern racial prejudices and practices, "widely reprinted" the *Herald*'s smears (Rubin 1969: 171). The homage Twain pays in that 1895 letter to Cable should have been paid a decade earlier, and in public.

And something more is at stake here than (to quote what Jim says so memorably to Huck) a friend putting dirt on the head of a friend. Currently one of the most fashionable ways to read the "evasion" chapters of *Huck Finn* is "as a satirical indictment of the virtual re-enslavement of free blacks in the South during the 1880s" (Fishkin 1997: 97). According to this "growing consensus about the meaning of the last portion of *Huckleberry Finn*" (p. 197), the "episode where Tom & Huck stock Jim's cabin with reptiles, & then set him free," the piece that set off "long rolls of artillery-laughter" in the white audiences who came to see the Twins, is actually making the same point as Cable's "Freedman's" essay. It's not hard to understand why this interpretation is so attractive at this moment, when *Huck Finn* is under attack from civil rights groups who want it banned from the schools as racist. At its best *Huck Finn* is a subtle, ironic, and subversive analysis of American racism; but, like Hank's impersonation of a mighty wizard, Twain's performance of the novel, both onstage and on the page, made it very difficult for his audience to suspect any attack on their prejudices. To me, the most important lesson we can learn from his relationship with Cable is how much he needed the undivided, unconflicted attention of the public for whom he wrote the novel. During and after the tour there were plenty of occasions for Twain to say something about his partner's indictment of the re-enslavement of blacks under segregation, or at least to defend his partner when he was so harshly attacked for his stand against discrimination. What we hear instead is the delighted laughter of those audiences listening to him perform the novel's ending. That's where our attempts to understand what *Huck Finn* and "Mark Twain" meant should start.

NOTES

1 This phrase appears in Cable's speech at the Memorial Ceremonies for Mark Twain (1910). This speech, and most of the primary sources cited in my essay, are available online at my website, *Mark Twain in his Times: An Electronic Archive* (http://etext.lib.virginia.edu/railton). Also to be found here is an extensive collection of materials relating to the "Twins

of Genius" lecture tour, including over 50 newspaper reviews of Twain's and Cable's performances.

2 The two *Herald* articles were published May 7 and May 10, 1885; Cable's letters in reply were written May 12 and May 14. My account of this affair follows Cardwell (1952), Turner (1955a), Fatout (1969), and Rubin (1969).

REFERENCES AND FURTHER READING

Bikle, Lucy Leffingwell Cable (1928). *George W. Cable: His Life and Letters*. New York: Scribner.

Cable, George W. (1885). *The Silent South*. New York: Scribner.

Cable, George W. (1889). *The Negro Question*. New York: Scribner.

Cable, George W. (1910). "Eulogy." In *Memorial Ceremonies for Mark Twain*. New York: American Academy of Arts and Sciences.

Cardwell, Guy A. (1952). "Mark Twain's 'Row' with George Cable." *Modern Language Quarterly* 13, 363–71.

Cardwell, Guy A. (1953). *Twins of Genius*. Lansing: Michigan State College Press.

Fatout, Paul (1969). *Mark Twain on the Lecture Circuit*. Carbondale: Southern Illinois University Press. (First publ. 1960.)

Fishkin, Shelley Fisher (1997). *Lighting Out for the Territory: Reflections on Mark Twain and American Culture*. New York: Oxford University Press.

Kaplan, Justin (1966). *Mr. Clemens and Mark Twain: A Biography*. New York: Simon & Schuster.

Lorch, Fred W. (1966). "Cable and his Reading Tour with Mark Twain in 1884–1885." *American Literature* 23, 471–86.

Lorch, Fred W. (1968). *The Trouble Begins at Eight: Mark Twain's Lecture Tours*. Ames: Iowa State University Press.

Paine, Albert Bigelow (1912). *Mark Twain: A Biography. The Personal and Literary Life of Samuel Langhorne Clemens*, 3 vols. New York and London: Harper & Bros.

Pond, James B. (1900). *Eccentricities of Genius*. New York: Dillingham.

Rubin, Louis D., Jr. (1969). *George W. Cable: The Life and Times of a Southern Heretic*. New York: Pegasus.

Smith, Henry Nash (1979). "Introduction." In Mark Twain, *A Connecticut Yankee in King Arthur's Court*, ed. Bernard L. Stein. Berkeley: University of California Press.

Turner, Arlin (1955a). "Mark Twain, Cable, and 'A Professional Newspaper Liar.'" *Tulane Studies in English* 5, 5–27.

Turner, Arlin (1955b). "George W. Cable's Revolt against Literary Sectionalism." *New England Quarterly* 28, 18–33.

Turner, Arlin (1960). *Mark Twain and George Washington Cable: The Record of a Literary Friendship*. Lansing: Michigan State University Press.

Turner, Arlin (1966). *George W. Cable: A Biography*. Baton Rouge: Louisiana State University Press.

Twain, Mark (1966). *The Autobiography of Mark Twain*, ed. Charles Neider. New York: Harper Perennial. (First publ. 1959.)

Twain, Mark (1979). *Mark Twain's Notebooks and Journals*, vol. 3: *1883–1891*, ed. Robert Pack Browning, Michael B. Frank, and Lin Salamo. Berkeley: University of California Press.

Twain, Mark, and Howells, William Dean (1968). *Selected Mark Twain–Howells Letters*, ed. Frederick Anderson, William M. Gibson, and Henry Nash Smith. New York: Atheneum.

Webster, Samuel Charles (1946). *Mark Twain, Business Man*. Boston: Little, Brown.

Wecter, Dixon (1947). *The Love Letters of Mark Twain*. New York: Harper & Bros.

Wilson, Edmund (1966). *Patriotic Gore: Studies in the Literature of the American Civil War*. New York: Oxford University Press. (First publ. 1962.)

13

Mark Twain, William Dean Howells, and Realism

Peter Messent

Brander Matthews reviewed *Adventures of Huckleberry Finn* enthusiastically in 1886. He remarked that "There is scarcely a character . . . who does not impress the reader at once as true to life . . . Mr. Clemens draws from life, and yet lifts his work from the domain of the photograph to the region of art" (Matthews 1892: 160–1). He particularly praised "the skill with which the character of Huck Finn is maintained":

> We see everything through his eyes – and they are his eyes, and not a pair of Mark Twain's spectacles. And the comments on what he sees are his comments . . . not speeches put into his mouth by the author. One of the most artistic things in the book . . . is the sober self-restraint with which Mr. Clemens lets Huck Finn set down, without any comment at all, scenes which would have afforded the ordinary writer matter for endless moral and political and sociological disquisition. (pp. 153–4)

William Dean Howells is the writer most closely identified with the development of American realism in the 1880s and early 1890s. Critics who have explored the Twain–Howells connection have rightly noticed "the absence of this term from Twain's [own] critical vocabulary," an absence that appears to have "the force of a deliberate avoidance" given the campaign then being waged by his "closest literary friend" (Bell 1993: 45). They have also identified the awkwardness of the fit between Twain's fiction and Howells's realist theory, noting that Twain's writings paradoxically "undermined realism even while serving to define it" (Daugherty 1996: 15). I explore such paradoxes as I proceed. But Matthews's response to *Huckleberry Finn* clearly suggests a relationship between Howells's theory and Twain's fictional practice, and also the extent to which Howells's thinking permeated the critical assumptions of his contemporaries.

For Matthews echoes Howells's own praise for (other) realist texts. Most obviously we are reminded of the latter's dislike of authorial intrusions, such as those of a Trollope "so warped from a wholesome ideal as . . . to stand about in his scene, talking it over with his hands in his pockets, interrupting the action, and spoiling the illusion in which alone the truth of art resides" (Howells 1973: 170). The distinction Matthews makes between photography and art in Twain parallels that Howells draws between science and art in Zola (and between "mapping" and "picturing" elsewhere): "[Zola] fancied himself working like a scientist who has collected a vast number of specimens . . . But the fact is, he was always working like an artist, [building up] every sugges- tion of experience and observation . . . into a structure of fiction" (p. 393).[1]

Matthews praises the way Twain lets us "see [Huck] from the inside" (Matthews 1892: 155), and his use of Huck's first-person voice: "the comments of an ignorant, superstitious, sharp, healthy boy" (p. 153). He does not then make the further step we might expect and explicitly comment on the use of the vernacular. It was Howells himself who would associate "the use of dialect" with "the impulse to get the whole of American life into our fiction" (Howells 1973: 233), and would celebrate its value in one of his best-known assertions of realist tenets. Though Howells is generalizing here, he might have been writing with *Huckleberry Finn* in mind:

> But let fiction cease to lie about life; let it portray men and women as they are, actu- ated by the motives and the passions in the measure we all know; let it leave off paint- ing dolls and working them by springs and wires . . . ; let it speak the dialect, the language that most Americans know – the language of unaffected people everywhere. (Howells 1959: 51)[2]

Twain, Realism, and the Literary Context

Twain's best-known novel can, then, certainly be read in a realist context. More gen- erally, too, it would seem perverse not to class Twain in the ranks of American real- ists. He "took up arms in the ongoing battle between romance and realism, joining passionately – indeed good-humoredly – in what . . . [his] friend and sponsor, William Dean Howells, called 'banging the babes of romance about'" (Krauth 2003: 23). "Romance" here had a wide range of connotations, conflating high cultural form (that practiced by a previous generation of American writers), genteel sentimentalism, and sensationalist popular fiction. Twain attacks the sentimental from the start of his career, and quite independently of Howells.[3] That he did so indicates the extent and range of the realist impulse during the period. As David Shi says,

> A realistic outlook seeped into every corner and crevice of intellectual and artistic life during the second half of the nineteenth century . . . Realists of all sorts . . . muscled their way onto center stage of American culture and brusquely pushed aside the genteel timidities, romantic excesses, and transcendental idealism then governing affairs of the mind. (Shi 1995: 3)[4]

As Twain's career progressed and his close friendship with Howells developed, he could hardly have avoided being influenced in some way by the latter's realist campaign.[5] So, when Twain wrote about literature he judged it according to the same stylistic criteria as Howells: the need for an "accurate, unromanticized observation of life and nature . . . [an] insistence on precise description, authentic action and dialogue" (Sundquist 1998: 502).[6] Twain's attacks on Cooper are notorious, and Edwin Cady calls "Fenimore Cooper's Literary Offences" "a major critique in the mode of negative realism" (see Howells 1973: 231). Less well known are "A Cure for the Blues" and "The Curious Book Complete," published as twinned texts in *Merry Tales*. Twain here anticipates the essays on Cooper, and establishes the aesthetic and representational failures of the genteel romance as his critical target.

The Enemy Conquered; or, Love Triumphant ("The Curious Book Complete") is a direct reprinting of a short 1845 pamphlet romance by S. Watson Royston – though Twain changes the authorial name to G. Ragsdale McClintock. Twain had first come across the text in 1884 when George Washington Cable was recovering from illness at his home, and both men were much tickled by the sentimental and inflated nature of its language and the resulting unintentional humor. "A Cure for the Blues," placed immediately before this reprinting, is Twain's critical assault on the story, and shows him taking considerable delight in targeting its high-flown rhetoric, illogical plotting, and generic determinants. He focuses especially on the author's style, which "nobody can imitate . . . not even an idiot" (Twain 1892a: 83): the "jingling jumble of fine words [that] seemed to mean something; but it is useless . . . to try to divine what it was" (p. 90). The alliterative simile "like the topmost topaz of an ancient tower" has, he says, not "a ray of sense in it, or meaning to it" (p. 80). Twain describes the names of McClintock's fictional characters as ones which "fantastically fit his lunatics" (p. 83), and draws particular attention to that of the heroine, Ambulinia Valeer, which "can hardly be matched in fiction" (p. 89). He pillories, too, the inconsistencies and absurdities of the plot. So when Elfonzo and Ambulinia, the two lovers, hide among the members of the orchestra to avoid being seen together at a village show, Twain writes: "This does not seem to be good art . . . [O]ne cannot conceal a girl in an orchestra without everybody taking notice of it" (p. 99).

Underpinning and motivating this essay, as well as the later, more vehement attacks on Cooper, is Twain's belief in a realist aesthetic. Howells described realism's aim as "to picture the daily life in the most exact terms possible" (Trachtenberg 1982: 186), and Henry James praised Howells's own writing for its "art of imparting a palpitating interest to common things and unheroic lives," adding that "truth of representation . . . can be achieved only so long as it is in our power to test and measure it" (Howells 1965: ix). Twain critiques *The Enemy Conquered* for its complete divergence from just such principles:

> The reader must not imagine he is to find in it . . . purity of style . . . , truth to nature, clearness of statement, humanly possible situations, humanly possible people, fluent narrative, connected sequence of events – . . . or logic, or sense. No; the rich, deep, beguiling charm of the book lies in the total and miraculous *absence* from it of all these qualities. (Twain 1892a: 78)

Twain's literary principles and practices, then, certainly share a number of key elements with the larger realist movement. And critics who have written about his major novels have regularly consigned them to this category. Brook Thomas calls Twain "one of the most important practitioners of realism" (Thomas 1997: 196), speaks of *Huckleberry Finn* as the work that established him as a realist (p. 5), and praises his "active presentation of reality" (Thomas's word "active" has a particular force here) in *Pudd'nhead Wilson* (p. 229). Richard Brodhead calls *Huckleberry Finn* one of the "classic texts" of American realism (Brodhead 1998: 474). Michael Davitt Bell defines Hank Morgan, in *A Connecticut Yankee*, as "a fictional embodiment of the 'realist'" (Bell 1993: 58) – though Eric Sundquist complicates things by describing the same novel as a "visionary wor[k] of nineteenth-century realism" (Sundquist 1998: 512).

As the ambiguous nature of the last of these comments suggests, the verdict is far from unanimous. Sarah Daugherty, taking her lead from James Cox and Alfred Habegger, says that Twain is "no realist" (Daugherty 1996: 12). Phillip Barrish, writing about Howells's major protagonists, speaks of "the clear eyedness that they bring to hard realities" (Barrish 2001: 39), such as the urban poverty and the violence of the streetcar strike in *A Hazard of New Fortunes*. This reminds us that none of the three novels by Twain mentioned in the previous paragraph offers any direct representation of contemporary America and its social problems – a vital component in Howells's own realist art. *A Connecticut Yankee* is a fantasy. Everyday reality is turned upside down, within its pages, by the introduction of another and obviously *unreal* scenario: an alternative and different world to set against Hank Morgan's (and Twain's) everyday America. *Pudd'nhead Wilson* – particularly if considered with its twin text, *Those Extraordinary Twins* – veers from farce to tragedy and, with its flattened characters and strongly determining circumstances, seems as close to allegory as to any other mode.

Critics are startlingly divided as to Twain's relation to realism, and make all kinds of twists and turns as they look to position him. David Shi calls him "a truant member" of the "realistic 'school'," "an idiosyncratic fellow traveler to his friends among the professing realists" (Shi 1995: 107). Lee Clark Mitchell seems to lose his way as he refers to literary careers (Twain's among them) that "resist classification" when they had "otherwise seemed straightforwardly realist" (Mitchell 1998: 531). Things do not get much easier when we turn to Twain experts who write explicitly on the Howells–Twain connection. Richard Lowry says that Howells wielded a "profound influence" on Twain. Acknowledging their significant differences, he nonetheless sees Howells using his critical writings about Twain to identify him, in a "remarkable" way, with his own agenda. Thus he manages to make "Twain *his*, a realist who, despite – indeed, perhaps because of – his mass appeal, wielded a moral authority over the democratic masses who nourished his vision" (Lowry 1996: 46). Louis J. Budd says just the opposite. He quotes passages from Howells's 1910 memoir, *My Mark Twain*, which refer to its eponymous subject as "at heart . . . romantic" and working in an "essentially histrionic" mode. Budd then continues: "Howells unavoidably realized how far Twain's fiction differed from, and for some readers, worked against the mode of novels he was developing." He does, though, also quote Howells's response to *Tom Sawyer* as "realistic in the highest degree . . . [giving] incomparably the best picture of life in that region as yet known to fiction."[7]

The fissure that opens up here may have something to do with the fact that in 1910 Howells was re-evaluating his earlier critical opinions; but there is more to it than this. For there are ways of agreeing with both judgments. Even as realism was being used as a rallying cry for postbellum writers and artists it remained a somewhat indeterminate and elastic concept, and one that came to contain a number of different and sometimes incompatible meanings (aesthetic, ethical, social, and ideological). Amy Kaplan indicates something of this when she refers to realism as "an anxious and contradictory mode" (Kaplan 1988: 9). Realism, she suggests (including even Howells's own), "can be examined as a multifaceted and unfinished debate re-enacted in the arena of each novel and essay . . . rather than as a monolithic and fully formed theory" (p. 15).[8]

As I stir these already muddied waters, one further issue needs raising: the relationship of realism to the literary movements from which it supposedly departs. There are always problems in periodizing literature and imposing generic categories upon it. Richard Brodhead usefully reminds us "how illusory the separation is that we erect between pre-Civil War and postwar American authors" (Brodhead 1986: 86). He carefully charts how Howells was powerfully influenced by Hawthorne, his apparent polar (Romantic) opposite, who was "strongly present to Howells in the making of his novels" (p. 83). Indeed, he argues that Howells's whole realist project (of "trying to formulate a contemporary social ethic and to enforce its reign within his culture") is in part undermined by a skepticism that pervades the fictions he writes. "This skepticism," Brodhead concludes, "is Hawthorne's legacy to Howells" (p. 103).

Taking Twain as his subject, Leland Krauth similarly illustrates how, despite the biting quality of his attacks on "the romantic in its various forms" (Krauth 2003: 24), Twain was – and remained – deeply indebted to sentimentalism. The use of the "sentimental in order to drive home a moral point," he rightly argues, is "a fundamental gesture in his writing" (p. 38). It is Twain's "shared . . . outlook" with an earlier generation of "sentimentalists" that enables Krauth then to describe *Huckleberry Finn* as "often as sentimental as it is realistic" (pp. 37–8).[9] Philip Fisher lists the distinguishing traits of the Sentimental Novel (his capitalization), at its most influential as a cultural form in the years before 1860, and epitomized by Stowe's *Uncle Tom's Cabin*:

> The extended central scenes of dying and deathbeds, mourning and loss, the rhetorical treatment of the central theme of suffering, the creation of the prisoner as the central character, the themes of imprisonment, the violation of selfhood, power relations in the intimate and familiar territory, freedom, the centrality of the family, and the definition of the power of literary representation in terms of tears. (Fisher 1986: 93)

To read this account of the "sentimental procedure" is to realize the affinities between Twain and this branch of his literary predecessors. There is further work to be done on the way he adapts, subverts, and departs from such mechanisms. But Twain is certainly highly aware of this arsenal of sentimental effects and uses them – sometimes with ironic intent, sometimes (in Emily Dickinson's word) "aslant," but sometimes in all seriousness – throughout his writing career. Fisher himself recognizes this, speaking of Twain as one of a series of writers whose "works . . . preserved the core of sentimental technique even in the process of adapting it to later conditions or obscuring it beneath a veil of toughness, elegance, or self-irony" (pp. 93–4).

The Case of *Huckleberry Finn*

All I have just said threatens, at first glance, to reduce the term "realism" to meaninglessness. And a number of recent critics have chosen to accept that implication, either avoiding the term completely or bypassing some of the generic distinctions (between realism and naturalism, for example) previously current. Realism is, however, still a useful and a valid generic category. I proceed to investigate some of its various connotations as I explore the connections, and the differences, between Twain and Howells.

Before I go further, but as a step in that direction, I briefly return to *Huckleberry Finn* to show how it both fits and fails to fit the realist category, depending on the particular criteria applied. Realism as an aesthetic makes a claim to transparency, appearing to offer a clear window outward onto the solid world it represents. June Howard describes this in terms of a "privileged relationship to [the] assumed extratextual world, invoking an ability to embody 'reality' . . . as constitutive of the genre itself" (Howard 1985: 11–12). Thus Twain uses Huck, his first-person narrator, to provide a seemingly direct depiction of the immediate world through which he moves.

Twain, indeed, out-realists Howells in his use of this first person-vernacular voice. Phillip Barrish analyses a complicated dynamic in *The Rise of Silas Lapham* by which the crude tastes and values of Lapham and his daughter Irene are subordinated to the more cultivated taste of Tom and Penelope. But that cultivated taste is itself defined by its ability to appreciate (from a position of cultural superiority) Lapham's and Irene's "vernacular" qualities. In other words, for Howells, an "alignment *with* the simple and the natural always precludes any preferential taste *for* the simple or natural" (Barrish 2001: 29). And it is the latter, not the former, which he automatically privileges. Such a discrepancy is considerably diminished in Twain's more genuinely democratic art.[10] Twain relies on Huck's voice to take us "transparently" through to a solidly framed historical context, the small-town antebellum Old Southwest and river life on the Mississippi. It is this regional and historical reality we are asked to take for granted, together with the range of social practices, racial distinctions, and cultural codes that compose it. Such an assumption, and the details that reinforce it, provide the realistic glue holding the whole novel in place.

One (other) definition of realism is in social and ethical terms, focusing on the relationship between the human subject and his or her surrounding environment, and the moral potential of that subject. At this time (the 1880s), Romantic beliefs in the authority and autonomy of the sovereign self were no longer easily tenable. Realist texts accordingly looked to firmly embed their protagonists in a larger social context, and focused on such areas as dress, manners, occupations, community practices, and connections as ways of doing this. The closeness of the connection between the individual and the material details and social practices of everyday life lay at the very core of the genre (when defined within this framework). Despite the increasing press of environment on character in the post-Civil War American world, realist authors assumed the essential wholeness and coherence of the human subject. Indeed, the genre is commonly described in terms of the *balance* it represents between the individual and his or her social world, and the ability of that individual to act as a free moral agent despite the increasing complications and determining networks of the larger world. Thus Lee Clark Mitchell loosely groups Twain, James, and Howells as realists, identifying a shared key concern in the fact that "They all presented characters as "subjective selves" who possessed clear capacities for constraint and responsibility . . . Realist authors enforced a moral perspective on narrative action, a perspective involving the same considerations of intention and responsibility we habitually project on each other (and onto fictional characters as well)" (Mitchell 1989: xii).

Huckleberry Finn works as a realist text according to such criteria. Huck can be seen as a unified subject, a sympathetic and freely speaking – in the sense, at any rate, that he speaks the text – young boy, making his way through a difficult world but responding to it with a clear-seeing and pragmatic eye. The fabric of the antebellum Southwestern world provides the backdrop against which Huck's negotiations with the established social order occur. Huck's decision to choose hell rather than allow Jim back into Miss Watson's hands is for many critics the climax of the book, and can be read – in realist terms – as an act of individual moral responsibility that counters the determining tendencies of the larger social environment. This reading of the novel, when taken alongside the comments I make on Brander Matthews's review in my opening section, clearly explains why so many commentators have read the novel as a realist text.

But there are other ways of approaching the book that call this reading into question. If we focus on plot rather than point of view, for example, Twain's one-time idea of having Huck visit a circus and then escape on an elephant might suggest that any reading of the book in terms of Howells's "fidelity to experience and probability of motive" may be tricky. Such random incidents as the boarding of the *Walter Scott*, the hiding of gold in Peter Wilks's coffin, and the shenanigans of the "evasion" routine all amount – especially when combined with the book's insistent strain of burlesque – to a failure to conform to realist criteria. At another level, the possibility of escaping social determinants in independent moral action (Huck's decision) is deeply undermined by Miss Watson's prior actions (Jim has already, in fact, been freed), by the negative quality of Huck's choice, and by his consequent position as Tom Sawyer's minion.[11] The very idea of the intending and coherent subject is, moreover, questioned by the extent to which Huck's own language and thought are inevitable products of his larger society, and by the textual play on disguise and identity slippage which necessarily subverts any notion of fixed selfhood. Finally, approaching the text from a different – and contradictory – perspective, the mythic and symbolic structures that permeate the novel, and its debt to a Romantic tradition of unfettered individualism, also work against its classification as realist. Jane Tompkins pinpoints the way in which the novel, in this way too, defies any easy categorization:

> *Adventures of Huckleberry Finn* has for a long time stood as a benchmark of American literary realism, praised for its brilliant use of local dialects and its faithfulness to the texture of ordinary life. Twain himself is famous for his scoffing attacks on the escapism of sentimental and romantic fiction. But . . . the events of *Huckleberry Finn* enact a dream of freedom and autonomy that goes beyond the bounds of the wildest romance. (Tompkins 1985: 175)

I am happy here, though, to revert to my earlier position. Realism is not a coherent and unified genre. Some aspects of Twain's novel undoubtedly fit its criteria, while others do not. Tensions and ambiguities in the novel stretch it in a number of generic directions. Daniel Borus usefully sums up such instabilities in his more general comment:

> The realists . . . violated their theoretical premises as often as they observed them. Fidelity to everyday life and to probability of motive were easier to theorize about than to realize. The classic texts of American realism boast more than their share of intruding narrators, improbabilities and coincidences, and cataclysmic or heightened moments of life deployed as plot devices. In addition to these textual qualities often associated with romanticism, realism also pointed ahead to modernism with the use of subjective narration, a stress on the fragmented self, and forays into symbolism and impressionism, all of which contradicted the realist dictum of an anchored reality. (Borus 1989: 17)

Realist Writing, Literature, and the Marketplace

Recent studies of realism have introduced another factor into an already complicated field by focusing on the changing relationship between literature and the marketplace in the period, and the stresses and accommodations that resulted. Howells and Twain both, in their different ways, adjusted to market demands and sought to define their cultural roles accordingly. As they did so, similarities, but also some highly significant differences, appeared between them.

Richard Lowry introduces his valuable discussion of Twain and Howells by situating them in the context of the complicated relationship between culture and capital prevailing at the time (Lowry 1996: 4–5). Most commentators on the period stress the extraordinary rapidity of the modernization process, "the bewildering social transformations of industrial capitalism" (Kaplan 1988: 6) and its related effects. Realist writers saw one of their main tasks to be the use of modern scientific techniques, with their "stress on observation and exactness," to produce "a living map of the new society" (Borus 1989: 9 and 19). One of a whole new range of experts – sociologists, city planners, business managers and the like – "the literary novelist . . . emerged . . . as an expert in a field of knowledge described loosely as 'real life,' which he . . . mapped with assiduous care both to material and to ideological detail" (Lowry 1996: 7).

Gender role was a significant issue in this self-conception. Unlike an earlier generation of American writers, the realist saw his role in terms of masculine authority, central rather than marginal to the business of the nation. Thus Brodhead compares Howells with Hawthorne. "In sharp contrast with early Hawthorne, 'for a good many years, the obscurest man of letters in America,' Howells became a somebody" when he became an editor for the *Atlantic Monthly* in 1866 (Brodhead 1986: 87). This recognized "authority in the literary sphere" was, though, just a prelude to the part he then figured for himself in the larger social and cultural whole.

The relationship between the realist writer and business took another, and more immediate, form. Such factors as the greater organization of markets and distribution systems, the more efficient production and more attractive presentation of books, and – most especially – the increasing size of the reading public and developing needs of a new "mobile society" led to what Daniel Borus calls the rise of a "literature industry" by 1900 (Borus 1989: 38). As book markets grew, so fiction especially flourished, and "the boundaries that separated literature from business, nineteenth-century tastes from twentieth-century practices" started to collapse (Rohrbach 2002: 76). Writers measured their success in terms of financial profit. So Howells, acutely aware of the literary market and its demands, kept careful check on the revenue his various literary activities brought in (see Rohrbach 2002). Twain "pursued the business of authorship" with, if anything, even more enthusiasm (Lowry 1996: 46). His writing habits, when they needed to be, were rigorously disciplined, and when in "business" mode he was – quite literally – aware of the worth of every word he wrote. His professionalism was "essential to his sense of masculinity," as was the rhetoric he used: that of "the literary entrepreneur who cornered markets and waged military marketing campaigns" (p. 85).

Twain wrote for the *Atlantic* magazine under Howells's editorship, largely as a result of his friend's encouragement. But the two men differed sharply in the type of work they produced and in their readership. It is here that Howells's particular conception of the relation between the realist writer and a newly available and potentially vast audience (see Corkin 1996: 25) ran into problems. Howells believed in "the authority and legitimacy of serious fiction as a serious enterprise" and in the beneficial social effects thereby produced (Trachtenberg 1982: 193). The realist novel, mapping this new society, had – in his view – a moral and educative purpose, providing its readers with a secular "guide to life in the late nineteenth century" (Borus 1989: 113):

> In a modern society afflicted by isolation and atomization, the mass-circulated novel held out the promise of a new common currency that would promote a new unity . . .
> The goal of this new discourse was to provoke in readers a new sense of their common-

ality both as readers and as citizens and to stimulate an active participation in social life. (pp. 172, 133)

There were a number of problems with this agenda that became increasingly obvious as time passed. These had to do both with the nature of Howells's audience and with the larger social and historical context he engaged. The issues are interrelated but at this point I focus on the former. The serious cultural product Howells wanted to sell (fiction as a guide to life) was *not* one that suited a heterogeneous mass market, and he realized this. His "cultural program to make [one] type of literature preeminent" was mainly directed at the middle and upper classes (Corkin 1996: 24–5). For, like it or not (and he did not), Howells knew that "the common people do not hear [the man of letters] gladly or hear him at all" (Howells 1959: 308). The American reading public was hugely fragmented, and the "common people" tended to read not serious fiction but rather dime novels, cheap magazines, and sentimental and sensationalist fictions. Many of his target audience, too, shared a taste for such "adventure and romance" (Corkin 1996: 26). Howells waged literary war against such "injurious" stuff, condemning it as "the emptiest dissipation," a form of "opium-eating," that "drugged the brain and [left] the reader 'weaker and crazier for the debauch'" (Trachtenberg 1982: 199). But the battle was lost almost before it began, for, as Borus puts it: "Invariably the novels that flooded the market were standardized, deficient in craftsmanship, and lacking in serious purpose. As realists surveyed the results of the literary marketplace, they saw an incessant demand for instant gratification rather than enlightenment, and a fiction that justified itself as a relief from boredom" (1989: 57–8).

Howells's vehement attacks on such popular forms were a measure of his own "sense of calamity" that his own version of literary taste and function was not widely shared (Corkin 1996: 26). Literary art, for him, had the status of "special communication." For too many of his intended readers, it was mere "merchandise" (Borus 1989: 58). His sense of a realist mission, and the success of his own central cultural role in pursuing it, consequently fell further and further apart as the century advanced.

It might seem difficult to connect this version of literature with Mark Twain, except to recognize the two men's shared sense of professionalism in the literary marketplace. But Twain did share aspects of Howells's thinking. In the 1880s Howells's battle against the harmful nature of sentimental and dime fiction was still being strongly waged, and Twain's "A Curious Experience" (1881) endorsed much the same message about poor reading habits. For the story effectively dramatizes the "deepest, most unsettling fears" of Howells and other "respectable critics": "that for the young readers of such sensational and fantastic fiction, the line between fiction and real life might indeed be entirely obliterated" (Trachtenberg 1982: 197).

"A Curious Experience" is a lengthy narrative that works as a type of hoax. The story concerns young Robert Wicklow, a drummer boy who enlists on the Union side at Fort Trumbull, Connecticut, during the Civil War. His mysterious activities and the letters he writes eventually lead his commanding officer – the main teller of this tale – to judge him a Confederate spy. The lives both of the Fort and of the local community are disrupted as this occurs. Finally, though, this narrative of mystery, betrayal, and rebellion turns out to lack all substance, to be a product of Wicklow's invention alone:

> It turned out that [the boy] was a ravenous devourer of dime novels and sensation-story papers – therefore, dark mysteries and gaudy heroisms were just in his line. Then he had read newspaper reports of the stealthy goings and comings of rebel spies in our midst, and of their lurid purposes . . . till his imagination was all aflame on that subject . . . Ah, he lived in a gorgeous, mysterious, romantic world during those few stirring days, and I think it was *real* to him, and that he enjoyed it clear down to the bottom of his heart. (Twain 1892a: 139, 141)

The only thing to fear, then, has been a boy's imagination and his bad reading practices.

That Twain seems here directly to dramatize Howells's warnings about "sensation-story" fiction may not be surprising, given the closeness of their friendship. His critique is, moreover, in line with repeated attacks throughout his work, from a realist perspective, on fraudulent sentimentality and romance. Nonetheless, there is something strange about one of America's best-known humorists criticizing popular forms of entertainment, and their injurious appeal.[12] I will return to this reflection shortly.

"About Play-Acting" (1898), a much later Twain essay, is also relevant here. In this piece, Twain indicates his acceptance of Howells's view that the writer has a "higher function" than that of mere entertainer (Borus 1989: 88), and that serious fiction could act as an educative tool, with "a certain kind of authority in and over culture" (Lowry 1996: 45). Indeed, many of Twain's *non-fictional* pieces were undoubtedly spurred by the same belief. Neither the form nor the setting of the "remarkable" Austrian play Twain has seen in Vienna (*The Master of Palmyra* by Adolf von Wilbrandt) is "realistic" in a Howellsian sense – it does not comply with his "vigorous insistence that realism directly confront the moral and material problems of society" (Sundquist 1998: 507). But its main theme certainly conformed to Twain's own developing view of reality, showing "what a silly, poor thing human life is; how childish its ambitions, how ridiculous its pomps, how trivial its dignities . . . how wearisome and monotonous its repetition of its stupid history through the ages" (Twain 1900: 242–3). As I awkwardly use the words "realistic" and "reality" in different ways, we catch something both of the ambiguities and instabilities surrounding the term and of the reason for Howells's own growing dissatisfaction with aspects of his original limited premise.

It is not, though, only the metaphysics of von Wilbrandt's play that interested Twain. For he used his essay to comment generally on a lack of seriousness in the American theater, and criticized its audience accordingly:

> You are trying to make yourself believe that life is a comedy, that its sole business is fun . . . . America . . . neglect[s] what is possibly the most effective of all the . . . disseminators of high literary taste and lofty emotion – the tragic stage. To leave that pow-

erful agency out is to haul the culture-wagon with a crippled team . . . What *has* come over us English-speaking people? . . . Comedy keeps the heart sweet; but we all know that there is wholesome refreshment for both mind and heart in an occasional climb among the pomps of the intellectual snow-summits built by Shakespeare and those others. Do I seem to be preaching? It is out of my line: I only do it because the rest of the clergy seem to be on vacation. (Twain 1900: 248–51)

This plea for "high literary taste and lofty emotion" and its benefits for a wide audience – who at present see the theater (and analogously the novel) as a source only of "fun" – accords more or less exactly with Howells's conception of the role and function of a serious, yet widely influential, art.

Twain here does seem to be considerably influenced by Howells's realist program. But at this point we should remember his very different place in that literary market for which both men wrote. Twain was a humorist whose appeal included the mass audience that had so little time for Howells and his reservations about fiction that "aims merely to entertain" (Howells 1959: 48). Twain, as is well known, had a highly ambiguous attitude to his own comic art. He remarked on his first book, *The Jumping Frog of Calaveras County, and Other Sketches*, that "I don't know that it would instruct youth much, but it would make them laugh" (Twain 1979: 543). But elsewhere, and often, he would insist on exactly that "preaching" he half-mocks above: the "deep seriousness" which he saw as "an absolutely essential part of any real humorist's native equipment" (Krauth 1999: 6). His work veered from playful relativism to the straightforwardly ludicrous to the clearly serious and moralistic, sometimes containing all these elements within a single text. Famously, he wrote to Andrew Lang around 1890 that he wrote not "to help cultivate the cultivated classes [but] always hunted for bigger game, the masses . . . the Belly and the Members . . . [T]he cultured classes . . . could go to the theatre and the opera, they had no use for me and the melodeon."[13] In his various moves between "genteel culture" and populist entertainment, instruction and amusement, a reliance on and the burlesque of popular forms, there lie a series of persistent and irreconcilable tensions at the root of Twain's artistic identity.

Twain, then, sympathized to some degree with Howells's notion of realism as a cultural force, and endorsed it in some of his work. But his own comic art was multidimensional in kind, and could not be contained by Howells's narrow definitions. Twain had no need to reconcile his contradictory feelings about the relationship of art to the mass market. Nor, as a corollary, did he need to commit himself to a particular cultural program – to find a common ground of value that could provide a basis for the responsible exercise of American citizenship (though this was undoubtedly sometimes his intention). Twain marketed his literary merchandise, with great success, across class lines. His serious essays rode on the back of a massive popularity, established through his fiction, travel writing, and lecturing, and confirmed by his celebrity. Twain may have had some sympathy with Howells's desire to offer the readers of his fiction a guide to life in turbulent and changing times, but neither the latter's artistic methods nor his (initial) ideological certainty suited him.

The realist novel would, for Howells, "be anchored in its own place and time, accord psychologically mimetic attention to the customs and actions of common people, and rely on observation and a 'neutral' dramatic method of narration" (Sundquist 1998: 504). Twain made use, as he needed, of fantasy, adventure, sentiment, romance, the tall tale, burlesque, and farce (among other modes) in his work, and never directly addressed the problems of his own time in his major novels. Howells sought – often unsuccessfully, as it happens – to reconcile social differences in his work. Twain's fiction was more likely to accept social fragmentation, inequality, and personal alienation as the unalterable "realities" of late-nineteenth-century American life. It is now accepted that, in *Huckleberry Finn, Connecticut Yankee*, and *Pudd'nhead Wilson*, Twain *was* approaching immediate social concerns (race and Reconstruction, modernization and its effects, class difference, concerns about masculinity, personal agency, law) but in a highly indirect way. The seriousness and contemporary relevance of such issues are, though, generally thickly disguised by the genres and settings he uses, and by his comic forms. For, ultimately, his cultural identity and success relied on his humor, and not on his increasingly bleak view of human nature and of American life at the century's end.

Howells described the attraction of the "unthinking multitude" to the kind of writing he called "melodrama, impossible fiction, and the trapeze," and accepted that the "highly cultivated person," too, will occasionally revert to such "barbarian" moments (Howells 1973: 113). Twain played his melodeon for anyone who cared to listen, and did not establish the same kind of cultural hierarchies and boundaries as his friend – or, at least, not in any consistent way. In chapter 22 of *Huckleberry Finn*, Huck enjoys a "bully circus," with clowns, and lady horse-riders "dressed in clothes . . . just littered with diamonds" (though no trapeze is mentioned) immediately after Colonel Sherburn has killed Boggs. Twain takes us from an entirely "serious" incident, and one that harshly, if implicitly, criticizes the inhumanity and violence at the heart of the Southern social system both before and after the Civil War, to the enjoyable entertainment of the circus, with whatever gaudy misrepresentations of reality (those diamonds) it contains (see, too, Krauth 2003: 232). This move might stand as a metaphor for Twain's art. Sympathetic to Howellsian realism and sharing some of its aspects, his work extends far beyond its relatively narrow limits.

The Limits of Realism

Realism, to summarize, is a flexible term, and one that can be approached in a number of ways – in terms, for instance, of aesthetic practice, cultural role, and ideological belief. Any analysis of the genre must recognize the slipperiness of the boundaries between realism and its bordering literary movements.[14] Howells is the single figure round whom all the various strands of late nineteenth-century American realism interweave, but Twain was sympathetic to aspects of his program. Howells would seem to have had a direct influence on Twain, though some of the latter's realist practices were developed independently.

Eric Sundquist writes that "no one strategy of 'realism' seemed adequate to portray the effects of capitalism across the spectrum of American life" (Sundquist 1998: 520).[15] Phillip Barrish comments similarly that "what comes to count as most real" in the texts produced in this period "not only changes from literary work to literary work but also shifts within individual works" (Barrish 2001: 8). His phrase, "what . . . count[s] as most real," draws attention to the way that "reality" – as it is represented in a text – is always already mediated, produced by the particular social position of the writer, along with her or his motivating values and beliefs and particular angle of vision. The indeterminacy of such definitions does not, however, reduce the term to meaninglessness. Realism attacks sentimental forms. It emerges from – and measures and reflects – the rapid and dramatic changes in American social conditions in the years following the Civil War. It is informed by a particular conception of the subject, and her or his capacity for moral action. And it is identified by a set of formal and stylistic practices which aim towards the type of transparency lacking both in romance (with its conspicuous use of allegory and symbol) and in modernism (with its explicit attention to the shaping hand of the artist). Though such descriptive boundaries may be crossed and muddied within and between individual texts, this does give us a base from which to work.

My comments on the way "reality" is textually produced lead to one further strand of my argument in terms of the Howells–Twain relationship. I have indicated something of the narrowness of Howells's conception of realism, and Twain's move beyond such limits. I now expand on this to show how Howells's *changing* view of reality affected his novelistic practice. Following Daugherty, I suggest that there are clear signs that Howells realized the limitations of his earlier position, and that it may indeed – and unexpectedly, given traditional readings of the two men's relationship – have been Twain who (to some degree at least) "liberated Howells from his own most restrictive canons" (Daugherty 1996: 21).

The contradiction and flaw at the heart of Howells's realist credo lies within his statement that "every true realist . . . is careful of every fact, and feels himself bound to . . . indicate its meaning" (Howells 1973: 83). For it is the relation between fact and meaning that haunts and finally explodes his whole project. Facts, Howells rightly implies, cannot speak for themselves. But as soon as larger meanings are indicated, so the ideological preconceptions of the artist necessarily distort any conception of "the real." To put this slightly differently, Howells saw the realist as a type of scientist, who through his "precision of vision accurately and objectively observes the world, records its facts, and draws out clearly their ramifications. Such a 'science' of composition would simply capture the fact of the world and present it" (Corkin 1996: 27). But – returning to the early distinction between mapping and picturing, photography and imaginative art – he also saw the realist writer as performing a "shaping function" (Borus 1989: 93), using his "designing . . . intelligence" (p. 95) to arrange and order the materials of the text. That designing intelligence, though, necessarily *re*-presented (represented) reality in a *subjective* and ideologically loaded way.

The first stage of Howells's realist career was to falter as the particular shaping vision he brought to his fiction failed to match the unfolding facts of late nineteenth-century history. As he lost confidence in the possibility of objectively recording the version of "America" in which he believed, so he modified his earlier realist practice. The first part of this argument is now a standard critical reading. Howells, in the heyday of his realist campaign, had a particular view of his contemporary American world. Anxious about the troubling social problems of the time, he nonetheless believed that they could be contained. Realist fiction would represent different classes and types of Americans to each other and in doing so would "create 'solidarity'" (a key word for Howells), "pave a common ground between diverse social groups through the recognition of the essential likeness of individuals in all social classes" (Kaplan 1988: 22). The ideological agenda of his realist art was to shape the reality he represented to emphasize what all Americans shared, rather than the countervailing sense of fragmentation and division – while yet recognizing those divisions within his texts. The novel form itself, with its orderly and coherent plot, thus mirrored the solid orderliness that cohered, in this vision, in "reality" itself (Borus 1989: 154). Howells, then, "envisaged realism as a strategy for containing social difference and controlling social conflict within a cohesive common ground" (Kaplan 1988: 23).

From an early point, however, this never quite worked. Howells's anxieties concerning the shape and direction of contemporary society were never fully resolved either in his mind or within his fictions. There are all kinds of "gaps and rifts" that unbalance and disrupt the desired sense of coherence and ordered resolution in his novels. His use of "contrived devices" and "arbitrary plotting" (Trachtenberg 1982: 192) gives the lie to the well-balanced "picture" of American social reality he seeks to represent. Howells was faced with two problems, neither of which his realist program could resolve. The first was the fact that developing social conditions denied his vision of any shared common ground, for "intense and often violent class conflicts" actually "produced fragmented and competing social realities" (Kaplan 1988: 9). The other (to return to my previous argument) concerned markets and audiences. A fracturing of the literary marketplace, an increasingly marked gap between high and mass culture and between serious novels and forms of popular entertainment, threatened to fatally undermine Howells's own literary aim, to provide serious social and moral instruction for a significant part of the national audience.[16]

In his 1894 novel *A Traveler from Altruria*, Howells would turn away from realism and, ironically, back to romance as he set out to expose "the social indifference, corruption, and cruelty at the heart of the American class system" (Krauth 2003: 81). But we can see a series of shifts occurring before that point. He increasingly lost confidence in his ability to artistically contain the fracturings in American social life, and to link individual moral perception and action to the larger social ground (both foundation stones of his realist beliefs); and, as a corollary of this, a growing sense of subjective instability and relativistic uncertainty came to trouble his fiction. Howells continued to work within a realist mode in terms of topic and setting. The sense of social engagement and dialogue at its heart remained central to his attempt to address questions of how American life worked, and what its meanings might be. There are indications, however, that as the beliefs that initially underpinned his fiction gradually eroded, so his use of the genre became – to a significant degree – inhabited by doubts and hesitations. I use the work of three recent critics as the most economical way of (selectively) charting some of these changes. I then return to Twain, to bring him finally back into the frame of my argument.

Amy Kaplan shows how "the elaborate balancing act" (Kaplan 1988: 46) of Howells's realism starts to crack in *A Hazard of New Fortunes*. Lindau, the German socialist, views America as a class battleground: "der *iss* no Ameriga anymore!" (Howells 1965: 285). He thus gives a voice to what Kaplan calls "the centrifugal force of realism" (Kaplan 1988: 57), and, despite the ways in which his voice is undermined and Lindau himself necessarily killed off, his message cannot be completely cast aside. Similarly, in the last stages of the novel, despite Howells's shift from "background" (the violence and social division of the New York streetcar strike) to "foreground" (the social intercourse between his main characters), he cannot altogether bypass "the abyss of conflict and fragmentation" (Kaplan 1988: 63) his text has revealed. The final problems in closing the novel – Kaplan speaks of its combination of "too many different finite and limited conclusions" (p. 61) – again suggests how Howells's realist needs for "picture" and "form" are being stretched to their very limit. He does find ways to combat such disruptions, but the fissures in his earlier conception of realism are clear.[17]

Phillip Barrish continues to see Howells in realist terms, but gives the genre a particularly negative and ironical turn in his focus on the *separation* of the subject from the larger social whole. Barrish concentrates on realism's "intellectual orientation towards various sorts of negativity" (Barrish 2001: 5). He shows how, in the late 1880s and 1890s, Howells focuses on "the intractabilities, impossibilities and ironies" that "cluster around America's socioeconomic system" (p. 31), and illustrates the "clear-eyedness" his protagonists now bring to the "hard realities . . . the irreducible complexities . . . of America's social problems" (pp. 38–9). There is, for Howells, no longer the possibility of finding "common ground" between members of different social classes. Indeed, an "inescapable *lack of transparency*" (my emphasis) means that they necessarily see each other through "distorting lenses of one sort or another" (p. 36). America's "bottom-line 'real'" now becomes "a taste for contingency." Barrish uses the work of Richard Rorty to explain further: "All facets of a given culture, from language to widely accepted social practices to a specific individual's deepest commitments, are *contingent*. That is, they are produced by multiple factors of history and chance and hence cannot be legitimately grounded either in universal nature, in the supernatural realm (God), or in abstractions such as absolute justice" (p. 43).

Intellectual distinction accordingly becomes, for Howells, the ability to empathize with members of other social groups but also to recognize "the unfixable brokenness of both self and world." A series of internal and external factors will always block the Basil Marches of this world (the liberal middle-class character who is most like Howells himself) from "effective action" (Barrish 2001: 47). Laughter has a special place in this reading of the world, as "a bodily index of . . . balance and perspective" (p. 40), the sign of an awareness both of self and world and of the impossibility of matching vision to action.

What we see here is a gradual move away from that confident sense of a solid and shared reality conveyed in Howells's earlier fictions and critical work. Sarah Daugherty further explores this loss of "grounding" in the later Howells with her analysis of his growing uncertainties over his realist program and the humanism that sustained it. She suggests that "his lingering hope for a moral order based on shared values" gives way before a sense of "psychological and verbal insecurity" (Daugherty 1996: 22), an abandonment of a "faith in objective truth," and a displacement of the "belief in a common reality" by an acceptance of "the play of differences" (p. 13).[18] This shift runs alongside a developing recognition of the instability of selfhood, and a collapse of confidence in the unified and morally responsible subject as the very source of meaning and action. She illustrates this changing conception of the subject by referring to a rather astonishing passage in *A Boy's Town* (1890) where Howells talks of the instability of a boy's identity, and the way that, when he gets to be a man, "he may turn out to be like an onion . . . nothing but hulls, that you keep pulling off, one after another, till you think you have got down to the heart, at last, and then you have got down to nothing" (see Daugherty 1996: 23). Daugherty never quite develops her argument as fully as she might, and we might challenge just how far the instabilities and uncertainties she identifies affect Howells's later literary works, taken as a whole. Nonetheless, her indications of the changes in Howells's vision, his increasing skepticism and development of a sense of relativistic uncertainty, are significant.

How, then, does this relate to Twain? Howells's darkening vision was undoubtedly a result of increasing evidence of unbridgeable social divisions in his America, and of his (much-discussed) personal crisis following the 1886 Haymarket Riot and its aftermath. The changes in his work identified above, though, suggest noticeable parallels with Twain's artistic practice. Given Howells's close engagement with Twain's work, it is reasonable to suggest an influence here – or, at the very least, two writers working on parallel tracks.

Twain (in *Huckleberry Finn* and *Pudd'nhead Wilson*) is more concerned with race than class. But Brook Thomas's reading of the latter novel is pertinent: "Pudd'nhead's triumph . . . signals the formation of a larger community of fools, Northern and Southern, who united after the war by collectively selling down the river blacks' efforts to integrate into the national community" (Thomas 1997: 224). We can read in both novels a disguised message: hear Twain too effectively saying, "der *iss* no Ameriga anymore." We can interpret *Connecticut Yankee* similarly, though here issues of labor, class, and region replace that of race. Twain, however, is more skeptical as to whether there ever *was* such a unified America as Howells implies. And, within *Pudd'nhead Wilson* at least, he makes little attempt to counter the grim quality of his vision.[19] Conflict and fragmentation were always central facets of Twain's vision. *Huckleberry Finn* is composed of a whole range of types and levels of social language, fiercely battling it out for authority (even despite Huck's overall narrative control). White is ranged against black, father against son, class against class, and neighbor against neighbor in this fictional world. *Connecticut Yankee* ends with the Battle of the Sand Belt. The possibility of finding "a moral order based on shared values," or a form to mirror the solid orderliness of the larger socio-historical world, looks in that novel to be a very bad joke indeed.

Barrish's description of the sense of contingency, too, could almost be written with Huck Finn in mind. In his clear-eyed way, Huck adopts a series of necessary social roles but "keeps those . . . roles from sticking" (Thomas 1997: 281), retaining "a space of emptiness" which enables him to preserve a distance from, and a "reflective self consciousness" (p. 283) about the world through which he moves. Again, Barrish's comments on laughter as an index of "balance and perspective" in engagement with a complex and irony-filled world fit Twain's art exactly.

Twain undermined the notion of the unified subject and of secure identity throughout his writing career. In *Pudd'nhead Wilson*, the only way of telling Tom and Valet apart is through their fingerprints. When, in chapter 5 of the novel, Tom comes back from Yale to have his "fancy Eastern graces" mocked by "the old deformed negro bell-ringer," we see an old black man imitating his young white (social) superior. This young white man, though, is a fraud; he is in fact a young "black" man – the "real" Valet, who ironically is not black at all – imitating a young white man (the "real" Tom). The "real" young white man now in turn imitates his "black" counterpart. If my word "imitate" implies an intention which is in some part absent, this sequence still indicates the spiraling dizziness that tends to inhabit concepts of distinct identity in Twain.

Twain's fictions are marked from the first by relativistic uncertainty and the play of differences. And as he continued writing, such a sense of pervasive instability, the lack of any reliable ground on which to establish any fixed or final "truth," would only increase. One has only to think of his late fictional meditations on telling – or failing to tell – dream from reality, or of "Three Thousand Years Among the Microbes," where human life is miniaturized and parodied in the microbic universe represented. The failure of objective certainty, and the indeterminacy that results from that failure, is illustrated in *Connecticut Yankee* in the story of the prisoner viewing the world through an arrow-slit, and the limited (and false) perspective given by that single frame.

My conclusions are tentative, and there is more work to be done here. But Howells and Twain did apparently come to share elements of a similar view of the world, and of man's place in it. Twain, though, developed his vision early, and followed it into much darker spaces than his friend. From the first, too, Twain conveyed his views of what "reality" was through the play of a number of literary forms. Indeed, it was only by *retreating* from any transparent representation of immediate reality that these views could be conveyed. Twain acknowledged his own difficulties with the traditional realist novel when he wrote to Howells in late 1899: "Ah, if I could look into the insides of people as you do, & put it on paper, & invent things for them to do & say, & tell *how* they said it, I could write a fine & readable book now" (Twain and Howells 1960: 710). Rather, he used any literary tactic at his disposal to convey his desired message: in *Connecticut Yankee*, fantasy; in *No. 44, The Mysterious Stranger*, an extraordinary mixture of defamiliarizing effects, including a boisterous jokester who takes

human time and history and reverses and rearranges them, replays conversations backwards, and throws the difference between dream and reality, self and world into utter
doubt. Howells, for the most part, remained much more committed to the conventional "realist" model.[20] Finally, though, Twain's example may have shown him that
to move beyond such realist practices – "objectively observ[ing] the world, record[ing]
its facts, and draw[ing] out clearly their ramifications" – did not necessarily entail a
lack of engagement with contemporary social problems and concerns: indeed, quite
the opposite.

One of Twain's great strengths as a writer is his constant resistance to easy categorization, his ability to stretch our literary definitions to their limits. This is true of
his relation to realism. While his work certainly shares a number of key realist attributes, it also escapes the boundaries of the genre at almost every turn.

NOTES

1   See Borus on the distinction between picturing and mapping, and some of the paradoxes
then raised (1989: 93–6). Edwin H. Cady
defines Howells's view of the photographic as
"what *realism* is not because realism is not
mechanical or cartographic but an art like
painting" (see Howells 1973: 5).

2   I approach my topic indirectly, by way of
Brander Matthews, since the language he
uses so clearly accords with realist practice.
Howells himself wrote extensively on Twain,
and in "Mark Twain: An Enquiry" (1901) he
recognized both the importance of the vernacular in *Huckleberry Finn* and the essentially
democratic nature of the book: "The probable and credible soul that the author divines
in the son of the town drunkard is one which
we might each own brother, and the art
which portrays this nature at first hand in the
person and language of the hero, without pose
or affectation, is fine art." But the problems
Howells would always have in fitting Twain
into his preferred critical scheme of things are
clear here. He first tentatively defines Twain
as a "romancer," then talks about this particular novel as picaresque rather than romance,
only to qualify further: "still it is more poetic
than picaresque, and of a deeper psychology."
Once more revealing his definitional uncertainties, he continues: "In the boy's history
the author's fancy works *realistically* to an end
as high as it has reached elsewhere if not

higher" (Howells 1973: 343, my emphasis).
Daniel H. Borus identifies realist writing
with "dialect rendered as exactly as possible"
(1989: 23) and uses *Huckleberry Finn* as his
primary example.

3   See e.g. my analyses of "Lucretia Smith's
Soldier" (December 1864) and "The Launch
of the Steamer 'Capital'" (November 1865)
in Messent (2001). Twain's comedy, however,
undermined realist assumptions of stable
subjectivity, representational authority, and
ontological certainty from the start.

4   This raises the issue of how we distinguish
realism as a broad and sweeping intellectual movement from the literary movement linked specifically to the career and
influence of William Dean Howells – "the
centre and circumference of realism in
America" (Sundquist 1998: 503). Though I
focus here on the Twain–Howells connection,
I suggest answers to this question as I proceed.

5   My argument here generally runs counter
to that of Michael Davitt Bell (1993).
I would resist the narrow limits of Bell's
definitions and conclusions as he argues, to
my mind perversely, that it is in *A Connecticut Yankee*, and not *Huckleberry Finn*, that
Twain identifies most strongly with realist
values.

6   Though Twain would often fail to conform to
such principles in his own fiction. Again, I
return to this later.

7 Louis J. Budd, "W. D. Howells and Mark Twain Judge Each Other 'Aright.'" My thanks to my co-editor both for permission to quote from this yet unpublished piece, and for his helpful comments on the draft version of my own essay. Thanks, too, to Forrest Robinson who helped clarify aspects of my thinking, and reminded me of a key quotation, in private conversation.

8 Howells's own critical vocabulary is full of large-scale abstractions and troublingly paradoxical statements which hinder as much as they help is in constructing a working definition of the "realism" for which he argued. "The novelist's main business," he writes in a particularly unenlightening sentence, "is to possess his reader with a due conception of his characters and the situations in which they find themselves" (Howells 1973: 67). Other phrases scattered through his essays – "good form without formality" (p. 77), "fidelity to experience and probability of motive" (p. 83), "the faithful representation of life" (p. 87), "to know and to tell the truth" (p. 115) – either raise questions as to their exact meaning or leave the reader with a series of unanswerable questions: if all artists (surely), in one way or another, seek to know and tell the truth, what then is so distinctive about the realist project? For the crucial paradox in his version of realism, see the final section of this essay.

9 Gregg Camfield (1994) was the first to explore this area in depth in his important book.

10 Though we should note Lowry's reading of Twain's novel as an "ideological drama of literacy": "Huck resists the incorporating fictions of others by empowering himself as the subject of his own discourse, yet his autobiographical strategy is itself the product of his submission to an education that reforms him into a literate subject" (Lowry 1996: 119).

11 The problem of individual moral responsibility in a world where the subject's engagement within the larger determining social network was increasingly binding was one that haunted realist authors. It often becomes very difficult to separate out independent moral action from dependent social conditioning. Thus the end of Howells's *Silas Lapham* is commonly read in terms of Lapham's "moral

rise . . . the victory of self-regulation over temptation, of rural values over urban" as he refuses to act dishonestly in business (Sundquist 1998: 506). But it can be viewed differently, and more deterministically, with Lapham as the "victim of his own premodern ideology." His Boston years then become "an anomaly, a period where the decentralised production of goods by small, family-owned concerns had access to major urban markets . . . . [T]his moment soon [necessarily] passed, as American industry entered an age of mass production and distribution" (Corkin 1996: 47, 49). See also note 19.

12 A further irony lies in the fact that Twain's most famous novel, *Huckleberry Finn*, was attacked by at least one early reviewer as "being no better in tone than the dime novels which flood the blood-and-thunder reading population." See Fulton (1997: 54). Fulton's Bakhtinian analysis of Twain's "ethical realism," and its search "for a nonsystemic, nonrelativistic ethics that would serve as a kind of . . . practical morality" (p. 7), provides another useful approach to the topic.

13 Quoted in Messent (2001: 117). Leland Krauth gives a slightly different version of the letter, and continues quoting to show that, later in it, Twain "endorses the idea of literature [for the masses] as a way to cultural improvement" (Krauth 1999: 15).

14 I have written elsewhere on Twain's links with naturalism, and the limited nature of that fit. See e.g. Messent (1985).

15 Though – keeping Twain's works in mind – I might wish to modify his "effects of capitalism" to "changing conditions and social relationships" (in which the effects of capitalism would be one crucial element). In a forthcoming article in *Emerson Studies Quarterly*, David Zimmerman brilliantly shows how the signifying properties of money and language are bound together in "The Man That Corrupted Hadleyburg" and how the story as a whole works to challenge the very premises of realism. This essay will contribute significantly to the debate about Twain and realism and I thank the author for allowing me to read it.

16 The "top-down" nature of Howells's work, the fact that he wrote for a particular class

audience that did not include the working-class "mass," further and necessarily compromised his intentions.

17   If, as Kaplan suggests, the fissures can (just about) still be contained within "realist" space, the novel is very close to falling apart at its seams. In her words, "by the end of the novel, the paint threatens to fly off the surface of Howells's largest novelistic canvas" (Kaplan 1988: 63).

18   Both Barrish and Daugherty (see my next paragraph) make a bridge from realism to post-structuralism/postmodernism. One could equally connect Twain's use of irony and of defamiliarization techniques with modernism, his spiraling relativism with the postmodern. Such connections are valid in their suggestion that both Twain and Howells saw beyond the limits of realism, and foreshadow, in their representations of the instabilities and uncertainties of a late nineteenth-century world, more recent social and intellectual preoccupations. The readings of Howells I follow here present one particular view of his artistic development.

19   Though the antebellum setting of the text masks its contemporary relevance, the picture of racism and racial division in the novel is nonetheless unrelenting.

Brook Thomas's discussion of "the question of agency" (Thomas 1997: 270) in the work of Twain and other realist writers is a stimulating one and suggests the individual capacity for meaningful engagement even in a world where surrounding and conditioning social and economic forces press increasingly on the human subject. He relies here on Hannah Arendt's distinction between sovereignty ("the ideal of a free will, independent from others") and freedom (which "resides not in control over action but in action itself") (p. 272). "Free agents," in Thomas's view, "retain the capacity to produce actions that are not totally controlled by the forces that create the conditions in which action occurs" (p. 279). *Pudd'nhead Wilson* remains for Thomas a realist text, largely (it seems) due to Twain's own authorial role. "Even though Twain works with material and voices made available to him by his culture, when that material passes through his imagination it is translated [a key word for Thomas] into a different form" (p. 280). While this may be true, the internal message of the text is less positive. Thomas's statement that "the realists . . . work to find a form that will be true to the contingency of events" (p. 275) matches Barrish's view of the later Howells, but shares, to my mind, something of its "often paralyzing" implications (Barrish 2001: 47). See, too, my later comments on *Huckleberry Finn*.

20   Though see Krauth (2003: 78–86) for a useful comparison and contrast of the two writers' use of the figure of the stranger (Howells's in *A Traveler from Altruria*) to launch "grim and angry assaults on the ills, wrongs and injustices they learned to see in life at the very beginning." (Krauth suggests their Western backgrounds helped to shape their final visions.)

References and Further Reading

Barrish, Phillip (2001). *American Literary Realism, Critical Theory and Intellectual Prestige, 1880–1995*. Cambridge, UK: Cambridge University Press.

Bell, Michael Davitt (1993). *The Problem of American Realism: Studies in the Cultural History of a Literary Idea*. Chicago: University of Chicago Press.

Borus, Daniel H. (1989). *Writing Realism: Howells, James, and Norris in the Mass Market*. Chapel Hill: University of North Carolina Press.

Brodhead, Richard H. (1986). *The School of Hawthorne*. New York: Oxford University Press.

Brodhead, Richard H (1993). *Cultures of Letters: Scenes of Reading and Writing in Nineteenth-Century America*. Chicago: University of Chicago Press.

Brodhead, Richard H. (1998). "Literature and Culture." In Emory Elliott (ed.), *Columbia Literary History of the United States*, 467–81. New York: Columbia University Press.

Camfield, Gregg (1994). *Sentimental Twain: Samuel Clemens in the Maze of Moral Philosophy.* Philadelphia: University of Pennsylvania Press.

Corkin, Stanley (1996). *Realism and the Birth of the Modern United States: Cinema, Literature, and Culture.* Athens: University of Georgia Press.

Daugherty, Sarah B. (1996). "William Dean Howells and Mark Twain: The Realism War as a Campaign that Failed." *American Literary Realism* 29: 1, 12–28.

Denning, Michael (1987). *Mechanic Accents: Dime Novels and Working-Class Culture in America.* London: Verso.

Eble, Kenneth E. (1985). *Old Clemens and W.D.H.: The Story of a Remarkable Friendship.* Baton Rouge: Louisiana State University Press.

Fisher, Philip (1986). *Hard Facts: Setting and Form in the American Novel.* New York: Oxford University Press.

Fulton, Joe B. (1997). *Mark Twain's Ethical Realism.* Columbia: University of Missouri Press.

Howard, June (1985). *Form and History in American Literary Naturalism.* Chapel Hill: University of North Carolina Press.

Howells, William Dean (1959). *Criticism and Fiction and Other Essays by W. D. Howells*, ed. Clara Marburg Kirk and Rudolf Kirk. New York: New York University Press.

Howells, William Dean (1965). *A Hazard of New Fortunes.* London: Oxford University Press. (First publ. 1890.)

Howells, William Dean (1973). *W. D. Howells as Critic*, ed. Edwin H. Cady. London: Routledge & Kegan Paul.

Kaplan, Amy (1988). *The Social Construction of American Realism.* Chicago: University of Chicago Press.

Krauth, Leland (1999). *Proper Mark Twain.* Athens: University of Georgia Press.

Krauth, Leland (2003). *Mark Twain & Company: Six Literary Relations.* Athens: University of Georgia Press.

Lowry, Richard S. (1996). *"Littery Man": Mark Twain and Modern Authorship.* New York: Oxford University Press.

Matthews, Brander (1892). "Of Mark Twain's Best Story." In *Americanisms and Briticisms Etc.*, 151–61. New York: Harper.

Messent, Peter (1985). "Toward the Absurd: Mark Twain's *A Connecticut Yankee, Pudd'nhead Wilson* and *The Great Dark*." In Robert Giddings (ed.), *Mark Twain: A Sumptuous Variety*, 176–98. London: Vision; Totowa, NJ: Barnes & Noble.

Messent, Peter (2001). *The Short Works of Mark Twain.* Philadelphia: University of Pennsylvania Press.

Mitchell, Lee Clark (1989). *Determined Fictions: American Literary Naturalism.* New York: Columbia University Press.

Mitchell, Lee Clark (1998). "Naturalism and the Languages of Determinism." In Emory Elliott (ed.), *Columbia Literary History of the United States*, 525–45. New York: Columbia University Press.

Rohrbach, Augusta (2002). *Truth Stranger than Fiction: Race, Realism and the US Literary Marketplace.* New York: Palgrave.

Shi, David E. (1995). *Facing Facts: Realism in American Thought and Culture, 1850–1920.* New York: Oxford University Press.

Sundquist, Eric J. (1998). "Realism and Regionalism." In Emory Elliott (ed.), *Columbia Literary History of the United States*, 501–24. New York: Columbia University Press.

Thomas, Brook (1997). *American Literary Realism and the Failed Promise of Contract.* Berkeley: University of California Press.

Tompkins, Jane (1985). *Sensational Designs: The Cultural Work of American Fiction 1790–1860.* New York: Oxford University Press.

Trachtenberg, Alan (1982). *The Incorporation of America: Culture and Society in the Gilded Age.* New York: Hill & Wang.

Twain, Mark (1892a). *Merry Tales.* New York: Charles L. Webster.

Twain, Mark (1900). *The Man That Corrupted Hadleyburg and Other Stories and Essays.* New York: Harper.

Twain, Mark (1979). *Early Tales and Sketches*, vol. 1: *1851–1864*, ed. Edgar Marquess Branch and Robert H. Hirst. Berkeley: University of California Press.

Twain, Mark, and Howells, William Dean (1960). *Mark Twain–Howells Letters: The Correspondence of Samuel L. Clemens and William Dean Howells, 1872–1910*, 2 vols., ed. Henry Nash Smith and William M. Gibson. Cambridge, Mass.: Belknap.

PART III
Mark Twain: Publishing and Performing

14

"I don't know A from B": Mark Twain and Orality

Thomas D. Zlatic

Definitions

A few years since, when the steam-engine was harnessed into the service of the print-ing press, we were ready to conclude that oral instruction would have to yield the palm, without dispute, to written literature . . . [W]e began to think that speaking intellect had seen its best days . . . We even imagined . . . that the ear . . . would retire on a pension, and that the eye . . . would literally become the most perfect of the senses. (*Harper's Monthly*, 1856, quoted in Scott 1983)

Within Mark Twain's writings, orality can be analyzed as a topic, theme, method, style, and mindset. Studying the oral in Mark Twain thus can involve several approaches, including historical analysis of how the availability and choice of media influenced Twain's thinking and literary production; aesthetic, psychological, and genetic analysis of how Twain was influenced, both consciously and unconsciously, by the oral tradition and of how he manipulated it in his fiction; and stylistic analysis and generic studies of oral features in his writing. It can also entail rhetorical analy-sis of the oral in his writing and platform performance, and thematic and philoso-phical considerations to do with contrasts between the oral and the literate, particu-larly relating to phenomenological and metaphysical properties of the spoken versus the written.[1] A complicating factor is the lack of agreement regarding the meaning of crucial terms, including "orality" itself.

In this discussion "oral" means more than being voiced. It is not always equiva-lent to spoken utterance: an academic lecture, for instance, may be less "oral" than a letter dictated by a nonliterate person to a scribe. "Speech" is not interchangeable with "orality," nor "writing" with "literacy": the set of terms "speech/writing" refers to modes of communication, whereas the pair "orality/literacy" refers to the habits of mind that are fostered by such modes (Heckel, quoted in Welch 1999: 66). This dis-tinction is easy to ignore, particularly because "oral" can refer either to speech (a mode of communication) or to orality (habits of mind), and it can also be used to define a style, whether in writing or speech. But failing to acknowledge the distinction can muddy arguments about the "oral" in Mark Twain's life and works. Finally, "orality" is an umbrella term that must be subdivided into such categories as "primary orality," "residual orality," and "secondary orality" in order to distinguish the complex interfaces that exist between oral, literate, and electronic media.

Orality studies explore both the distinct patterns of communication and thought that may be manifested in nonliterate cultures and the interactions between oral and other modes of communication. Among the most cited writers on the topic within a literary/humanistic framework is Walter Ong, who investigates the impact exercised on human consciousness by stages of communications technology, including oral–aural interactions, writing, print, and electronic media. He argues that technologies of the word can influence what is thought, what is said, and how it is said.[2]

"Primary orality" refers to the habits of thinking and communication that commonly pertain in cultures that have been exposed to writing or print either not at all or only marginally. In a primary oral economy where human memory is the only record for what is known, preservation rather than creation of knowledge is of primary importance. A tendency toward conservative, traditional, and communal thinking is a natural response. Experience is not only recorded mnemonically but processed mnemonically. Patterning, balance, repetition, antithesis, rhythm, sound devices, proverbs, commonplaces, epithets, and formulary devices are functions not just of expression but of intellectual processing. Stories with formulaic plots and stereotyped characters convey the knowledge, history, and values of the culture. Oral noetics places less value in formal abstract knowledge; thinking tends to be concrete and situational, rooted in concerns of the human life-world. Peoples in an oral culture are not less intelligent or less reasonable than those in literate cultures, but they may be reasonable in different ways. The attainment and management of knowledge tend to be more communal and participatory in nature, rather than private and objective investigations.

Writing and, later, print, are involved in a restructuring not only of communication but of culture and consciousness. By storing information outside human consciousness, writing can alter social structures and relationships and enable a greater degree of objectivity, introspection, and analysis. Ong argues that writing is alienating and thereby humanizing: it separates knower from known, provides a private domain for knowledge apart from communal interaction, encourages an "inward turn" that leads to deepening of the self, and enables the methods of modern science. By altering relationships with self, others, and knowledge, writing can promote a different type of consciousness, a different sense of being in the world, from that experienced by those in oral cultures. For instance, the visualization and spatialization of thought processes that are encouraged by writing, and more so by print, make it easier to conceptualize knowledge not as an interaction among human beings but as a commodity-as-information or data to be manipulated.

Several scholars, including Ong himself, warn against overly deterministic models of cultural change. No communications technology produces inexorable and identical changes in cultures or individuals, and any changes that do occur result from a wide variety of forces in society. Also, the influences of communications technology are not independent of one another. There are no "great divides" that isolate stages of communication.[3] In order to impact on human consciousness, word technologies must be "interiorized," that is, used without reflection as part of the ordinary way of organizing and responding to reality. Such interiorization takes place at both a cultural and an individual level, and is interrelated with other technological, historical, and social developments (educational systems, transportation, location, political structures, religion, values, etc.), and it can take hundreds of years for habitual ways of organizing perception, thought, and communication to be absorbed into an unnoticed world-view.

As an example, the phenomena of reading, writing, and printing do not serve the same intellectual, social, and psychological functions in all times and in locations. Writing for many years remained closely bound up with the oral, a craft rather than a requirement for education. Only gradually did writing become interiorized, developing its own conventions and discourse, internalized as a different way of organizing and communicating facts, ideas, and emotions. The interiorization of reading also was slow to develop: silent reading spread very gradually, and through the Middle Ages reading aloud both publicly and privately was common. This explains why there are no great gulfs or insurmountable divides between different stages of communications technology. What usually are most interesting in orality studies are the "interfaces of the word," the interactions of the oral, literate, and now electronic in response to specific local and temporal conditions. "Residual orality" refers to the continuation of oral patterns and frameworks within literate cultures.

In the world of Mark Twain we can find examples of such shifting ratios between communications technologies. Again, reading is not an invariant experience, always involving the same mental operations and orientations. Extending as late as 1850 in America, and in some cases beyond, the mindset of "traditional reading" involved the slow savoring and frequent rereading of a limited number of widely circulated books, with reading itself being taught (often independently of writing) by reading aloud (Hall 1983: 23–4). Also, even more than writing, the printing press was an agent of change that promoted new social, psychological, and political structures, but it too was not a monolithic force exercising the same influence in all places at the same time. The influence exercised by print in American culture at the beginning of the nineteenth century was radically different from that at the century's end, when the village printer gave way to the mass marketing of national printing, establishing different social relationships among writers, publishers, readers, and the general population as a new sense of community evolved (Hall 1983: 3; Barrow 1991: 37–40, 80–119). After the Civil War a new mentality emerged, entailing a new conception of knowledge as rapid consumption of "information" and "fact." This emphasis on speed and commodification of fact was not unrelated to the emergence of electric communications technology, the telegraph and telephone, presaging what Ong and others have seen as another shift in consciousness toward a "secondary orality" – a re-emerging participatory orality, but one enabled by print.

Mark Twain's life spanned rural orality, the waning of traditional reading, the development of national printing and mass marketing, the professionalization and rationalization of society, and the development of electric communications technologies. Indeed, he himself was an active force in many of these transformations. His fiction returns frequently to worlds of primary orality, and he lived in a culture that was quickly shaking off its oral past. Orality studies provide a framework for the exploration of "relationism," the connections between communications media and other cultural forces as they impinge on the methods and themes of Twain's works, including the interaction of oral and literate modes of thought and communication, conscious and unconscious artistry, primitivism and progress, and vernacular versus genteel values. Such studies do not resolve but add resonance to discussions of many central themes in Twain's life and work.

Roots and Reading

> Orion's boyhood was spent in that wee little log hamlet of Jamestown up there among the knobs — so called — of East Tennessee, among a very sparse population of primitives who were as ignorant of the outside world and as unconscious of it as the other wild animals were that inhabited the forest around. (*Mark Twain's Autobiography*)

Mark Twain did not have a theory of orality and in fact very seldom even used the terms "oral," "literate," or "illiterate," but he had significant first-hand experience with the oral tradition, with both nonliterate and semi-literate populations, and with the verbal transmission of oral tales by literates. As a boy in rural Missouri he was raised in a living tradition of orality, as exemplified in the religious revivals and "Arkansas gossips" depicted in *Adventures of Huckleberry Finn*. Growing up, he was entranced by oral stories in slave kitchens delivered by Uncle Dan'l — a fascination that continued into adult life, as shown by his appropriation of Auntie Cord's narration in "A True Story." Later he participated in oral traditions on Midwestern river boats and at camp fires and mines in the West. He encountered indigenous populations and cultures where a majority of people still moved in a largely oral milieu, early in his career in the United States, Hawaii, Europe, and the Middle East, and later, on his round-the-world-lecture tour, in places such as Australia and Africa.

Twain was sensitive to the unique socio-psychological characteristics of these oral cultures. The "Raftsmen Passage" deleted from *Huckleberry Finn* is an evocative boyhood reverie of a bygone world: a residually oral keelboat subculture, in which drinking and brawling braggarts told stories around a fire, exchanging folk wisdom and spurious explanations of nature and society while engaging in male polemic taunting and ritualistic fighting. Similarly, in *Personal Recollections of Joan of Arc* he depicts oral performance in a primary oral milieu in which the bard educates, entertains, and inspires his nonliterate audience, who do not sit passively but participate with their whole bodies in the manner typical of an oral "verbomotor" culture: "the tears came and flowed down their cheeks, and their forms began to sway unconsciously to the swing of the song, and their bosoms to heave and pant; and moanings broke out, and deep ejaculations" (Twain 1896: 29).[4]

Ironically, residual orality was promoted not only within low culture but within high culture as well. During the nineteenth century a significant shift in educational theory took place in American universities as classical-based rhetorical education was supplanted by a more practical and modern course of study. The earlier, orally toned educational system, with its Latin-based instruction, oral examinations, exclusion of women, and celebration of a male-agonistic rhetorical world, had promoted oral/rhetorical forms of thought and communication that preserved an oral cast of thinking within highly literate culture (Ong 1982: 116). But oratorical education was not inculcated in the universities alone. In the elementary schools, the highly influential McGuffey reader taught language arts through "sound-conscious," elegant, and uplifting declamatory literature meant to inspire mid-Victorian faith in civil religion. Reading was not a private activity directed toward analysis or even meaning, but a group event (Lynn 1973: 20). "Oratory was *the* . . . educational medium for creating 'public sentiment'" (Lynn 1973: 20–1; and see Ong 1982: 115–16). A culture of oratory flourished, as evidenced by platform lecturing, the lyceum system, and an elocutionist movement that emphasized expressive readings of texts. This is the milieu for the great success of Dickens's, and later Mark Twain's, public readings of their works, and for the family- and community-based readings within households. In a letter he wrote to Livy before their marriage, Twain opined, "[I]t is unsatisfactory to read to one's self anyhow," a comment which prompted Gribben's observation, "Like many of his nineteenth-century contemporaries, he came to think of reading as ideally an *oral* pastime" (Gribben 1976: 49). Apparently, Twain both wrote for, and read with, the "mind's ear" (Blair 1981). Of course solitary, silent, and analytical "extensive reading" was more common for the extremely well-read Mark Twain, but he still exhibited lingering traits of "traditional reading," returning frequently to beloved texts such as Cervantes, Malory, Lecky, and Suetonius, and slowly savoring those he most valued. For example, Twain was unable fully to appreciate a Howells passage when he heard the author read it aloud, but he could grasp the subtleties when he himself read it at a leisurely pace: "When I catch it in the magazine, I give a page 20 or 30 minutes in which to gently & thoroughly filter into me" (Twain and Howells 1960: vol. 1, 408).

In addition to his exposure to living and academic traditions of oral thought and expression, Twain was sensitized to oral practice and noetics through his readings of the Southwestern humorists, Western tall tale artists, and medieval authors such as Malory, and through his study of history and popular anthropology, which speculated about a generalized "savage" or "primitive" mind. Though appreciative of the "oral," Twain was more skeptical about "orality." William Hartpole Lecky, who "without question had the most significant impact on Twain's philosophy of morality and history" (Fulton 2000: 29), tried to ascertain, in *The Spirit of Rationalism*, "the leading characteristics that mark the belief of civilised ages and nations as compared with barbarous ones, and of the most educated as compared with the most illiterate classes" (Lecky 1955: vol. 1, xvii). Lecky asserted that the course of human development is determined not by arguments but by mentalities: that is, "mental habits" or predis- positions resulting from "intellectual type" (p. x). These mental habits are shaped in part by the communications technologies of writing and print: "in a period when the intellectual discipline of reading is unknown, the mind is incapable of grasping con- ceptions that are not clothed in a pictorial form" (vol. 2, p. 203). "Civilized man" not only knows more because of books but, unlike the "savage," has "an intellectual strength, a power of sustained and patient thought and abstraction" (vol. 1, p. 207). Other authors read by Twain – Schoolcraft on the American Indian, Smyth on the aborigines of Victoria, and Taine on early Anglo-Saxons – similarly associate a lack of writing with situational concrete thinking and with a lack of reflection, abstract thinking, and the art of reasoning.

The point here is not to claim that such ethnocentric analyses were accurate (often they were not), but to provide insights into Mark Twain's frameworks of thinking as regards oral populations. In *Following the Equator* Twain defines "Aborigine, Pacific Islander, Maori, and South African as 'savage' in exactly that ahistorical and reduc- tive manner which is typical of those who would see other (tribal) cultures and social systems mainly as static entities" (Messent 1993: 74). It was not uncommon during Twain's time to see history and geography as functions of one another: traveling to less developed regions was comparable to moving back in time, so that, for instance, the Scottish highlands could be taken as a living laboratory to plot the progress of other "primitives" such as American Indians. Hank Morgan's sixth-century Camelot is based not so much on Malory's fifteenth-century England as on eighteenth-century Scotland, and, in this synchronic historical view, Arthurians, Scots, and Comanches are interchangeable (Fulton 2000: 37, 56–7).

Twain in his fiction thematizes these contrasts between oral–aural and literate psy- chodynamics that he had encountered in his personal experiences and reading. Two stories that deal with cultures in which the peasants live in worlds close to primary orality provide contradictory reflections on the oral mind. In *A Connecticut Yankee in King Arthur's Court*, illiteracy is a primary impediment to human progress; in *Joan of Arc* it is a prerequisite for moral victory.

Oral Gentility/Literate Vernacular

> I know of governors of palaces, and seneschals of castles, and sheriffs of counties, and many like small offices and titles of honor, but him you call the Science of Optics I have not heard of before; peradventure it is a new dignity. (Mark Twain, *A Connecticut Yankee in King Arthur's Court*)

In *A Connecticut Yankee* an oral–literate struggle is projected onto two worlds, those of sixth-century England and nineteenth-century America, whose respective values, educational practices, societal structures, and forms of expression are conditioned by technologies of communication (Zlatic 1991b). Because of his literate perspective, Hank identifies characteristics but does not understand the logic of oral–aural psychodynamics, and thus can conclude only that the people of Camelot are ignorant idiots with questionable morality. Hank's judgment "that these animals didn't reason; that *they* never put this and that together; that all their talk showed that they didn't know a discrepancy when they saw it" (Twain 1889: 65), exemplifies his literate misunderstanding of oral noetics and his lack of appreciation for multiple intelligences.

Chapter 25 of the novel, "A Competitive Examination," appears to have been written deliberately as a case study to contrast the modes of thinking Lecky identified for oral and literate cultures; between knowledge rooted in the life-world and knowledge as an abstract body of facts collected into a science. Hank stages a rigged or culturally biased contest to determine who will lead the King's army: the oral lords steeped in traditions of honor and chivalry, or the literate products of the Boss's manufactory who are professionalized in the "science of war." The Boss attempts to embarrass a lord by exposing his inability to engage in abstract thinking, presenting him with an absurd legal–logical problem involving persons A, B, C, and D, but the lord begs off, acknowledging both the complexity of the issue and the fact that he does not know either the people or their situation: "Wherefore I beseech you let the dog and the onions and these people of the strange and godless names work out their several salvations from their piteous and wonderful difficulties without help of mine" (Twain 1889: 323–4). Thinking for Hank means being able to process decontextualized information, to dispassionately employ fact in abstract ratiocination. The people of Camelot, in contrast, exhibit concrete situational thinking that is interpersonal, participatory, and rooted in the human life-world.

It is curious, though, that while Hank is unequivocal in his denunciation of oral psychodynamics, it is Sandy, an exemplar of oral thinking, whom he marries. Hank discovers there is more to life than discursive reasoning, and that the childlike, unconscious innocence of the nonliterate can be endearing. Though Twain frequently railed against the Middle Ages and heaped vituperations on its nineteenth-century prophet, Walter Scott (ironically, the writer who had mesmerized him as a young man), he nonetheless had a deep fascination with the period, returning to it in four books and a number of shorter works (Moreland 1996: 28–76). Malory remained a lifelong favorite writer, one from whom Twain read aloud in bed (Paine 1912: vol. 3, 891; vol. 4, 1445).

Four or five years after *A Connecticut Yankee*, when Twain wrote about the analytic capabilities of another unlettered pre-modern military leader, he represented literacy as more of a hindrance than an asset (Zlatic 1992). When Joan of Arc is being questioned by her captors, echoes from Hank's "A Competitive Examination" resonate in her answers. To underscore the point, the narrator, de Conte, begins with the reminder, "As I have told you, she could not read." He continues: "One day they harried and pestered her with arguments, reasonings, objections, and other windy and wordy trivialities, gathered out of the works of this and that and the other great theological authority." Frustrated, Joan rebukes them: "I don't know A from B; but I know this: that I am come at the command of the Lord of Heaven to deliver Orleans from the English power and crown the King of Rheims, and the matters ye are puttering over are of no consequence!" (Twain 1896: 125).

It is true that writing is associated now not with science but with scholastic theology; still, ratiocination and the ability to distinguish "A from B" are clearly foreign to this woman whom Twain ranked at the front of the procession of the entire human race. Whereas for Hank writing is a precondition for education, progress, and democracy, for Joan it is associated with sterility, alienation, and duplicity (Twain 1896: 362). Though Joan "had had no opportunity to study the complex arts of war" (Smith 1962: 235), there is no doubt in Mark Twain's mind that Hank's West Point cadets would be no match for the untutored passion that marks her dependency upon an oral world.

One strategy that might be used to untangle the contradictions here is to explore how orality is related to the "vernacular" and "genteel" paradigms, as Henry Nash Smith defines them. Smith identified two mentalities in conflict: the genteel, with its ideality and elevated, albeit artificial, language and feelings; and the vernacular – the colloquial, possibly vulgar, but ultimately authentic expression of democratic values (Smith 1962: 20). A clearer understanding of the range of relationships that can pertain in Mark Twain's fiction between the literate and oral, vernacular and genteel, reveals not just dichotomies but a variety of intersections.[5]

The barely literate Huck Finn helps substantiate the expected connection between orality and the vernacular. Many of Mark Twain's vernacular characters, however, are extremely literate, and though they may choose to express themselves in colloquial idiom, they can rise to eloquence as needed, whether in rapture or sarcasm, to meet the desires of the consuming public. Hank Morgan, an archetypal proponent of vernacular talk and values, is also prototypically literate and in fact is intensely hostile to the oral mindset of Camelot. In Hank's attempt to civilize medieval England, writing is the introductory course taught in his "man-factory" (Twain 1889: 161). In contrast, a noble of Camelot is insulted when asked if he can read: "Takest me for a clerk?" (p. 323). Ironically, the representatives of gentility are the nonliterate populace such as this lord and Alisande – oral but not vernacular characters. Particularly instructive is that the medieval page-turned-administrator, Clarence, evolves into a vernacular character *after* he learns to read. Originally Clarence typified the oral mind, fearful about the magical power of spoken words and copious in his narrations, but Hank charts in him the transformation of mentalities related to communications media: "Already he had doubled himself in one way; he talked sixth century and wrote nineteenth" (p. 121).

Another problem arising from the alignment of orality with the vernacular, of course, is the nonliterate "vernacular" character who does not display the appropriate humanistic and democratic values, Pap Finn being an obvious example. In the tradition of Mike Fink and the Southern roustabouts, this illiterate is "exasperatingly oral" and his behavior can be explained within oral psychodynamics (Beaver 1987:

82–3). Contrast him, though, with Joan of Arc. Both are unschooled and unread, but one is among the most degraded of all Twain characters, while the other is elevated above "any other person whose name appears in profane history" (Twain 1896: 461).

The terms "illiterate," "nonliterate," and "pre-literate" distort orality by defining it in terms of something that post-dates it – similar to thinking of a horse as "a car without wheels." Although "oral" and "illiterate" denote the same lack of writing, "illiterate" is pejorative, implying ignorance, poverty, and perhaps moral question-ability. An illiterate is in a deficient relationship with a dominant and alienated culture. Pap's orality is transformed into illiteracy only when literate modes of think-ing and organization prevail (Barrow 1991: 57–69). What is particularly telling is that sometimes within the same persons there are dramatic and even unrealistic shift-ings of characterization as they vacillate between the unspoken labels of "oral" and "illiterate." The illiterate King Arthur is an oaf, but the oral King is a Walter Scott hero. Jim is a father figure within oral tradition, but he is betrayed as an illiterate minstrel "darky" when contextualized within the white man's literacy.

Thus, the vernacular characters include the literate and sometimes ironic (Hank, Pudd'nhead Wilson, the travel literature narrators), the semi-literate/residually oral (Huck, the narrator of *No. 44, The Mysterious Stranger*), the illiterate (Pap), and the oral (Jim and Joan of Arc). The oral and the vernacular are not always synonymous. Huck is mainly oral and vernacular, whereas Hank is literate and vernacular. Sandy is oral but not vernacular; Pap is illiterate, and vernacular in language but not in values. Joan is oral and genteel; Arthur is both illiterate and oral but not vernacular, and Jim is both oral and illiterate as well as vernacular.

To turn the screw one more time, the highly literate, genteel culture, as repre-sented by Scott, Cooper, and Longfellow, also bears the stamp of orality – a residual academic orality. For orality was preserved not only through the living traditions of the lower classes but also through academia. When Leo Marx identifies a "vernacular tradition in American literature," his critique of Longfellow's gentility (Marx 1988: 3–17) parallels Twain's demolition of Cooper in "Fenimore Cooper's Literary Offences": the targets are the residually oral features of elevated, imprecise language, commonplace and generalized descriptions, epithets, episodic structure, formulaic plots, stereotyped and two-dimensional "heavy" characters, and miraculous heroic action (see Ong 1982: 33–6, 69–71). A refined orality is one component of the escapism of the medieval revival.

A simple dichotomy of oral/literate, then, does not illuminate the complexity of orality within Mark Twain's writings and world. A literate vernacular and a genteel-ized orality reflect different social, historical, and psychological orientations, but they can interact in a variety of ways as a result of both conscious and unconscious forces. Twain manipulated a tradition when responding to a market interested in oral and vernacular topics and methods; but calculated self-promotion alone does not explain his immersion in the oral, nor the cultural forces that created the market in the first place.

Re-presented Orality

"All text is pretext." (Walter J. Ong, "Technological Development and Writer–Subject–Reader Immediacies")

All of the above oral influences being acknowledged, Mark Twain himself, of course, had thoroughly interiorized literate perspectives. His career was bound up intricately not only with writing but with publishing and print technology, beginning at the age of 11, and his "world-view" was deeply influenced by the spatialization of thought and communication associated with print, as reflected perhaps in the rigid determinism of his later years (see Zlatic 1991a). And though he popularly is associated with frontier freedom and intuitive, folkloric wisdom, Mark Twain was entrenched in literate, sentimental, domestic, and genteel culture (see Camfield 1994).

Though entangled with residual orality, both from a living popular oral tradition and from a fading academic one, Twain was a highly conscious craftsman who laboriously forged the oral into print and who "re-presented" the oral on the platform. This was not primary or residual orality but a reconstructed or "represented orality," a conscious attempt to appropriate the oral for the needs and pleasure of a literate audience. Such a fabricated orality does not spring from the same psychodynamics as primary and residual orality, but the conscious recreation of oral features is not independent of oral influences acting upon the culture.

Some parallels might be found in the ambivalence toward orality in eighteenth-century Scotland. In her analysis of Scot and Ossianic literature, Fielding posits a "good orality" and a "bad orality," as perceived by literate culture. High Scottish culture regarded orality in the highlands as illiteracy and ignorance, to be feared when it found expression in popular print as "vile greasy scrawl." But once Celtic orality was processed through literacy, it was sanctioned as culturally acceptable; once it had been tamed for a genteel, romantic audience it could be used to celebrate nationalistic pride (Fielding 1996: 10, 24–45). This "romance of orality" is a sentimental "literary reclamation" of the oral, and is itself a product of an intellectual processing very different from that associated with oral psychodynamics.

A somewhat similar anxiety appears in Southwestern humor, in the problem of containment of the oral vernacular. Despite its vernacular dialect, Southwestern humor is highly literate, the vernacular being captured within the literate. With a hypersensitivity to contamination by the marginal and inferior, the Southwestern humorists created a frame to distance themselves from their rude, low-class, unlettered comedic speakers. A formal, elegant, Latinate style enclosed, and mocked, their backwoods characters (Schmitz 1983: 33–57). Again, this was an orality produced by literates for the enjoyment of literates: "the 'vernacular perspective' was a point of view constructed *within* literate culture to represent those on the linguistic margins" (Lowry 1996: 13).

Among Mark Twain's artistic breakthroughs was the removal of the frame in *Huckleberry Finn*, allowing the vernacular character, Huck, to speak directly for himself. The change did not altogether remove the comic status of the character, but blended it with a romanticized portrayal of a sound heart in conflict with a repressive civilization. Huck's narration is an oral performance (Beaver 1987: 83), but Twain's creation of Huck's performance is a literate one. Mark Twain also had to reclaim the oral within the written. Not only Huck's vernacular dialect but also his orality is fabricated, sanitized, recreated, idealized, bowdlerized, and simulated. His thought patterns, dialect, and oral style are literary renderings, a self-consciously and meticulously reconstructed orality modified and adapted for his literate audience.[6]

Though Twain was not simply an amanuensis for an oral tradition speaking through him, that does not mean that his every artistic decision was premeditated. While consciously reconstructing the tradition he was still within the tradition, conscious in his craftsmanship but not necessarily entirely so in motivation. Even a represented or "tamed" orality apparently was meeting some unspoken psychic and emotional needs of a culture in which oral traditions were being devalued by industrialization, professionalization, urbanization, rapid travel, mass marketing, technology, and other forces altering a more traditional sense of community.

Stage/Presence

And then there is the immortal "My word!" . . . I saw it in print several times on the Pacific Ocean, but it struck me coldly, it aroused no sympathy. That was because it was the dead corpse of the thing, the soul was not there – the tones were lacking – the informing spirit – the deep feeling – the eloquence. But the first time I heard an Australian say it, it was positively thrilling. (Mark Twain, *Following the Equator*)

Though the two constructs are interrelated, resituating the oral from orality/literacy construct to the speech/writing construct opens up new issues and philosophical problems, with less focus on historical conditions and more on the phenomenological and metaphysical properties of sound and sight, speech and writing.

As one of America's most gifted platform lecturers, Twain recognized distinctive characteristics of writing and speaking. Though he championed writing and print as inventions that created and sustained modern civilization, he frequently commented on the impoverishment of the written word. He associated life, soul, and eloquence with the spoken word; death, sleep, coldness with the written. Writing is the word's corpse. Bringing that corpse to life was a lifelong fascination for Mark Twain.

Though a naturally gifted oral performer, Twain was also a technical craftsman who carefully studied tricks for turning the written into the oral, and vice versa. Writing systems focus on the semantic content of a communication, having only a paltry ability to indicate tone, pitch, stress, loudness, hesitation, and silence. To remedy that deficiency when, for instance, he read Browning to a women's study group, Twain "'scored' [it] . . . in order to give the eye instant help in placing & shading emphases" (Gribben 1976: 51). But still he found that writing is but an excerpt of spoken language, and spoken language itself captures only a snippet of an experience, even with all associated paralinguistics. The oral–aural communication event is not just auditory but involves all the senses as speakers and hearers share a common circum-ambient reality that clarifies, limits, and extends the communication. According to Twain, the interactivity of oral–aural communication with its immediate feedback was particularly important in the pause, the length of which was never predetermined but was based upon the faces of the audience. The difference between the spoken and written extended beyond the revoicing of the text; vocalization of the written word brought it closer to the fullness of life, but not close enough. Twain learned that in order to be able to revivify reductively encoded experiences when he gave readings of his own and others' texts, he had to memorize the written words, but not verbatim. The text needed to be absorbed and then reissued, with deletions and modifications; rendering the written into the spoken was a task of transformation (Twain 1940: 224).

The oral and written were juxtaposed not only in the de-composing and re-composing of oral delivery, but also in composition. It is in his frequent explanations of the method of his *Autobiography* that he is most reflective about media bias, about the implications of choosing to communicate oral or written form. Twain rejected a text outline for his autobiography, choosing instead to dictate it, using a written text or a conversation to inspire free associative meditations that united past and present, diary and history. As many have recognized, the *Autobiography* is thus oral in flavor, with its conversational style, extemporaneous structure, and a proclivity for exaggeration that justify some comparison to a genre rooted in oral tradition, the tall tale.[7]

Twain is explicit about the superiority of the oral over the written:

> Narrative *writing* is always disappointing. The moment you pick up a pen you begin to lose the spontaneity of the personal relation, which contains the very essence of interest. With shorthand dictation one can talk as if he were at his own dinner-table – always a most inspiring place. (Paine 1912: vol. 4, 1268)

Such a method was a response to the problems Twain faced in creating autobiography by more traditional writerly methods. For he realized that writing is necessarily linear, logical, theme- or thesis-directed, ordered by a preconceived idea that is abstracted both from "personal relation" and from the plenum of reality:

> Within the last eight or ten years I have made several attempts to do the autobiography in one way or another with a pen, but the result was not satisfactory; it was too literary . . . With a pen in the hand the narrative stream is a canal; it moves slowly, smoothly, decorously, sleepily, it has no blemish except that it is all blemish. It is too literary, too prim, too nice; the gait and style and movement are not suited to narrative. (Twain 1924: vol. 1, 237)

Oral narration, on the other hand, conforms to neither law nor logic. It revels in *copia*, an endless flow of words, unconcerned about direction or prescribed destination, responsive to the current environment and situation:

narrative should flow as flows the brook down through the hills and the leafy wood-
lands, its course changed by every bowlder. . . . a brook that never goes straight for a
minute, . . . but always *going*, and always following at least one law, always loyal to that
law, the law of *narrative*, which *has no law*. (Twain 1924: vol. 1, 237)

Twain's pronouncements on oral composition and delivery and his denigration of
writing make it tempting, in our postmodern milieu, to jump to psychological and
metaphysical conclusions about his desire for an unmediated connection between
thought and language, a search for "presence," a return to unalloyed pristine orality,
or the achievement of a zero degree of writing (see Marotti 1990). But Twain's thrust
here is more rhetorical and aesthetic than philosophical:

> Written things are not for speech; their form is literary; they are stiff, inflexible, and
> will not lend themselves to happy and effective delivery with the tongue – where their
> purpose is to merely entertain, not instruct; they have to be limbered up, broken up,
> colloquialized, and turned into the common forms of unpremeditated talk – otherwise
> they will bore the house, not entertain it. (Twain 1940: 216)

Writing and speech have their own economies. Writing is not merely a record of
speech; speech is not simply voiced text. It is important to notice that Twain has
limited his claims about the superiority of speech over writing to narrative. It is entertainment, not instruction, that is at issue. Writing and reading do have educational
value; it is just that "they only get at the intellect of the house, they don't get at its
heart" (Twain 1940: 225). Likewise, the primary motivation for dictating the *Autobiography* is to keep it interesting – for both the writer and his audience. Twain is not
espousing a phonocentrism or claiming that writing is an inferior vehicle for all com-
municative purposes.

In fact, in both Twain's oral performances and his dictations, the oral is mediated
through writing. Though oral, the dictated autobiography is not backward-looking
toward an ideal oral tradition. The speaker clearly values literate modes of thought
and expression. Print sources are employed as *aides-memoires* and are incorporated into
the text. Dictation is predicated on a gramophone or a stenographer's pen, and editing
follows transcription, as subsequent radically different editions have demonstrated.
The *Autobiography* is a literate orality, "programmed spontaneity," reaching not toward
the past but toward secondary orality, the oral mediated through literacy (Ong 1982:
135). Twain's preference in some situations for the "oral," that is, for speaking over
writing, does not translate into a preference for "orality" over literacy. Again, modes
of communication and mindsets are not equivalent.

Similarly, oral delivery is not a quest for unmediated reality. Twain's performances
were text-based, whether from books or notes. In fact, his route for "getting to the
heart" is through a tunnel of deception, and writing is a tool to achieve naturalness.
The effect Twain hoped to achieve in his audiences was based on "studied fictions":
"fictitious unconscious pauses," "fictitious unconscious side remarks," "fictitious
unconscious embarrassments," "fictitious unconscious emphases" – all these are in
the arsenal of "artful fictive shades" which give to a recited tale the "captivating

naturalness of an impromptu narration" (Twain 1940: 224). The "art" of speaking
depends on literacy. Artificiality is not a problem in essence, only in effect. Twain
ridiculed Cable's elocution training not because his performance was thereby phony
but because it appeared phony: "[H]e was so well and thoroughly educated that he
was merely theatrical and artificial and not half as pleasing as he had been in the splendid days of his ignorance" (p. 216).

Twain was not a primitivist, in philosophy or in art. Though as he aged he became
increasingly skeptical about civilization, he nonetheless regarded literacy as more of
a gain than a loss. On the other hand, he did respond with almost religious fervor to
the power of oratory, the spoken word. Oral and moral intersect in verbal eloquence,
an age-old locus for unresolved tensions in residually oral speakers: sincerity and simplicity were indicators of authenticity and character, but both of the latter seemed
irreconcilable with artfulness. Aesthetics and ethics become intertwined here. But
Twain's passion for spoken eloquence does not mean an unqualified endorsement of
orality as a mindset. He was not willing to exchange his self-analytical awareness,
guilt-ridden as it might be, for the unconscious and spontaneous simplicity he associated with unlettered or naïve speakers.

"Unconscious" has a number of meanings for Twain. He relished tall-tale deadpan
poses, the simulated unconscious demeanor of the storyteller pretending ignorance.
He acknowledged the "unconscious and profitable cerebration" that nourished his
creative process (Twain 1940: 197). "Unconscious" implies the natural unpreten-
tiousness emanating from character, as reflected in his mother, and the "unstudied and
unconscious pathos [which] was her native speech" (Twain 1924: vol. 1, 117). "Unconscious" could also mean "instinctual" or "ignorant," and though this ignorance could
have charm, as in Huck Finn or the Paladin (from *Joan of Arc*), it was seldom removed
from the condescension reserved for children and the illiterate. Even if naïve or foolish,
they are at least authentic.

This value Twain attached to authenticity, I think, helps to explain the anomaly
of Joan of Arc: that is, Twain's infatuation with her, his fanatical and illogical adulation, and his complete failure of critical acumen in judging the book as his best work
(Paine 1912: vol. 3, 1034). Such a judgment, in defiance of his foundational literary,
religious, philosophical, and historical beliefs, must be deeply rooted in something
more than a quest for Victorian respectability. Issues of orality and literacy may
provide a key here.

Joan is the epitome of unconscious sincerity and native intelligence. Mark
Twain is emphatic about this: that she embodied "sweetness and simplicity and unconscious eloquence . . . whose source was the heart, not the head" (Twain 1896: 106,
125):

> And how it beggars the studied eloquence of the masters of oratory. Eloquence was a
> native gift of Joan of Arc; it came from her lips without effort and without preparation.
> Her words were as sublime as her deeds, as sublime as her character; they had their
> source in a great heart and were coined in a great brain. (p. 382)

She "disconcerted the sciences of the sages with her sublime ignorance – an ignorance which was a fortress; arts, wiles, the learning drawn from books, and all like missiles rebounded from its unconscious masonry" (p. 124–5).

Joan's inspiration is derived not from texts but from "voices." Her words are her actions and her character. Literacy, on the other hand, promotes cleavage, separation of self from knowledge, audience, and self. Such distancing is instrumental for mental and psychological growth, but – apparently – self-reflection would strip Joan of her greatness. Her unconsciousness and artless eloquence could not survive a reading lesson. Her sublime achievement is a function of her sublime ignorance, of her oral patterns of thought and communication. History would not remember a literate Joan of Arc (see Zlatic 1992).

Illiterate characters in Twain tend to be ignorant and dirty. Oral characters – children, slaves, medieval villagers – have a charm that derives from unconsciousness, but there is also a patronizing if not comic attitude taken toward them, even toward the minimally literate Huck Finn. In Joan, oral performance is not that of the cantankerous Pap, nor that of the bumptious raftsmen, or the blowhard Paladin, or the rousing but ignorant jongleurs; nor is it that of literate story-tellers in their simulated unconsciousness, or of mannered elocutionists such as Cable, or of such studied orators as the wily rhetoricians who besieged Joan. She does not represent a return to a pristine orality, which Twain had previously found to be a romantic concoction. His canonization of her is based on her integration of oral authenticity with an intellectual rigor that had been identified previously only with literacy. This was an innocence that was not to be patronized, a nonliterate character who was more than charmingly natural. No wonder Twain wished to turn back history and substitute her for a prelapsarian Eve facing the blandishments of the silver-tongued serpent (Paine 1912: vol. 4, 1546). Twain never ceased to insist on the historicity of his depiction of Joan, but his decision to tell her story through de Conte – a pre-Gutenberg narrator who has not fully interiorized writing as a perspective – indicates that at some level Twain may have been aware that his hagiography could not withstand scrutiny from a print-oriented age such as his own.

The participatory and interpersonal encounters of oral–aural communication remained for Mark Twain among life's peak moments, and spoken eloquence may be as close as the aging, cynical author came to religious experience. But his informal and professional oral performances were based on a substratum of writing. Orality as a mindset could be sentimentally charming in children and childlike unlettered adults, but it could be celebrated without qualifications only in the singularity of wish-fulfillment that is Joan of Arc.

NOTES

1   Among the many works dealing with orality/literacy in Twain, see the representative studies by Barrow (1991), Beaver (1987), Brown (1987), Hoffman (1988), Hurm (2003), Lowry (1996), Marotti (1990), Schmitz (1983), Wonham (1993), and Zlatic (1991a, 1991b, 1992).

2   The following discussion is based upon Ong's work, with specific reference to *Orality and Literacy* (Ong 1982); for related works see the bibliography there, and in Welch (1999), Foley (2002), and Hurm (2003).

3   Theories regarding autonomous or "strong" models of orality sometimes have been mistakenly attributed to Ong, who has pointedly rejected claims that he espouses an impassable cultural or cognitive gap between orality and literacy, or that he argues for an autonomous model of cultural change in which communications technologies influence individuals and societies independently from other cultural, historical, political, and technological forces. Ong states instead that his studies investigate not causation but "relationism": not how communications technologies determine change, but how they are related to all the cultural/historical forces that help to shape societies and individuals. Partly to avoid such misunderstandings, Ong late in life proposed "oralism" as an alternative to "orality."

Within Twain criticism the most vocal critic of Ong is Hurm, who rejects what he sees as an "essentialism" in orality studies, mistakenly using "Ong" as a code name for such an approach. Hurm provides some interesting readings of Twain, but he frames his analysis upon a misreading of Ong and Derrida, dichotomizing them around voice and text. Already in the 1950s Ong had rejected a spurious "corpuscular epistemology" – what Derrida later named "logocentrism" – and Derrida's deconstruction of a "metaphysics of presence" is unrelated to the sense of presence discussed by Ong (1982: 165–70). A more judicious reappraisal of orality studies can be found in Foley (2002).

4   Verbomotor culture is discussed in Zlatic (1992).

5   See Camfield: "sentimental gentility, rather than being alien to vernacular culture, was part of it" (1994: 18).

6   A number of critics have commented on this: see e.g. Beaver (1987), Hurm (2003), and Wonham (1993).

7   See e.g. Brown (1987), who demonstrates as well the "intertwining of oral and printed yarns."

References and Further Reading

Barrow, David (1991). "Mark Twain and the Oral Economy: Digression in the Age of Print." Ph.D. diss., Duke University.

Beaver, Harold (1987). *Huckleberry Finn*. London: Unwin.

Blair, Walter (1981). "Mark Twain and the Mind's Ear." In Sam B. Girgus (ed.), *The American Self: Myth, Ideology, and Popular Culture*, 231–39. Albuquerque: University of New Mexico Press.

Brown, Carolyn S. (1987). *The Tall Tale in American Folklore and Literature*. Knoxville: University of Tennessee Press.

Camfield, Gregg (1994). *Sentimental Twain: Samuel Clemens in the Maze of Moral Philosophy*. Philadelphia: University of Pennsylvania Press.

Fielding, Penny (1996). *Writing and Orality: Nationality, Culture, and Nineteenth-Century Scottish Fiction*. Oxford: Clarendon.

Foley, John Miles (2002). *How to Read an Oral Poem*. Urbana: University of Illinois Press.

Fulton, Joe B. (2000). *Mark Twain in the Margins: The Quarry Farm Marginalia and* A Connecticut Yankee in King Arthur's Court. Tuscaloosa: University of Alabama Press.

Gribben, Alan (1976). "'It is unsatisfactory to read to one's self': Mark Twain's Informal Readings." *Quarterly Journal of Speech* 62, 49–56.

Hall, David D. (1983). "Introduction: The Uses of Literacy in New England, 1600–1850." In William L. Joyce, David Hall, Richard D. Brown, and John B. Hench (eds.), *Printing and Society in Early America*, 1–47. Worcester, Mass.: American Antiquarian Society.

Heckel, David (1988). "Ong and Derrida: Orality, Literacy, and the Rhetoric of Deconstruction." Paper presented at the Conference on College Composition and Communication, St. Louis, March.

Hoffman, Andrew Jay (1988). *Twain's Heroes, Twain's Worlds: Mark Twain's Adventures of Huckleberry Finn, A Connecticut Yankee in King Arthur's Court, and Pudd'nhead Wilson*. Philadelphia: University of Pennsylvania Press.

Hurm, Gerd (2003). *Rewriting the Vernacular Mark Twain: The Aesthetics and Politics of Orality in Samuel Clemens's Fictions*. Trier: Wissenschaftlicher Verlag Trier.

Lecky, W. E. H. (1955). *History of the Rise and Influence of the Spirit of Rationalism in Europe*, 2 vols. in 1, intr. C. Wright Mills. New York: George Braziller. (First publ. 1878.)

Lowry, Richard S. (1996). *"Littery Man": Mark Twain and Modern Authorship*. New York: Oxford University Press.

Lynn, Robert Wood (1973). "Civil Catechetic in Mid-Victorian America: Some Notes about American Civil Religion, Past and Present." *Religious Education* 68, 5–27.

Marotti, Maria Ornella (1990). *The Duplicating Imagination: Twain and the Twain Papers*. University Park: Pennsylvania State University Press.

Marx, Leo (1988). *The Pilot and the Passenger: Essays on Literature, Technology, and Culture in the United States*. New York: Oxford University Press.

Messent, Peter (1993). "Racial and Colonial Discourse in Mark Twain's *Following the Equator*." *Essays in Arts and Sciences* 22, 67–84.

Moreland, Kim (1996). "Mark Twain: An Ambivalent Yankee in King Arthur's Court." In *The Medievalist Impulse in American Literature: Twain, Adams, Fitzgerald, and Hemingway*, 28–76. Charlottesville: University of Virginia Press.

Ong, Walter J. (1982). *Orality and Literacy: The Technologizing of the Word*. London: Methuen.

Paine, Albert Bigelow (1912). *Mark Twain: A Biography. The Personal and Literary Life of Samuel Langhorne Clemens, with Letters, Comments, and Incidental Writings Hitherto Unpublished; Also New Episodes, Anecdotes, Etc.* 4 vols. New York: Harper & Bros.

Schmitz, Neil (1983). *Of Huck and Alice: Humorous Writing in American Literature*. Minneapolis: University of Minnesota Press.

Scott, Donald M. (1983). "Print and the Public Lecture System, 1840–60." In William L. Joyce, David Hall, Richard D. Brown, and John B. Hench (eds.), *Printing and Society in Early America*, 278–99. Worcester, Mass.: American Antiquarian Society.

Smith, Henry Nash (1962). *Mark Twain: The Development of a Writer*. Cambridge, Mass.: Belknap/Harvard University Press.

Twain, Mark (1924). *Mark Twain's Autobiography*, 2 vols., ed. Albert Bigelow Paine. New York: Harper & Bros.

Twain, Mark (1940). *Mark Twain in Eruption*, ed. Bernard DeVoto. New York: Harper & Bros.

Twain, Mark, and Howells, William Dean (1960). *Mark Twain–Howells Letters: The Correspondence of Samuel L. Clemens and William D. Howells, 1872–1910*, 2 vols., ed. Henry Nash Smith and William M. Gibson. Cambridge, Mass.: Belknap/Harvard University Press.

Welch, Kathleen E. (1999). *Electric Rhetoric: Classical Rhetoric, Oralism, and a New Literacy*. Cambridge, Mass.: MIT Press.

Wonham, Henry B. (1993). *Mark Twain and the Art of the Tall Tale*. New York: Oxford University Press.

Zlatic, Thomas D. (1991a). "Mark Twain's View of the Universe." *Papers on Language and Literature* 27, 338–55.

Zlatic, Thomas D. (1991b). "Language Technologies in *A Connecticut Yankee*." *Nineteenth-Century Fiction* 45, 453–77.

Zlatic, Thomas D. (1992). "'The Seeing Eye and the Creating Mouth': Orality and Literacy in Mark Twain's *Joan of Arc*." *Clio* 21, 285–304.

15

Mark Twain and the Profession of Writing

Leland Krauth

The Emerging Professional

In "The Turning Point of My Life," an essay published in *Harper's Bazaar* in February 1910, just two months before he died, Mark Twain denied that there was any turning point in his life – or in anyone's. Playfully defying the premise of the *Harper's* series, the idea that the lives of famous authors were shaped by pivotal moments, he insisted that everyone's life was determined by an inevitable sequence of events, an inexorable "chain" that shackled the individual to his or her destiny. Tracking his own chain, he humorously traces his professional origin this way and that, back to Adam and Eve, at one far-fetched extreme, and to catching the measles, at another. While he thus spoofs causality and avoids any taint of self-importance, Twain does in fact acknowledge the center of a life that had no turning point. "To me," he writes, "the most important feature of my life is its literary feature. I have been professionally literary something more than forty years" (Twain 1992b: 931). The avowal that he has been a professional writer seems appropriate enough, indeed obvious; but, as his autobiographical reminiscences make clear, he had led other lives as well: journeyman typesetter, riverboat pilot, silver miner, stock speculator, hopeful inventor, part-time politico, confident publisher, intrepid entrepreneur, and devoted family man. Twain saw it all, as his friend and literary sponsor William Dean Howells recalled, as a "fairy" tale, an "Arabian Nights story," one that he never tired of telling (Howells 1910: 10). Nonetheless, marvelous as these other lives may have been, in the end Twain knew that his life had revolved around the profession of writing.[1]

Twain's final account of his literary life in "The Turning Point" is especially notable for what it ignores: the long first phase of early amateur and professional newspaper work. For of course Sam Clemens wrote and published long before Mark Twain – his famous persona – came into being. Sam's early efforts, frequently topical, generally slight, often comic, arose, on the one hand, from what was deepest in him, a creativity that insisted on expressing itself, and, on the other, from the working world in which he grew from boyhood to maturity. He was impelled toward the profession of writing by emergent genius and dire happenstance. After his father's death, when Sam was apprenticed to Joseph P. Ament, publisher of the *Missouri Courier*, he entered, at the lowest level, a world of words in which an author was a figure who mattered. When Twain came to recall this time in 1886 in a talk to the Typothetae (an association of master printers), he would remember chiefly his drudgery as a cub who built fires, fetched water, swept the floor, redistributed type, cleaned the rollers, washed the forms, and folded and delivered the paper (Twain 1910: 182–5). But there, in the print shop, he witnessed the force and magic of the written word. He saw at first hand its power to convey facts, mock foolishness, shape opinion, advance ideas, advocate causes, enlarge perspectives, demolish pettiness, celebrate greatness, honor the past, herald the future, and, perhaps most beguilingly, entertain. Seeing all this, he was enticed to write.

Although they have been insufficiently examined, Twain's early newspaper writings form the gateway to his career as a professional writer. The world in which Sam Clemens grew up was a hardscrabble, frontier one, but it valued books, reading, and writing, recognizing that literacy along with a smattering of learning was a likely way to both prosperity and prominence. Twain's early newspaper pieces do not in themselves foretell the brilliant writer to come, but they do reveal his gradual movement toward authorship as a profession. Having published letters and sketches, off and on, from 1851 to 1861, Twain turned professional journalist in the West in 1862 when he joined the staff of the Virginia City *Territorial Enterprise*. His Western writing generally falls into four categories: local news items, special political reports (most often factual, occasionally satiric), hoaxes, and humorous sketches centered on real or fictive experience. In penning all these he practiced the craft of writing. He worked for steady wages as a reporter and for piecemeal pay as a contributor to journals, chiefly the *Golden Era* and the *Californian*. A key foundation for his future life as a writer was laid in this Western journalism: he worked for money. For him, writing was first of all a trade, a way of making a living. He came to and remained in the profession of writing not as a man of leisure indulging an avocation, but as a person of practical need earning a living by skill.

In the West, Twain became a competent journalist and a skilled writer of short, humorous fictions. However, there is some uncertainty about when he committed himself to the profession of writing. His first biographer maintained that even after the publication of *The Innocents Abroad* in 1869 Twain did not think of himself as a literary man, and that at that point he had no plans for another book (Twain 1917: vol. 1, 162). One of his recent biographers has insisted to the contrary that as early as 1860 Twain desired and expected to achieve fame through his writing (Hoffman 1997: 57). While an exact date may remain elusive, it is clear that, though he flirted with notions of other jobs, once he arrived in the East in 1867 he became a professional writer with breakneck speed.

In 1867 Twain published *The Celebrated Jumping Frog of Calaveras County and Other Sketches*. In 1869 he became an editor of and writer for the *Buffalo Express*, and in the same year he published *The Innocents Abroad*, the travel book that made him famous (and somewhat rich). In 1870 he signed a contract with the American Publishing Company to write a second book, which eventually became *Roughing It*, thereby inaugurating what would become a recurrent interest in sequels (see Emerson 2000: 71). He undertook at the same time to write a monthly column for the *Galaxy* magazine. In 1873 he brought out his first novel, *The Gilded Age* (co-authored with Charles Dudley Warner). In 1874 he published *Mark Twain's Sketches, Number One* (the "Number One" promised more numbers to come) and launched a dramatized version of *The Gilded Age* in New York. In 1875 he began his "Old Times on the Mississippi" series in the *Atlantic Monthly* and brought out Mark Twain's *Sketches, New and Old*. Most significantly, in 1876 he published *The Adventures of Tom Sawyer*. Whatever divergent inclinations he might have had, and whatever misgivings, he was by 1876 firmly established as what he would be for the rest of his life: a professional writer who worked in multiple genres and published in venues that ranged from the humdrum to the influential.

Twain and the Business of Writing

In 1899 Twain published "My Début as a Literary Person" in the *Century* magazine. With a characteristic combination of play and truth he recalled that début as a fiasco. He claims that when, in 1866, he published in *Harper's Monthly* his account of the *Hornet* shipwreck and those who survived it and six weeks at sea in their lifeboat, he was expecting to be "famous," so famous he could afford to give a "banquet." But his plans miscarried and there was no celebration, since *Harper's* had misread his signature as "Mike Swain," not "Mark Twain." The result, he says, was that he was "a Literary Person" who was "buried alive." Perhaps the most interesting revelation in this comic sketch is Twain's insistence that "a person who published things in a mere newspaper could not properly claim recognition as a Literary Person: he must rise away above that; he must appear in a magazine" (Twain 1996b: 84–5).

Twain thus acknowledged in retrospect what he knew at the time: that there was a clear hierarchy in the varied profession of writing. At the bottom was writing for newspapers, above that was writing for magazines (how far above depended on the particular journal), and at the top was writing for publication in a book. Twain wanted to move up in the profession of writing.[2] He had acquired in his earliest years, as a part of the ethos of his small-town world, the ineradicable belief (by no means an incorrect one, for the talented) that writing was a way of advancing not only economically but also socially. And Mark Twain was nothing if not upwardly mobile.

The world of writing Twain entered was exploding. As period histories make clear, the decades from the Civil War to the First World War were marked by an unprecedented expansion in print media. Developments in production, distribution, communication, advertising, and even managerial techniques made the printed word more readily and widely available than ever (at lower costs than ever), and the market for writers' work expanded correspondingly. These familiar changes need to be recalled here to put into perspective the burgeoning profession Twain entered. In the 1870s the number of newspapers in America almost doubled to about 7,000, and the growth continued through the 1880s until by 1890 there were over 12,000 newspapers in the country. The number of magazines published in America increased phenomenally, from 200 in 1860 to 1,800 by the turn of the century. The publication of books expanded dramatically from about 1,000 new titles a year in the 1830s to over 3,000 a year in the 1870s and an astonishing 6,000 a year at the turn of the century. In the second half of the nineteenth century the United States had the largest literate population of any country up to that point in history. It is important to note, also, that this vast audience for the written word was not one community but many. Writing, from newspapers to magazines to books, catered to different groups defined by class, race, region, ethnicity, and gender (Brodhead 1993). And while the market for the written word was large, it was also chancy, for there were significant economic depressions in Twain's time – one from 1873 to 1879, another from 1893 to 1897.

Twain announced his urge to move up socially as well as economically via the hierarchy of writing frequently and with characteristic certitude. He actually enjoyed all three media – newspapers, magazines, and books – while being well aware of clear distinctions among them. Twain knew the enormous power of the press in his time, but it was a power that lacked prestige. Although he could upon occasion criticize the press for lies, slander, and ignorance (see Twain 1992a: 551–5), he more often celebrated it as a check on social pretension and political tyranny, on the one hand, and as a spur to free thought, liberty, and democracy, on the other (see chapter 10 of *The American Claimant*, for instance). He wrote for newspapers at the beginning of his career, and he never stopped writing for them or, in his later years, giving them interviews. (His newspaper writing lacks an extended critical study; for illuminating brief commentaries see Budd 1981a; Fishkin 1985.) But as early as 1870 he was explaining to Mary Mason Fairbanks, his friend, sometimes editor, and social mentor from the *Quaker City* excursion, that he would prefer to write for magazines:

> I needed a *Magazine* wherein to shovel any fine-spun stuff that might accumulate in my head, & which isn't entirely suited to either a daily, Weekly, or *any* kind of newspaper. You see I often feel like writing something, & before I set down the first word I think, "No, it isn't worth while to write it – might do for a magazine, but not a newspaper." (Twain 1995: 95)

But no sooner had he declared his intention to abandon newspaper publication for magazines than he complained of "cheapening" himself by "periodical dancing before the public" (p. 350). He announced with seeming determination that he would "write no more for any periodical." Despite, he said, being offered "great prices," he would "simply write books" (p. 338).

There was in fact no decisive, final step for Twain up what he saw as the ladder of professional prestige. He continued to write for newspapers even as he entered the magazine world, and to write for magazines even as he turned out books. As a professional writer, Twain sent his work every which way. He wrote so copiously and so variously that he needed multiple outlets for his work.

Who read Mark Twain? The easy answer – and an accurate one – is many people. He hoped to reach a large audience, but he certainly understood the difference between the *Atlantic* readership and that of the New York *Tribune*. In a well-known letter to the English critic Andrew Lang he declared that he wrote for "the Belly and the Members" – that is, the lower classes, not the "cultivated classes" (Twain 1917: vol. 2, 525, 527); but reviews of his works make it clear that the cultivated also took note of Mark Twain. If he entertained what he once called "the kitchen & the stable," at the same time he amused "the drawing room" (Twain and Howells 1960: 193). In time, as his fame spread, he could command appearance in the most prestigious magazines, the *Atlantic Monthly*, *Harper's Monthly*, and the *Century*, for instance; in less exalted but very popular ones, such as *St. Nicholas Magazine*, *Cosmopolitan*, and *Collier's*; and in relatively obscure ones, such as *Forum*, the *New Princeton Review*, and the *Pennsylvania Magazine*. Though a piece here and there was rejected, on the whole Twain eventually had ready access at any time to one or another of the many magazines that flooded the country. Declaim as he might about a magazine as the appropriate organ for his "fine-spun stuff," Twain was interested in the money he could make, and he did not hesitate to haggle over prices for his work (Budd 1981b: 38–9).

More men than women read newspapers, but when one looks at magazines, the gender of the readers varies from journal to journal. The readership for books, potentially the most lucrative market, is especially important, but controversial. Thinking principally of novels, Nina Baym has maintained that women's fiction was "by far the most popular literature of its time [1820–1870]" and that "on the strength of that popularity, authorship in America was established as a woman's profession and reading as a woman's avocation" (Baym 1978: 11). In his provocative study *Gender, Fantasy, and Realism in American Literature*, Alfred Habegger also argues not only that the predominant audience was female but also that the profession of writing was gendered female. This leads him to discuss the personal gender difficulties Howells and James faced in their commitment to the literary profession (Habegger 1982: ss. III and IV). However, other studies have seen a masculinizing of the profession, especially in the closing decades of the nineteenth century (Wilson 1985: 58, 61–2). While the profession of writing may have been demonstrably female when Twain thrust himself into the print world at all levels, he was confidently male in his writing and completely untroubled by any notion of female dominance in the profession. The reason for this was threefold: first, he came to writing via the print shop, a male enclave; second, he learned his craft as a journalist, another largely male preserve; and finally (and perhaps most importantly) he initially made his way as a humorist writing in a roughshod male mode.

One significant sea-change clearly underway at this time, though its depth is difficult to sound, was a shift from writing governed by a didactic aesthetic to writing shaped by an entertainment aesthetic (Newbury 1997: 3–4). Everyone thinks of Mark Twain as a great, perhaps *the* great entertainer of his time; but he was also a didactic moralist, a social critic, a commentator on the drift of civilization itself, making his general appeal as double as his pseudonym. (In his autobiography he insisted in long retrospect that he had always preached.) By serendipity, calculation, or instinct, he wrote in many popular – and profitable – genres. From his travel books to his topical satires, in his boy adventures, his mysteries, his historical romances, and even his philosophical and religious commentaries, he was attuned to the interests of his time. In his versions of these forms he typically created an idiosyncratic amalgamation of realism, sentimentality, and humor. Softening realism with sentiment, or tempering sentimentality with realism, he bridged the great divide between feminized literature and stark realism. Working in one popular form after another, Twain rode the high tides of his profession.

As the demand for writing soared, payments to authors rose, royalties increased, and authorship achieved new prominence. But if the Gilded Age suddenly seemed a golden one for writers, there were also serious dislocations. The very idea of authorship changed, both diminishing and empowering the writer. Writing was commercialized, and literature, once a rare and treasured gem of culture, was commodified, becoming a product to be produced, traded, and consumed. On the one hand, this profound change brought with it for the writer the chance (a relatively new one) of economic prosperity. On the other, it gave editors and publishers, the middlemen in the new market, increasing power to tell the author what was wanted: that is, what would sell. Financial gain was thus countered by a loss of authorial independence. In one sense, a writer was a lesser figure by virtue of market direction; but in another, by virtue of increased readership a writer was more important than ever.

One response to this welter of shifts was the professionalization of authorship itself. In Twain's time American culture in general underwent a new professionalization (see Bledstein 1976). Religion, law, and medicine solidified their standing as professions, and education, science, and authorship began to acquire the same firm footing. Sociologists have defined the creation of any profession as the result of a combination of multiple cultural forces and imaginings. The most determinant among them are special education, skill, or training; an exclusionary mystique; and a social positioning apart from the mainstream. Such forces came into play for authors in Twain's time, altering writing for ever; but in this development, as with so many aspects of writing, Twain himself was something of an anomaly.

To begin with, he did not worry much about the status of an author. For him, writing was a very respectable but not supremely exalted endeavor; he saw it as work that paid and as a way to improve his social standing. He loved literature and revered some classic authors with an almost schoolboy enthusiasm, while detesting others with a kind of adolescent fervor, but he had no quarrel with the commodification of literature, and he found his audience through his humor and his instinctive exploitation of popular genres. He welcomed the anonymous masses whose salience left other writers in dismay. While for many authors the trade-off of increased income for reduced personal control engendered a sense of impotence, Twain suffered no such feeling – far from it.

For Twain associated professional writing with power. One key to his sense of empowerment was his mode of book publication. When asked in 1867 by Elisha Bliss of the American Publishing Company to write a book based on his *Quaker City* travels to Europe and the Holy Land, Twain entered the world of subscription publishing – and, as it turned out, would never leave it. That world was far from the realm inhabited (or aspired to) by most serious writers of literature. It was for the most part a domain governed by capital investment, market demands, and profit returns. Subscription publishing flourished from just before the Civil War to the turn of the century, and its success was, in large measure, the result of its unconventional tactics. A subscription publisher typically contracted for a book, calculated its size, format, and illustrations, put together a prospectus, advertised it in newspapers and trade journals, then solicited canvassers for it, who were sent out to sell the book house to house, flat to flat, farm to farm; only finally – after a sufficient number of buyers had signed on to buy it – did the publisher actually begin to print it. Subscription publishing reached a large audience, one that did not normally have access to bookstores, but it often marketed items of dubious quality. Still, by the end of the nineteenth century many reputable trade houses had a subscription branch, often offering fancy collected editions of famous English and American authors. Some cultural historians have surmised that such collections were valued as bric-a-brac, but (whatever the cause) many of them sold very well.

After the subscription success of *The Innocents Abroad*, Twain became a lifelong devotee of the process. He believed in it because he profited from it – and perhaps because he believed in reaching a general public. He continued to bring out his works through subscription, arranged for some friends (Bret Harte and Dan De Quille, for instance) to be published by subscription, repeatedly urged Howells to take that route, and actually made it pay for Grant. Most importantly, he eventually established his own subscription house, Charles L. Webster & Company. (This alone makes Twain a unique figure in the American profession of writing.) Webster & Company had both foreseen and unexpected consequences for Twain. He did make money for his firm (over $200,000 for Grant's *Memoirs* alone), but he also lost money. He became something of an expert on subscription publishing, and his expertise positioned him a long way distant from the usual writer. Even though it failed (and contributed to his bankruptcy), his venture into publishing along the roughest but potentially most profitable path bolstered his sense of personal power as a professional. He reveled in the idea that subscription publishing involved "an enormous lot of machinery," and envisioned it in telling military metaphors:

> It is easy to see, when one travels around, that one must be endowed with a deal of genuine generalship in order to maneuver a publication whose line of battle stretches from end to end of a great continent, & whose foragers & skirmishers invest every hamlet & besiege every village hidden away in all the vast space between. (Twain 1995: 41)

While some writers felt increasing impotence, personal diminishment, and loss of control, Twain as self-publisher felt just the opposite. And insofar as society was giving the writer ever more cultural clout, Twain dealt in spades. He was an author in control of all aspects of his craft and its dissemination (or so it seemed), and he was a prominent public figure. Even after the collapse of his publishing firm, his fame (and marketability) guaranteed that his wishes as a writer would be respected. His imagined – and real – authority as a writer was immense. Twain was something of a Titan in the field.

But even as such, Twain chose not to stand alone. Throughout his career he thought of himself as a part of a community of writers. Early on, he was a newspaper journalist among other journalists, but even as he moved up in the stratified world of letters, he continued to think of himself as a member of a confederation of writers. Revealingly, when he recalled his life's vocation in "The Turning Point of My Life," he defined himself as a member of "the literary guild" (Twain 1992b: 935). Although authorship had been variously figured in the antebellum period in relation to modes of production (Newbury 1997: 5), for Twain to figure himself as a guild member seems at first glance surprising. It is, however, natural, since the print-shop world he knew as an apprentice compositor was organized around the practices of craft guilds.

Twain not only thought of himself as a part of a "literary guild" – a professional writer among other professionals – but also undertook or planned a notable number of joint literary ventures. He co-authored *The Gilded Age* with Charles Dudley Warner, wrote a play with Bret Harte and planned several with Howells, co-edited with Howells a library of humor, toured the lecture circuit with George Washington Cable, collaborated on a comedy with the playwright Siegmund Schlesinger, and promoted a composite novel to be written in separate chapters, as he put it, by various "big literary fish" (Twain and Howells 1960: vol. 1, 60). These associations are finally less important for the works they created (or failed to create) than for what they suggest about Twain as a professional author: his deep and constant sense of himself as a writer working alongside other writers in a shared craft. Although some studies have begun to explore this area, the full extent of Twain's literary associations remains to be studied.

Pragmatist that he was, Twain aligned himself with other writers on an issue of special concern to all literary professionals, one that troubled Twain in particular throughout his career: copyright. He suffered incalculable financial losses from pirated editions of his works (though these bastard texts did spread his fame), and he went to great lengths to protect himself. He arranged as often as he could to have his books published first in England, thereby securing British copyright; he hired lawyers to challenge Canadian pirates; and he enjoined his own American publishers to derail unauthorized printings of his works. But when he spoke in behalf of extended copyright (he was in favor of copyright in perpetuity but welcomed any extension of it) he spoke for *all* writers as a member of what he repeatedly called the "trade" of making "the literature of the land" (Twain 1910: 314–21). Advocating extended copyright, he spoke out stridently – and humorously – as a professional writer concerned for all writers.

Twain's use of the term "trade" is an honest expression of the way he conceived of his work. It puts him at odds with most of his contemporaries, certainly with those genteel writers who imagined themselves the high priests of culture, but even with the more original and powerful writers who forged American realism, like Howells and James. Howells is the most illuminating case in point. In 1893, in a now famous essay, he discussed "The Man of Letters as a Man of Business." Howells had by then been at the epicenter of American letters for over 25 years, and his essay acknowledged the radically altered conditions of the professional writer by making it clear that the writer had become a businessman. But while summoning enough of his democratic fervor to concede that "the author is, in the last analysis, merely a workingman" (Howells 1959: 307), Howells did not really countenance the new role. He opens his essay with an old-fashioned notion that is really his deepest conviction:

> I do not think any man ought to live by an art. A man's art should be his privilege, when he has proven his fitness to exercise it, and has otherwise earned his daily bread; and its results should be free to all. There is an instinctive sense of this, even in the midst of the grotesque confusion of our economic being; people feel that there is something profane, something impious, in taking money for a picture, or a poem, or a statue. Most of all, the artist himself feels this. (Howells 1959: 298)

Howells felt it; he understood that the professional writer had of necessity become a businessman, but he clearly regretted it. Twain understood that change too, but he not only accepted it, he drew strength – and pleasure as well as profit – from it. Though often frustrated, vexed, or infuriated by the business of writing, at bottom he reveled in it, for, as he told Howells, with some truth as well as a lot of good humor: "I take a vile, mercenary view of things" (Twain and Howells 1960: vol. 1, 92).

The Resisting Writer

In an early *Galaxy* piece, "My First Literary Venture" (1871) Twain reminisced about, and fictionalized in playful ways, some of his earliest writing. The sketch is slight but intriguing. He recalls a one-week stint editing his uncle's newspaper (actually his brother Orion's) in which he first made fun of the editor of a rival paper and his failed resolve on suicide after being jilted, then attacked another editor in a parody of "Sir John Moore," followed that with lampoons of "two prominent citizens," and finally capped his play with a send-up of a local dandy, a "simpering coxcomb," via a sentimental poem that spoofed the lady-killer as it parodied Robert Burns. Multiplying his fun, he also created fictional responses to his own pieces. He claimed that his "First Literary Venture" provoked threats of "dissection," "tomahawking," "libel," and having his uncle's "head shot off" (Twain 1996a: 93–5). Loosely factual and firmly comic, the sketch nonetheless discloses fundamental impulses in Twain's writing. The account reveals not only his irresistible desire to be funny but also the aggression latent in his humor. It suggests even more. On the one hand, it shows his inveterate urge to attack pretension and debunk sham, and on the other, it signals his curiously recurrent inclination to turn against literature itself, or at least some kinds of literature. For Twain not only assails social types but also parodies literary forms.

Throughout his career Twain turned, often gently, sometimes sharply, against literature. His resistance to his own profession as a maker of literature shows up in multiple ways. The most obvious is just what his 1871 sketch reveals: an inveterate urge to burlesque, denigrate, or slight some forms of literature. To be sure, making fun of one kind of literature is often a writer's way of dealing with a troubling precursor or just dismissing what the nascent writer takes to be the facile in order to make way for the authentic. (One thinks at once of Fielding's parody of the sentimental, domestic novel, or Austen's spoof of the gothic.) When Twain began writing in the West, literary burlesque was something of a stock comic device. What is striking in his case, though, is how broad and persistent his impulse to burlesque was. Perhaps no other major American writer has had such an inclination to laugh at the creations of the profession he practiced. He mocked news reports, fashion items, social columns, and celebrity features as well as temperance literature, French novels, Shakespearean tragedy, fairy tales, gothic novels, autobiographical success stories, love romances, and sentimental fictions. His impulse to laugh at popular literary forms was so deep-seated that it persisted throughout his career. Even the last piece published in his lifetime, "The Turning Point of My Life," originally began with a burlesque (his daughter Jean and biographer Paine talked Twain into omitting it from the final version). This lifelong obsession with subverting literary forms is usually seen as a dislike of feeble, outworn modes or as an easy means of broad humor. But Twain's recurrent attacks on a wide range of literature may also reveal some doubt about literature itself – and about those who create it.

Embedded in each of Twain's important works is a notable resistance to his own text. His works contain moments, small and large, of self-subversion, moments in which he turns against the very kind of literature he is writing. As he writes his travel narrative, *The Innocents Abroad*, he parodies the form. He exploits the sensational love story in *The Gilded Age* and yet mocks it. Even more notably, as he writes a bad-boy story in *The Adventures of Tom Sawyer* he spoofs the genre, and after creating boy adventure in *Adventures of Huckleberry Finn* he ends by burlesquing the form itself. Even *A Connecticut Yankee in King Arthur's Court* begins as a mockery of the combat-driven, pathos-laden medieval romance only to become one, thereby undercutting its comic form. The impulse to resist the very writing he is doing seems endemic in Twain.

Even more obvious is his quarrel with his own creative process. Perhaps every writer struggles in the act of writing, but Twain seems to have suffered more than most. Indeed, he most often cursed his way through the creation of a book. He worried as he wrote *The Innocents Abroad*, railed against *Roughing It*, wanted to cut "Old Times," pigeonholed *Tom Sawyer* while in the middle of it, fumed as he tried to shape *A Tramp Abroad*, hated the work of padding out *Life on the Mississippi*, dawdled for eight years in writing *Huckleberry Finn* (and said along the way that he might "burn the MS when it is done" [Twain and Howells 1960: vol. 1, 144]), battled his way through *A Connecticut Yankee*, performed, by his own account, a desperate caesarian operation to give birth to *Pudd'nhead Wilson*, and felt he was in "hell" as he wrote *Following the Equator* (Twain and Howells 1960: vol. 2, 690). And, of course, he never finished *The Mysterious Stranger*, though he worked on it off and on for almost 11 years, sometimes feeling exhilarated by it – "an intellectual drunk" – and sometimes finding it "perfectly horrible – and perfectly beautiful" (Twain and Howells 1960: vol. 2, 698–9). One might argue that the only notable book Twain enjoyed writing was *The Prince and the Pauper*, since even *Joan of Arc*, a book he cherished, caused him trouble as he felt obliged to extend his original narrative of Joan's life through her military triumphs to include her trial and death. While his volatile temperament no doubt led him to exaggerate his tribulations as a writer, there is surely some fire beneath all the smoke.

His aversion to his own creative process was usually a private matter, recorded only in his notebooks and in letters to his friends, most notably Howells. But in December 1877, in a very public forum, he may have been airing his reservations when he gave his now famous Whittier birthday speech. The occasion was an august one. Sponsored by the *Atlantic*, the dinner honored John Greenleaf Whittier on his seventieth birthday, but it also celebrated the *Atlantic* itself, New England literary culture, and – most importantly here – the profession of writing in America. The often-analyzed speech seems to attack – overtly or covertly, depending on how one reads it – not just the genteel writers it playfully misrepresents (Longfellow, Emerson, and Holmes), but the profession of writing itself and Twain himself as a writer. Placing the speech in the context of professional writing, Lowry points out that Twain "profaned" the "burden of reverence" surrounding authorship in America (Lowry 1996: 29). Although the particular occasion garnered considerable publicity, Twain's inclination to diminish the act – and significance – of writing was an abiding one, though not usually as visible as in this moment. At just the time writing was becoming professionalized to ensure its importance, Twain set himself against the current, demystifying the profession he practiced so successfully.

Twain rarely wrote about writing or literature in any extended way. Compared to Howells or James in this regard, he is virtually mute. But when he did, here and there, mention his craft he tended to democratize it; he insistently transformed it from an esoteric art into ordinary work. "Every day," he told a friend, "I nerve myself, & sieze [*sic*] my pen, & dispose my paper, & prepare to buckle on the harness & *work*!" (Twain 1995: 70). He chafed under the harness but knew the need to pull. Writing was work, and Twain often put it on a par with other forms of labor: "Every man must *learn* his trade – not pick it up. God requires that he learn it by slow and painful processes. The apprentice-hand, in black-smithing, in medicine, in literature, in everything, is a thing that can't be hidden" (Twain 1917: vol. 1, 322).

He talked about writing in a workman's terms. Style was bricklaying; inspiration was tank-filling; imaginative space was a builder's shipyard. And he said he "shoveled" his work into one newspaper or periodical after another. In 1883 in *Life on the Mississippi* he described himself as just a scribbler, a unimportant hack, and even in

1894 – after over 30 years as a professional writer – he called himself a jackleg, a mere novice.

Unlike most writers, Twain threatened time and again to quit writing altogether. In 1874, early in his career, he avowed that he would "quit authorizing in a minute to go piloting" (Twain and Howells 1960: vol. 1, 50). In 1889, midway along in his life as a writer, he announced that *A Connecticut Yankee* was his "swan-song," his "retirement from literature permanently" (Twain and Howells 1960: vol. 2, 610–11). Although he made such disavowals of his work off and on throughout his career, most of them were prompted by some specific circumstance. In the first instance just cited he is more interested in trumpeting his past experience as a pilot (about which he was then writing) than in dismissing his profession as a writer. And his announcement of "retirement" from literature is provoked by his anticipation of making a fortune from the Paige typesetter. After his bankruptcy in 1894 Twain had to write to recover financially, and after the death of his daughter Susy in 1896 he found refuge from his grief in his writing. Yet as late as 1899, when his finances were restored and his grief lessened, Twain told Howells that he had harbored the desire to quit writing: "For several years I have been intending to stop writing for print as soon as I could afford it" (vol. 2, 698).

For one reason or another Twain did often stop writing. Perhaps his pauses were welcome insofar as he found writing trying, bothersome, at times even hateful, but in any case he repeatedly stopped, restarted, and then abandoned one project after another, short or long. Critics have often lamented this and just as often seen his sporadic writing, his fits and lapses, as signals that he was essentially a flawed writer, one who could never tell the good from the bad, the likely from the impossible. But his stop-and-start, forget-and-finish, hit-and-miss mode of literary creation seems to me to suggest something quite different. On the one hand, it does reveal a resistance to his professional work; but on the other, it discloses his astounding creative energy. Envisioning one literary work after another, Twain exerted an enormous, wide-ranging imaginative talent. Far from indicating confusion or ineptitude, his helter-skelter work as a writer, his ceaseless, literary scheming, signals – perhaps more than anything else – how deeply he was enthralled by the profession of writing. Complain though he did about it, the resisting writer simply could not resist writing.

The Consummate Professional

Each of the three previous sections of this essay has begun with one of Twain's own sketches about his work as a writer. Together, they virtually span his career, running from 1871 to 1899 to 1910. They demonstrate that he thought self-consciously about himself in his profession as he practiced it. Despite deploring many forms of literature, despite making fun of the very modes he employed, and despite complaining about the trials of creating his own works, Twain was a consummate professional writer.

Unusual as he was as a writer, Twain's way of doing things paid off not just in popularity, money, fame, and personal satisfaction (punctuated by annoyance) but ultimately in recognition. A lifelong believer in the suitability of subscription publishing for his work, he also knew that the traditional trade outlets bestowed more status. He was conflicted: on the one hand, he felt that "a book in the trade is a book thrown away, as far as money-profit goes" (Twain 1917: vol. 2, 579); on the other, he understood that "Mighty few books that come strictly under the head of *literature* will sell by subscription" (quoted in Hill 1964: 11). He knew that high-class books came from trade houses, and he wanted to be ranked with the high-class at the same time he wanted to be widely read by the middling sorts. And in the end (or near end) he had it both ways. Complex arrangements eventually made his collected works available by subscription through the American Publishing Company in America but also through one of the most elite of American trade houses, Harper & Brothers. In England he was brought out anew by his long-time publisher, Chatto & Windus, in a deluxe edition. In short, by the turn of the century, when he returned from his decade-long exile in Europe, Mark Twain was available by subscription, or through trade houses, in popular, deluxe, and library collected editions. He had made himself both a popular and a respectable author, both lowbrow and highbrow. No other author of his time came close to this achievement.

Some time ago James M. Cox made what still seems the essential point about Mark Twain as a professional writer. When one examines Twain in this capacity, beneath, or rather alongside, his multiple roles as lecturer, publisher, politico, entrepreneur, and even inventor, what one finds is finally "a Mark Twain who emerges before us as nothing but writing. To read his notebooks is to see him turning everything at hand into writing. If he is traveling, it is never to take a vacation to get away from his 'profession' but to turn every trip and every observation into a book" (Cox 1984: 101). Paradoxical as it seems, Twain's many-sided life was not a distraction from but the groundwork for his writing. And writing was the be-all and end-all of his creative identity. Compared to any of his contemporary fellow writers, Twain was more savvy about every aspect of his profession – from the trials of creation, to the apparatus of publication, to the location of audience, to the public relations of selling, to the quicksands of reviewing, to the marketing of the writer himself. In all of this, Twain is clearly the first modern American professional writer.

He took himself seriously as a writer but refused to be seen doing so. In the context of his time, he is something of an odd man out. While most serious writers looked for publication through reputable publishing houses, he embraced subscription publishing; while other writers clung to – or tried to create – a grand view of the writer, he cast himself as just a craftsman working at his trade; while many writers deplored the commercialization of literature in the emerging culture of consumption, he welcomed it, sought ways to capitalize on it, and delighted in the profits it provided. He made more money from his writing, and reached a wider audience, than any other important writer of his time. As a professional writer, he was an anomaly in his era, perhaps most so because he wrote some of the most important literature of his time, while pretending not to. When Howells memorialized him as "sole, incomparable" (Howells 1910: 101) he was, to use a phrase Twain would have approved of, right on the money.

NOTES

1 The seminal study of Twain and authorship is Lowry (1996). Emerson (2000) provides a useful, detailed account of Twain's writing and publishing.

2 Twain thought as early as 1865 of writing a book about the Mississippi, and a year later he was contemplating turning his letters from the Sandwich Islands into a book. One of the first things he did when he arrived in New York in 1867 was to try to arrange book publication of a collection of his short pieces. Clearly, he aimed for the highest status in the profession he was approaching.

REFERENCES AND FURTHER READING

Baym, Nina (1978). *Women's Fiction: A Guide to Novels by and about Women in America, 1820–1870*. Ithaca, NY: Cornell University Press.

Bledstein, Burton (1976). *The Culture of Professionalism: The Middle Class and the Development of Higher Education*. New York: Norton.

Brodhead, Richard H. (1993). *Cultures of Letters: Scenes of Reading and Writing in Nineteenth-Century America*. Chicago: University of Chicago Press.

Budd, Louis J. (1981a). "Color Him Curious about Yellow Journalism: Mark Twain and the New York City Press." *Journal of Popular Culture* 15: 2, 25–33.

Budd, Louis J. (1981b). "Mark Twain and the Magazine World." *University of Mississippi Studies in English* 2 (n.s.), 35–42.

Charvat, William (1968). *The Profession of Authorship in America, 1800–1870*, ed. Matthew J. Bruccoli. Columbus: Ohio State University Press.

Cox, James M. (1984). "*Life on the Mississippi* Revisited." In Sara deSaussure Davis and Philip D. Beidler, eds., *The Mythologizing of Mark Twain*, 99–115. Tuscaloosa: University of Alabama Press.

Emerson, Everett (2000). *Mark Twain: A Literary Life*. Philadelphia: University of Pennsylvania Press.

Fishkin, Shelley Fisher (1985). *From Fact to Fiction: Journalism and Imaginative Writing in America*. Baltimore: Johns Hopkins University Press.

Habegger, Alfred (1982). *Gender, Fantasy, and Realism in American Literature*. New York: Columbia University Press.

Hill, Hamlin (1964). *Mark Twain and Elisha Bliss*. Columbia: University of Missouri Press.

Hoffman, Andrew (1997). *Inventing Mark Twain: The Lives of Samuel Langhorne Clemens*. New York: Morrow.

Howells, William Dean (1910). *My Mark Twain: Reminiscences and Criticisms*. New York: Harper & Bros.

Howells, William Dean (1959). "The Man of Letters as a Man of Business." In Clara Marburg Kirk and Rudolf Kirk, eds., *Criticism and Fiction and Other Essays*, 298–9. New York: New York University Press.

Lowry, Richard S. (1996). *"Littery Man": Mark Twain and Modern Authorship*. New York: Oxford University Press.

Newbury, Michael (1997). *Figuring Authorship in Antebellum America*. Stanford: Stanford University Press.

Sheehan, Donald (1952). *This Was Publishing: A Chronicle of the Book Trade in the Gilded Age*. Bloomington: Indiana University Press.

Twain, Mark (1917). *Mark Twain's Letters*, 2 vols., ed. Albert Bigelow Paine. New York: Harper & Bros.

Twain, Mark (1995). *Mark Twain's Letters*, vol. 4: *1870–71*, ed. Victor Fischer and Michael B. Frank. Berkeley: University of California Press.

Twain, Mark (1996a). *Mark Twain's Sketches, New and Old*. New York: Oxford University Press. (First publ. 1875.)

Twain, Mark (1996b). *The Man That Corrupted Hadleyburg and Other Stories and Essays*. New York: Oxford University Press (First publ. 1900.)

Twain, Mark, and Howells, William Dean (1960). *Mark Twain–Howells Letters: The Correspondence of Samuel L. Clemens and William Dean Howells*, 2 vols., ed. Henry Nash Smith and William M. Gibson. Cambridge, Mass.: Harvard University Press.

Wilson, Christopher P. (1985). *The Labor of Words: Literary Professionalism in the Progressive Era*. Athens: University of Georgia Press.

16

Mark Twain and the Promise and Problems of Magazines

Martin T. Buinicki

Mark Twain's varied career has lent itself to numerous narrative constructions over the years: the lecturer turned man of letters, the humorist turned novelist, the printer turned writer/publisher, and any number of other combinations and permutations. Largely missing from the diverse assortment of critical and biographical examinations is the story of Mark Twain the magazine writer. With the notable exception of Louis J. Budd, critics have treated the author's connection to the vibrant world of nineteenth-century periodicals only peripherally. Lamenting this fact in his article "Mark Twain and the Magazine World," Budd notes: "For Mark Twain we generally stick to his books written once he achieved that stage in his career" (Budd 1981: 35). This critical tendency perhaps results in part from the difficulty of synthesizing Twain's often contradictory statements regarding magazine writing. It is the purpose of this essay to build on Budd's work and to explore what might be learned from examining how the amateur magazine writer "S.L.C." – who first appeared in the Boston weekly *The Carpet-Bag, A Literary Journal: Published Weekly, For the Amusement of Its Readers* in 1852 – came to publish material from his autobiography in 1907 in the *North American Review*, one of the country's oldest and most distinguished magazines. Analysis of the author's dealings with periodicals can provide a vivid and detailed illustration of the developing magazine market of the second half of the nineteenth century. Study of Twain's views concerning magazine publication can also reveal a great deal about his attitudes toward his audience and his craft. For Twain, magazines were promotional tools of which he took advantage with great frequency, as well as sources of income and prestige, and they ultimately served as a vehicle through which he could shape his legacy. At the same time, however, writing for magazines appears to have been burdensome to the author. These varying objectives and views illustrate the ambivalence that strongly characterized Twain's relationship to the magazine world.

Publicity

Twain's earliest work in *The Carpet-Bag*, "The Dandy Frightening the Squatter," fore-shadows few of these concerns. The short tale is largely a local color piece that shows a river-town denizen getting the better of a snobbish steamboat passenger. While it reveals little of the author's future promise, the story does reveal some of the limita-tions of the periodical press and the distance that both Twain and magazines would travel over the next 50 years. Twain's piece is nearly lost on the crowded page, which is structured in long columns. Shoehorned between an article lamenting the torture of "Tight Boots" – "Tell me not of the horrors of the Inquisition . . . [N]o way com-parable are such endurances to the keen torment of being encased in a pair of *tight boots!*" – and an "Extract from a Private Letter" detailing the travels of a prominent European dissident, Twain's story, whose header proclaims that it was "Written for the Carpet-Bag," seems just one more piece of random filler (Twain 1852: 6). The format and the hodge-podge of topics add to the anonymity of the contributors, and few readers at the time would have been able to make much of the initials "S.L.C." printed at the bottom of the story.

Of course, anonymity was not the only obstacle that Twain confronted at the outset of his magazine career. Equally vexing were the regional limitations placed upon the periodical press: few journals could reach a broad readership (Mott 1938: 102). The difficulty of transporting magazines affordably, not to mention the sectional griev-ances that pervaded the country before, during, and after the Civil War, combined to make it difficult for authors – especially Western writers – to establish a national reputation. The *Overland Monthly*, for instance, the distinguished California magazine edited by Bret Harte for which Twain wrote articles in 1868, is a consciously "Western" magazine, even as it tries to position itself for a broader readership. Anx-ieties over its identity as a regional text are evident in Harte's address to readers in the first issue:

> Why, for instance, is this magazine called "The *Overland* Monthly?" . . . I might explain how "Pacific Monthly" is hackneyed, mild in suggestion, and at best but a feeble echo of the Boston "Atlantic." . . . The bear who adorns the cover may be "an ill-favored" beast whom "women cannot abide," but he is honest withal. Take him if you please as the symbol of local primitive barbarism. (Harte 1868: 99)

The apparent pride of place is belied by the reluctance to appear "but a feeble echo" of the *Atlantic*, as well as by the writer's self-deprecation and the suggestion that the Californian "bear" has met with disapproval. Remarks such as these suggest that, sep-arated as he was from the "elite" readers of the East, Harte was sensitive and vulner-able to the regional attitudes and prejudices prevalent at the time.

While Twain's experiences in the West inevitably propelled his success, the limited audience that he could reach writing for Western periodicals was one more obstacle to overcome. Twain was fortunate in this regard to be writing for the *Overland*, for, as

Frank Luther Mott writes, it was "the only [Western magazine] which attracted eastern attention" (Mott 1938: 58). However, in spite of the magazine's unusually high profile, its practice of publishing articles anonymously did not help Twain to build his Eastern reputation, particularly not in the shadow of Bret Harte, whose name was actively sought out by prominent New England publishers (p. 404).

Still, the man whose life was book-ended by Haley's comet was the beneficiary of good timing. As he rose to prominence, both marketing and distribution made considerable advances, among them the publication of authors' names. This trend was just beginning in the 1860s and, "when the *North American Review* began publishing the names of its authors in 1868, it delivered a staggering blow to the ancient tradition of the anonymous review" (Mott 1938: 19). In this way, Twain's writing career dovetailed nicely with a growing sense of the power of publicity in publishing. By the late 1860s, when Twain's success as a platform speaker and travel writer made him an attractive draw for magazines, the practice of anonymity was giving way to the trumpeting of recognizable names. Nowhere is this more evident than in Twain's first contract with an Eastern magazine. When Twain accepted an invitation to write a series of "Memoranda" for the *Galaxy* in 1870, the editors plastered the front covers with the announcement of the humorist's inclusion (McElderry 1961: ix). The importance of name recognition would only increase in the years ahead. As Richard Lowry notes, "By the 1870s, not only was a name essential for economic success, a work had virtually no *literary* value unless it was known by its author" (Lowry 1996: 32). In this regard, Twain's books, his platform performances, and his writings for the periodicals were symbiotic, each feeding the others and raising his public profile.

If the *Galaxy* helped Twain to establish name recognition, it also helped him to reach a national audience. Although it was published in New York, it went further than its Eastern predecessors in deliberately marketing itself to a larger readership. Bruce McElderry notes:

> The *Galaxy* aimed to be a national magazine, instead of a sectional organ, as the *Atlantic* was thought to be . . . Among contributors of fiction . . . secured . . . during the twelve years it survived were Henry James (twelve stories), Rebecca Harding Davis, John William De Forest, John Esten Cooke, Rose Terry Cooke, and Constance Fenimore Woolson. Six stories by Turgenev appeared. (McElderry 1961: xv)

As this list of contributors suggests, the magazine was reaching beyond New England and a stable of regional writers or thinkers and, with a list of subscribers that numbered over 21,000 at its peak (p. xv), it gave Twain access to a steady pool of readers early in his career.

Furthermore, the proliferation of rail lines combined with other technical innovations during the Civil War helped nurture a national audience for periodical literature. Arthur John sums up vividly some of the dramatic changes taking place during the period:

The railroads were gathering the regions together. Advances in printing, stereotyping, and engraving processes were underway. Distribution techniques kept pace with production innovations; the American News Company, founded in 1864, assured a wider and more economical sale of periodicals by taking from the publishers the problems and credit risks of doing business with newsdealers in all parts of the country. Under these favorable circumstances, American periodicals, exclusive of newspapers, grew from about 700 in number in 1865 to more than 1,200 in 1870. (John 1981: 13)

Not only were there substantially more venues in which to publish after the Civil War, but these periodicals were reaching more readers than ever before. Between 1850 and 1870, *Harper's Monthly*, for example, tripled its list of subscribers to 150,000 (p. 13). Ten years after its founding, *Scribner's Monthly* had increased its subscription roll from 40,000 to over 100,000 (p. 45). Magazines were truly becoming a national medium.

Pleasure vs. Pain: The Problems of Magazine Writing

While increasing his renown was always a concern for Twain, he was also interested in improving his reputation as a "serious" writer. The *Galaxy* was useful to him in both regards. Upon agreeing to write and edit the "Memoranda" for the magazine, he wrote to his friend Mary Fairbanks:

> And now I will disclose to you that I am going to edit a department in the "Galaxy." They are not to advertise that it will be a *Humorous* department, but simply *a* department. The humor shall be relieved all along by serious paragraphs, dainty bits subtracted from your letters, poetry, pathos, statistics – *every*thing that an artistic taste may suggest for effect. They pay me a good salary & let me have my trash again after they have used it in the magazine. I just came to the conclusion that I would quit turning my attention to making money especially & go to writing for enjoyment as well as profit. I needed a *Magazine* wherein to shovel any fine-spun stuff that might accumulate in my head, & which isn't entirely suited to either a daily, weekly, or *any* kind of newspaper. You see I often feel like writing something, & before I set down the first word I think, "No, it isn't worth while to write it – might do for a magazine, but not a newspaper". Do you see? I can make a *living* without any trouble, & still write *to suit myself* – & therefore wouldn't *you* do as I am doing if you were me? (see McElderry 1961: xi–xii)

The ranking of magazines over newspapers is evident here, a hierarchy that would last throughout Twain's career, and while it is clear that Twain is pleased with the "serious" nature of his writing for the magazine, it is equally important to recognize that the author emphasizes both the "good salary" and the fact that he would retain possession of his work. The magazine will allow him to write "for enjoyment as well as profit." This is important, for, despite his later statement to Mrs. Fairbanks that he "would rather write for a magazine for $2 a page than for the newspaper at $10" (see Budd 1981: 37), Twain never completely set aside financial concerns, and there would come a time only a few years later when pecuniary matters would have a much greater impact on his publishing decisions. Still, even when forced by necessity to take remuneration more prominently into account when choosing venues for his work, Twain's preference for magazines over newspapers was unwavering.

While Twain's arrangement with the *Galaxy* initially appeared to be ideal, he soon became disenchanted. When his brother Orion wrote to him suggesting he might contribute to a projected magazine Orion planned to edit for Twain's publisher Elisha Bliss, Twain replied in a scathing letter of March 1871:

> I have suffered damnation itself in the trammels of periodical writing, and I will *not* appear once a month, nor once in *three* months, in the Publisher, nor any other periodical . . . Haven't I risked cheapening myself sufficiently by a year's periodical dancing before the public but must continue it? . . . I am plainly and *distinctly* committed to those shuffling gentlemen of the Galaxy for *Frequent* articles, and I tell you I wouldn't write them a single paragraph for $25.00 a word. (Twain 1967: 57–8)

This seems to be a dramatic reversal of his feelings only a few months earlier. McElderry has suggested that the reason for this change of heart lies in the timing. Twain was working on *Roughing It* and "was renouncing journalism. He was becoming an Author" (McElderry 1961: x). While such an interpretation lends itself nicely to a narrative in which the young apprentice journalist blossoms into the professional writer of books, it seems untenable when one considers Twain's ongoing engagement with periodical writing.

It does, however, seem apparent that Twain was becoming more sophisticated in his ideas regarding publicity, and was wary of appearing before the public too often. His fear of "cheapening" himself has less to do with writing for the "lesser" form of magazines and more to do with his notion that relative scarcity would make him a more valuable commodity: "I tell you I mean to go *slow*. I will 'top' Bret Harte again or bust. But I can't do it by dangling eternally in the public view" (Twain 1967: 58). This idea of rationing his appearances in the periodical press in order to preserve his book profits would remain throughout his career. Much later, in answer to the question "as to whether it were beneficial for an author to have his work run in serial form through a good magazine," Twain answered: "[I]f I were running a serial, I'd like to get it into some nice obscure publication that nobody ever saw. Then, you see, it would not interfere with the subsequent sale of the work in book form" (Twain 1895–1900).

Although Twain craved publicity, he always feared that ubiquity would lead to decline in both profits and quality. Early in his career, this reservation was expressed as a reluctance to face undue criticism. He wrote to William Dean Howells in 1874: "I am seriously afraid to appear in print often – newspapers soon get to lying in wait for me to blackguard me. You think it over & you will see that it will doubtless be better for all of us that I don't infuriate the 'critics' to [*sic*] frequently" (Twain and Howells 1960: 44).

This seemed all the more true to him 21 years later when he faced financial ruin. As he considered ways to raise money to support his family, he wrote to his friend Henry Huttleston Rogers in 1895:

> This last item would be quite easy if I might venture to raise it by magazine articles, but that is dangerous & to be avoided if possible. A man who is on the downgrade must not print too often – he must keep out of the public view as much as he can; & when he prints to be sure he is not printing anything that is not up to his very best. (Twain 1969: 119)

Here the dangers of appearing too often in print converge with what Twain saw as other hazards of magazine writing: the inflexible time deadline, the potential for sloppy work, and the overexposure to pitiless critics.

It also appears that what Twain initially viewed as an opportunity to write for both pleasure and profit ceased to deliver enjoyment fairly quickly. He had described himself as suffering "damnation itself in the trammels of periodical writing" in his letter to Orion in March 1871. In a subsequent letter to Bliss, his language became more specific:

> Do you know that for seven weeks I have not had my natural rest but have been a night-and-day sick-nurse to my wife? And am still – and shall be for two or three weeks longer – yet must turn in now and write a damned *humorous* article for The Publisher, because I have *promised it* – promised it when I thought that the vials of hellfire bottled up for my benefit *must* be about emptied. (Twain 1967: 60).

The opportunity for publishing whatever pieces of writing came to his mind – and earning an adequate income at the same time – had quickly become a burden, a commitment that had to be met regardless of the circumstances of his personal life. In later years, facing the arduous task of working his way out of bankruptcy, he considered a contract for a series of articles and lamented:

> I can write a *subscription* book of travels without any effort, but to write travels for *serial* publication is hideous hard work. I am not committed to any magazine yet – and I believe it will be wisest to remain unfettered. The Century people actually proposed that I *sign a contract to be funny* in those 12 articles. That was pure insanity. Why, it makes me shudder every time I think of those articles. I don't think I could ever write one of them without being under the solemnizing blight of that disgusting recollection. (Twain 1969: 152)

He added a few days later: "I never *could* write those mag. articles to my satisfaction, for I would always be trying to write them according to Mr. Scott's [President of Century Publishing Company] requirement – whereas I have never written with chains on, in my life, and wouldn't know how to manage it" (p. 153). By this time Twain appears to have forgotten his days chained to his desk for the *Galaxy*, but the sentiment, nearly 25 years later, is the same. Too often, he felt, magazine writing demanded that he put his true feelings aside to produce what was needed for immediate periodical publication; and inevitably took a toll, demanding a great deal of time for only a slight reward: "Magazining is difficult work because every third page represents 2 pages that you have put in the fire; (because you are nearly sure to *start* wrong twice) and so when you have finished an article and are willing to let it go to print it represents only 10 cents a word instead of 30" (Twain 1917, vol. 2: 748).

The "mighty difficult work" of Magazines

The author used an even more surprising formulation to describe the relative difficulty of writing books and articles when he wrote to a correspondent in 1895: "My objection is that magazine-writing is mighty difficult work, whereas book-writing isn't any trouble."[1] For many, this might seem counter-intuitive, considering the energy required to produce a lengthy volume. Twain always seemed to feel the reverse was true: what consumed time and effort was confining himself to the constraints of the periodicals. As we have seen, he chafed under the time pressures placed upon him by periodical publication schedules, but it also appears that the shorter form itself gave him trouble. Prior to traveling abroad in 1891, Twain made a deal with *McClure's* to write travel letters for the magazine. Once he had begun, he started to reconsider, writing to his business partner Frederick Hall:

> The 6 McClure letters are the only ones I am going to send from Europe . . . To write a big book of travel would be less trouble than to write 6 detached chapters. Each of these letters require the same variety of treatment and subject that one puts into a book; but in the book *each* chapter doesn't have to be rounded and complete in itself. I have a fourth letter finished, but it takes longer to trim and fix and *edit* a letter than it does to write it . . . I shall write rafts of travel over here, but for a *book*, not serial publication. (Twain 1967: 282–3)

This is reminiscent of Twain's decision to cease publishing articles in the "Old Times on the Mississippi" series for the *Atlantic* many years earlier. He wrote to Howells in 1875, "The piloting material has been uncovering itself by degrees, until it has exposed such a huge hoard to my view that a whole book will be required to contain it if I use it" (Twain and Howells 1960: 62). Elaborating a short time later, he added, "There is a world of river stuff to write about, but I find it won't cut up into chapters, worth a cent. It needs to run right along, with no breaks but imaginary ones" (p. 85). For Twain, magazine writing precluded "imaginary breaks," forcing him to confine his thoughts and shape them into a coherent unity in too brief a time. While he could write tight prose and carefully plotted narrative, his repeated declarations regarding the difficulty of magazine writing suggest that he found the short form of articles far more demanding than the arguably larger task of book writing.

Vexing as the time and space constraints were, perhaps the highest hurdles Twain had to clear were editorial and audience demands concerning style and subject matter.

He was always aware of his audience's expectations of him, but the demands of the magazine public seem to have been particularly burdensome. In 1898 he wrote to Edward Bok, editor of *Ladies Home Journal*, concerning the publication of portions of his autobiography: "[A] good deal of it is written in too independent a fashion for a magazine. One may publish a *book* & print whatever his family shall approve & allow to pass, but it is the Public that edit a Magazine, & so by sheer necessities of the case a magazine's liberties are rather limited" (Budd 1981: 37).

Budd notes of this statement, "The distinction here probably distorted and certainly oversimplified the realities of marketing his own books, but at least it restated his ponderous regard for the world of periodicals" (1981: 37–8). Twain's feelings seem to have resulted from his apparent belief that the opinion of the editor reflected that of the public, and, as one reads his correspondence, one finds many examples of editors acting on their audiences' behalf. Richard Watson Gilder, editor of the *Century* in 1884, begged for permission to publish portions of *Adventures of Huckleberry Finn* – with one small caveat: "There are some few expressions 'not adapted to our audience' (I do not find many) that we would wish the liberty of expunging, and a good deal would have to be omitted on acct. of space – and in omitting we might also have a regard for our audience" (Gilder 1884). Twain's correspondence with his friend William Dean Howells while the latter was editor of the *Atlantic Monthly* contains many similar examples. In response to a satirical attack Twain had written on a popular novelist, Howells informed his friend in 1876, "You use expressions there that would lose us all our book-club circulation" (Twain and Howells 1960: 165); and, in critiquing a travel piece in 1877, Howells wrote, "This number of the Bermudas is delicious. But you can't put a health-officer's heart on a fork in The Atlantic Monthly. None of our readers have ever heard of such a thing" (p. 207). As statements like these suggest, Howells' editorial remarks were sometimes made with an eye as much to the taste of his readers as to the development of his friend's artistic potential.

In this regard, Twain was right to view the public as his editors when writing for the magazines. As more magazines emerged and the market became increasingly competitive, editors paid ever closer attention to their desires and preferences. Ellery Sedgwick argues that, as a result,

> Magazines have always been more vulnerable and therefore more sensitive to public displeasure than books . . . First, while most books were bought and read by an individual, general magazines like the *Atlantic* were considered "family reading." In the middle-class nineteenth-century American family there was a wide discrepancy between what was deemed appropriate for men and women and younger folk. Second, magazine subscribers have on-going control over their purchase and can choose to terminate at any point. This gives them a sense of proprietary power, and many will write letters to the editor criticizing a decision while they would not think of complaining to a publisher or author of a book. (Sedgwick 1994: 57–8)

The readers' influence was reflected both in the editors' sensitivity to their tastes and in the more direct manner of reader participation that Sedgwick notes. Thus, in spite of the personal views and aspirations of the founders of magazines like the *Atlantic* and the *Galaxy*, editorial choices were often driven in some degree by the preferences of subscribers. This could require a delicate balancing act, as Sedgwick explains:

> While [Howells] was personally squeamish, especially concerning sex, and sometimes timid about offending the *Atlantic* audience, especially concerning religion, he was highly conscious of the need to build a new readership, particularly among women and among readers beyond New England, not just to shore up the *Atlantic's* dwindling circulation, but more specifically for realism and for the authors who practiced it in its early years. His editorial record shows that he was both willing to expose audiences to constant doses of realism in order to build a readership and willing to make strategic compromises with those audiences to avoid alienating them. (1994: 148)

Twain provided Howells with material that would allow him to forward both of these aims.

While this situation was apparently advantageous to the editor, Twain occasionally seems to have been ambivalent about writing for this audience. Howells wrote to Twain with some advice as the author began working on the second article in the "Old Times on the Mississippi" series: "Don't write *at* any supposed Atlantic audience, but yarn it off as if into my sympathetic ear. Don't be afraid of rests or pieces of dead color. I fancied a sort of hurried and anxious air in the first" (Twain and Howells 1960: 46). As we have already seen, however, Howells was the surrogate for the *Atlantic* audience, as Twain himself seems to have realized despite the distinction Howells tried to make between his "sympathetic ear" and the imagined readers. Twain replied, "It isn't the Atlantic audience that distresses me; for *it* is the only audience that I sit down before in perfect serenity (for the simple reason that it don't require a 'humorist' to paint himself striped and stand on his head every fifteen minutes)" (p. 49). This may or may not have been an accurate description of the *Atlantic's* readership, but it is an undeniably accurate description of Howells. Just as Howells worked to identify his own tastes with those of his readers (by at once catering to them and trying to influence them), Twain seems to have elided Howells with the *Atlantic* subscribers. Thus, Howells's recognition that a humor writer can be more than a painted clown became Twain's view of the broader readership.

Twain was not always so at ease with his *Atlantic* audience – at least, not with its size and elitism; nor was he always content with the amount of money that the small subscription list enabled Howells and the publisher to offer him. In 1875, as he considered where to publish *Tom Sawyer*, he turned down his friend's request to "advertise" the book by publishing it in the *Atlantic* (Twain and Howells 1960: 90–1). He wrote, "I would dearly like to see it in the Atlantic, but I doubt if it would pay the publishers to buy the privilege, or me to sell it . . . You see I take a vile, mercenary view of things – but then my household expenses are something almost ghastly" (p. 92). In 1880, as he considered the potential advantages of the unregulated reprinting of his short pieces versus publishing in the *Atlantic*, he took a similarly "mercenary" view:

I would rather the N.Y. Times & all the other journals *would* copy my stuff – it keeps a body more alive & known to the broad & general public, for the Atlantic goes to only . . . the select high few. Yes, I would rather write for the modester wage of one whose articles increase not the subscription list, & then be copied in the general press; for I should find my vast reward in the augmented sales of my books. However, maybe they *do* copy – hope they do. (p. 320)

This letter indicates that Twain was developing a more nuanced view of publicity and how the *Atlantic* could further his aims. Despite the best efforts of his friend, the readership of the *Atlantic* had fallen from its all-time high of 50,000 subscribers, due in large part to the increase in competition from illustrated magazines (Sedgwick 1994: 113). As a result, Twain appears to have reached a conclusion that he was perhaps doing more for the magazine's subscription list than the magazine was doing for him. In this he was mistaken, although he was correct in his assessment of the strategy. Howells wrote in 1907:

We counted largely on [Mark Twain's] popularity to increase our circulation when we began to print the piloting papers; but with one leading journal in New York republishing them as quickly as they appeared, and another in St. Louis supplying the demand of the Mississippi Valley, and another off in San Francisco offering them to his old public on the Pacific slope, the sales of the *Atlantic Monthly* were not advanced a single copy, so far as we could make out. (Twain and Howells 1960: 48n.)

In an even more defeated tone, Howells wrote, "*The Atlantic Monthly* languished on the news stands, as undesired as ever" (Howells 1968: 268). So, while Twain was correct regarding at least one of the motives for his appearance in the *Atlantic*, he seems to have overestimated his effect.

Twain, Books, and Magazines

As we have already seen, throughout his career Twain regarded magazine publication as secondary to his book publishing. As a result, some came to believe that Twain not only was dismissive of magazines, but refused to write for periodicals altogether. A writer for the *Examiner*, a San Francisco paper, wrote in 1891:

While almost every other writer of the time seeks his audience first through the medium of the newspapers and magazines, and then binds up his serials into books, Mark Twain invariably launches his writings in volume form from the first. He does so because it pays, for Mark Twain is a not a sentimentalist, but a businessman. Most writers say that there is no money in books – that final publication in book form is only an esthetic gratification after the author has made his profit from the periodicals. But Mark Twain makes enormous profits from his books – so enormous that newspapers and magazines have been staggered at the idea of paying him enough for the privilege of first publication to make it worth his while to concede it.

The picture of Twain as an author so successful that he could escape the normal habits of his peers is one that the author himself seems to have embraced. At roughly the same time this article appeared, he wrote the following to the editor of *Truth* magazine in reply to a request for a submission:

> My great trouble is, that I can't find any publication rich enough to buy my miscellaneous matter. You see, as I write only one such article a year, I'm obliged to charge the same as if it took me the whole year to write it. Why, it looks perfectly fair, divinely fair; & yet these magazines all rise up with enthusiasm & say my system's a swindle. The consequence is, that my last article has been floating around for nearly thirteen years, now, trying to bankrupt some periodical, & I reckon the rags of it will arrive at your door in time. (Letter of 1891 in Twain 2001)

Lurking behind the humor is Twain's own assessment of his value, and it is clear that he felt it transcended the resources of most magazines. It also appears that profit has become the sole motivation for magazine publication, and these statements give the impression that there was no longer profit to be found there.

In spite of these public and private repudiations of magazine publication, however, Twain was still the businessman, never afraid to take a "mercenary view" of things. A letter to Gilder in 1892 makes this plain: "Well, you see, what little I have written lately was kind of forced into the syndicates because they seduce a person by the large wage they pay, which is double & treble what the magazines grant to the laborer in the literary field. Naturally I prefer to be in the magazines, but you see how it is" (Letter of 1892 in Twain 2001).

Although the longstanding hierarchy that reigned in Twain's conception of publication throughout his career remained in place, he was not opposed to writing even for the newspapers – provided the price was right, of course. In fact, even as the press was reporting that Twain was the rare author who premiered his work only in book form, he was making arrangements to publish *The American Claimant* as a serial in a newspaper: "Won't you appoint a meeting with Col. Cockerill managing editor of the World," he wrote to Hall, "and see if you can sell him the use of this 70 or 75,000 word story for $10,000? If not, ask for his best terms" (Twain 1967: 273). As if to emphasize that he has reversed his common practice, he wrote to Hall several months later, "You are going to issue the 'American Claimant' as a $1 book the moment it is finished as a syndicate-serial, aren't you? At any rate you are going to issue it as a *book*" (p. 305). This last statement seems an almost plaintive appeal for book publication, an acknowledgment that, despite the financial benefits of periodical publication, Twain's first and last choice remained the book form.

At this stage in his career, it appears, he would abandon book publication of his longer works only when the financial incentive was irresistible. As he wrote to Hall in 1892 regarding "Those Extraordinary Twins," "The price is not very important on a miscellaneous article, but if I publish 'Those Extraordinary Twins' serially the price must be high. It is going to be a full-sized novel, and longer than the American

Claimant" (Twain 1967: 326). Regardless of the reports of the press or his own preferences, the author was constantly printing and promoting his works in and through periodicals. Considering the number of times he complained of the difficulty of writing for magazines, the emotional price that Twain paid to produce these pieces easily matched the price paid by the publishers.

Prestige

Given the obstacles that confronted Twain when he wrote for periodicals, and in light of his own statements, one is forced to ask if Twain ever felt there was anything to gain from the magazines beyond profit and publicity. Was there any sort of appeal in the magazines for Twain after those first heady months writing for the *Galaxy*? Scholars have long noted the pleasure that he took from his appearance in the *Atlantic*. Indeed, many critics have cited his first publication in the magazine, the short story "A True Story. Repeated Word for Word as I Heard It," as a dramatic turning point for him, marking the transition from Twain the Western humorist to Twain the serious author. Howells seemed to feel this was true, writing in 1907, "It was finally decided to give the author twenty dollars a page, a rate unexampled in our modest history . . . I myself felt that we were throwing in the highest recognition of his writing as literature, along with a sum we could ill afford" (Twain and Howells 1960: 25–6n.). Twain appears to have felt the same way, writing that while the pay might have been disappointing, "the awful respectability of the magazine makes up" (see Kaplan 1966: 181). When Howells wrote a favorable review of his collection of stories *Sketches, New and Old*, Twain wrote with delight, "Yours is the recognized critical Court of Last Resort in this country; from its decision there is no appeal; & so, to have gained this decree of yours before I am forty years old, I regard as a thing to be right down proud of" (Twain and Howells 1960: 107). Twain was right to be pleased. From its inception, the *Atlantic*'s editors had felt that "the democratic age needed intellectual, moral, and aesthetic leadership and that the magazine should contribute to that cultural leadership by addressing itself to the 'discerning minority,' which in turn could educate the tastes of the broader majority" (Sedgwick 1994: 26). While publishing Twain helped Howells reach out to that "broader majority," it also clearly presented the author to readers as a serious literary figure.

The *Atlantic* was not the only magazine that inspired Twain's respect and admiration. As Budd points out, "Throughout [his] career he never ridiculed either the quality or the cultural mission of the triumvirate that dominated literate households – the *Atlantic, Harper's Monthly*, and the *Century*" (Budd 1981: 36). Indeed, in 1885 Twain described the task of writing for the *Century* with a kind of awe: "There is a restraint about writing for the Century, somehow. It is not intemperate language to say it is the best magazine that was ever printed; & so, what would read quite fairly elsewhere, loses force & grace in the company of so much derned good writing" (Twain 1945: 23).

The *Century* was a publishing powerhouse at this time, with a list of subscribers reaching 250,000 (John 1981: 129). Still, when one considers the magnitude of the author's success by 1885, it is easy to see the amount of respect for the *Century* that is reflected in Twain's comment. His statement also indicates another positive aspect of magazine writing: the circles within which it allowed him and his work to circulate. While most books sold by subscription were not considered to be of great literary merit by the intelligentsia – indeed, the *Atlantic* generally paid almost no attention to these books at all (see Twain and Howells 1960: 4) – Twain joined the canonical figures of his time between the covers of the magazines like the *Century*.

Periodical publication also allowed him to associate with these literary lions personally. After publishing only two pieces in the *Atlantic*, "A True Story" and the first article in the "Old Times on the Mississippi" series, he was invited to attend a dinner for contributors. As noted in the Twain–Howells correspondence, "It was even more striking that Clemens was asked to speak in an after-dinner program whose Bostonian character was authenticated by the recital of an occasional poem by Dr. Holmes" (Twain and Howells 1960: 53n.). There is no denying that Twain's travel writing and his platform performances made him immensely popular, but it was his magazine writing, and the reviews of his works that appeared in those magazines, that helped to cement his identity as more than a Western humorist. In the ephemeral pages of the periodical press, Twain was able to establish a longlasting literary identity.

Understanding this can shed light on the author's decision near the end of his life to forgo publishing his autobiography in book form and instead to allow chapters of it to appear in the *North American Review*. As we have already seen, he showed reluctance to publish this material as early as 1898, fearful of the editorial censorship required to make it suitable for subscribers. There was also the familiar reluctance to go about editing the by-now voluminous amount of material that Twain had amassed into concise and publishable magazine "chapters." In 1906 George Harvey, editor of the venerable *North American Review*, overcame these objections, and Twain seems to have been thrilled by the prospect of appearing in the magazine. He wrote several friends about it, the letters all couched in similarly enthusiastic language. He explained what had happened to his daughter Clara:

> Col. Harvey arrived from Europe & we straightened out our snarl in five minutes. He next told me of his great plan: to turn the North American Review into a *fortnightly* the 1st of Sept. introduce into it a purely *literary* section, of high class, & in other ways make a great & valuable periodical of it. He was always icily indifferent to the Autobiography before, but thought he would like to look at it now, so I told him to come up. He arrived 3 days ago, & has now carefully read close upon a hundred thousand words of it (there are 250,000). He says it is the "greatest book of the age," & has in it "the finest literature."
>
> He has done some wonderful editing; for he has selected 5 installments of 5,000 words each; & although these are culled from here & there & yonder, he has made each seem to have been written by itself – & without altering a word. At 10,000 words a month we shall place about 110,000 or 120,000 words before the public in 12 months. (Letter of 1906 in Twain 2001)

What is most readily apparent in this letter is how the problem of editing has been solved. He has not had to "alter" a word for his audience, nor has he had to go through the effort of making each chapter a unified whole.

More striking, however, is the almost insistent reference to literary quality in the letter. Both the magazine and the autobiography are mentioned in terms of high praise, and Twain gives greatest emphasis to the fact that the magazine will have a "purely *literary* section, of high class." He echoes this language in a letter to Howells: "Harvey will go hence with [the autobiography], to you, to-morrow. He is going to volley it at the public in the new N. A. Review, which I think is going to be the greatest of the periodicals, & the most conspicuous in America" (Twain and Howells 1960: 817). To another friend, he wrote, "I think it will be a great magazine, & I'm charmed. You must be, too – do you hear?" (Twain 1961: 39).

As one of the nation's oldest periodicals, the *North American Review* carried significant prestige, but it had also gone through a variety of transformations and difficult times. In 1878 it had moved to New York and reinvented itself. Mott notes, "It was almost as close to current events as a newspaper" (Mott 1938: 250). While this increased its subscription list for several years, its circulation suffered a decline in the 1890s (p. 256). Harvey, who also edited *Harper's Weekly* from 1901 to 1913 (p. 256), was working to revitalize the magazine, and securing Twain's work was an important step. By placing portions of his autobiography in the newly re-emergent *North American Review*, Twain presented himself to the public once more not simply as a humorist, but foremost as a *literary* figure. He felt the new literary section of the magazine was "just the place for [his] Autobiographical chapters" (Letter of 1906 in Twain 2001). His life had always been a fundamental source for his fiction, and now the story of his life itself was being deemed "the finest literature." While we now have reason to question his enthusiasm regarding the magazine's prospects – it lasted only one year as a fortnightly publication (Mott 1938: 258) – Twain would have been well familiar with the long history of the *North American Review* and its distinguished line of editors and contributors, a list that included Charles Eliot Norton, James Russell Lowell, and Henry Adams (p. 31). Once more, near the end of his life, Twain found prestige and a reaffirmation of his artistic value in the pages of a magazine.

Conclusion

It is tempting to put Mark Twain's career as a magazine writer into an easy narrative framework: one might suggest the symmetry of the young author first achieving literary respectability and acclaim in the pages of the *Atlantic*, and then confirming his canonical status once more at the end of his career in the pages of the *North American Review*. Alternatively, one could describe a successful ascent, the author climbing up from the obscurity of *The Carpet-Bag* to achieve the eminence of the most respected journals of the nation. While there are some elements of truth in both of these accounts, they are finally incomplete and misleading. Both suggest a committed magazine writer who, like nearly all of his contemporaries, viewed periodicals as the medium of choice for authors in nineteenth-century America seeking profit and prestige.

The truth is that, throughout his career, Twain viewed magazines as tools: as promotional channels to exploit in order to sell books, and as sources of literary credibility. They could provide significant profits, but these almost always proved to be smaller than those that could be gained through book publication. They could be outlets for his inexhaustible energy, and they could be a burden, shackling him to his desk and forcing him to pump out humorous material regardless of his state of mind. They could force him to tame the torrents of his creativity only to pour them into what he felt to be inadequately small vessels. These ambiguities offer ample material from which to construct a number of narratives regarding the writer and the magazine world, and they can support a number of views regarding Twain's preferred image of himself as an author and his opinions of and capacities for differing forms and genres. The challenges that confront scholars examining Twain's magazine career also ultimately offer an opportunity to gain a greater understanding of Twain's unique approach to his craft and to the profession of authorship in the rapidly evolving literary marketplace of the late nineteenth century.

NOTES

1   Unless otherwise noted, the Mark Twain letters quoted here appear in Twain (2001).

REFERENCES AND FURTHER READING

Branch, Edgar Marquess (1966). *The Literary Apprenticeship of Mark Twain, with Selections from his Apprentice Writings*. New York: Russell & Russell.

Budd, Louis J. (1981). "Mark Twain and the Magazine World." *University of Mississippi Studies in English* 2, 35–42.

Gilder, Richard Watson (1884). Letter to Mark Twain. In the Mark Twain Papers, Bancroft Library, Berkeley, Calif.

Harte, Bret (1868). "Etc." *Overland Monthly* 1, 99.

Howells, William Dean (1968). *Literary Friends and Acquaintance*, ed. David F. Hiatt and Edwin H. Cady. Bloomington: Indiana University Press. (First publ. 1900.)

John, Arthur (1981). *The Best Years of the "Century": Richard Watson Gilder, "Scribner's Monthly," and the "Century" Magazine, 1870–1909*. Urbana: University of Illinois Press.

Kaplan, Justin (1966). *Mr. Clemens and Mark Twain: A Biography*. New York: Simon & Schuster.

Lowry, Richard S. (1996). *"Littery Man": Mark Twain and Modern Authorship*. New York: Oxford University Press.

McElderry, Bruce R. (1961). "Introduction." In *Contributions to "The Galaxy": 1868–1871 by Mark Twain*. Gainesville, Fla.: Scholars' Facsimiles and Reprints.

Mott, Frank Luther (1938). *History of American Magazines*, 5 vols. Cambridge, Mass.: Harvard University Press.

San Francisco Examiner (1891). See Scrapbook 26, Mark Twain Papers, Bancroft Library, Berkeley, Calif.

Sedgwick, Ellery (1994). *The Atlantic Monthly: 1857–1909*. Amherst: University of Massachusetts Press.

Twain, Mark (1852). "The Dandy Frightening the Squatter." *The Carpet-Bag* 2: 5 (1 May), 6.

Twain, Mark (1895–1900). Scrapbook 27. Mark Twain Papers, Bancroft Library, University of California, Berkeley.

Twain, Mark (1917). *Mark Twain's Letters*, 2 vols., ed. Albert Bigelow Paine. New York: Harper & Bros.

Twain, Mark (1945). "Letter from Mark Twain." *Mark Twain Journal* 6, 23.

Twain, Mark (1961). *Mark Twain's Letters to Mary*, ed. Lewis Leary. New York: Columbia University Press.

Twain, Mark (1967). *Mark Twain's Letters to his Publishers 1867–1894*, ed. Hamlin Hill. Berkeley: University of California Press.

Twain, Mark (1969). *Mark Twain's Correspondence with Henry Huttleston Rogers, 1893–1909*, ed. Lewis Leary. Berkeley: University of California Press.

Twain, Mark (1988). *Mark Twain's Letters*, vol. 1: *1853–1866*, ed. Edgar Marquess Branch, Michael B. Frank, and Kenneth M. Sanderson. Berkeley: University of California Press.

Twain, Mark (2001). *Microfilm Edition of Mark Twain's Previously Unpublished Letters*, 8 vols., prepared by Anh Quynh Bui, Victor Fischer, Michael B. Frank, Robert H. Hirst, Lin Salamo, and Harriet Elinor Smith. Reels 4, 6 and 7. Berkeley, Calif.: Bancroft Library.

Twain, Mark, and Howells, William Dean (1960). *Mark Twain–Howells Letters: The Correspondence of Samuel L. Clemens and William Dean Howells, 1872–1910*, 2 vols., ed. Henry Nash Smith and William M. Gibson. Cambridge, Mass.: Belknap.

17

Mark Twain and the Stage

Shelley Fisher Fishkin

As a theatergoer, theater critic, friend of actors and producers, sometime actor in family entertainments, author of books that others reshaped into plays, and as an aspiring playwright, Mark Twain was intrigued by the stage all his life.[1] He expressed his strong opinions through drama reviews, theatrical parodies, and personal correspondence. He could pan a production mercilessly or champion it tirelessly, demanding that all of his friends attend. The stage left an indelible mark on virtually every phase of his career as a writer. And although the success he sought as a playwright eluded him during his lifetime, a recently rediscovered zany, cross-dressing comedy he wrote in 1898 may yet bring him some of the recognition that he craved.

During his childhood in Hannibal, Missouri, showboats that plied the Mississippi exposed young Sam Clemens to theatrical entertainments ranging from Shakespeare's plays to minstrel shows. These forms would figure in his most famous novel, *Adventures of Huckleberry Finn*, where the amateur thespians, the king and the duke, would improvise mangled scenes from Shakespeare, and where some of the pacing and rhetorical moves of minstrel shows – minus minstrelsy's racist derogation of blacks – may be detected in conversations between Huck and Jim.

After leaving home at the age of 17, Clemens attended his first professional theatrical productions in New York, Philadelphia, St. Louis and Keokuk, Iowa. In October 1853 he wrote his sister, Pamela, about a performance by Edwin Forrest on Broadway in the title role of *The Gladiator*. Although Clemens did not find all of the play to his liking, he praised the ending: "I did not like parts of it much, but other portions were really splendid. In the latter part of the last act, where the 'Gladiator' (Forrest) dies at his brother's feet (in all the fierce pleasure of gratified revenge), the man's whole soul seems absorbed in the part he is playing" (Twain 1988: 16).

Did Mark Twain recall this early impressive theatergoing experience when faced with the challenge of finding something new to say about the original scene of real gladiatorial combat, the Coliseum, in chapter 25 of *The Innocents Abroad*? "What is there in Rome for me to see that others have not seen before me? . . . What is there for me to feel, to learn, to hear, to know, that shall thrill me before it pass to others? What can I discover? – Nothing. Nothing whatsoever." Mark Twain makes up in part for his sense of being destined to be derivative and belated by finding "among the rubbish of the ruined Coliseum the only playbill of that establishment now extant." A section of the document reads:

ROMAN COLISEUM.

UNPARALLELED ATTRACTION!

NEW PROPERTIES! NEW LIONS! NEW GLADIATORS

Engagement of the renowned
MARCUS MARCELLUS VALERIAN!
For six nights only!

The management beg leave to offer to the public an entertainment surpassing in magnificence any thing that has heretofore been attempted on any stage. No expense has been spared to make the opening season one which shall be worthy the generous patronage which the management feel sure will crown their efforts . . .

Twain goes on to find "a stained and mutilated copy of the *Roman Daily Battle-Ax*, containing a critique upon this very performance" – a gambit which allows him both to take pot-shots at the level of "civilization" that characterized the glory that was Rome ("A matinee for the little folks is promised for this afternoon, on which occasion several martyrs will be eaten by the tigers"), and to domesticate and demystify the august landmark of classical civilization, showing that what went on at that intimidating site was not unlike the extravagantly hyped lowbrow small-town traveling shows familiar to his readers (and again the king and duke come to mind). It also allows him to poke some pointed jabs at theater critics: he concludes this section with the comment, "I have been a dramatic critic myself in my time, and I was often surprised to notice how much more I knew about Hamlet than Forrest did; and it gratifies me to observe, now, how much better my brethren of ancient times knew how a broadsword battle ought to be fought than the gladiators" (Twain 1869: 278–83).

Twain had first wrought humor from the world of the stage more than a decade before he set sail on the voyage that would be memorialized in *Innocents Abroad*, in pieces he contributed to newspapers in Iowa. On 28 February 1855, with heavy-handed sarcasm, Twain wrote a snide squib about an amateur production of *The Merchant of Venice* performed by a thespian society called the Young Men's Dramatic Association in the Varieties Theater in St. Louis. "I had always thought that this was a comedy, until they made a farce of it," he quipped in the correspondence section of the Muscatine *Tri-Weekly Journal*: "The prompters found it a hard matter to get the actors on the stage, and when they did get them on, it was harder still to get them off again. 'Jessica' was always 'thar' when she wasn't wanted, and never would turn up when her services were required. They'll do better next time." He signed the letter "S.L.C." ([Clemens] 1855).

Less than two years later, the 20-year-old country-boy-cum-sophisticate – confident that he knew enough about how plays ought to be performed to send a letter on the subject to a paper in Muscatine after attending a performance in St. Louis – wrote a parody of someone in exactly the same situation for a paper in Keokuk. The correspondent to the Keokuk paper who identified himself as "Thomas Jefferson Snodgrass" is not at all like "S.L.C." – with the exception of the fact that both writers are smugly certain that their descriptions of performances of Shakespeare in St. Louis theaters will be of interest to readers back home in Iowa. Thomas Jefferson Snodgrass's letter to the *Keokuk Saturday Post* in 1856 about a production of *Julius Caesar* in St. Louis is Twain's first spun-out parody set in the theater – but this time the object of ridicule is not the inept actors, but the ignorant, arrogant, and incongruously proud country bumpkin who is in the audience. "MISTER EDITORS, I want to enlighten you a leetle," Snodgrass begins inauspiciously: "I've been to the Theater – and I just want to tell you how they do things down here to Saint Louis . . ." ([Twain] 1856). The humorous Snodgrass letters are slight and would likely be forgotten were it not for the fact that Snodgrass, unlike Huck in so many ways, nonetheless prefigures aspects of Huck's limitations and of the potential humor to be found therein. He also represents the first sustained effort by Twain to tell an extended story in print in a vernacular voice (a voice that happens to speak a variant of Pike County dialect – another link to Huck). One can easily imagine Huck coming out with a description of a scene from *Julius Caesar* similar to the one Snodgrass provides:

> Pretty soon a little bell rung, and they rolled up the side of the house with Alexandria on it, showin a mighty fine city, with houses, and streets, and sich, but nary a fire plug – all as natural as life. This was Rome. Then a lot of onery lookin fellers come a tearin down one of the streets, hurrayin and swingin their clubs, and said they were going to see Julius Cesar come into town. ([Twain] 1856)

Mark Twain quickly became a more knowledgeable and versatile theater critic than "S.L.C." or Thomas Jefferson Snodgrass had been. Virginia City, Nevada, where he lived in the early 1860s, had several flourishing theaters where touring companies performed mainly romantic and burlesque comedies and farces, and in 1863 Maguire's Opera House, a theater as elegant as any in San Francisco, opened its doors. The newspaper on which Twain worked, the *Territorial Enterprise*, devoted so much space to its theater coverage that the Opera House routinely reserved a section of front-row seats for *Enterprise* reporters. Twain and his pals on the paper, Joe Goodman and Dan De Quille, would attend a play together, each write his own review, have late-night debates about their various reactions, and then decide what to publish – often an amalgam of their responses (Schirer 1984: 12).

In San Francisco, where he worked as a reporter in the mid-1860s, surrounded by actors, actresses, and aspiring playwrights, Twain attended the theater regularly, occasionally sent reviews back to the *Territorial Enterprise*, and is believed to have contributed theater reviews to the irreverent and satirical San Francisco *Dramatic Chronicle* (none are extant). Sometimes a particularly unimpressive production could inspire

Twain to write a theatrical parody of his own. The four-act burlesque *Il Trovatore* that he wrote in 1866, for example, was his response to a poor production of the opera of the same name at Maguire's Opera House in San Francisco. He had (earlier) reacted similarly to the overdone, heroic romanticism of a production of Friedrich Hahn's *Ingomar, the Barbarian* at Maguire's Opera House in Virginia City in 1863 by publishing a burlesque, "'Ingomar' over the Mountains," in the *Territorial Enterprise* and the *Golden Era* (Krause 1967: 47). Twain similarly had little patience with productions like *The Black Crook*, a play he saw in New York, which in his view was simply a rather transparent excuse for presenting near-nudity on the stage (the show, a musical based on a play by Charles M. Barras, grossed $1,100,000 over the course of a sixteen-month run of 475 performances, each of which lasted about six and a half hours [Krause 1967: 39]). Twain viewed the fate of the legitimate theater as precarious if "girlie shows" like *The Black Crook*, or preposterous extravaganzas such as the production of *Mazeppa* featuring a body-suited, nude-appearing Adah Isaacs Menken, kept packing in audiences.

Throughout his life Twain would continue to write dramatic criticism – both parodic and serious – and to attend plays for his own pleasure, in New York, London, Vienna and elsewhere. Although he disliked the theater's efforts to pander to prurient tastes, a broad range of productions from popular to highbrow appealed to him. He could enjoy the vaudeville shows laced with ethnic humor at Harrigan's theater in New York as well as a tragedy like Wilbrandt's *The Master of Palmyra* in Vienna (which prompted Twain to excoriate American theatergoers for failing to demand more drama of this serious nature).

Twain was friends with a number of actors, including Sir Henry Irving, who provided him with a special pass that admitted him to any play in which he was performing (Fishkin 2003: 228). When actors were treated badly or in need of assistance, Twain quickly leaped to their aid. When a minister refused to read a burial service for George Holland because he was an actor, Twain was outraged, and launched into an impassioned defense of the acting profession in the February 1871 issue of *Galaxy* magazine. He was still defending actors more than three decades later when, in 1907, he was the leading celebrity supporter of a fair to raise funds for indigent actors. Twain was also a founding member of the Players' Club, created by actor Edwin Booth in 1888 as "a place where actors would be able to meet artists of other professions, and laymen interested in the arts and the theatre" (Frohman 1935: 82). Twain stayed there frequently when he was in New York.

Twain allowed dramatists to produce stage versions of a number of his books, including *Roughing It* (although Augustin Daly's production of that title had in fact little to do with Twain's book), *Tom Sawyer*, *The Prince and the Pauper*, and *Pudd'nhead Wilson*. And he avidly participated in plays privately performed for friends and relations – everything from family stage versions of *The Prince and the Pauper* (in which he himself played Miles Hendon) to an amateur production of James R. Planche's *Loan of the Lover* (in which he played the leading role). Sir Henry Irving once remarked that Twain had missed his calling by not becoming an actor himself (Paine 1912: vol. 2, 571).

The runaway success of a burlesque by Twain's friend Charles Henry Webb, at the San Francisco Academy of Music, opened Twain's eyes to the moneymaking potential of the theater, and may have suggested to him that writing a play was, potentially at least, a route to vast wealth (Schirer 1984: 12–13, 23–4). Playwriting did turn out to be a route to wealth for Twain once in his career. But he could never make it happen again.

In 1874, the year after they published their collaborative novel *The Gilded Age*, Twain and Charles Dudley Warner heard that an unauthorized dramatization of the work starring comic actor John T. Raymond was being mounted in San Francisco, produced by G. B. Densmore, co-owner and drama critic of the San Francisco *Golden Era*. Twain soon learned that Densmore's production was "a one-character play" – like comic actor Joe Jefferson's famous performance as Rip Van Winkle in a play by Dion Boucicault (a role in which Jefferson starred almost continuously from 1866 until 1904) (Twain 2002: 129). The one fresh character showcased in the production was Twain's irrepressible Colonel Sellers. Nothing by Warner had made it into the play. When Twain proposed that they split their copyright, each retaining dramatic rights to the characters he alone had created, Warner agreed. Together they persuaded Densmore to close his pirated production, and Twain began writing his own version of the play, finishing it in a month. He kept little of Densmore's language, but retained much of his plot (Paine 1912: vol. 1, 518; Thomason 1991; Thomason and Quirk 1995).

The play opened at the Park Theater in New York on 16 September after some upstate New York try-out performances with Raymond playing the title role of Colonel Sellers, a role that made his career. Twain never thought much of *Colonel Sellers* as a play ("It is simply a setting for the one character, Col. Sellers, and as a *play* I guess it will not bear a critical assault in force," he wrote Howells), and he was never happy with how Raymond interpreted the role. But it was hard to argue with success (Twain 2002: 127–9, 233). The indefatigable Sellers's determination to make his fortune in steamboats or mules or hogs or congressional appropriations or liniment for sore eyes gave the phrase "There's millions in it!" to American popular culture (Frohman 1911: 49; Schirer 1984: 56). The play would become one of the biggest hits of the decade, and at one point would bring Twain more annual income than all of his books combined (Schirer 1984: 56). The *Tribune* called it "excessively thin in texture" while Odell's *Annals of the New York Stage* later dubbed it "a wretched thing" (p. 45). However, the play's one original character, the upbeat and self-assured speculator Colonel Sellers, managed to offset the weak dialogue and insipid romance plot and win over even the most impatient critics. Twain bragged to his brother-in-law Charlie Langdon in March that "in Brooklyn, Baltimore, Washington, Cincinnati, St. Louis & Chicago, the play paid me an average of nine hundred dollars a week. In smaller towns the average is $400 to $500" (Twain 2002: 420). And that was only Twain's half of the earnings; the other half went to Raymond. For the rest of Twain's life the memory of the money that *Colonel Sellers* brought him regularly lured him back into writing for the stage.

Of his next effort as a playwright – *Ah Sin*, a collaboration with Bret Harte – the less said, the better.[2] Colonel Sellers may have been "a wretched thing," but at least it made money. *Ah Sin* was even more wretched, and was a financial flop. The play exploited the figure of "the Heathen Chinee" from Harte's popular poem, "Plain Language from Truthful James," and also built on Harte's moderately successful popular drama, *Two Men of Sandy Bar*. Harte came to Hartford in the fall and winter of 1876 to write the play with Twain. Before they were done, personal animosities would explode into a bitter feud that would last the rest of their lives. The comedy–melodrama they wrote is so embarrassingly bad that it is very tempting to attribute as little of it as possible to Twain. Twain himself claimed that Harte wrote it while he himself played billiards, with Twain later going "over it to get the dialect right," but that probably overstates the case (Paine 1912: vol. 2, 587; Schirer 1984: 51, 62; Scharnhorst 2000: 124–9; Twain and Harte 1961). The play opened in Washington, at the National Theater, on May 7, 1877, and closed in a week. On opening night in New York, Twain gave a speech after the play which struck the audience as infinitely more amusing than the comedy that had just been performed. The more Daly had cut, Twain said, "the better the play got. I never saw a play that was so much improved by being cut down; and I believe it would have been one of the very best plays in the world if his strength had held out so that he could cut the whole of it" (Daly 1917: 235–6).

Only one other play Twain wrote was produced professionally – if a one-night stand by an elocutionist can, indeed, be considered a "production." His 1883 play, *Colonel Sellers as a Scientist*, was – like *Ah Sin* – an ill-fated collaboration, this time with his friend William Dean Howells. It was an effort to spin off a sequel to his profitable earlier venture by featuring the same character that had made that play such a success (Twain and Howells 1960b: 205–41). The play was filled with gimmicks – beginning with the flame-throwing "fire-extinguisher" that accompanied Colonel Sellers's entrance. But John Raymond, who had brought Colonel Sellers to life in the earlier play, refused to have anything to do with this one, both because of animosity that had developed between him and Twain, and because he disliked the play (Goldman 1985: 123).[3] And since the role was so closely identified with Raymond, no other actor of any standing would touch it. Howells eventually turned over his rights in the play to Twain, who paid theatrical manager Daniel Frohman $1,000 *not* to produce it (Frohman had rented the Lyceum theater to Twain before it had become clear that the play was unlikely to succeed). Twain then leased the rights to an elocutionist and impersonator named A. P. Burbank (Frohman 1937: 107–8). The play opened and closed in New York on the same day.

Twain percolated with real and hypothetical dramatic projects from the 1860s on, experimenting with dramatic sketches, fragments, one-acts, and occasional longer plays as well. There is his burlesque *Hamlet*, which adds a running commentary on every scene in Shakespeare's drama from a book agent named Basil who is trying to get members of the Danish royal family to sign up on his subscription list (thereby providing an endorsement for the book he is touting). And there is Twain's leaden parody of Alan Pinkerton's detective stories, "Cap'n Simon Wheeler, The Amateur Detective" (Twain 1967). There is also a fragment about a hard-working, hard-drinking reporter involved in a love triangle (*Beau Brummel and Arabella*); a set of notes for a play about the Franco-German war of 1870–1; a bilingual playlet, *Meisterschaft*, written for a German class made up of his friends; and *The Death Wafer*, a deadly one-act melodrama about Oliver Cromwell. Twain's jottings in his journal are filled with other ideas as well, such as: "Speak to Howells about Dramatizing Don [Quixote]" (see Fishkin 2003: 151, 210–11). Twain and Howells also discussed the possibilities of collaborating on an abolition spy drama and a play set in the Sandwich Islands: "If we should ever let ourselves loose on the drama we could write a pile of plays," Howells effused. Howells and Twain each published prolifically over the years, but nothing came of these projected collaborations (Fishkin 2003: 151, 210–11; Schirer 1984: 72, 30).

During the winter of 1897–8, when Twain moved his family to Vienna to allow Clara Clemens to pursue her piano studies with the renowned Professor Theodor Leschetizky, he suddenly found himself in the most theater-obsessed city on the planet. As Stefan Zweig notes, "the first glance of the average Viennese into his morning paper" in *fin-de-siècle* Vienna "was not at the events in parliament, or world affairs, but at the repertoire of the theater, which assumed so important a role in public life as hardly was possible in any other city" (see Dolmetsch 1992: 111). The city's dozen or so major resident repertory companies would present as many as 75 different works in a given season, characterized generally by extremely high standards of performance in productions that spared no expense. Twain's excellent German allowed him to take full advantage of the city's rich theatrical offerings. He attended plays constantly, and also cultivated the theaters' managers, directors, and leading actors. The vitality of the theater world he encountered in Vienna fired his ambition to write for the stage again, as did his conversations with Austrian playwright Siegmund Schlesinger, with whom he collaborated on several plays – none of which survive (Fishkin 2003: 152–4, 211; Dolmetsch 1992: 109–31; Schirer 1984: 94–101).

By the start of the new year, 1898, Twain was able to put his draining bankruptcy behind him: the plan his friend Henry Huttleston Rogers had devised for satisfying creditors had worked (Paine 1912: vol. 2, 1056). And although Twain still grieved the death a year and a half earlier of his daughter Susy, and would continue to do so for the rest of his life, the freshness and rawness of that grief were beginning to fade. Twain decided to put those bleak and dreary days of debt and mourning behind him by starting to write a new play of his own – a wild, over-the-top, cross-dressing farce set in France that celebrated his embrace, once again, of the world of the living.

On January 20, Twain wrote his friend and financial advisor, Rogers:

Since we began to pay off the debts I have abundant peace of mind again – no sense of burden. Work is become a pleasure again – it is not labor, any longer. I am into it up to my ears, these last 3 or 4 weeks – and all *dramatic*. (I always believed I couldn't write a play that would *play*, but this one will that I am putting the finishing touches to).

He had high hopes for success. "Yes," he continued jocularly, "I shall want seven rooms in the eleventh story of the new building next year, to conduct my dramatic business in. Please have them frescoed. Put in a billiard table. I will send you further details as they occur to me" (Fishkin 2003: 206; Twain 1969: 316). Two days later, on January 22, he wrote Howells:

> I have made a change lately – into dramatic work – & I find it absorbingly entertaining. I don't know that I can write a play that will play; but no matter, I'll write half a dozen that won't, anyway. Dear me, I didn't know there was such fun in it . . . I get into immense spirits as soon as my day is fairly started. (Twain and Howells 1960a: vol. 2, 670)

On February 5, Twain wrote Rogers that he had written a comedy entitled *Is He Dead?* – "I put on the finishing touches to-day and read it to Mrs. Clemens, and she thinks it is very bully" (Twain 1969: 318). Twain thought it was pretty good, himself.

Is He Dead? is Twain's best play – the one play that may yet bring him posthumously the popular success as a playwright that he craved. Twain based it explicitly on a short story ("Is He Living or Is He Dead?") that appeared in *Cosmopolitan* in September 1893. But his first effort to work through the ideas that would come together in *Is He Dead?* shows no signs of the *élan* that he would bring to the play he wrote five years later. The play revolves around an international group of artists in Barbizon, France – friends and pupils of Jean François Millet, who is himself struggling in obscurity. An unctuous and usurious art dealer named André is in love with a young Frenchwoman named Marie who has just turned him down for the last time because she is in love with Millet. André, who has the power to ruin Millet and all of his associates, vows to do just that and, indeed, manages to push them to the brink of starvation and suicide. In a scene directly reminiscent of one in Dion Boucicault's play *The Poor of New York*, a resourceful and inventive American in the group (named Chicago) bursts into the room in which the gas had been turned on, throws open the door for air, and announces that his friends do not have to die! Or at least that *all* of them don't have to die . . . Recognizing that the price of an artist's work tends to skyrocket after his death, Chicago proposes that Millet die – or *seem* to die – pointing out that the prices that his paintings will thereafter command will feed and house the whole group for the rest of their lives. They decide that Millet must reappear in drag as his sister, the Widow Tillou – a disguise that will allow the real Millet to remain very much alive, and to continue to produce valuable paintings.

The result of all this is an exuberant, over-the-top farce that prefigures aspects of films involving cross-dressing such as *Some Like It Hot* or *Tootsie*, and blends them with some of the lunacies familiar to readers of Twain's fiction. The play is a satire on how the art world assigns value to paintings – and also an extended dig at the French, whose misplaced pride and tolerance for injustice, in Twain's view, knew no bounds. During the same month that Twain wrote *Is He Dead?*, French writer Émile Zola published *J'Accuse*, his scathing attack on French anti-semitism as manifested in the

Dreyfus trial. Twain admired Zola as much as he hated the French in general, and welcomed the opportunity to satirize in this play the French propensity for never admitting an error: as the Widow/Millet puts it at the play's climax, "When France has committed herself to the expression of a belief, she will die a hundred thousand deaths rather than confess she has been in the wrong" (Twain 2003: 143; Fishkin 2003: 154–86, 212–25).

From the 1870s through the turn of the century, Americans were obsessed with Millet – so much so that they earned a reputation in England for being "Millet-mad," as one contemporary observer put it (Hubbard 1912: 85). Given the massive interest his countrymen had in this painter, Twain may well have believed that, from a purely commercial standpoint, a play about Millet was destined to be a hit. American industrialists who collected Millet's work saw in his weary peasants a nod to the nobility of the everyman idealized by American democracy. None of Twain's contemporaries drew comparisons between his work and Millet's art. That is unsurprising, since Twain's work was still relatively new and undigested, its larger significance often missed until the twentieth century. But looking back on these two towering figures today, a parallel is striking: both men made great art out of subjects that their predecessors had viewed as too ignorant or poor or simply unimportant to be worth delineating in paint or print – including French peasants, American slaves, and the poorest of poor whites. Twain and Millet were, in this respect, kindred spirits – a fact which may help explain the sincerity and passion that inform the appreciation of the painter conveyed in *Is He Dead?*

Twain maintains fidelity to the growing consensus in the United States in the 1890s about both Millet's character as a man and his talent as an artist. Millet was known for being kind, generous, intelligent, warm-hearted, and underappreciated during his lifetime; and he was respected for having painted resonant, powerful, and moving works of "noble simplicity" – "no fuss, no feathers, no tricks of color, no theatricals," as Chicago puts it in the play. In his painting *The Angelus*, Chicago sees

> just that solemn half-light, and those brooding distances for the chimes to wander through, and those two humble figures, so poor outside, so rich with the peace of God in their hearts. Dutchy I'd rather be the painter of that picture than – look here, that picture's going to make a strike to-day – you'll see. (Twain 2003: 21)

By the time Twain wrote those words, that picture *had* made "a strike" – and not just any strike: it had sold for more than any painting in past history, inaugurating the modern age of the extravagant art auction. Twain knew that viewers of the play would be aware of that fact; he could assume that this dramatic irony would add to the play's appeal.

The subjects Twain tackled in this play, and many of the "shtiks" as well, were familiar (recycled from "The Legend of the Capitoline Venus," *Tom Sawyer*, "Encounter with an Interviewer," and other works); but he combined them in fresh and engaging ways. Thematically, *Is He Dead?* reprises aspects of "The Legend of the

Capitoline Venus," a six-chapter "condensed novel" Twain published in 1869. The creator of the highly valued art in "The Capitoline Venus" is presumed to be many centuries dead rather than recently so (as the creator of *The Angelus* in *Is He Dead?*), but in both cases the basic principle is the same: living artists starve while the work of dead artists fetches fortunes. Both works satirize the process by which value is assigned to a work of art. *Tom Sawyer* comes to mind in the scene in which Chicago asks the Widow whether she is going to Millet's funeral, and she responds: "No I'm not. The idea of a man attending his own funeral. I never heard of such a thing" (Twain 2003: 117). (Twain reworks this imaginative gambit in *Is He Dead?* with enough style to gratify even Tom Sawyer, who surely would have loved to watch all the crowned heads of Europe pay their respects.) Some of the zaniness of the Widow's encounter with three elderly Frenchwomen who come to pay their condolences in *Is He Dead?* may be found in "An Encounter with an Interviewer," a sketch Twain published in 1874. And *Is He Dead?* was not Twain's first tale to involve male cross-dressing.

Is He Dead? has relatively little in common with Twain's other plays, but a handful of parallels are worth noting. Both *Colonel Sellers* and *Is He Dead?* began in another genre, as prose fiction. Twain wrote each in a matter of weeks. And Colonel Sellers himself is as ebullient and self-confident as Chicago will be. But beyond these fairly trivial connections, the plays are very different from each other. The dialect spoken by Li-Hung-Chang in *Is He Dead?* is not totally unlike that of the title character in the play *Ah Sin*, but there the parallels with that embarrassing disaster end.

In *Is He Dead?* Twain combined aspects of some of the nineteenth century's most popular theatrical traditions – vaudeville, melodrama, and cross-dressing comedy – in his attempt to craft a play that might potentially appeal to a large popular audience. Some of the ethnic accents he tries to evoke in the play may be indebted to his visits to the Garrick Theater in New York, where Edward ("Ned") Harrigan starred in vaudeville-style shows in which dialect humor was central, and often involved Irish and German characters. *Is He Dead?* also captures the spirit of vaudeville on those three occasions when Chicago and his fellow artists and art students erupt into spontaneous celebratory dances. These moments of jubilant *élan* set to music remind us of the vaudeville stage at its silly, exuberant best. André's greed and villainy, the victimization of the innocent Leroux family and Millet, the attempted suicide involving carbon monoxide fumes from a lit charcoal-heater, and Millet's eventual triumph, would have struck turn-of-the-century audiences as redolent of popular melodrama – particularly of plays by the versatile Dion Boucicault. In addition to the similarities between the near-suicide scenes in *The Poor of New York* and *Is He Dead?*, Boucicault's play features a villainous lovestruck banker who tries to squeeze his victims dry on technicalities, much as André tries to find legal loopholes that allow him to ruin Millet, his sweetheart, and the other artists. The plot of *Is He Dead?* is activated by the Manichean "clash of virtue and villainy," as Peter Brooks characterizes the engine that drives melodrama (Brooks 1976: 34–6). André is the embodiment of evil, while Marie, her family, and Millet and his fellow artists are good, kind, persecuted innocents. The play's happy ending invites the kind of audience response that the authors of nineteenth-century melodramas typically sought: "We rejoice at [the hero's] luck, share vicariously in his triumphs, and leave the theatre ready to tackle the world single-handed and win" (Gerould 1983: 10–11; Smith 1973: 19). Twain wrote *Is He Dead?* at precisely the moment he managed to extricate himself from the burdens of heavy debt. It is certainly possible that some of the pleasure he took in writing the play came from his identification with his characters' escape from penury and debt, as well.

Female impersonators were stock figures in pantomimes, minstrel shows, burlesque, vaudeville, and popular comedies, as well as in amateur theatricals (Schirer 1984: 7; Senelick 2000; Fishkin 2003: 191–6, 226–8). Indeed, male cross-dressing was central to the play that was probably the biggest worldwide hit of the 1890s, Brandon Thomas's *Charley's Aunt*. Charles Frohman brought that play to New York in October 1893, after a London run of 1,469 consecutive performances, and it quickly became the talk of the town. By the time it opened in New York, the playwright's son recalled, "*Charley's Aunt* had become a craze. All kinds of souvenirs were made in its honor – there were *Charley's Aunt* paper-knives, ink bottles, nibs, dolls, pen wipers" (Brandon-Thomas 1955: 180). It would become the most popular British play of the nineteenth century and, in one critic's view, "one of the most successful plays of all time" (Huberman 1986: 116).

Charley's Aunt was precisely the kind of theatrical success to which Twain himself aspired. When it opened in New York, Twain was living at the Players' Club, attending the theater regularly and spending a substantial portion of his time dining, drinking, and playing billiards with actors and producers including, quite likely, the star of *Charley's Aunt*, who frequented the Players' Club as well. Twain could not have missed the barrage of glowing reviews of the play that filled the New York papers when the play opened, or the notices attesting to its worldwide success throughout the 1890s (Fishkin 2003: 194–6, 227–8).

Charley's Aunt and *Is He Dead?* are set in different times (Oxford, England, in the 1890s; Barbizon, France, in the 1840s), and have very different sets of characters. *Is He Dead?* embraces more social satire, and explores more serious issues than *Charley's Aunt*. Yet similarities remain. Both plays involve groups of young men who find themselves in a crisis that can be resolved only by one of their group donning women's clothes and impersonating a widow. The cross-dressing males have trouble in both cases remembering how women are expected to carry themselves, speak, and act. They both shock people around them by their habit of smoking. Both are pursued by unwanted suitors. And both are befuddled about how to respond to questions about their children. Perhaps the greatest similarity between *Charley's Aunt* and *Is He Dead?* lies in the character, demeanor, and carriage of the cross-dressed protagonist. Brandon Thomas said approvingly of W. S. Penley, the actor who inaugurated the title role in his play, "He is unerring refinement" (see Brandon-Thomas 1955: 155). Twain clearly sought a similar portrayal of his own cross-dressed protagonist when he specified that the Widow Tillou should be, despite her accidents and awkwardnesses, "a lady" (Twain 2003: 3). The phenomenal success of *Charley's Aunt* in England, in America, and around the world in the 1890s may well have helped inspired Twain to write his own farcical comedy in which a cross-dressing character played a central role.

Soon after Twain finished *Is He Dead?* he sent it off to Bram Stoker, who had agreed, some time earlier, to be his dramatic agent in Britain. Unbeknown to Twain, his timing could not have been worse. On February 18, 1898, the storage unit for Stoker's Lyceum Theatre caught fire, and 260 scenes for 44 plays, more than 2,000 pieces of scenery, along with the corresponding costumes and props, all insured for vastly less than their worth, went up in flames (Ludlum 1962: 116–17; Stoker 1906: vol. 2, 297–303; Belford 1996: 278–9). Twain took Stoker's lack of encouragement at face value, apparently unaware of the devastating loss that might have made him reticent, at the time, about any future project on the stage. Twain then asked two of his friends, Henry Huttleston Rogers and Dr. C. C. Rice, to help him try to place the play in the United States. They failed. Twain had come along at the tail-end of a bubble that had burst: farcical comedy had run its course during the 1890s on both sides of the Atlantic. Twain's play was original – even the theatrical syndicate that sent a rejection letter had to admit that the idea of the play was "certainly unique" – but its moment had passed. The supply of farces had outstripped the demand, and the saturated market stopped buying. In Britain, naturalistic foreign plays, Shavian comedy, and "problem plays" were in ascendance; farce was out. The situation was much the same in New York where, in the wake of the Spanish–American War (as Twain heard in June 1898), "war-plays" were currently all the rage.[4] Even authors of many of the successful farces of the early 1890s could not get their new plays on stage by 1898 (Huberman 1986: 132).

Twain's response to his failure to place *Is He Dead?* was to give up on the theater, largely abandoning the dream he had had since the 1870s of writing another hit play.[5] Another obstacle to Twain's attempts to have his play produced may have been its treatment of a revered cultural icon. Although Millet/The Widow is portrayed respectfully, traditionalists might have felt that presenting the great painter in drag was inappropriate, no matter how refined the lady was. Neither in Britain nor in the United States had any of the Widow's cross-dressing predecessors in either legitimate theaters or more popular venues portrayed real historical figures. They were always invented characters. Twain's decision to cast a towering figure in the arts like Jean-François Millet in drag, and to show him engaging in demonstrations of affection – however feigned – with a repulsive male art dealer, may well have been too audacious and transgressive for 1898.

Although *Is He Dead?* may have been out of step with the theater trends of the late 1890s, today we are free to see the play for the surprising work that it is. In terms of the arc of Twain's life and career, *Is He Dead?* is particularly interesting because its high-spirited energy runs counter to the dominant image of Twain's writing during this period – a time when he produced, according to the conventional wisdom, mainly works of dark, brooding pessimism and grim determinism. Rather than reflecting a world ruled by determinism, nihilism, and despair, *Is He Dead?* evokes a world in which imagination, chutzpah, and collective action trump malevolence and abusive power. There is something inspiring about the fact that Twain was able to emerge from his slough of mourning and gloom with the resilience to write a play as zany and exuberant as this one. This neglected work also gives us a new perspective on the engagement with debates about authenticity and artifice that resonate throughout Twain's writings. Questions of who and what one really "is" come into play in *Is He Dead?* when Millet realizes, as he is about to "return" as a young painter who is a "marvelously successful imitator of the late lamented" great French artist, that he is destined to spend his life as an "imitator of myself" (Twain 2003: 128). Might a Mark Twain who often felt constrained to present to the world familiar versions of himself that the public held dear have also felt like an imitator of himself at times? The question of authenticity and artifice in people is not unrelated to the questions of originals and copies in art that the play raises frequently, as Millet paints fresh copies of his most famous paintings and sells them as "originals." Who is the "real" Millet? Which is the "real" *Angelus*? Who is authentic, and who is the imposter or claimant?[6] And will the "real" Mark Twain/Samuel Clemens please stand up? *Is He Dead?* complicates, in interesting ways, a theme that runs through virtually everything Twain ever wrote: the riddle of identity.

Also striking is the play's contribution to the Twain œuvre of a memorable and distinctive character. In the Widow Daisy Tillou, Twain has created a "female character" who is sensitive, astute, smart, kind, and outspoken; a libidinous heterosexual male impeccably attired as a proper Victorian matron; a man pretending to be a woman, who both chafes under the restrictions of the role and revels in the opportunities for intimacy with his sweetheart that it affords him; a good-hearted leader of a band of talented young men, and a sympathetic female friend of a young woman in mourning; a ditzy nonsense-spewing eccentric old lady, and a woman who rises to heights of eloquence usually reserved, on the Victorian stage, for men. But what does it mean that, during the rise of the "New Woman," one of the most interesting female characters Twain created is really a man? This latter question intersects with a number of debates in the academy today – about the significance of drag, the nature of gender, the complex meanings of cross-dressing. "If essence of gender can be simulated through wigs, props, gestures, costumes, cross-dressing implies that it is not an essence at all, but an unstable construct," Senelick writes, for example, in *The Changing Room* (2000: 3).[7] While some critics accept the idea that cross-dressing can be a useful tool in the project of subverting gender stereotypes, others focus on drag's more potentially retrograde underside, suggesting that it always reinforces male power – or at least, that it sends inherently mixed signals (Fishkin 2003: 231–2). Twain's engaging, cross-dressing Millet/Daisy Tillou should provide new grist for this debate.

Is He Dead? may have been too "out there" for the Victorian 1890s, but twenty-first-century audiences might be ready to enjoy the play's ingenuity, ebullience, and sheer loopiness. They might appreciate its celebration of male friendship and its send-up of hype in the art world. And they might have fun watching Twain masterfully reprise some of his favorite comic gambits. The play has been optioned by veteran Broadway producer Bob Boyett, who is now trying to bring it to the stage. Twain's dream of writing "a play that would play" may be fulfilled yet – nearly a hundred years after his death.

NOTES

1 Portions of this essay draw heavily on the author's recent study of Mark Twain's experiences in the theater (Fishkin 2003).
2 For a particularly lucid and helpful analysis of the play, see Woo (2003).
3 For Twain's notes on the saga of *Colonel Sellers as a Scientist*, see Twain 1979: 2, 13 n. 21, 33 n. 60, 35, 37–9, 195 n. 46, 226, 237–9, 334, 337 n. 106, and 342.
4 Twain wrote as part of a letter to Bettina Wirth, "war-plays are all the go [in New York], these days" (Fishkin 2003: 239). This comment is supported in part by a facsimile of a page of theater advertisements from "a New York newspaper" of 7 May 1898 that Twain reprints in his essay "About Play-Acting." The page features advertisements for "The Man-o'-War's Man" at the Fourteenth Street Theater; "Battles of Our Nation" at the Academy of Music; and "War Bubbles," followed by "An

Original Patriotic Extravaganza," at the Olympic Music Hall (Twain 1996: 237).
5 The only play Twain wrote after *Is He Dead?* was *The Death Wafer*, an eminently forgettable and dull dramatization of his story "The Death Disk." It was written in 1900, runs to 58 pages in manuscript, and was performed informally at the Carnegie Lyceum. (The manuscript is in the Mark Twain Papers at the Bancroft Library, Berkeley.) Twain remained an avid theatergoer, however. On one occasion he persuaded many of his friends to attend a remarkable production of *The Prince and the Pauper* performed by Jewish immigrant children at the Educational Alliance, a Lower East Side settlement house.
6 For a lucid consideration of the issue of imposture and identity in Twain's work, see Gillman (1989).
7 Senelick adds: "the transvestite in the theatre does not confute or elude categories; it creates new ones" (2000: 11).

REFERENCES AND FURTHER READING

Belford, Barbara (1996). *Bram Stoker*. New York: Knopf.
Boucicault, Dion (1968). *The Poor of New York* (first publ. 1857). In *The Character of Melodrama: An Examination through Dion Boucicault's "The Poor of New York" including the text of the play*, ed. William Paul Steele, 59–101. Orono, Maine: University of Maine Press.
Brandon-Thomas, Jevan (1955). *Charley's Aunt's Father: A Life of Brandon Thomas*. London: Douglas Saunders/MacGibbon & Kee.
Brooks, Peter (1976). *The Melodramatic Imagination*. New Haven: Yale University Press.
[Clemens, Samuel] "S.L.C." (1855). "Correspondence." http://www.twainquotes.com/Muscatine/18550228.html (accessed Jan. 16 2005).
Daly, Joseph F. (1917). *The Life of Augustin Daly*. New York: Macmillan.

Dolmetsch, Carl (1992) *"Our Famous Guest": Mark Twain in Vienna*. Athens: University of Georgia Press.
Fishkin, Shelley Fisher (2003). "Introduction" and "Afterword." In Mark Twain, *Is He Dead? A Comedy in Three Acts*, ix–xii, 147–232. Berkeley: University of California Press.
Frohman, Daniel (1911). *Memories of a Manager*. London: Heinemann.
Frohman, Daniel (1935). *Daniel Frohman Presents: An Autobiography*. New York: Claude Kendall & Willoughby Sharp.
Frohman, Daniel (1937). *Encore*. New York: L. Furman.
Gerould, Daniel C., ed. (1983). *American Melodrama*. New York: Performing Arts Journal Publications.
Gillman, Susan (1989). *Dark Twins: Imposture and Identity in Mark Twain's America*. Chicago: University of Chicago Press.

Goldman, Robert (1985). "Mark Twain as a Playwright." In Robert Giddings (ed.), *Mark Twain: A Sumptuous Variety*, 108–131. Totowa, NJ: Vision/Barnes & Noble.

Hubbard, Elbert (1912). *Little Journeys to the Homes of Eminent Painters, Book Two*. East Aurora, NY: Roy Crofters.

Huberman, Jeffrey H. (1986). *Late Victorian Farce*. Ann Arbor: UMI Research Press.

Krause, Sydney J. (1967). *Mark Twain as Critic*. Baltimore: Johns Hopkins University Press.

Ludlum, Harry (1962). *A Biography of Dracula: The Life Story of Bram Stoker*. London: Fireside Press/W. Foulsham.

Paine, Albert Bigelow (1912). *Mark Twain: A Biography. The Personal and Literary Life of Samuel Langhorne Clemens*, 3 vols. New York and London: Harper & Bros.

Scharnhorst, Gary (2000). *Bret Harte: Opening the American Literary West*. Norman: University of Oklahoma Press.

Schirer, Thomas (1984). *Mark Twain and the Theatre*. Nürnberg: Hans Carl.

Senelick, Laurence (2000). *The Changing Room: Sex, Drag and the Theatre*. New York: Routledge.

Smith, James L. (1973). *Melodrama*. London: Methuen.

Stoker, Bram (1906). *Personal Reminiscences of Henry Irving*, 2 vols. New York: Macmillan.

Thomas, Brandon (1935). *Charley's Aunt: A Play in Three Acts*. New York: Samuel French. (First publ. 1892.)

Thomason, Jerry (1991). "'Colonel Sellers': The Story of his Play." Ph.D. diss., University of Missouri, Columbia. Abstracts International, DA9133640. 52 (6): 2145A.

Thomason, Jerry, and Quirk, Tom (1995). "Introduction" to "Colonel Sellers: A Drama in Five Acts." *Missouri Review* 18: 3, 111–12.

[Twain, Mark] (1856). Thomas Jefferson Snodgrass, "Correspondence." *Keokuk Saturday Post*, Nov. 1, 1856. http://www.twainquotes.com/Keokuk/18561101.html (accessed Jan. 6, 2004).

Twain, Mark (1967). *Mark Twain's Satires and Burlesques*, ed. Franklin R. Rogers. Berkeley: University of California Press.

Twain, Mark (1969). *Mark Twain's Correspondence with Henry Huttleston Rogers, 1893–1909*, ed. Lewis Leary. Berkeley: University of California Press.

Twain, Mark (1979). *Mark Twain's Notebooks and Journals*, vol. 3: *1883–1891*, ed. Robert Pack Browning, Michael B. Frank, and Lin Salamo. Berkeley: University of California Press.

Twain, Mark (1988). *Mark Twain's Letters*, vol. 1: *1853–1866*, ed. Edgar Marquess Branch, Michael B. Frank, and Kenneth Sanderson. Berkeley: University of California Press.

Twain, Mark (1995). "Colonel Sellers: A Drama in Five Acts." *Missouri Review* 18: 3, 113–51.

Twain, Mark (1996). *The Man That Corrupted Hadleyburg and Other Essays and Stories*. New York: Oxford University Press. (First publ. 1900.)

Twain, Mark (2002). *Mark Twain's Letters*, vol. 6: *1874–1875*, ed. Michael B. Frank and Harriet Elinor Smith. Berkeley: University of California Press.

Twain, Mark (2003). *Is He Dead? A Comedy in Three Acts*, ed. Shelley Fisher Fishkin. Berkeley: University of California Press.

Twain, Mark, and Harte, Bret (1961). *Ah Sin, A Dramatic Work*, ed. Frederick Anderson. San Francisco: Book Club of California.

Twain, Mark, and Howells, William Dean (1960a). *Mark Twain–Howells Letters: The Correspondence of Samuel L. Clemens and William D. Howells, 1872–1910*, 2 vols., ed. Henry Nash Smith and William M. Gibson. Cambridge, Mass.: Belknap/Harvard University Press.

Twain, Mark, and Howells, William Dean (1960b). *Colonel Sellers as a Scientist*. In *The Complete Plays of W. D. Howells*, ed. Walter J. Meserve, 205–41. New York: New York University Press.

Woo, Miseong (2003). "The Racial Frontier: *Ah Sin*, a Play by Bret Harte and Mark Twain." *Journal of American Studies* [Korea] 35: 3, Winter, 230–51.

18

Mark Twain on the Screen

R. Kent Rasmussen and Mark Dawidziak

Despite the fact that Mark Twain was a consummate showman and master of timing, the timing of his death was not quite perfect. He had the misfortune of making his final exit just as motion pictures were going through their birth pangs. He lived just long enough to see the first primitive adaptations of his writings to the screen, and even saw himself on a screen, but he did not live quite long enough to see anything like a major film adaptation of one of his works.[1] Always fascinated by new technologies, he would certainly have followed the development of motion pictures with interest. He would also have enjoyed knowing how future films would reintroduce his works to one generation of filmgoers after another.

Film and television adaptations of Twain's writings have helped keep interest in his books alive. For proof, one has only to watch the Mark Twain shelves in bookstores or monitor sales-rank figures on Amazon.com and Barnesandnoble.com and note the vanishing stock and sales spikes every time a new Mark Twain film or television program comes along. That much is clearly for the good.

It is also true that the author's works are better known to the world through their movie and television versions than they are through Twain's own written words. *The Adventures of Tom Sawyer* (1876), perhaps his most popular book, provides a case in point. That novel has gone through more than 1,300 editions and been translated into at least 57 different languages (see Rodney 1982: 265). Nevertheless, for each person now living who has read the novel, probably two or more have seen at least one of its many screen adaptations. Tom Sawyer is an iconic figure in American culture, but the Tom that most people know is more likely a character from a film than the Tom of the novel.

Film representations of Tom Sawyer do not always depart radically from Twain's own depiction, but the same is not true of other characters, especially Huckleberry Finn. Among the dozen or so screen adaptations of *Adventures of Huckleberry Finn*, it is difficult to find more than one or two Hucks who bear a family resemblance to the Huck described in the novel. Thanks to the power of the screen, Tom and Huck are virtually interchangeable in the popular mind. Indeed, it might not be going too far to say that in the most recent adaptation, Disney's 1993 *The Adventures of Huck Finn*, Huck morphed almost completely into Tom, retaining only his own name and family history. Proof of this transformation appears the moment the movie begins, in Huck's voiceover narration: "My name's Huck. Huck Finn! And this story's about me and a slave named Jim. And it's mainly the truth. Oh sure, there's a few stretchers, here and there. But, then, I never met anybody who didn't lie a little when the situation suited 'em."[2]

After contradicting the premise of the novel by establishing that Huck is a liar, the film opens with the totally misconceived scene of Huck fighting another boy on a riverbank, as friends cry out, "Go for the glory, Huck!" It is a sobering thought that more people living today may have seen this travesty than have read the original book.[3]

An example of a Mark Twain work from near the other end of the popularity scale is *Roughing It*. Though scarcely a minor work, it is now read by only a tiny fraction of the numbers of people who read *Tom Sawyer* and *Huckleberry Finn*. A few tens of thousands of readers may be familiar with the superb University of California Press edition of *Roughing It* prepared by the editors of the Mark Twain Project. Contrast that number with the millions of cable television viewers introduced to *Roughing It* in March 2002, when the Hallmark Channel aired an original two-part adaptation of the book, featuring James Garner as a 55-year-old Clemens looking back on his time in the Far West. Part one of the mini-series drew a Nielsen rating of 1.6 (million households tuned in). Though minuscule by the standards of network television, this was the highest rating the Hallmark Channel had received to that date for any original program.[4] Assuming a conservative average of at least two viewers per household, more than three million people watched the first telecast of *Roughing It*. It is likely that far more people have seen Hallmark's production than have read the book throughout its entire existence.

It is undeniable that Mark Twain's works are better known to the world through the screen than they are through his own words – and, further, that as literacy retreats before movies, television, videos, the internet, and video games, that imbalance will grow larger. Teachers and other champions of the written word can do little to halt or even slow this trend. What matters is understanding how screen adaptations are shaping contemporary views of Mark Twain, how they can be used to attract people to read his books, and what can be done in the classroom to counter the typically distorted versions of both the author and his books that viewers absorb from movies and television.

Professional reviews of films and television programs often provide literate insights into treatments of Twain's works and their place in contemporary culture. More intriguing, perhaps, are the views of average moviegoers and television watchers. One can tap into these views through several public forums which, not surprisingly, can be found on the internet. In addition to providing nearly exhaustive listings of films – along with detailed credit lists – the Internet Movie Database (www.imdb.com) encourages its users to post comments on individual films. Amazon.com and

Barnesandnoble.com are known primarily as online booksellers, but they also sell video cassettes and DVDs and encourage customers to post reviews of those products. Individual film titles occasionally elicit surprisingly large numbers of amateur reviews on these sites. To a greater extent, perhaps, than in professional reviews, user comments reflect the impact that screen adaptations are having on audiences.[5] This comment on Hallmark's *Roughing It* posted on Amazon.com by a Missouri schoolteacher is a representative example:

> After completing The Adventures of Tom Sawyer and The Celebrated Frog of Caleveras [sic] County, I decided to show Roughing [It] to my 8th grade students. Some students had enjoyed Tom Sawyer, but there were quite a few that found the vocabulary very difficult. Many of them were apprehensive, and thought it might be BORING, but the classroom was silent during this film. I ask students after they have watched a film if they would recommend showing [it] to future students. All of them said they would watch it again, at home, if they had the movie.

The fact that 13- and 14-year-old eighth-graders in Clemens's Missouri find the vocabulary of *Tom Sawyer* "very difficult" is distressing, but it merely underlines the unlikelihood of these students ever knowing *Roughing It*, or indeed any other Mark Twain work, through a medium other than the screen. Moreover, like it or not, screen adaptations are increasingly finding their way into literature classrooms.

Hollywood as an Ally

The film and television industries have been valuable allies in keeping Twain's stories alive over the past century, while dozens of other literary stars have slipped out of print and dropped off the celebrity radar. Indeed, few authors have served more consistently as a source of script material than he has. In return for the use of his stories, film and television producers have turned his characters into iconic, sometimes archetypal, figures. Even those who have never read *Tom Sawyer* probably have an image of the wily young fellow and know about his enterprising method of whitewashing a fence. Most Americans would have a difficult time picking out Herman Melville or Henry David Thoreau in a line-up. However, thanks in large part to movies and television, Twain is an instantly recognizable figure, and the mere mention of his name summons a veritable parade of Americana. This would have pleased this man who took great delight in being recognized while strolling down a street or walking across a hotel lobby.

   Film and television productions also have aided and abetted in keeping Twain himself alive as an iconic figure – and as something of an American folk hero. He was played by an Academy Award-winning actor, Fredric March, in *The Adventures of Mark Twain*, a glossy Hollywood film biography released by Warner Bros. in 1944. On March 6, 1967, 30 million people saw him in the person of Hal Holbrook, who performed his celebrated one-man stage show on CBS-TV that night. In 1985 he was a claymation character, with James Whitmore's voice, in a film also titled *The Adventures of Mark Twain*. In 1991 he was portrayed by another Oscar-winning actor, Jason Robards, in the Disney television movie *Mark Twain and Me*. In 2002 he was the subject of a Ken Burns documentary on PBS. His many other screen incarnations over the years have included appearances as characters in such popular television programs as *Bonanza*, *The Rifleman*, *Death Valley Days*, *Father Murphy*, and *Star Trek: The Next Generation*.

Although Twain would have been pleased by what films and television have done to spread his fame, he would certainly have hated the many sanitized, minimized, Hollywood-ized, compromised, modernized, devitalized, and bowdlerized adaptations of his writings. While the cornucopia of Clemens cinema is not short of quantity, it is sadly lacking in quality. One or two adaptations are generally conceded to be sturdy efforts, but not a single one in the bunch is generally considered a masterpiece.[6]

Film producers are notorious for butchering literature, but Hollywood has served some writers well. The outstanding example is Charles Dickens, one of the few prose writers more frequently adapted than Clemens. Almost all of Dickens's major novels and several of his shorter works have been filmed – and in these, along with quantity, there has been an abundance of quality. Since the early 1930s, almost every decade has seen at least one acknowledged masterpiece adapted from a Dickens work, ranging from director George Cukor's *David Copperfield* in 1935 to Douglas McGrath's *Nicholas Nickleby* in 2002. A handy measure of film quality is film historian Leonard Maltin's rating system. His annual movie guide assigns four stars, his highest rating, to at least a half-dozen Dickens adaptations. By contrast, not a single Mark Twain adaptation earns that status. Why is it that film-makers seem unable to miss with Dickens and yet unable to score a hit with Mark Twain? One possible explanation is that none of the finest American directors has ever tackled a Mark Twain work. The directors responsible for masterly adaptations of writers such as Dickens, John Steinbeck, and Dashiell Hammett read like a Hollywood hall of fame: John Ford, George Cukor, David Lean, John Huston, Lewis Milestone, and Elia Kazan. Not one of them ever tried his hand at a Mark Twain story.

On the few occasions when Mark Twain characters have landed in classy company, the results have been above average. For example, *Gone with the Wind* producer David O. Selznick, also responsible for the 1935 *David Copperfield*, was the Hollywood power behind 1938's *The Adventures of Tom Sawyer*. In 1985 the esteemed PBS series *American Playhouse* presented an *Adventures of Huckleberry Finn* mini-series, in which Patrick Day played Huck and Samm-Art Williams played Jim. Those two productions are generally recognized as the best adaptations of the Mark Twain works on which they are based. Unfortunately, others attaining similar standards have been rare.

Given that most people now know Mark Twain's work primarily from what they see on screens, what kinds of pictures are they getting? For the most part, the answer has to be: distorted ones. *Tom Sawyer* adaptations, for example, typically project eternal Norman Rockwell summers, populated by characters blissfully unaware of the novel's intriguing undercurrents. In the case of Twain himself, the icon, not the man, pre-dominates – a grandfatherly white-haired figure in a white suit, ever puffing on a cigar. Staying true to facts or to the spirit of Twain's writing rarely has been a matter of concern for those carrying his works into the cinematic and video realms. This is not to say that there have not been adaptations that remain true to the spirit of the original stories. Selznick's team certainly captured much of the charm, humor, exu-berance, and even the sense of menace in *The Adventures of Tom Sawyer*. In 1989 David Birney made an admirable effort to blend two works in his *The Diaries of Adam and Eve* on PBS-TV. In 1994 comedian Paul Rodriguez cleverly recast "The £1,000,000 Bank-Note" in modern East Los Angeles in *A Million to Juan*. Rodriguez naturally took broad liberties with the story's details, but he remained faithful to its spirit.[7]

The 1944 Warner Bros. biopic *The Adventures of Mark Twain* was as sentimental as it was unreliable in its characterization of Twain (Fredric March). By contrast, play-wright Horton Foote's 1960 drama for television's *Playhouse 90*, *The Shape of the River*, managed to reveal the complex man behind the popular image by emphasizing the profound tragedies occurring during the last 15 years of the author's life. Holbrook's Twain impersonation on CBS-TV's 1967 broadcast (*Mark Twain Tonight!*) was nothing less than sublime television. Finally, *Mark Twain: Beneath the Laughter*, a December 1979 PBS drama with Irish actor Dan O'Herlihy as Twain, was another television production that cannot be accused of playing to a stereotype. However, these fine pro-grams have been seen by too few people to counterbalance the more folksy and genial Mark Twain images trotted out through the mass media.

If it is true, as Shelley Fisher Fishkin argues in *Lighting Out for the Territory*, that "Mark Twain has indelibly shaped our view of who and what the United States is as a nation and who and what we might become" (Fishkin 1997: 7), then it is also true that Hollywood has indelibly shaped our view of Mark Twain. Moreover, that image is part American myth, similar to the folk-hero status conferred on Benjamin Franklin, Davy Crockett, and Abraham Lincoln. It is a process that makes fascinating person-ages seem larger than life but, at the same time, less fascinating and less lifelike. The Mark Twain represented in *The Shape of the River* and *Mark Twain: Beneath the Laugh-ter* is far more heroic than *The Adventures of Mark Twain*'s pale imitation, and that is simply because those two productions allow him to be more human. However, Fredric March's Twain has been seen by many more people and has had a far greater impact.[8]

Quibbles about screen depictions of Twain's life are minor compared to concerns about adaptations of his work. Although film and television producers have adapted a wide variety of material, they return with great regularity to four titles: *The Adven-tures of Tom Sawyer* (1876), *Adventures of Huckleberry Finn* (1885), *The Prince and the Pauper* (1881), and *A Connecticut Yankee in King Arthur's Court* (1889). Since the earli-est known film adaptations in 1907, more than one hundred movies and television shows have been adapted from about 21 of Twain's books and short stories. Roughly 60 of these are adaptations of the four named works. Why, we might ask, has no acknowledged classic been made from this gang of four?

Tom Sawyer and *The Prince and the Pauper* would seem easy to adapt. Both have plots and characters that can be fully realized in a two-hour movie, much as David Lean scaled down *Oliver Twist* and George Cukor reduced *David Copperfield* without damage to the books' themes. Only Selznick's *Tom Sawyer*, however, comes close to doing the same. Far more difficult are the challenges presented by *A Connecticut Yankee* and, most especially, *Huckleberry Finn*. With its Camelot setting, twisting plot, grand turns, dark social criticism, and inexplicable contradictions, *Connecticut Yankee* probably would have been best suited for the kind of extended mini-series treatment popular during the 1970s and 1980s. The same might be said of *The Gilded Age* (1873), which Clemens co-wrote with Charles Dudley Warner. However, in neither case did this happen. Instead, we have been left with only a sad line of frivolous *Connecticut Yankee* adaptations that have stressed silly slapstick stuff, all but ignoring the novel's savage satire. For its part, *Huckleberry Finn* has presented more than a raft of trouble to those who would steer that story into television and film tributaries. Even PBS's solid *American Playhouse* mini-series had difficulty depicting the book's most dramatic and powerful moments. The fundamental failings of *Huckleberry Finn* adaptations are probably due to the fact that the novel's most poignant struggles unfold within Huck's mind and are expressed through his guileless narration. Visual media have trouble grasping such power, preferring strong visual images to strong words. Moreover, even when movies use voiceover narration, they are still inclined to get things wrong – as is the case with *The Adventures of Huck Finn*.

The only book-length study of any aspect of Mark Twain films is Clyde V. Haupt's engaging *"Huckleberry Finn" on Film: Film and Television Adaptations of Mark Twain's Novel, 1920–1993* (1994). Haupt points out that "virtually all novels adapted to film" are at odds with the films made from them. He points out that "if a novel is powerful, a faithful adaptation of it should also be powerful – as well as profitable" (Haupt 1994: 1). Since the many versions of *Huckleberry Finn* have all employed traditional film and television storytelling techniques, it is small wonder that the book has defied adaptation. Routine screen approaches simply do not work in its case, and this is the principal reason why American film-makers have failed to make a great movie out of one of the greatest American novels. They fight against the current of Twain's mighty narrative skills, foolishly drifting off in directions that lead them astray. Haupt adds that:

> typical *Huck* adapters avoid most of Twain's novel. They prefer their own imaginations to the novel's strength and content. Consequently, most *Huck* films are works of cinematic taxidermy: Twain's story line is broadly preserved, the native life of the novel is displaced, and the remaining carcass is stuffed with someone's special agenda; after which attempts are made to breathe a new, albeit strange, life back into the remains. (p. 1)

One *Huckleberry Finn* adaptation that has gloriously met the challenge of dramatizing the searing emotions within Huck's head came to life, not on the screen, but on stage: country singer Roger Miller's musical play, *Big River*. Miller's play opened on Broadway in 1984 and won seven Tony awards. Miller understood that songs – basically musical monologues – are ideal for expressing *Huckleberry Finn*'s strongest emotional moments. Might a movie version of *Big River* transfer that magic to the screen as effectively as, say, *Oliver!* did for Dickens's *Oliver Twist* in 1968? Of course, the mere transformation of *Huckleberry Finn* into a musical film does not guarantee success. The 1974 Reader's Digest/United Artists production of *Huckleberry Finn* was a musical, yet failed to capture the novel's themes. While no producer has yet turned a Clemens story into a cinematic masterpiece, that is not for any lack of trying. Film adaptations of Mark Twain stories began appearing before Hollywood's first film studio even opened for business.

The Silent Film Era

During Twain's last years, American film production was in the process of centering its operations in Hollywood. In 1910 – the year in which he died – Hollywood was absorbed into the city of Los Angeles. Twain himself never went near Hollywood. Even so, he had already forged spiritual and archaeological links with the movies that John Seelye explored in *Mark Twain in the Movies* (1977). Seelye describes Twain as an American star whose "mixture of charisma and chutzpah" showed the way for the galaxy of Hollywood stars who were to follow him as cultural icons, dubbing him "homo movens . . . the original Kineman" (Seelye 1977: 5). If Twain took notice of the handful of silent film adaptations of his work released during his lifetime, he left behind no scraps of what certainly would have been valuable early examples of movie criticism. The first of these adaptations, *A Curious Dream*, a Vitagraph production based on an 1870 sketch, and a highly condensed *Tom Sawyer*, were released in 1907.

Given Twain's fascination with inventions and patents, one suspects that he gave at least passing thought to the commercial possibilities of these flickering images. Toward the end of his life, he paraded before one of Thomas A. Edison's motion-picture cameras at his Stormfield home and, for $150, his Mark Twain Company licenced Edison's company to film *The Prince and the Pauper* (to which the Stormfield footage was attached). D. W. Griffith directed *The Death Disc: A Story of the Cromwellian Period*, from a Twain short story, for Biograph in 1909. In 1910 Edison made *A Mountain Blizzard*, based on *Roughing It*'s blizzard episode. The following year saw the release of *Science*, an adaptation of Twain's anti-vivisection story "A Dog's Tale," and starring Mary Pickford. Each of these early films was probably no longer than a single reel – about ten minutes. The first adaptation that might be considered a "feature film," another version of *The Prince and the Pauper*, was released in 1915 by Famous Players (later Paramount) with 32-year-old stage actress Marguerite Clark playing both Prince Edward and Tom Canty.

In 1916, Alan Hale played Tom Driscoll to Theodore Roberts's Wilson in *Pudd'nhead Wilson*. The following year, Jack Pickford, Mary's brother, had the title role in director William Desmond Taylor's *Tom Sawyer*. With Robert Gordon as Huck, this 44-minute film followed the first half of Twain's novel closely, and most of the dialogue printed on the title cards that appeared on the screen came straight from the book. The film was sufficiently successful for Taylor to complete his adaptation of the novel with the 45-minute sequel, *Huck and Tom*, in 1918. When Paramount followed the success of Taylor's *Tom Sawyer* films by having him direct *Huckleberry Finn* in 1920, Lewis Sargent played Huck, with George Reed also featured as Jim. As the earlier films, the designers made a special effort to match the look of costumes and sets with the illustrations of the original book. Although substantial cuts in content were made, the film's running time being only 78 minutes, Taylor was intent on exploring the book's major themes. Despite some uncomfortable moments and an ending that has Huck return to Mary Jane Wilks, Sargent and Reed delivered earnest performances that underscored the characters' dignity.[9] Also in 1920, the Hungarian director Alexander Korda released his version of *The Prince and the Pauper*, which imitated the 1915 film by having one actor, Tibi Lubinsky, play both Tom and Edward.

One of the most intriguing lost films of the silent era was director Emmett J. Flynn's *A Connecticut Yankee* (1921), in which Harry Myers had the title role.[10] Establishing several precedents for the many *Connecticut Yankee* adaptations to come, this version put a high premium on physical comedy and ignored the book's savage attacks on slavery, monarchy, and established religion. A *New York Times* critic called it "broad comedy at its broadest."[11] Since then, *Connecticut Yankee* adaptations have tended to update the story's starting point to whatever year is the present, and then use contemporary gadgets and technology to generate gags.

No further major Twain adaptations were produced in Hollywood through the remainder of the silent era. Meanwhile, Richard Rodgers and Lorenz Hart scored a stage hit with a musical adaptation of *Connecticut Yankee* that opened a long Broadway run in November 1927. That production demonstrated intriguing possibilities for translating a Mark Twain work into musical comedy, but it has not yet been adapted to the big screen.

The Coming of Sound

In 1930, Paramount returned to the Mark Twain well with a sound version of *Tom Sawyer*. It featured popular child star Jackie Coogan as Tom, Junior Durkin as Huck, and Mitzi Green as Becky Thatcher. *New York Times* critic Mordaunt Hall wrote that Coogan played Tom "with an uncanny appreciation of what is wanted of him," and called the film "an extraordinarily faithful conception of the book."[12] At the same time, however, he praised a fight between Tom and Joe Harper for its "fidelity to Mark Twain's description," even though, in the novel, Tom is pitted against the new boy in town, Alfred Temple – not his pal Joe. Of the major dark themes of *Tom Sawyer*, the one that has most frequently survived to the screen is the menacing presence of Injun Joe, and the 1930 film actually intensifies this menace by having Joe chase Tom into the cave, where the former eventually falls to his death. The 1938 film version would carry this departure from the novel even further by having Tom cause Joe's fatal fall. Cromwell's *Tom Sawyer* proved so successful that Paramount reunited its cast a year later to make a sound version of *Huckleberry Finn*. Coogan was the only member of the cast with real box-office power, and this resulted in the ludicrous decision to put Tom on the raft along with Huck and Jim – the latter well played by Clarence Muse, despite a poor script.

A somewhat better film from this period was the 1931 *Connecticut Yankee*, with Will Rogers as Hank. Like the 1921 film, this version stressed broad comedy and took substantial liberties with the original story. Nevertheless, it is an entertaining film that gives Rogers ample opportunities to display the wit for which he was noted. Since Rogers was viewed as an American humorist in the Mark Twain mold, his presence as Hank seems somehow fitting.

Six years later, Warner Bros. made its first entry into the field with *The Prince and the Pauper*, starring Errol Flynn as Miles Hendon, and identical twins Billy and Bobby Mauch as Tom Canty and Prince Edward. Released exactly one week before George VI was crowned monarch of the United Kingdom, this film about a sixteenth-century British king garnered considerable publicity. The Mauch brothers, who were charmers in the title roles, even made the cover of *Time* magazine. But again big plot changes were the order of the day. One of the biggest was having Hertford (Claude Rains) discover Tom's real identity early in the story and sending a man to murder Edward so that he could manipulate Tom and rule England himself.[13] *The Prince and the Pauper* may not be a major work, but it does treat a theme important to Twain – that of forlorn claimants, people who make claims that they can persuade no one else to believe. Much of the novel's dramatic tension and fun are lost by having other characters know who they truly are prematurely.[14]

The most outstanding Mark Twain adaptation of the early sound era was Selznick's *The Adventures of Tom Sawyer* (1938), the first color film of a Twain story. Ten-year-old Tommy Kelly won the title role after a nationwide talent search. Selznick's director on this film was Norman Taurog, who had directed Paramount's *Huckleberry Finn* in 1931. Selznick's *Tom Sawyer* was scarcely a model of fidelity, but it does retain the novel's major plot elements and remains true to its spirit. Also during 1938, Paramount released the only screen version of *Tom Sawyer, Detective* ever made. Billy Cook played Tom and a 13-year-old Donald O'Connor played Huck. This film is a short and entertaining adaptation of a slight mystery tale that serves as a kind of carefree encore for Tom and Huck – which is precisely how director Louis King treats it. The next year saw the third major film version of *Huckleberry Finn*. Directed by Richard Thorpe, this MGM production starred Mickey Rooney of "Andy Hardy" fame as Huck, and Rex Ingram as Jim. While the film takes pains to explore the friendship between Huck and Jim, it often plays too much like "Andy Hardy Goes Rafting." This is primarily the fault of Hugo Butler's script, which was ground through the studio's notorious factory system.

Hollywood's next major Mark Twain project also took liberties – this time, not with a story but with the author's life. As the lead in *The Adventures of Mark Twain*,

Fredric March shows flashes of a Twain who might have provided a more compelling center to this 1944 Warner Bros. production; but the film mangles the facts of Twain's life. As is often the case with a Mark Twain film gone wrong, the lead actor is not at fault. Two broad problems afflict the Warner Bros. biopic. First, it tends to sentimentalize Twain almost to the point of emasculation, particularly in having his wife, Livy (Alexis Smith), repeatedly encourage him to crank out more treacle to make the world a happier place. When the film finally reaches Twain's death, his spirit rises from his body and heeds Tom and Huck's call to run off and play. A second great flaw is the film's almost aggressive insistence on getting the biographical facts wrong. For example, the film has Twain give up piloting in the hope of striking it rich in the West so he can marry Olivia (Livy) Langdon (whom he had not, at that point, even met). He then returns east on the outbreak of the Civil War (which started, in fact, before he went west). The Warner Bros. writers seemed to believe they could improve on the incredible drama of his real life. Moreover, just as Hollywood adaptations of Mark Twain stories so often get things wrong when it would just as easy to get them right, so too does *The Adventures of Mark Twain*, and for no apparent reason. One might argue that such details do not matter, so long as a film conveys the correct spirit of its subject, but a film with as many howlers as this cannot possibly achieve such a purpose.

In 1948 Columbia released the low-budget *Best Man Wins*, an adaptation of the jumping frog story that was so loose that Clara Clemens tried to get her father's name removed from the film. Nevertheless, Columbia trumpeted its production as being based on "Mark Twain's funniest story." There is not much of the jumping frog tale to celebrate in this film, but it is a mildly entertaining trifle, in which Jim Smiley (Edgar Buchanan) is a shiftless gambler trying to win back his estranged wife. Another wrong note struck during the late 1940s was Bing Crosby's *A Connecticut Yankee in King Arthur's Court*. This cheerful 1949 Paramount musical features several pleasing James Van Heusen and Johnny Burke tunes, including "Busy Doing Nothing." However, its weak script drains the novel's substance, leaving only amiable gags and light musical numbers. As Hollywood musicals of the era go, it was decent second-tier stuff, but as an adaptation of *Connecticut Yankee* it was about as dependable as Merlin's magic.

The Emergence of Television

During the late 1940s television broadcasting began in earnest, so it was probably not a coincidence that virtually all major screen adaptations of Mark Twain works produced between then and 1960 were made for this medium. One exception was United Artists' *Man with a Million*,[15] an uneven 1954 adaptation of Twain's "The £1,000,000 Bank-Note." The same story also appears to have been the first Mark Twain work adapted to television, in a 30-minute episode of Arthur Shields's *Your Show Time* in 1949. The 1954 film starred Gregory Peck as Adams, the penniless American who is given the use of a one-million-pound banknote for one month by two strangers.

The 1950s are remembered as a golden age of television drama, and many Mark Twain productions appeared in such distinguished weekly anthology series as *Studio One*, *Kraft Television Theatre*, and the *US Steel Hour*. This is not to say, however, that the individual productions themselves were necessarily distinguished. The adaptations of *Huckleberry Finn* were especially poor. In *"Huckleberry Finn" on Film*, Clyde Haupt lumps the five television and film adaptations made between 1955 and 1978 under the collective heading of "Royal Nonesuches" because of their common tendency to elevate the importance of the king and the duke to that of Huck and Jim and thereby reduce the productions to low comedy (Haupt 1994: 71). In what may have been the worst of this bunch, the adaptation on television's *Climax!* in 1955 put Tom on the raft with Huck and omitted Jim altogether. Other stories adapted to television during the medium's early years included three versions of *Connecticut Yankee*, four of *Tom Sawyer*, and one of *The Prince and the Pauper*. Compressed into 30- or 60-minute time slots, most of these productions could not pretend to be full adaptations of their stories. An exception was the 90-minute musical version of *Connecticut Yankee* made for *Max Liebman Presents* in 1955. In that production, Boris Karloff played Arthur,[16] and Eddie Albert played the Boss, Hank Martin. The 1950s ended with MGM's *The Adventures of Huckleberry Finn* (1960), the only major feature film of that period. It curiously inverts the novel's narrative by reversing the order of some of its episodes. The film was further flawed by the casting of Eddie Hodges as Huck. At 13, Hodges was the correct age, but he looked much younger and was too aware of his own cuteness to be taken seriously. A more appropriate casting choice was boxer Archie Moore as Jim, projecting the strength and dignity of Twain's character.

The year 1960 saw one of the most distinguished dramatic takes on Twain's life: Horton Foote's *The Shape of the River* on *Playhouse 90*. That moving examination of Twain's last years was broadcast only once, however, and would now be forgotten, had not an original script and videotape been recently rediscovered (see Dawidziak 2003: 1–4). Virtually all the Mark Twain adaptations of the 1960s were made for television. They include four largely forgettable versions of *The Prince and the Pauper*, a version of *Tom Sawyer* on *Shirley Temple Theatre*, and two partial adaptations of *Roughing It*. The year 1968 saw the launching of a 17-episode French television series based on *Tom Sawyer* and *Huckleberry Finn* and an American series, *New Adventures of Huckleberry Finn*, which mixed live action with animated sequences. In 1970 an Australian company made animated films of *Connecticut Yankee* and *The Prince and the Pauper* for television. The first is of some interest because it addresses some of the darker themes that have been neglected in other film adaptations.

Return to Big-Screen Productions

After two decades of being adapted mostly to television productions, Mark Twain's works began receiving renewed attention from the feature-film industry during the 1970s. In 1972 a major production of *Huckleberry Finn* was made in the Soviet Union, where Twain's books had long been popular. The following year saw *Tom Sawyer* return to the big screen in America in the Reader's Digest/United Artists musical titled *Tom Sawyer*. Johnnie Whittaker played Tom, and future Oscar-winner Jodie Foster played Becky Thatcher. This production earned no rave reviews but did well enough for Reader's Digest to follow up with a musical production of *Huckleberry Finn* the next year. Jeff East reprised his role as Huck and Paul Winfield played Jim, but Harvey Korman's and David Wayne's king and duke were the true stars – as noted above, Clyde Haupt called this a "Royal Nonesuch" version of *Huckleberry Finn*.

Meanwhile, ambitious new television adaptations were also coming out. Universal and Hal Roach Productions produced a full-length television version of *Tom Sawyer* in 1973, and ABC Circle produced a curious version of *Huckleberry Finn* for television in 1975. The latter starred 21-year-old Ron Howard as Huck and his *Happy Days* co-star Danny Most as Tom, while Antonio Fargas – straight from playing the hip Huggy Bear in *Starsky and Hutch* – made perhaps the least plausible Jim in screen history.

The year 1979 saw two Mark-Twain-inspired productions that are notable for contrary reasons. PBS's one-hour drama *Mark Twain: Beneath the Laughter* explored the last months of Twain's life, with actor Dan O'Herlihy playing a weary Clemens reflecting on his life after learning of the death of his daughter Jean. In addition to moving re-enactments of moments from the author's life, the drama offered scenes from *Huckleberry Finn* as powerful as any ever filmed, and even a dramatization of "The War Prayer." At the other end of the quality scale that year was Disney's *The Spaceman and King Arthur* (also known as *Unidentified Flying Oddball*), in which an American astronaut (Dennis Dugan) goes off course and lands in King Arthur's time. This dismal production is representative of the growing tendency to twist *Connecticut Yankee* to fit contemporary interests and fads.

In 1989, NBC-TV broadcast a new two-hour production titled *A Connecticut Yankee in King Arthur's Court*. This film follows some of the novel's plot elements, but its Yankee is a 12-year-old black girl from modern Hartford. Played by Keshia Knight Pulliam of *Cosby Show* fame, Karen Jones is shocked to find Camelot in disarray, with Merlin and Mordred plotting to kill King Arthur. Armed only with a Polaroid camera and a portable cassette-player, Karen wins Arthur's trust. She then works to reform the kingdom, while introducing aerobics and martial arts to the women of the court. The trend toward reducing the age of the *Connecticut Yankee*'s protagonist continued in 1995 with two similar productions: a Canadian film titled *A Young Connecticut Yankee in King Arthur's Court*, with Philippe Ross as Hank, Michael York as Merlin, and Nick Manusco as King Arthur, and another Disney feature, *A Kid in King Arthur's Court*, with Thomas Ian Nicholas as the kid, Joss Ackland as Arthur, and Ron Moody as Merlin. True to their titles, both films are about modern young boys cast into Arthur's time.

Disney's 1998 television film, *A Knight in Camelot*, contributed yet another dimension to modern retellings. This 90-minute production offers a quasi-feminist take on Twain's story, featuring comedian Whoopi Goldberg as a computer scientist. Thrust back to Arthur's time, she uses her laptop computer and boombox to impress the natives by passing off science as magic – much as Hank Morgan does in the novel. Her real strength, however, is being able to fast-talk people into almost anything. After being dubbed "Sir Boss," she promotes reforms for peasants and introduces modern plumbing in the royal castle. Goldberg's film has a faint kinship to the 2001 theatrical release *Black Knight*, starring another black comedian, Martin Lawrence. This film acknowledges no debt to *Connecticut Yankee*, but it clearly draws on the premise of Twain's novel, by now something of a public-domain fairy-tale. Lawrence plays a fast-talking, streetwise modern American who is sent back in time by a knock on the head.

A Mark Twain story that has more fully entered the realm of the fairy-tale is *The Prince and the Pauper*. The original novel has many ingredients of the genre, and the story has found its way to the screen, in one form or other, at least 16 times. A big-budget international adaptation hit screens in 1978 under the title *Crossed Swords*, directed by Richard Fleischer. Mark Lester, who played the title role in *Oliver!*, played both Tom and Edward, and Oliver Reed, *Oliver!*'s Bill Sikes, played Miles Hendon. Adaptations made from around that time have tended to move further and further from their source material. For example, a 1976 television play titled *P. J. and the President's Son* recast the story in a modern American political setting, and in 1999 the theme was given a modern southern Californian twist in *The Prince and the Surfer*. There is even a feature-length video called *Barbie as the Princess and the Pauper* (2004), part of an animated series about the famous doll.

A New Golden Age of Television

Apart from Will Vinton's fascinating *The Adventures of Mark Twain* (1985), no new film adaptations reached theater screens during the 1980s. However, the decade saw an unprecedented number of significant television productions. Vinton's film has nothing in common with the 1944 Warner Bros. biopic except its title. It is an animated film lasting nearly 90 minutes and employing a skillfully crafted and complex form of stop-motion photography called claymation. Evidently inspired by the premise of *Tom Sawyer Abroad*, the film has Twain piloting a giant balloon craft in a quest to meet his destiny with Halley's Comet. He is joined by three stowaways: Tom Sawyer, Huck Finn, and Becky Thatcher. As their voyage progresses, moments from Twain's life and writings are played out in cleverly executed animated scenes, including amusing extracts from the Adam and Eve diaries, "The Chronicle of Young Satan," and "Captain Stormfield's Visit to Heaven" – works rarely, if ever, seen on the screen. Often displaying surprising insights into Twain's mind, the film is one of the most imaginative ever made about Mark Twain.

The most important Mark Twain productions to come out of the 1980s were a remarkable series of television plays broadcast on PBS-TV, mostly for PBS's *American Playhouse*. That series was an earnest attempt to present a wider range of Mark Twain works to the public than are usually seen, but several productions were badly flawed – though not in ways that average viewers would notice. The series began promisingly in 1980 with *The Man That Corrupted Hadleyburg*. Robert Preston played the stranger and helped move the largely static story along by staying almost continuously on camera as a narrator. This gimmick did an effective job of conveying the savage irony of the original story. Less successful was that same year's *Life on the Mississippi*. A condensation of Clemens's colorful memoir about his cub piloting experiences, the 90-minute production starred David Knell as the cub pilot and Robert Lansing as his mentor, Horace Bixby. Failing to evoke the grandeur of steamboating, the production scrambled events and wrongly attributed passages of dialogue.

PBS's *The Private History of a Campaign that Failed* (1981) is an appropriately thoughtful and moody interpretation of Twain's largely fanciful Civil War memoir. Tacked on to the end of this 90-minute production is a dramatization of "The War Prayer." Twain wrote the latter piece in 1905, 20 years after his Civil War story. He intended it as a protest against the rise of American imperialism, but the fact that it works so well alongside the Civil War story demonstrates its universality. The next contribution to PBS's *American Playhouse* was 1982's *The Mysterious Stranger*, a reasonably faithful adaptation of Twain's posthumously published *No. 44, The Mysterious Stranger* (not the bowdlerized *Mysterious Stranger* of 1916). The following year's entry in the series was *The Innocents Abroad*, a 90-minute production undermined by perhaps the least convincing Mark Twain to appear on screen, in the person of Craig Wasson, and a script that largely trivialized the book.

American Playhouse's production of *Pudd'nhead Wilson*, first broadcast in 1984, with Ken Howard in the title role, was the first screen adaptation of that novel since 1916. That earlier film is now lost, and one might wish the same fate for this later version, whose script is almost a travesty. This production's treatment of Roxy (Lise Hilboldt) is particularly misguided. In the original novel, the former slave sacrifices her freedom by allowing her worthless son – who is passing as her former master's son, Tom Driscoll – to sell her back into slavery to raise money to pay his gambling debts. One of the most powerful moments in any of Twain's writings comes when Roxy discovers that her son has betrayed her by selling her to a plantation *down* the river. After she escapes, she tracks down Tom and confronts him with his treachery. The television production presents the confrontation scene much as Twain wrote it, but with one crucial difference: until that moment, the screen Tom does not know Roxy is his natural mother. That tiny alteration in the story flattens the entire production's power and leaves one wondering, once again, why film producers so often get things wrong, when it would be just as easy to get them right.

The most impressive contribution to the *American Playhouse* series came in 1986, with the broadcast of the four-hour production of *Adventures of Huckleberry Finn*, which starred Patrick Day as Huck and Samm-Art Williams as Jim. This production was not without its shortcomings, but no other attempt to translate *Huckleberry Finn* to the screen approaches its fidelity to the original story and its themes. If any screen version of *Huckleberry Finn* must be shown to students to help explain the novel, it should be this version – and only this version – until something finer comes along. Alternatively, if students were to view *both* the PBS production and Disney's *The Adventures of Huck Finn* and then compare the two versions and analyze how each relates to the novel, they would likely gain better understandings of both what the novel is really about and how literature is transformed when it moves to the screen. Since visual media will demand an ever-greater share of our attention in the future, our best strategy is not to fight this trend but to devise methods of using it to assist in winning new converts to Mark Twain's works and in teaching them effectively.

NOTES

1 Clemens saw Thomas A. Edison's one-reel *The Prince and the Pauper* film in Bermuda in 1909 and was impressed by footage of himself smoking a cigar. That footage was from a movie that had Edison shot at Stormfield earlier the same year. See Marian Schuyler Allen, "Some New Anecdotes of Mark Twain," *The Strand Magazine*, 46 (Sept. 1913), 218–24. Cited in Tenney (1979: 197).

2 This passage should be compared to the novel's opening paragraph.

3 The film had a domestic gross of $24,103,594. At the average US ticket price in 1933 of $4 (children's tickets may have been cheaper), that translates into at least six million tickets sold. Many ticket buyers doubtless saw the film more than once, but the number of people who have seen it rises well above six million when foreign ticket sales, multiple screenings on television, and video and DVD viewings are factored in.

4 The rating number comes from several different websites. The show's relative popularity can probably be attributed to Garner's appearance in it.

5 In January 2005, for example, Amazon.com's page for *The Adventures of Huck Finn* contained 40 customer reviews. Many raved about the film's youthful star, Elijah Woods, but others were thoughtfully composed comments on connections between the novel and the film – which most reviewers seemed to prefer.

6 Among the 40 reviewers of *The Adventures of Huck Finn* on Amazon.com, a half-dozen

called it their favorite movie; one called it "one of the greatest movies ever made"; another simply said, "You can't improve on perfection."

7 See Fishkin (1997: 141). The 1983 Eddie Murphy–Dan Ackroyd film *Trading Places* also owes something to the same story.

8 Broadcast only once, on May 2, 1960, *The Shape of the River* has not been publicly available in any form since then. *Mark Twain: Beneath the Laughter* has been broadcast multiple times and has been available to schools in 16mm prints. By contrast, *The Adventures of Mark Twain* enjoyed a successful run on its initial release and has since become a television staple that is also available on video cassette.

9 See *New York Times*, February 23, 1920; Haupt (1994: 20).

10 Only a few of the film's five or six reels still exist, and they are not accessible to the public.

11 *New York Times*, March 16, 1921.

12 *New York Times*, December 20, 1930.

13 The Hallmark Channel's 2001 version of the story uses the same plot device.

14 Disney's 1962 television mini-series of *The Prince and the Pauper* also flattens the claimant theme by having Hendon (Guy Williams) accept Edward's claim almost immediately and then struggle to help Edward regain his throne.

15 Released in Great Britain as *The Million Pound Note*.

16 Karloff earlier played Merlin in a 1952 television production.

REFERENCES AND FURTHER READING

Ashley, L. F. (1971). "Huck, Tom and Television." *English Quarterly* 4 (Spring), 57–64.

Britton, Wesley A. (1993). "Media Interpretations of Mark Twain's Life and Work." In J. R. LeMaster and James D. Wilson (eds.), *The Mark Twain Encyclopedia*, 500–4. New York: Garland.

Budd, Louis J. (1995). "Mark Twain as an American Icon." In Forrest G. Robinson (ed.), *The Cambridge Companion to Mark Twain*, 1–26. New York: Cambridge University Press.

Dawidziak, Mark (2003). *Horton Foote's "The Shape of the River": The Lost Teleplay about Mark Twain with History and Analysis*. New York: Applause.

Fishkin, Shelley Fisher (1997). *Lighting Out for the Territory: Reflections on Mark Twain and American Culture*. New York: Oxford University Press.

Frank, Perry (1985). "*Adventures of Huckleberry Finn* on Film." In M. Thomas Inge (ed.), *Huck Finn among the Critics: A Centennial Selection*, 293–313. Frederick, Md.: University Publications of America.

Frank, Perry (1991). "The Adventures of Tom Sawyer on Film: The Evolution of an American Icon." Ph.D. diss., George Washington University.

Haupt, Clyde V. (1994). "*Huckleberry Finn*" on Film: Film and Television Adaptations of Mark Twain's Novel, 1920–1993. Jefferson, NC: McFarland.

Irwin, Robert (1967). "The Failure of *Tom Sawyer* and *Huckleberry Finn* on Film." *Mark Twain Journal* 13: 4, 9–11.

Langman, Larry (1986). *Writers on the American Screen: A Guide to Film Adaptations of American and Foreign Literary Works*. New York: Garland.

Limbacher, James L. (1979). *Haven't I Seen You Somewhere Before? Remakes, Sequels, and Series in Motion Pictures and Television, 1896–1978*. Ann Arbor, Mich.: Pierian.

Magill, Frank N. (1980). *Cinema: The Novel into Film*. Pasadena, Calif.: Salem Softbacks.

Maltin, Leonard (2004). *Leonard Maltin's Movie Guide 2005*. New York: Signet.

New York Times (1968). *New York Times Film Reviews, 1913–1990*. New York: New York Times/Arno.

Nowlan, Robert A., and Nowlan, Gwendolyn Wright (1989). *Cinema Sequels and Remakes, 1903–1987*. Jefferson, NC: McFarland.

Peary, Gerald, and Shatzkin, Roger, eds. (1977). *The Classic American Novel and the Movies*. New York: Ungar.

Rodney, Robert M., ed. (1982). *Mark Twain International: A Bibliography and Interpretation of his Worldwide Popularity*. Westport, Conn.: Greenwood.

Seelye, John (1977). *Mark Twain in the Movies: A Meditation with Pictures*. New York: Viking.

Tenney, Thomas (1979). "Mark Twain: A Reference Guide Third Annual Supplement." *American Literary Realism* 12: 2, 175–276.

PART IV
Mark Twain and Travel

19

Twain and the Mississippi

Andrew Dix

The Matter of the River

The visit paid by the young Mississippi pilot Samuel Clemens to a New Orleans fortune-teller in 1861 was not striking in its predictive accuracy. According to Madame Caprell's somewhat clouded crystal ball, Clemens would marry twice, father ten children, and ultimately settle in the South. Nevertheless, Caprell's opening words, as her client recorded them in a letter to his brother Orion, have a suggestiveness not matched by those later attempts at substantive detail: "Yours is a watery planet; you gain your livelihood on the water" (Twain 1988: 108). Given Twain's own testimony in both correspondence and *Life on the Mississippi* (1883) regarding the privileged caste status of river pilots in the heyday of steamboat travel, it might not have been insurmountably difficult for Caprell to find signs of her visitor's profession in his appearance and demeanor. We may push her remarks, however, beyond this relatively banal reading of surfaces, and take them as evoking Twain's complex engagement with water on a more fundamental level.

In *Water and Dreams*, Gaston Bachelard proposes that each of the four elements has its "faithful followers" (Bachelard 1983: 5). One of these rival modes of "material imagination" or "the imagination of matter" is what he names the "hydrous," a sensibility especially energized by the element of water. I resist certain aspects of Bachelard's thought, in particular his implication that literary representations of this element are unvarying across time rather than constantly reshaped by historical and geographical circumstance. To be effective in interpreting texts like Twain's, such watery poetics urgently needs supplementing by a *politics* of water attuned to worldly concerns. Nevertheless, I am still interested in considering Twain as another instance of primarily "hydrous" imagination alongside Bachelard's key representatives, such as Edgar Allan Poe.

The movements of Twain's "watery planet" can be tracked across much of his writing. One thinks, for example, of the description of the Atlantic crossing in *The*

Innocents Abroad (1869) or of contrasting episodes from *Roughing It* (1872) such as visiting toxic Mono Lake in California and watching native surfers off the Sandwich Islands. Despite Twain's engagement by such different spaces as ocean, lake, and bay, however, it is accurate to characterize his watery imagination as chiefly *riverine* (although we shall see that a politically and culturally adequate account of the Mississippi River in his work entails its reconnection to larger geographical flows). As his friend, the Reverend Joseph Twichell, wrote to a mutual acquaintance: "Mark is a queer fellow. There is nothing he so delights in as a swift strong stream" (see Tanner 1965: 165).

Twain was resourceful in discovering such streams not only across America, but also beyond its borders. *A Tramp Abroad* (1880), for instance, describes a voyage by raft down the Neckar in Germany. In 1891, seeking not only new literary materials to help ease financial distress but also what he termed a pleasing "extinction from the world and newspapers," he temporarily abandoned his family in Switzerland, bought a flat-bottomed boat, and hired a steersman to conduct him on a ten-day river trip through the south of France from Lake Bourget to Arles (Kaplan 1966: 313).[1] In Twain, however, such rivers inevitably tend to register as displaced versions of – or inadequate substitutes for – his key river, the Mississippi itself.

We should, of course, be cautious about centering Twain's work on the Mississippi, since this risks producing static, nostalgic, merely regionalist versions of the author and takes him out of those complex national, even international geographies that have been the focus of some of the most exciting criticism in recent years.[2] While acknowledging this caveat, it still needs to be stressed that there is an insistent, many-stranded discourse of the Mississippi in his writing that not only runs through a familiar quartet of texts – *The Adventures of Tom Sawyer* (1876), *Life on the Mississippi*, *Adventures of Huckleberry Finn* (1885), and *Pudd'nhead Wilson* (1894) – but also is articulated by *The Gilded Age* (1873), co-authored with Charles Dudley Warner, and the fragmentary Tom and Huck writings, as well as many of Twain's personal letters, journals, and notebooks. This discourse manifests itself throughout his literary career. An adolescent sketch, "The Dandy Frightening the Squatter" (1852), sets up the kind of cultural collision in the Mississippi Valley of which Twain would later make such literary capital as it describes the quarrel between a local woodsman and a passenger arriving by steamboat at Hannibal, Missouri. And at the end of his life, as if by repetition-compulsion, Twain was still revisiting the scenes of river childhood and piloting during the autobiographical dictations.

Twain's imaginative dependency upon the Mississippi has, of course, long been recognized. In his own lifetime, the reviewer of *Life on the Mississippi* for the *New York Tribune* wrote that "He clings to the Mississippi as Byron says that hoarse Fitzgerald clung to the Phoenix. He beams on every wood pile and he vaults over every snag" (Budd 1999: 241).[3] The unprecedented stylistic revisions of this text which Twain undertook in 1908 have led one critic to conclude that he may have been intending it to become the first volume in a collected works, thereby reinforcing a sense of the Mississippi's priority in his literary achievement (Kruse 1981: 127). Certainly, Henry Nash Smith seems justified when, by analogy with "the Matter of Troy or the Matter of Britain" that offered a ready-made, indeed essential topic for medieval writers of romance, he speaks of "the Matter of the River" which Twain obsessively returns to and exploits (Smith 1962: 72).

Twain constructs the river, however, not by a single idiom but through multiple, discontinuous registers that include the navigational code of his first pilot's notebook, stock poetic formulae in *Tom Sawyer*, vernacular idyll in *Huckleberry Finn*, and the mixture of hydrography, sociological report, and anecdote in *Life on the Mississippi*. He revisits it imaginatively during different phases not merely of personal but of regional and national crisis. While the topic of the Mississippi is indeed recurrent in Twain, it is thus by no means always comforting or familiar. Indeed, his encounters with the river are, at times, properly uncanny in their merging of intimacy and estrangement. As befitting the fluidity of its referent, Twain's Mississippi is protean and restless in its significances. The instability of his river representations accords with the profile that Bachelard draws of "the hydrous psyche": "Water is truly the transitory element . . . A being dedicated to water is a being in flux" (Bachelard 1983: 6). While leaning upon Bachelard's sense of the radical fluctuations of a poetics drawn to water, I also want to depersonalize this approach somewhat, and to argue that the liquid meanings of Twain's Mississippi are evocative not only of his own psychobiography – fascinating though that is in itself as a topic – but of larger American contradictions, desires, even traumas in the closing decades of the nineteenth century.[4]

The Duplicity of the Mississippi

While Twain's Mississippi writings often follow Melville's *The Confidence-Man* (1857) in making the river's steamboat culture the scene of fraudulent manipulations, including slave-selling, medical charlatanism, and card-sharping, I do not intend "duplicity" here in this sense of the deceitful. Instead, I borrow the term, with its implications of doubleness and complexity, from the work of the cultural geographer Stephen Daniels. Along with others in his discipline, Daniels has been instrumental in rescuing for radical use the seemingly unpromising analytic category of "landscape." Although there is a long tradition of rendering landscape a static object so as "to dissolve or conceal" conflicts in its meaning, it is better understood as something open, unfinished, a scene of ongoing political struggle (Daniels 1989: 196). For Daniels, any landscape does not simply reflect the interests of oppressive power, but should also be surveyed for its progressive potentials: "Landscape may be seen, as Adorno sees culture generally, as a 'dialectical image,' an ambiguous synthesis whose redemptive and manipulative aspects cannot finally be disentangled" (p. 206). It is the task of any interpreter of place "to abide in its duplicity," rather than resolving these contradictions and characterizing the landscape in question as either purely emancipatory or purely coercive in its political effects (p. 218).

Twain's riverscapes require precisely this double reading. As we review scholarly discussion of his representations of the Mississippi, however, we often find critics choosing between their "redemptive" or "manipulative" aspects, rather than dwelling productively on their contradictory political meanings. Utopian assessments of Twain's Mississippi tend to take *Huckleberry Finn* – or rather, selected moments from it – as their preferred text. They might fairly be represented by Lionel Trilling's introduction to the novel, first published in 1948 and echoed by T. S. Eliot's own prefatory essay two years later, and then by critical writings including Tony Tanner's *The Reign of Wonder*. Although Trilling begins by acknowledging that the world of *Huckleberry Finn* is marked by conflict between "the river-god" and "the money-god," his account favors the Mississippi's sublime natural processes and largely sets aside its economic and social life. In terms of the distinction with which Twain opens *Life on the Mississippi*, he privileges the river's "physical history" over "its historical history – so to speak" (Twain 1883: 25). While he recognizes danger on the river, this emerges largely from the vagaries of current itself. By virtue of its "sunlight, space, uncrowded time, stillness" (Trilling 1981: 110), the Mississippi, in Trilling's reading, becomes a pure alternative to the acquisitive economics and pervasive injustice of antebellum America.

A more recent strain of Twain criticism has properly highlighted risks of mystification and abstraction from worldly concern in such assessments of his riverscape. One unfortunate by-product of these corrective readings, however, is that they sometimes turn away prematurely from the more progressive, liberatory aspects of his representation of the river. No longer Trilling's untrammeled natural space, the Mississippi in such work bears all the inscriptions of capitalist process (as well as of white and masculine supremacy). I will return later to the links Stephanie LeMenager makes between Huck's floating down the river and the circulation of white-owned capital in the Mississippi Valley. For the moment, however, in order to assess the political limits as well as gains of anti-utopian constructions of Twain's river, I wish to focus on Howard Horwitz's work on *Life on the Mississippi*.

Taking as his key topic the steamboat pilot, Horwitz critiques what he terms Twain's "romance of the free self" (Horwitz 1991: 111). Where Twain mystifies the pilot as "the only unfettered and entirely independent human being that lived in the earth" (Twain 1883: 166), Horwitz valuably repositions him in a determinate socioeconomic context by stressing such factors as corporate ownership of steamboats and the labor conditions in an often cut-throat industry. Thus, not only after the diminishing of the steamboat trade by Civil War and railroad competition, but even earlier, the pilot's relationship to the Mississippi is cause for ideological pessimism. Indeed, if we revisit *Life on the Mississippi* via Horwitz's demystificatory approach, episodes in the piloting experience that previously seemed part of benign reminiscence look appreciably darker. The principles of "water-reading" (p. 112) that Twain describes himself learning from Horace Bixby register less as the means of the pilot's intimate, sensuous enfolding with the river than as the reproduction of techniques which will further open up the Mississippi to exploitation (by other frontier pioneers besides steamboat entrepreneurs). Even the pilot's fabulous memory comes to look uncannily like that extreme development of a specialized bodily function produced by techniques of industrial mass-production then spreading across America: "Give a man a tolerably fair memory to start with, and piloting will develop it into a very colossus of capability. But *only in the matters it is daily drilled in*" (p. 155).

Nevertheless, there is a danger that Horwitz's reading flattens out the complex ideology of the Mississippi pilot. To note the pilot's loss of perfect autonomy in the socioeconomic structures of the river is not thereby to turn him into a mere unthinking drudge of the system. Horwitz has grounds for regarding the Pilots' Benevolent Association – extolled by Twain in *Life on the Mississippi* – as less a form of resistance to the *laissez-faire* capitalism of the period than an extension of its logic (Horwitz 1991: 103–4). But if this fraternity of pilots looks ahead to the "emergent" tendencies of advanced capital, it also takes the "residual" form of a craft guild convinced of the civic virtue of its labor: "the sense of republicanism as the fundamental orientation should be clear: these were workers who saw their work not as oppressed or oppressive, but as the source of their dignity" (Camfield 2002: 113).[5]

We need to be alert, more generally, to the disparate ideological meanings of Mississippi steamboating in Twain. His writing, for example, often characterizes the steamboat as belonging to a pastoral landscape violated by the brute force of technology: "the unholy train comes tearing along . . . ripping the sacred solitude to rags and tatters with its devil's warwhoop and the roar and thunder of its rushing wheels" (Twain 1883: 569). Other moments in his work, however, complicate his own myth of a fall, and bear out historians' claims that it was not the railroad but actually the steamboat itself which "gave the predominantly rural population of the western country its first experience . . . with industrial machinery," including its terrifying hazards and accidents (Hunter 1969: 271). For evidence of the steamboat's disturbance of traditional social and economic forms, think not only of its smashing the raft in *Huckleberry Finn*, but of the horrific impact made in *The Gilded Age* by this new machine's "fierce eye of fire" and "tall duplicate horns" (Twain and Warner 1873: 36–7). If, in Jim's words, a raft "doan' *make* no track" (Twain 1885: 70), a steamboat does, its itineraries commodifying and routinizing travel on the Mississippi: in *Pudd'nhead Wilson* one passes Dawson's Landing "every hour or so" (Twain 1894: 19), while no sooner has the first boat appeared in *The Gilded Age* than "here comes another one up the river!" (Twain and Warner 1873: 39).[6] Yet it is indicative of the divided ideology of steamboating in Twain that between these terrifying first appearances in *The Gilded Age* and the catastrophic explosion of the *Amaranth* during a race, Squire Hawkins and his family experience their voyage as "a royal progress through the very heart and home of romance, a realization of their rosiest wonder-dreams" (p. 41). There is authentic magic here – briefly liberating this impoverished rural group from practical and psychological constraints – not wholly dispersed by admonitions to attend to the economics of steamboating or to the industry's poor safety record.

From the steamboat, Hawkins's family looks out on a scene apparently free from social and economic inscriptions: "the curving expanses of the river sparkling in the sunlight" (Twain and Warner 1873: 41). It is Horwitz's most disturbing argument, however, that *any* kind of gaze upon the Mississippi in Twain is liable to be complicit with the interests of capital. Despite Twain's reference in *Life on the Mississippi* to the first 150 years after the river's discovery by white explorers as a time when it was regarded only with curiosity – remaining "out of the market and undisturbed" (Twain 1883: 30) – Horwitz argues that even such seemingly noninstrumental perception evokes property relations: "To admire the river's sublimity, even to notice the river at all, means already to have understood its economic potential" (1991: 92). By this argument, not only the view of the river from the steamboat, but even, say, Huck's closer engagement with it, is liable to be a mode of economic colonization.

Is it the case, however, that any form of sensuous involvement with the Mississippi in Twain takes place, finally, under the sign of capital? To arrive at a provisional answer to this question, I want to consider briefly the politics of swimming in his work. My example from the many descriptions he gives of the pleasures of Mississippi swimming comes from *Tom Sawyer*:

> After breakfast they went whooping and prancing out on the bar, and chased each other round and round, shedding clothes as they went, until they were naked, and then continued the frolic far away up the shoal water of the bar, against the stiff current, which latter tripped their legs from under them from time to time and greatly increased the fun. And now and then they stooped in a group and splashed water in each other's faces with their palms, gradually approaching each other, with averted faces to avoid the strangling sprays and finally gripping and struggling till the best man ducked his neighbor, and then they all went under in a tangle of white legs and arms and came up blowing, sputtering, laughing and gasping for breath at one and the same time. (Twain 1876: 134–5)

The "stiff current" and "strangling sprays" are reminders of the river's ever-present dangers: a little earlier, Huck recalls "last summer, when Bill Turner got drownded" (p. 125). Nevertheless, any radical politics should have to reckon with the kind of sensuous immersion in the world exemplified by the boys' swimming. Contrast their sportive, unconstrained bodily movements with, say, the training and exploitation of the pilots' mnemonic muscles under the most disciplinary aspects of steamboating. It is going too far to say, as Tanner does, that water in Twain is "the uncivilizable element" (1965: 164) and thereby somehow nonsocial. Besides yielding to steamboat timetables, this particular river is, as both *Life on the Mississippi* and *Huckleberry Finn* make clear, subject to political demarcation, its very turns between states delivering a slave either into or out of freedom. Even so, the aquatic sport of *Tom Sawyer* evokes a way of being in nature radically at odds with the instrumental, appropriative logic of an increasingly potent American capitalism. Rather than being rejected as "that useless river," as Twain called it in a late autobiographical dictation (Twain 1940: 18), the Mississippi here figures Utopia in its very resistance to economic "use."

But, just as to overlook the utopian dimension of Twain's Mississippi is to forgo valuable political resources, so to see *only* the utopian in the river is a kind of blindness with respect to actually existing social and economic inequalities. While the swimmers in the episode above are drying off, they notice that "their naked skin represented flesh-colored 'tights' very fairly" (Twain 1876: 135), and this leads them away from the water and into playfully staging a circus. Here the body falls from some-thing sufficient and relishable in itself into mere cultural currency. Mention of a circus also raises thoughts specifically of that emerging "leisure ethic" in the United States which William Gleason has shown did not evoke an alternative to the capitalist order – as did earlier kinds of play – but, rather, functioned within it as a means of divert-ing the worker and renewing him or her for productive labor.[7] Even the seemingly free swimming throughout *Tom Sawyer* might be reinterpreted as not wholly divorced from leisure of this more organized sort, since it tends to occur in circumscribed periods and within sight of St. Petersburg. To a degree, at least, it is like the com-munity's picnic at the caves: that is to say, a limited, temporary excursion into the natural, rather than abandonment altogether of propertied and unequal society.

The boys in *Tom Sawyer*, as in *Huckleberry Finn* and *Tom Sawyer's Conspiracy*, alter-nate energetic swimming with periods of indolence by the river. Such "loafing" and "lazying" also has an ambiguous political value. If it is indeed a form of (non)motion opposed to the corporeal discipline required by a capitalist productive mode, then its critical potential is compromised by its also expressing a kind of social privilege. In his assault particularly on the cultural status of *Huckleberry Finn*, Jonathan Arac chal-lenges perceptions of Huck as demotic hero, linking him instead to "the 'sensitive spectator' of literary narrative" (Arac 1997: 159). We do not have to agree entirely with Arac to concede that even the outcast Huck is placed quite advantageously in Mississippi culture. If we look again at the group of swimmers, we see strict limits on precisely whose bodies can circulate in and near the water. The group is not only all-male, but also racially coded as "a tangle of white legs and arms."[8] Any utopian sense of play upon the Mississippi is vitiated by this exclusion of female and African American subjects – to whose rather different locations on Twain's river I now turn.

Maternal Water

Nineteenth-century American usage often casts the Mississippi in terms of a genera-tive masculine force, referring to it as "the Father of Waters" (see e.g. Budd 1999: 247). The "river-god" invoked by Trilling in his response to *Huckleberry Finn* is sim-ilarly not neuter, but masculinized (1981: 103). Despite these suggestions, however, the gendered status of the Mississippi across Twain's writing actually proves to be diffuse and ambiguous. If specific female subjects are often lacking in his riverscape, symbolic traces of the feminine are nevertheless strongly present, serving to compli-cate any narrative of male mastery over this space.

As itself a form of territorial representation, Twain's writing about the Mississippi may be vulnerable to both prongs of the critique launched by Gillian Rose against the "masculinism" of the geographical imagination. In the first instance, she chal-lenges the subdiscipline of "time-geography" for its modeling of space in a way that tends to reflect men's historically greater freedom of movement and to efface women's more constrained, often domestic trajectories (Rose 1993: 29–39). Considered from this perspective, Twain's own time-geography of the Mississippi indeed appears constituted by the traditionally male activities of rafting, steamboat piloting, even swimming. Female figures decisively involved with the river itself in his work are rare. In *Pudd'nhead Wilson*, Roxy goes "chambermaiding" on a steamboat and, more encouragingly, later escapes in a canoe (Twain 1894: 93, 231–2). In *Life on the Mississippi*, Mrs. Trollope and several other women figure among precursor travel writers named by Twain. Women in his Mississippi writings tend, however, to be distanced from the water itself and to be most conspicuously repositioned as decorators of those sentimental domestic interiors typified by the Grangerfords' home in *Huckleberry Finn* and "The House Beautiful" in *Life on the Mississippi*.

Such withdrawals of the feminine leave the river itself in Twain's work as a domain of masculine activity, even control. A spectrum of male aquatic operations can be constructed that extends from boys swimming to Army engineers ambitiously seeking, after the Civil War, to discipline and direct the river's flow. Twain frequently celebrates single-sex gatherings on the river: think, for example, of the admiring "male coterie" of pilots gathered around Bixby as he negotiates a particularly tricky crossing (Twain 1883: 95–101; and see Stoneley 1992: 66). Although we should note the recent interest within geography in exploring "queer" topographies,[9] it is perhaps still not advisable to speak of a gay Mississippi in Twain. Instead, even such episodes as Huck and Jim's naked raft-trip belong with the hothouse of male pilots, at the homosocial rather than homoerotic end of the continuum of same-sex interactions. All these instances share in an attempt to configure the river as space of both work and play for men only.

A larger cultural politics is at stake in any such "masculinization" of the Mississippi Valley. Written, of course, in the wake of the Civil War, *Life on the Mississippi* often seems less interested in tactfully devising means of national reconciliation than in identifying pockets of the feminine in Southern culture still to be eradicated by the "masculine" forces that Twain identifies as vital for American progress. Faced with the historical obsolescence of rafting, even steamboat piloting, he fights his gender war in the book's second half on the ground of modern, industrializing Northern cities like Burlington, Dubuque, and St. Paul (the latter's strength lying "in her commerce – I mean his commerce" [1883: 584–5]). Given his faith in more artisanal forms of production, there are good reasons why he does not get close enough to these factories by the Mississippi to represent in detail the lives of their male workers. Fully as much as Twain's interest in rafting and steamboating, however, the description of such advanced manufacturing shares in what Peter Stoneley calls his "masculinist counter-aesthetic" (1992: 56).

Yet the Mississippi in Twain's work is too unstable in gender terms to provide a basis for this project to masculinize – or remasculinize – America. As we read his river texts, we find not only confident assertions of masculine identity but also signs of unease. While, for example, a letter of 1866 describes the river pilot as an embodiment of "genuine *manliness*" (Twain 1988: 358), it is unclear what happens to such "manliness" during the routinization of the steamboat trade, and whether it can be replicated anyway by the male travel writer, the persona Twain adopts when visiting the river in his research trip of 1882. Even from his own piloting days, there is a nice emblem of the Mississippi's complex gendering in the fate that befell the first note-book of navigational marks he kept. After he left it with his mother for safekeeping when he headed west with Orion, she "used its blank pages to record household income and expenditures" (Twain 1975: 60–1). Rather than keeping them apart, the notebook thereby brings into adjacency two discourses respectively gendered as mas-culine and feminine. It offers a figure of how Twain's life on the Mississippi exem-plifies not only oedipal mastery but also possibilities of regression and imprisonment by the feminine. In particular, of course, the notebook speaks allegorically of a con-nection between the Mississippi and the mother.

Indeed, as we evaluate the space of Twain's river psychoanalytically, we find it par-tially configured in terms of maternal geography. Bachelard speaks suggestively, if still in ahistorical terms, of "maternal water" (1983: 115–32); he adds that, because of its liquid enfolding of the subject, "Water gives us back our mother" (p. 131). There are possible affinities here with Rose's politicized geography. In developing the second, more far-reaching strand of her critique of the sexual politics of the geographical imag-ination, Rose argues that landscape generally – not only a watery environment – tends to be construed by its perceiver in feminine terms. Specifically, it registers as "the fan-tasized maternal Woman" (Rose 1993: 57), as a recollection of the primal mother's body experienced by the infant. Just as time-geography bases itself upon characteristi-cally male itineraries, so this feminization of landscape is also troubling for Rose because it seems to underwrite forms of male fantasy and control over space.

However, Rose's work is most suggestive for us where it allows for crisis rather than straightforward mastery in the male perception of any landscape (such as the Mississippi in Twain). She writes that place seems to stand for "nothing other than the inaccessible plenitude of Mother" (1993: 60), but goes on to concede that the per-ceiving subject's sense of this may be as much anxious as desiring: "Landscape can then be not the welcoming topography of nurturing mother but terrifying maternal swamps, mountains, seas, inhabited by sphinxes and gorgons" (p. 106). Even if Twain's river is deficient in such mythical beasts, its maternal geography still encompasses horror as well as a sense of pleasurable immersion. This becomes clear if we attend for a moment to representations of drowning in Twain's work. It is well known that in 1876 he wrote to his boyhood friend and fellow pilot Will Bowen cautioning against too much Mississippi reminiscence, which he describes as "simply moral & mental masturbation" (Twain 1941: 24). Less familiar, however, are his words to Bowen's widow in 1893: "I should like to call back Will Bowen and John Garth and the others, and live the life, and be as we were, and make holiday until 15, then all drown together" (quoted in Powers 1999: 88). Even allowing for Twain's sympathetic intent, this passage is striking for its commitment to precisely that regression warned about in the earlier letter. Politically, too, it figures an immersion in Southern cul-tural topography very different from the narrative of national modernization which Twain tells in the second half of *Life on the Mississippi*.

Drownings elsewhere in Twain, however, evoke those more disturbing aspects of maternal geography referred to by Rose. *Life on the Mississippi* itself reads at least partly as a Mississippi Book of the Dead, its many fatalities including two childhood friends who drowned in circumstances still recalled with horror. Set against Twain's own mobility, not only nationally but also internationally, such episodes allegorize the danger – rather than romance – of submergence in the world of the Mississippi. In this context, note also a traumatic discovery made by Twain in the summer of 1847. Swimming with friends, he was confronted by the body of a murdered runaway slave, Neriam Todd, which, freed by the current, rose up in front of them (Powers 1999: 108–9). While the final section of this chapter will show Twain offering some restitution by imagining African Americans instead in dynamic, even liberated situations on the Mississippi, such an event gives drowning an urgent political significance rather than a romantic aura.

For Bachelard, "maternal water" is also liable to be what he calls, more darkly, "funeral water" (1983: 77). In his estimation, "All rivers join the River of the Dead" (p. 75). Again I am less interested here in the generalization than in its specific suggestiveness with regard to Twain. Without speaking melodramatically, it is possible to say that the Mississippi sometimes registers in his work as precisely this kind of deathly geography. The river as image of uterine security turns into a space in which the subject is altogether annihilated. From this perspective, Twain's lifelong imaginary returns to the Mississippi resemble that compulsion to repeat in which the later Freud reads evidence of the death-instinct. Within particular texts, too, we can identify a frequent association between the river and death-wish. As well as instances of drowning noted above, consider how the protagonists in *Tom Sawyer*, *Tom Sawyer, Detective*, and *Huckleberry Finn* are all drawn in states of melancholy to the Mississippi because of the possibilities it offers of self-erasure. Even if Tom's wish for drowning, in particular, is exposed as unsurprisingly bookish – "He wandered far from the accustomed haunts of boys, and sought desolate places that were in harmony with his spirit" (Twain 1876: 39) – these narrative moments still hint at how powerfully in Twain the Mississippi may be associated with regression and extinction rather than ongoing worldly processes.

The reasons for Twain's thanatoid geography of the river are again more than simply personal. If, in Freudian theory, the death-instincts aim at reducing to zero all of a subject's tensions and at restoring some more harmonious, original state of being, then Twain's repeated emphases upon death by drowning in the Mississippi may take on political significance. Given the conflicts in the United States both preceding and outlasting the Civil War, they figure a desire for return to an earlier society without divisions and crises. Less positively, the recurrence of drowning could stand for that danger of inundation by Southern culture which, at least at times, Twain views as a threat to national progress. Yet if he repetitively projects either desire for or fear of drowning in the Mississippi, he also counters this vigilantly at other moments in his writing. This is perhaps nowhere more clearly seen than when, in *Life on the Mississippi*, he takes a cruise very near the mouth of the river. With the proximity of the sea, the moment promises an even more complete liquefaction of both self and the everyday world than is possible in the normal river environment. However, Twain writes that he was recalled from such reflections by the cries of the boat's pet parrot, which were "always this-worldly, and often profane" (1883: 480). There is here a parable of his own project and mode of operation. Rather than continuing into the desocialized space of the ocean, Twain turns back and orients his writing instead toward the actually existing tensions of his world. Chief among these crises, of course, is the state of American race relations.

Reconstructing the Mississippi

Near the beginning of *The Gilded Age*, Twain describes a Mississippi sunset: "When the sun went down it turned all the broad river to a national banner laid in gleaming bars of gold and purple and crimson" (Twain and Warner 1873: 42). Given the extent, however, to which both the river's material resources and its symbolic value were an object of struggle in the Civil War (see Anderson 1925: 17–18), it is often unclear in Twain just how effectively it can serve as an emblem of national unity. Where the sentence describes an actual spectrum of gold, purple, and crimson, it also raises the question – speaking racially now – of how varied are the colors of Twain's Mississippi.

In Lawrence Howe's reading of *Life on the Mississippi*, Twain successfully reconstructs the river so that, in the aftermath of the Civil War, it signifies an America which is racially and culturally heterogeneous. Drawing upon both Freud and Bakhtin, Howe argues that Twain struggles with various father-figures in this text – including the river pilot Isaiah Sellers, and Sir Walter Scott as a presiding influence in the South – in order to resist their implied lack of commitment to pluralism. Where they stand for "political monism," Twain's version of the Mississippi is marked instead by that cultural multiplicity Bakhtin terms "heteroglossia" (Howe 1991: 438). Certainly, as we read his river writings, we find evidence of such enthusiastic response to cosmopolitan variety. Although in *The Gilded Age* St. Louis still embodies provincial uniformity – so that the novel finds diversity away from the Mississippi Valley altogether in Washington, DC (Twain and Warner 1873: 217) – polyglot cultures in Twain are more usually located on the Mississippi itself, especially in New Orleans. As early as May 1857, when just beginning his steamboat career, he wrote excitedly to his family about seeing many different ethnicities thronging the city's marketplace. Almost 30 years later, this primal animation by the cosmopolitanism of New Orleans recurs in *Life on the Mississippi* itself, particularly in Twain's description of a cockfight where the (admittedly single-sex) crowd still contains males "of all ages and all colors, and of many languages and nationalities" (Twain 1883: 457).

Nevertheless, aspects even of his representation of New Orleans may resist appropriation by a progressive racial politics. If the crowd at the cockfight is ethnically diverse, for example, the handlers of the opposing birds themselves – "A negro

and a white man" (Twain 1883: 458) – still offer a stark tableau of American racial
conflict. The broader suggestion that *Life on the Mississippi* emerges from a position
generally of white privilege is supported when we look again at Twain's idea of including four pages of the New Orleans directory so as to show the city's "variegated nationalities."[10] Even though this plan was not finally acted upon, it is still taken by critics
like Howe as evidence of Twain's cosmopolitan Mississippi. Such cosmopolitanism,
however, may have strict limits: Twain speaks of the directory testifying "to white
political liberty" in New Orleans, and the examples he gives at this point in the
text of ethnic variety are "Germans and Frenchmen," not Indians and African
Americans.

While much work has been done recently on the complex racial signifiers of Twain's
language – notably, of course, in Shelley Fisher Fishkin's *Was Huck Black?* (1993) –
his voice in *Life on the Mississippi* itself perhaps remains more narrowly "white." The
textual diversity that extends to white raftsmen, pilots, professors, and salesmen never
incorporates significant black voices. Two conversations that Twain overheard and
transcribed on his research voyages of 1882 – respectively involving several African
American deckhands, and a black laundress and her subordinate – do not survive into
the published text. Even in Twain's unobserved eavesdropping and subsequent transcription here, there is an indication of unequal racial power.

This episode invites us to consider larger discrepancies in white and black experience on the river. Describing the effects of mud carried down from the Missouri, Twain
refers in *Life on the Mississippi* to "this water's mulatto complexion" (Twain 1883: 252).
Culturally, however, just how "mulatto" can the Mississippi be in Twain? For
Sherwood Anderson, in his novel *Dark Laughter*, Twain is relatively uninterested in
the evidence of miscegenation on the river. By contrast, his own protagonist when
visiting New Orleans makes a point of noticing changes in the features and skin tones
of African Americans, "getting the race lighter and lighter" (Anderson 1925: 73).
While this topic may indeed be effaced in *Life on the Mississippi*, it is of course central
to *Pudd'nhead Wilson*. At a level of exchange below sexual relationship, Twain also
notably explores the possibility of cultural miscegenation in *Huckleberry Finn*, where
Huck and Jim's raft offers a specialized place of multiracial contact. Stephanie
LeMenager has recently identified Huck's mobility on the river with the economic
situation of "middling speculators and small riverside plantation owners." In this
provocative reading, his floating down the Mississippi recapitulates "the same international networks of capital and power that sponsored the slave trade" (LeMenager
2004: 416, 409).[11] However, this restricts the analogical force of Huck's trip on the
raft: if it indeed repeats the movements of white-owned capital in the Mississippi
Valley, it also allows a white character – albeit briefly – to perform the more desperate, covert motion of fugitive slaves.

Yet even conceding such examples of reciprocity across racial boundaries, Twain's
river is still often a space experienced and traveled through differently by white and
black. He writes in *Life on the Mississippi* that "We were getting down now into the

migrating negro region" (1883: 326). This reference to migration away from the Mississippi Valley altogether during the 1880s serves to underscore a generally restricted black mobility on the river itself. African Americans circulating on the Mississippi earlier in the nineteenth century were themselves, of course, most likely to be slaves in transit – a process Twain narrates not only in major texts like *Huckleberry Finn* and *Pudd'nhead Wilson*, but in the sketch "Jane Lampton Clemens," which recalls slaves on the wharf at Hannibal at the beginning of their enforced journeys. These limited itineraries contrast with the diverse, privileged forms taken by white movement on the Mississippi. LeMenager shows how, as well as serving as the transport route for relocated slaves, the river was more generally "a carrier of economic desire" (2004: 405), a means of passage for other kinds of white capital. Particularly after the Louisiana Purchase of 1803, the Mississippi functioned, too, as a conduit of white exploration in America, the colonization of its own space leading to a larger, often racially coded "national-imperial possession of 'our' continent" (Arac 1997: 211). Later in the nineteenth century, such forms of privileged mobility were joined by tourism, which Twain notes regarding the caves in *Tom Sawyer* (Twain 1876: 254) and practices himself in *Life on the Mississippi*.

These inscriptions of a sustained white power on the Mississippi are hard for even a well-intentioned writer to erase. Certainly, Twain tracks changes in the river's racial demographics just as he does shifting cultural and industrial practices. Even here, however, his writing cannot be construed as straightforwardly contributing to a program of "literary Reconstruction" (Howe 1991: 436). In *Life on the Mississippi*, for instance, proper weight is given to the fact that one of Twain's boyhood residences in Hannibal is now occupied by "colored folk" (Twain 1883: 537), denoting a fuller incursion of African Americans into formerly white-controlled spaces on the river than can be narrated in the pre-Civil War settings of *Huckleberry Finn* or *Pudd'nhead Wilson*. Earlier in the same text, however, Twain describes how the "poison-swilling Irishmen" of the St. Louis waterfront – part of a coarse yet vibrant culture – have been replaced by "a few scattering handfuls of ragged negroes, some drinking, some drunk, some nodding, others asleep" (p. 256). Far from incarnating national progress, African Americans are imaged here by Twain – from a tourist's distance – as the passive casualties of history.

At times in Twain there is a quietist racial politics that leaves the norms of white power in the Mississippi Valley substantially unchallenged. That this is a matter not merely of historical interest but of abiding cultural significance may be gauged, finally, by considering the current tourist economy raised upon Twain's representations of the river. Fishkin describes a visit to Hannibal in which she finds all evidence of racial conflict and injustice erased by the town's self-presentation. The blander sequences of *Tom Sawyer* are privileged as the tourist industry's preferred text; the cruise which Fishkin takes to the actual counterpart of Jackson's Island draws attention to flora and fauna, but not to its setting for what she terms "one of the most hopeful and positive black–white relationships in American literature" (Fishkin 1997: 65). Faced with this touristic packaging, Fishkin offers an alternative, radical geography: for example, she reactivates a sense of the river as contested social space in Twain by visiting a site near Hannibal associated with the Underground Railroad (pp. 53–7).

Nevertheless, even Fishkin's valuable corrective work is open to question, since it risks stabilizing the turbulences and fluctuations of Twain's representation of the river. Even within particular texts, as well as across the full range of his work, the Mississippi is indeed duplicitous – not sufficiently coherent or unilinear to serve as Fishkin's model for a progressive vision of America, but marked also by durable inequalities of class, gender, and race. If such a conservative politics is especially visible in *Tom Sawyer*, it is not fully displaced by Twain's other Mississippi writings either. To this extent, the touristic construction put upon his river is not so much wrong as itself another instance of partial reading. Now from a retrograde rather than radical perspective, it similarly homogenizes the space. Without resting complacently in the piling-up of plural meanings, we need, by way of alternative, to recognize that the Mississippi in Twain is and continues to be a contested object. How exactly his river is read and how its divergent meanings are negotiated is a matter that bears upon the construction of America generally – not merely in the past but in the future also.

NOTES

1 "Down the Rhone," an abridged account of this journey, was posthumously brought to publication by Twain's biographer and literary executor, Albert Bigelow Paine (Kaplan 1966: 313–14).

2 See e.g. increased attention given to Twain's critical posture regarding American empire. Zwick's essay in Fishkin (2002) repositions the writer in the context of global anti-imperialist struggle. It is my contention, however, that Twain's Mississippi, freed of more parochial readings, is *already* national, indeed international, in its implications.

3 The allusion is to Byron's campaign against the minor poet William Thomas Fitzgerald (c.1759–1829). Twain's reviewer appears to be making a mild observation about an affective closeness between writer and topic rather than satirizing cliché as Byron does.

4 This extrapolation echoes Lawrence Howe's argument that Twain stages a series of encounters with emblematic father-figures in *Life on the Mississippi* so as to convert "personal oedipality into a culturally representative complex" (Howe 1991: 434). However, my account of his relationship to the Mississippi

differs from Howe's in also stressing regression.

5 For discussion of "emergent" and "residual" forms, see Williams (1977: 121–7).

6 The traceable nature of Mississippi steamboat travel allows Twain new possibilities of pursuit narrative in *Tom Sawyer, Detective* (1896) and the unfinished *Tom Sawyer's Conspiracy* (c.1897–1900).

7 Gleason places steamboat racing itself at the borders between an older sort of carnival and more regimented, quantified "leisure" (1999: 82–3).

8 There is an example of multiracial, but not yet unisex, swimming in *Pudd'nhead Wilson*, when white boys admire the diving of "Chambers," racially categorized as black (Twain 1894: 59–60).

9 See e.g. Bell and Valentine (1995).

10 For this and further quotations in this paragraph, see Twain (1984: 335–6). This material does not appear in the "Oxford Mark Twain" edition.

11 I am grateful to Professor LeMenager for supplying me with a copy of her essay in advance of its journal publication.

REFERENCES AND FURTHER READING

Anderson, Sherwood (1925). *Dark Laughter*. New York: Boni & Liveright.

Arac, Jonathan (1997). Huckleberry Finn *As Idol and Target: The Functions of Criticism in our Time*. Madison: University of Wisconsin Press.

Bachelard, Gaston (1983). *Water and Dreams: An Essay on the Imagination of Matter*, trans. Edith R. Farrell. Dallas: Pegasus Foundation. (First publ. 1942)

Bell, David, and Valentine, Gill, eds. (1995). *Mapping Desire: Geographies of Sexualities*. London: Routledge.

Branch, Edgar M. (1985). "Mark Twain: The Pilot and the Writer." *Mark Twain Journal* 23: 2 (Fall), 28–43.

Budd, Louis J., ed. (1999). *Mark Twain: The Contemporary Reviews*. Cambridge, UK: Cambridge University Press.

Burde, Edgar J. (1978). "Mark Twain: The Writer as Pilot." *PMLA* 93: 5, 878–92.

Camfield, Gregg (2002). "A Republican Artisan in the Court of King Capital: Mark Twain and Commerce." In Shelley Fisher Fishkin (ed.), *A Historical Guide to Mark Twain*, 95–126. New York: Oxford University Press.

Cummings, Sherwood (1988). *Mark Twain and Science: Adventures of a Mind*. Baton Rouge: Louisiana State University Press.

Daniels, Stephen (1989). "Marxism, Culture, and the Duplicity of Landscape." In Richard Peet and Nigel Thrift (eds.), *New Models in Geography*, 196–220. London: Unwin Hyman.

Fishkin, Shelley Fisher (1997). *Lighting Out for the Territory: Reflections on Mark Twain and American Culture*. New York: Oxford University Press.

Fishkin, Shelley Fisher, ed. (2002). *A Historical Guide to Mark Twain*. Oxford: Oxford University Press.

Gleason, William A. (1999). *The Leisure Ethic: Work and Play in American Literature, 1840–1940*. Stanford: Stanford University Press.

Horwitz, Howard (1991). *By the Law of Nature: Form and Value in Nineteenth-Century America*. New York: Oxford University Press.

Howe, Lawrence (1991). "Transcending the Limits of Experience: Mark Twain's *Life on the Mississippi*." *American Literature* 63, 420–39.

Hunter, Louis C. (1969). *Steamboats on the Western Rivers: An Economic and Technological History*. New York: Octagon.

Kaplan, Justin (1966). *Mr. Clemens and Mark Twain: A Biography*. New York: Simon & Schuster.

Kruse, Horst H. (1981). *Mark Twain and* Life on the Mississippi. Amherst: University of Massachusetts Press.

LeMenager, Stephanie (2004). "Floating Capital: The Trouble with Whiteness on Twain's Mississippi." *ELH* 71, 405–32.

Marx, Leo (1963). "The Pilot and the Passenger: Landscape Conventions and the Style of *Huckleberry Finn*." In Henry Nash Smith (ed.), *Mark Twain: A Collection of Critical Essays*. Englewood Cliffs, NJ: Prentice-Hall.

Powers, Ron (1999). *Dangerous Water: A Biography of the Boy Who Became Mark Twain*. New York: Basic Books.

Rose, Gillian (1993). *Feminism and Geography: The Limits of Geographical Knowledge*. Cambridge: Polity.

Sattelmeyer, Robert (2001). "Steamboats, Cocaine, and Paper Money: Mark Twain Rewriting Himself." In Laura E. Skandera Trombley and Michael J. Kiskis (eds.), *Constructing Mark Twain: New Directions in Scholarship*, 87–100. Columbia: University of Missouri Press.

Smith, Henry Nash (1962). *Mark Twain: The Development of a Writer*. Cambridge, Mass.: Belknap/Harvard University Press.

Stoneley, Peter (1992). *Mark Twain and the Feminine Aesthetic*. Cambridge, UK: Cambridge University Press.

Tanner, Tony (1965). *The Reign of Wonder: Naivety and Reality in American Literature*. Cambridge, UK: Cambridge University Press.

Trilling, Lionel (1981). *The Liberal Imagination: Essays on Literature and Society*. Oxford: Oxford University Press. (First publ. 1950.)

Twain, Mark (1940). *Mark Twain in Eruption*, ed. Bernard DeVoto. New York: Harper & Bros.

Twain, Mark (1941). *Mark Twain's Letters to Will Bowen*, ed. Theodore Hornberger. Austin: University of Texas Press.

Twain, Mark (1975). *Mark Twain's Notebooks and Journals*, vol. 1: *1855–1873*, ed. Frederick

Anderson, Michael B. Frank, and Kenneth M. Sanderson. Berkeley: University of California Press.

Twain, Mark (1984). *Life on the Mississippi*, ed. James M. Cox. Harmondsworth: Penguin.

Twain, Mark (1988). *Mark Twain's Letters*, vol. 1: *1853–1866*, ed. Edgar Marquess Branch, Michael B. Frank, and Kenneth M. Sanderson. Berkeley: University of California Press.

Weinstein, Cindy (1995). *The Literature of Labor and the Labors of Literature: Allegory in Nineteenth-Century American Fiction*. Cambridge, UK: Cambridge University Press.

Williams, Raymond (1977). *Marxism and Literature*. Oxford: Oxford University Press.

20

Mark Twain and the Literary Construction of the American West

Gary Scharnhorst

The first major American writer born west of the Mississippi, Mark Twain did not discover the American literary West. This distinction rightly belongs to such California writers as Louisa Amelia Clapp, Alonzo Delano, and Bret Harte, or perhaps such humorists as Artemus Ward (a.k.a. Charles Farrar Browne) and John Phoenix (a.k.a. George H. Derby). But Twain's literary construction of the trans-Mississippi West, particularly in his early California sketches and his satirical travelogue *Roughing It* (1872), was more durable than theirs. "Mark Twain" was literally a product of the literary West, Samuel Clemens first adopting his pseudonym as a reporter in Virginia City in February 1863. More to the point, Twain from the beginning of his writing career constructed an ironic West or satirized the mythic West that Harte and others had depicted through a soft lens or veil of nostalgia. In the preface to his first important book, *The Luck of Roaring Camp and Other Sketches*, for example, Harte declared his intention to record "an era replete with a certain heroic Greek poetry" and to gather materials for a Western epic, "the *Iliad* that is yet to be sung" (Harte 1870: n.p.). Mark Twain, on the other hand, always debunked this imaginary West by portraying the region as a nest of snares for the unwary, ripe with fraud, and peopled by confidence men and hucksters. "Rather than sustaining a romantic view of the West as a natural escape," as Joseph Coulombe suggests (2003: 116), Twain regarded it as a series of traps.

Among his first notable writings after arriving in Nevada in August 1861 were a pair of widely reprinted hoaxes that gulled the readers of local Washoe newspapers. In "Petrified Man" (1862), one of the first pieces he published in the Virginia City *Territorial Enterprise*, Twain announced the discovery of a fossilized human body in the Nevada mountains. He was weary, he later wrote, of the recent "mania" about "extraordinary petrifactions" found in the region and decided to burlesque it with "a very delicate satire" (Twain 1992a: 389). The joke, lost upon most readers, was that the stone figure Twain described was thumbing his nose. "From beginning to end the 'Petrified Man' squib was a string of roaring absurdities," he reminisced, "told with an unfair pretence of truth that even imposed upon me to some extent" (pp. 390–1). A year later, he invented gory details of an ostensible massacre near Carson City: a father had killed his wife and children, scalped and mutilated their bodies, and then committed suicide – all after losing the fortune he had earned in the mines because "the San Francisco papers exposed the game of cooking dividends" on stocks (Twain 1992a: 58). Once again, Twain ridiculed the mythology of the pastoral lives of the red-shirt miners and the easy wealth they earned in the gold fields. "[I]n all my life I never saw anything like the sensation that little satire [the "Massacre at Empire City"] created," he later admitted. "It was the talk of the town, it was the talk of the Territory" (Twain 1992a: 393). Never mind how ludicrous the story, Twain's readers took the tale at face value. But he had struck a theme he would exploit and a pattern he would repeat for years to come: ridiculing the hypocrisy and pretensions of the pioneers and exposing the deceptions of the mythic West.

While Twain was living in the West, first in Virginia City and later in San Francisco, few groups provoked his ire more than the Society of California Pioneers and the native tribes. He scorned them both for similar reasons: he thought they had been romanticized beyond recognition. Members of the Society of Pioneers, who were required to prove they had arrived in the territory in 1849 or '50, were an easy target. After all, many of them had come west a step ahead of the law or because they had been unable to make a living in "the States." Some of them had abandoned families and remarried in the West. "The less said about the motives of some of our pioneers the better," as Harte warned in 1866 (1992: 88). In "The Pioneers' Ball" the previous year, Twain had lampooned the Forty-Niners' pomposity in general and the conspicuous display of their trophy wives in particular. One woman was "attired in an elegant *pate de foi gras*," he noted, while another "was attractively attired in her new and beautiful false teeth" (Twain 1992a: 184).

For better or worse, the so-called "Wild Humorist of the Pacific Slope" turned the same jaundiced eye upon Native Americans. In a letter written for publication from the West in 1862 he claimed to describe the local tribes from "personal observation," not in terms "gleaned from Cooper's novels." He insisted that a "typical" Indian ate the lice from his own body; others, he said, ate grasshoppers. Indian women were normally ugly hags who ate soap and traded their children (Branch 1950: 233–7). Similarly, in "The Noble Red Man" (1870), Twain disputed the depiction of Indians in books as "tall and tawny, muscular, straight, and of kingly presence," with "generous impulses" and "knightly magnanimity." For "[s]uch is the Noble Red Man in print" alone (Twain 1992a: 442–3). Instead, Twain insisted, the natives were ignoble miscreants. They are "little, and scrawny, and black, and dirty; . . . thoroughly pitiful and contemptible, . . . base and treacherous" (pp. 443–4), and descriptions of "their favorite mutilations cannot be put into print" (p. 446). Again Twain claimed his characterization was based upon first-hand experience in the West: "I did not get him from books, but from personal observation" (p. 445). In fact, he groused about Cooper's portrayal of Indians throughout his career, most famously in "Fenimore Cooper's Literary Offences" (1895). "Cooper's Indians never notice anything," he noted there. "Cooper thinks they are marvellous creatures . . . but he was almost always in error about his Indians. There was seldom a sane one among them" (Twain 1992b: 185). In all, as Helen L. Harris says, "Twain found it easier to be liberal toward the Blacks, the Chinese or any other relative newcomer to America than to be liberal toward the Indian" (Harris 1975: 504).

To his credit, as a news reporter in San Francisco Twain repeatedly challenged the status quo and earned a reputation as an iconoclast, in keeping with his refusal to submit to Western custom and law. He defended the Chinese immigrants to California, who were often scorned as "inscrutable" and denied equal justice. He remembered to the end of his days how in 1864 the editor of the San Francisco *Call*, after reading in galley proof a piece he had written on police indifference to anti-Chinese violence, had "ordered its extinction" (Twain 1940: 256). The article would have angered Irish readers, who hated the Chinese, the editor explained. As late as 1880 Twain referred derisively in a letter to his friend W. D. Howells to "that degraded 'Morning Call,' whose mission from hell & politics was to lick the boots of the Irish & throw brave mud at the Chinamen" (Twain and Howells 1960: 326). As the San Francisco correspondent of the *Territorial Enterprise* in 1865–6, moreover, Twain was a self-appointed vigilante, waging a one-man crusade against police corruption. His articles "What Have the Police Been Doing?" and "The Black Hole of San Francisco" indicted police brutality and exposed the mismanagement of the city police court. In retaliation, he was threatened with a libel suit and once jailed overnight on a charge of public drunkenness. He planned to deliver a public lecture in February 1866 on "Spiritualism and the San Francisco Police." As late as November 1866 he was hauled into court and the receipts for his Sandwich Islands lecture were seized in revenge for his efforts "to reform the Police force." Hence his diatribe in *Roughing It* about the "policemen and politicians" in San Francisco, "the dust-licking pimps and slaves of the scum" (Twain 1872: 397). He wrote Jervis Langdon, his future father-in-law, in December 1868 that "much of my conduct on the Pacific Coast was not of a character to recommend me to the respectful regard of a high eastern civilization" (Twain 1990: 327).

Twain placed his first significant publication in an Eastern venue, the New York *Saturday Press*. "Jim Smiley and His Jumping Frog" (1865) was based on a tall tale he heard in Calaveras County, and organized around a series of the tricks or practical jokes traditionally characteristic of Southwestern humor. The narrator has been directed by Artemus Ward to call upon Simon Wheeler, a Western yarn-spinner. Wheeler barricades the narrator in a corner and reels off the story of Jim Smiley, a Western miner victimized by a Yankee stranger, who fills Smiley's frog Daniel Webster (named for the US senator discredited for supporting the Compromise of 1850) with quail-shot so that he loses a jumping contest with a rival frog. Though often read simply as a humorous sketch in the Western vein, the sketch is also political satire, implicitly demeaning Webster and valorizing Smiley's ferocious dog, Andrew Jackson, named for the first President born west of the Appalachians. As Sydney J. Krause concludes, "The events of the tale bring to mind some of the leading facts associated with the names of Jackson and Webster. Specifically, the bull-pup evokes the ironies of Jackson's reputation as a frontiersman, while the frog evokes the various flip-flops that characterized Webster's career" (Krause 1964: 568). But above all, the sketch reinforces the image of the West as a nexus of deceit and deception. The narrator, no less than Smiley, has failed to read or heed the signs of danger.

Roughing It, Twain's account of life among the rowdies in Nevada and California, fudges or obscures many of the specific details normally associated with literary realism. For example, Twain invented from whole cloth his visit with Brigham Young, who was absent from Salt Lake City on the days he passed through the city with his brother Orion, as well as the chapters in which he and his mining partner discover a "blind lead." He nowhere names the luxurious hotel where he lived in San Francisco (the Lick House), the newspaper for which he worked there (the *Call*), or the theaters he frequented (among them, Platt's Hall, the Metropolitan, and the Academy of Music), not even the one where his delivered his first lecture (Maguire's Opera House). He mentions the "queer earthquake" that struck the city "on a bright October day" in 1865 as he was "coming down Third Street"), but his anecdotal account consists largely of gossip about the disaster (Twain 1872: 421–7). He betrays no hint of the reasons for his hasty departure from Virginia City (he had riled several fellow citizens with a facetious editorial written while he was drunk). Of the six years he lived in the West, the most eventful year – 1866, when he warred with the San Francisco police, was briefly jailed, and contemplated suicide – is dismissed in scarcely two pages. In the penultimate chapter, the narrator returns from his "luxurious vagrancy" (p. 558) in Hawaii to inaugurate his career as a platform speaker in San Francisco. Once more Twain's version of events distorts the historical record, however. Though the narrator claims to fear his lecture will fail and the hall will be empty, in fact the San Francisco papers puffed his appearance for days in advance and indeed reported on the morning of the lecture that all the tickets had been sold. The narrator's pro-fession of surprise when he discovers that the "house was full, aisles and all!" (p. 562) is at best disingenuous. At the beginning of chapter 52 – the only chapter in the book which is documentary in purpose, describing in technical detail methods of silver mining in the Comstock – Twain pauses to make this offer: "Since I desire, in this chapter, to say an instructive word or two about the silver mines, the reader may take this fair warning and skip, if he chooses" (p. 376). That is, he invites the reader to ignore the most realistic chapter in the book. In short, the fictionalization of his expe-riences throughout the book is distinctly, sometimes radically, at odds with the bio-graphical record. "The myth-making power of his imagination is in evidence in this book," as Gladys Bellamy remarks (1950: 272). Twain "dramatized many episodes that seemed a little tame, touched up others, and invented others outright when the narrative demanded it. He fictionalized himself, too, and his own adventures" (p. 274). Even Twain's official hagiographer, Albert Bigelow Paine, allowed that *Roughing It* "was not accurate history, even of the author's own adventures. It was true in its aspects, rather than in its details" (Paine 1912: 454–5).

Put another way, *Roughing It*, published the same year the overland railroad opened the nation to Western migration and tourism on a greater scale than ever before, systematically reinvented the literary West. Twain satirized in the narrative such genteel Western travelogues as Washington Irving's *A Tour of the Prairies* (1835), Francis Parkman's *The Oregon Trail* (1849), Samuel Bowles's *Across the Continent* (1865), and A. D. Richardson's *Beyond the Mississippi* (1867); sentimental Western novels such as Emerson Bennett's *The Prairie Flower* (1850); and frontier melodrama – in short, all the works and authors who insisted on viewing the West "through the mellow moonshine of romance" (Twain 1872: 149). Twain's West, replete with desperados and confidence men, is as terrifying as it is entertaining. Not coincidentally, he competed with his sometimes friend and rival, Bret Harte, in exploiting the West for literary material. As he boasted to his brother Orion in March 1871, as *Roughing It* was in press, "I will 'top' Bret Harte again or bust" (Twain 1995: 351). In *Roughing It* he sought to demythologize the romantic "Wild West" of ruthless outlaws, red-shirted miners, noble Indians, and hardy pioneers which Harte had popularized. Written in the same satirical voice as *The Innocents Abroad* (1869), the travelogue is structured according to the same pattern of repeated disillusionment, disappointment, and failure that organized his earlier book. Whereas in *Innocents* the narrator is a western American who voyages east until he reaches the site of early Christendom, here the narrator is an eastern innocent who treks west to the very frontier of civilization (and even across the Pacific to Hawaii). If, in the first book, the churlish narrator is disillusioned by the paintings of the Old Masters and Turkish baths, here he is dismayed by barren alkali deserts and frustrated by his failure to strike it rich. If, in the first book, he is the stranger who bedevils his fellow "pilgrims," here he is the naïf who must earn his spurs.

"Mark Twain," the narrator of *Roughing It*, purports on the first page to be "young and innocent," even asserting he "never had been away from home." In truth, Twain was 25 years old in 1861 when the narrative opens, and had worked for eight years as a journeyman printer and as a pilot on the Mississippi River. During his planned "three-months excursion" in the West, the narrator expects to see "buffaloes and Indians, and prairie dogs, and antelopes, and have all kinds of adventures, and may be get hanged or scalped, and have ever such a fine time, and write home and tell all about it, and be a hero" (Twain 1872: 19). The West also offers the mythic possibility of striking it rich in the gold fields of California or in the Comstock silver mines, and the narrator imagines how even the most casual tourist might "go about of an afternoon" while at leisure "and pick up two or three pailfuls of shining slugs, and nuggets of gold and silver on the hillsides" (p. 19). His dream of wealth will eventually turn to ashes, of course, but first he must run a gauntlet of traps and temptations.

The narrator's first lesson in Western etiquette occurs just west of St. Joe. He overhears a cowboy's demand at dinner in a stagecoach station: " 'Pass the bread, you son of a skunk!' No, I forget – skunk was not the word; it seems to me it was still stronger than that." His first encounter with "the vigorous new vernacular of the occidental

plains and mountains" (Twain 1872: 45) neatly foreshadows the scene early in Owen
Wister's *The Virginian*, written over a generation later, when the narrator hears the
villain calls the hero a "son of a bitch," and the hero responds by laying his pistol on
the poker table and replying, "When you call me that, *smile!*" That is, just as the tenderfoot narrator of *Roughing It* learns in his second day on the road something about
the force of the robust Western vernacular, the tenderfoot narrator of *The Virginian*
discovers on his first day in Wyoming that the tone in which one utters a (similar)
coarse epithet is crucial, that "the letter means nothing until the spirit gives it life"
(Wister 2002: 29).

This episode in *Roughing It* leads directly into a parable about the differences
between Eastern polite behavior and the social code of the West. The narrator medi-
tates on the character of the coyote, "a living, breathing allegory of Want" with "a
general slinking expression" (Twain 1872: 49). But in a race with a "swift-footed dog,"
a domesticated pet, the dog is doomed to defeat, taken in by this "entire stranger"
with his "gently swinging . . . deceitful trot" and "fraudful smile" cast over the shoulder (p. 50). Finally, unable to ever quite catch his rival and "more and more incensed"
at being so "shamefully . . . taken in," the dog "jogs back to his train, and takes up a
humble position under the hindmost wagon." And "for as much as a year after that,"
when tempted to chase a coyote, the dog will "apparently observe to himself, 'I do
not think I want any of the pie'" (p. 51). The coyote, an old-timer indigenous to the
West, effectively defeats the town dog, the uninitiated interloper. Or, as Henry Nash
Smith concludes, this anecdote

> involves a tenderfoot . . . with a higher opinion of himself than he can make good in the
> Far West environment; a veteran who looks disreputable by town-bred standards but is
> nevertheless in secure command of the situation; and the process by which the tender-
> foot gains knowledge, quite fresh and new knowledge, at the cost of humiliation to
> himself. (Smith 1962: 55)

Like the dog inured to genteel convention, the narrator of *Roughing It* must gradually
learn a new code of conduct.

Nowhere is the narrator's anomie in his new environment more apparent than when
he encounters the desperado Slade, west of Fort Laramie. As Jeffrey Melton has
observed, Slade epitomizes "the new western type" (2002: 102) and "serves as an ideal
romantic figure of the West" (p. 54). He also represents a morally ambiguous figure
who, as the narrator notes, "was at once the most bloody, the most dangerous, and
the most valuable citizen that inhabited the savage fastnesses of the mountains" (Twain
1872: 79). The narrator approves the primitive justice meted out by Slade as a necessary evil. Though technically a criminal who has murdered 26 men, he has also
"restored peace and order to one of the worst divisions of the road," a "very paradise
of outlaws and desperadoes" (pp. 82–3). When the narrator encounters Slade in the
flesh, he is struck by his mild-mannered appearance, in stark contrast to the legend:
he was the "most gentlemanly-appearing, quiet, and affable officer we had yet found

along the road . . . Here was romance – and I sitting face to face with it!" (p. 87). After Slade is arrested and, weeping on the gallows, hanged for his crimes, the ambivalent narrator does not dispute the necessity of *lex talionis* or primitive justice. Yet neither can he unravel the paradox that Slade represents, and finds the peculiar composition of "this bloody, desperate, kindly-mannered, urbane gentleman . . . a conundrum worth investigating" (p. 96).

The lack of connection between myth and reality becomes more complex the further west the narrator travels. In Salt Lake City, the capital of Mormonism – initially nothing less than "a land of enchantment, and goblins, and awful mystery" (Twain 1872: 108) – the narrator realizes that a "Mormon Destroying Angel," entrusted with maintaining doctrinal purity (if necessary by murdering apostates), was "nothing more than a loud, profane, offensive old blackguard!" (p. 106). The institution of polygamy, or "celestial marriage," seems titillating to the "feverish" narrator until he meets actual Mormon wives. Then he realizes that the man who marries one of "these poor, ungainly, and pathetically 'homely' creatures" has performed "an act of Christian charity" and "the man that marries sixty of them has done a deed of open-handed generosity" (pp. 117–18). The *Book of Mormon*, supposed holy writ, the narrator regards as a transparent fraud, "a pretentious affair," "an insipid mess of inspiration," "chloroform in print," and "a tedious plagiarism of the New Testament" (p. 127).

Western topography is no less a hazard than thieves and confidence men, for even nature seems to conspire against the uninitiated. From a distance, the narrator contemplates "the majestic panorama of mountains and valleys spread out below us" (Twain 1872: 140). But he soon realizes that the "poetry was all in the anticipation – there is none in the reality" (p. 143). Once again expectations are disappointed. The vagabonds cross an alkali desert, hardly the "virgin land" or "new world garden" of popular myth, and the dust "cut through our lips . . . persecuted our eyes and made our noses bleed and *kept* them bleeding – and truly and seriously the romance all faded away, and disappeared, and left the desert trip nothing but a harsh reality – a thirsty, sweltering, longing, hateful reality!" (p. 144)

Once settled in Virginia City, the narrator and a partner take an excursion to Lake Tahoe, a trip over the mountains from Carson City, that turns into slapstick comedy. Staking their claim beside the "marvelous beauty" of the lake, the boys – intending "to take up a wood ranch or so ourselves and become wealthy" (Twain 1872: 168) – make no more than a token attempt at building a fence and shanty. After completing the latter, however, they inadvertently set the woods on fire and watch as their fence and house are consumed by flame. To add insult to injury, they are suddenly drenched by a thunderstorm, and consequently freeze "all the night through" (p. 177). Stubbornly remaining at the lake, they fish "a good deal," but despite seeing trout "by the thousand" in the waters beneath "did not average one fish a week" (p. 175) – defeated, presumably, by the crystal-clear water of the lake. Not only do they fail as fishermen, upon returning to Carson they find they must pay damages for starting the fire (p. 177).

Just as the narrator fails to read nature aright, so he must revise his opinions of the concept of "natural man," the expectations based on his reading, in line with his actual frontier experiences. Before arriving in the West, he claims, he had been a "disciple of Cooper and a worshipper of the Red Man – even of the scholarly savages of *The Last of the Mohicans*" (Twain 1872: 149). But he is surprised and disgusted by the so-called "Goshute" Indians he encounters, "very considerably inferior to even the despised Digger Indians of California" rather than noble figures. The "Goshutes" are "always hungry, and yet never refusing anything that a hog would eat, . . . [and] manifestly descended [like the "African bushmen"] from the selfsame gorilla, or kangaroo, or Norway rat, whichever animal-Adam the Darwinians trace them to." Indians of every tribe, he concludes, "deserve pity, poor creatures." "[A]nd they can have mine," he adds, "– at this distance. Nearer by, they never get anybody's" (p. 149). As Helen Harris comments, "In *Roughing It*, Twain described the desert Indians much as he had done in 'The Noble Red Man'" (1975: 498).

The narrator's next failures occur as he first buys a horse, then mines for gold. Of course, he knows nothing about either horseflesh or mining, so again he is an easy mark. Set up by an auctioneer and his shill in the audience, he buys a "genuine Mexican plug," a "bloody old foreign relic," for $27, as much as he would have paid for a respectable horse. The Mexican plug, however, is utterly untamed and incorrigible. The narrator tries to sell him, to no avail, then to give him away, but again without success. His livery bill for his six weeks of ownership amounts to over $250 – most of it for hay, because the "Genuine Mexican Plug had eaten a ton." In the end, the only way to rid himself of the horse and its livery costs is to find an even more guileless victim, "a passing Arkansas emigrant" (Twain 1872: 178–84). Undeterred by this experience, he heads for the gold fields, expecting "to find masses of silver lying all about the ground . . . glittering in the sun on the mountain summits" (p. 204). Instead, he gathers bushels of mica or fool's gold, only to learn from a grizzled prospector of its worthlessness: "So vanished my dream. So melted my wealth away. So toppled my airy castle to the earth and left me stricken and forlorn" (p. 208). As Melton observes, Twain describes a series of failures "due to ignorance combined with hubris" (2002: 116). In his "Roughing It" lecture, delivered dozens of times during the 1870–1 season alone, Twain had made exactly the same point about his gullibility:

> I had supposed in my innocence that silver mining was nice, easy business, and that of course silver lay around loose on the hillsides, and that all you had to do was to pick it up, and that you could tell it from any other substance on account of its brightness and its white metallic look. Then came my disappointment; for I found that silver was merely scattered through quartz rock. (Twain 1976: 55)

Nevertheless, the tenderfoot has yet to plumb the depths of his utter incompetence. In chapter 31 of *Roughing It*, Twain ridicules the notion of moral self-reform as he satirizes Bret Harte's "The Outcasts of Poker Flat" (1869), itself loosely based on the Donner Party disaster of the winter of 1846–7. The gambler and prostitutes in Harte's story, trapped by a blizzard, behave nobly and courageously before they "hand in [their] checks" (Harte 1870: 36). Twain burlesques such sentimental depiction of sinners-with-hearts-of-gold. Also lost and blinded by a blizzard, the narrator and his two companions wander in circles in the snow. They try to follow the example of the "common book fraud about Indians and lost hunters making a fire by rubbing two dry sticks together," but of course fail. One of the men desperately fires a revolver into a stack of sticks he has gathered, to light them this way, but merely "blew the pile clear out of the country!" Their horses shy at the gunshot and disappear into the blizzard. Finally, convinced they will not survive the night, the narrator and his companions resolve to reform their lives before they die. One pledges to abstain from whisky, another swears off card-playing, and the narrator himself throws away his pipe – whereupon "[o]blivion came. The battle of life was done" (Twain 1872: 237). The punch-line inevitably comes the next morning when the men discover that, "not fifteen steps from us, were the frame buildings of a stage station, and under a shed stood our still saddled and bridled horses!" (p. 238). Of course, within a page or two, each of the men has returned to his vice. Unlike Harte's romanticized West, where gamblers reform and prostitutes share their victuals with ladies, Twain's West is the locus of neither moral rejuvenation nor life-changing experience.

This episode represents a turning point in the narrative. The narrator has learned his lessons; or at least, he has been sufficiently assimilated into the community of "roughs" that he is rarely again the victim of their practical jokes. Indeed, in the sequel to his experience in the blizzard, he turns the tables and is among the perpetrators of a hoax. He explains that "the older citizens of a new territory look down upon the rest of the world," and the boys, the narrator among them, accordingly have fun in "the shape of a practical joke" (Twain 1872: 241) at the expense of a newcomer to the region. The miners construct a legal puzzle. In a landslide, Dick Hyde's ranch has been covered by Tom Morgan's ranch to the depth of 38 feet. Hyde persuades General Buncombe, recently exiled to Nevada to serve as US attorney, to defend his property rights in court. All the evidence and the whole direction of the case goes in the plaintiff, Hyde's, favor. And when Buncombe finishes his summation, he is convinced "Morgan's case was killed." But the judge reasons that "Heaven, in its inscrutable wisdom, has seen fit to move this defendant's ranch for a purpose," and so he rules in Morgan's favor, though stipulating that Hyde could still excavate his ranch. Incredulous, the general pronounces the judge "a miraculous fool, an inspired idiot" – and it was not until two months later that "the fact that he had been played upon with a joke had managed to bore itself, like another Hoosac Tunnel, through the solid adamant of his understanding" (pp. 245–7). This hoax on Judge Buncombe may well have inspired the trick Wister has his hero play on a self-righteous preacher, similarly puncturing his pretensions, in chapter 21 of *The Virginian*.

The narrator of *Roughing It* weaves his most elaborate fiction in the subsequent "blind lead" episode, which restages his early prospecting failure. He and his partner Calvin Higsbee purportedly strike a "blind lead" rich with ore and overnight become paper millionaires. By law, however, they need to work the claim within ten days of filing it. Both, though, are (each unbeknown to the other) called out of town and, failing to work the lead, relinquish their claim to it. As the narrator laments, "We would have been millionaires if we had only worked with pick and spade one little day on our property and secured our ownership!" (Twain 1872: 291). Twain even dedicated *Roughing It* to Higsbee "in memory of the curious time when we two were millionaires for ten days." Trouble is, the episode never occurred. Just as Twain made up his visit with Brigham Young in Salt Lake City, so he completely invented the "blind lead" episode. So even the dedication works as a type of practical joke – this one on the reader. "As a metaphor for the West itself," Melton concludes, "the blind lead *leads* nowhere because the tourist is blind to the true depth and complexity of the region and of making a home there" (2002: 117). And so ends the first half of the narrative.

In the second half, his initiation more or less complete, the narrator becomes a newspaper reporter. Though his perspective shifts from miner to journalist, from participant to observer, he continues to describe various get-rich-quick schemes and other hazards in the mining camps. For example, he explains how to "salt" a wildcat mine with nuggets of silver and "sell out while the excitement was up." To do this, one simply locates a "worthless ledge," sinks a shaft, dumps some rich ore into it, and sells the claim "to a simpleton" (Twain 1872: 311). Ironically, the opposite is also true: some aspiring nabobs unknowingly sell "feet" in claims that turn out to be rich, and so – rather than unearthing a fortune – "drift back into poverty and obscurity again" (p. 325).

Twain wrote the latter half of *Roughing It* in a chastened narrative voice for the same reasons that he tamed some of the vulgar excesses of his *Alta California* letters before submitting the manuscript of *The Innocents Abroad* to his Eastern publisher. In a style that may be described as a reformed vernacular, the narrator in the latter chapters begins to identify with polite society and subtly condescends to the old-timers. As the salaried "city editor" of the *Territorial Enterprise*, he discards his mining clothes and his revolver for "a more Christian costume" (Twain 1872: 295). In the description of Buck Fanshaw's funeral, the narrator restages the coyote vs. town dog conflict, but with a difference: now the Western veteran is the buffoon. Fanshaw, a saloon-keeper and so a prominent citizen in Virginia City, commits suicide "in the delirium of a wasting typhoid fever." His friend Scotty Briggs, a "stalwart rough," arranges the "obsequies" with a minister, "a fragile, gentle, spirituel new fledgling from an Eastern theological seminary" (and so a figurative town dog), in a conversation that illustrates comically the difference between colloquial and genteel speech:

> ". . . one of the boys has gone up the flume –"
>   "Gone where?"
>   "Up the flume – throwed up the sponge, you understand."
>   "Thrown up the sponge?"
>   "Yes – kicked the bucket –"

"Ah – has departed to that mysterious country from whose bourne no traveler returns."

"Return! I reckon not. Why pard, he's *dead*!"

In the end, Fanshaw's funeral – complete with "plumed hearse," brass bands, and processions of secret societies, political officials, and military battalions – sets the local standard for such ceremonies. For "years afterward," the narrator reports, "the degree of grandeur attained by any civic display in Virginia was determined by comparison with Buck Fanshaw's funeral"(Twain 1872: 329–37). The fact that the narrator then says that in "after days it was worth something to hear the minister tell" this story (p. 330) suggests that he both gleans the tale from the minister and now identifies more with the polite classes than with the "stalwart roughs."

From this more polite perspective of the latter chapters of *Roughing It*, the narrator criticizes the unwashed masses and uncouth mob. Having been ambivalent about the outlaw Slade when en route to the West early in the book, he is now scathing about the corrupt elections and compromised juries endemic to the region, and here endorses vigilante justice without qualification. The jury system, he protests, has been perverted into "the most ingenious and infallible agency for *defeating* justice that human wisdom could contrive" (Twain 1872: 341). That is, it "puts a ban upon intelligence and honesty, and a premium upon ignorance, stupidity, and perjury" (p. 343). Qualified jurors – e.g. a minister, a mining superintendent, a quartz-mill owner – were routinely dismissed. Instead, the courts would impanel "two desperados, two low beerhouse politicians, three barkeepers, two ranchmen who could not read, and three dull, stupid, human donkeys!" (p. 349). As a result, as Twain ironically reports, "[t]rial by jury is the palladium of our liberties." Despite "dozens, perhaps hundreds" of murders in Nevada, "only two persons have suffered the death penalty there" (p. 351). The narrator's argument anticipates Judge Henry's argument in defense of vigilante justice in Wister's *The Virginian*:

> And so when your ordinary citizen . . . sees that he has placed justice in a dead hand, he must take justice back into his own hands where it was once at the beginning of all things. Call this primitive, if you will. But so far from being a *defiance* of the law, it is an *assertion* of it. (Wister 2002: 356)

In 1864 Twain moved to San Francisco from the Washoe, ostensibly because he was "tired of staying in one place so long" (Twain 1872: 398). During his first months there he enjoyed a "butterfly idleness" (p. 419) – or so he claimed. Fired for laziness from the San Francisco *Call*, however, in the next two months he "did not earn a penny, or buy an article of any kind, or pay my board. I became a very adept at 'slinking'" (p. 428) – a term, now used in a derogatory sense, reminiscent of the coyote's gait back in chapter 5. Eventually hired to tour Hawaii as a correspondent of the *Sacramento Union*, and launching out as a lecturer on his return, he becomes the target of a final indignity. Flush with the box receipts from his lecture in Gold Hill, he is accosted by a gang of highwaymen and robbed. To his relief, the "whole thing was a practical joke, and the robbers were personal friends of ours in disguise." But as a result of the chill in the air while he is "in a perspiration" he comes down with a "troublesome disease" which cost him "quite a sum in doctor's bills. Since then I play no practical jokes on people and generally lose my temper when one is played on me" (pp. 567, 569). Both the debunking narrative, and the narrator's experiences in the treacherous West, end with this resolution, as if to suggest he will never again be a dupe to illusion.

The increasingly popular "performed West" – plays such as Dion Boucicault's *Horizon* (1871) and Joaquin Miller's *First Families of the Sierras* (1876) – appealed primarily to vicarious tourists residing in the East and in Europe. Twain was eager to tap this market. He reminisced in his autobiographical dictation that Harte's Western melodrama *Two Men of Sandy Bar* (1876) "would have succeeded if anyone else had written it" (Twain 1940: 275). When Harte proposed in the fall of 1876 that they write a Western comedy together "& divide the swag" (Twain and Howells 1960: 157), they agreed to build the play around a minor character in *Two Men*, a Chinese laundryman. The result was the most disastrous collaboration in the history of American letters. The finished script was mostly Twain's, though neither writer ever included *Ah Sin* among his collected works, and for good reason – for even the tangled plot defies brief synopsis. The title character exists mostly in the margins of the story, which consists of the stock elements of melodrama. During rehearsals, Twain insisted to an interviewer that Charles Parsloe, the white actor who starred in the title role, "was a lost and wandering Chinee by nature" whose two front teeth were "just separated far enough to give him the true Mongol look" (Gath 1877: 438). As such a dubious claim to verisimilitude suggests, Twain's version of the "heathen Chinee" is a grotesque caricature, a thieving coolie. Despite his earlier sympathy for the long-suffering Chinese laborers in California, he mocks them in the play as a "moral cancer" and an "unsolvable political problem" (Twain and Harte 1961: 11). As Twain declared in his curtain speech in Washington on opening night, "The Chinaman is going to become a very frequent spectacle all over America, by and by, and a difficult political problem, too. Therefore it seems well enough to let the public study him a little on the stage beforehand" (quoted in Ferguson 1943: 269). Twain wrote Howells in August 1877 that the play was "a-booming at the Fifth Avenue" theater in New York (Twain and Howells 1960: 191), and Parsloe toured with the play in upstate New York in October. It closed, though, not with a bang but a whimper in Pittsburgh in November. To judge from reviews, the failure of the play had nothing to do with the characterization of the Chinese laundryman and everything to do with the weaknesses of its plot.

Twain revisited his satirical version of the West in his "Whittier birthday speech" in December 1877, apparently written to beat Harte – with whom he was feuding – at his own game. Stopping at "a miner's lonely cabin in the foothills of the Sierras," the narrator learns that he is the "fourth littery man" to visit within the past day. The others – Ralph Waldo Emerson, Henry Wadsworth Longfellow, and Oliver Wendell

Holmes – were, it turns out, drunken, flea-bitten tramps. Emerson "was a seedy little bit of a chap," Longfellow "was built like a prizefighter," and Holmes was "as fat as a balloon" (Twain 1992a: 695–9). They cheat at cards, attempt to steal their host's boots, and repeatedly misquote their own poetry. Though the speech became a *cause célèbre* because Emerson, Longfellow, and Holmes were all in attendance at the Brunswick Hotel, the controversy should not disguise a larger point: Twain presumed to ridicule the brightest stars in the American literary pantheon by casting them as low Western figures, much as he had ridiculed the sacred cows of the Forty-Niners in "The Pioneers' Ball." As ever, Twain demythologized the West, picturing it through a comic lens.

In the final chapter of *Huckleberry Finn*, Tom proposes to "go for howling adventures amongst the Injuns" (Twain 1885: 365). His idea becomes the premise of a little-known and critically neglected sequel to the novel, a fragment entitled "Huck and Tom Among the Indians," first published in 1989. Though narrated by Huck, the story is little more than a single strained joke about Indians. Here, the bookish Tom says that

> they're the noblest human beings that's ever been in the world . . . . [I]f an Injun tells you a thing, you can bet on it every time for the petrified fact; because you can't get an Injun to lie, he would cut his tongue out first . . . You take an Injun and stick him full of arrows and splinters and hack him up with a hatchet, and skin him, and start a slow fire under him, and do you reckon he minds it? No sir; he will just set there in the hot ashes, perfectly comfortable, and *sing*, same as if he was on salary. (Twain 1989: 35–6)

The remainder of the fragment is designed to puncture such positive ("noble savage") myths. Huck, Tom, and Jim (though he is soon written out of the story) meet a family moving west by wagon across the northern plains and befriend their daughter Peggy, another type of Becky Thatcher. When the company is unexpectedly attacked by Indians, most of the family is massacred, though Peggy is captured and carried away. Tom and Huck are joined in pursuit of Peggy by her fiancée Brace Johnson, an Indian-hater, the type of morally ambiguous stock character often featured in the fiction of William Gilmore Simms. The brief plot actually anticipates by some 70 years the John Ford movie *The Searchers*, with John Wayne in the role of Brace Johnson and Natalie Wood in the role of Peggy. More to the point, Huck finally asks Tom where he learned about Indians – "how noble they was and all that." Tom replies, "Cooper's novels" (p. 50). The fragment breaks off when Tom, Huck, and Johnson come across four stakes in the ground, evidence that Peggy has been gang-raped. Tom and Huck's dream of the pastoral West ends in atrocity and horror. Twain never resumed the narrative. How, indeed, could he?

In *Pudd'nhead Wilson* (1894), Twain not only exploits elements of the classical detective story in which the hero solves a mystery and unmasks the villain, but also anticipates the formula Western. Epitomized by Wister's *The Virginian* (1902), the Western is set, as John Cawelti explains, at a "point of encounter between civilization and wilderness, East and West, settled society and lawless openness" (1977: 193). In this symbolic setting on the cusp of civilization, the hero mediates or incarnates the tension between social order and anarchy. Dawson's Landing, where Twain's novel is set, is another version of Hannibal, on the western shore of the Mississippi, literally (at the date at which the novel is set) on that symbolic frontier. Pudd'nhead Wilson settles into a house "on the extreme western verge of the town" (Twain 1894: 27) that "looked westward over a stretch of vacant lots" (p. 30). He also mediates conflict as when, in these fields, he acts as Judge Driscoll's second in his duel with Luigi, a form of justice more medieval than modern (that is, executed most often in a state of nature). In that same space, too, the villain Tom Driscoll learns the secret of his birth in slavery, the illegality of his status as a gentleman, and the fiction of law that allows such crimes to occur. His mother Roxy reveals the secret in a haunted house "three hundred yards beyond Pudd'nhead Wilson's house, with nothing between but vacancy" (p. 112), before extorting money from him. It is this crime of patrimony that Wilson, both detective and Western hero, corrects by the end of the novel. He may resolve the conflict at court, rather than by gun-play (as in *The Virginian*), but make no mistake: Pudd'nhead maintains social order by siding with the agents of civilization and defeating the outlaw – and, like the Virginian, he is rewarded for his service with public acclaim and a promotion.

After leaving San Francisco in 1867 Twain returned to the city only once, to secure copyright of his *Quaker City* dispatches to the San Francisco *Alta California* and to write the first draft of *The Innocents Aboard*. He never went back to California again, not even when the itinerary of his North American lecture tour in 1895 took him to Portland, Seattle, and Vancouver. Significantly enough, however, the formal news of his bankruptcy was first reported in an interview with him in the San Francisco *Examiner*, no doubt as a favor to the interviewer, Twain's nephew Samuel Moffett, who worked for the paper. Still, it is somehow appropriate that the news was telegraphed to the world from the West. For this was where he had first "gone bust" (in the mines); where, too, he had launched his literary career, refined his style, and earned his first reputation.

References and Further Reading

Bellamy, Gladys (1950). *Mark Twain as a Literary Artist*. Norman: University of Oklahoma Press.

Branch, Edgar Marquess (1950). *The Literary Apprenticeship of Mark Twain, with Selections from his Apprentice Writings*. Champaign: University of Illinois Press.

Cawelti, John G. (1977). *Adventure, Mystery, and Romance*. Chicago: University of Chicago Press.

Coulombe, Joseph (2003). *Mark Twain and the American West*. Columbia: University of Missouri Press.

Ferguson, DeLancey (1943). "Mark Twain's Lost Curtain Speeches." *South Atlantic Quarterly* 2, 262–9.

Gath [George Alfred Townsend] (1877). "Mark Twain and his Chinaman." New York *Daily Graphic*, May 3, 438.

Harris, Helen L. (1975). "Mark Twain's Response to the Native American." *American Literature* 46, 495–505.

Harte, Bret (1870). *The Luck of Roaring Camp*. Boston: Fields, Osgood.

Harte, Bret (1992). *Bret Harte's California: Letters to the Springfield Republican and Christian Register 1866–67*, ed. Gary Scharnhorst. Albuquerque: University of New Mexico Press.

Krause, Sydney J. (1964). "The Art and Satire of Twain's 'Jumping Frog' Story." *American Quarterly* 16, 562–76.

Melton, Jeffrey Alan (2002). *Mark Twain, Travel Books, and Tourism: The Tide of a Great Popular Movement*. Tuscaloosa and London: University of Alabama Press.

Paine, Albert Bigelow (1912). *Mark Twain: A Biography. The Personal and Literary Life of Samuel Langhorne Clemens*, 3 vols. New York and London: Harper & Bros.

Smith, Henry Nash (1962). *Mark Twain: The Development of a Writer*. Cambridge, Mass.: Belknap/Harvard University Press.

Twain, Mark (1940). *Mark Twain in Eruption*, ed. Bernard DeVoto. New York: Harper & Bros.

Twain, Mark (1976). *Mark Twain Speaking*, ed. Paul Fatout. Iowa City: University of Iowa Press.

Twain, Mark (1989). *Huck Finn and Tom Sawyer among the Indians and Other Unfinished Stories*. Berkeley: University of California Press.

Twain, Mark (1990). *Mark Twain's Letters*, vol. 2: *1867–1868*, ed. Harriet Elinor Smith and Richard Bucci. Berkeley: University of California Press.

Twain, Mark (1995). *Mark Twain's Letters*, vol. 4: *1870–1871*, ed. Victor Fischer and Michael B. Frank. Berkeley: University of California Press.

Twain, Mark, and Harte, Bret (1961). *Ah Sin: A Dramatic Work*, ed. Frederick Anderson. San Francisco: Book Club of California.

Twain, Mark, and Howells, William Dean (1960). *Mark Twain–Howells Letters: The Correspondence of Samuel L. Clemens and William D. Howells, 1872–1910*, 2 vols., ed. Henry Nash Smith and William M. Gibson. Cambridge, Mass.: Belknap/Harvard University Press.

Wister, Owen (2002). *The Virginian*. New York: Simon & Schuster. (First publ. 1902.)

21

Mark Twain and Continental Europe

Holger Kersten

For nineteenth-century Americans, Europe was a fixed reference point in matters of history, culture, and politics. It represented the cultural richness of the past, but it was also a place that suffered from monarchic despotism, poverty, corruption, and other social and political ills. From this contrast emerged a basic ambivalence in which an appreciation of Europe's cultural treasures struggled with a scorn for what appeared to be an outmoded political system. Despite these shortcomings, however, the Old World exerted a fascination on a growing number of Americans who were attracted by unfamiliar scenery, strange customs, spectacular architecture, and other sights – to say nothing of the leisurely sea-voyage and the continental spas with their reputation for restoring good health. There were also those Americans who traveled to Europe in the hope of escaping, at least temporarily, from the restraints of nineteenth-century America's Victorian conventions. To them, Europe represented "diversity as contrasted with conformity, play as contrasted with work, pleasure contrasted with duty" (Dulles 1964: 4). All of these factors are mirrored in the career of Samuel Clemens, in whose personal life and literary endeavors Europe occupied an important place. From a young age, he was aware of and interested in European history; he visited the Old World and wrote travel books about it; he used European settings and characters in *The Prince and the Pauper*, *A Connecticut Yankee in King Arthur's Court*, and *Joan of Arc*, as well as in his short fiction and his essays; and his personal correspondence and notebooks are filled with observations and comments about Europe.

Although Clemens grew up in Hannibal, Missouri, a frontier settlement remote from the cultural centers of nineteenth-century America, he was not isolated from the Old World. Newspapers, periodicals, and especially the tremendously popular travelogues on Europe provided American readers with a steady flow of information about it (Thorp 1948: 830ff.). Even first-hand experience with Europeans was possible through encounters with immigrants, whom Clemens met almost everywhere he went in America.[1] Throughout his life, further information and insights about Europe came from friends and neighbors, many of whom were experienced travelers. Clemens's own immediate experience with the Old World started in 1867 when he boarded the *Quaker City* on its first pleasure cruise to Europe and the Holy Land. For him, it was the beginning of a series of trips to Europe that continued over the next 40 years.

From the *Quaker City*'s arrival in European waters on June 29 to its departure on October 25 from Cadiz (Spain), Clemens and the ship's passengers visited several European countries, most of them located on the Mediterranean. Their first stop was the French port of Marseilles (July 4), from where Clemens traveled the next day to Paris, where he remained until July 11. Having returned to Marseilles, the group reached Genoa, in Italy, on July 14. They remained in Italy until August 11, briefly visiting a number of cities including Milan, Venice, Florence, Pisa, Rome, and Naples. After a very short stop in Greece, where Clemens defied the quarantine regulations to pay a night-time visit to the Acropolis, the *Quaker City* continued its voyage to Constantinople (August 17–19), and then sailed on to Russia, with stops in Sevastopol (August 21), Odessa (August 22–24), and Yalta (August 25–28). The next stretch of the trip took them to the Middle East, the Holy Land, and Egypt. The party returned to Europe on October 13 for a brief stop in Cagliari, Sardinia, and spent the final days of the trip in Spain (October 18–25).[2]

In April 1878, Clemens returned to the European scene. In contrast to his first Old World trip, this was not a tourist excursion designed to cover as much territory as possible within a limited period of time, but a leisurely voyage with prolonged stays in Germany, Switzerland, and France. In Germany, Heidelberg (May 6–July 23) and Munich served as a base for visits to various places of interest, ranging from the immediate vicinity to more distant destinations. For four weeks (August 12–September 16) the Clemenses visited Switzerland, and then moved on to Italy for the fall (September 16–November 14), staying in Milan, Venice, Florence, and Rome. After spending the winter in Munich (November 15–February 27), Clemens and his family again changed quarters to Paris, where they lived from the end of February until July 10. Traveling for slightly more than a week (to July 19) through various Belgian and Dutch cities, including Brussels, Antwerp, Rotterdam, and Amsterdam, they reached the final destination of their European sojourn, England. Here they spent most of their time in London, but also visited the Lake District before finally boarding the steamer *Gallia* in Liverpool on August 23 to return to the United States.[3]

Financial pressures and health issues prompted the Clemens family to return to Europe in June 1891. Their first place of residence was France, where they spent about a month before visiting Germany and Switzerland briefly in August and September, returning to France in the fall to see Arles and Nîmes. From mid-October to the end of February 1892 they lived in Berlin, a stay that afforded Clemens the honor of dining with the German emperor, William II. April and May were spent traveling through the south of France and Italy before the family settled in Nauheim, Germany, while Clemens briefly returned to the United States for business. After his return to Europe, the family found convenient accommodation near Florence, where they lived for more than seven months (from late September 1892 to mid-June 1893). During most of 1893 and 1894, the Clemens family made their residence in different European cities, among them Berlin, Munich, Rouen, and Paris, but Clemens's never-ending financial troubles at home required him to travel back to the United States several times. Sometimes members of the family accompanied him on these trips, but more often than not they remained behind. In May 1895 Clemens and his family briefly returned to the United States together before he, Livy and Clara took off on Clemens's world lecture-tour.

When the global tour ended in October 1896 (and after the tragedy of daughter Susy's death), Clemens and his family decided to remain in Europe. In late July 1897 they moved from England to Switzerland to spend the summer in the little town of Weggis before continuing on to Vienna in late September. Vienna's newspapers proudly announced Clemens's arrival and quickly turned him into a local celebrity: "The Clemens apartments at the [Hotel] Metropole were like a court, where with those of social rank assembled the foremost authors, journalists, diplomats, painters, philosophers, scientists, of Europe, and therefore of the world" (Paine 1912: 1052). At the end of May 1898 the Clemenses moved into a summer house in the village of Kaltenleutgeben, whence they returned to Vienna for another prolonged stay from mid-October 1898 to May 26, 1899). After a series of brief visits to Budapest (March 23–29) and Prague (May 26–30), the health of their youngest daughter, Jean, prompted them to seek special treatment for her, first in London and then in Sanna, Sweden, where the family arrived in early July 1899. Here, where they stayed until September, Clemens developed an intense enthusiasm for Sweden's sunsets: "America? Italy? The tropics? They have no notion of what a sunset ought to be. And this one – this unspeakable wonder! It discounts all the rest" (Paine 1912: 1088). They spent the remainder of their extended European sojourn in London before returning to the United States in October 1900.

Not quite four years later, Clemens and his family returned to Europe yet again. Ten years after their pleasant stay in Italy, the Clemenses decided in October 1903 to go back to Florence, vainly hoping to improve Olivia's failing health. Her death, on June 5, 1904, marked the end of Clemens's European sojourns, although he did return to the Old Continent once more in the summer of 1907 – to receive an honorary degree from Oxford University.

This brief summary of biographical facts regarding Clemens's travels to the Old World shows that his experience in Europe was extensive and varied. He set foot in all three countries that a contemporary had described as the "leading nations of Europe, – the French, the English, and the German" (Anon. 1861: 548) and he also caught glimpses of "minor" European destinations. He gave little attention in his commentaries to Spain, visited during the *Quaker City* cruise, though he spent seven days traveling through the country with stops in Seville, Cordova, Cadiz, and a number of villages in Andalusia. What he saw on this excursion remains unknown, since none of the impressions gathered there were ever published: "The experiences of that cheery week were too varied and numerous for a short chapter," explained the narrator of *The Innocents Abroad*, "and I have not room for a long one. Therefore I shall leave them all out" (Twain 1869: 637). As noted above, a quarantine during the *Quaker*

City's stopover in Greece reduced Clemens's opportunities for sightseeing to a clandestine visit to the Acropolis. Despite this very limited exposure to Greece, the narrator describes the country as "a bleak, unsmiling desert," and its people as living in "poverty and misery" (p. 370). Belgium and Holland, on the other hand, two countries which Clemens saw in the final days of his 1878–9 European sojourn, left a more positive impression on him. A notebook entry characterized Brussels as "a dirty, beauful [*sic*] (architecturally) interesting town," and the organ music he heard at the local cathedral impressed him as "majestic." In the Netherlands, a country "so green & lovely, & quiet & pastoral & homelike," Clemens recorded enjoyable sights and registered the appealing nature of the country, with its cleanliness, "lovely country seats," and attractive girls (Twain 1975b: 328ff.).

While Spain, Belgium, and the Netherlands were only summarily treated in Clemens's travelogues, his longer sojourns in France, Italy, Germany, Switzerland, and Austria gave him more opportunities to observe the national customs and comment on the inhabitants' life as it appeared to him.

Clemens's first encounter with France and its people came during his Mediterranean cruise in 1867, when he visited Marseilles and spent nearly a week in Paris. His initial impressions were positive. He enjoyed the sights and "was impressed by French precision, neatness, and the beauty of the land culture, and people" (Rasmussen 1995: 300). The narrator in *The Innocents Abroad* spoke of the "noble city of Marseilles" (Twain 1869: 93) and "magnificent Paris" (p. 112). Even the French emperor made a positive impression on him: Napoleon III was "the representative of the highest modern civilization, progress, and refinement" (p. 126). But although the narrator exclaimed in ecstasy, "Verily, a wonderful land is France!" (p. 113), readers can never be fully convinced that the rapture was genuine. The comments on "extravagant honesty" (p. 113), the disillusioning and painful experience at the barber's shop (pp. 114ff.), the "harmless and unexciting" wines (p. 116), the annoying experience with a guide (p. 123), and the encounter with the Cathedral of Notre Dame, "the brown old Gothic pile . . . clustered thick with stony, mutilated saints" (p. 130), raise doubts about how deep the admiration and enthusiasm really were.

Clemens had an opportunity to renew his acquaintance with France during his second extended European visit in 1878–9. His letters and notebooks covering the period of his sojourn in Paris from February through mid-June 1879 show an intensive mental engagement with the country. In his attempt to compose *A Tramp Abroad*, his forthcoming travel book and second travelogue about Europe, Clemens produced a significant number of manuscript pages dealing with France but ultimately decided not to use them. For reasons that are not entirely clear, Clemens was developing a strong distaste for French morality. Experiencing the "cancan" for the first time, the narrator in *The Innocents Abroad* had simply stated that "French morality is not of that straight-laced description which is shocked at trifles" (Twain 1869: 136). The 1879 notebook, however, did not employ such diplomatic rhetoric, containing sentences such as " 'Tis a wise Frenchman that knows his own father" (Twain 1975b: 309), "France has usually been governed by prostitutes," and "France has neither winter nor

summer nor morals" (p. 318). To Clemens, France appeared as a "nation of savages"
(p. 321), and not even the French language was exempt from his diatribes: "It is the
language for lying compliment," he noted, "for illicit love & for the conveying of
exquisitely nice shades of meaning in bright graceful & trivial conversations"
(p. 320).[4]

Despite his negative attitude, Clemens returned to France on several occasions. In
June 1891 he and his family passed through Paris on their way to Aix-les-Bains, a
health spa which helped soothe Clemens's rheumatic pain. He praised the beneficial
effect in "Aix, the Paradise of the Rheumatics," but said nothing to revise his former
and probably persisting rejection of the French way of life. Other brief trips that same
year provided opportunities for the Clemens family to visit Arles and Nîmes, and in
March 1892 they spent three weeks in Menton, a resort town on the Mediterranean
(Rasmussen 1995: 156). The fragment "Down the Rhone" came out of his travel to
the south of France, but went unpublished until after Clemens's death (when it
appeared in the collection *Europe and Elsewhere*). It contains nothing substantial about
France or the French: just a few complaints about unsatisfactory cream, dark wall-
paper, and houses built of stone which, according to Clemens, breed "melancholy
thoughts in people used to friendlier and more perishable materials of construction"
(Twain 1963: 604). In the mid-1890s he returned to France once more, spending most
of his time in Paris, but none of his impressions found public expression in any of his
writings.

Despite Clemens's five visits to Italy, which added up to more than a year and a
half of his life, the country does not figure largely in his writings. Two humorous
essays, "Italian without a Master" and "Italian with Grammar," describe the narrator's
strenuous efforts to deal with the Italian language (Twain 1906: 171–85, 186–96).
The most comprehensive treatment of selected sights in Italy came out of his brief
initial encounter with the country during the *Quaker City* cruise, although the months
spent in Italy in 1892–3 and 1903–4 must have familiarized him much more fully
with Italian life and culture.

Clemens's attitude toward Italy is not easily summarized. Although he found a
great deal to like there, he was of two minds about Italians (Scott 1969: 55). The passages dealing with the different Italian cities the *Quaker City* tourists visited create an
incoherent picture. Genoa, their first stop in Italy, struck the narrator as "a stately
city" with attractive people and unusually beautiful women (Twain 1869: 160).
Immediately afterwards, however, the narrator qualifies his praise by pointing out that
"the palaces are sumptuous inside, but they are very rusty without" (p. 162). His
reports on Genoa epitomize another pattern to be found in his reports about the Old
World – his interest in the new, for items that signaled material progress and technological advance. Railroads and highways captured his attention much more than
the well-known cultural treasures of the countries he visited (Ganzel 1968: 128).

Clemens's narrator did not shy away from mentioning the aspects of Italy that
struck him as unpleasant. He found "deformity and female beards . . . too common in
Italy to attract attention" (Twain 1869: 199). More important was his political obser-

vation regarding the clash between the splendor of the church buildings and the poverty of the mass of the people: "for fifteen hundred years, [Italy] has turned all her energies, all her finances, and all her industry to the building up of a vast array of wonderful church edifices, and starving half her citizens to accomplish it," the narrator commented, adding a sweeping generalization, "She is to-day one vast museum of magnificence and misery . . . It is the wretchedest, princeliest land on earth" (p. 258). His encounter with Italian art triggered a similar response. For Clemens, these artworks were a constant reminder of a strictly hierarchical society that cared little for the average citizen but benefited the rich and the mighty, regardless of their moral record. The narrator deplored the connection between the immoral and exploitative aristocratic patrons of art and the dependent artists who sold their talent to them: "I keep on protesting against the groveling spirit that could persuade those masters to prostitute their noble talents to the adulation of such monsters as the French, Venetian and Florentine Princes of two and three hundred years ago" (p. 260).

Venice did not live up to this American traveler's expectations either. "This Venice," he stated, "is fallen a prey to poverty, neglect and melancholy decay" (Twain 1869: 217). His remark may have reflected the actual state of affairs in Venice at the time, but it may also have been influenced by the time constraints that marred the visit. Under pressure to write about five thousand words a day for the travel letters to be sent to the *Alta California*, he simply may not have had enough leisure to indulge in the beauty of the city (Ganzel 1968: 143). This, and a host of other factors, prevented Clemens from producing a comprehensive written record documenting what he saw and how he reacted toward it. The gaps in his reporting do not necessarily reflect a lack of interest in, or an attitude of indifference toward, the sights that were there to be admired. Similarly, it was the loss of letters and notebooks containing detailed information on Florence and Rome, rather than Clemens's supposed impatience with the treasures of art upon which their reputation rested, that led to an inadequate representation of these cities in *Innocents Abroad*. The loss of notes taken to keep track of the many sightseeing opportunities was particularly unfortunate because the *Quaker City*'s tight schedule produced such a quick succession of impressions that it was hard to remember the numerous events with sufficient precision in the absence of such *aides-memoires*. After a full day of sightseeing the sensory overload produced disorienting psychological effects at night: the travelers went to bed "with drowsy brains harassed with a mad panorama that mixes up pictures of France, of Italy, of the ship, of the ocean, of home, in grotesque and bewildering disorder" (Twain 1869: 201).

Of the various places Samuel Clemens visited in Europe, the German-speaking countries had the most profound impact on him. For one thing, his life in America had provided many opportunities for contact with German immigrants and German Americans. Additionally, he had prepared for his sojourn in Germany and Austria many months before his departure on the 1878 trip by taking German lessons and collecting information about the place that would become his temporary home. As a result, he knew much about the country, its people, and its culture before he set foot on German soil for the first time.[5] The most comprehensive literary record of his sojourn in Germany is *A Tramp Abroad*. However, while this book contains the largest number of pages written about the subject, it is not a comprehensive rendition of the impressions and experiences gathered during the 1878–9 visit. Clemens saw different regions and visited various cities in Germany, but his travel account concentrates on Heidelberg and the Neckar region. Despite this limited scope, the prospectus produced to advertise the new publication informed potential buyers that *A Tramp Abroad* was "a gossipy record of the author's pedestrian tour through Germany and other parts of Europe." Calling Clemens "perfectly familiar with the whole country he visited and the people he met," it cast him as an expert on German affairs.[6]

Readers who took seriously Twain's direct reference to *The Innocents Abroad* in an interview given to reporters in New York City (in which he said that the new book was "entirely solemn in character, like the 'Innocents Abroad,' and very much after the general plan of that work" [Budd 1982: 50]) might have been disappointed by the way in which *A Tramp Abroad* differed from its predecessor. The "Mark Twain" in this latter book limited his observations to the more or less traditional pattern of the American travel account on Europe, focusing mainly on the landscape and the people. According to the narrator's view, Germany, in the summer, was "the perfection of the beautiful" (Twain 1880: 126). He spoke positively about the German people, who appeared to him "warm-hearted, emotional, impulsive, enthusiastic, their tears come at the mildest touch, and it is not hard to move them to laughter" (p. 93). The numerous remarks about the German language, both in the travel account and in the appendix, "The Awful German Language," testify to the interest Clemens took in it. While learning German was portrayed as a frustrating endeavor for the narrator, the language itself received praise for its expressiveness. It was deemed "surpassingly rich and effective" in words which describe pathos, love, home life, outdoor nature, and the creatures and the marvels of fairyland (p. 615). The seriousness of this statement is borne out by the fact that the German language occupied a special place in the life of the Clemens family: they organized a German-language class in their Hartford home, their children were partially reared by German nursemaids, and Samuel Clemens wrote affectionate notes to his wife and children in German (see Kersten 1998: 203–4). The last entry in his notebook was in German (Hill 1973: 265), and when, on the occasion of his wife's burial, he chose what was perhaps one of the most meaningful phrases of his life, he determined to express his final benediction in German.[7]

While the impressions recorded in *A Tramp Abroad* convey a very incomplete picture of Germany in the late 1870s, Clemens's notebooks indicate that he was paying attention to a broad range of issues of current and historical interest, including political events and questions of social importance. Ultimately, however, his notes must have appeared too provocative to him to be included in the final version of the book. There was no way for Clemens to publish in print what he wrote privately in a letter to W. D. Howells: namely, that the German empire, ruled by Bismarck's strong hand, impressed him with its prosperity, its "genuine freedom," and its "superb government" (Twain and Howells 1968: 109).[8] It also seems doubtful that many of his countrymen would have appreciated seeing Emperor William I, the personification of the German monarchy, equated with Abraham Lincoln, America's foremost democratic hero. Clemens, however, apparently thought nothing of mentioning the two men in the same sentence: "It is worth something to be a Lincoln or a Kaiser Wilhelm," he wrote to Bayard Taylor, "and it gives a man a better opinion of the world to see it show appreciation of such men – & what is better, love of them" (Schultz 1936: 49).

Such comments grew out of Clemens's increasing dissatisfaction with America. If Clemens had ever had an unequivocal sense of America's superiority over the Old World, by the late 1870s it was crumbling. At this point in his life, America did not live up to its claim to be the land of the free, the antipode to a Europe governed by ruthless autocrats. In fact, to him, political freedom in the United States seemed weaker than anywhere else in the world. "[W]e are ruled by a King just as other absolute monarchies are," he wrote in a fragment of the *A Tramp Abroad* manuscript. "His name is The Majority . . . Our King rules with a rod of iron. Ours is an Absolute Monarchy" (Scott 1969: 96–7). Such a belief made it difficult to produce the "sharp satires on European life" Howells had encouraged him to write (Twain and Howells 1968: 120). Without a sense of America's moral superiority, it was pointless to criticize Europe's political system. Ultimately, however, Clemens decided not to include any of these powerful and explosive statements in the travel book he was writing, mainly for economic reasons. Any hint of what might have been construed as an unpatriotic position would certainly have harmed his reputation, his popularity, and, by extension, his economic success as a writer. Consequently, his narrator retained the role of an inoffensive observer engaged in a private pedestrian tour.

Clemens and his family returned to Germany in 1891–2. But despite the fact that he came into contact with a significant number of prominent people, including the Prince of Wales and the German emperor, the literary record of this sojourn is limited to a few articles written for the New York *Sun* (Scott 1969: 171–2). "The German Chicago" was a journalistic piece devoted to Berlin, painting a positive picture of life in that city. "At the Shrine of St. Wagner" described his visit to Bayreuth, the site of the Wagner music festival. And "Marienbad, a Health Factory," prompted by his visit to this well-known Bohemian spa, collected a variety of general, rather disconnected impressions gathered during his time there.

The 1878–9 European sojourn also included a stay in Switzerland: the first of three visits to this country which added up to a total of approximately four months spent in its different towns and villages. The most detailed literary reflection on Switzerland is found in the second half of *A Tramp Abroad*. Most of the chapters dealing with the experiences of the protagonist and his traveling companion, however, consist of burlesque adventures in the mountains. The reader finds few specific comments on life in Switzerland, and no political remarks at all. Although the narrator described the country as "simply a large, humpy, solid rock, with a thin skin of grass stretched over it" (Twain 1880: 483), the tone of the chapters conveys a sincere enthusiasm for Switzerland's impressive peaks, beautiful valleys, lakes, rivers, and waterfalls.

Clemens's next visit to Switzerland, in 1891, found a brief reflection in a letter he wrote for the New York *Sun*. The title of the piece, "Switzerland, the Cradle of Liberty," announced a political focus but, very much like the other travel letters written during this period, it simply strung together a series of more or less unrelated observations. The introductory section, however, does emphasize the exemplary character of the Swiss political system: "It is healing and refreshing to breathe in air that has known no taint of slavery for six hundred years," Clemens wrote, distinguishing Switzerland from the neighboring monarchies. The high degree of morality he observed there emerged, he concluded, from the fact that political struggles in this country had always been "in the interest of the whole body of the nation, and for shelter and protection of all forms of belief." Such moral rectitude, the letter-writer thought, was "worthy to be taught in schools and studied by all races and peoples" (Twain 1963: 111).

The last of Clemens's three visits to the Alpine republic occurred in 1897 and took the writer and his family back to Weggis, where he worked on a number of unfinished projects. None of them dealt with the village, or with Switzerland. That he enjoyed the sojourn, however, is clear from the letters he wrote to his friends in America. He told his Hartford friend Joseph Twichell that Weggis was "the charmingest place we have ever lived in for repose and restfulness" (quoted in Paine 1912: 1045). Despite this positive environment, Clemens's literary endeavors did not progress much. None of the four or five books he was working on at the time was completed. Perhaps the limited social life led to a feeling of frustration and prompted him to complain that beautiful Weggis "was wasted on the 'ignorant, poor, good-hearted jabbering animals' who lived there" (Scott 1969: 232).

At the end of September 1897 Clemens and his family left Weggis for Austria, where they would stay for 22 months. In contrast to the quiet atmosphere in Switzerland, life in Vienna put him in touch with a large number of prominent public figures. He enjoyed the hospitality extended to him by the Austrian aristocracy, the attention that was lavished upon him by Vienna's diplomatic community, and the intellectual stimulation that came from his contacts with prominent journalists, literary authors, and other celebrities. It may have flattered him and thus contributed to his general appreciation of life in the Austrian capital that Vienna lionized him to such an extent that he became "a privileged character" there (Paine 1912: 1051). The time Clemens spent in Vienna was a tonic that helped him overcome the disappointments and emotional pressures that had marred the previous years. Much of what he saw there fed his intellectual curiosity and stimulated his thinking and writing in a variety of ways. Some of his experiences may have alerted him to new subject matter, new ideas, new ways of looking at life; others appealed to him because they confirmed, reinforced, or expanded ideas he himself had nourished for some time (Dolmetsch 1992: 15). At any rate, it was a period full of creative energy, a time in which Clemens wrote more prolifically than in almost any other phase of his long career, although little of what he composed during this period was published during his lifetime.[9]

The time spent in Austria was undoubtedly an inspiration to Clemens, and yet few of the ideas and thoughts spawned there relate to or reflect his actual sojourn in Vienna and Kaltenleutgeben. There were occasional journalistic pieces that described and commented on contemporary issues (e.g. "Stirring Times in Austria" and "The Memorable Assassination"). The setting of *No. 44, The Mysterious Stranger*, it is true, is medieval Austria, and its themes were doubtlessly influenced by the Viennese background (Dolmetsch 1992: 297); but it is not a story about Austria or Austrians. It is, rather, "a psychic adventure, a journey into the deeper mind and beyond" (see Twain 1982:). Nothing of what Clemens wrote in Austria is comparable to the type of travel description supplied in *The Innocents Abroad* and *A Tramp Abroad*.

Regardless of how intensely European scenes and events found their way into Samuel Clemens's writing, there can be no doubt that his exposure to Europe had a significant influence on him. In official statements, however, Clemens tried to downplay its impact, and he tended to repeat what his narrator had stated in the conclusion to *A Tramp Abroad*: "Europe has many advantages which we have not, but they do not compensate for a good many still more valuable ones which exist nowhere but in our own country" (Twain 1880: 580). The underlying notion that, for Clemens, life in America was preferable to that in Europe has become a widely accepted truth in Twain scholarship. Recently, Jeffrey Melton has refreshed the image of Clemens as an irreverent traveler: "Touring eastward in *The Innocents Abroad* and *A Tramp Abroad*," he writes, "Mark Twain repeatedly snubs the grandiose pretensions of the cultures he encounters." But if Samuel Clemens was convinced of "the failure of the Old World civilizations" (Melton 2002: 59), the question remains why he returned to them so often.

The reasons why Clemens went to Europe were always complex. To some extent, the journeys leading to the writing of *The Innocents Abroad* and *A Tramp Abroad* were motivated by a professional impulse. The *Quaker City* excursion seemed attractive because it promised "a vast amount of enjoyment for a very reasonable outlay" (Twain 1975a: 301) and because such a trip was supposed to make it easier for the aspiring author to earn his living as a writer of travel letters for the San Francisco *Alta California* (Ganzel 1968: 7–8). The second trip to Europe was also undertaken in the hope of stimulating his literary creativity. The plan to write a new book for the subscription market obviously had a financial dimension, and it tied in with Clemens's desire to economize: "We are in Europe mainly to cut down our expenses," he explained in a letter to Mary Mason Fairbanks (quoted in Kaplan 1966: 213). Psychological reasons may also have played a role in his decision to put some distance between himself and his homeland (and particularly his feelings of guilt and humiliation following the Whittier birthday dinner). This combination of economic and psychological pressures may have affected Clemens's mood in such a way that he saw going to Europe as an escape and a liberation. "Life has come to be a very serious matter with me," he wrote his mother in early 1878 (Twain 1920: 177), and he gloomily recorded the hope that his absence might numb his pain: "To go abroad has something of the same sense that death brings," he wrote in his notebook, "I am no longer of ye – what ye say of me is of no consequence" (Twain 1975b: 64). This general feeling of frustration may explain an even more striking entry in his notebook: "One feels so cowed, at home, so unindependent, so deferential to all sorts of clerks and little officials, that it is good to go and breathe the free air of Europe and lay in a stock of self-respect and independence" (p. 56).

That he associated freedom and independence with Europe was an indication that Clemens's opinion of his home country had reached a low point in the late 1870s. How else could such a comment be explained in America, whose self-definition hinged on the idea that it was, in contrast to Europe, "the land of the free"? In Europe "man is a ward under guardianship," an anonymous reviewer had written in 1861, "a pupil under discipline at school, a pauper to be cared for, a vagabond to be put in the pound, a thing to be looked after and watched; but not a man who can take care of himself, provide for his own safety and interests, and get his own living generally" (Anon. 1861: 539). But none of these received notions about personal and political freedom seemed valid for Clemens at this stage of his life. He evidently wanted to put some distance between himself and the daily hassles and cares of his life in Hartford, and he looked for a way to vent his frustration and disillusionment with America. Europe seemed to be the environment in which he might achieve this.

The contrast between Clemens's public statements about the advantages of life in America, on the one hand, and the privately held view that something was seriously wrong with his country, on the other, points to the ambivalence that is ubiquitous in his writings about Europe too. His depiction of Europe and his attitude toward it cannot be easily summarized and categorized. More than once the voices represented in his books admitted that it was impossible to give an adequate rendition of impressions collected abroad. The full travel schedule of the first European tour led to bodily and mental exhaustion which affected the traveler's capacity for perception and evaluation. "How the fatigues and annoyances of travel fill one with bitter prejudices sometimes!," exclaimed the narrator in *The Innocents Abroad*, going on to point out the arbitrary nature of single impressions: "I might enter Florence under happier auspices a month hence and find it all beautiful, all attractive" (Twain 1869: 247). In *A Tramp Abroad*, the narrator conceded that much of what he had written might actually be incorrect. Comparing notes with his travel companion, he noticed "that each of us by observing and noting and inquiring, diligently and day by day, had managed to lay in a most varied and opulent stock of misinformation" (Twain 1880: 165). Even in his antipathy toward the French, Clemens admitted that the narrow basis for statements about things seen in a foreign country militates against a definitive truth: "I generalize with intrepidity from single instances," he wrote in his notebook. "When I see a man jump from the Vendome column, I say, 'They like to do that in France'" (Twain 1975b: 318).

Additionally, the time gap between the actual visit and the act of writing and revising influenced the rendition of things seen and events experienced. Whenever Clemens was unable to use the travel letters and notes from his European trip as a basis for the chapters he was writing because they had been lost, he found himself in a difficult situation. It was simply impossible for him to recreate the experience in his mind many months after the event. The conclusion to *The Innocents Abroad*, written a year after the *Quaker City* trip had ended, displays the narrator's awareness of the fact that the time elapsed between the original event and the literary account had mitigated the emotional response to the excursion: "I am moved to confess," the narrator says, "that day by day the mass of my memories of the excursion have grown more and more pleasant as the disagreeable incidents of travel which encumbered them flitted one by one out of my mind" (Twain 1869: 648).

It is also important to remember, despite the claim that *The Innocents Abroad* represents Europe seen freshly with the narrator's own eyes, that its composition and publication were heavily influenced by economic factors. "Every book [Twain] ever wrote," Kenneth Andrews stated, "was constructed with its prospective sale as the important condition of its composition" (Andrews 1950: 156–7). By Clemens's own estimate, the most profitable way to sell books was the subscription book market. In 1881 he explained that a subscription book "will sell two or three times as many copies as it would in the trade, and the profit is bulkier because the retail price is greater" (Twain 1999: 134). By calculating how he might address his books to the widest audience, he had to cater to the tastes of subscription book buyers – his financial success depended upon it. Against this background, his writing may be said to be as much a reflection of what he thought his audience wanted to read about Europe as a faithful rendition of his own observations.

As he found out to his dismay, his reputation as a humorist also circumscribed the range of his literary creativity: "Even when . . . he is in a serious mood and would like to talk sense on grave topics," one reviewer noted, "the despotic public won't let him." At the same time, Clemens's humor and his writing style left readers "at a loss to determine whether Mark is indulging in a vein of sarcasm, or whether he is fairly describing something that he really saw" (see Budd 1999: 190). Those familiar with the conventions of Western humor, however, would no doubt have noticed, and enjoyed, the "odd mixture of sober truth, droll exaggeration, and occasional buffoonery, all mixed up together in the most incongruous way" (Budd 1999: 191). This was, after all, his trademark style: layered, ambivalent, even self-contradictory. Stringing together incongruities and absurdities in a wandering and sometimes purposeless way, Clemens produced many vignettes which captured individual aspects of life observed in different European countries at different points in time – but this technique makes it difficult to extract an unambiguous image of Europe from the record he left behind. His writings were never intended to produce a coherent whole, and since they were produced over a long stretch of time, it is perhaps only natural that they changed and developed with the expanding mind of their author. Clemens knew that it was impossible to encapsulate the essence of a nation within the confines of a story, an essay, or even a book. "When a thousand able novels have been written," he declared, "there you have the soul of the people, the life of the people, the speech of the people; and not anywhere else can these be had. And the shadings of character, manners, feelings, ambitions, will be infinite" (Twain 1897: 188).

While it is beyond doubt that Samuel Clemens's writings contain critical remarks about the Old World, these self-conscious observations imply that his position toward Europe was too complex to be reduced to the single adjective "irreverent."

His substantial travel experience effectively undermined the notion that some people or nations might be superior to others. He realized early on that being exposed to other cultures did achieve an important effect in that it "rubs out a multitude of . . . old unworthy biases and prejudices" (Twain 1976: 35). Indeed, as time went on, Clemens became convinced that all humans, regardless of their national background, were equally corrupt. During his sojourn in Vienna, this conviction culminated in the conclusion that it was enough to know "that a man is a human being, . . . he can't be any worse" (Twain 1996b: 253–4).

In the final analysis, Europe was much more to Clemens than an easy target that allowed him to affirm a sense of American self-confidence. Considering that his periods in Europe were prompted by attempts to find the leisure for his literary endeavors, to improve his financial situation, and to restore the health of himself or other members of his family, one might suggest that he came to Europe in search of remedies for his artistic, economic, and health-related problems. For his career as an author, the Old World was a source of inspiration, suggesting settings, characters, and topics to be used in his writing. On a more abstract level, it may have offered him "a convenient staging ground for exploring his fears, desires, and ideas about women, men, and their relations with each other" (Stahl 1994: 177). In his private life, it was a tonic applied to bring about his own and his family's mental and bodily regeneration. It also provided him with a much-needed distance from his own country, allowing him to think about and express his reservations against life in America. Ultimately, traveling and living in Europe proved to be a formative element in Samuel Clemens's personal and literary life. Here he found both the leisure and the critical distance he needed to complement and balance his development as a person and a writer.

Notes

1 In *Life on the Mississippi*, Clemens claimed that during his training as a Mississippi pilot he "got personally and familiarly acquainted with about all the different types of human nature that are to be found in fiction, biography, or history" (Twain 1883: 217). His encounters with German immigrants and German Americans are documented in Kersten (1993).

2 For a detailed itinerary of the *Quaker City* trip see Twain (1996b: 392ff.).

3 Detailed information about the 1878–9 sojourn is supplied in Twain (1975b: 41ff.).

4 A portion of this material was later published under the title of "The French and the Comanches" (Twain 1962: 181–90). See also Twain (1975b: 323ff.).

5 See Kersten (1993, 1998).

6 Quotes from the prospectus of *A Tramp Abroad* (Mark Twain Papers, Bancroft Library, University of California, Berkeley; hereafter MTP).

7 The simple marker at Olivia Clemens's grave bears the inscription "Gott sei dir gnädig, O meine Wonne!" [God be merciful to thee, O my joy!]. See Paine (1912: 1223).

8 Even Clemens's nephew, Samuel Moffett, mentioned "Bismarck's gagging laws" in a letter to his mother: Samuel Moffett to Pamela Moffett, 21 March 1879 (MTP).

9 Among the projects he worked on were *What is Man?*, the *Mysterious Stranger* manuscripts, sections that would become part of his autobiography, portions of *Christian Science*, and "The Man That Corrupted Hadleyburg."

REFERENCES AND FURTHER READING

Andrews, Kenneth R. (1950). *Nook Farm: Mark Twain's Hartford Circle*. Seattle: University of Washington Press.

Anon. (1861). "Travel in Europe." *North American Review* 92: 191 (April), 529–51.

Budd, Louis J., ed. (1982). *Critical Essays on Mark Twain, 1867–1910*. Boston: G. K. Hall.

Budd, Louis J., ed. (1999). *Mark Twain: The Contemporary Reviews*. Cambridge, UK: Cambridge University Press.

Dolmetsch, Carl (1992). *"Our Famous Guest": Mark Twain in Vienna*. Athens: University of Georgia Press.

Dulles, Foster Rhea (1964). *Americans Abroad: Two Centuries of European Travel*. Ann Arbor: University of Michigan Press.

Ganzel, Dewey (1968). *Mark Twain Abroad: The Cruise of the "Quaker City"*. Chicago: University of Chicago Press.

Hill, Hamlin (1973). *Mark Twain: God's Fool*. New York: Harper & Row.

Kaplan, Justin (1966). *Mr. Clemens and Mark Twain: A Biography*. New York: Simon & Schuster.

Kersten, Holger (1993). *Von Hannibal nach Heidelberg: Mark Twain und die Deutschen*. Würzburg: Königshausen & Neumann.

Kersten, Holger (1998). "Mark Twain and the Funny Magic of the German Language." In David E. E. Sloane (ed.), *New Directions in American Humor*, 284–305. Tuscaloosa: University of Alabama Press.

Melton, Jeffrey Alan (2002). *Mark Twain, Travel Books, and Tourism: The Tide of a Great Popular Movement*. Tuscaloosa: University of Alabama Press.

Paine, Albert Bigelow (1912). *Mark Twain: A Biography. The Personal and Literary Life of Samuel Langhorne Clemens*, 3 vols. New York: Harper & Bros.

Rasmussen, R. Kent (1995). *Mark Twain: A to Z. The Essential Reference Guide to his Life and Writings*. New York: Facts on File.

Schultz, John Richie (1936). "New Letters of Mark Twain." *American Literature* 8: 1, 47–51.

Scott, Arthur L. (1969). *Mark Twain at Large*. Chicago: Regnery.

Stahl, John D. (1994). *Mark Twain, Culture and Gender: Envisioning America through Europe*. Athens: University of Georgia Press.

Thorp, Willard (1948). "Pilgrims' Return." In Robert E. Spiller, et al. (eds.), *Literary History of the United States*, 827–42. New York: Macmillan.

Twain, Mark (1920). *Letters of Mark Twain*, ed. Albert Bigelow Paine. London: Chatto & Windus.

Twain, Mark (1962). *Letters from the Earth*, ed. Bernard DeVoto. New York: Harper & Row.

Twain, Mark (1963). *The Complete Essays of Mark Twain*, ed. Charles Neider. Garden City, NY: Doubleday.

Twain, Mark (1975a). *Mark Twain's Notebooks and Journals*, vol. 1: *1855–1873*, ed. Frederick Anderson, Michael B. Frank, and Kenneth M. Sanderson. Berkeley: University of California Press.

Twain, Mark (1975b). *Mark Twain's Notebooks and Journals*, vol. 2: *1877–1883*, ed. Frederick Anderson, Lin Salamo, and Bernard L. Stein. Berkeley: University of California Press.

Twain, Mark (1976). "The American Vandal Abroad." In *Mark Twain Speaking*, ed. Paul Fatout, 27–36. Iowa City: University of Iowa Press.

Twain, Mark (1982). *No. 44, the Mysterious Stranger*, ed. John S. Tuckey. Berkeley: University of California Press.

Twain, Mark (1990). *Mark Twain's Letters*, vol. 2: *1867–1868*, ed. Harriet Elinor Smith and Richard Bucci. Berkeley: University of California Press.

Twain, Mark (1996a). "What Paul Bourget Thinks of Us" (first publ. 1898). In *How to Tell a Story and Other Essays*, 181–209. New York: Oxford University Press.

Twain, Mark (1996b). *The Man That Corrupted Hadleyburg and Other Stories and Essays*. New York: Oxford University Press. (First publ. 1900.)

Twain, Mark (1996c). *The $30,000 Bequest and Other Stories*. New York: Oxford University Press. (First publ. 1906.)

Twain, Mark (1999). *The Selected Letters of Mark Twain*, ed. Charles Neider. New York: Cooper Square.

Twain, Mark, and Howells, William Dean (1968). *Selected Mark Twain–Howells Letters*, ed. Frederick Anderson, William M. Gibson, and Henry Nash Smith. New York: Atheneum.

22

Mark Twain and Travel Writing

Jeffrey Alan Melton

In early June of 1867, while waiting to embark on America's first tourist cruise across the Atlantic, Mark Twain wrote his mother: "All I do know or feel, is, that I am wild with impatience to move, move – *Move*! Half a dozen times I have wished I had sailed long ago in some ship that wasn't going to keep me chained here to chafe for lagging ages while she got ready to go" (quoted in Twain 1990: 49–50). Frustrated by the problems specific to the departure of the *Quaker City* Pleasure Excursion, Twain here also betrays his growing eagerness to get on with his life. In his early thirties, unsettled personally and professionally, Twain was eager to "move," indeed.

The letter also carries a tone of self-reprobation for his tendency to misbehave while standing still, so his desire to get on with the cruise derives from both his wariness of the temptations of idleness and his failure yet to secure a sense of purpose to his life. Caught in the doldrums, little could he know that his passionate urge to "move" would eventually lead him not only to the four corners of the globe but also to a literary and cultural status far removed from the relative smallness of the mid-nineteenth-century Missouri of his youth. His restlessness would have been, like that of so many other young men, unfulfilled, however, had it not been for his ability to render his experiences attractive to readers worldwide. Mark Twain wanted to "move" out into the world; travel writing would allow him to claim his prominent place in it.

For readers in the late nineteenth century, Mark Twain was first and foremost a travel writer rather than a novelist. He earned the greatest patronage from his contemporaries not as the author of *Adventures of Huckleberry Finn* and *The Adventures of Tom Sawyer*, as most modern readers assume, but as the endearing narrator of *The Innocents Abroad*, his most popular work and the best-selling travel book of the century. He ultimately published five travel books: *The Innocents Abroad* (1869), *Roughing It* (1872), *A Tramp Abroad* (1880), *Life on the Mississippi* (1883), and *Following the Equator* (1897).[1] These popular narratives record an incomparable 30-year reign as America's premier traveling spokesperson.

It was no coincidence that Twain made such extensive use of the genre, but this choice of professional direction came about by fits and starts. Twain recognized that being a "roving correspondent" was profitable in the nascent days of his journalistic life in Nevada and California, but it was only after the runaway success of *The Innocents Abroad* that he fully understood the lucrative sales potential of travel books as decidedly separate from travel sketches. A writer of periodical travel pieces could make a living; a writer of travel books could make a career. In its first three years, *The Innocents Abroad* sold over 100,000 copies, just over 70,000 of them in the initial 12 months (Hill 1964: 39).[2] *Roughing It* sold over 76,000 copies in its first two years and 96,000 by 1879 (p. 63), and *A Tramp Abroad* sold 62,000 in its first year (p. 152). By comparison, *Life on the Mississippi* struggled somewhat, selling around 32,000 in its first year (see Twain 1967: 164).[3] *Following the Equator* sold between 20,000 and 30,000 copies in its first few months; this brisk pace, however, did not hold, and Twain was characteristically disappointed that the numbers were not significantly higher.[4] Twain insisted on subscription publishing for *Following the Equator* while simultaneously shifting to Harper's to publish *Personal Recollections of Joan of Arc* and other works, convinced that bookstore readers were "surfeited" by travel narratives but that the market remained strong among "the factory hands and the farmers" (Twain 1969: 249).[5] Perhaps he had finally overestimated the viability of the genre, its popularity stretched by a glut of travel books toward the century's close. Nevertheless, the consistently favorable reviews for *Following the Equator*, along with the lecture tour that served as its structural frame, ensured Twain's emergence from bankruptcy with an unprecedented and unparalleled status as a cultural icon. His repeated return to travel narratives throughout his career indicates in no uncertain terms his confidence in the genre and his ability to please readers. Despite the tendency of following generations to define his career primarily by the Mississippi River novels featuring Huck and Tom, readers of the late nineteenth century loved him most endearingly as the quintessential American on the move.

The Popularity of Travel Writing

No other genre of American literature enjoyed a greater popularity or a more enduring prominence in the nineteenth century than travel writing. Essential to the development of America's literary identity, the passion for traveling, both as tourist and as reader, touched most sectors of American life by the mid-nineteenth century. Curiosity about faraway lands, combined with the increasing availability of quicker and cheaper transportation, created a boom in foreign travel. Physically and economically, more Americans were able to travel abroad, and as the number of commercial and passenger ships sailing the Atlantic Ocean multiplied, so did the number of tourists who could afford to make the trip to the Old World. Christof Wegelin, in tracing the steady but undramatic rise in tourists from 1820 to 1849, points out how those numbers had exploded by 1860. US citizens returning yearly to Atlantic and Gulf ports, according to Wegelin, "rose from 1,926 to 2,659" in the three decades following 1820, but in 1860 the number returning to the four largest Atlantic ports alone amounted to 19,387 (Wegelin 1962: 307).[6] With the dramatic technical advances in steam-powered ships, voyages between the continents became commonplace. In *The United States Magazine and Democratic Review*, Henry Tuckerman noted, "steam is annihilating space . . . The ocean, once a formidable barrier, not to be traversed without long preparation and from urgent necessity, now seems to inspire no more consideration than a goodly lake, admirably adapted to a summer excursion" (Tuckerman 1844: 527). By the post-Civil War era, the travel contagion had become a full-fledged social upheaval. *Putnam's Magazine* observed:

> [I]f the social history of the world is ever written, the era in which we live will be called the nomadic period. With the advent of ocean steam navigation and the railway system, began a travelling mania which has gradually increased until half of the earth's inhabitants, or at least of its civilized portion, are on the move. (Anon. 1868: 530–1)

Indeed, Americans were "on the move" in unprecedented numbers, and as an inevitable result supply and demand economics gradually took hold as the industry and ancillary business ventures responded to public interest. For the first time in history, tourism was going mainstream, and traveling became associated with economic forces more often than aesthetic ones.[7]

The corresponding interest in travel literature swelled as well, both for readers who planned to make their own journeys and for those who simply wanted to gain the experience vicariously. Behind every actual tourist lurked hundreds more who were fascinated by reading travel books. In *Trubner's Bibliographic Guide to American Literature*, Benjamin Moran writes, "this would seem to be the age of *travel literature*, judging from the many narratives now published, and the general excellence of such works. No nation has given more good books of this class to the world since 1820 than the United States, considered with regard to styles or information" (Moran 1859: lvi). Sales figures encouraged writers and publishers to fill the seemingly insatiable demand aggressively, and the result was a plethora of travel texts with a wide array of points of interest and narrative styles. Harold Smith, whose *American Travellers Abroad: A Bibliography of Accounts Published before 1900* is the only attempt to provide a comprehensive listing of travel narratives, cites just under two thousand travel books published in the United States (Smith 1999). Although this number is astounding, it is actually quite conservative, since Smith excludes all books concerned with journeys made within the modern continental 48 states (whether or not the states existed as such at the time of publication), a body of narratives that constituted a substantial portion of the genre. Moreover, virtually all periodicals and newspapers featured travel sections that served as outlets for travel writers throughout the nation – Mark Twain, of course, being one of them.

Conventions of Travel Writing

Travel literature is a varied genre in which overlapping elements of journalism, autobiography, fiction, history, anthropology, and political analysis, among others, combine into a smorgasbord narrative. As a composite literary form, it resists neat categorization. It does, however, exhibit certain conventions that set it apart from other more focused forms of writing with which it shares characteristics.[8] In essence, travel writing is a nonfictional narrative form that evinces a strong sense of *self* and *place*. The travel book is a first-person account of the narrator's venture into the unknown, an experience from which he or she ostensibly learns. The form begs indulgence, as readers follow an outwardly personal journey that is physical, intellectual, and emotional all at once. The presence of a self-conscious narrator is the essential quality that separates a travel book from a guidebook, or from history or journalism proper. Yet the self has to go to some place to distinguish the narrative from memoir. The trip could be around the world or just down the road, as in Thoreau's *Walden*. The interaction between self-conscious, even self-absorbed, narrators and the realities or fancies of unfamiliar places creates narrative tension. Because travel writing offers an essential conflict between a narrative self and a foreign place, it allows modern readers a valuable window not only into a world of destinations but also into the psychological nuances of American tourists.

Twain readily accepted and even embraced standard travel-book formulas. But he was by no means simply a conventional writer. Rather, he chose often to manipulate expectations for his readers' entertainment and his own satirical interests. He thus achieves a tenuous balance between following form and snubbing it. Twain was an effective conventional writer in many ways; he incorporated established formulas into his narrative tours, and he dutifully fulfilled the standard obligations facing travel writers by offering instruction, amusement, and comfort to his readers at home. Such adherence by no means represents a lack of skill or interest; rather, it reveals a successful writer at work. William Dean Howells, in a review of *A Tramp Abroad*, captures the essence of Twain's effective use of convention:

> Every account of European travel, or European life, by a writer who is worth reading for any reason, is something for our reflection and possible instruction; and in this delightful work of a man of most original and characteristic genius "the average American" will find much to enlighten as well as amuse him, much to comfort and stay him in such Americanism as is worth having, and nothing to flatter him in a mistaken national vanity or stupid national prejudice. (Howells 1880: 688)

Although Howells sidesteps Twain's ability to "flatter" readers' national complacency, he correctly recognizes his craft, his remarkable balance, and his ability to fulfill the reading expectations of "the average American." The travel book is a specific genre that generated expectations among its readers, and, for them, conventions were both necessary and commendable. This is not to say, however, that these same readers could not respond favorably to fresh approaches. Twain developed the best of both approaches by carefully following certain patterns while also manipulating them to suit his humorous and critical inclinations. In so doing, he offered his contemporary readers familiar yet often innovative approaches to the art form, and his five travel books represent the work of a master travel writer who recognized the vagaries of a rapidly changing world.

His ability to work within and without conventional expectations served Twain well, but it was the holistic balance of self and place that drew forth his gifts. In short, travel writing was a perfect fit for Mark Twain, an inherently keen cultural observer. A travel writer can hold forth on just about anything and still be within the bounds of the genre, a freedom highly suitable to Twain. Richard Bridgman, in his insightful *Traveling in Mark Twain*, points out that the features of travel writing allowed Twain to tap into his native talent: "All that the form demanded Twain had in abundance: curiosity, a reactive intelligence, and stamina" (Bridgman 1987: 3). Bridgman explores how travel encouraged Twain's powerful associative ability, which in turn led him to produce his most compelling writing, fully exploiting the basic tenets of self and place. Likewise, in *Return Passages: Great American Travel Writing, 1780–1910*, Larzer Ziff, offering a strong overview of Twain's travel books, complements Bridgman by emphasizing Twain's personal recollections, noting that "travel writing was a perfect vehicle for Twain's imagination" (Ziff 2000: 174). What these critics and others reveal is Twain's ability to explore the world and his imagination in a consistently compelling way. This combination of observation and introspection informs his travel writing and records the tumultuous changes that catapulted a nation into prominence at the dawn of a modern age. Twain's five-book series thus provides a textured mosaic of Mark Twain's America, as well as of Mark Twain's world.

The Roving Correspondent

The master of late nineteenth-century American travel writing began inauspiciously with occasional sketches for a variety of newspapers. The apprenticeship helped him forge an early understanding of the potential of not only reporting about place but also creating a self. As a roving correspondent of sorts for the *Sacramento Union*, Virginia City *Territorial Enterprise*, and San Francisco *Alta California*, among others, Twain was able to dabble in travel sketches from time to time. His first significant break into the genre came from the *Union*, which sent him to the Sandwich Islands (as Hawaii was then known) from March until June 1866 to write a series of travel sketches. While on assignment, Twain produced 25 letters totaling around 90,000 words (see Twain 1966: x). He attempted to publish the letters in book form but was unable to secure a deal, which left the material available later for him to work into *Roughing It*.[9] The letters fulfill the basic demands of any travel writing, offering a wealth of information balanced by an engaging narrative voice. The most significant aspect of this narrative play is the use of "Mr. Brown," a persona that helped Twain toy with point of view and distance. Twain used Brown as a simple, sometimes vulgar, observer, and as such he provided cover for the author as he put down his coarser reactions to local custom and history.

Twain's second important series of travel letters recorded his return east to New York via Nicaragua, the assignment that would extend to his first and innovative travel book, *The Innocents Abroad*. Soon after returning from Hawaii, Twain contracted with the *Alta California* for travel letters from his trip to New York. This second series built on his successful experience in Hawaii and led directly to his signing on to the *Quaker City* Pleasure Excursion, thus enlarging his role as the paper's traveling correspondent and setting the stage for the full-length narrative to follow.[10] Twain continued to prove himself a keen observer, again using Brown as his skeptical sidekick. As Twain worked these letters into *The Innocents Abroad*, however, Brown receded. Juggling dual personas, manageable in short letters, now proved too distracting. With his power as an astute travel writer ascending, Mark Twain would carry the travel books on his own.

"A Brave Conception": *The Innocents Abroad*

In the preface to *The Innocents Abroad* Twain offers "no apologies for any departures from the usual style of travel-writing" (Twain 1869: 5), implying that his narrative does indeed take its own course. This implicit claim, however, itself bows to convention. *The Innocents Abroad* does serve as a watershed in the history of American travel writing – but for different reasons. As a "record of a pleasure excursion," the first transatlantic cruise, it marks the beginning of a new age, and neither Twain nor American tourism at large would be the same afterwards. Americans were moving onto the world stage, and they were eager to make an impression.[11] The actual tour, of course, changed Twain for ever, giving to him an opportunity that led to financial and literary status he could never have obtained as a sketch writer, journalist, or newspaper editor. *The Innocents Abroad* launched Mark Twain as a consummate travel writer who would construct an American perspective on the world, and place himself as its leading mouthpiece.

The excursionists on board the *Quaker City* began their tour on 8 June 1867, embarking on an itinerary Twain called "a brave conception" (Twain 1869: 20). Indeed, the trip's program was ambitious: a five-month tour around the Mediterranean Sea, with options for a variety of excursions into southern Europe, Asia Minor, the Holy Land, and Egypt. Although in the formal address to the Russian royal family, Twain – along with other members of the committee that drafted the address – described the tourists as "traveling simply for recreation," claiming that they did so "unostentatiously" (p. 403), the scheme was bold and showy. Much of the country followed the trip via his letters, along with those of other tourists on board, but it was *The Innocents Abroad* that would define the travelers' "brave" entrance into the world stage. It was successful, and Twain captured the overall confident mood of the "handful of private citizens of America" in his letter to the New York *Herald* (published 20 November 1867 and included in the book) upon the return of the *Quaker City*. Even though he likened the tour to a funeral without a corpse, Twain was certain that the tourists nonetheless impressed upon the people of the Old World that there was a new force to be reckoned with: "The people stared at us every where, and we stared at them. We generally made them feel rather small, too, before we got done with them, because we bore down on them with America's greatness until we crushed them" (p. 646).

Twain asserts nationalism throughout the tour, snubbing the grandiose pretensions of the cultures he encounters. He shows readers that the Old World, if viewed honestly through definitively American eyes, falls far short of common overblown expectations. A natural and logical theme of any travel book centers on the inevitable differences between expectations and realities, and Twain employs the disappointment caused by those variances as a touchstone throughout the tour. Although such descriptions are staples of travel writing, Twain's narrative captures a uniquely American reintroduction to the world. *The Innocents Abroad* became, as Fred Kaplan calls it, "a pilgrimage that touched on core issues of identity and belief" (Kaplan 2003: 195). Peter Messent concurs, noting that the narrative works "to debunk European cultural authority and, simultaneously, to define America's own cultural identity" (Messent 1997: 29). In this context, Twain's promise in his preface, to see with his "own eyes," stands as an assertive statement of nationality in the bustling aftermath of the American Civil War. The consistency of independent thought that permeates *The Innocents Abroad* illustrates Twain's reinvention of the American self as a defining participant in a new world order. Although the narrative offers much reverence and even sentiment – at Versailles, Athens, Jerusalem, and Egypt – its irreverence captivated readers and subsequent generations of critics. This says, and continues to say, as much for the needs of readers as it does for Twain's engaged response to the Old World with all of its grace and history, its ornaments and shams.

"Variegated Vagabondizing": *Roughing It*

If Mark Twain's travels to the Old World typify a quest for an American identity in contrast to antiquity, his follow-up narrative looks westward into the New World to establish an American identity in consort with destiny. In *Roughing It*, Twain consciously attempts to follow up *The Innocents Abroad* with a logical companion, "The Innocents at Home,"[12] yet the narrative does not derive from a specific, self-contained trip like the *Quaker City* Pleasure Excursion. Rather, it covers a series of "vagabondizing" adventures that occurred several years before the idea of the narrative itself emerged. It thus resembles memoir, influenced by nostalgia for the material on which it is based. Yet its final form reveals Twain's recognition of the narrative's qualifications, and thus its economic potential to the author, as a travel book proper. Twain specifically constructed and manipulated this autobiographical clay and molded it to fit the conventions of the genre, transforming memoir into travel book.

While built around the same travel-book formulas that worked so well in *The Innocents Abroad*, *Roughing It* remains a work of more distant memory, a text separated from the actual travels not by weeks or months, but by years. In July 1861 Twain had accompanied his brother, Orion, to Nevada, ostensibly to serve as his secretary. But Twain soon began dabbling in an assortment of activities to make money, and eventually stayed in the West for over five years. He had from this episode no body of published letters (other than the "Sandwich Islands" letters), nor any specific itinerary to provide an organizing framework for a travel book. Eager to relive the success of *The Innocents Abroad* – rather than to provide any exact recollection of Nevada and California – Twain fundamentally revised his material relating to his past life and presented it as a "pleasure excursion." Unique within Twain's travel-writing canon in its subject matter if not in its structure, *Roughing It* presents youthful meanderings remembered by the older, more settled man. Though it depends often on Twain's (and Orion's) partial reconstructions of distant travels, *Roughing It* is presented, nonetheless, as a conventional travel book. In constructing *Roughing It*, Twain was not so much nostalgic as shrewd in remaking his past into travel narrative, into a tour of the mythic West.

Here the same critical eye that skewered the pretensions of the Old World is applied to the New World. *Roughing It* captures the always confident and sometimes desperate American attempt to impose its self upon the promising but ultimately unforgiving landscape of the West. *Roughing It* offers a satirical look at how delusions of self and illusions of place work together to create a failure in America's manifest aspirations. Romantic expectations are created not by historical association but primarily, as Twain illustrates, by dreams of the future. Touring the Old World gave Euro-American tourists a glimpse into the past. Touring the West delivered a chance to make the future. Twain thus participated in the winning of the mythic West while demonstrating its deceptiveness, recording not so much a clear destiny as a chaotic present.[13] The result is a narrative that pretends to record an emigration wherein Twain attempts to transform himself into a local citizen, and re-enacts both the winning and the squandering of the West.

Twain claims in the preface that the book offers "information concerning an interesting episode in the history of the Far West" and, as he had with *The Innocents Abroad*, refers to his "eyes" for their honest perspective (Twain 1872: iv). This time, however, the eyes are those also of a man who was "on the ground in person" during the Nevada Silver Rush. As such, Twain becomes the prototypical American seeking his fortune on what would become wholly American soil. In a cautionary tale rife with comic failure, the fault lies not with the West but with the man who, in the end, proves to be of "'no account'" (p. 570). Despite the comic buffoonery of his "variegated vagabondizing," Twain's experience as defined within *Roughing It* makes one point absolutely clear. The West, as a place, was wide open to such rambling and would be subdued whether or not the men who did it were of any account at all. The process, however, would not be orderly, and Twain's constant struggles to define himself in the indeterminacy and tumult that was the West make an astute commentary on a land in transition. Only a travel book could provide the narrative space for Twain to imagine the variety and cacophony of the American West with such precision.

"The Spectacle": *A Tramp Abroad*

A Tramp Abroad is a natural extension of *The Innocents Abroad* as a travel narrative – a return to the Old World. Like *Roughing It*, it serves as another sequel. As a valuable cultural document, it is also a natural continuation of the expanding American presence in the Old World. In the eleven years that had elapsed since publication of *The Innocents Abroad*, both Twain and the United States had increased in confidence and influence, a change that Twain connotes in the movement from "innocent" to "tramp" in the title. Mark Twain returned to Europe and to the travel book out of professional necessity, eager to save money by living abroad and to make money by turning the experience into a travel book. After the auspicious beginning provided by his first two travel books, his career seemed stagnant, with disappointing sales from his fictional works *The Gilded Age* (1873, with Charles Dudley Warner) and *The Adventures of Tom Sawyer* (1876), and he needed to rejuvenate his image in the public eye.

In April 1878 Twain traveled to Europe on the *Holsatia* for a trip that would last 16 months. Among his fellow passengers was Bayard Taylor, arguably the only contemporary American travel writer who rivaled Twain in popularity. Taylor's first travel book, *Views A-Foot* (1846), was a runaway bestseller and, like Twain's, had established the beginning of a remarkable career. *Views A-Foot* recorded a two-year walking tour of Europe "with knapsack and staff." It is likely that Twain was making a bow to Taylor in his opening chapter in explaining his plan to walk across Europe. He used the adventurer context so endemic to Taylor's tramp as backdrop to his own, but the joke was that within the narrative Twain would rarely walk at all, avoiding such exercise with seeming indifference to the legitimacy of his actions (or lack thereof). This narrative frame also allowed Twain to further define the American impact in the Old World and reflect the new reality that Americans with money were remaking the cultural map of Europe.

A Tramp Abroad, unlike Twain's first foray into Europe, has no distinct itinerary, no grand program. There is nothing brave in its conception at all. Though for some readers the narrative suffers as a result of such lack of focus, the rambling structure does indeed accurately capture the changing emphasis for American tourists at large, a move away from *seeing* the world to *being* at the center of it. Twain's condition matches that of the nation on the whole – more settled, more affluent, more experienced. Twain returned to Europe with his own entourage, traveling the continent at will and always in comfort, a luxury paid for from his own pockets rather than those of the *Alta California*. Not surprisingly, the theme of expectation versus reality, so prominent in *The Innocents Abroad*, is practically nonexistent in its sequel. The focus, more often, is on Twain himself, the leisured tourist-artist, student of the German language, mountain-climbing adventurer. The satire and parody within the narrative, then, depend not on what he sees but on what he does (or fails to do). The "spectacle" in *A Tramp Abroad* is not Europe; it is Twain himself.

"A Standard Work": *Life on the Mississippi*

In a letter to his wife, Olivia (November 27, 1871), long before commencing on the narrative, Twain indicated his early plans for a book about the Mississippi: "When I come to write the Mississippi book, *then* look out! I will spend 2 months on the river & take notes, & I bet you I will make a standard work" (Twain 1995: 499).[14] Flush with renewed interest   in the Mississippi River of his childhood, Twain eventually returned as favorite son in April 1882 to tour for a month to gather material for his planned book. *Life on the Mississippi* was published a year later, in May 1883. Like *Roughing It*, *Life on the Mississippi* challenged Twain as a travel writer to explore a sense of self inextricably tied to place. Twain faced the difficulty of visiting his past in the process of creating a travel narrative; aspiring to see the life on the river as both tourist and native, he was attempting to inhabit two diametrically opposed selves. He would have been wise to take the excited statement from the letter to Livy – "look out!" – as a warning to the author who would undertake such a daunting task. *Life on the Mississippi*, a vital part of Twain's canon, has rewarded readers for generations, but the successes of the narrative, perhaps, derive from its distinctive character as a thoroughly nonstandard work.

As a result of the basic conflict within *Life on the Mississippi*, the narrative proves problematic also for readers, who must sense the ambivalence that often haunts their guide. The two mantras of the travel writer – *self* and *place* – are here taken beyond their normative constraints and contexts. As a result, the self – as tourist, as travel writer, as autobiographer, as historian – is confused from the beginning because it is unclear which voice should dominate. The fusion of past and present blurs the narrator's eyes throughout as Twain comes upon conflicting images from the Mississippi of 1882 to set against those of his own past, his own childhood.

The title itself, *Life on the Mississippi*, indicates the perspective within the narrative proper that will make this travel book unique in Twain's canon. Unlike his other travel-book titles, *Life on the Mississippi* does not foreground the tourist's perspective as the center and true subject of the text. This narrative does not derive from the eyes of an "innocent" or a "tramp"; it does not record Twain "roughing it" or "following the equator." Rather, this title focuses on the place itself and the "life" that defines it. As a result, *Life on the Mississippi* is intermittently both the most intensely personal of his travel books and the most passionless and distant. While readers are made well aware of Twain's emotional connection to this place, he rarely lets them into his various psyches for very long – not even through his use of comic forms – preferring to retreat frequently into the objective cover of the historian.

Twain is forced to take readers along not only on his journey down and up the river but also on his journey into the past and into the full meaning implied by the Mississippi River's history and culture. Therein lie both the beauty and the failure of *Life on the Mississippi*: Twain's heartfelt love for the river is not altogether sustainable within the theoretically objective historical account. All in all, Twain, perhaps aware of the dangers of simultaneously traveling to the river and writing a "standard" book about it, blends his two often competing impulses to generally good effect, producing an ostensibly dispassionate record spliced with highly personalized touches. It offers what a travel book in the nineteenth century should – that is, a little bit of everything. The general organization tells of his struggle in writing it. Twain does not provide a personal preface (as in *The Innocents Abroad* and *Roughing It*), nor does he include an authorial introduction and justification in the opening paragraphs of the first chapter (as in *A Tramp Abroad* and *Following the Equator*). *Life on the Mississippi* stands alone in omitting such travel-book conventions.

Life on the Mississippi is Twain's most personal travel book, but for many readers it is the most difficult to appreciate. The traveling narrator, with his conflicted perspectives mired in the past and flustered by the present, seems overwhelmed by the vastness of Mississippi culture and history and underwhelmed by how his own life fits within (and without) it. Chapter 4, "The Boys' Ambitions," is emblematic of Twain's ambivalence. In recounting how the townspeople of Hannibal in his childhood reacted to the arrival of a steamboat, Twain also provides an analogous appraisal of his identity in *Life on the Mississippi*: "Before events, the day was glorious with expectancy; after them, the day was a dead and empty thing" (Twain 1883: 63). The long-awaited "expectancy" of writing a standard work, of touring the Mississippi, of seeing his home again is initially thrilling. Disappointment, however, soon sets in and deflates his buoyancy. The autobiographer seems unable to face the changes caused by the ebb and flow of the mighty river, and the historian becomes distracted. Twain's only recourse is to his incomparable imagination, reassuring himself that "after all these years I can picture that old time to myself now, just as it was then" (p. 63).

The "Power of Thought": *Following the Equator*

Mark Twain ended his travel-writing career in much the same way as he began it, producing a successful narrative based on a highly publicized tour with a specific itinerary – a farewell tour for America's most popular travel writer. *Following the Equator* is Twain's most conventional travel book, in form and in tone, and it provides a fitting closing bookend to his canon. Almost 30 years after his initial astounding success, with *Following the Equator* Twain offered his readers yet another companion to *The Innocents Abroad*, illustrating for a final time his recognition of the vagaries and idiosyncrasies of the genre. Still, *Following the Equator* is in many parts the least readable of his travel books and never matches the humor and energy of its predecessors. It has comic moments, but its humor is more likely to garner a smirk or bemusement than the boisterous laughter evoked by the other books. As such, the narrative may be less like a formal closing to a century of "innocent" travel and more like a sad, if cynical, acknowledgment of what is to come: a watershed narrative marking an end to willful ignorance of the dark imperialistic context necessarily intertwined with all nineteenth-century travel writing.

In an ambitious effort to crawl out of bankruptcy, Twain left from Elmira, New York, in mid-July 1895, making a slow overland tour of America for a series of lectures, and setting sail for the south seas in late August from Vancouver. The main stopovers for the tour were New Zealand and Australia, India and South Africa. The writer finished the tour in England a year later, buoyed up by the tremendous level of adoration he had received throughout the journey but exhausted nonetheless. Added to the burden of producing a lengthy travel book under financial duress, Twain had to endure the tragic death of his eldest daughter, Susy, while he was in England. Not surprisingly, then, *Following the Equator* emanates a distinctively somber mood throughout, the humor too rare and too slight to lift it. He explained his struggle to William Dean Howells in April 1899:

> I wrote my last travel book in hell; but I let on, the best I could, that it was an excursion through heaven. Some day I will read it, & if its lying cheerfulness fools me, then I shall believe it fooled the reader. How I did loathe that journey round the world! – except the sea part and India. (Twain and Howells 1960: 690)

We cannot know if he ever read through *Following the Equator* with this point in mind, but the fact that he would characterize it as cheerful may simply describe that depth of his darkness at the close of the century.

This final narrative, in addition, is Twain's most ethically conflicted travel book. Twain could no longer ignore his inevitable connection to the misdeeds of an aggressively imperialistic culture and his complicity as a prominent tourist. As the travel writer, he could no longer salvage such experiences in anodyne words. If there was no social or political escape from the imperialistic context for mass tourism, then nor was there any refuge for the writer in his craft. The problem is that the act of touring is implicitly an act of escape from one's home, but is also inescapably a political act. Mary Louise Pratt, in a seminal work on travel writing and imperialism, *Imperial Eyes*, coins the term "contact zone," referring to "social spaces where disparate cultures meet, clash, and often grapple with each other, often in highly asymmetrical relations of domination and subordination" (Pratt 1992: 4). On the political level, the imperial culture spreads its influence throughout the world, and travel writers participate not only by touring but by promoting such travel in their narratives. On the personal level for the tourist and travel writer, the act of sightseeing is also an act of domination, no matter the intention or comprehension of the tourist, since the "sights" are subordinated to the primary goal of pleasing tourists. In an imperialistic context, such movement, in any mode, can have unforeseen and dire consequences. *Following the Equator*, though his last travel narrative, is actually Twain's first to try to reconcile this basic dilemma in a substantive fashion.[15] He methodically assesses the effects of the "contact zones" on indigenous peoples in Australasia, India, and South Africa and is appalled by the results.

The most powerful instance of such awareness, but mediated via – and commenting on – Twain's own boyhood experience, occurs in chapter 38 of the book, when Twain witnesses a German supervisor striking an Indian servant (Twain 1897: 351). Twain observes and marvels at his own thinking process, and how his mind constructs experiences beyond immediate physical restrictions. As he witnesses the violence, he travels mentally back to the Missouri of his youth. He describes honestly and with clear self-awareness the slavery he saw but could not comprehend as a child. The well-known passage is a stirring exploration of Twain's understanding of self:

> It is curious – the space-annihilating power of thought. For just one second, all that goes to make the *me* in me was in a Missourian village, on the other side of the globe vividly seeing again these forgotten pictures of fifty years ago, and wholly unconscious of all things but just those; and in the next second I was back in Bombay, and that kneeling native's smitten cheek was not done tingling yet! Back to boyhood – fifty years; back to age again, another fifty; and a flight equal to the circumference of the globe – all in two seconds by the watch. (p. 352)

Twain writes of "all that makes the *me* in me" and moves free from physical realities and restrictions; emotional and mental gymnastics characterize his reaction to the violence he sees. The German was, in effect, punishing the Indian on Twain's behalf, since both the supervisor and the servant were, after all, serving him. The affirmative part of the experience comes from Twain's thoughtful and empathetic response. He understands that the slaves of his childhood and the Indian of his maturity bear the same burdens; and that he, once again, is of the privileged race (and class). This is a compelling moment for readers, as Twain offers a candid glimpse into an unpleasant moment from his past that is also a reminder of the continuing racial strife that defines so much of the world. The time-travel has only a tangential relationship to India, which the present experiences abroad had sparked.

Yet this is gripping travel writing, not simply because it offers a shameful memory of antebellum Missouri, but because it brings the past forward into Twain's current life. The two pictures, one an Indian scene, the other an American one, are variations on the same theme of racism. In both, Twain, the little boy or the older man, is a spectator who is nonetheless associated with the violence, whether he comprehends it or not. The travel writer recognizes the synchronicity and tries to give both pictures – as one image – to readers. No matter the gloom that pervades the narrative or its lack of sustained humor; this particular moment stands as a monument to Twain's mastery of his craft.

America's Travel Writer

Mark Twain remade travel writing in his own image. He followed and exploited the long-established conventions of the genre and adapted them to his native talents, evolving intellectual curiosity and emotional maturity. In the 30-year process he created a body of travel writing that has no peer in its depth and versatility. His five-book canon captures a vital part of an American culture as it saw itself and the world. In doing so, he transformed a vibrant genre and in the process also defined an ever-changing and adapting American identity.

NOTES

1 All of these titles and dates refer to publication in the United States. Publication in England often involved different forms, timetables, and even content, thus complicating the authorized publication history of each work. Routledge published the authorized edition of *The Innocents Abroad* and a two-volume edition of *Roughing It* in 1872. Chatto & Windus published *A Tramp Abroad* and *Life on the Mississippi* with similar dates, titles, and content to the American editions. The British edition of *Following the Equator*, however, was titled *More Tramps Abroad* and contained significantly more of Twain's text, some of which had been deleted by publisher Frank Bliss from the American edition. British editions consistently offered far fewer illustrations.

2 Hill provides accurate sales figures, pointing out that Twain and Bliss commonly inflated the numbers of actual sales for the publicity value. Budd notes that even as late as 1905–7, *The Innocents Abroad* sold 46,000 copies, which was 5,000 more than *Adventures of Huckleberry Finn* in the same period (Budd 1983: 30).

3 The numbers for *Life on the Mississippi* are low in comparison to the other travel books but not necessarily lower than sales of Twain's fiction. Indeed, his three fictional works of the same period as his first four travel books sold substantially less well. *The Gilded Age* (1873), co-written with Charles Dudley Warner, took over six years to sell 56,000 copies (Kaplan 1966: 167–8), and *The Adventures of Tom Sawyer* (1876) sold only 24,000 copies in its first year (p. 200). *The Prince and the Pauper*, published in 1882, sold around 18,000 copies in its first few months, according to Twain's estimate, but sales dropped off dramatically soon after the brisk start and became so disappointing that Twain was tempted to abandon subscription sales and dump the work on the trade market (Salamo 1979: 17).

4 In a letter to Rogers (April 20, 1898), Bliss states that the company had shipped 28,500

copies and 10,000 more were being printed (see Twain 1969: 346).

5 The comments appear in a letter to Henry H. Rogers in November 1896 (Twain 1969: 249). He also mentions that he expected to earn "$30,000 in the first six months," an ambitious expectation that helps to explain his dejection over less than stellar sales.

6 Wegelin derives his figures from cited government publications and extrapolates the totals for the four major ports: Boston/Charlestown, New York, Philadelphia, and Baltimore. He lists totals for the remainder of the century: 25,202 for 1870; 36,097 for 1880; 81,092 for 1890; 108,068 for 1900; and 144,112 for 1901.

7 See Buzard (1993, esp. 47–8).

8 For a more comprehensive discussion of travel-book conventions, see Melton (2002: 16–58) and Stowe (1994: 3–15).

9 The letters would be published as a unit 100 years later. See Twain (1966: x). Day notes that Twain used 30,000 words from the letters and added 5,000 words more of new material to work into chapters 74–78 of *Roughing It*.

10 The original letters from this series were collected in two books. See Twain (1940), which contains his letters before the *Quaker City* departure, and Twain (1958), which includes the letters from the excursion originally published in the *Alta California*, New York *Herald*, and New York *Tribune*.

11 See Messent (1997: 22–43). Messent discusses the importance of the emerging financial power of American tourists as they spread across the Old World.

12 See Smith (1993: 797–911). Smith notes that an early title for the narrative was "Flush Times in the Silver Mines, and Other Matters," but Elisha Bliss, Twain's publisher, copyrighted "The Innocents at Home" on August 3, 1871 (p. 862, n. 190). Bliss later copyrighted "Roughing It" on December 6, 1871 (p. 871, n. 220). British publication by Routledge came out in two volumes, the first as "Roughing It," the second as "The Innocents at Home" (pp. 876–7).

13 For an extended discussion of this point, see "*Roughing It* and the American West" in Messent (1997: 44–64).

14 For a helpful discussion on the plans for *Life on the Mississippi*, see Kruse (1981, esp. 1–19).

15 Throughout his travel-writing career Twain mocked bad tourist behavior that intruded upon local custom or betrayed decency, yet the application of such a perspective in *Following the Equator* takes on a far more serious context, well beyond admonishing the mischievousness of individual tourists (or himself) and into implicating his culture at large.

References and Further Reading

Anon. (1868). "Going Abroad." *Putnam's Magazine*, 1, 530–38.

Bridgman, Richard (1987). *Traveling in Mark Twain*. Berkeley: University of California Press.

Budd, Louis J. (1983). *Our Mark Twain: The Making of his Public Personality*. Philadelphia: University of Pennsylvania Press.

Buzard, James (1993). *The Beaten Track*. New York: Oxford University Press.

Dulles, Foster Rhea (1964). *Americans Abroad: Two Centuries of European Travel*. Ann Arbor: University of Michigan Press.

Hill, Hamlin (1964). *Mark Twain and Elisha Bliss*. Columbia: University of Missouri Press.

Howells, William Dean (1880). "Mark Twain's New Book." *Atlantic* (May), 686–8.

Kaplan, Fred (2003). *The Singular Mark Twain*. New York: Doubleday.

Kaplan, Justin (1966). *Mr. Clemens and Mark Twain: A Biography*. New York: Simon & Schuster.

Kruse, Horst H. (1981). *Mark Twain and Life on the Mississippi*. Amherst: University of Massachusetts Press.

Melton, Jeffrey Alan (2002). *Mark Twain, Travel Books, and Tourism: The Tide of a Great Popular Movement*. Tuscaloosa: University of Alabama Press.

Messent, Peter (1997). *Mark Twain*. New York: St. Martin's. (Modern Novelists.)

Moran, Benjamin (1859). "Contributions Towards a History of American Literature." In *Trubner's Bibliographical Guide to American Literature*, xxxvii–civ. London: Trubner.

Perry, Lewis (1993). *Boats against the Current*. New York: Oxford University Press.

Pratt, Mary Louise (1992). *Imperial Eyes*. New York: Routledge.

Salamo, Lin (1979). "Introduction." In Mark Twain, *The Prince and the Pauper*. Berkeley: University of California Press.

Smith, Harold F. (1999). *American Travellers Abroad: A Bibliography of Accounts Published before 1900*. Lanham, Md.: Scarecrow.

Smith, Harriet Elinor (1993). "Introduction." In Mark Twain, *Roughing It*, 797–911. Berkeley: University of California Press.

Stanley, Hiram (1898). Review of *Following the Equator*. *The Dial*, March 16, 186–7.

Stowe, William W. (1994). *Going Abroad*. Princeton: Princeton University Press.

Tuckerman, Henry T. (1844). "The Philosophy of Travel." *United States Magazine and Democratic Review* 14, 527–39.

Twain, Mark (1940). *Mark Twain's Travels with Mr. Brown*, ed. Franklin Walker and G. Ezra Dane. New York: Knopf.

Twain, Mark (1958). *Traveling with the Innocents Abroad*, ed. Daniel Morley McKeithan. Norman: University of Oklahoma Press.

Twain, Mark (1966). *Mark Twain's Letters from Hawaii*, ed. A. Grove Day. New York: Appleton-Century.

Twain, Mark (1967). *Mark Twain's Letters to his Publishers 1867–1894*, ed. Hamlin Hill. Berkeley: University of California Press.

Twain, Mark (1969). *Mark Twain's Correspondence with Henry Huttleston Rogers, 1893–1909*, ed. Lewis Leary. Berkeley: University of California Press.

Twain, Mark (1990). *Mark Twain's Letters*, vol. 2: *1867–1868*, ed. Harriet Elinor Smith and Richard Bucci. Berkeley: University of California Press.

Twain, Mark (1995). *Mark Twain's Letters*, vol. 4: *1870–1871*, ed. Victor Fischer and Michael B. Frank. Berkeley: University of California Press.

Twain, Mark, and Howells, William Dean (1960). *Mark Twain–Howells Letters: The Correspondence of Samuel L. Clemens and William Dean Howells, 1872–1910*, 2 vols., ed. Henry Nash Smith and William M. Gibson. Cambridge: Belknap.

Wegelin, Christof (1962). "The Rise of the International Novel." *PMLA* 77, 305–10.

Ziff, Larzer (2000). *Return Passages: Great American Travel Writing 1780–1910*. New Haven: Yale University Press.

PART V
Mark Twain's Fiction

23

Mark Twain's Short Fiction

Henry B. Wonham

Mark Twain's reputation as one of the world's great writers has little to do with his achievement in the art of short fiction. Although he published sketches, tales, and stories throughout his long career, and produced numerous volumes of collected shorter works during his lifetime, critics have paid relatively little attention to his efforts in this vein, and Twain himself was never entirely at home with the short story as a literary form.[1] Collapsing aesthetic and financial considerations into a single statement on the subject, he complained to a friend that "the short story is the worst paid of all forms of literature." A poor story "isn't worth printing," whereas a good story is actually "a novel in the cradle." Any writer with a lick of business sense would "take it out of the cradle to play with it . . . & *raise* it." "In the cradle it is . . . worth a few hundred dollars – maybe a thousand. Raised, it can be worth (Huck Finn is a case in point) forty-eight thousand."[2]

Beyond a few unencouraging remarks of this sort, Twain had little to say about his surprisingly vast and diverse output of stories, tales, and sketches. He did not – like Henry James, Anton Chekhov, or James Joyce – articulate a theory of literary short fiction, and for all his experimentation with dialect and perspective, he cannot be considered a serious innovator of the genre, like Edgar Allan Poe or Charles Chesnutt. Critics often cite his most famous essay, "How to Tell a Story," as a source for Twain's views on the construction of short narratives – but this, as its title indicates, has more to tell us about oral performance than about literary aesthetics.

Another obstacle to assessing Twain's achievement as a writer of short fiction is the sticky question of genre. In fact, among the hundreds of pieces he published in magazines and collections during his lifetime, only a handful would qualify as short stories under a strict generic definition. Taken together, according to Justin Kaplan, the impressively heterogeneous body of work generally cobbled together under the rubric of Twain's short fiction "practically exhausts the genre vocabulary: sketches, yarns, tales, fables, folk tales, tall tales, fairy tales, ghost tales, fantasies, allegories, incidents, anecdotes, hoaxes, domestic comedies, animal stories, and short short stories" (see Quirk

1997: 5). Kaplan simply ran out of breath, for he could have extended this list to include burlesques, farces, jokes, aphorisms, Socratic dialogues, detective stories, and more.

The staggering formal variety of Twain's shorter writings stemmed from his belief that every story, incident, or event chooses its own form, the one most appropriate to its telling, regardless of whether an author sets out to write one particular kind of narrative or another. This openness to experiment was one of his greatest assets as a writer, but the unevenness that necessarily resulted makes it difficult to compare Twain's shorter works with those of America's greatest practitioners of the short story proper, such as Nathaniel Hawthorne, Sherwood Anderson, Ernest Hemingway, Flannery O'Connor, or Raymond Carver. Comparisons of this sort – the stock-in-trade of literary criticism – are oddly irrelevant in the case of Twain, who, according to Charles Neider, "wrote primarily to satisfy an audience rather than the requirements of a genre" (see Quirk 1997: 5). The writer and critic William Dean Howells, a close friend of Twain's, had much the same idea in mind when he commented that Mark Twain was "the most unliterary" of literary men, explaining that he wrote "as if no one had ever written before" (Howells 1910: 17).

Howells was right: Twain's short fiction is unprecedented and incomparable. He refused to play by the accepted rules, and his brash literary independence produced a great deal that is hardly worth the trouble to read, as well as a great deal that can be called, simply, masterly. This is the conundrum of Twain's shorter work. While he scoffed at the short story as a mere underdeveloped novel, neglected by its authorial parent, and while the quality of his sketches and tales was undeniably mixed, most readers agree that his finest efforts resulted in some of greatest short fiction ever written by an American. This claim cannot be substantiated, of course, for it implies a comparison that I have already called irrelevant. I offer it anyway as a clumsy way of beginning to gesture toward the elusive power of Twain's best short pieces.

Many of these are now available in Louis J. Budd's two-volume Library of America edition of *Collected Tales, Sketches, Speeches, and Essays*, an anthology that wisely side-steps questions of generic definition by including anything and everything that might qualify as a short work, from advice literature ("How to Cure a Cold") to Washoe journalism ("Doings in Nevada") and selected maxims. One might point to representative texts almost anywhere in these lengthy volumes, but the opening pair of sketches, written in 1852, more than ten years before Sam Clemens adopted his famous sobriquet, provides a suggestive point of departure.

"The Dandy Frightening the Squatter" and "Historical Exhibition – A No. 1 Ruse" are the hackwork of a bored and mischievous typesetter, but these two pieces are also oddly suggestive of the qualities that pervade Twain's mature writing. The second of the pair describes the showing in a small frontier town of an art exhibition entitled "Bonaparte Crossing the Rhine" (Twain 1992a: 3). "Jim C.," watched by a group of local boys, eagerly pays the five-cent admission to see a representation of the famous event and to hear a lecture "explaining its points, and giving the history of the piece." Jim cannot contain his excitement over this rare opportunity to encounter high culture in the backwoods, and he pleads with the impresario, "Quick, Mr. Curts, I want to see it the worst kind." "Well, you shall see it," responds Curts, "and I hope by this show to impress upon your young minds, this valuable piece of history, and illustrate the same in so plain a manner that the silliest lad amongst you will readily comprehend it." With this austere introduction, Mr. Curts pulls from his drawer "the bony part of a hog's leg" and holds it before the bewildered crowd. He then produces a three-inch piece of hog's rind and begins slowly, with great solemnity, passing the bone across the skin. "[Y]ou see, boys, this is the 'bony part crossing the rind,'" he explains. "You have now learned a valuable lesson" (Twain 1992a: 4–5).

"The Dandy Frightening the Squatter" is another frontier episode that hinges on defeated expectations. A well-to-do dandy "with a killing moustache" plans to impress his fellow steamboat passengers by frightening a local man who stands on the shore (Twain 1992a: 1). With a bowie knife in his belt and a pistol in each hand, the dandy approaches the unsuspecting woodsman "with an air which seemed to say – 'The hopes of a nation depend on me.'" Aiming his pistols at the squatter, he declares: "Found you at last, have I? You are the very man I've been looking for these three weeks! Say your prayers . . . [Y]ou'll make a capital barn door, and I shall drill the key-hole myself!" The squatter responds by planting his enormous fist between the eyes of his "astonished antagonist," and the story closes with the champion's brief but impressive speech: "I say, yeou, next time yeou come around drillin' key-holes, don't forget yer old acquaintances!" (Twain 1992a: 2).

These two crude sketches, written by a teenager without literary ambitions, give little indication of Sam Clemens's potential as a writer, but they do curiously anticipate some of the major tendencies of what would become Mark Twain's art. Both sketches describe a staged performance, an entertainment devised for bourgeois tastes, and in both the show is interrupted and transformed by a potent, unexpected element, a latent force associated with material reality and actual experience. The Dandy's fraudulent display of power is met with the real violence of the squatter, much as the historical sense of the phrase "Bonaparte crossing the Rhine" is exploded by an earthy, grotesque redeployment of the very same syllables. The "lesson" taught in each sketch is really the same: beneath the complacent rituals of middle-class entertainment there lies something real and powerful, something rooted in democratic values and vernacular style, something capable of breaking through at the least provocation. It would be many years before Sam Clemens, and later Mark Twain, would realize the full potential of the stylistic confrontation that unfolds so abruptly in these early sketches, but readers will recognize a pattern of joking that reappears over and over in Mark Twain's more polished works, such as "Jim Smiley and His Jumping Frog" (1865), "A True Story" (1874), and "The Man That Corrupted Hadleyburg" (1899). Thematically, these classic stories share little in common with one another, and each comes from a significantly different phase of Twain's tumultuous career. Nevertheless, they all describe the hijacking of a staged performance by an unexpectedly vigorous creative intelligence, the disruption of entertainment-as-usual by an arch-entertainer; and in this fundamental respect Mark Twain's best-known short stories recall Sam Clemens's earliest efforts as a writer.

Of course, the showdown between an effete dandy and a vulgar squatter was already a traditional motif in American writing long before Sam Clemens began scribbling his own version of the encounter shortly after midcentury. As far back as the 1830s, Southwestern humorists such as Augustus Baldwin Longstreet had popularized this sort of frontier comedy, setting the wild antics of rural characters against genteel standards of speech and behavior. Sam Clemens's efforts in this vein were perfectly conventional, except that he seems always to have conceived of the contest as, at heart, a matter of language. Other writers might have understood the squatter's knockout punch as the appropriate climax of his encounter with the dandy, but for Clemens the squatter's triumph is secure only when he taunts his adversary by lingering over the pronoun "Yeou," repeating it twice to add emphasis to the insult. Mark Twain relished physical comedy as thoroughly as any of his Southwestern precursors, but the site of his humor is language, the discursive zone where "Bonaparte" becomes "bonypart," and a world of expectations is overturned in the process.

All of this is just another way of saying that while the humor of Twain's early sketches is undeniably coarse, his fascination with the *sound* of spoken English sets him apart from the Phunny Phellows and literary comedians who anticipated his brand of comedy. The difference I am pointing to can be hard to measure, but Twain's sensitivity to the nuances of verbal performance helps to explain why a story such as "Jim Smiley and His Jumping Frog," a perfectly conventional frontier sketch in most respects, became a national sensation when it was published by a New York newspaper in 1865, establishing Mark Twain as a leader of the "Western School" of humorous fiction.[3] Twain first heard the frog story while pocket mining at Angel's Camp in Calaveras County, where on rainy days he and his partner, Jim Gillis, listened to an old-timer named Ben Coon tell meandering stories about nothing in particular. From the beginning, it was Coon's mode of connecting images and ideas in a non-sequential narrative collage, rather than any particular theme or dramatic action, that fascinated Twain, who jotted down a few perfunctory notes for future use: "Coleman with his jumping frog – bet a stranger $50 – stranger had no frog, & C got him one – in the meantime stranger filled C's frog full of buckshot & he couldn't jump – the stranger's frog won" (Twain 1981: 263).

This, in a nutshell, is the frog story, and yet in Twain's artful retelling of the tale and its performance the unfair contest of frogs becomes something much more, a pretext for social drama and populist satire. Twain casts himself as a pedantic snob who has paid a call on "good-natured, garrulous old Simon Wheeler" to inquire about the friend of a friend, the Reverend Leonidas W. Smiley (Twain 1992a: 171). Instead of responding to Mr. Twain's request, Wheeler backs his auditor into a corner and regales him with a "monotonous," "interminable narrative" about a former acquaintance, Jim Smiley, a miner and compulsive gambler. The comedy here follows the pattern of "Historical Exhibition," in that an over-eager listener has been led to expect the wrong kind of performance, and the price of his mistake is the annoyance and humiliation he experiences upon finding himself subject to Wheeler's endless ramblings. Of course, there is a "lesson" here as well: one that is all the more amusing because it is so completely lost on Wheeler's primary audience. Jim Smiley's motley animal friends, the 15-minute nag and the little bull-pup, Andrew Jackson, share a notable affinity, namely that although they appear worthless and incompetent, each possesses hidden power. The diminutive pup, in fact, remains undefeated in battle until an even more pitiful-looking contender, a dog without hind legs, denies him his favorite hold.

Smiley profits handsomely by betting on these unlikely champions, until a stranger arrives and beats him at his own game. "Well – I don't see no points about that frog that's any better'n any other frog," declares the stranger upon his introduction to Daniel Webster, Smiley's latest contender (Twain 1992a: 175). As the stranger understands even better than Smiley, appearances can be deceptive, and the outward expression of strength and prowess may actually work against a competitor. In his eagerness to win a sure bet, Smiley places himself on the wrong side of another contest between apparently unequal athletes.

The narrator, Mark Twain, listens to this disjointed parable about strength, style, deception, and humiliation without a trace of awareness that the story also concerns himself. Addressing the reader in a polished legalese that conveys social standing and professional legitimacy, he carefully notes the "dilapidated" condition of Wheeler's working-class surroundings and goes on to describe the storyteller as "fat and bald-headed," with "an expression of winning gentleness and simplicity upon his tranquil countenance" (Twain 1992a: 171). Basing his pronounced feelings of superiority strictly on appearances, Twain allows himself to be trapped in a bar-room corner, immobilized like the unfortunate Daniel Webster, while Wheeler's more limber intelligence fills him with riotous images and magnificently improbable metaphors. Andrew Jackson, when the money is on him, becomes a different dog: "his under-jaw'd begin to stick out like the for'castle of a steamboat, and his teeth would uncover, and shine savage like the furnaces" (p. 173). Smiley's 15-minute nag, at the fag end of the race, would "get excited and desperate-like, and come cavorting and spraddling up, and scattering her legs around limber, sometimes in the air, and sometime out to one side amongst the fences" (p. 173). And when Daniel Webster finds himself unable to budge, he "give a heave, and hysted up his shoulders – so – like a Frenchman, but it wasn't no use" (p. 176). It is difficult to say exactly how a Frenchman hysts his shoulders, but one can almost imagine Smiley's educated and overconfident frog doing just that.

Mark Twain remains deaf to the sound and sense of Simon Wheeler's fantastic homespun poetry, and he flees the scene before Wheeler can launch into another episode about "a yaller one-eyed cow that didn't have no tail only just a short stump like a bannanner" (Twain 1992a: 177). Yet most readers, by this point, have been so thoroughly charmed by the storyteller's command of language and of the social situation that it is hardly necessary to illustrate once again, as the yaller cow surely will, that appearances can be deceiving, that weakness and affliction may be turned to advantage. Mark Twain has the last word, as he condescendingly bids the old man farewell, but Simon Wheeler has won our attention and our respect.

Wheeler's eccentric vernacular style is full of colorful surprises, and yet, like animal fables from cultures around the world, his stories serve to illustrate the most elemental qualities of human nature, such as vanity, pride, greed, and credulity. This exploration of basic human tendencies by means of a highly idiosyncratic narrative voice is the recipe for many of Twain's finest literary performances, from *Adventures of Huckleberry Finn* (1885) to the less well-known, but no less masterly, "Jim Baker's Blue-Jay Yarn" (1880). Jim Baker is another miner from "a lonely corner of California," and like Simon Wheeler he appears "simple-hearted" and quaintly naive (Twain 1880: 36). In the story's opening frame, Mark Twain remembers Baker as the one man he ever met who "believed he could accurately translate any remark" made by the animals who are his only neighbors. With this set-up, one might expect another lopsided confrontation between literary smugness and vernacular artistry, but Twain does not develop the stylistic contrast this time, preferring to allow the storyteller to have the stage all to himself. This paring down of the literary frame allows Baker to emerge even more fully than Simon Wheeler as a believable and sympathetic character, a wise hermit, whose exclusive contact with animals and birds has resulted in a profound, if unusual, understanding of human nature.

Baker's favorite animal friends are the blue-jays, and he admires them because they are gifted and incessant talkers: "mind you, whatever a blue-jay feels he can put into language. And no mere common-place language, either, but rattling, out-and-out book-talk – and bristling with metaphor, too – just bristling! And as for command of language – why you never see a blue-jay get stuck for a word. No man ever did. They just boil out of him!" (p. 36).

With their abundant verbal resources, Baker's friends demonstrate a full range of human emotions and sensibilities. They love gossip and scandal, they can swear more profanely than a miner, they plan and reason, and – perhaps most remarkably – "a jay knows when he is an ass just as well as you do – maybe better" (Twain 1880: 37). Baker's story of a blue-jay who makes a fool of himself by trying to fill up a house with acorns serves ostensibly to demonstrate his point that "a jay is everything a man is," but this fantastic premise doesn't capture the magical quality of the tale. With their quick appreciation for "the whole absurdity of the contract," Baker's blue-jays are really more nimble-witted and "human" than most of us, who cling to feelings of moral righteousness and intellectual superiority as defenses against laughter (p. 41). A jay is capable of "guffawing" at himself and at the silliness of the habits, convictions, and instincts that propel him and his kind toward sometimes ridiculous extremes of attitude and behavior. Two key attributes – the command of a vibrant idiom and the ability to laugh at absurdity – distinguish humans and, more convincingly, blue-jays from the rest of creation, according to Baker's philosophy, which in its genial and unassuming way begins to foreshadow the more misanthropic writings of Twain's older age, products of what he called the "pen warmed-up in hell." To be human, he would later conclude, is to lack precisely this inclination toward joyous, profane self-criticism. Jim Baker reveals none of Mark Twain's brewing anger toward the damned human race, but one is justified in wondering why, if "a jay is everything a man is," he lives alone in a remote cabin with only birds and animals for company.

The most compelling feature of stories such as "Jim Smiley and His Jumping Frog" and "Jim Baker's Blue-Jay Yarn" is the leisurely, seemingly spontaneous, subtly ironic "*manner* of the telling," rather than what Twain called the "*matter*" of the tale (Twain 1992b: 201). In fact, some of his most entertaining stories contain little or no "*matter*" at all. Style is substance, for example, in "Jim Blaine and His Grandfather's Ram" (1872), a magnificently woven shaggy dog story by a drunken raconteur who never arrives at his titular subject. After a promising beginning, the forgetful storyteller loses track of his theme, and what follows is merely his captivating talk: "There never was a bullier ram than he was. Grandfather fetched him from Illinois – got him of a man by the name of Yates – Bill Yates – maybe you might have heard of him; his father was a deacon – Baptist – and he was a rustler, too" (Twain 1872: 384). And so on, until we hear about Miss Jefferson, who loaned her glass eye to Miss Wagner to receive company in, though "it warn't big enough, and when Miss Wagner warn't noticing, it would get twisted around in the socket, and look up, maybe, or out to one side, and every which way, while t'other was looking as straight ahead as a spy-glass" (p. 385). Blaine's wildly colorful detours and stream-of-consciousness segues suggest a virtuosity that has tempted some critics to think of Twain as an early modernist, though he understood the technique as simply "American." The "humorous story," he explained, as "created in America," may be "spun out at great length, and may wander around as much as it pleases, and arrive nowhere in particular" (Twain 1992b: 201). Blaine's story arrives nowhere, to be sure, but rather peters out when the teller drifts off into a drunken sleep. As so often in Twain's finest short pieces, there is no plot worth mentioning, and thus no ending; the story is simply over when we no longer hear the engrossing sound of the speaker's voice.

Although it reads perfectly well as a discrete story, "Jim Blaine and His Grandfather's Ram" first appeared in *Roughing It* (1872), Twain's semi-autobiographical account of his travels and adventures in the American West. Another story interpolated into *Roughing It*, "Buck Fanshaw's Funeral," illustrates a different side of his preoccupation with language and verbal style. The narrator explains that Buck Fanshaw, a fireman and former barkeeper in Virginia City, has died. His close friend Scotty Briggs visits the minister, "a fragile, gentle, spirituel new fledgling from an Eastern theological seminary," in order to make arrangements for the funeral (Twain 1872: 330). These two speakers from different ends of the social spectrum proceed to "discuss" the situation for six or seven hilarious pages, neither one understanding a word spoken by the other. A short excerpt of their conversation will convey the basic joke, though readers should not cheat themselves of the chance to see Twain at his best in this episode, which occurs in chapter 47 of the book. Scotty begins "in lugubrious tones":

> "Are you the duck that runs the gospel-mill next door?"
> "Am I the – pardon me, I believe I do not understand?" . . .

"Why you see we are in a bit of trouble, and the boys thought maybe you would give
us a lift, if we'd tackle you – that is, if I've got the rights of it and you are the head
clerk of the doxology-works next door."
"I am the shepherd in charge of the flock whose fold is next door."
"The which?" (Twain 1872: 331–2)

There are no winners or losers in this confrontation of upper- and lower-class speakers, for the dandy figure in *Roughing It*'s version of Twain's perennial showdown is just
as well armed with flashy metaphors as his ruffian counterpart. The comedy here, as
in Jim Blaine's tale, is all about style, and although the narrator concludes the episode
by explaining that Scotty later became a Sunday-school teacher, the story (if we can
call it that) is once again really over when Twain's mutually bewildered speakers get
tired of talking.
   Twain occasionally embedded this sort of comedy of verbal incongruity within a
more elaborate plot structure, as in "Barnum's First Speech in Congress" (1867), where
the language of huckster advertising becomes an unlikely (though oddly prescient)
idiom for political oratory. The vernacular of lawmakers creates a different kind of
dissonance when a group of snowbound legislators finds itself reduced to savagery in
"Cannibalism in the Cars" (1868):

   Mr. Halliday of Virginia: "I move to further amend the report by substituting Mr.
   Harvey Davis, of Oregon, for Mr. Messick. It may be urged by gentlemen that the hardships and privations of a frontier life have rendered Mr. Davis tough; but, gentlemen,
   is this a time to cavil about toughness? . . . No, gentlemen, bulk is what we desire –
   substance, weight, bulk – these are the supreme requisites now – not talent, not genius,
   not education. I insist upon my motion." (Twain 1992a: 273–4)

The senators and congressional representatives continue to bicker over parliamentary maneuvers until Mr. Harris of St. Louis is elected as the dinner meal, with only
his own vote cast in dissent. Unlike "Buck Fanshaw's Funeral," where irreconcilable
idioms meet directly in conversation, here the verbal friction is more subtly implied
by the striking inappropriateness of legislative jargon as a vocabulary for discussing
bloodthirsty actions. Nevertheless, in both stories – and in many of the pieces I have
mentioned already – plot serves as a mere pretext for exploring the comic possibilities of verbal dissonance.
   The effect of this dissonance was often a raunchy form of comedy, designed to appeal
primarily to middle-class male audiences. Yet Twain could play many of the same notes
in a sentimental key, as he showed in his first contribution to the *Atlantic Monthly*, the
nation's leading literary periodical. "A True Story, Repeated Word for Word as I Heard
It" (1874) opens with a piece of deliberate stagecraft, as "Misto C—," or Mr. Clemens,
explains that he was sitting with his family on the farmhouse porch one summer
evening, while "Aunt Rachel" sat "respectfully below our level, on the steps, – for she
was our servant, and colored" (Twain 1992a: 578). Comfortable with what he takes to
be a natural state of inequality, Misto C— joins the family in poking fun at Aunt

Rachel, who lets off "peal after peal of laughter " and shakes "with throes of enjoyment which she could no longer get breath enough to express." Interpreting her laughter as the sign of a carefree disposition, he goes on to ask good-naturedly: "Aunt Rachel, how is it that you have lived sixty years and never had any trouble?" This ill-considered remark provokes an astonished look from Aunt Rachel, who launches into a powerful story about her life under slavery, the dispersal of her family, and the miraculous recovery years later of her youngest son. Aunt Rachel herself seems to expand in dignity and authority as the tale progresses, rising from her subservient position on the steps until "she towered above us, black against the stars" (p. 579). Misto C—'s conspicuous silence at the end of story, where the frame narrator conventionally reappears, can be taken as a sign of his humiliation and regret over the gross misreading of her character.

When Twain submitted the manuscript of "A True Story" for consideration at the *Atlantic Monthly*, he declared half-apologetically that there was "no humor in it" (Twain and Howells 1960: vol. 1, 22). This was true in the main, for Aunt Rachel's story is clearly designed to play on the heart-strings rather than the funny-bone. Yet the shift from a raucous to a sentimental mood required surprisingly little modification of the basic patterns that characterize even Twain's crudest sketches. As in "Historical Exhibition – A No. 1 Ruse" and any number of other early anecdotes, the key moment in "A True Story" occurs when Aunt Rachel, the featured performer, begins speaking, and what comes out of her mouth is nothing like what her immediate audience expects. Of course, the situation is significantly reversed, in that whereas Jim C. hopes to attend a serious exhibition that turns out to be a crude joke, Misto C— expects Aunt Rachel to share her limitless joy with the family but instead hears a tale of unimaginable suffering, delivered "without even a smile" (Twain 1992a: 578). The effects of these two stories are completely different, of course, and yet both generate excitement from the shock of defeated expectations and the verbal resourcefulness of an underrated and misunderstood vernacular speaker. Whether it is laughter or moral seriousness that provides the charge of surprise, Twain achieves his most powerful effects by disrupting a staged performance so that a seemingly more authentic, truthful, and captivating voice can break through.

For all its structural similarity with Twain's irreverent comic sketches, the appearance in 1874 of "A True Story" in the eminently respectable *Atlantic Monthly* announced the emergence of a new, more serious Mark Twain. This realignment of his already famous persona continued in subsequent works of short fiction contributed to the *Atlantic Monthly* and other leading periodicals, including *Harper's Monthly* and *Century* magazine. Some of these stories begin to reveal Twain's penchant for philosophizing over ethical, theological, and metaphysical questions, a tendency that would become more pronounced in later works, but that is already clearly apparent in a story such as "The Facts Concerning the Recent Carnival of Crime in Connecticut," published in the *Atlantic Monthly* in 1876. In this amusing but somewhat labored *doppelgänger* tale, Mark Twain confronts his own conscience, embodied as a grotesque dwarf. Their interaction produces some moments of comedy and psychological intrigue, but the story is primarily interesting for its anticipation of Twain's treatment of conscience in *Adventures of Huckleberry Finn*, which he was just beginning to write, and for its very deliberate borrowing from the ethical philosophy of W. E. H. Lecky.[4] Critics have enjoyed a carnival of their own speculating about the story's significance as a statement of Twain's emerging philosophical position, and yet Tom Quirk hits the nail on the head – with no insult intended toward utility players or kitchen lieutenants – when he asserts that "[a]s a philosopher, Twain would have made a good third baseman; as a metaphysician, a first-rate pastry-chef" (Quirk 1997: 65). While the story provides an important index to Twain's thinking about conscience and social responsibility during one of the most productive periods of his career, "The Carnival of Crime" is finally more memorable for its zany comedy than for its ethical profundity.

A more successful attempt to explore the phenomenon of guilt and the idea of moral complicity appeared ten years later, when Twain was invited to contribute an essay to *Century* magazine's "Battles and Leaders of the Civil War" series. Sam Clemens had fought in no battles, and he certainly was not a military leader, but at the outbreak of war in 1861 he had served briefly with the Marion Rangers, an informal Confederate militia unit in Missouri. His essay in *Century* is a masterly blend of fiction and autobiography, in which a naïve and overconfident boy is confronted by the reality of violence and the moral burden of his own participation in bloodletting. The story again hinges on defeated expectations and the sudden eruption of feelings, both physical and emotional, for which the narrator is utterly unprepared, though here the effect is neither humorous nor sentimental. Rather, "The Private History of a Campaign That Failed" (1885) is a fictional confession and a powerful statement of hopelessness and moral outrage at the horrors to which the young soldier and the nation itself are fast succumbing. As in *Adventures of Huckleberry Finn*, where Huck can think of no other way to preserve his innocence than by fleeing to the Territory, the narrator of "The Private History" finally deserts his unit and heads west: "It seemed to me that I was not rightly equipped for this awful business; that war was intended for men, and I for a child's nurse. I resolved to retire from this avocation of sham soldiership while I could save some remnant of my self-respect" (Twain 1992a: 880).

This retreat to a less complicated and compromising environment is the characteristic gesture of Twain's imagination, which perpetually lights out for the Territory "ahead of the rest" in the hope of preserving what is left of innocence (Twain 1885: 366). Such an escape is part of a fantasy that Twain himself loved to ridicule, and indeed his entire literary output might be understood as an assault against innocence and naïve complacency. Yet if, as we have so often seen, his most effective stories operate by relentlessly exploding innocent expectations, they do so in order to recover a profounder innocence. The narrator of "The Private History" says as much when he closes his memoir – ostensibly an account of moral awakening – by boasting that he knows "more about retreating than the man that invented retreating" (Twain 1992a: 882).

If "The Private History of a Campaign That Failed" vents Mark Twain's growing rage at the inhumanity of what passes for civilized behavior, it does so with more shame than bitterness. This ratio was to change in later years, as it became increasingly difficult for Twain to imagine what he called a "refuge of the derelicts," a safe haven for life's defeated people, outcasts and vagabonds who have failed to find a place in the civilized world (Twain 1972: 157). Huck's Territory is one such refuge, and Twain worked hard to reimagine its possibility in works written during the last 20 years of his life, but with greater and greater difficulty. The major stories of this long and generally unhappy phase, such as "Which Was the Dream?" (1897) and "The Great Dark" (1898), tend to emphasize the impossibility of escape from a perpetually benighted human condition, except through death or under the influence of dreams and supernatural phenomena.

Readers brought up on the boisterous irreverence of Twain's earlier writings often balk at the dark mood that characterizes his later years, but his anger at the human race occasionally erupted in fits of comedy and social satire that bear comparison with anything he had written as a young man. The most celebrated story from this period, and perhaps the story for which Twain is best known to the world, is "The Man That Corrupted Hadleyburg" (1899), a tale about the festering hypocrisy of a small town renowned for the honesty of its citizens. Virtue turns out to be skin-deep when a stranger with a grudge against the town returns to test Hadleyburg's famous righteousness against the more profound human instincts of greed and envy. The story is bitter, like the mysterious stranger (one of many in Twain's late fiction) who orchestrates the town's undoing, and yet "Hadleyburg" ends with a reaffirmation of community, a new community built out of laughter, song, and self-knowledge. With the public exposure of one after another of its leading citizens, the delighted townspeople join in a chorus of derision, singing their satirical refrain to a tune from Gilbert and Sullivan's *Mikado*. The event everyone had expected to witness, the naming of Hadleyburg's most virtuous individual, has degenerated into a riot of self-mockery, and by the story's end all but one doomed pair stand revealed. "The Man That Corrupted Hadleyburg" is by no means a cheerful tale, but the town's sham honesty is ultimately replaced with something more like the bemused self-understanding of Jim Baker's blue-jays, who *know* when they are asses, "just as well as you do – maybe better" (Twain 1880: 37). In this knowledge lies at least some hope for a viable human community.

"Hadleyburg" is Twain's most frequently anthologized tale, in part because of its powerful satire, and in part because it looks and reads more like a conventional short story than any of the pieces I have mentioned so far. These may be ample justifications for its reputation as a great work, but I hope to be forgiven for asserting that the real gem among Twain's late stories is "Extract from Captain Stormfield's Visit to Heaven" (1909). Like so many of his short pieces, the "Extract" is difficult to categorize, for during most of its nearly 40-year gestation Twain thought of Stormfield's tale as a novel-in-progress, or at least a novella.[5] He had begun writing it in 1868 and amassed as many as 40,000 words before turning to other projects. He returned to the manuscript intermittently during the next 30 years, and then took it up again in earnest around the turn of the century. The novelistic project conceived as *Captain Stormfield's Visit to Heaven* was never completed, but in 1907 and 1908

Twain published chapters 3 and 4 of the larger manuscript in *Harper's Monthly*, calling them "Extracts." In 1909 Harper's combined the two published installments into a slender Christmas volume entitled *Extract from Captain Stormfield's Visit to Heaven*, and this "book" – less than 40 pages long as it appears in the Library of America edition – was the last to be issued during Twain's lifetime.

Reviewing "Captain Stormfield" in 1910, shortly before Twain's death, Clarence Gaines called it "nearly the most perfect thing the author has written: so much of him expressed in so short a space" (Gaines 1910: 583). Indeed, for all its interest in death and the afterlife – central preoccupations of Twain's last years – the story reads like the work of a much younger author. Stormfield, the last of Twain's great vernacular speakers, delivers his rollicking tale in a slangy idiom that recalls the informal poetry of Simon Wheeler, Jim Baker, Aunt Rachel, and, perhaps most of all, Huck Finn. The Captain is more full of swagger than Huck, but, like the runaway orphan who feigns his own death before launching out on the river, Stormfield feels "dreadful lonesome" and "so down-hearted and homesick I wished a hundred times I never had died" (Twain 1992b: 835). Feelings of isolation and homesickness may underlie the tale, but they never become morose. The irrepressible Captain remains confident, defiant, and cleverly resourceful even in death, as he turns his 30-year journey to heaven into a magnificent race with the comets. Sam Clemens seems to have rediscovered some of the happiest moments of his life as a riverboat man when Stormfield approaches a fast-moving comet piloted by a competitive crew:

> Well, I boomed along another hundred and fifty million miles, and got up abreast his shoulder, as you may say. I was feeling pretty fine, I tell you; but just then I noticed the officer of the deck come to the side and hoist his glass in my direction. Straight off I heard him sing out –
>   "Below there, ahoy! Shake her up, shake her up! Heave on a hundred million billion tons of brimstone!" (Twain 1992b: 827)

When Stormfield arrives in heaven, he is surprised to discover that very little conforms to the expectations he was trained to accept as a citizen of the earth. Once again, as in the case of Mr. Curts's fraudulent "Historical Exhibition," a culturally sanctioned and conventional representation of reality turns out to be grossly unlike the actual thing, and Twain's humor turns on the difference. Heaven is a delightful place, Stormfield finds, "though it's about as different from the one I was brought up on as a live princess is different from her own wax figger" (p. 839).

This is Mark Twain's joke, the same joke he told a thousand times in a thousand wonderfully various ways during his long career as a writer and platform entertainer. Although nothing kills a joke more effectively than repetition, most readers of "Captain Stormfield" concur that this one remains as fresh and entertaining in its 1909 version as it was when an unknown printer's apprentice began publishing anecdotes in 1852. Reality bears little resemblance to our ideas about reality, Stormfield's journey confirms, and the best we can do on earth is to laugh at each other and ourselves, acknowledging that we are asses, like Jim Baker's blue-jays. For all the immense variety of his forms, his themes, his characters and their many idioms, Twain's short fiction never wavers from this view of our world and of ourselves.

NOTES

1 Twain published seven volumes that can be identified as short-story collections during his lifetime: *The Celebrated Jumping Frog of Calaveras County, and Other Sketches* (1867), *Sketches, New and Old* (1875), *The Stolen White Elephant, Etc.* (1882), *Merry Tales* (1892), *The $1,000,000 Bank-Note and Other New Stories* (1893), *The Man That Corrupted Hadleyburg and Other Stories and Essays* (1900), and *The $30,000 Bequest and Other Stories* (1906). He also published many short pieces separately in newspapers and magazines, and some of his longer stories appeared independently in book form, such as *A Double-Barreled Detective Story* (1902), *A Horse's Tale* (1907), and *Extract from Captain Stormfield's Visit to Heaven* (1909). A full catalogue of Twain's short fiction would also necessarily include many stories interpolated into works of travel, such as *Roughing It* (1872), *A Tramp Abroad* (1880), and *Following the Equator* (1897), as well as stories and sketches published posthumously. For the purposes of this essay, I have taken the liberty to range freely among representative texts from a variety of sources without addressing impor-

tant questions pertaining to the circumstances of composition and publication. For a more concentrated analysis of Twain's story collections, see Messent (2001). Quirk (1997) offers an excellent overview, and Wilson (1987) provides detailed information about the publication history of many individual stories.

2 These statements are from an 1897 letter to Henry Loomis Nelson, quoted at more length in Messent (2001: 3).

3 "Jim Smiley and His Jumping Frog" first appeared in the New York *Saturday Press* on November 18, 1865, and was reprinted ten times during the following decade. For a full publication history, see Wilson (1987: 163–4).

4 Many critics have examined the influence of Lecky's *History of European Morals from Augustine to Charlemagne* (1869) on Twain's story. See especially Baetzhold (1970: 58), Emerson (1984: 90–1), and Wilson (1987: 101–2).

5 The composition and publication history of "Extract of Captain Stormfield's Visit to Heaven" is thoroughly presented in James A. Miller's "Afterword" to the Oxford University Press edition. See also Wilson (1987: 83–6).

REFERENCES AND FURTHER READING

Baetzhold, Howard G. (1970). *Mark Twain and John Bull: The British Connection.* Bloomington: Indiana University Press.

Emerson, Everett (1984). *The Authentic Mark Twain: A Literary Biography of Samuel L. Clemens.* Philadelphia: University of Pennsylvania Press.

Gaines, Clarence H. (1910). "Mark Twain the Humorist." *Book News Monthly* 28, 583–88. Repr. in Louis J. Budd (ed.), *Critical Essays on Mark Twain, 1867–1910*, 221–25. Boston: G. K. Hall, 1982.

Howells, William Dean (1910). *My Mark Twain: Reminiscences and Criticisms.* New York: Harper & Bros.

Kaplan, Justin (1985). Introduction to *Mark Twain's Short Stories*, ed. Justin Kaplan. New York: Signet.

Messent, Peter (2001). *The Short Works of Mark Twain: A Critical Study.* Philadelphia: University of Pennsylvania Press.

Neider, Charles (1957). "Introduction." In *The Complete Short Stories of Mark Twain*, ed. Charles Neider. New York: Doubleday.

Quirk, Tom (1997). *Mark Twain: A Study of the Short Fiction.* New York: Twayne.

Twain, Mark (1972). *Mark Twain's Fables of Man*, ed. John S. Tuckey. Berkeley: University of California Press.

Twain, Mark (1979). *Early Tales and Sketches*, vol. 1: *1851–1864*, ed. Edgar Marquess Branch and Robert H. Hirst. Berkeley: University of California Press.

Twain, Mark (1981). *Early Tales and Sketches*, vol. 2: *1864–1865*, ed. Edgar Marquess Branch and

Robert H. Hirst. Berkeley: University of California Press.

Twain, Mark, and Howells, William Dean (1960). *Mark Twain–Howells Letters: The Correspondence of Samuel L. Clemens and William Dean Howells, 1872–1910*, 2 vols., ed. Henry Nash Smith and William M. Gibson. Cambridge, Mass.: Belknap/Harvard University Press.

Wilson, James D. (1987). *A Reader's Guide to the Short Stories of Mark Twain.* Boston: G. K. Hall.

24

The Adventures of Tom Sawyer and The Prince and the Pauper as Juvenile Literature
Linda A. Morris

Two of Mark Twain's many full-length novels were clearly intended for a young audience. A third, *Adventures of Huckleberry Finn*, has also been read and appreciated by young readers since its initial publication, but its canonical stature in adult American fiction takes it beyond the reach of this investigation. The two novels in question, *The Adventures of Tom Sawyer* and *The Prince and the Pauper*, are so markedly different from one another that on the surface the only threads that seem to tie them together are the facts that Twain intended them to be read by young readers (and by adults as well) and that they have indeed been perennial favorites of adolescents. Why this is so will be taken up in the pages that follow. The differences between them, however, are legion. In *Tom Sawyer* Twain drew upon his memories of his own childhood, growing up along the Mississippi River before the Civil War; *The Prince and the Pauper*, set in sixteenth-century England, was based on his reading and research into English history. *Tom Sawyer* has been understood within the tradition of moral instruction in juvenile literature, although the novel belongs to the "bad boy" end of that spectrum, while *The Prince and the Pauper* is more readily appreciated as historical fiction. However, different as they are in their tone and subject matter, both feature young male protagonists as the heroes, and both tap into universal childhood fears and fantasies. Examining the two together, with an emphasis on the novels as juvenile literature, ultimately offers us an opportunity to appreciate yet one more facet of Twain's distinguished career.

The Adventures of Tom Sawyer

To identify *The Adventures of Tom Sawyer* as "juvenile literature" is not to deny its appeal to adult readers. Indeed, in the century and a quarter since its publication it has been read with pleasure by both adults and children, and no doubt reread by adults who read it initially as juveniles. Such a dual audience reflects in part the dual narrative perspective at the core of the novel – those times when Twain seems to enter into the mind of the boy with remarkable freshness and clarity, and those times when he looks down upon the boy's antics from a wholly adult perspective. As scholars have noted, from the beginning Twain wavered between believing he had written a "boy's" book and believing his forthcoming book was written only for adults and would "only be read by adults" (Twain and Howells 1960: 91).[1] After his friend William Dean Howells read the manuscript, he insisted that "it's altogether the best boy's story I ever read": "But I think you ought to treat it explicitly *as* a boy's story. Grown-ups will enjoy it just as much if you do; and if you should put it forth as a study of boy character from the grown-up point of view, you'd give the wrong key to it." (pp. 110–11). Twain was persuaded by Howell's argument, seconded by Livy Clemens: "Mrs. Clemens decides with you that the book should issue as a book for boys, pure & simple – & so do I. It is surely the correct idea" (p. 112).

In the end, it was never quite so simple, however. Howells's review of the book, published in the *Atlantic* in advance of the American release of the novel, walks a thin line between calling the book a boy's book and calling it a book for adults: "throughout there is scrupulous regard for the boy's point of view in reference to his surroundings and himself," which, Howells says, "adds immensely to the grownup reader's satisfaction in the amusing and exciting story" (Budd 1999: 157). Twain instructed his publisher at the American Publishing Company to "make a Boy's Holiday Book of it," but the salesman's prospectus developed for *Tom Sawyer* excluded any quotations from the English or American reviews that would lead the readers to believe it was "a book *for* boys" (Twain 1980: 25 n. 53). In point of fact, most of the English reviews did emphasize that *Tom Sawyer* was a boy's book; in so doing, they revealed a fascination with the view of American boy-life that it embodied:

> The human nature is boys' human nature all the world over. Tom Sawyer is a true boy, up to all sorts of adventure, however risky; more precocious than a boy of the same age would be in England, as is natural in a country where boys of eighteen consider that the "old man" is behind the age and doesn't know much, but likeable boys for all that: frank, fearless, mischievous, and as full of tricks as monkeys. (Budd 1999: 160)[2]

American reviewers, perhaps taking their cue from Howells, were more cautious about labeling the book a boy's book. The Hartford *Times* reviewer says, ambiguously, that "those who imagine this to be a tame story for little boys will discover their mistake on reading it" (Budd 1999: 161). Another Hartford paper insisted that "the stories of boy-life have ever an interest for those to whom mature years have brought the cares, ambitions, struggles and hopes of full-grown men" (p. 163). The New York *Evening Post* captured a paradox still sometimes imagined to be at the heart of the novel: "Certainly it will be in the last degree unsafe to put the book into the hands of imitative youth, and as certainly every grown reader will enjoy it heartily" (p. 166). Finally, the Hartford *Christian Secretary* lamented that Tom had "grave faults, some of which you almost wish had been omitted . . . One cannot help regretting that so fine a fellow as Tom lies and smokes, but the intention was not to describe a model boy. Yet these traits solely detract from the hero" (p. 166).

Tom Sawyer was not the first piece Twain wrote that can be categorized as juvenile fiction, although the earlier pieces are more properly comic burlesques than fiction written from a boy's perspective. Among those earlier works is an unfinished sketch given the title "Boy's Manuscript" (1870) by Albert Bigelow Paine, Twain's first biographer and literary editor. Henry Nash Smith characterized the fragment as "the germ of *The Adventures of Tom Sawyer*" (Smith 1962: 81). Unlike *Tom Sawyer*, the story is written in the first person, from the perspective of the protagonist, Billy Rogers. It rehearses the "courtship" of Bill and Amy that anticipates Tom's romantic attachment for Becky; as in the latter story, even though Billy purportedly speaks in his own voice, the hero's perspective is much closer to an adult's view of children's attachments than that of an adolescent boy. More interesting, from my point of view, is Twain's comic exaggeration in "Boy's Manuscript," centering on medical remedies administered to Billy by his mother: ipecac, calomel, tea, "blue mass pills," Epsom salts, hot water at the feet, "socks full of hot ashes on my breast, and a poultice on my head," and rhubarb "to regulate my bowels" (Twain 1980: 423–4).

Even earlier than "Boy's Manuscript," Twain wrote a series of short pieces that burlesqued the "Bad Boy" and "Good Boy" stories then in vogue.[3] The first of these, "Advice for Good Little Boys," written in 1865, was clearly intended for the amusement of adults; it contained sets of contrary advice such as "you ought never to take anything that don't belong to you – if you can't carry it off" (Twain 1992a: 163). At that same time he also wrote a parallel story for "Good Little Girls," offering advice such as "Good little girls ought not to make mouths at their teachers for every trifling offense. This kind of retaliation should only be resorted to under peculiarly aggravating circumstances" (Twain 1992a: 164). Clearly Twain was working his way, albeit unconsciously, toward Tom Sawyer's world by creating exaggerated stories that set the usual expectations for juvenile fiction on their ear: bad boys are not punished by fate for their bad deeds and instead grow up to become respected members of the Legislature, and "good little boys" are repeatedly punished for their good deeds, as in the case of Jacob Blivens ("The Story of the Good Little Boy Who Did Not Prosper") who is blown to smithereens by nitro-glycerin (Twain 1992a: 378).

Most likely in the year following his experimentation with "boy stories," Twain recorded in his notebook a series of superstitions that he recalled from his childhood. Because of its concreteness, its grounding in the imaginative and daily life of young boys, it is this list that strikes me as the real "germ" of *Tom Sawyer*:

Superstition.
Whence come the wise saws of the children?
Wash face in rain water standing on fresh cow dung to remove freckles.
Wash hands in rain water standing in old rotten hollow stump to remove warts.
Stick pin in wart, get blood, then stick in another boy will transfer your warts to him.
Split a bean, bind it on wart [&] wait till midnight & bury at X roads in dark of the moon. (Twain 1975: 160)

The fidelity to actual childhood memories, and the universality of superstitions such as these, lead inexorably toward the world of *Tom Sawyer*, which continues to be appreciated by young boys and adults alike – as Twain hoped, by "any man *who has ever been a boy*" (Gribben 1985: 151).

Granting that *The Adventures of Tom Sawyer* is a boy's book (and a book for adults), we would do well to ask if "boy" in this instance should be understood as a generic term for all children or as gender-specific. Gillian Brown has made a convincing argument that in nineteenth-century children's fiction – i.e. fiction in which "children inhabit their own world" – boys' and girls' play is gendered:

> As nineteenth-century accounts of boyhood advance the values of pleasure and careless-
> ness in childhood, accounts of girlhood present another, now equally familiar, notion of
> childhood and child's play as preparation for adulthood . . . The unremarked significance
> of the gendering of play, I think, lies in the fact that the sexual division of play simul-
> taneously promotes two distinct but closely related ideals of play: play as re-enactment
> of the past and play as rehearsal for the future. (Brown 2000: 89–90)

The Adventures of Tom Sawyer enacts precisely this distinction in its depiction of Tom and Becky Thatcher. Becky is represented only in terms of the future – as an object of courtship – and, when lost in the cave with Tom, as a timid, wholly dependent creature.

Francis Molson argues that *Tom Sawyer* is a "touchstone for children's fiction" because its hero's "winning portrait is one of the most richly conceived and drama-tized in children's literature" (Molson 1985: 269). The novel, Molson says, meets all but one of 13 previously identified hallmarks of good children's literature. These include "games and play as both incident and intrinsic element in the plot," "great gifts of improvisation in work, adventure, and play," an "opportunity to experience known dangers vicariously," and "various threats and promises which correspond to children's basic fears and hopes" (pp. 264–7). It is this last characteristic to which I wish to turn, for in it lies, I believe, the enduring appeal of the novel, and simulta-neously its biggest problem for modern readers: Injun Joe as an avatar, as an outcast, as the book's embodiment of evil.

Modern readers of *Tom Sawyer* cannot help being troubled by its representation of Injun Joe – as, indeed, by the depiction of American Indians wherever they appear in other works by Twain, such as *Roughing It* and "Huck and Tom Among the Indians." Yet Injun Joe is a central figure in the unfolding of the drama, an actor who drives the plot at critical points, and a figure who represents real danger to Tom and Huck. He inhabits a ghostly, shadow world that haunts the novel to its conclusion. As Cynthia Wolff has observed, "no other adult male plays so dominant a role in the novel as Injun Joe" (Wolff 1980: 648). More dramatically, Wolff says of Injun Joe, "it is as if one element in Tom's fantasy world has torn loose and broken away from him, roaming restlessly – a ruthless predator – genuinely and mortally dangerous" (p. 647). This is an essential point. Injun Joe is the embodiment of childhood fears, or night-mare visions; such a figure is a readily identifiable trope in juvenile fiction, which frequently depends upon the presence of some terrifying and threatening force. As twenty-first-century readers we are made uncomfortable not by the fact that Twain created a powerful figure of evil incarnate, but by the fact that he created a "half-breed" as the figure who haunted Tom's life and dreams.

If we reflect upon it for a moment, it is not difficult to imagine why Twain reached for the figure of a Native American: the mere presence of Indians evoked fear (and admiration) from the beginning of America's history, persisting in popular literature and film well into the twentieth century. One has only to think of James Fenimore Cooper, of Beadle's dime novels, or of John Wayne films. As well, there was a "real" Injun Joe in Samuel Clemens's Hannibal, although he was a much more benign figure than his fictional counterpart. Shelley Fisher Fishkin has recently argued that Joe Douglas, part Osage Indian, was also part black. According to Fishkin, he was a man "who should have been honored as hard working and enterprising [but] was unjustly remembered as the model for a murderous villain in the most famous novel by the town's most famous native son" (Fishkin 1997: 44). As a "half-breed," the fictional Injun Joe existed at best on the margins of St. Petersburg society, living essentially beyond the reach of the town's control, but nonetheless a familiar figure to its inhabitants. Tim Hirsch, while arguing that the book should be taught to children, readily admits to finding the "blatant anti-American Indian racism in the book" deeply troubling, indeed "offensive" (Hirsch 2002: 1). But rather than ignore the conflicts inherent in the novel, Hirsch argues for assigning the book because "it forces us to address innumerable unsavory features of American history" (p. 7). It surely is a novel that has to be understood in its historical context; at the same time, we also want to understand the depths that it mines.

For a juvenile book, *The Adventures of Tom Sawyer* is remarkably "dark," both literally and figuratively. Many key dramatic adventures take place at night, and/or in the dark (in the instance of the cave, in impenetrable darkness). More than this, however, a figurative, psychological darkness casts its shadow over the book. To begin with, Tom is an orphan, being raised by his mother's sister, so the experience of death lies just behind the storyline. The boys Tom and Huck are eye-witnesses to grave-robbing and a murder, and Muff Potter is nearly convicted of a murder he did not commit. Tom has numerous death fantasies, and the whole town reasonably assumes that Tom, Huck, and Joe Harper have been drowned in the Mississippi River. At the literal center of the novel lies the funeral for the three boys, which although it ends in triumph and jubilation, nevertheless draws the whole town into mourning for the lost boys (see Cox 1966: 136–40). Tom and Becky have a very real scrape with death when they are lost for three days and three nights in McDougal's cave, where they are plunged into complete darkness. Finally there is Injun Joe, who commits the murder in the graveyard, who haunts the streets of St. Petersburg in disguise, and who appears in Tom's dreams. He plots revenge on the Widow Douglas for treatment he received at the hands of her husband, threatening to tie her to her bed and slit her nostrils and notch her ears – like a sow's. In the depths of the cave, where he ultimately dies a terrible death, he appears like a satanic figure before Tom's astonished eyes.[4]

As I indicated earlier, a major part of the appeal of the novel to young readers is precisely its darkness and dangers, and the way that Tom triumphs over them.[5] The novel taps into universal childhood fantasies, but also, perhaps more dramatically, it has no doubt shaped childhood fantasies in the century and a quarter since its publication. The most salient of these fantasies, I have been assured by more than two generations of college students, has been that of escape to an island where the young heroes can be self-sufficient and live as they wish, without any adult presence. Students speak, too, of imagining themselves roaming a small town after dark, exposing a cruel teacher in public, or leading a band of young boys (and girls). They reminisce about imagining themselves dead or dying, and how much they would be missed and mourned by members of their families who did not properly appreciate them. A few even confess to wondering what it would be like to attend their own funeral.

Few, however, report wish-fulfillment fantasies about being lost in a cave and enduring the darkness for days and nights. Herein might lie the true genius of the novel, for in the McDougal cave episode Twain exceeded most childish fantasies and instead entered a deeper, even more universal world: a hero's descent into the underworld – the final and most significant trial of the mythic hero. As Fred See has so cogently argued, in the "magnificent scenes in McDougal's Cave," Tom "penetrates past the familiar and romantic portals of selfhood, beyond what can ever be communal, beyond the power of authority to claim and define, even beyond his own ability to chart" (See 1985: 252, 265). Tom and Becky move through the familiar, the known, the explored parts of the cave to the unfamiliar, moving deeper and deeper into the labyrinth. When they realize they are lost, and when their supply of candles and cakes dwindles, Tom must face the test of his life. He also comes face to face with evil itself as embodied in Injun Joe, and, while he flees from the specter, he has literally faced his greatest fear:

> Tom got down on his knees and felt below, and then as far around the corner as he could reach with his hands conveniently; he made an effort to stretch yet a little further to the right, and at that moment, not twenty yards away, a human hand, holding a candle, appeared from behind a rock! Tom lifted up a glorious shout, and instantly that hand was followed by the body it belonged to – Injun Joe's! Tom was paralyzed; he could not move. He was vastly gratified, the next moment, to see the "Spaniard" take to his heels and get himself out of sight. (Twain 1876: 245).

Tom triumphs, too, over the all-too-real danger of his own death, and Becky's, because he persists against all odds in finding a way out of his entombment. He emerges from the cave in a symbolic re-enactment of his birth:

> Tom lay upon a sofa with an eager auditory about him and told the history of the wonderful adventure, putting in many striking additions to adorn it withal; and closed with a description of how he left Becky and went on an exploring expedition; how he followed two avenues as far as his kite-line would reach; how he followed a third to the fullest stretch of the kite-line, and was about to turn back when he glimpsed a far-off

speck that looked like daylight; dropped the line and groped toward it, pushed his head and shoulders through a small hole and saw the broad Mississippi rolling by! (Twain 1876: 249)

"Born again upon his beloved river, Tom has earned his reward" (Wolff 1980: 650), returning to St. Petersburg as a hero for having saved Becky's life, and his own, and soon to be additionally rewarded by finding Injun Joe's hidden treasure in the depths of the cave. His less tangible reward for having descended into the underworld and survived is that he is ready to take his place as a leader in St. Petersburg society.

Here the child's and the adult's sensibilities may part company, for while young readers may glory in Tom's exalted position in the town, and the power of his money (properly shared with Huck), many modern adult readers have expressed dissatisfaction about the person Tom becomes at the end of *The Adventures of Tom Sawyer*.[6] This discomfort is exacerbated by reading backwards from *Adventures of Huckleberry Finn*, in which Tom's final role in freeing the already free Jim is problematic at best. Twain himself famously distanced himself from the Tom Sawyer he created in the first book bearing his name: "If I went on, now, & took him into manhood, he would just be like all the one-horse men in literature & the reader would conceive a hearty contempt for him" (Twain and Howells 1960: 91).

If the novel seems remarkably dark for a book for young people, it also embodies many of the comic techniques that were the hallmarks of Twain's other novels, and it does so with a deft hand. For instance, the practical joke, so critical to earlier stories by Mark Twain, is never more adroitly engineered than in the boys' triumphal return to their own funeral. As with all others, this practical joke requires for its effect a mastermind, a "victim," and a surprise. What seems especially remarkable about this joke played upon the whole community is that in the end both the mastermind and the victim are jubilant:

Aunt Polly, Mary and the Harpers threw themselves upon their restored ones, smothered them with kisses and poured out thanksgivings . . . Suddenly the minister shouted at the top of his voice: "Praise God from whom all blessings flow – SING! – and put your hearts in it!"

And they did. Old Hundred swelled up with a triumphant burst, and while it shook the rafters Tom Sawyer the Pirate looked around upon the envying juveniles about him and confessed in his heart that this was the proudest moment of his life.

As the "sold" congregation trooped out they said they would almost be willing to be made ridiculous again to hear Old Hundred sung like that once more. (Twain 1876: 146–7)

In one of the most delightful comic moments in *The Adventures of Tom Sawyer*, Mark Twain attributes human characteristics to an animal, as he did so many other times throughout his career. This time the animal is Peter the cat, to whom Tom feeds the painkiller his aunt has been giving him:

"Don't ask for it unless you want it, Peter."

But Peter signified that he did want it.

"You better make sure."

Peter was sure.

"Now you've asked for it, and I'll give it to you, because there ain't anything mean about *me*; but if you find you don't like it, you mustn't blame anybody but your own self."

Peter was agreeable. (Twain 1876: 109)

In the aftermath of receiving the tonic, Peter's antics are described in terms ordinarily reserved for people. He gave "a war-whoop," he pranced "in a frenzy of enjoyment, with his head over his shoulder and his voice proclaiming his unappeasable happiness." He "thr[e]w a few double summersets," and "deliver[ed] a final mighty hurrah" (p. 110). Tom, for his part, "lay on the floor expiring with laughter."

Other comic techniques abound in *Tom Sawyer*. One of these is the use of burlesque to make fun of familiar literary forms, as exemplified in the "original" composition by the young ladies at the school celebration:

Each in her turn stepped forward to the edge of the platform, cleared her throat, held up her manuscript (tied with dainty ribbon), and proceeded to read, with labored attention to "expression" and punctuation. The themes were the same that had been illuminated upon similar occasions by their mothers before them, their grandmothers, and doubtless all their ancestors in the female line clear back to the Crusades. (Twain 1876: 170)

Not content merely to describe the compositions, Twain first quotes one of the "examinations," then two stanzas from "A Missouri Maiden's Farewell to Alabama," and finally a piece entitled "A Vision," which he calls a "nightmare" sermon, "so destructive of all hope to non-Presbyterians that it took the first prize" (p. 173). What is unusual about this series of burlesques is that Twain admits at the end of the chapter that he was quoting actual "compositions" rather than imitating them. In effect, then, they were mock-burlesques, a form for which he had a particular fondness.

Although Twain never took Tom Sawyer into adulthood, he did return to him as a central character over the next decade, most famously, of course, in *Adventures of Huckleberry Finn*. Beyond that, however, Tom Sawyer was the hero of two novellas, *Tom Sawyer Abroad* (1893–4) and *Tom Sawyer, Detective* (1896), as well as one unpublished fragment, "Huck and Tom Among the Indians."[7] In all three, Huck narrates and Tom stars. *Tom Sawyer Abroad*, published in the prestigious periodical for young people, *St. Nicholas Magazine*, is a science fiction fantasy in which the two protagonists, plus Jim, set out to travel around the world in a balloon. *Tom Sawyer, Detective* revolves around a complicated plot featuring Silas Phelps from *Huckleberry Finn*, and allows Tom to show off his deductive powers and save an innocent man from hanging. In "Huck and Tom Among the Indians," the boys and Jim head west to live with Indians, supposedly Noble Savages, but this apparently friendly group end up killing and scalping most of the white adults in Huck and Tom's party and abducting Jim and a young white woman whom they clearly brutalize. Only one of the tales, *Tom Sawyer Abroad*, can be said to be unequivocally a story for juveniles, but in all Twain seeks to capitalize upon the success of *Huckleberry Finn* and Tom's dominant personality as exhibited at the end of that novel.

The Prince and the Pauper

In contrast with *The Adventures of Tom Sawyer*, *The Prince and the Pauper: A Tale for Young People of All Ages* (1881) was intended primarily for a young audience. So it was received, and so it has remained. The novel has been continuously in print since its initial publication, and remains one of Twain's most successful works, if not a favorite of Twain scholars. Begun in 1876, the year of the publication of *Tom Sawyer*, *The Prince and the Pauper* adopted a noticeably different narrative strategy, one much more in keeping with the juvenile audience for whom it was intended. As we shall see, like *Tom Sawyer*, it is a novel filled with "dark" elements that play into childhood fears and fantasies, and it, too, features a young hero who is subjected to multiple trials before he is ultimately fit (literally) to lead his people. It is a much more "serious" novel than *Tom Sawyer*, and although it is not without its humorous moments, and a great deal of play with language, it employs many fewer of the comic techniques for which Twain was already famous.

Twain had a juvenile audience in mind from the beginning as he wrote his tale of a sixteenth-century English prince (Edward VI, son of Henry VIII) and a pauper (Tom Canty) who exchange places and undergo a series of personal trials until the prince is restored to his rightful place and crowned king of England and Tom Canty is spared the fate of returning to life as a pauper. The novel was dedicated to his two daughters, Susy and Clara (Jean was not born until the manuscript was substantially complete, in 1880), who, along with his wife Livy, were his first audience:

> Each afternoon or evening, when he had finished his chapter, he assembled his little audience and read them the result. The children were old enough to delight in that half real, half fairy tale of the wandering prince and the royal pauper: and the charm and simplicity of the story are measurably due to those two small listeners, to whom it was adapted in that early day of its creation. (Paine 1912: 662–3)[8]

Having an immediate, intimate, audience may explain in part why Twain, rather uncharacteristically, professed to have delighted in writing the novel, even toward its conclusion. In February 1880 he wrote to his brother, Orion Clemens, "I am grinding away now, with all my might, & with an interest which amounts to intemperance, at the 'Prince and the Pauper'" (Twain 1946: 143). Ten days later he told Howells of his "jubilant delight" in writing the novel, and the next week wrote that "I take so much pleasure in my story that I am loath to hurry, not wanting to get it done" (Twain and Howells 1960: 290–1).

Long after the publication of the novel, it remained a favorite of the Clemens family. As a surprise for her husband, in March 1885 Livy created a stage version of it with the parts of the central characters played by Susy, Clara, and the neighborhood children. The neighbors were all invited to the production:

> There was but one hitch in the performance. There is a place where the Prince says, "Fathers be alike, mayhap; mine hath not a doll's temper."
>
> This was Susy's part, and as she said it the audience did not fail to remember its literal appropriateness. There was a moment's silence, then a titter, followed by a roar of laughter, in which everybody but the little actors joined. They did not see the humor and were disturbed and grieved. Curiously enough, Mrs. Clemens herself, in arranging and casting the play, had not considered the possibility of this effect. The parts were all daintily played. The children wore their assumed personalities as if native to them. Daisy Warner played the part of Tom Canty, Clara Clemens was Lady Jane Grey (Paine 1912: 789)

Twain "was deeply moved and supremely gratified" (p. 789). That night he wrote to his friend James B. Pond:

> My boy, you ought to have been here tonight to see Susie & Clara & a dozen of the neighbors' children play half a dozen stirring scenes from the Prince & the Pauper – one of the prettiest private thatrical [_sic_] performances I have ever seen. Audience of 25 neighbors. Mrs. Clemens has been drilling these kids 3 or 4 weeks in their parts, & to-night the thing was sprung on me as a surprise. When it is repeated, you must run up & see it. (Twain 2001: reel 2, 14 March 1885)

According to Paine, "the play was repeated, Clemens assisting, adding to the parts, and himself playing the role of Miles Hendon" (1912: 789).

Other factors point to a juvenile audience for the novel. Twain initially offered the book to _St. Nicholas Magazine_, edited by Mary Mapes Dodge, then essentially withdrew the offer for fear that publishing the novel serially would hurt its sales when it was later sold by subscription.[9] William Dean Howells, when asked to read the manuscript, identified passages whose suitability for young people he questioned:

> I send some pages with words queried. These and other things I have found in the book seem rather strong milk for babes – more like milk-punch in fact. If you give me leave I will correct them in the plates for you . . . I don't think such words as devil, and hick (for person) and basting (for beating,) ought to be suffered in your own narration. I have found about 20 such. (Twain and Howells 1960: 375)

The next day, Howells wrote to Twain that he had marked specific passages "which I don't think are fit to go into a book for boys . . . I hope you wont think I'm meddling." Twain immediately replied: "slash away, with entire freedom; & the more you slash, the better I shall like it & the more I shall be cordially obliged to you. Alter any and everything you choose – don't hesitate" (p. 376). Twain also read portions of the manuscript to the young Girls' Club of Hartford, "half a dozen chapters at a time . . . They profess to be very much fascinated with it; so do Livy & Daisy Warner" (Twain 1949: 218). Finally, the book received its imprimatur as juvenile fiction from Twain's most distinguished Hartford neighbor: "'I am reading your *Prince and Pauper* for the fourth time,' Harriet Beecher Stowe was to tell Clemens in 1887, pressing his hand in hers and speaking with such fervor it brought the tears to his eyes, 'and I *know* it is the best book for young folks that was ever written'" (Kaplan 1966: 240).

As Victor Fischer has so cogently and succinctly argued, the book represents, for young readers,

> the working out of a universal fantasy – what if I were he and he were I? Along the way, universal childhood fears are encountered and overcome: the death of a parent, cruel substitute parents, abandonment, lost identity, kidnap, unjust punishment and imprisonment. The rewards for confronting such fears are greater understanding, compassion, maturity, and ultimately, elevated estate. (Twain 1983: xv)

Beyond the very child-centered essence of the story, certain scenes in the book seem designed to appeal directly to young readers. One brief moment, almost a throwaway line, is illustrative: Miles Hendon coerces a constable into turning a blind eye so he and Edward can escape from captivity, instructing him "to count to a hundred thousand, slowly" (Twain 1881: 291). In its context, the line is silly, but young children, who universally engage in extravagant counting rituals, are bound to be delighted by this touch. Other extended episodes seem designed for no other apparent purpose than to thrill and delight a youthful audience. Consider, for instance, the episode in which Edward lies down to sleep in a pitch-dark barn and imagines at first, then knows with certainty, that something mysterious and soft is touching him in the darkness. The vignette is a skillful piece of storytelling, of the oral tradition brought to bear on a written work:

> Then, just as he was on the point of losing himself wholly [in sleep], he distinctly felt something touch him! He was broad awake in a moment, and gasping for breath. The cold horror of that mysterious touch in the dark almost made his heart stand still. He lay motionless, and listened, scarcely breathing. But nothing stirred, and there was no sound . . . So he began to drop into a drowse once more, at last; and all at once he felt that mysterious touch again! It was a grisly thing, this light touch from this noiseless and invisible presence; it made the boy sick with ghostly fears. (p. 231)

The prince finally convinces himself that he has to reach out his hand to solve the mystery:

> his hand lightly swept against something soft and warm. This petrified him, nearly, with fright – his mind was in such a state that he could imagine the thing to be nothing else than a corpse, newly dead and still warm. He thought he would rather die than

touch it again. But he thought this false thought because he did not know the immortal strength of human curiosity. In no long time his hand was tremblingly groping again – against his judgment, and without his consent – but groping persistently on, just the same. (Twain 1881: 232)

At last he perceives that the "grisly thing" is a slumbering calf, and he is ashamed for having been so frightened. The narrator, however, says he had no reason to feel shame: "for it was not the calf that frightened him but a dreadful non-existent something which the calf stood for; and any other boy, in those old superstitious times, would have acted and suffered just as he had done" (p. 233).

In creating a vivid picture of this remote historical time, Twain employs adjectives that are uncharacteristically general, intended specifically for a juvenile audience. Most often this is true of adjectives used to evoke images of royalty. For example, when describing Tom's first view of Westminster, Twain writes:

> Tom stared in *glad* wonder at the *vast* pile of masonry, the *wide-spreading* wings, the *frowning* bastions and turrets, the *huge* stone gateway, with its gilded bars and its *magnificent* array of colossal granite lions and other . . . signs and symbols of English royalty. . . . *Splendid* carriages with *splendid* people in them and *splendid* servants outside were arriving and departing by several other *noble* gateways that pierced the royal enclosure . . . Within [one of these] was a comely boy, tanned and brown with sturdy out-door sports and exercises, whose clothing was all of *lovely* silks and satins, shining with jewels; at his hip a little jeweled sword and dagger; *dainty* buskins on his feet, with red heels, and on his head a *jaunty* crimson cap with *drooping* plumes fastened with a great sparkling gem. Several *gorgeous* gentlemen stood near, – his servants, without a doubt. (Twain 1881: 38–9, emphasis added)

Other descriptions of the royal quarters and state ceremonies – "a gorgeous fleet," bells that "shook out tiny showers of joyous music," furniture that was "all massy gold, and beautified with designs" – are accompanied by similar adjectives designed to evoke wonder in a young audience, especially a listening audience such as Susy and Clara or the Hartford Girls' Club.

A similar impulse governs some of Twain's descriptions of the horrors Edward encounters as he tries to make his way back to the palace. They work to the same effect, as in the following passage which records Edward awakening to behold the gathering of criminals surrounding him:

> A *grim* and *unsightly* picture met his eye. A bright fire was burning in the middle of the floor, at the other end of the barn; and around it, and lit weirdly up by the red glare, lolled and sprawled the *motliest* company of *tattered* gutter-scum and ruffians, of both sexes, he had ever read or dreamed of. There were *huge*, stalwart men, brown with exposure, long-haired, and clothed in *fantastic* rags . . . (Twain 1881: 208–9, emphasis added)

As the description goes on, however, Twain seems to warm to his subject and perhaps even forget for a moment his intended audience, for the prose becomes more vivid and specific:

there were middle-sized youths, of truculent countenance, and similarly clad; there were blind mendicants, with patched or bandaged eyes; crippled ones, with wooden legs and crutches; there was a villain-looking peddler with his pack; a knife-grinder, a tinker, and a barber-surgeon, with the implements of their trades; some of the females were hardly-grown girls, some were at prime, some were old and wrinkled hags, and all were loud, brazen, foul-mouthed; and all soiled and slatternly; there were three sore-faced babies; there were a couple of starveling [*sic*] curs, with strings about their necks, whose office was to lead the blind. (p. 209)[10]

As the novel progresses, and as Edward encounters more of the violence and poverty at large in his kingdom, the story's dark side, as in *The Adventures of Tom Sawyer*, becomes more prominent. Because the novel is set in the sixteenth century, and because Twain was careful to be truthful in his portrayal of "those old superstitious times," there is a kind of gothic quality about the violence in it. Or, as Victor Fischer observes, "set in sixteenth-century England, with great attention to historical detail, it has all the grace, charm, and unreasoned violence of an ancient folk tale" (Twain 1983: xv). The list of violent actions, both on stage and off, so to speak, is long. Four women are burned at the stake, with Edward witnessing two of the executions; severed heads are displayed on pikes on London Bridge, with one falling off during a mob scene; people are threatened with being boiled in oil; accused criminals have their ears cut off; men and women are enslaved, and branded as slaves; and at almost every turn people are beaten, among them Miles Hendon, who takes a public lashing in Edward's stead. John Canty murders the good priest, Father Andrew, who befriended the young Tom and taught him to read (and to dream), and a mad hermit binds and gags Edward, intending to murder him.

The purpose of all the violence is similar to its purpose in *Tom Sawyer* – and in the terms of juvenile literature generally – only this time the hero is a real leader who must undergo significant trials in order to learn to lead his kingdom wisely. On his quest to return to London, and to regain his place in the palace, Edward is educated about the cruelties of his father's laws, and about the poverty in his kingdom, at the peril of his life. He is, however, in many respects a remarkably slow learner. Repeatedly he stands his ground by insisting loudly and boldly that he is the king, no matter how rough the response. He will not modify his behavior, and he is nearly killed for it. Unlike Tom Sawyer, who survives his descent into the underworld by his own wits, Edward has a protector, Miles Hendon, who sees him through almost every peril he faces, except the mad hermit's real threat to stab him to death. Edward is rescued from that last fate, ironically, by the man who believes he is his father, the cruel John Canty.[11] Remarkably, the original illustration of the mad hermit, hovering over the prostrate figure of Edward on the bed, is nearly identical to the illustration of Injun Joe threatening Tom (in his dreams) with a knife. In each instance, the young boy is on a bed, and hence extremely vulnerable, and in each instance a fiendish male figure is poised to plunge his long dagger into the heart of the helpless hero.[12] The major difference is that Tom Sawyer's danger is a manifestation of his imagination, of his nightmares, while Edward's danger is real, brought about, at least indirectly, as a consequence of his father's dissolution of the Catholic monasteries. In the final section of the novel, during his short reign as king, Edward is depicted as a lenient and merciful ruler, who ultimately did learn from his trials and suffering as a pauper.

Lest we forget, however, there are two heroes in *The Prince and the Pauper*, and Tom Canty, like Edward, also undergoes a series of trials. If a young reader were to have identified with Tom rather than Edward, he or she would be taken through a fantasy world in which a young boy escapes from his terrible father, and the abject poverty in which his family is mired, and literally lives the life of a prince – pampered, waited on, honored, and obeyed. Unlike Edward, Tom is a reasonably quick study. Prepared for his role by his own earlier role-playing, and by his tutor, Father Andrew, Tom comes to enjoy his position as prince and heir apparent. In his brief reign, he shows himself to be a benign ruler; as Edward acknowledges: "Thou has governed the realm with right royal gentleness and mercy" (Twain 1881: 394). He is not, however, returned to his "rightful" place if that means returning to Offal Court. Instead, Edward rewards him with a place of honor at Christ's Hospital:

> "this boy shall dwell there, and hold the chief place in its honorable body of governors, during life. And for that he hath been a king, it is meet that other than common observances shall be his due; wherefore, note this dress of state, for by it he shall be known, and none shall copy it; and wheresoever he shall come, it shall remind the people that *he hath been royal, in his time*, and none shall deny him his due of reverence or fail to give him salutation. He hath the throne's protection, he hath the crown's support, he shall be known and called by the honorable title of the King's Ward." (Twain 1881: 394–5, emphasis added)

Unlike Edward VI, Tom "lived to be a very old man, a handsome, white-haired old fellow, of grave and benignant aspect. As long as he lasted he was honored" (p. 401).

Finally, as in *Tom Sawyer*, there are comic elements in *The Prince and the Pauper*, but here they play a much lesser role. Aside from the play with language, which is everywhere in the novel, the primary comic technique Twain relies upon is comic exaggeration, centering on Tom's experience as a member of the royal court who is not allowed to do anything for himself – fancily dressed servants do everything for him. Besides the royal Diaperer,

> my lord d'Arcy, First Groom of the Chamber, was there, to do goodness knows what, but there he was – let that suffice. The Lord Chief Butler was there, and stood behind Tom's chair, overseeing the solemnities, under command of the Lord Great Steward and the Lord Head Cook, who stood near. Tom had three hundred and eighty-four servants beside these, but they were not all in that room, of course, nor the quarter of them; neither was Tom aware yet that they existed. (Twain 1881: 90)

Although little humor accompanies Edward on his perilous journey, there is nonetheless considerable laughter. That laughter, however, is almost always derisive, mocking the boy who insists he is king. Fully half of the times in the novel when people laugh, it is at the boy's expense. In contrast, people laugh at Tom only once. At the end of the story, when the two boys have resumed their proper places, someone asks Tom what he had used the royal seal for, and he admits he used it to crack nuts: "Poor child, the avalanche of laughter that greeted this, nearly swept him off his feet. But if a doubt remained in any mind that Tom Canty was not the king of England and familiar with the august appurtenances of royalty, this reply disposed of it utterly" (Twain 1881: 380).

This is the laughter of relief, laughter that signals that all is once again right with the world of the prince and the pauper.

NOTES

1 See e.g. Kaplan (1966), Fiedler (1966), and Stone (1961).

2 In a similar vein, the *Spectator* asserted that "altogether, Tom Sawyer's lot was cast in a region not so tamed down by conventionalities, as is that in which English boys are doomed to live. Hence he had rare opportunities, and saw rare sights, actually tragedies, which our tamer life is content to read about in books" (Budd 1999: 161).

3 This issue has been examined in detail by critics such as John C. Gerber in his introduction to Twain (1980), Stone (1961), Fetterley (1971), Gribben (1985), Mailloux (1989), and Messent (1997).

4 Injun Joe's role in the novel as a force of evil, as a frightening figure, was underscored by True Williams's original illustrations for the novel. In chapter 24, in which we learn that Injun Joe "infested" all of Tom's dreams, Williams drew a larger-than-life image of a crazed-looking Injun Joe, dagger in hand, hovering over the vulnerable body of Tom asleep.

5 For a compelling argument about the role of physical punishment in the novel, see Messent (1997).

6 See especially Fetterley (1971) and Robinson (1984).

7 The two novellas have been published in Twain (1980), while the fragment appears in Twain (1989).

8 As several critics have noted, Twain also asked his friends Joseph Twichell, William Dean Howells, and Edwin Pond Parker to read the manuscript to their children and to send their comments back to him. See e.g. Lin Salamo's introduction to Twain (1979: 7).

9 For an extended discussion of the state of children's literature in the 1870s, and for the role of such magazines as *St. Nicholas*, see Stone (1961: 102–9).

10 Albert E. Stone notes that among the many books Twain read in preparation for writing *The Prince and the Pauper* was "an old seventeenth-century history of vagabonds, criminals, and gypsies" by Richard Head and Francis Kirkman (Stone 1961: 113).

11 For an extended discussion of the roles of fathers and sons in *The Prince and the Pauper*, see Lulofs (1984: 52–94).

12 See Twain (1876: 190; 1881: 260).

REFERENCES AND FURTHER READING

Brown, Gillian (2000). "Child's Play." *Differences: A Journal of Feminist Cultural Studies* 11: 3, 76–107.

Budd, Louis J., ed. (1999). *Mark Twain: The Contemporary Reviews*. Cambridge, UK: Cambridge University Press.

Cox, James M. (1966). *Mark Twain: The Fate of Humor*. Princeton: Princeton University Press, 136–40.

Fetterley, Judith (1971). "The Sanctioned Rebel." *Studies in the Novel* 3: 3, 293–304.

Fiedler, Leslie A. (1966). *Love and Death in the American Novel*, rev. edn. New York: Stein & Day. (First publ. 1960.)

Fishkin, Shelley Fisher (1997). *Lighting Out for the Territory: Reflections on Mark Twain and American Culture*. New York: Oxford University Press.

Gribben, Alan (1985). "'I Did Wish Tom Sawyer Was There': Boy-Book Elements in *Tom Sawyer* and *Huckleberry Finn*." In Robert Sattelmeyer and J. Donald Crowley (eds.), *One Hundred Years of Huckleberry Finn: The Boy, his Book, and American Culture*, 149–70. Columbia: University of Missouri Press.

Hirsch, Tim (2002). "Banned by Neglect: *Tom Sawyer*, Teaching the Conflicts." In Nicholas J. Karolides (ed.), *Censored Books II: Critical Viewpoints, 1985–2000*, 1–9. London: Scarecrow.

Kaplan, Justin (1966). *Mr. Clemens and Mark Twain: A Biography*. New York: Simon & Schuster.

Lulofs, Timothy (1984). "Fathers and Sons in Mark Twain's Fiction." Ph.D. diss., University of California at Davis.

Lynn, Kenneth S. (1959). *Mark Twain and Southwestern Humor*. Boston: Little, Brown.

Mailloux, Stephen (1989). *Rhetorical Power*. Ithaca, NY: Cornell University Press.

Messent, Peter (1997). *Mark Twain*. Basingstoke: Macmillan.

Messent, Peter (1998). "Discipline and Punishment in *The Adventures of Tom Sawyer*." *Journal of American Studies* 32: 2, 219–235.

Molson, Francis (1985). "Mark Twain's *The Adventures of Tom Sawyer*: More than a Warm Up." In Perry Nodelman (ed.), *Touchstones: Reflections on the Best in Children's Literature*, 262–69. West Lafayette, Ind.: Children's Literature Association.

Paine, Albert Bigelow (1912). *Mark Twain: A Biography. The Personal and Literary Life of Samuel Langhorne Clemens*, 3 vols. New York and London: Harper & Bros.

Robinson, Forrest G. (1984). "Social Play and Bad Faith in *The Adventures of Tom Sawyer*." *Nineteenth-Century Fiction* 39, 1–24.

See, Fred G. (1985). "Tom Sawyer and Children's Literature." *Essays in Literature* 12: 2 (Western Illinois University), 251–71.

Seelye, John (1994). "What's in a Name: Sounding the Depths of Tom Sawyer." In Eric J. Sundquist (ed.), *Mark Twain: A Collection of Critical Essays*, 49–61. Englewood Cliffs, NJ: Prentice-Hall.

Smith, Henry Nash (1962). *Mark Twain: The Development of a Writer*. Cambridge, Mass.: Belknap/Harvard University Press.

Stone, Albert E., Jr. (1961). *The Innocent Eye: Childhood in Mark Twain's Imagination*. New Haven: Yale University Press.

Twain, Mark (1946). *Mark Twain, Business Man*, ed. Samuel Charles Webster. Boston: Little, Brown.

Twain, Mark (1949). *Mark Twain: To Mrs. Fairbanks*, ed. Dixon Wecter. San Marino, Calif.: Huntington Library.

Twain, Mark (1975). *Mark Twain's Notebooks and Journals*, vol. 1: *1855–1873*, ed. Frederick Anderson, Michael B. Frank, and Kenneth M. Sanderson. Berkeley: University of California Press.

Twain, Mark (1979). *The Prince and the Pauper*, ed. Victor Fischer and Lin Salamo. Berkeley: University of California Press.

Twain, Mark (1980). *The Adventures of Tom Sawyer; Tom Sawyer Abroad; Tom Sawyer, Detective*, ed. John C. Gerber, Paul Baender, and Terry Firkins. Berkeley: University of California Press.

Twain, Mark (1983). *The Prince and the Pauper*, ed. Victor Fischer. Berkeley: University of California Press.

Twain, Mark (1989). *Huck Finn and Tom Sawyer among the Indians and Other Unfinished Stories*. Berkeley: University of California Press.

Twain, Mark (2001). *Microfilm Edition of Mark Twain's Previously Unpublished Letters*, 8 vols. Prepared by Anh Quynh Bui, Victor Fischer, Michael B. Frank, Robert H. Hirst, Lin Salamo, and Harriet Elinor Smith. Berkeley, Calif.: Bancroft Library.

Twain, Mark, and Howells, William Dean (1960). *Mark Twain–Howells Letters: The Correspondence of Samuel L. Clemens and William D. Howells, 1872–1910*, 2 vols., ed. Henry Nash Smith and William M. Gibson. Cambridge: Belknap.

Wolff, Cynthia Griffin (1980). "*The Adventures of Tom Sawyer*: A Nightmare Vision of American Boyhood." *The Massachusetts Review* 21, 637–52.

25

Plotting and Narrating "Huck"

Victor Doyno

The long-lost "first half" of Twain's original manuscript of *Huckleberry Finn* (1885) was only rediscovered in 1990 (see Twain 1996: xiii–xiv). In this essay I explore the now complete set of manuscript materials to reveal more of the process of composition of this great novel. My particular interest here is in the development both of narrative voice and of plot as the author made his episodic way through his fiction.

The first compositional tasks Twain had, in what would become the opening five chapters of *Huckleberry Finn*, involved imagining the village or town of St. Petersburg from Huck's point of view and – importantly – establishing Huck's narrative voice. Twain had to imagine Huck within the Widow Douglas's home, and struggling with Miss Watson. It was important for him that Huck, as early as page 9 of the manuscript version of the novel, considered going to hell, deciding – in his original words – to "keep dark and go for the other place" (MS 9 [all references in this essay are to the pages of Twain's original manuscript: see Twain 2003]). This early allusion to religious damnation went hand-in-hand with other Christian references, most especially the early mention of Moses and the issues of separation from parental love, travel, exile, self-creation in difficult circumstances, biblical slavery, oppression, and liberation thus implicitly raised.

After enduring the conflicting ways of Miss Watson and the Widow Douglas, Huck needs to get away. The child seems of an indeterminate age, but leaning toward the younger side, around nine or ten in the first chapter. Twain's uncertainty about tone is evident in the first stages of his writing, for when Huck hears Tom me-yowing to call him out for night-time pranks, Huck's first "That was jolly!" was changed by Twain to "That was good!" – a less clichéd, much less "bully" and bookish phrasing. The more Twain wrote, the terser Huck's voice became, and the pace of the narrative increased accordingly.

The first compositional break in the manuscript occurred when Twain decided, seven lines down on MS sheet 15, to reach for a new sheet to start his second chapter. This seems consistent with the entry of a new character, Tom Sawyer, and with a shift of action, from the stifling house to a stimulating outside space of night-time adventure. But it is important to recognize that Twain was apparently in no hurry to get Huck away from the village for a while – actually, for 94 manuscript sheets. No evidence exists of any early pressure toward movement downriver. Twain, rather, contentedly writes from incident to incident, prank to prank, within the St. Petersburg setting, as he does so establishing Huck's voice and his character as a naïve literalist, an unsophisticated but active boy who listens pragmatically to adults' talk about religion and to his friend Tom's bookish, unrealistic talk about "adventures."

But as Huck speaks to *us* (the readers), we realize his need to test pragmatically whatever he hears, his recognition of a similarity between "Sunday-school" teachings and Tom's deceptive books of adventure when it comes to knowing how the world really works. Huck seems to know when he has been told a "whopper," even when that falsehood is socially approved, and he learns to keep his silence about the fictions he hears and is expected to believe. The boy reveals a lot to his readers, although he is usually (apparently) a largely silent presence among those who immediately surround him.

Twain needed to have a motive for Huck to leave his familiar village, to set off on an indefinite "voyage to other lands." Pap Finn had been first mentioned when Twain was writing *The Adventures of Tom Sawyer* (1876). It was he, rather than Muff Potter – though most readers do not know this – who had been the original accomplice for Injun Joe's murder of the Doctor in the cemetery in that novel. In its early manuscript version, Tom and Huck go to the graveyard, become frightened when they hear noises, then watch as Injun Joe and pap Finn approach with the Doctor to disinter a body. (In the *Huckleberry Finn* manuscript Twain generally used a capital letter for the nickname "Pap," but he changed the printed version to "pap" for all uses except at the conventionally capitalized beginning of a sentence.) Twain based Huck's father on the Hannibal drunk, Jimmy Finn.

The earliest reference to Huck's father in the *Huckleberry Finn* manuscript occurs when the boys in Tom Sawyer's Gang complain that Huck does not have a relative to be killed. Attention is redirected to him on MS sheet 45, when Huck says that he had not seen his father for more than a year and mentions a rumor about a drowned person, who some supposed to have been pap.

While writing MS sheets 45 to (about) 60, Twain was apparently primarily engaged in a village-based satire about Huck and the follies of school and "civilization," with Tom Sawyer's delusions about reading as a particular target. At the top of page 60, he began to write, "One morning . . . ," but then wiped away the wet ink and wrote what we now know as the second paragraph of chapter 4: a long, balanced treatment of what Huck had learned at the Widow Douglas's, including the important and favorable statement that the Widow said "she warn't ashamed of me." For Huck's world will function in terms of shame (and shame avoidance), rather than in terms of guilt. Once this summary of Huck's progress was written, Twain again began, "One morning . . . ," with Huck's overturning of the salt-cellar at breakfast, and the "bad luck" sure to ensue, a continuing motif in the text. Twain then prepared for pap's appearance with suspenseful writing about the mysterious, distinctive heelprint, with the cross "to keep off the devil." Twain knew he was leading up to pap Finn, but most first-time readers do not.

Twain explored the possibilities, and maintained suspense, by having Huck visit two very different trusted, and smart, men: Judge Thatcher and Jim. In the manuscript Jim's future importance is implicitly signaled by the fact that Huck's consultation with him takes up a complete, separate chapter (MS chapter 5). At this point, however, the comic aspects of the scene belie any clear idea of a plot development which might involve the twinned destinies of these two figures: man and boy, black and white.

And it is pap who is the major figure in Huck's life at this point. Once Twain had Huck under pap's control in the isolated shanty, he could then explore and recreate pap Finn's hatreds and abusiveness. The novel now briefly becomes an alcohol-influenced, European American variant of a captivity narrative, and it will return to this somewhat static imprisonment genre again at its conclusion, when Jim is similarly held as a prisoner in Arkansas. Although Huck is locked securely inside pap's cabin, Twain knew relatively early on that Huck would have to escape from pap's control and cruelty on his own.

He did not, however, know where Huck would go or by what means. Twain had Huck express preliminary thoughts about going off across the state of Illinois – and, if that possibility had held, his adventure would have taken the form of a road-journal (or a swamp-book!) instead of a river-book. Huck's plans for escape are expressed, in manuscript version, as follows:

> I thought it all over and I reckoned I would walk off with <one of> [pap's] gun<s> and some <fishing> lines, and take to the woods when I run away. I guessed I wouldn't stay in one place, but just tramp right across the country, mostly night-times, and hunt and fish to keep alive, and so get so far away that the old man nor the widow couldn't ever find me any more. (MS 103–4)

By MS pages 121–2, however, Twain began to remember the river's "June rise," and by MS 123 a drifting canoe comes along down the river, and Huck's – and Twain's – plans change:

> But when I got to shore Pap wasn't in sight yet, and as I was running her [the canoe] into a little creek like a gully, all hung over with vines and willows, I struck another idea; I judged I'd hide her good, and then, <in>'stead of taking to the woods when I run off, I'd go down the river about fifty mile and camp in one place for good, and not have such a rough time tramping on foot. (MS 124)

Interestingly, when writing this passage Twain seems to have become excited, for he began to use a lot of "running-script" – a form of handwriting where he did not raise the pen from the paper as he swiftly moved from word to word. His right hand just sped along, with only the occasional lifting of pen from the page. We can render

Twain's "running script" typographically as: "Butwhen Igottoshore/Papwasn't in sight yet;/andas Iwas runningher/. . . andnothave such a rough time tramping on foot." Twain appears to have used this handwriting when, on occasion, he was composing very rapidly, or when he had a very clear idea of what he wanted to happen next or, as in this case (as I believe), when he had become excited about the direction his story was taking. Often, after a plot-swerve of this type, Twain had several pages of heavy revision. But at this point he likely still did not have a clear notion of plot in his mind; did not know that Huck would go far downriver. Certainly, though, once Twain remembered the Great Flood of 1847 and the empty canoes which then floated down the river, the ease and convenience of such a method of continuing Huck's journey must have appealed to him.

In a state of some excitement, after the frightening episode of pap's delirium tremens and Huck's discovery of the canoe, Twain began to hatch the plan of the boy faking his own death, fabricating the idea that a fictional stranger might have broken into the shanty, based on Huck's excuse to his father about why he had the gun pointed toward the door. Huck ruminated and Twain projected:

> I got to thinking that if I could fix up some way to keep Pap and the widow from trying to follow me, it would be a <more> certainer thing than trusting to luck to get far enough off before they missed me; you <see, the canoe might up set> see, all kinds of things might happen. (MS 126)

Twain here has, I infer, the next episode, of Huck faking his own death, clearly in mind. The running-revision toward open-ended phrasing, "all kinds of things might happen," could however, be self-reflexive – Twain's musing to himself about a continued longer-term plot-uncertainty.

Jackson's Island and Jim

After Huck does escape from his father's shanty, and first lands at Jackson's Island, Twain thought of having him stay there for a while. On MS sheet 157 he inserted a new "Chap. 9" heading and began to describe the place in more detail. A careful reader can almost feel Twain's prose shift from boredom to exploration and to reminiscence:

> But the next day I went exploring down through the island. I was boss of it; it all belonged to me . . . so to speak, and I wanted to know all about it; but mainly I wanted to put in the time. I found no end of strawberries, ripe and good and I found green summer-grapes, and green raspberries; <and green> yes, and the green blackberries were just beginning to show. They would all come good and handy by and by, I <thought> judged.

I find this writing touching: Twain creatively plants enough not-quite-ripe fruit to feed the boy in the near future and, as his imagination began to recall the various specific fruits, his particular enthusiasm or nostalgia led him to write the manuscript not in Huck's voice but in that of Clemens's/Twain's own memory: "yes," as if he – like Molly Bloom – wished to elicit our assent, our own recognition of such sensuous recalls, and our concurrence. Apparently Twain felt no compulsion to hurry his plot, or to move his adventurer away to other settings.

The passage suggests that Twain at first might have planned to have Huck stay on Jackson's Island for some time (and possibly to have Huck sneak back into the village, as he had Tom Sawyer return in his earlier book, to visit when people thought that he was dead). Instead, it is the presence of the other inhabitant of the island that now comes to drive the plot. When Twain had Huck come across the (revealing) campfire, he might not have thought much further than this; might not have already intended to attach an identity to this sign of human presence. He certainly felt excitement, though, in writing about Huck's reactions to the campfire, and he echoes Cervantes and Shakespeare as Huck, in flight and fright, then looks back to mistake a tree-stump for a human being: "I <moved> slunk along further, then listened again; and so on, and so on; if I saw a stump, I took it for a man; if I trod on a stick and broke it, it <most> nearly took my breath away" (MS 159–60). I think Twain himself enjoyed the utter surprise of the discovery, and the heart-pounding moments of fleeing the campfire; but as yet he may not have seen beyond this narrative point.

What should Huck and Twain now do? In manuscript pages 160–3 Huck's scare leads to his flight to the Illinois shore. After Twain had quickly got him off the island to this relatively safe, but unknown, setting, the boy overhears a fragmentary conversation between two horsemen. This, however, leads nowhere in plot terms. It is the mysterious presence on the island that prompts a return to that spot. I am inferring, from the large number of changes in the manuscript around this section, that Twain's narrative intentions were still confused. It is only now, as he rewrites the campfire scene, that Huck's approach is given more efficiently, differently; and that Jim now enters the textual equation:

> But by and by, sure enough, I catched a glimpse of fire, away through the trees. I went for it, cautious and slow. <When I was in about twenty yards of it, I took to my hands and knees.> By and by I was close enough to have a look, and there laid a man on the ground. My heart <was just a jumping.> fell to thumping. The man had a blanket around his head, and his head was <most> nearly in the fire. I set there behind a clump of bushes, within six <feet> foot of him and kept my eyes on him steady <a <a->looking with all the eyes I had.> It was getting gray with daylight, now. Pretty soon the man stretched himself and hove off the blanket, and it was Miss Watson's Jim! I bet I was glad to see him. (MS 165–7)

I think Twain – like Huck – was immensely relieved to find out who it was! He wrote, with running script, "I betIwas glad tosee him." The writer's suspenseful compositional process had led Twain to find a perfect companion for Huck.

Twain already knew how Jim spoke and how he related to people. He could enjoy Jim's appearance and listen as Jim tells his own story of betrayal and escape. Also,

Jim's surprising presence could provide a continuing reason for travel, for flight down the river. The combination of a very smart, older but powerless man with a smart, naïve, unschooled boy led, too, to countless plot possibilities and to great dialogue and conversation. It is unlikely, though, that Twain realized, at the moment of discovering Jim on the island, how hard, complex, or important it would ultimately be to write about an escaping slave traveling downriver with a white boy.

The Move Downriver toward Cairo

Twain's writerly imagination was drawn to repetition (and the variations then necessarily implied), and – as his narrative moved on – he quickly involved his new pair of travelers in two naked-cadaver episodes: Jim's telling of his being frightened by a cadaver that moved (MS 199–214) and Jim covering pap Finn's corpse in the House of Death (MS 218). The former would later be dropped. I would emphasize, though, that Twain apparently felt no immediate pressure to move the pair downstream. As long as he could write from episode to episode he was apparently content to let the long-range plot fend for itself.

By MS sheet 216 Twain had provided Huck and Jim with a raft, and by MS 232 he has Huck think, "it was getting sl<o>ow and dull, and I wanted to get a stirring up, some way." The Mrs Loftus episode then follows. Twain wrote many parts of this sequence very rapidly, using the dialogue to provide a convenient partial summary of his novel's development to that point. The hasty departure from the island, and the crucially important commitment to the move downriver, immediately follows.

We then have one of the crucial episodes in terms of the Huck–Jim relationship as their separation in the fog leads Huck to trick Jim. The river debris on the raft, the "trash," becomes – as Jim responds – an analogous marker for Huck's social class. Jim's astonishingly direct and contemptuous statement that "trash is what people is dat puts dirt on de head er dey fren's en makes 'em ashamed" (Twain 1885: 121), surprisingly (given normative racial dynamics) leads to Huck's heartfelt apology to Jim – a major step in Huck's personal development. Could we ever imagine characters/ personalities such as pap Finn, or Tom Sawyer, or the king uttering such an apology?

The raftsmen's episode (MS 309–62) began as an attempt by Huck to find out where he and Jim were on the river, but Twain characteristically soon became more interested in the sequence itself, and in describing the figures involved, than in larger, long-range plot concerns. After he completed that episode, he made several notes to himself, writing at a sideways slant across the top of the manuscript sheet. These seem to be jottings about possible future individual episodes, not plans for long range plot possibilities. The notes read: "negro sermon Twichell's clothes – p. 58 80 80 A town ball 46 Home 236 Remarks at a funeral." And the top of the next page, which begins a new chapter in the manuscript, also has notes: "Eddy" "Child with rusty unloaded gun *always* kills" (MS 363). I interpret "Eddy" as a note about the recently concluded raftsmen's section; the "child" note likely hints toward a proposed incident not then used. (Twain may have intended a fictional version of an accidental shooting involving his young in-law, Charles Webster, who, when he was ten years old, had killed a three-year-old girl. If this was so, his personal consideration for Webster may have stopped him proceeding in his direction.)

At this stage of the narrative, Huck and Jim's exact location (above or below Cairo) on the river Twain once knew so well remained fictionally uncertain. The section from MS 362 to 384 was apparently written as a unit and deals with Jim's excitement about being almost free. In Twain's imagination, Huck suffers extreme moral discomfort because he knows he is defying conventional racial attitudes, but nonetheless he suddenly – and with great social intelligence and autonomy – decides to deceive, with his tale of smallpox, the two slave-hunters who wish to search the raft. Moral, interpersonal, and thematic issues intertwine here. Sam Clemens, whose father John Marshall Clemens served on a jury that sent abolitionists to prison, could now write (through his authorial persona Mark Twain) about a white boy deliberately assisting a slave's escape. Married to Olivia Langdon, daughter of Jervis Langdon (a northern supporter of the Underground Railroad), he could now write sympathetically about a child's tormented, clever, unselfish, and brave moral action to protect another person, a powerless African American, the considerate, and smart, father of two children.

The Break (and Resumption) in Composition: The Feud

For years, scholars assumed that Twain stopped working on his novel in 1876 after the moral crisis just described, and at the point when the raft was hit by a steamboat. According to the standard interpretation, this was because Twain's book was changing on him: the ethical struggles, resulting from the sequence running from Huck's apology to Jim through to his clever concealment of Jim from the slave-hunter, created an uncomfortably difficult book, too uncomfortable for Twain then to continue. Consequently – so the explanation then goes – Twain reacted by running a steamboat over the raft, stopping dead his supposedly conflict-filled creative engagement for several years. This theory, though, is factually wrong, despite its apparently impressive explanatory value. For Twain continued writing after the steamboat crash, right on into the Grangerford episode.

Moreover, Twain certainly knew from the beginning of the Grangerford section that he would be writing about a feud; and he developed the episode with full, even lavish, attention to the setting and to the characters. Twain, in fact, kept writing right to the moment where Huck and Buck discuss what a feud is; where Huck asks, and Buck replies:

> "What's the feud?"
> "Why where was you raised? Don't you know what a feud is?"
> "Never heard of it before – tell me about it." (MS 446)

Then Twain stopped writing, after putting down only six lines on the page, setting the manuscript aside for about three years.

Why he stopped in the middle of this expository dialogue seems, at first, puzzling. Three possible hypotheses may, however, be advanced. It is, of course, possible that Twain's imaginative well was empty: that he felt a lack of inspiration, and simply stopped writing. I consider that possibility unlikely, however, since his episode was rolling along with a strong cast of well-established characters and a highly dramatic situation. A second, more probable, likelihood is that Twain felt drawn toward this new satiric target, but thought that a full development of the feud would have derailed his plan to have the boy proceed on the "voyage to other lands." A final plausible explanation involves the technical and narratological difficulty of having Huck see the extremely dangerous events of a feud from close up, while still living to escape and relate the events he had witnessed. How could a realistic novelist get his narrator into, and safely out of, such extreme danger? This problem could give even those writers who make intricate and careful long-range plans reason to pause. However, though this is possible, it is unlikely that Twain would worry excessively about such a detail – simply on the basis that he usually composed from incident to incident, from action to action. There were, though, other related imaginative dilemmas at stake. How might the feud end? What, in the meantime, had happened to Jim? Would Huck find him? Where would Twain's/Huck's story go? And what underlying reason would there be for such a movement?

Whatever the reasons for the compositional break, after about three years Twain resumed work on the story. He reread at least from manuscript pages 408–46, making a note on MS 439: "Sophia, Last Link." He then continued writing on different, smaller paper in a purple ink. The possibility of the love-elopement scenario had already been planted when he had previously written of Harney Shepherdson not shooting at Buck Grangerford on MS 443. Now Twain quickly explained more about the feud; and he brought Huck and Jim back together by MS 466. He then did some explaining, though in an awkward and patchy fashion:

> "Why didn't you tell my Jack to fetch me here sooner, Jim?"
>
> "Well, 'twarn't any use to 'sturb you, Huck, tell we could do su\<f\>mfin – but we's all right, now. I been a-buyin' pots \<and\> en pans \<and\> en vittles, as I got a chanst, \<and\> en a-patchin' up \<our ole\> de raf', nights when –"
>
> "*What* raft, Jim?"
>
> "*Our* ole raf'!"
>
> "You mean to say our old raft \<wasn't\> warn't smashed all to flinders?" (MS 470–1)

This retroactive salvation of the raft may well strike modern readers as improbable, a highly creaky prop/plot device, but it did restore to Huck and Jim their familiar method of escape. Moreover, Twain might have felt some relief that the adventures would be able to resume with some combination of his picaresque plotting and character mobility among more familiar river settings.

Twain solved the problem of having Huck see horrific violence from up close and still remain safe – although traumatized – by having him go toward the shooting, but then climb into a tree, and conceal himself accordingly. It is here that Twain's knowledge of the art of omission becomes so clear. Twain allows Huck to say, of the latter stage of the feud: "I ain't agoing to tell *all* that happened – it would make me sick again if I was to do that. I wished I hadn't ever come ashore that night, to<o> see such things. I ain't ever going to get shut of them – lots of times I dream about them" (MS 488–9). Twain knew human savagery, and apparently knew that the combination of a child's point of view and the physical violence and reality of a bitter feud seen from close-up could cause nausea. His use of self-restraint and of the child's voice pay real literary dividends here.

The Continued Journey and the King and the Duke

After Huck and Jim escape from the feud's bloodshed, the novel drifts for a while. Twain did not feel compelled to have a new plot-action start right away. MS sheets 498 and 499 preserve how Twain's exploratory process developed, as his unusual use of verbs and adjectives introduces us imaginatively to the described setting:

> Two or three days and nights went by; I reckon I might say they *swum* by, they slid along so quiet and smooth and lovely. Here is the way we put in the time. – It was a monstrous big river down there – sometimes a mile and a half wide; we run nights, and laid up and hid, daytimes; soon as <day> night was . . . most gone, we <would quit> stopped navigating and tied up – nearly always in the dead water under a tow-head; and then cut young cottonwoods and willows and hid<e> the raft with them. <But I'll <tll> tell what we done and what we saw for *one* day and night, and that will do for all – for all the days and nights was about alike.
>   Well, we hid in a towhead >. (MS 498–9)

This passage – developed with some uncertainty – sounds as though Twain were speaking the lines; practicing them out loud with his authorial voice. The following 15 manuscript pages are devoted to a detailed, leisurely description of daybreak and a full narration of daily, restful, reflective activities. The emotional pressure of Buck's death gives way here to an altered pace, and a change of intensity from frantic, frightening, murderous action in the feud to a restful sense of slow peacefulness.

But it is when Huck goes off canoeing for berries one morning, on MS sheet 515–16, that Twain introduces his next plot device. Here Huck views another fascinating and mysterious entrance, as two men come running: "here comes a couple of men tearing up the path as tight as they could foot it. I thought I was a goner, for whenever anybody was after anybody, I judged it was *me* – or maybe Jim" (MS 516–17). Huck's constant and anxious insecurity is evident here, but he acts cleverly to save these two unknown men. Twain now had to listen as his imagination allowed these two men – who had just run into his text, and possibly into his imaginative mind too – to tell him who they were, and what were their personalities. As they build their false claims of competing European aristocratic backgrounds, Twain, in a way, permits himself to turn the control of his plot over to this tricksy and immoral pair of scoundrels. The two thieves allowed him to draw upon his recent trip to Europe and to satirize the widespread – and anti-democratic – American esteem for, and deference to, "noble birth." Much of this part of the novel can be interpreted as a form of satiric revenge by an author/citizen of a colonized country on the styles and thefts of the previous exploiters. Obviously Twain enjoyed using these two comical drifters, grifters, and scammers as embodiments of comic shabbiness and "royal ways." Importantly, on the level of narrative progression, because these rogues take over the raft, the voyage must now continue deeper into the South.

An early incident that now follows is the two frauds' arrival at a town downriver, where they exploit, spontaneously and cleverly, the resources offered by a local printing-shop, a setting Twain knew well. After the Dred Scott decision and the fugitive slave laws but prior to the Civil War, it was possible for slave-hunters to come to a free state, closely observe a free black person, and then write a detailed description to be sent back to be printed in a Southern newspaper as an escaped-slave notice. Once the printed notice was then mailed North, the "slave-catchers" – or kidnappers – could then apprehend or abduct the black person, with total federal protection. A judge would be paid $10 if he found the person to be an escaped slave, but only $5 if he determined that the person was free. The black person was not allowed by law to call witnesses or testify. The duke's creation of an escaped-slave notice for Jim serves both as convenient plot device and as a covert form of historically based social criticism. Twain writes: "Then he showed us another little job he had printed and hadn't charged for because it was for *us*. It had a picture of a runaway nigger, with a bundle on a stick, over his shoulder, and '$200 *Reward!*' under it. The reading was all about Jim, and just described him to a dot" (MS 604–5).

When the passage was printed the emphasis on "us" had disappeared, lessening the tonal variation and (just possibly) generalizing the word to suggest a national audience. In print the text states "$200 reward" without the capital letter or exclamation point, a less emphatic, less attention-drawing, and more ordinary version. The counterfeit escaped-slave notice could provide plot-cover, a reason for these rafters to explain why they were drifting downriver. The printing of the notice begins, too, the process of slave appropriation as these two white male scoundrels begin to take control of Jim. Jim's situation grows more and more desperate as the raft goes downriver, and he knows it.

The extended manuscript version of the episode of the king's clever scam at a camp-meeting originally had a more complex satiric target. Twain originally wrote about a black woman at the camp-meeting hearing the preacher's words, "'One more shake and your chains is broke – ah!' [*Glory hal-lelujah!*]" (MS 587), and thinking – quite reasonably – that the ending of her slavery was coming. But her genuinely Christian attempts to hug the surrounding white people in a spirit of happiness and forgiveness are not reciprocated. Put alongside the motif of the escaped-slave notice, this episode highlights the dramatic contrasts at play among notions of slavery, freedom, and renewed captivity.

The king's and duke's need to flee the various angry townspeople they have bilked, by moving the raft on down the river, begins to drive the narrative and helps to conceal the improbability of a slave (Jim) trying to escape that condition by fleeing further South. Their counterfeit escaped-slave notice would provide cover for this travel, while hinting at the power of the two fraudulent thieves to take over, not just the raft, but the (assumed) legal control of Jim himself. As the two men act out – for comic purposes – their mock-aristocratic attitudes, they also repeat a parodic version of supremacist values. Huck and Jim are made to be their servants and the costume they have Jim wear, and the ropes with which they bind him, act as clumsy and infuriating ways of depriving him once more of dignity, as well as of freedom.

Colonel Sherburn

The Colonel Sherburn episode is bracketed within the "king and duke" section of the novel. Twain here takes the real town of Council Bend as his model for the small town he describes, using it to build a picture of poverty, squalor, and a restless desire for excitement. Boggs's drunken violation of a Southern Colonel's "honor," and Sherburn's unjust execution of Boggs that results, concluded Twain's work on the novel for about three years. His notes on the manuscript indicate his authorial dilemma. After the townspeople storm toward Colonel Sherburn's place, with lynching on their minds, the text reads: "Well, by and by somebody said Sherburn ought to be lynched. In about a minute everybody was saying it; so away they went, mad and yelling, and snatching down every clothes line they come to, to do the hanging with. But they was too late. Sherburn's friends had got him away, long ago" (MS 663).

However, Twain wrote a note to himself on the page, contradicting that script: "No, let them lynch him." Clearly, he felt undecided about the episode's outcome. It might conceivably be possible to narrate the lynching of a white man, but if so, it would give the book an extremely harsh edge and an explicit tone of social criticism. In all likelihood, it would also antagonize some of his Southern readers. (Twain had previously cancelled a chapter in *Life on the Mississippi* because it too sharply criticized the New Orleans political habit of one-party Democratic, anti-Republican registration.) Perhaps, too, at some deep level, a link was made in the author's mind between the possible representation of a white man's lynching and the increase of lynchings of African Americans at the time of his writing. Racial discrimination in the post-Civil-War period is the specter that haunts this text.

Once more, then – perhaps as a result of his failure to resolve the Sherburn plot – Twain set the manuscript aside, letting his creative processes ferment. In 1880 he still did not have a finished book. He had instead an interesting and humane narrator, an escaped slave way below the Ohio River and far from any reasonable or plausible chance of freedom, two scoundrels in charge of the raft, and a river still inevitably flowing south. His chances of finishing a saleable novel looked, at that point, slim.

The resumption of the composition in 1883 began with Colonel Sherburn's critique of the lynch mob. The particularities of this scene need emphasizing. In the part of the manuscript composed in 1880, the fictional mob had come after Sherburn in daylight and without masks. That indeed is how most Southern lynchings, or killings, of whites, slaves, or freedpeople were conducted prior to the end of the Civil War. Only after the South was militarily defeated and after Federal troops had been stationed there for a while did the use of masks prevail, especially during the Ku Klux Klan days. But in the portion of the manuscript composed in 1883 Colonel Sherburn refers repeatedly (and in a historically inaccurate way) to the Southern habit of using masks. In the compositional pause, we can see postwar social and racial issues bubbling beneath the surface of the novel and in the author's imaginative life.

In the 1883–4 portion of the manuscript Twain developed his plot with longer episodes, and more complex satiric targets, as indicated in my *Writing Huck Finn* (Doyno 1991). Certainly he was bound by more constraints. At the start of a chess game, many moves are possible; by the two-thirds point, possibilities have become severely limited as a result of earlier moves. So, too, with Twain's novel.

Tom Sawyer's Return

Tom Sawyer had disappeared from the novel a lot earlier: by the end of chapter 3, on about MS 57 and 58. But the success of *The Adventures of Tom Sawyer* had always made the prospect of writing a companion novel appealing. If only a half of those readers who bought *Tom Sawyer* would buy *Huckleberry Finn*, the large sales would give Twain a wonderful head-start for his new publishing company, Webster & Co. Twain had also conducted an ongoing campaign against the piratical copying of his earlier books. If he could now appeal to many of his *Tom Sawyer* readers, including those who had purchased pirated editions, then the linking of the two books could be seen and thought of as a type of long-term financial victory for him.

Twain could decide that Tom Sawyer had to reappear, but he did not have to like him. Twain knew that Tom was the wrong kind of child – and he could prove it, in detail! In the long Phelps's farm section Tom enacts a supremacist attitude, automatically assuming great power over Huck and Jim, setting rules and regulations, all to plot the escape of a man who Tom knew had already been freed by Miss Watson's act of manumission. Twain signals Tom's knowledge of Jim's freedom during the first conversation between Huck and Tom, when Huck has gone out to meet Tom on the road. On manuscript sheets from the second half of the novel (originally numbered 497, 498, and 499, but later renumbered 493 through 495) we find the revealing passage of dialogue between Tom (who speaks first) and Huck that shapes the book's next major plot-swerve:

"All right; <I'm William.> <Go on."> but wait a minute.

<"Now t> There's one more thing – a thing that *nobody* don't know but me. And that is, there's a nigger here that I'm a trying to steal out of slavery – and his name is *Jim*. – old Miss Watson's Jim . . . . <You'll say it's dirty low-down business >

He says: "What! Why Jim is –"

He stopped, and went to studying. I says:

"*I* know what you'll say. You'll say it's dirty low-down business, but what if it is? – *I'm* low-down; and I'm agoing to steal him, and I want you to keep mum and not let on. Will you?"

His eye lit up, and he says:

"I'll *help* you steal him!"

Well, I let go all holts, then, like I was shot. It was the most astonishing speech I ever heard in my life – and I'm bound to say Tom Sawyer fell considerable, in my estimation. Only I couldn't quite believe it. Tom Sawyer a *nigger stealer*!

"Oh, shucks," I says, ["]You're joking."

"I ain't joking, either."

"Well, then," I says, "joking or no joking, if you hear anything said about a runaway nigger, don't forget to remember that *you* don't know nothing about him, and I don't know nothing about him."

Clearly Twain had decided at this point that Tom Sawyer would already know about Jim's freedom during the novel's final sequence. Tom, then, certainly is lying when he says he "ain't joking" about helping Huck "steal" Jim. Twain gives Tom the duplicity that will permit him to reassert his own power over both Huck and Jim by withholding any and all information about Jim's emancipation. Unfortunately, Tom was not the only American who treated a free man in this way, as becomes clear with any look at the stories about African Americans kept in forms of slavery long after the Civil War was over, and after full emancipation had been declared.

The idea of writing a parody of literature about European nobility and prison escapes may have seemed funny and nationalistic (or, at least, anti-European) to Twain, but the countless soldiers who had fought in the American Civil War and suffered in prison camps a relatively short time earlier, as well as the many families of soldiers who had died there, might not think the topic inherently amusing. Twain had first thought and planned to have the boys get away from the Phelpses without consequences, for Note C-10 reads, "Steal guns and get away under a volley of blank cartridges." But his realism apparently led him to rethink this plot line, resulting in an exciting night-time escape from a cabin, with a group of white male Southerners shooting at those in flight: the young, bookish white boy (Tom), his unsophisticated and considerate friend (Huck), and the legally free, but still despised and vulnerable, African American (Jim). Such night attacks, chases, and shootings occurred throughout the South during the "outrages" of the time when Twain was writing his book. I would suggest that to read the novel's ending in, say, 1885, when the newspapers, magazines, and telegraphs carried stories about such night attacks, would be to read a book with unusual but particular resonances.

In all likelihood Twain did not plan or plot deliberately how this novel would end. Instead, he managed to treat a boy with a bullet in his leg as a compelling, realistic reason to have the games finally stop. The action could then return to a state of Southern normalcy after Jim had proved his devotion and humanity by immediately giving help to the wounded Tom. The flexibility of Twain's earlier plottings was a form of freedom, and the novel – similarly – concluded with both a superb sense of order restored, and also a sense of pause, as an exhausted trio of adventurers come to a halt before resuming the adventures of "Huck and Tom Among the Indians." There, out West, in the Territory and beyond, they would explore, under Twain's observant and skeptical eyes, other American expectations, settings, literary delusions, romanticisms, and dangerous stereotypes. And, of course, Jim would also be re-enslaved there, too.

References and Further Reading

Beaver, Harold (1987). *Huckleberry Finn*. London: Unwin.

Blair, Walter (1960). *Mark Twain and Huck Finn*. Berkeley: University of California Press.

Carrington, George C., Jr. (1976). *The Dramatic Unity of Huckleberry Finn*. Columbus: Ohio State University Press.

Doyno, Victor (1991). *Writing "Huck Finn": Mark Twain's Creative Process*. Philadelphia: University of Pennsylvania Press.

Doyno, Victor (2002). *Beginning to Write "Huck" Finn: Essays in Genetic Criticism. Huck Finn: The Complete Buffalo and Erie County Public Library Manuscript – Teaching and Research Digital Edition.* CD-ROM. Buffalo and Erie Public Library.

Fischer, Victor (1983). "Huck Finn Reviewed: The Reception of *Huckleberry Finn* in the United States, 1885–1897." *American Literary Realism* 16 (Spring), 1–57.

Fishkin, Shelley Fisher (1993). *Was Huck Black? Mark Twain and African-American Voices*. New York: Oxford University Press.

Leonard, James S., Tenney, Thomas A., and Davis, Thadious, M., eds. (1992). *Satire or Evasion?*

Black Perspectives on Huckleberry Finn. Durham, NC: Duke University Press.

Sattelmeyer, Robert, and Crowley, J. Donald, eds. (1985). *One Hundred Years of Huckleberry Finn: The Boy, his Book, and American Culture*. Columbia: University of Missouri Press.

Schmitz, Neil (1971). "Twain, Huckleberry Finn, and the Reconstruction." *American Studies* 12 (Spring), 59–67.

Smith, Henry Nash (1962). *Mark Twain: The Development of a Writer*. Cambridge, Mass.: Belknap/Harvard University Press.

Twain, Mark (1996). *Adventures of Huckleberry Finn: A Comprehensive Edition*, foreword and textual addendum by Victor Doyno. New York: Random House.

Twain, Mark (2002). *Adventures of Huckleberry Finn*, ed. Victor Fischer and Lin Salamo. Berkeley: University of California Press.

Twain, Mark (2003). *Huck Finn: The Complete Buffalo and Erie County Public Library Manuscript – Teaching and Research Digital Edition*. CD-ROM. Buffalo and Erie Public Library.

26

Going to Tom's Hell in
Huckleberry Finn

Hilton Obenzinger

After Tom Sawyer is shot in the leg during the "evasion," Huck, lying one more time for the sake of survival, seeks the help of a doctor. This time, though, it is Tom's life that's at stake. "How'd you say he got shot?" the doctor asks, and Huck replies in desperation, "He had a dream . . . and it shot him." "Singular dream," the doctor replies, a sarcasm that stands as one of the few moments of intentional irony voiced by a character in the novel (Twain 1885: 347). Often overlooked, Huck's response constitutes a revelatory moment, a high point almost as "singular" as his earlier refusal to betray Jim – "All right, then, I'll *go* to hell" (p. 272). Throughout the novel, Huck persistently (and adroitly) lies in order to survive, and the few times he consciously does not dissemble or fabricate fictions, he incurs the wrath of the adult world or he faces great danger: "I reckon a body that ups and tells the truth when he is in a tight place, is taking considerable many resks . . ." (p. 240).

So, in appealing to the doctor, Huck once again attempts to construct a credible fabrication to accomplish a goal, this time to save Tom's life. Huck, though, is inadvertently telling the doctor the truth. Tom has in fact been shot by his dream: the delusional play-world of the "evasion" and all that it has come to represent. As Jim says, "*{N}obody* kin git up a plan dat's mo' mixed-up en splendid" (Twain 1885: 344) than Tom Sawyer, and a bullet in his calf is the high point of his mixed-up, splendid dream of romance; the bullet serves as material evidence of the efficacy of his fantasies, the truth content of "Tom Sawyer's lies" (p. 33) that have completely enveloped Huck and Jim. It is also the beginning of the end of Huck's world of invented identities along the river, and soon the entire truth (or as close to truth as the social consciousness of the characters will allow) of Tom's plot, Jim's status, and pap's death will be revealed. As the journey downriver reaches its end in the farcical "evasion," a wide range of social terms become exhausted, including various lies of "silent assertion" (a concept Twain would explain years later) – particularly "the silent assertion [about slavery] that there wasn't anything going on in which humane and intelligent people were interested" (Twain 1992b: 440). Slavery and the logic of racial supremacy that would extend into post-Reconstruction society are revealed as hypocrisies or deadly delusions, along with other socially determined structures of authority, including religion, masculinity, and certain forms of literature. "Don't you reckon that the people that made the books knows what's the correct thing to do?" (Twain 1885: 27), Tom hectors Huck early in the book. The whole force of the novel answers: No. Readers, like Huck himself, are left to determine "the correct thing" for themselves.

By the time of the "evasion" Huck has – to a certain degree – thrown in his lot with Jim, and both of them interrogate Tom's plans for "when a prisoner of style escapes" (Twain 1885: 337), resisting the most outrageous elements of his overcooked conspiracy and wringing out some concessions from the obsessed fantasist. Tom, on the other hand, thinks it so much fun that he wishes "we would keep it up all the rest of our lives and leave Jim to our children to get out" (p. 313). In the first part of the novel, Tom is merely a child whose play is rendered irrelevant by the horrific reality of pap's abuse which Huck must face. When Tom reappears at the end, he is both an unexpected ally and a menace, engineering an "evasion" that merely reaffirms inequality, despite his knowledge of Jim's manumission, and provoking violence where none existed (not just the bullet in his leg, but the fact that Jim is very nearly lynched). Tom is so deluded, so caught up in the romance, that he seems completely unaware of the cruel consequences of his fantasy. In Tom's dream life, Jim remains a slave, an object for his own gratification, a projection in a dream-world based on supremacy and subordination. His fantasy is not just playful; his play is toxic.

Who is this Tom Sawyer? And over what realm does he rule? Certainly, he is not the same character depicted in the earlier novel bearing his name, despite striking similarities. I suggest that this latter Tom Sawyer is an incarnation of what I call "the bad-boy deity," a type of character who fascinated Twain throughout his career. And through his "evasion" he transforms the Phelps plantation section of the novel into a type of social hell. When seen alongside the vogue in "bad-boy books" at the time *Adventures of Huckleberry Finn* was published, Twain's fascination with this bad-boy prodigy can illuminate the novel, particularly its ending. The last section has confounded many readers, especially after Ernest Hemingway's famous comment in *Green Hills of Africa* about the "real end" of Twain's book (where "the Nigger Jim is stolen from the boys") and the "cheating" that follows (Hemingway 1935: 22). This comment has done much to convince many readers, and it is a legitimate interpretive stance to find fault with the novel's ending. Still, while the prose of the last third of the book may not seem as brilliant as the rest, it certainly appears odd that "the best book we've had," according to Hemingway, is so fatally flawed that he advises tossing it aside before finishing it. I offer another view, one which revolves around understanding the Phelps plantation as a form of hell presided over by Tom Sawyer, and which shows how the ending resolves the novel's narrative logic and completes its social satire.

Huckleberry Finn appeared as part of the post-Civil War boom in "bad boy" books inaugurated by Thomas Bailey Aldrich's *The Story of a Bad Boy* (1869). The pranks of Aldrich's bad boy are mischievous but mild compared to the sadistic practical jokes

George Peck's Bad Boy inflicts in episode after episode on the father in *Bad Boy and His Pa* (1883). Tom in Twain's novel, like Aldrich's and Peck's creations, acts out the popular notions of child psychology arising in the post-Civil War period. As argued by the prominent contemporary psychologist G. Stanley Hall, the child, especially a boy, "is in the primitive age. The instinct of the savage survives in him" (see Bederman 1995: 78). The savage boy recapitulates the evolutionary development leading to the civilized man – "normal children often pass through stages of passionate cruelty, laziness, lying, and thievery" (see Mailloux 1989: 112) – and parents were urged to indulge much of the wildness, even "semicriminality," of boys as a way to offset the danger of neurasthenia or nervous exhaustion facing overcivilized, too-refined adult men in an industrializing society. So Tom, as a middle-class boy des-tined to join the ruling class, is expected to be mischievous, and even his cruel practical joke at Jim's expense can be regarded as a normal exercise in learning gender roles. When questioned by Aunt Sally on why he wanted to set Jim free, "seeing he was already free," he responds, "Well, that *is* a question, I must say; and *just* like women! Why, I wanted the *adventure* of it; and I'd a waded neck-deep in blood to –" (Twain 1885: 361). His explanation is interrupted by the entrance of Aunt Polly, but no more needs to be said: Tom is all boy, a boy's boy, and he authorizes his gender definition through the pursuit of his savage fantasy-quest.

We can situate Tom's role within yet another phenomenon of American culture of the time: the minstrel show.[1] Mark Twain, like many, was a devoted fan of minstrelsy (see e.g. Mailloux 1989: 84–5), and a quick overview of the form reveals how deeply it influences the language, dialogues, antics, and structure of *Huckleberry Finn*.

The minstrel show was typically organized in three parts. After the walkabout, the entry of the troupe, there was a series of songs and comic dialogues, most of them between the interlocutor, the master of ceremonies who typically spoke in standard English and put on refined airs, and Bones and Tambo, the "end-men" who sat on either end of the procession of marchers, dancers, and singers as they arrayed them-selves in a semi-circle. The end-men faced the audience and spoke in dialect, their puns and malapropisms and wit often undermining the respectable interlocutor. This was followed by the olio, a variety show of magic acts, acrobatics, musical numbers, parodies, stump speeches, and more. The final section was often composed of a one-act play of domestic nostalgia about life on the plantation invoking "Home Sweet Home." After the Civil War, this tended to reinforce the notion that blacks were better off as slaves and, analogously, should accept subordination under Jim Crow rule. The final section might also, though, be a burlesque about plantation life.

Twain's novel roughly follows the same form, with the first section revolving around antics and comic dialogues between Huck and a succession of other charac-ters. Huck also sometimes plays the role of end-man (for example, with Aunt Sally and with Tom) or interlocutor (with Jim). Twain's minstrel dialogues involve philo-sophical debate, and they expose various limitations of thought and language. The dialogues between Jim and Huck in the book's first section enhance Jim's status as a man, as Huck concedes, in a statement ringing with unconscious irony (and as he feebly attempts to maintain his sense of white superiority), that he "has an uncom-mon level head, for a nigger" (Twain 1885: 107). And as the "King Sollermun" and "*Polly-voo-franzy*" (p. 113) debates with end-man Jim show up the illusory nature of interlocutor Huck's superiority, he can only assert his authority by appeal to white privilege as last resort: "[Y]ou can't learn a nigger to argue" (p. 114).

Huck encounters different versions of truth in the first section, all regularly under-mined by his naïve reportage: the widow's restrictive morality endorsed by Bible stories; Tom Sawyer's romance "lies"; pap's enraged rant on the "govment" and the "mulatter" professor (a Fredrick Douglass type who is clearly more educated and capable than the disgusting "fish-belly white" drunk – splattered with mud, as if in blackface himself); and the code of honor which leads the Grangerfords and Shepherd-sons to their endless and murderous feud. Grotesque realism and the fantastic merge as Huck first engineers his escape and then comes upon Jim. For the alliance between the marginalized white boy and the escaped slave quickly creates a situation almost beyond credibility in the antebellum South. "They're after us!" (Twain 1885: 92), Huck exclaims, after his disguise as a girl is exposed by Judith Loftus, and in his words a new bond is spoken. From this point, the bond between the two deepens, climaxing initially in Jim's plain-speaking after Huck's prank in the fog, when he removes his mask to address Huck directly as an equal, and calls him "trash" (p. 121). In this extra-ordinary world, the film of white supremacy peels back, and Huck responds on an entirely new level. The logomachies (wars of words) between Huck and Jim extend throughout the book (see Chadwick-Joshua 1998). Jim progressively reveals his humanity, intelligence, even cunning ("I's a free man, en I couldn't ever ben free ef it hadn't ben for Huck" [p. 124]), and Huck responds with empathy, friendship, and understanding despite the color line ("I do believe he cared just as much for his people as white folks does for their'n. It don't seem natural, but I reckon it's so" [p. 201]).

These developments unfold on the sometime utopian site of the raft drifting down the river. On either bank there is violence and compulsive if unconscious delusion. Meanwhile, the unlikely version of a father–son bond ripens on the flux of the river itself. Utopian possibility, though, is cut off with the olio, which begins with the entrance of the king and the duke, and the various cons they perform, such as their "missionarying," the ludicrous hodgepodge of Shakespeare, the Royal Nonesuch, and the final extended climax of the funeral "orgies" at the Wilks farm (aimed at defraud-ing that family's surviving daughters of their inheritance). These episodes and others enact the humbuggery, duplicity, and idiocy of life along the river – and reveal how the many fools encountered there deserve their diddlers! All this highlights how Huck and Jim's utopia is undermined by these usurpers.

The final section of the novel can be read as a blend of the two styles of minstrelsy's plantation endings. It is both a sentimental invocation of home (family life on the Phelps plantation, in which Huck is "born again" as Tom Sawyer) and a burlesque of plantation life.

This tripartite form is not static; it is not simply three independent sections loosely related to each other by the continuity of characters. There is a progression, in which the forceful and cumulative ironies undermine the expectations of the minstrel-show form. The final plantation burlesque then stands as a revelatory re-enactment of social relations. Under the mixed-up, splendid direction of Tom Sawyer, the evasion becomes a burlesque of a burlesque, one in which the re-enslavement and freedom of one black man can be read as a semi-allegorical parody of the cruelly absurd post-Reconstruction reality that in effect re-enslaves the former slaves – compelling them to live in their "place," on terms acceptable to white supremacy. The ending thus exposes accepted, "normal" Jim Crow social categories as more "lies of silent assertion."

In order to fully elucidate this point, I would contrast the tripartite structure of the minstrel show with another enduring narrative structure – specifically a journey to the underworld – shaped by the literary tradition of the menippean satire. The critic Mikhail Bakhtin has traced both the roots of this literary form in classical antiquity and its modern manifestations in such writers as Dostoevsky. Menippea is a highly comic form involved in a quest for truth which employs adventure, fantasy, extraordinary situations, eccentric behavior, abnormal psychology, dreams, inappropriate speeches, scandals, and other violations of norms and etiquette, all "for the provoking and testing of a philosophical idea, a discourse, a truth" (Bakhtin 1984: 114). It is a genre of "ultimate questions" (p. 115) in which high-flown symbols and exalted religious ideas are often mixed with lower-class experiences and vernacular idiom, the lofty with the low, the abstract with the concrete. These ultimate questions are often debated within a narrative form that combines "philosophical dialogue, lofty symbol-systems, the adventure-fantastic, and slum naturalism" (p. 115). The menippea often includes notions of "social utopia incorporated in the form of dreams or journeys to unknown lands" (p. 118), and it is particularly concerned with movement to the threshold of the world after death.

These are just a few of the elements of this particularly rich genre, but it should already be evident how much *Huckleberry Finn* conforms to such patterns. In particular, I want to underscore how the journey downriver can be seen as a voyage to hell. Certainly, for Jim as for any slave, traveling further and further downriver meant moving further from freedom in the North. Drifting "downriver" also meant joining what one scholar calls the "Second Middle Passage," the movement of slave labor to the nightmarish conditions on the labor-short cotton and sugar plantations of the Deep South. The horror of being "sold downriver," for example, is what motivates Roxy's conspiracy in *The Tragedy of Pudd'nhead Wilson*.[2]

We get a clear indication that we are entering the nether world when Huck, arriving at the Phelps's place, senses death in the "Sundaylike" stillness:

> [T]here was them kind of faint dronings of bugs and flies in the air that makes it seem so lonesome and like everybody's dead and gone; and if a breeze fans along and quivers the leaves, it makes you feel mournful, because you feel like it's spirits whispering – spirits that's been dead ever so many years – and you always think they're talking about *you*. As a general thing it makes a body wish *he* was dead, too, and done with it all. (Twain 1885: 277)

Death is regularly invoked – and witnessed – throughout the journey, but death particularly haunts the Phelps plantation, where it is closely associated with domesticity and supernatural incarnations: "I reckon the world is coming to an end" (p. 318), Aunt Sally exclaims during the strange goings-on of the evasion. Here Huck allows Aunt Sally to assume what she would about him, going with the flow – "I'd noticed that Providence always did put the right words in my mouth, if I left it alone" (p. 278) – and when he discovers he is mistaken for Tom Sawyer, responds: "[I]t was like being born again, I was so glad to find out who I was" (p. 282). When he then meets Tom, Huck explains to the boy (who believes he's seen a ghost): "I hain't come back – I hain't been *gone*" (p. 284), which, in a way, is correct – since the "death" of this place is only an intensification of the world from which he had fled.

Huck has not been resurrected or saved, despite being "born again" – although he has been "gone" from the constraints of social convention. Having left the world of life-as-moral-death, he has become truly alive and morally independent in his decision to go to hell to free Jim. Indeed, almost immediately after his momentous decision, he does in fact go to hell, albeit one in the form of a plantation ruled by Tom, the *deus ex machina*, to whose dreams Huck becomes a willing captive. Jim, now bound in chains, reverts to a submissive role for survival's sake. Any semblance of utopian escape fades from view, and they return to the horrors of life within Mississippi riverbank slave-holding society. Huck had already encountered "awful thoughts, and awful words" when he resigned himself to going to hell – "And for a starter, I would go to work and steal Jim out of slavery again; and if I could think up anything worse, I would do that, too; because as long as I was in, and in for good, I might as well go the whole hog" (Twain 1885: 272). While Huck speaks of an invisible, spiritual hell, it is the material, social hell to which he is in fact then relegated.

That Huck would join Tom in hell is anticipated even in the very first chapter of the novel. When Miss Watson indicates to Huck that Tom would go to hell, Huck is relieved: "I was glad about that, because I wanted him and me to be together" (Twain 1885: 20). But when Tom agrees to help free Jim, Huck is incredulous that he would join him in hell, to be sent to spiritual damnation for committing a socially proscribed sin: for "[h]ere was a boy that was respectable, and well brung up; and had a character to lose" (p. 295). Tom's uncharacteristic behavior – "I'm bound to say Tom Sawyer fell, considerable, in my estimation" (p. 285) – reinforces the fact that Huck, having vowed to go to hell, has in fact arrived in what seems to be a topsy-turvy underworld in which Tom is master of pandemonium, even though he does not recognize it as such. This hell is also a familiar one: the Phelps place is "one of these little one-horse cotton plantations; and they all look alike" (p. 277). It serves as a concentration of riverbank social relations in which apparent morality and domestic warmth actually mask the terror which white supremacy fuels.

The vicious hypocrisy that fills this subterranean moral realm is cued early in the final section, when Huck, inventing his story of arriving by steamboat, without knowing from which direction, "struck an idea, and fetched it out":

"It warn't the grounding – that didn't keep us back but a little. We blowed out a cylinder-head."

"Good gracious! anybody hurt?"

"No'm. Killed a nigger."

"Well, it's lucky; because sometimes people do get hurt. Two years ago last Christmas, your uncle Silas was coming up from . . ." (Twain 1885: 280)

As a shrewd, improvisational scriptwriter/performer, Huck knows his audiences well, and he is always aware of how to formulate his appeal or engineer a distraction. Thus here Huck prevents Aunt Sally from asking too many questions by diverting her into a long, comic digression about a white man who also died in an engine blowout ("He turned blue all over, and died in the hope of a glorious resurrection" [Twain 1885: 280]). Her unselfconscious, even innocent obliviousness to the death of a black man – in fact, her inability even to recognize African Americans as "people" – is juxtaposed with her rambling, digressive concern about a white-man-turned-blue, and a man – at that – of whom she had heard only third-hand. The reader squirms at the excruciating irony, even though Huck and Aunt Sally are completely unaware of it, sealed in the hellish depths of their society. "It shows how a body can see and don't see at the same time" (p. 293), Huck later comments on Tom's "detective" work in locating the hut where Jim is imprisoned. Yet such a comment describes the contradictions revealed by layered ironies throughout the entire evasion sequence.

The horror continues, even as the burlesque becomes increasingly frenetic. When Jim and Huck resist Tom's plan, their leader exclaims in exasperation, "It ain't no use to try to learn you nothing" (Twain 1885: 308). "It ain't right, and it ain't moral," Tom finally complains, when he relents and decides to use a shovel instead of case knives. "Now you're talking!" Huck responds:

"Picks is the thing, moral or no moral; and as for me, I don't care shucks for the morality of it, no-how. When I start in to steal a nigger, or a watermelon, or a Sunday-school book, I ain't no ways particular how it's done so it's done . . . [A]nd I don't give a dead rat what the authorities thinks about it nuther." (p. 310)

Again, the transposition of morality is highlighted. The authority of literary romance is regarded as moral, but the obvious immorality of slavery is ignored, underscored by Huck's equating a man, a fruit, and a prayer book as different forms of the same thing (property).

The commonplace violence of white folks continues with the wild, gossipy talk of Mrs. Hotchkiss and the other "farmers and farmers' wives" after Jim's escape. As they consider how "the nigger was crazy," they discuss the strange events of the "evasion": "I lay I'd skin every last nigger on this place, but *I'd* find out who done it . . . 'n' as for the niggers that wrote it ["secret writ'n" on a shirt], I 'low I'd take 'n' lash 'm t'll –" (Twain 1885: 350–1). Only an interruption stops her from completing her account of such intended torture. And when Jim is returned, the men "wanted to hang Jim, for an example to all the other niggers around there, so they wouldn't be trying to run away, like Jim done" – until dissuaded by the fact that the runaway is someone else's property. Huck observes that "the people that's always the most anxious for to hang a nigger that hain't done just right, is always the very ones that ain't the most anxious to pay for him when they've got their satisfaction out of him" (p. 356). The educated doctor, testifying to Jim's faithful care of Tom, can say, "I never see a nigger that was a better nuss or faithfuller, and yet he was resking his freedom to do it" (p. 357). Moral judgments, however, again quickly recede before property value, for the seemingly enlightened doctor's conclusion is that "a nigger like that is worth a thousand dollars – and kind treatment, too" (p. 357). In response, the lynch mob "softened up a little, too . . . Then they all agreed that Jim had acted very well, and was deserving to have some notice took of it, and reward" (p. 358). Again, the ironies should make the reader squirm, since their "reward" amounts merely to a promise "that they wouldn't cuss him no more" (p. 358).

All of this echoes earlier encounters where racial assumptions are acted out with no apparent awareness. Tom and Huck treat Jim as a plaything. Pap, in his rant about the educated, free mulatto, resorts to the refuge of his own white skin. Judith Loftus, for all her cunning and her kindness to Huck, has no qualms in guiding her husband in the hunt for the runaway slave. And everywhere – at the Grangerford plantation or where the lynch party runs after Colonel Sherburn or at the Wilks farm – black eyes witness from the background or at a cautious distance the inflated self-regard and self-destructive violence of white folks: "there was nigger boys in every tree, and bucks and wenches looking over every fence; and as soon as the mob would get nearly to them they would break and skaddle back out of reach" (Twain 1885: 189). The white characters are oblivious, mired in their sense of superiority, corrupt and vicious. And even the more educated or sophisticated among them are either ineffectual, such as the judge who seeks to reform pap, and Doctor Robinson, who warns the Wilks family of the king and duke's "soul-butter and hogwash" (p. 213), or self-deluded frauds. Colonel Grangerford may be "a gentleman all over" (p. 143) and his family well-to-do, each with "their own nigger to wait on them" (p. 144), but they are fools, driven by an irrational code of honor. When Huck praises Jim – "I knowed he was white inside" (p. 345) – the terms in which he does so are suffused with the most biting irony for the alert reader. It is, in fact, about the worst thing he could say about him.

Colonel Sherburn is one of the few characters who can stand outside – or at least above – social conventions. "Do I know you?" he rhetorically questions the lynch mob from his rooftop: "I know you clear through. I was born and raised in the South, and I've lived in the North; so I know the average all around" (Twain 1885: 190). He is the closest to Twain himself – reconstructed Southerner transformed by the West and hammered into respectability by the North. And like the author, "who told the truth, mainly" (p. 17), he is flawed (although, unlike the author, unaware of it). While he can talk down a lynch mob, he is nonetheless a cold-blooded murderer of a drunken but harmless loudmouth. Even so, Colonel Sherburn taunts the mob to show him a "man" with backbone and courage, and he points to their leader Buck Harkness as merely "half-a-man." He manages to drive the mob back, but his question remains: who, in this novelistic world, is a complete, courageous man or woman?

Huck is merely a boy, a bad boy at that, and not a "man." He is not endowed with Tom's powers, but consistently acts with compassion, although usually limited by his education and social standing. Huck follows a type of golden rule applied so broadly as to include even murderers. When he attempts to save the outlaws on the sinking steamboat, he rationalizes: "I begun to think how dreadful it was, even for murderers, to be in such a fix. I says to myself, there ain't no telling but I might come to be a murderer myself, yet, and then how would *I* like it?" (Twain 1885: 103). Despite the impositions of the king and the duke, he can empathize when he sees the scoundrels run out on a rail in tar and feathers: "Well, it made me sick to see it" (p. 291). And he concludes with the ultimate understatement of the book: "Human beings *can* be awful cruel to one another" (p. 291).

Huck's sense of morality arises from contingent circumstances, since his sympathies tend to run counter to the prevailing standards. At an early stage of the novel, when Huck is tempted to betray Jim but decides against it, he rationalizes: "Well, then, says I, what's the use you learning to do right, when it's troublesome to do right and ain't no trouble to do wrong, and the wages is just the same? I was stuck. I couldn't answer that. So I reckoned I wouldn't bother no more about it, but after this always do whichever come handiest at the time" (Twain 1885: 128). And what comes handiest is to follow the impulse of friendship and kindness – even if such an impulse leads to spiritual damnation, to hell.

Still, Huck does not escape the confines of his social conditions. He never takes a stance against the normal assumptions of life, never becomes an abolitionist, and his declaration that he would go to hell is no denial of the entire social order that created Jim's situation in the first place. Readers who expect Huck to turn against the entire slave system, to become an abolitionist through a sort of spontaneous moral enlightenment, are reaching too far. Huck remains a creature of plantation society, engulfed by its racial assumptions. He is only willing to go to hell for stealing someone's "property" because of his personal contact with one individual. The reader can articulate a broader response, what Eric Auerbach has called "creaturality," a sense of commonality arising from the realization that all humans must face suffering and death in similar ways – but Huck entertains such a sensibility only unconsciously (through the rough golden rule by which he works).

Tom, even though a boy, has the intelligence and courage of a "man," but he does not act with human compassion. He is a leader, a kind of Nietzschean superman spawned by settler–colonial plantation society. And his morally oblivious playfulness has its source in a fascination Twain entertains over the course of his career with what I call the bad-boy deity.

Twain first found expression for his fascination with this figure in the apocryphal Infancy Gospel of Thomas, excerpts of which he incorporates in his 1867 *Alta California* articles – then adapted (in fact, censored) for *The Innocents Abroad* (1869).

The mischievous Jesus reappears at the end of Twain's career as a model for Philip Traum/Satan/No. 44 in The *Mysterious Stranger* manuscripts, and Gladys Bellamy, William Gibson, and Bruce Michelson have examined the Infancy Gospel as a source for these manuscripts. The fact that this extraordinary, amoral character appears both early and late in Twain's career highlights the importance of the bad-boy deity: it provides a kind of frame or bracket for an insistent fascination with an excessive type of male character throughout much of his work, including Hank in *A Connecticut Yankee in King Arthur's Court*, along with the character of Tom in *Huckleberry Finn*.[3]

In the Infancy Gospel, the boy Jesus is marked by his magical powers. Twain, in *The Innocents Abroad*, quotes selected summaries of its chapters to illustrate the boy's extraordinary abilities. For example:

> Chapter 16. Christ miraculously widens or contracts gates, milk-pails, sieves or boxes, not properly made by Joseph, he not being skilful at his carpenter's trade. The King of Jerusalem gives Joseph an order for a throne. Joseph works on it for two years and makes it two spans too short. The King being angry with him, Jesus comforts him – commands him to pull one side of the throne while he pulls the other, and brings it to its proper dimensions.
>
> Chapter 19. Jesus, charged with throwing a boy from the roof of a house, miraculously causes the dead boy to speak and acquit him; fetches water for his mother, breaks the pitcher and miraculously gathers the water in his mantle and brings it home.
>
> Sent to a schoolmaster, refuses to tell his letters, and the schoolmaster going to whip him, his hand withers. (Twain 1869: 537–8)

In the *Alta California* correspondence, he concludes his description of the schoolmaster's torment: "and he dies" (Bellamy 1950: 352–3). In other Gospel passages, some clearly recognizable as models for parts of *The Chronicle of Young Satan* (Twain 1969: 50), Jesus makes clay figures with his playmates, alarms them and their parents by bringing them to life, then, bored with his game, wipes them away, thoughtlessly killing the inhabitants of his miniature world. One verse quoted by Twain in his *Alta California* correspondence is pointedly left out of the travel book: "Then said Joseph to St. Mary, Henceforth we will not allow him out of the house; for everyone who displeases him is killed" ([Hone] 1820: First Gospel, 20: 16). Twain concludes his account for his California readers with the wry comment that "His society was pleasant, but attended by serious drawbacks" (Twain 1940: 252–3).

In *The Other Gospels: Non-Canonical Gospel Texts*, Ron Cameron explains that the Infancy Gospel depicts Jesus "as an *enfant terrible*, always clever and mischievous, often intractable and even malicious . . . , portrayed simply as a child of the gods, a *Wunderkind* in whose life are manifested epiphanies of the divine." Despite this distinctly un-Christian quality, the *Infancy Gospel* "was extremely popular in the first centuries and appears translated in many languages" (1982: 123). As Willis Barnstone in *The Other Bible* explains, "For modern apologists, the work is an ethical embarrassment, for the little Jesus is not only a child prodigy but a child terror, performing nasty miracles" (1984: 397). Modern translators of the text regard the representation of

Jesus as "a classic example of the influence of the Hellenistic 'divine man' concept" (p. 398) popular in antiquity. This was a tradition that affirmed the miraculous capabilities of the god–hero with legends of his wildly capricious divine powers.

Versions of the "divine man" and "savage boy" emerge in different forms in American culture (including the Davy Crockett legends and other tall tales), but it is enough here to see how this character fuses into the figure of that savage boy considered necessary by Hall and others for the healthy development of the white ruling-class male, even if his magic is more mundane. Today we might view Tom as an "ethical embarrassment," though not a spiritual being; neither devil nor god. The episodes at the Phelps plantation enact a social hell, not a Christian one. Yet Tom is both master and dramaturge. His plan to free Jim has "style, and would make Jim just as free a man as mine would, and maybe get us all killed besides" (Twain 1885: 294). He is loyal to his "dream," loyal even unto death, because "there's more honor in getting [Jim] out through a lot of difficulties and dangers" (p. 301) than in liberating him as simply as possible. Huck cannot understand how Tom, obsessed with "honor," would "stoop to this business," and when Tom's secret knowledge of Jim's actual status is finally revealed, the fact that Tom has merely engaged in adventure for the sake of adventure also becomes clear. Tom never goes beyond the sanctions of society, never threatens the status quo.

Throughout the novel, Tom is the gold standard for adventure and male "style." Tom knew how to "throw in the fancy touches" (Twain 1885: 57), Huck observes, as he engineers his own fake death. "Do you reckon Tom Sawyer would ever go by this thing?" Huck exclaims, approaching the wrecked steamboat: "Not for pie, he wouldn't. He'd call it an adventure – that's what he'd call it; and he'd land on that wreck if it was his last act. And wouldn't he throw style into it?" (p. 97). Even Jim uses Tom as his standard, declaring that he would stay beside the side of the wounded boy to await the doctor: "Ef it wuz *him* dat 'uz bein' sot free, en one er de boys wuz to git shot, would he say, 'Go on en save me, nemmine' bout a doctor f'r to save dis one? Is dat like Mars Tom Sawyer? Would he say dat? You *bet* he wouldn't" (p. 345). We have to take Jim at his word, since nowhere else in the novel does Tom act in a selfless manner. However, despite Huck and Jim's constant struggle against the more preposterous aspects of Tom's evasion, they still regard him as a master. Tom, if his plan succeeded, would have had "adventures plumb to the mouth" of the Mississippi – taking Jim to the bottom of hell – paying off the freed slave "for his lost time" (p. 364). And, in the end, he does pay Jim "forty dollars for being prisoner for us so patient" (p. 365). His gesture demonstrates how property relations define (or contain) the virtue of patience. So long as Tom has the cash, his responsibility for Jim's agony can be absolved. His callous generosity may make Tom like a "divine child," unaware that a brush of his hand could wipe out his plaything, but it does not mark him as a fully developed, compassionate human.

On the other hand, although uneducated, Jim is as much a "man" as it is possible to be, although in order to survive as a slave he is constantly forced to hide behind his mask of willing subservience. I have already noted several junctures at which Jim reveals himself: through the dialogues with Huck; through his desire to buy his wife and children out of bondage, or even steal them; the way he gets "low and homesick" (Twain 1885: 201) when he thinks about his wife and children; his heart-rending account of how he learned that his daughter was deaf (pp. 201–2). In a world of absent or abusive fathers, Jim stands out as an exception to the normal white rule.

At the same time, Jim can be read as possessing a type of wily intelligence only fully revealed at the very end of the novel. Early in their journey, Jim warns away Huck from looking at the face of the dead body in the house floating down the river – "it's too gashly" (Twain 1885: 77) – but at the very end he explains that pap "ain't a comin' back no mo'" because "dat wuz him" (pp. 365–6). Huck makes no response, but clearly, if Jim were to have told him that pap was dead earlier, Huck might have had no cause to join Jim on the raft. Huck was Jim's means of escape, and the runaway slave had purposely hidden the truth in order to keep the white boy on the raft as his protective cover. The novel would have abruptly ended with Huck turning back to collect his money and live free from the abuse of his father, and Jim would very likely have been captured and returned. So Jim not only displays his agency here, but indeed controls the unfolding of the entire plot.

Nonetheless, Jim too is constrained by his own understanding of social conventions. Jim "couldn't see no sense" in Tom's evasion, "but he allowed we was white folks and knowed better than him" (Twain 1885: 313). True, if Tom decides to secure his freedom, and if he has his unexpected support, then he might as well concede whatever he must to accomplish his goal. But Jim is also deluded by white conceptions of property relations. "Yes – en I's rich now, come to look at it," he exclaims to Huck on his initial escape. "I owns mysef, en I's wuth eight hund'd dollars. I wisht I had de money, I wouldn't want no mo'" (p. 73). If only his value as chattel could be separated from his humanity – but the harsh contradiction of slavery is that it cannot be. At the very end, his good luck – Tom's forty dollars plus his freedom – seems to resolve this contradiction. "[S]igns is *signs*" (p. 365), Jim declares, remembering the earlier good omen of his hairy chest. But he still cannot comprehend that the whole semiology of slavery, and particularly the sign that equates black skin with property, is still in place, needing to be overthrown.

There is yet another character, often overlooked, who should be examined here. At the very beginning of the narrative, Huck introduces this person – in fact the reader – with the words: "You don't know about me . . ." (Twain 1885: 17). The second-person form is hardly used in the novel (the passage when Huck reaches the Phelps plantation is a rare moment in which it is employed) but the reader is constantly called upon to make crucial judgments, to participate actively in order to comprehend the dramatic ironies produced by the narrative. This "You" is constantly being challenged – and constructed – and it is this reader's capacity (or lack of it) to understand the multiple meanings of the narrative which troubles many critics. Huck is a naïve, deadpan narrator – he finds little that is funny or ironic in the events he describes – and he speaks with "dense simplicity," as Twain describes the talk of the black boy in his sketch "Sociable Jimmy" (Twain 1994: 77). It is up to the reader to peel back the multiple meanings that Huck delivers unaware. "The novel works," Stephen Mailloux observes, "not as a formal unity but as a rhetorical performance in which the reader must participate in order to read at all" (Mailloux 1989: 98).

Many readers in 1885 uncritically accepted the stereotypes of the minstrel show, along with the presumptions of white supremacy and black subordination, and it was very difficult for such readers to comprehend the author's ultimate subversion. "Twain fitted Jim into the outlines of the minstrel tradition," Ralph Ellison observes, "and it was from behind this stereotype mask that we see Jim's dignity and human capacity – and Twain's complexity – emerge" (see Fishkin 1993: 80). Twain had few other means available to him to create an authentic black character – and new, realist conventions would arise in part from the burlesque of previous forms. If readers accept racial stereotypes or cannot go beyond the "fun" of the minstrel show, it may be hard to participate in this satirical performance. But there are a number of scenes, particularly those involving theatrical performances of one sort or another, in which Twain trains the reader, passages where he offers the reader examples of "how a body can see and don't see at the same time" (Twain 1885: 293).

"I went to the circus" (Twain 1885: 191), Huck says immediately after he flees Colonel Sherburn's challenge with the rest of the lynch mob. This jump-cut (in cinematic terms) underscores the dream-like quality of the narrative, as a switch occurs, with little explanation, to an altogether different episode. But the circus, like the lynch mob scene, is a type of theater, in which audience and participants overlap and where judgments about meanings and significance need to be made. The circus is one of the few places where Huck enjoys himself with abandon – "It was the splendidest sight that ever was" (p. 192). But most readers soon become aware that Huck does not understand that the drunken man who jumps up on a horse is in fact part of the act in progress. Even when he pulls off his clothes and reveals himself to be one of the ring-master's "own men," Huck doesn't fully "see": "He had got up that joke all out of his own head, and never let on to nobody. Well, I felt sheepish enough, to be took in so, but I wouldn't a been in that ring-master's place, not for a thousand dollars" (p. 194). Huck only partially understands the circus routine, where the ring-master appears to be the butt of a practical joke. Nonetheless, he is well entertained, thoroughly delighted, despite his inability to see the full import of the ruse: that it is the audience that has been toyed with and not the ring-master (who remains very much in control).

Mark Twain is the ring-master of this novel, although speaking through the medium of Huck's "dense simplicity." It is up to "You" to decide whether to laugh at the surface, and perhaps misunderstood, jokes, or to respond to the deeper incongruities of the human comedy. Shelley Fisher Fishkin has demonstrated how Twain employs "the indirect, double-voiced variety of satire known as 'signifying'" (Fishkin 1993: 55), a mode adopted from and rooted in African American culture. But perceptive readers not familiar with African American forms can still respond to Twain's multiple meanings. The farcical evasion – filled with shackles, talk of prisoners, and abuse – echoes the bleak conditions blacks faced after the defeat of Reconstruction:

mass arrests for chain-gang convict labor on trumped-up charges, peonage under the sharecropping system, loss of effective political power, and the imposition of crushing segregation. Fishkin asks: "Is what America did to the ex-slaves any less insane than what Tom Sawyer put Jim through in the novel? . . . What is the history of post-Emancipation race relations in the United States if not a series of maneuvers as cruelly gratuitous as the indignities inflicted on Jim in the final section of *Huckleberry Finn?*" (pp. 199–200).

Although Mark Twain was primarily a writer who relied on intuition and the force of narrative rather than didactic exposition – I suspect that he was only partially conscious of the full import of his depiction of Tom's antic hell – his reaction to the "silent assertion" not only of slavery but of white supremacy comes through clearly to any contemporary reader attuned to his ironies. The irony of Tom's wish that Jim could keep up his game of the evasion "all the rest of our lives and leave Jim to our children to get out" becomes even harsher, more bitter, when he adds, "for he believed Jim would come to like it better and better the more he got used to it" (Twain 1885: 313). Decades later, during the Civil Rights movement, the descendants of Tom Sawyer would decry outside agitators for stirring up trouble among Southern Negroes who were "content" in their "place." Twain's ear was well attuned to similar pronouncements made in the post-Reconstruction period. Tom would gladly give Jim his freedom, on terms of continued white supremacy and in his own good time. He could not contemplate, much less accept, the idea that Jim himself could take his freedom. The reader ("You") is called upon to perceive all of the presumptions of racial superiority throughout the novel, so that Huck's final invocation, "YOURS TRULY," becomes even more poignant. Dear Reader, what exactly is "true" in this tale or in the society it dramatizes? While the dark satire clearly targets the delusions of racial supremacy, its thrust goes beyond racial categories to all texts or structures of authority that seek to impose their own "preforeordestination" (p. 148) upon life.

This is signaled in an inverted way in the "Notice" that precedes the narrative. "[P]ersons attempting to find a motive in this narrative will be prosecuted . . . to find a moral in it will be banished . . . to find a plot in it will be shot" (Twain 1885: 5), the "Author" admonishes in the prefatory "Notice" before the voice of Huck takes up the story. Fishkin notes how many readers take Twain "at his word" and read it as a boy's book, a novel of comic adventures and humorous antics. "But," as Fishkin notes, "such a limited reading denies the corrosive satire of white society (and of the many 'texts' that undergird its position of alleged racial superiority) that is at the book's core" (Fishkin 1993: 63). Once aware of the full breadth of the novel's subversive performance, the reader can return to this Notice to "see" it in two other ways. The perceptive reader who has been prosecuted, banished, and shot, or who can empathize with those who have been, will readily discover the true motive, the moral, and the plot of *Huckleberry Finn*. At the same time, if "You" really do understand the motive, the moral, and the plot, you are in grave danger – you may indeed be prosecuted, banished, and shot in a larger society that protects its "dreams" of racial supremacy with total and unselfconscious violence.

NOTES

1 Others have commented on the relationship with minstrelsy. See e.g. Berret (1986).

2 Conditions were so harsh on the sugar plantations of Louisiana (for instance) that the death rate of slaves far exceeded the birth rate. See Berlin (2003: 161–209).

3 For further examination of Twain's fascination with Jesus as a bad boy in the *Infancy Gospel* see Obenzinger (1999); Obenzinger (forthcoming).

REFERENCES AND FURTHER READING

Bakhtin, M. M. (1984). *Problems of Dosteovsky's Poetics*, trans. Caryl Emerson. Minneapolis: University of Minnesota Press.

Barnstone, Willis (1984). "The Infancy Gospel of Thomas (Christian Apocrypha)." In *The Other Bible: Jewish Pseudepigrapha, Christian Apocrypha, Gnostic Scriptures, Kabbalah, Dead Sea Scrolls*. San Francisco: HarperCollins.

Bederman, Gail (1995). *Manliness and Civilization: A Cultural History of Gender and Race in the United States, 1880–1917*. Chicago: University of Chicago Press.

Bellamy, Gladys (1950). *Mark Twain as a Literary Artist*. Norman: University of Oklahoma Press.

Berlin, Ira (2003). *Generations of Captivity: A History of African-American Slaves*. Cambridge, Mass.: Belknap.

Berret, Anthony J., S.J. (1986). "Huckleberry Finn and the Minstrel Show." *American Studies* 27: 2, 37–49.

Cameron, Ron (1982). *The Other Gospels: Non-Canonical Gospel Texts*. Philadelphia: Westminster.

Chadwick-Joshua, Jocelyn (1998). *The Jim Dilemma: Reading Race in Huckleberry Finn*. Jackson: University Press of Mississippi.

Fishkin, Shelley Fisher (1993). *Was Huck Black? Mark Twain and African American Voices*. New York: Oxford University Press.

Fishkin, Shelley Fisher (1997). *Lighting Out for the Territory: Reflections on Mark Twain and American Culture*. New York: Oxford University Press.

Hemingway, Ernest (1935). *The Green Hills of Africa*. New York: Scribner.

[Hone, William] (1820). *The Apocryphal New Testament, Being All the Gospels, Epistles, and Other Pieces Now Extant, Attributed in the First Four Centuries to Jesus Christ, His Apostles, and Their Companions, and Not Included in the New Testament by Its Compilers*. London: William Hone.

Lhamon, W. T., Jr. (1996). "Ebery Time I Wheel About I Jump Jim Crow: Cycles of Minstrel Transgression from Cool White to Vanilla Ice." In Annemarie Bean, James V. Hatch, and Brooks McNamara (eds.), *Inside the Minstrel Mask: Readings in Nineteenth-Century Blackface Minstrelsy*, 275–84. Hanover, NH: Wesleyan University Press/University Press of New England.

Lott, Eric (1996). "Blackface and Blackness: The Minstrel Show in American Culture." In Annemarie Bean, James V. Hatch, and Brooks McNamara (eds.), *Inside the Minstrel Mask: Readings in Nineteenth-Century Blackface Minstrelsy*, 3–32. Hanover, NH: Wesleyan University Press/University Press of New England.

Mailloux, Stephen (1989). *Rhetorical Power*. Ithaca, NY: Cornell University Press.

Obenzinger, Hilton (1999). *American Palestine: Melville, Twain, and The Holy Land Mania*. Princeton: Princeton University Press.

Obenzinger, Hilton (forthcoming). "Better Dreams: Political Satire and Twain's Final 'Exploding' Novel." *Arizona Quarterly*.

Twain, Mark (1940). *Mark Twain's Travels with Mr. Brown*, ed. Franklin Walker and G. Ezra Dane. New York: Knopf.

Twain, Mark (1969). *Mark Twain's Mysterious Stranger Manuscripts*, ed. William M. Gibson. Berkeley: University of California Press.

Twain, Mark (1992c). "My First Lie and How I Got Out of It." In *Collected Tales, Sketches, Speeches, and Essays, 1891–1910*. New York: Library of America.

Twain, Mark (1994). "Sociable Jimmy." In *Tales, Speeches, Essays, and Sketches*, ed. Tom Quirk. New York: Penguin.

27

History, "Civilization," and *A Connecticut Yankee in King Arthur's Court*

Sam Halliday

On the highly civilized man there rests at all times a three-fold burden – the past, the present, and the future! the barbarian carries through life but one burden – that of the present; and in a psychological view, a very light one indeed; the civilized man is ever thinking of the past – representing, repeating, recasting, and projecting the experience of bygone days to days that are to come. (George Miller Beard, *American Nervousness: Its Causes and Consequences*)

A Connecticut Yankee in King Arthur's Court (1889) represents Mark Twain's most serious and sustained attempt to think about history. Through its time-travel plot, which involves the "transposition" of its hero from his native nineteenth-century Connecticut to sixth-century England (Twain 1889: 18), the novel brings together two otherwise disparate historic periods (one of which, of course, is Twain's own present) in order to measure them against one another, and, in the process, find one or the other wanting. Predictably enough, the results of this exercise tend, on the face of things at least, to overwhelmingly affirm the superiority of the late nineteenth century over its premodern adversary. However, as the novel's most perceptive critics have often noted, there is a deeper level at which this outcome is subverted – not only because the nineteenth century turns out to share all too many of the sixth century's deficiencies, but also because it suffers from several others of its own. In this essay, I re-examine some of the reasons for these two apparently contradictory outcomes, and, in so doing, seek to show the intricacy of the novel's engagement with history. To do this, I read Twain's novel alongside three other works that share many of its key concerns: George Miller Beard's *American Nervousness* (1881); Friedrich Nietzsche's *On the Genealogy of Morality* (1887); and, more briefly, Sigmund Freud's *Civilization and its Discontents* (1930). Two of these date from the same decade as *Connecticut Yankee* itself, the third from somewhat later. All four exemplify what Carl E. Schorske calls "thinking with history": an imaginative process whereby the past appears, not as an inert set of "facts," but as a set of materials to be arranged and rearranged in the service of a better understanding of the present (Schorske 1998: 3).

In this respect Twain's novel, no less than these other texts, exemplifies the intellectual temper of its time. As my epigraph from Beard's *American Nervousness* suggests, Americans and other nationals of Twain's generation were intensely concerned with the past, and had a habit of more or less systematically juxtaposing it with the present (to say nothing of the "future" [Beard 1881: 130]). As Beard's words also help to indicate, such habits were linked to a wider set of concerns – the nature of "civilization," the apparent "burden[s]" it imposes, and the strangely vexed relation between civilization and barbarism – of central importance to the period's self-understanding. Each of these concerns bulks largely in the texts I will consider, and nowhere to more bizarre or ultimately disturbing effect than in *Connecticut Yankee* itself, where the task of "representing, repeating, [and] recasting" the past is pursued with a comic panache that is, at bottom, deadly serious.

"The Excess of Yankee Curiosity": Twain with Beard

Before assessing *Connecticut Yankee*'s treatment of the past, however, we must first address the views of those for whom the novel is not "really" about the past at all. The *locus classicus* for all such readings is that of Henry Nash Smith. For Smith, the novel is of all Twain's books "the most urgently focused on the state of the nation and of the world at the moment of writing" (Smith 1964: 7). It follows that Twain's sixth-century setting is but a smokescreen behind which the novel's real business is conducted:

> It is true that Mark Twain professes to be rehearsing a dream about a far-away country, the Britain of King Arthur and his Round Table. But this medieval setting is obviously not meant to represent any actual place or time. It is a backdrop designed to allow a nineteenth century American industrial genius to show what he can do with an underdeveloped country. (p. 36)

On this reading, the heart of the novel lies with the efforts of its hero, Hank Morgan, to transform Arthurian England. As a "Yankee of the Yankees," Hank represents many of the most powerful social forces transforming nineteenth-century America: industry (before his removal to sixth-century England, Hank has been the foreman of an arms factory); technology (while there, he has "learned to make everything" from guns and engines to telephones); and entrepreneurial capitalism (as the only would-be "capitalist" in Arthur's kingdom, Hank not only devises a string of marketable goods, but also commissions them in his role as Arthur's prime minister, and tries to stimulate popular demand for them with advertising) (Twain 1889: 20). The basic procedure of the novel is thus to identify the most characteristic features of contemporary society and then have Hank "invent" them. As Smith concludes, the novel must therefore be reckoned "not a mere tall tale but a philosophical fable which sets forth a theory of capitalism and an interpretation of the historical process that has brought it into being" (Smith 1964: 37).

Other critics of the novel have generally either extended this analysis or evolved their own in complementary directions. Smith himself has contributed to another longstanding school of thought, seeing the novel as an exploration of intra-American North–South relations, with Arthurian England as a stand-in for the American South, and the "Yankee" (as his name suggests) as an exemplar of the North (Smith 1958). In a related fashion, some have seen the book's violent conclusion – in which Hank's deadly weapons are pitted against the massed ranks of Arthurian knighthood – as a re-enactment of the American Civil War (Aaron 1973). More recently, Hank's attempts to renovate Arthurian production methods have been read in the light of late nineteenth-century industrial reform, and the emergence of "scientific management" (see e.g. Messent 1997). Finally, the novel has been read as an allegory of imperialism, with Hank's sojourn in England standing for (or anticipating) American involvement in the Sandwich Islands, Cuba, and the Philippines (Rowe 2000; Kaplan 2002).

All these approaches constitute significant advances in our appreciation of the novel, and all grasp important elements of the truth. However, all may be faulted for systematically undervaluing Twain's interest in the past in its own right. Wherever Arthurian England is taken as the body-double for something else, in other words, the fact that it may also function as, quite simply, a representation of Arthurian England tends to get lost.[1] This is unfortunate, because it implies a false choice between the contemporary and the historical that Twain and his contemporaries would scarcely have recognized. As I have already suggested, members of this generation wasted few opportunities to juxtapose the past and present. But what must now be seen is that this habit was no whimsy, but rather the expression of a profound sense of the past's enduring potency: its presence, so to speak, *in* the present. To see this, we can turn directly to Beard's *American Nervousness*, and its relation to Twain's novel.[2]

We can begin by reconsidering my epigraph. As well as acting as a pretty good gloss on *Connecticut Yankee* itself – for Hank, there is indeed a "three-fold burden," as he seeks to drag the "past" into a "future" that is also his own "present" – Beard's comment functions both as a description of the people in whom he is interested, and as a précis of his own theoretical assumptions. Though Beard was a neurologist by profession, his contemporary fame stemmed less from his innovations in this field than in his extrapolation of its principles onto more general questions of culture and society. From the late 1860s onward, he became increasingly concerned by a disturbing rise in "nervous exhaustion" or "nervousness" among his middle- and upper-class patients in New York City, where he worked. Not only was this rise, he thought, "one of the most stupendous, complex, and suggestive" facts of its age, but it was one that, if correctly interpreted, could illuminate the contours of world history (Beard 1881: viii). *American Nervousness* is Beard's most sustained attempt to make this case to a lay audience. It begins by considering the factors distinguishing ancient and modern "civilization," arguing that it is in the transition from one to the other that the origins of "nervousness" reside: "The chief and primary cause of this development and very rapid increase of nervousness is *modern civilization*, which is distinguished from the ancient by these five characteristics: steam power, the periodical press, the telegraph, the sciences, and the mental activity of women" (p. vi).

As this rather startling taxonomy indicates, Beard's analysis is thoroughly "historical." It is by measuring contemporary civilization against its ancient counterpart that the characteristic features of the former may be identified. If this already suggests an affinity between Beard's approach and that of Twain in *Connecticut Yankee*, so too do the features by which modern civilization is characterized. Of the five on Beard's list, at least four – steam power, the periodical press, the telegraph, and the sciences – play a prominent role in Hank's attempts to renovate Arthurian England (the final factor, "the mental activity of women," may, on balance, be counted an exception).[3] And if, for Beard, the most salient effect of these developments is the creation of nervous illness (because, through constant stimulation of the nervous system, all such factors tend to deplete the body's native energies, thus causing "nervousness"), he nonetheless shares with Hank an underlying faith in the beneficence of "modern civilization." "The evil of American nervousness," he writes, "tends, within certain limits, to correct itself" (Beard 1881: ix). The cure for the disease thus lies in the very "civilization" that gives rise to it.

The homology between Beard's basic definition of "civilization" and Hank's reforms also extends to what Beard calls the "secondary and tertiary" causes of nervousness (Beard 1881: vi). Hank creates "a complete variety of Protestant congregations all in a prosperous and growing condition" (Twain 1889: 118); Beard refers to "the religious excitements that are the sequels of Protestantism" (Beard 1881: 99). Hank builds "an admirable system of graded schools", plus military and naval academies (Twain 1889: 118, 120); Beard notes the "extending complexity of modern education in and out of schools and universities" (1881: 100). Hank rationalizes the taxation system, abolishes slavery, and ensures equality before the law (Twain 1889: 513); Beard refers to "the political machinery of free countries" (1881: 99). And so on. All of this thus begs the question of what, if anything, is specifically *American* about the "civilization" both men anatomize: it is "*American* nervousness," after all, that Beard set as out to diagnose, and as a "Yankee of the Yankees" that Hank is identified.

To answer this question, Beard invokes the category of "curiosity": "[T]he curiosity of the Yankee, which, when harnessed, trained, and held in check, becomes the parent of invention, science, and ideas, inquiring into everything with eagerness, unrest, impatience, palpitating anxiety and breathlessness, draws heavily on the units of nerve force" (Beard 1881: 131). Thus, the American drive for innovation goes hand in hand with a propensity for nervous illness. But what really throws the significance of "curiosity" into clear relief is a contrast between "civilized" Yankees and "savage" Native Americans:

> The difference between civilization and savagery, and an impressive and instructive illustration of the cause of nervousness, is given us whenever any representatives of our Indian tribes visit the east. The utter want of curiosity in matters that do not come immediately home to them is a feature most noticeable and interesting, contrasting as it does

with the excess of Yankee curiosity. The barbarian cares nothing for the great problems
of life; seeks no solution – thinks of no solution of the mysteries of nature, and, after
the manner of many reasoners in modern delusions, dismisses what he cannot at once
comprehend, as supernatural, and leaves it unsatisfactorily solved for himself, for others,
and for all time. (Beard 1881: 130–1)

It is striking how well each of these accounts corresponds with Hank's narration
in *Connecticut Yankee*. Time and again, he contrasts his own invention and quick-
wittedness with the sloth, superstition, and sheer intellectual vacuity of Arthurians.
When a holy well dries up, for instance, the Arthurians are quick to blame some terrible curse, while Hank simply enters the well chamber, has a good look around, and
discovers the leak responsible "by natural means" (Twain 1889: 274). More significantly still, Hank follows Beard in associating Arthurian failings with "savages" or
"Indians," both of which terms he applies to the Arthurians themselves. Shortly after
arriving in Camelot, he calls a group of prisoners "white Indians" (p. 40). "Measured
by modern standards," he asserts, Britons are "merely modified savages" (p. 153). The
great Arthurian Round Table itself is but a "polished-up court of Comanches" (p.
178). These epithets suggest a systematic tendency – as much Twain's as it is Hank's
– to conflate "ethnic" or "racial" difference with national difference, on one hand, and
temporal difference, on the other (see Sollors 1995). Arthurian "savagery" thus takes
on a threefold signification: English, sixth-century, and pseudo-"Indian." This brings
us to a crucial point.

Ever since its "discovery," of course, America has been regarded as a "New World,"
distinct from the "Old World" represented by the Near East, Middle East, and Europe.
This idea, perhaps the most familiar in American cultural history, has as one of its
less-remarked corollaries a view of the past as something that continues to exist elsewhere. It exists, that is, as a determinate set of geographical locations, and is, as such,
a "place" that can be visited. Thus, in a long tradition of American travel writing –
to which Twain himself is an important contributor, with *The Innocents Abroad* (1869)
– travel to and through Europe and the Holy Land is represented as, quite literally,
a kind of time travel (see Leask 2002). American "present-ness" and Euro-Asian "past-
ness" are here coeval and mutually sustaining ideas.

Throughout the nineteenth century, meanwhile, these ideas were shadowed by a
similarly deep-rooted set of notions concerning the native inhabitants of North
America, and other "races" (see e.g. Takaki 1979). According to these, the people
Beard calls "Indian tribes" were just as obsolete, historically speaking (if not more so),
as any that a traveler might meet abroad. Not only were such people racially or ethnically distinct from "civilized" Americans, in other words, but they were *temporally*
distinct as well.

Clearly, these two sets of ideas are related, and it is as such that they are combined
in the period's historical imaginary. Here, the past assumes at least two substantial
forms, either one of which may be encountered in the present: one made accessible
by foreign travel; one made manifest by "racial" others. If the "civilized man" of

Beard's account "is ever thinking of the past," this is because he could scarcely help being reminded of it at every turn. And so it is that Beard himself, in seeking to substantiate his claim that nervousness is linked to the rise of "modern civilization," claims it "impossible to solve the problem of American nervousness without taking into our estimate the nervousness of other lands and ages" (1881: 14). In his very methodology, Beard recapitulates the turn towards the past that he notes in his contemporaries. And if, in practice, Beard says relatively little about "other lands and ages" – apart from noting the philosophical prestige of Germany, and the prodigious drinking habits of the English[4] – this matters little, for he can also say, quite consistently: "It is not necessary to go off the continent of North America . . . in order to demonstrate out of all dispute the proposition, that nervousness is a result and accompaniment and barometer of civilization." One need simply look to the Indian, the "Negro," or, for that matter, the contrast between the North and South (p. 186).

We are now in a better position to see what is happening when Hank calls Arthurians "Indians"; or when (as others have suggested) he notes affinities between the American South and sixth-century England. In each case, Twain is simply superimposing phenomena that, for Beard, remain related but distinct. The reason for this difference, of course, is that Twain is writing a self-consciously extravagant work of fiction, whereas Beard is writing a sober piece of socio-historical (and medical) analysis. Nonetheless, the two texts manifestly mirror one other, Twain's time-travel plot merely literalizing, so to speak, the kind of temporal disjuncture that Beard takes for granted. This is why Henry Nash Smith and his successors are doubtless right to see Twain's representation of the past as an expression of contemporary concerns. What we can now add, however, is that the converse is also true: Twain can use a sixth-century setting to articulate contemporary concerns precisely because, in his view, the problem with the present century is the recalcitrant presence in it of the sixth. Witness the fact that Hank, in Arthurian England, finds people who remind him of *contemporary* Southerners and "savages."

One can conclude this section by noting the several occasions in *American Nervousness* when Beard seems to have Twain himself in mind. These feature in the book's discussions of "American oratory, humor, speech, and language" (1881: ix), with all of which Twain was prominently associated. To illustrate American humor, Beard cites the stage version of *The Gilded Age* (adapted from Twain's and Charles Dudley's Warner's novel in 1875), noting its "absurdity and grotesqueness" (p. 83). Though Beard doesn't mention it, one may also note that the central themes of both play and novel – American capitalism and its psychological correlatives – are very close to being those of Beard himself. Finally, this raises the question of where, if anywhere, the category of "nervousness" fits into *Connecticut Yankee*. Though Twain wrote about "nervous" symptoms on at least one other occasion – in "Punch, Brothers, Punch!" (see Messent 2001) – he makes no obvious mention of them in the novel. Yet, taking Beard's analysis at its word, it is precisely in a "civilized" individual like Hank that one would most expect to find them. And though this may have something to do with Hank's ambiguous class position – neither thoroughly bourgeois nor proletarian, he fits uneasily into Beard's schema, in which only the middle and upper classes are truly "nervous" (see Beard 1881: 26) – there is another sense in which Hank *does* suffer from some "civilized" affliction. Beard's analysis, however, does not allow us to identify it. What, then, could this affliction be?

"The Joys of Cruelty": Twain with Nietzsche

As is well known, one of Twain's major sources for *Connecticut Yankee* was William Lecky's *History of European Morals* (1869). Here, Lecky opposes himself to utilitarianism – one of the major philosophical currents of its day – and its efforts to explain the origin of moral sentiments. To utilitarians, morality is best explained on practical grounds, our moral values simply reflecting those practices that have proved "useful" over time. Lecky's response to this was twofold: first, to assemble an exhaustive list of historical examples showing how, on the contrary, moral norms have often been opposed to self-interest; and second, to defend a view of morality as innate, rather than acquired.

Twain's reaction to this was itself distinctly "moral." Outraged by the evidence Lecky had assembled – which seemed to him conclusive proof of Europe's depravity throughout much, if not all, of its history – Twain set about mining the book for several key scenes in *Connecticut Yankee*. But what is of more immediate interest here is that Nietzsche, in his own essay *On the Genealogy of Morality* (published just two years before Twain's novel) should have chosen a starting point similar to Lecky's. Beginning with an attack on those "English psychologists" Lecky himself opposes, Nietzsche embarks on what is ultimately a far more radical critique; encompassing not only contemporary moral theory but also "civilized" morality itself (Nietzsche 1998: 11). Like Beard, Nietzsche sees signs of exhaustion everywhere in contemporary culture. Unlike Beard, however, he is profoundly hostile to "modern civilization," and has no faith whatsoever in its attempts to cure itself.[5] Nietzsche's attitude can be gleaned from a passage in the *Genealogy* that reads like nothing so much as an attack on *Connecticut Yankee*'s Hank: "*Hubris* today characterizes our whole attitude towards nature, our rape of nature with the help of machines and completely unscrupulous inventiveness of technicians and engineers" (p. 86). Taking Nietzsche's critique as a whole, is Hank a fitting target for such ire?

The answer, in short, is yes and no. On the one hand, Hank's identification with technocratic science makes him exemplary of trends Nietzsche always affected to detest.[6] Moreover, as we shall see, Hank's critique of Arthurian morality is made from the perspective of contemporary moral tastes that *Genealogy* especially attacks. On the other hand, however, aspects of Hank's behavior align him with figures Nietzsche admires. And some of Hank's (and Twain's) ideas on punishment have parallels with Nietzsche's own.

We can start to see this by examining the historic basis of Nietzsche's argument. Like *Connecticut Yankee*, *Genealogy* is predicated on a series of contrasts between the past and the present. However, Nietzsche's view of the past is more extensive, encompassing not only the early Judeo-Christian period, but also, crucially, pre-Christian antiquity. Just as crucially, Nietzsche inverts Twain's sympathies, finding the pre-Christian past far more attractive than the present. What Nietzsche really likes about this past is the ascendancy of *noble morality*, which he locates among the aristocracy of ancient Greece. This emerges "organically," as it were, from this class's experience of mastery, and simply renders their experience self-conscious: it "acts and grows spontaneously, seeking out its opposite only so that it can say 'yes' to itself even more thankfully and exultantly" (1998: 22). When it *does* seek out this opposite, however, the result is profoundly generative, creating what Nietzsche calls the "pathos of nobility and distance": "[a] continuing and predominant feeling of complete and fundamental superiority of a higher ruling kind in relation to a lower kind, to those 'below' – that is the origin of the antithesis 'good' and 'bad'" (p. 13). Psychologically speaking, then, this "pathos" merely intensifies the pleasurable feelings that accrue to the nobility as such. Axiologically speaking, however, Nietzsche believes that this accounts for nothing less than the emergence of the moral value "bad." It is in relation to this also that Nietzsche claims the nobles have "left the concept of 'barbarian' [*Barbar*] in their traces wherever they went," in order to designate those they subjugate (p. 25). This concept – whose bearers Beard had contrasted with "civilized man" – is here identified with conquest, and is a consequence *of* it.

It is here that we may situate Hank's impressions of the nobles he encounters in Arthurian England. Distinguished as these are by "high animal spirits, innocent indecencies of language, and happy-hearted indifference to [as we can now say, *modern*] morals" (Twain 1889: 108), Twain's Arthurian aristocracy have much in common with Nietzsche's self-congratulatory Greeks. To be sure, Arthur and his knights are somewhat doltish, but Nietzsche is attuned to this as well, noting "a certain lack of cleverness . . . by which noble souls down the ages have recognized one another" (1998: 23). The comparison may also be extended to the knights' feelings of superiority over the Arthurian populace, a hereditary version of Nietzsche's "pathos of nobility and distance." Thus, when traveling incognito, Arthur is incredulous at Hank's insistence that he should affect "brotherhood" with commoners: "Brother!" the King exclaims, " – to dirt like that?" (Twain 1889: 364).

But herein lies a complication. As we have seen, Hank sees Arthurians as "savages," not sparing the knights, whom he compares to "Comanches." This suggests that he, no less than Arthur, feels a "fundamental superiority" over his counterparts. In the very place, in fact, where he notes Arthurian nobles' "indifference to morals," he calls them "barbaric" – thus using a cognate of the term Nietzsche identifies with noble conquest (Twain 1889: 108). In this way, Hank enjoys his own version of "the pathos of nobility and distance," homologous with that of the Arthurian knights:

> Well, I liked the king, and *as* king I respected him – respected the office; at least respected it as much as I was capable of respecting any unearned supremacy; but as *men* I looked down upon him and his nobles – privately. And he and they liked me, and respected my office; but as an animal, without birth or sham title, they looked down on me – and were not particularly private about it either. (p. 103)

The pathos of historical difference and that of hereditary distance thus mirror one another, linking Hank and the knights in a contract of mutual contempt.

What is going on here, of course, is a conflict of "values" that is as much political and cultural as moral. This, of course, would be no surprise to Nietzsche, whose analysis of noble values is designed to show precisely how morality and politics are interlinked. But as *Genealogy* goes on to argue, noble values have themselves been displaced by "slave morality," the Judeo-Christian usurper that has, over the course of almost two millennia, all but dissipated the strength and vitality of ancient culture. In the form of Christianity, especially, this has been accomplished quite deliberately. For this is a religion that celebrates weakness rather than strength, and that says "no" rather than "yes" to life (see e.g. Nietzsche 1998: 21). As a testament to this, Nietzsche cites the "over-valuation of pity" among contemporary philosophers, and the "disgraceful modern softness of feeling" of contemporary culture in general (p. 7). This brings us on to Twain's own moral sensibility, which this analysis surely helps to specify. Here is Hank's reaction to a passing group of slaves: "something in their hearts was written in the dust upon their faces, plain to see, and lord how plain to read! for it was the track of tears . . . It hurt me to the heart to read that writing" (Twain 1889: 262). And later, when these slaves are encountered again: "The king was not interested, and wanted to move along, but I was absorbed, and full of pity" (p. 447). For Nietzsche, one may say, there can be nothing fortuitous about the access of such feelings in the company of slaves. What Hank expresses is, in effect, his *own* adherence to "slave morality."

It is, however, the tour of Morgan le Fay's dungeon that provokes Hank's most significant "pitiful" reaction, for it is here that he invokes his "conscience":

> I had had enough of this grisly place by this time, and wanted to leave, but I couldn't, because I had something on my mind that my conscience kept prodding me about, and wouldn't let me forget. If I had the remaking of man, he wouldn't have any conscience. It is one of the most disagreeable things connected with a person; and although it certainly does a great deal of good, it cannot be said to pay, in the long run; it would be much better to have less good and more comfort. (Twain 1889: 219)

Well, indeed. After all, Twain had said as much before; most notably in "The Facts Concerning the Recent Carnival of Crime in Connecticut" (1876), where a man performs a string of murders in "unalloyed bliss," having first killed his own conscience (Twain 1992a: 660). For Nietzsche, too, "conscience" is an essentially repressive agency, whose office is to curb the pleasure one would otherwise, quite "naturally," derive from violence. In *Genealogy*, Nietzsche explains the origins of this conscience in prehistoric modes of punishment, born of the discovery "that pain [is] the most natural aid to mnemonics" (1998: 41). Memory, on this account, proceeds from pain, and is, as such, coeval with "conscience" itself. "Bad conscience," it follows, is but an extended form of memory and an "internalization" of primordial pain (pp. 61 and *passim*). But let it not be thought that punishment arose in order to provoke "bad conscience" in its victims. Rather, Nietzsche argues, punishment arose from the *pleasure* its perpetrators must have taken in inflicting it, lacking, as they must have, any "conscience" of their own (pp. 43–6).

In *Connecticut Yankee*, this conclusion is echoed in the person of Morgan le Fay. As Hank's visit to her dungeon shows, Morgan takes the most naïve delight in what Nietzsche calls "the joys of cruelty" (Nietzsche 1998: 48), her eyes "light[ing] with pleasure" when she hears a prisoner being tortured (Twain 1889: 207). As Hank later discovers, some of these prisoners are kept "for no distinct offense at all, but only to gratify somebody's spite," thus emphasizing the hedonic basis for their capture (p. 223). Hank's wonderment at Morgan's untroubled conscience, then – expressed by his "surprise" at her unblemished beauty (p. 195) – reflects his failure to understand that, as Nietzsche could have told him, there is no reason she should have one. And yet Hank's discomfort with his *own* conscience (experienced, we recall, in Morgan's very dungeon) is a sign that he is not perhaps immune to "the joys of cruelty" himself. It is after all he who, when disgusted by the music at Morgan's banquet, gives her "permission to hang the whole band" (p. 206).

This apparently throwaway remark, though one of the novel's better jokes, cannot be written off as "just" a joke. For, as many readers feel, it exposes something fundamental about Hank and his Arthurian career. This remark foreshadows other acts of violence, culminating in the destruction of Arthurian knighthood at the novel's end. In doing so, it opens directly onto perhaps the most important thing that Twain and Nietzsche share: their profound appreciation of the violence that lies hidden under "civilized" morality and customs, even – and perhaps, especially – where "barbarous" violence is condemned. For Nietzsche, the lesson of history is not that "slave morality" has vanquished noble cruelty, but that cruelty continues to live on under the auspices *of* slave morality. Similarly, in *Connecticut Yankee*, nineteenth-century civilization does not so much efface sixth-century violence as provide it with a new means of expression. Hank's execution of the band thus offers a privileged glimpse of "how much blood and horror lies at the basis of all 'good things'!" (Nietzsche 1998: 42).

In this respect, a "Nietzschean" reading of Twain's novel reaches much the same conclusion as that arrived at via Beard: though *Connecticut Yankee* starts as an attempt to juxtapose the past and present, it ends up struggling to tell them apart. But whereas in Hank's "Beardian" view this confusion stems from the proximity of others ("Indians," the English), a second look at Hank, via Nietzsche, locates its sources in the self, and the sudden bursts of cruelty that punctuate "civilized" or "slave" morality. And so it is to Nietzsche, finally, that we should look to solve the question left hanging earlier, concerning Hank's "affliction." For Nietzsche, no less than for Beard, there is indeed something profoundly wrong with "civilized" humanity: quite simply, "man's sickness of *man*, of *himself*" (Nietzsche 1998: 62). Thus, Nietzsche tells his readers: "we have . . . lost our love for him, our respect for him, our hope in him and even our will to be man" (p. 27). If this is so, it may explain why Hank declares, "there are times when one would like to hang the whole human race" (Twain 1889: 395). For Morgan le Fay's band, we may now substitute the species.

"The Economics of our Happiness": Twain with Freud

In many respects, *Civilization and its Discontents* may be seen as a synthesis of Beard's and Nietzsche's analyses. It is perhaps the *ne plus ultra* of the tradition they represent. Like Beard, Freud sees a direct link between "civilization" and a pervasive malaise he identifies among his contemporaries. Like Nietzsche, he argues that this malaise is rooted in primal violence and the "bad conscience" it engenders (see especially Freud 1986: 315–26). Like both his predecessors, Freud develops this analysis by "thinking with history," firing off a host of historical examples to back up specific points. And, like them, he emphasizes the *historicity* of humankind – evolving a famous (if, in his view, ultimately unsustainable) analogy between the mind and ancient, archaeologically rich cities such as Rome (Freud 1986: 256–9).

Neither Beard nor Nietzsche is mentioned directly in Freud's essay, although Twain, in many ways a more surprising influence, is. Twain is recalled giving a public reading of his story "The First Melon I ever Stole," which Freud finds exemplary of the "enhancing of morality as a consequence of ill-luck" (1986: 318 n. 2). Notwithstanding this shared insight, however, we must look beyond this citation to find a still deeper affinity between *Civilization and its Discontents* and *Connecticut Yankee*: their interest in – and profound ambivalence toward – technology.[7]

This is not, of course, an entirely new subject. As we have seen, both Beard and Nietzsche count new technologies among the salient features of contemporary culture. Beard sees steam power and telegraphy as primary causes of "nervousness." Nietzsche rails at the hubris of "technicians and engineers." This identification of technology with "civilization" was lent powerful impetus throughout this period by Western imperialism, which we have already noted as a context for Hank's sojourn in England (and see Adas 1989). Given this, it comes as no surprise to find that Hank (who is, of course, a type of engineer himself) holds technology in especially high esteem. Here is his reaction when he finds a telephone office he has commissioned located in what had once been a hermit's den: "what a fantastic conjunction of opposites and irreconcilables – the home of a bogus miracle become the home of a real one, the den of a medieval hermit turned into a telephone office!" (Twain 1889: 303). In such technologies, the supposed antithesis between ancient and modern upon which Hank's world-view depends finds its most complete expression and apparent confirmation.

This is all very well, but for Freud, the pertinent question to ask of such technologies is not whether they perform their promised "miracles" (for, in their own terms, they surely do), but whether, in so doing, they make us *happy*. And here, Freud argues, the results are profoundly paradoxical.[8] On one hand, the telephone and telegraph ensure that he can "hear the voice of a child of mine who is living hundreds of miles away", or "learn in the shortest possible time after a friend has reached his destination that he has come through the long and difficult voyage unharmed" (Freud 1986: 276). On the other hand, however,

If there had been no railway to conquer distances, my child would never have left his native town and I should need no telephone to hear his voice; if travelling across the ocean by ship had not been introduced, my friend would not have embarked on his sea-voyage and I should not need a cable to relieve my anxiety about him. (pp. 276–7)

Though the benefits of telephony and other such technologies are real, therefore, the very need for them would be unthinkable had not *other* technologies created it. Thus, in Freud's wonderful simile, "the enjoyment" derived from such devices is comparable to that "obtained by putting a bare leg from under the bedclothes on a cold winter night and drawing it in again" (1986: 276). Taken as a whole, then, technology represents a decidedly mixed blessing, merely providing recompense for losses it itself has caused.

This is remarkable enough, but what one must also note here is the *retrospective* structure of Freud's thinking. Freud looks "back in time," both biographically (before his child had left) and, so to speak, "historically" (before the ship's or railway's introduction), thus linking technology to commemoration and historic reconstruction. (Here, one may again recall Beard's civilized man, "ever thinking of the past.") This, indeed, is not fortuitous; for, as Freud later suggests, certain technologies are "at bottom materializations of the power [man] possesses of recollection, [of] memory" (Freud 1986: 279). As examples of this, Freud adduces photography and the gramophone. Writing, too, he adds, "was in its origin the voice of an absent person" (p. 279).

These reflections lead us back to *Connecticut Yankee*, where – as we have seen – the telephone is prominent among Hank's innovations. But what has not yet been considered is the technology's *emotional* significance, arising from its association with a particular kind of person. This is the "Hello Girl" or telephone operator, who, in Hank's late nineteenth century, was (as the name implies) characteristically female, young, and single. Hank's attraction to such persons may be gauged from the strange mix of yearning and embarrassment with which he explains them to Sandy, the woman who will later be his wife (Twain 1889: 177–8; and see Lerer 2003: 477–9). Later still, Sandy names the couple's child "Hello Central," having, as Hank explains, "heard that imploring cry come from my lips in my sleep" and "conceiving it to be the name of some lost darling" (Twain 1889: 524). And while Sandy is wrong about this in actual fact (Hank has been dreaming of his nineteenth-century "past" more generally), there is a wider sense in which she is surely right. For what this strange career of the two words, "Hello Central," throughout the novel shows is that the past may be conflated with an absent person (especially a loved one), and that another (i.e. a child) may be symbolically appointed to their place.

It is around the telephone, then, that Twain's and Freud's ideas about technology converge. For both, the device is linked to recollection, and the attempt to compensate for remembered loss. These dispositions are, of course, related, as Freud discovers when his child's telephonic voice reminds him of the very loss for which it compensates. And so for Hank too, these dispositions coalesce around the telephonic couplet "Hello Central," which comes to signify not only a specific person (and type of person), but also the entire past from which that person springs, *and* a child who (via Sandy's appropriation of the phrase) perpetuates this past within the present.

Finally, we might consider how telephony relates to the generic status of technology in Twain's novel. For Freud, as we have seen, technology can never add to "the economics of our happiness," but only reimburse what it subtracts (Freud 1986: 276). Towards the end of *Connecticut Yankee*, trapped in a cave and separated from his wife and child, Hank offers what amounts to a positive spin on this idea:

> It was always my habit to write to Sandy every day . . . [i]t put in the time, you see, and was almost like talking; it was almost as if I was saying, "Sandy, if you and Hello-Central were here in the cave, instead of only your photographs, what good times we could have!" And then, you know, I could imagine the baby goo-gooing something out in reply . . . I could sit there in the cave with my pen, and keep it up, that way, by the hour with them. Why, it was almost like having us all together again. (Twain 1889: 549–50)

As Freud says, writing has its origin in "the voice of an absent person," though here it is Hank's own voice ("almost like talking") that his writing conjures up. This voice provokes another, albeit imaginary, in response, thus turning writing itself into a form of surrogate telephony. (This, of course, is only fitting, given that the voice is that of Hello-Central — *herself* a telephonic surrogate.) The presence of photography in this scene only strengthens the impression that, with all these technologies, Hank is guided by the same basic desire: namely, that of bringing "us all together again," or, in other words, *making things as they were*. And now we see why technology is so significant for Hank from a "Freudian" perspective, for this desire is none other than that which defines his entire career in Arthurian England. By trying to reproduce his nineteenth-century past in every detail — from technology and taxation to religion and newspapers — Hank is simply recapitulating what we might call the "telephonic" logic of commemorative compensation on the grandest possible scale.

Conclusion: The "Battle of the Sand Belt"

Why, then, does this project fail? At the end of *Connecticut Yankee*, Hank destroys the "civilization" he has so patiently built up, at the same time killing thousands upon thousands of Arthurian knights, and sowing the seeds of his own ultimate demise. Notwithstanding the obvious fact that Twain "needed" to provide some such conclusion in order to bring his novel into alignment with the received facts of history, one is tempted by the prospect of a more "philosophical" answer to this question. Very briefly, we may consider three alternatives, derived from Beard, Nietzsche, and Freud respectively.

We can begin with Freud, thus inverting our itinerary to date, for it is he who suggests the answer closest to the commonsensical one just offered. "If we want to represent historical sequence in spatial terms," Freud argues, "we can only do it by juxtaposition in space: the same space cannot have two different contents" (Freud 1986: 258). This is why Freud's own analogy between the mind and an ancient city, as previously mentioned, is said to be unworkable: "only in the mind" can two such contents coexist (p. 259.) Translating this formulation back into the terms of *Connecticut Yankee*, one might say that Twain's own "juxtaposition" of historic periods can only ever be a virtual, or mental one. Logically, physically – and, indeed, historically – Hank's project is untenable.

The answer suggested by Nietzsche, by contrast, is political. In Nietzsche's view, the sort of republican and democratic values espoused by Hank are, at bottom, expressions of the same slave morality that is leading contemporary "man" to ruin. Thus, he warns, "the democratic bias within the modern world" can wreak "havoc . . . once it is unbridled to the point of hatred" (Nietzsche 1998: 14). This certainly accords with the ferocious violence Hank unleashes in the "Battle of the Sand Bank", directed as this is at noble (therefore "anti-democratic") adversaries (Twain 1889: 549–65). The sting in the tail, however (as Nietzsche would surely have anticipated) is that Hank himself becomes a victim of this violence, his "democratic bias" leading ultimately to his own destruction.

And so we come back, finally, to Beard. In Beard's view, "American civilization" is all but destined to spread across the globe (Beard 1881: 14). However, this confidence is tempered by a sober recognition of just how easily civilization's path may be reversed: "All our civilization hangs by a thread; the activity and force of the very few makes us what we are as a nation; and if, through degeneracy, the descendants of these few revert to the condition of their not very remote ancestors, all our haughty civilization would be wiped away" (p. 96).

If it is not Hank's "degenerate" ancestors, but Hank himself, who causes civilization to be "wiped away" in Twain's novel, this only heightens the foreboding Beard expresses. For whatever the ultimate reason for the failure of Hank's project may be, it is clear that Twain's exploration of the "three-fold burden" carried by his narrator ends up finding little lasting satisfaction, and much to be afraid of, in the past, the present, and the future.

NOTES

1 This is not to say that Twain's representation of Arthurian England is any way "accurate." Clearly, it is governed rather by the supervening objective of generating salutary comparisons between the two periods concerned.

2 The first study to link Beard with *Connecticut Yankee*, to my knowledge, is Takaki (1979). There is now a large secondary literature on Beard: see e.g. Armstrong (1999).

3 Hank's plans include the introduction of "unlimited suffrage"; to be "given to men and women alike – at any rate, to all men, wise or unwise, and to all mothers who at middle age should be found to know nearly as much as their sons at twenty-one" (Twain 1889: 514). The limitations smuggled into this definition of "unlimited suffrage" seem indicative of Hank's indifference, at best, to the raft of contemporary

developments (not least, the ongoing campaign for truly unlimited female suffrage) comprehended under Beard's heading.

4   "To see how an Englishman can drink," Beard promises, "is alone worthy the ocean voyage" (Beard 1881: 34). This remark finds echo in *Connecticut Yankee*: see Hank's reaction to the amount of alcohol consumed at Arthurian banquets (Twain 1889: 39, 204).

5   For example, Nietzsche ridicules the "bedrest" cure of Silas Weir Mitchell, an American physician whose analysis is comparable to Beard's own (Nietzsche 1998: 17).

6   This is a theme in Nietzsche's writing from *The Birth of Tragedy* (1871) onwards.

7   This and other affinities are also noted by Girgus (1978). The seminal discussion of technology in *Connecticut Yankee* is Marx (1964).

8   The following account is indebted to Ronell (1989: 84–94). See also Armstrong (1999: 77–8).

References and Further Reading

Aaron, Daniel (1973). *The Unwritten War: American Writers and the Civil War.* New York: Oxford University Press.

Adas, Michael (1989). *Machines as the Measure of Man: Science, Technology, and Ideologies of Western Dominance.* Ithaca, NY: Cornell University Press.

Armstrong, Tim (1999). *Modernism, Technology and the Body: A Cultural Study.* Cambridge, UK: Cambridge University Press.

Beard, George Miller (1881). *American Nervousness: Its Causes and Consequences.* New York: G. P. Putnam's Sons.

Freud, Sigmund (1986). *Civilization and its Discontents* (first publ. 1930). In *Civilization, Society and Religion*, Penguin Freud Library, vol. 12, trans. and ed. James Strachey and Albert Dickson. Harmondsworth: Penguin.

Girgus, Sam B. (1978). "Conscience in Connecticut: *Civilization and its Discontents* in Twain's Camelot." *New England Quarterly* 51, 547–60.

Kaplan, Amy (2002). *The Anarchy of Empire in the Making of US Culture.* Cambridge, Mass.: Harvard University Press.

Leask, Nigel (2002). *Curiosity and the Aesthetics of Travel Writing, 1770–1840.* Oxford: Oxford University Press.

Lecky, William E. H. (1911). *History of European Morals: From Augustus to Charlemagne.* London: Watts. (First publ. 1869.)

Lerer, Seth (2003). "Hello, Dude: Philology, Performance, and Technology in Mark Twain's *Connecticut Yankee.*" *American Literary History* 15, 471–503.

Marx, Leo (1964). *The Machine in the Garden: Technology and the Pastoral Ideal in America.* New York: Oxford University Press.

Messent, Peter (1997). *Mark Twain.* Basingstoke: Macmillan.

Messent, Peter (2001). *The Short Works of Mark Twain: A Critical Study.* Philadelphia: University of Pennsylvania Press.

Nietzsche, Friedrich (1998). *On the Genealogy of Morality*, trans. Carol Diethe, ed. Keith Ansell-Pearson. Cambridge: Cambridge University Press. (First publ. 1887.)

Ronell, Avital (1989). *The Telephone Book: Technology, Schizophrenia, Electric Speech.* Lincoln: University of Nebraska Press.

Rowe, John Carlos (2000). *Literary Culture and US Imperialism: From the Revolution to World War II.* New York: Oxford University Press.

Salomon, Roger Blaine (1961). *Twain and the Image of History.* New Haven: Yale University Press.

Schorske, Carl (1998). *Thinking with History: Explorations in the Passage to Modernism.* Princeton: Princeton University Press.

Smith, Henry Nash (1958). "Mark Twain's Images of Hannibal: From St. Petersburg to Eseldorf." *Texas Studies in English* 37, 3–23.

Smith, Henry Nash (1964). *Mark Twain's Fable of Progress: Political and Economic Ideas in* A Connecticut Yankee. New Brunswick, NJ: Rutgers University Press.

Sollors, Werner (1995). "Ethnicity." In Frank Lentricchia and Thomas McLaughlin, eds., *Critical Terms for Literary Study.* Chicago: University of Chicago Press.

Takaki, Ronald (1979). *Iron Cages: Race and Culture in 19th-Century America.* New York: Oxford University Press.

28

Mark Twain's Dialects

David Lionel Smith

Mark Twain's masterpiece, *Adventures of Huckleberry Finn*, begins with an "Explanatory" regarding the language used in the book:

> In this book a number of dialects are used, to wit: the Missouri negro dialect; the extremest form of the backwoods South-Western dialect; the ordinary "Pike County" dialect; and four modified varieties of this last. The shadings have not been done in a hap-hazard fashion, or by guess-work; but pains-takingly, and with the trustworthy guidance and support of personal familiarity with those several forms of speech.
>
> I make this explanation for the reason that without it many readers would suppose that all these characters were trying to talk alike and not succeeding. (Twain 1885: 7)

The word "dialect," derived from a Greek word for conversation, refers to a regional variant of a language, having distinctive elements of vocabulary, grammar, and pronunciation that set it apart from other dialects and from the standard form of the language. On its most immediate level, this "Explanatory" functions as a promise of authenticity. Of course, very few readers, even a century ago, would know a "Missouri negro dialect" from any other negro dialect, and even in 1885, "South-Western" indicated a far different region from what it had meant in the 1840s. In any case, "South-Western" is a very large a category and probably too inclusive, especially compared with "Pike County," which Twain describes as having four variants. In practical terms, this "Explanatory" seems to function primarily as a declaration of the author's authority.

Let us assume for now that these dialects actually existed. Readers who knew them would not need this explanation; and all other readers could only take the author at his word. Twain purports to offer this gloss for the sake of the reader who might "suppose that all these characters were trying to talk alike and not succeeding." There are undoubtedly readers who are obtuse to this degree, but Mark Twain could hardly have been so naïve as to think that simple explanation could rescue such folk from error. Furthermore, he surely knew that no amount of explanation could compensate for the lack of first-hand knowledge regarding a particular dialect. His "Explanatory" is really not intended to be helpful to readers. Rather, he uses it to assert his own skill, knowledge, and assiduity.

Dialect occupies a peculiar position in American literary culture, and Mark Twain's relationship to dialect is especially intriguing, given this larger context. Appropriately, we understand dialect as a conversational mode of language. Literacy and hence respectability presuppose mastery of the standard language. Dialect may enter literary works for purposes of representational accuracy, but the expectation remains that a respectable author will have a mastery of the mainstream language. In the American literary context, dialect is always highly charged. Questions of social status and respectability are inherently connected with literary uses of dialect. Given the democratic traditions of the United States and the deep ideological commitment of Americans to the possibility of mobility between classes, the presentation of dialect can be emotionally and politically fraught. Typically in nineteenth-century American fiction, protagonists have mastery of Standard English, but they also are either conversant in some dialect or socially at ease with dialect speakers. As a convention of fictional style, the omniscient narrative is written in Standard English. Dialect speakers may be subsumed within the narrative. This allows for an unstated distinction to be made between the author, who is shown to be literate and thus respectable, and the characters, who may or may not be.

Mark Twain understood this perfectly well – he was himself, after all, a classic example of nineteenth-century American social climbing – but in *Adventures of Huckleberry Finn* he chose to write entirely in the first-person voice of Huck Finn. This is what actually necessitates his "Explanatory": it is not that he wants to spare his readers confusion, but rather that he wants to call attention to his difference from his protagonist. His "Explanatory" is the functional equivalent of a device commonly used on posters advertising minstrel shows. The performers would appear in formal attire, and opposite them their burnt cork alter egos would appear in their buffoonish Negro stereotypicality. The message, clearly, is that the performers are white gentlemen who ought not in any way to be conflated with their social inferiors, whom they portray onstage. A fine example of such a poster appears on the cover of Robert C. Toll's classic book, *Blacking Up*. Like these performers, Twain is anxious to ensure that the audience does not equate him with the characters he depicts.

Class status is not the only issue embedded within dialect. Dialect is a relational concept, and thus can easily be used to represent various kinds of binaries. In most periods, and especially in late nineteenth-century America, dialect is a nostalgic trope. That is, given the reality of American social mobility, whenever a specific dialect appears in a literary work, it is always already endangered. Dialect, after all, is by definition a regional, "in-group," conversational language. Its appearance in a literary work means either that at least one member of the group has become literate or that a literate outsider has entered the group and become conversant in its dialect. In either case, the geographical or social isolation that has allowed the dialect to be developed and sustained has been breached. The fact of literary publication is inherently an indicator of that rift.

Nostalgia is a sentimental trope, generally perceived as the antithesis of irony. Nonetheless, the case of dialect reveals an irony at the heart of nostalgia. Dialect writing appeals to readers or auditors who stand outside the dialect-speaking social group, and can prompt quite different, but paired, reactions. Either dialect reminds the listener, a former insider, of past associations, now disrupted by time or social distance; or dialect strikes the more privileged listener as an amusingly and reassuringly quaint manifestation of some other group's apparent difference from, and inferior status to, her or his own group. The irony in both cases is that the literary use of dialect necessarily bridges the social distance between the observers and the observed that dialect is assumed to represent. In other words, by understanding a dialect, the observer manifests his actual closeness to the group he observes, even though he may feel subjectively a smug reassurance of his own presumed superiority in the social pecking order.

Pudd'nhead Wilson represents a classic illustration of how painful and comic such irony can be. In the concluding chapter, after the trial has untangled Roxy's plot and the crimes of her son (the fraudulent Tom), the author describes the sad plight of the rightful heir, who has been raised as a slave:

> The real heir suddenly found himself rich and free, but in a most embarrassing situation. He could neither read nor write, and his speech was the basest dialect of the negro quarter. His gait, his attitudes, his gestures, his bearing, his laugh – all were vulgar and uncouth; his manners were the manners of a slave. Money and fine clothes could not mend these defects or cover them up; they only made them the more glaring and the more pathetic. The poor fellow could not endure the terrors of the white man's parlor, and felt at home and at peace nowhere but in the kitchen. The family pew was a misery to him, yet he could nevermore enter into the solacing refuge of the "nigger gallery" – that was closed to him for good and all. (Twain 1894: 301–2)

In the end, Chambers's dialect becomes the emblem of his total displacement and alienation within the social order, despite his legal restoration. Even more pungently ironic is the fate of the "real" Chambers, who has lived and transgressed in the guise of Tom. He is identified as a slave and treated not as a criminal but rather as a piece of property. In Mark Twain's astringent words: "As soon as the Governor understood the case, he pardoned Tom at once, and the creditors sold him down the river" (Twain 1894: 303). The bitterness of this irony is undoubtedly heightened by the fact that Samuel Clemens was himself struggling to raise money and to avoid the equivalent of Tom's fate at the hands of his own creditors, even as he wrote these words. Clearly, the charm of dialect and its social world dissipates when social mobility goes awry.

Unfortunately, social mobility too often goes awry. Perhaps this is why the fascination with dialect was so pervasive around the turn of the century. During this period, the forces of modernity exerted disruptive pressures on traditional ways of life. Agricultural workers sought industrial jobs, and young people raised on farms fled toward the siren songs of the cities. Excitement and anxiety romped hand in hand. Half a century earlier, Karl Marx had written the quintessential description of how

the triumphant voracity of an emerging capitalist economy shatters familiar patterns
of social life:

> The bourgeoisie cannot exist without constantly revolutionizing the instruments of pro-
> duction, and thereby the relations of production, and with them the whole relations of
> society. Conservation of the old modes of production in unaltered form, was, on the con-
> trary, the first condition of existence for all earlier industrial classes. Constant revolu-
> tionizing of production, uninterrupted disturbance of all social conditions, everlasting
> uncertainty and agitation distinguish the bourgeois epoch from all earlier ones. All fixed,
> fast-frozen relations, with their train of ancient and venerable prejudices and opinions,
> are swept away, all new-formed ones become antiquated before they can ossify. All that
> is solid melts into air, all that is holy is profaned, and man is at the last compelled to
> face with sober senses, his real conditions of life, and his relations with his kind. (Marx
> and Engels 1978: 476)

Though we may think of Marx and Mark Twain as representing different eras, the
two were contemporaries, born only 17 years apart. Samuel Clemens could easily have
been Karl Marx's younger brother. The explosive emergence of new technologies, the
rampant growth of capitalist enterprises, and the upheavals of social life that Marx
describes are also elements of Mark Twain's work. The excitement and disruption
created by modernity go hand in hand with the anxiety and nostalgia caused by the
demise of agrarian traditions. This double-edged energy pulses through *A Connecticut
Yankee in King Arthur's Court*, *Pudd'nhead Wilson*, and even parts of *Huckleberry Finn*.
To believe in the ultimate triumph of "sober senses" may require a revolutionary opti-
mism, but Mark Twain clearly relished the comic phantasmagoria of social orders
being constantly disrupted.

Dialect, obviously, is a convenient emblem of the past, and of ways of life that have
not yet been swept away by the homogenizing forces of modernity. The popularity of
dialect stories by George Washington Cable, Joel Chandler Harris, Thomas Nelson
Page, and others derived from this nostalgic sentimentality – the yearning for the safe
domesticity of "the good old days." Mark Twain wrote fondly of Cable and Harris (see
Twain 1883: ch. 47); and, having his own sentimental streak, he could write adeptly
in this nostalgic mode when he felt so inclined. "A True Story" is a fine example of
his skill at blending sentimentality and dialect. Primarily, however, he was an ironist.
The tension between these divergent aspects of his sensibility can be seen in all three
of the novels mentioned above.

In *Connecticut Yankee*, Mark Twain deploys a kind of dialect that we do not necessarily regard as dialect, because of its remote historical setting: the language of
Arthurian England. Strictly speaking, however, the extinct local Missouri dialects of
40 years past in *Huckleberry Finn* and the dialects of Arthurian England pose the same
kinds of issues for a historical linguist, except that no native speakers of the latter –
not even their children or grandchildren – remain alive. In both novels, the author
sets his narrative in a time and place where English is spoken in forms distinctly
different from contemporary Standard English. Interestingly, Twain does not treat

Arthurian English nostalgically. That dialect has no affective emotional charge for Mark Twain's audience, unlike the forms of speech associated with the world of the American frontier and, especially, the world of slavery just before the Civil War: worlds that stirred the emotions of Twain's readers then, and do so even now.

Nonetheless, dialect is used in *Connecticut Yankee*. We first see it in the pompous speech of the knights. When Hank awakens in the sixth century, he finds himself accosted by a knight in full armor:

> "Fair sir, will ye just?" said this fellow.
>   "Will I which?"
>   "Will ye try a passage of arms for land or lady or for –"
>   "What are you giving me?" I said. "Get along back to your circus, or I'll report you."
> (Twain 1889: 21–2)

This language is clearly English, but it is English of a strange sort that Hank understands only partially. Hank soon decides that its speakers are lunatics. This point is explicitly reinforced at the beginning of chapter 2:

> The moment I got a chance I slipped aside privately and touched an ancient common looking man on the shoulder and said, in an insinuating, confidential way –
>   "Friend, do me a kindness. Do you belong to the asylum, or are you just here on a visit or something like that?"
>   He looked me over stupidly, and said –
>   "Marry, fair sir, me seemeth – "
>   "That will do," I said; "I reckon you are a patient." (Twain 1889: 33)

It is striking that the use of dialect in this novel has no sentimentality or even sympathy associated with it. Indeed, this dialect is for Hank an emblem of bigotry and backwardness – what Marx calls a "train of ancient and venerable prejudices and opinions." Hank's Yankee sensibilities are outraged by the values, beliefs, and norms of this sixth-century world, and he immediately declares war on it. In fact, he assaults the culture of Arthurian England with a remorseless efficiency that rivals the impersonal forces of capitalism. Mark Twain's usual ambivalence is strangely muted, at least in the early stages of this novel, as Hank Morgan's willful, egocentric impositions of modernity overwhelm every countervailing tendency. The novel is anti-nostalgic with a vengeance.

The triumph of modernity in this novel is, however, finally presented ironically, as each manifestation of Hank's victory vanishes into ultimate defeat. At the end of the book, the armies of backwardness mount a massive insurrection against "The Boss." Naturally, tens of thousands of armored knights are no match for 54 men wielding modern Yankee technology. When 30,000 knights charge The Boss and his men, they ride directly into a booby trap and are instantly obliterated. As Hank describes it: "Why, the whole front of that host shot into the sky with a thunder-crash, and became a whirling tempest of rags and fragments; and along the ground lay a thick wall of smoke that hid what was left of the multitude from our sight." Then, The Boss follows with his *coup de grâce*: "I touched a button, and shook the bones of England loose from her spine! In that explosion all our noble civilization-factories went up in the air and disappeared from the earth" (Twain 1889: 554). As Marx says, "all that is solid melts into air."

A few pages later, The Boss electrocutes some of the remaining knights. He muses: "One terrible thing about this thing was the absence of human voices; there were no cheers, no war cries . . . [T]hey struck the fatal line and went down without testifying." These hapless men do not utter dialect; they do not utter any language at all. Moments later, Hank unleashes the full power of his electrical assault, and the result is different. "*There* was a groan you could *hear!* It voiced the death-pang of eleven thousand men. It swelled out on the night with awful pathos" (Twain 1889: 564). Hank is not gratified until he hears human sound from his victims, yet his intention is to obliterate their voices and all of the culture that their voices bespeak. The irony of this moment is troubling to contemplate. Nonetheless, despite his heartless gloating over this massacre, The Boss strangely lapses into uncharacteristic sentimentality and decides to aid the few wounded survivors of his onslaught. A vengeful knight stabs him and, subsequently, a disguised Merlin works a spell that dooms him to sleep for 13 centuries. The outrageous attempt to impose modern civilization on Arthurian England both triumphs and implodes as a result of Hank Morgan's egocentric acts. The ultimate symbol of this enterprise is Clarence, Hank's right-hand man, whom Hank has trained to speak The Boss's version of Standard English, not the dialect of his own time. In the end, Clarence completes Hank's manuscript of this narrative. This is, of course, the ultimate act of literacy and the clearest possible gesture of Clarence's alienation from his own culture. He has evolved from a dialect speaker to a literal destroyer of his own world.

In many ways, *Pudd'nhead Wilson* is a more ambivalent and thus a more ironic version of the same narrative situation. David Wilson is a thoroughly modern Yankee who enters the backward world of Dawson's Landing with friendly and benign intentions, but his ineptness in speaking the local dialect relegates him to a marginal status. Wilson speaks a modern dialect, a language of wit, ambiguity, and irony. Naïvely, he addresses the folk of Dawson's Landing with the intent of making a clever remark about a noisy dog. Being totally obtuse to irony (and, it seems, to all subtleties of perception), these witless citizens immediately brand him "a pudd'nhead," a title that precludes his preferred status of attorney for the next 20 years. Dawson's Landing conquers David Wilson in their first encounter. By contrast, though Hank Morgan is also conquered in his initial encounter, forced to surrender and to enter Camelot as the vanquished prisoner of a knight, he soon reverses his situation by using his knowledge of an impending eclipse to subdue Arthurian England. Wilson spends two decades trying to fit in, while Hank devotes a comparable amount of time to his technological missionary work, transforming many aspects of King Arthur's world. Both of them, however, are lonely figures of modernity, exiled in the backward (dialect) worlds that surround them.

Wilson eventually makes himself useful by solving a bewildering murder case and unraveling the tale of the two Toms. But he does not in any way alter Dawson's Landing. He is notable instead for his powers as an observer. He is, in effect, an anthropologist residing among a strange and entertaining tribe. His field notes include some shrewd observations about how dialect functions in Dawson's Landing. One July afternoon, Wilson's bookkeeping work is disturbed by two bantering voices outside his window:

"Say, Roxy, how does yo'baby come on?" This from the distant voice.

"Fust-rate; how does *you* come on, Jasper?" This yell was from close by.

"Oh, I's middlin'; hain't got noth'n' to complain of. I's gwine to come a-court'n' you biemby, Roxy."

"*You* is, you black mud-cat! Yah – yah – yah! I got somep'n' better to do den 'sociat'n' wid niggers as black as you is. Is ole Miss Cooper's Nancy done give you de mitten?" Roxy followed this sally with another discharge of care-free laughter.

"You's jealous, Roxy, dat's what's de matter wid *you*, you hussy – yah – yah – yah! Dat's de time I got you!" . . .

This idle and aimless jabber went on and on, both parties enjoying the friendly duel and each well satisfied with his own share of the wit exchanged – for wit they considered it. (Twain 1894: 30–1)

The latter comment by Mark Twain's omniscient narrator raises the question of wit once again, with the clear implication that "aimless jabber" such as this falls below the threshold of true "wit." Indeed, this exchange is in most ways an instance of stereotypical "darky" dialect, such as one might find in much popular fiction of the time. The important exception is that these two speakers are indulging themselves in self-conscious exaggeration and playfulness, which distinguishes them as subjects, not just objects, of humor. Theirs is a low humor, but because it is self-conscious and playful, it places them a notch above the stereotypical, dialect-spouting "darkies" of Thomas Nelson Page and his ilk. Indeed, this pair are also a notch above the white citizens Wilson encountered in the opening scene. The bumbling attempts by those towns-folk to analyze Wilson's joke are witless and devoid of critical self-consciousness. Though they deliberately make jokes, they show no signs of recognizing their own absurdity. They are strictly objects of satire. Mark Twain pokes fun at both the white and the black townsfolk, but in making the whites more ridiculous, he distinguishes himself from most of his literary contemporaries.

This point is amplified as Wilson begins to observe Roxy and Jasper carefully.[1] Jasper is described as "young, coal-black and of magnificent build," taking an hour's rest in his wheelbarrow before he supposedly begins his day's work. When Wilson steps out onto the street, Twain remarks, "Jasper went to work energetically, at once perceiving that his leisure was observed" (1894: 33–4). This behavior further illustrates Jasper's self-consciousness. He works when white people are watching. When they are not watching, he seeks his own pleasures. The author's description of Roxy is similarly revealing:

From Roxy's manner of speech, a stranger would have expected her to be black, but she was not. Only one sixteenth of her was black, and that sixteenth did not show. She was of majestic form and stature, her attitudes were imposing and statuesque, and her gestures and movements distinguished by a noble and stately grace. Her complexion was very fair, with the rosy glow of vigorous health in the cheeks, her face was full of character and expression, her eyes were brown and liquid, and she had a heavy suit of fine soft hair . . . Her face was shapely, intelligent and comely – even beautiful. She had an easy, independent carriage – when she was among her own caste – and a high and 'sassy' way, withal; but of course she was meek and humble enough where white people were (Twain 1894: 32).

By using the word "caste" rather than the usual American term, "race," Mark Twain indicates clearly that Roxy's inherently superior qualities are devalued only because of her position in the social pecking order. "Race" in America carries implications of inherent, qualitative group differences, while "caste" indicates that social convention defines group differences, not inherent qualities. In the subsequent paragraph the author argues this point about race explicitly, dismissing it as "a fiction of law and custom" (Twain 1894: 33).

This view of race pertains directly to the beginning of the passage quoted above, as Twain focuses on "Roxy's manner of speech." She speaks what listeners perceive as "negro dialect." This dialect creates expectations that the speaker will conform to racial stereotypes, but in fact, the author asserts, her dialect and her social status are the only things that identify her as African American. Twain's long and detailed listing of Roxy's virtues is a direct contradiction of the usual racial stereotype. Thus dialect is, in Roxy's case, a complicated and deceptive signifier. It accurately reveals her status as a slave, but it also entails many other expectations about appearance, character, intelligence, and behavior, none of which turn out to be true. In this instance, then, dialect is an ironic signifier.

In 1882 Mark Twain published an essay called "Concerning the American Language," which he described as part of a chapter dropped from *A Tramp Abroad* (1880). The piece is structured as an argument between Mark Twain and an Englishman who had complimented him on his English. Twain responds, "I said I was obliged to him for his compliment, since I knew he meant it for one, but that I was not fairly entitled to it, for I didn't speak English at all, – I only spoke American" (Twain 1992a: 830). His argument in the essay is that American has evolved into a different language from English, and he provides many examples of differences in vocabulary and pronunciation. He and the Englishman also argue over various points of regional dialect and class inflection. In essence, Twain's argument is that American is a distinct dialect of English, though he uses the word "language" rather than "dialect." In terms of linguistics, Mark Twain makes better arguments than his English admirer.

H. L. Mencken discusses this essay in his classic work, *The American Language* (Mencken 2003: 71, 351), and substantially agrees with Twain's position. But he, too, manifests the same move we see in Twain, from the argument in "Concerning the American Language" that "American" is a single language, distinct from "English," to the insistence, in the preface to *Huckleberry Finn*, on the particularity of regional dialects. Mencken elaborates the two sides of this contradiction in his discussion of dialect. On the one hand, he notes, "all the early writers on the American language remarked its strange freedom from dialects." That is, in contrast to England, there is very substantial consistency in how the American language is spoken throughout the country, largely as a result of the vastly greater social and geographical mobility of the American people, which works against the development of truly idiosyncratic local dialects. On the other hand, however, he does identify what are, strictly speaking, three major dialect groups in America (Western, New England, and Southern), as well as various local dialects based on English and other languages, such as German, Dutch, Yiddish, and Spanish (pp. 354–78). The Western dialect, Mencken notes, is the only one of the three that has actually expanded its range, rapidly evolving into Standard American English. The other two variants have, by contrast, become increasingly diluted and isolated. Twain and Mencken ultimately agree, then, in viewing the American language as evolving toward unity despite its colorful regional variants. Social mobility rapidly dissolves the linguistic habits developed through generations of isolation.

Mark Twain was himself a fine example of American social and geographical mobility – he interacted with people of all social classes, from slaves to robber barons – and, for this reason, his comments on language and dialect are especially interesting. His account of the American language as both one and various captures perfectly a central defining paradox of the United States.

The literary career of Mark Twain covered the same period as the local color movement, and sometimes he pretended to have a local colorist's fascination with dialects. As we have seen, however, Twain could not espouse the literalist dogmas of local colorists with a straight face. Admittedly, he spun out the voice of Huckleberry Finn with an obvious affection. At the same time, he frequently used dialect for comic and even for satirical purposes. Unlike those local colorists who fixated on dialect, making it a kind of fetish, Mark Twain used it in a variety of ways, with varying purposes and attitudes. Dialect was not more important than his characters, and narratives were not mere props to facilitate its representation. Rather, dialect was more like a set of chisels in his literary toolbox – carefully collected, finely honed, affectionately maintained, but tools nonetheless. His true purpose was the crafting of literary art.

NOTES

1   This scene might also be considered in terms of how Mark Twain himself listened to African American voices, a topic addressed in detail by Fishkin (1993). Fishkin is specifically concerned with how Mark Twain developed a literary language on the basis of such attentiveness. Interestingly, David Wilson listens perceptively but is not changed or influenced by his listening.

REFERENCES AND FURTHER READING

Fishkin, Shelley Fisher (1993). *Was Huck Black? Mark Twain and African American Voices.* New York: Oxford University Press.

Marx, Karl, and Engels, Friedrich (1978). *Manifesto of the Communist Party.* In *The Marx–Engels Reader*, ed. Robert Tucker, 469–500. New York: Norton. (First publ. 1848.)

Mencken, H. L. (2003). *The American Language*, 4th edn. New York: Knopf. (First publ. 1936.)

Toll, Robert (1974). *Blacking Up: The Minstrel Show in Nineteenth-Century America.* New York: Oxford University Press.

29

Killing Half a Dog, Half a Novel: The Trouble with *The Tragedy of Pudd'nhead Wilson* and *The Comedy Those Extraordinary Twins*

John Bird

Half a century ago, in 1955, a year before F. R. Leavis called attention to *Pudd'nhead Wilson* as "Mark Twain's Neglected Classic," Leslie Fiedler made this perceptive comment:

> The most extraordinary book in American literature unfortunately has not survived as a whole . . . What a book the original might have been, before *Those Extraordinary Twins* was detached and Pudd'nhead's *Calendar* expurgated – a rollicking atrocious melange of bad taste and half understood intentions and nearly intolerable insights into evil, translated into a nightmare worthy of America . . . All that the surrealists were later to yearn for and in their learned way simulate, Twain had stumbled on without quite knowing it. And as always (except in *Huckleberry Finn*) he paid the price for his lack of self-awareness; he fumbled the really great and monstrous poem on duplicity that was within his grasp. The principle of analogy which suggested to him linking the story of Siamese Twins, one a teetotaler, the other a drunk; Jekyll and Hyde inside a single burlesque skin – to a tale of a Negro and white baby switched in the cradle finally seemed to him insufficient. He began to worry about broken plot lines and abandoned characters, about the too steep contrast between farce and horror; and he lost his nerve – that colossal gall which was his essential strength as well as his curse. Down the well went the burlesque supernumeraries and finally out of the story; and the poor separated twins remain to haunt a novel which is no longer theirs. (Fiedler 1955: 220–2)

Astute as Fiedler is here, I disagree that Twain "lost his nerve." By publishing *Those Extraordinary Twins* as a supplement, in a twinned form with *Pudd'nhead Wilson*, Twain was able to have his cake and eat it. He did not lose his courage, but found a way to present a form of his strange story in the only way an audience of his time could have accepted it. But this book of twinned texts works only if we actually read and consider them together, and that is often not done. *Those Extraordinary Twins*, textually joined to *Pudd'nhead Wilson* (the novel that most critics and readers now rank second only to *Huckleberry Finn* in the author's œuvre), is assuredly among the overlooked works of Mark Twain. Critics of *Pudd'nhead Wilson* mention it only rarely and, when they do, usually disparagingly, dismissively, and in passing; or see it only as a way for Twain to pad out what would have been a slim novel to make a larger volume (which is indeed partly true).[1] I suspect, moreover, that teachers of the novel usually do not require their students to read it. I would insist, however, that the two are a single story: that Mark Twain intended for us to read them (it) as one, and that we cannot understand the main novel without its twin. Just as you cannot kill "half a dog," you cannot kill half a novel. *Those Extraordinary Twins*, while often ignored, overlooked, or seen merely as an interesting appendage to *Pudd'nhead Wilson*, is actually an integral part of its novelistic twin and illuminates not only that paired text, but also Mark Twain as a man and an artist, as well as the subject of fragmented identities at its (their) heart.

We meet here, though, the thorny problem of authorial intention. Uncharacteristically, Twain comments extensively (if not always accurately) about the composition of this novel. "A man who is not born with the novel-writing gift has a troublesome time of it when he tries to build a novel," he begins (Twain 1894: 309). He tells how what he was writing "changed itself from a farce to a tragedy"; that he found "it was not one story, but two stories tangled together." Then, in an arresting and revealing metaphor, he says, "I pulled one of the stories out by the roots, and left the other one – a kind of literary Caesarean operation" (p. 310). As James M. Cox argues in *Mark Twain: The Fate of Humor*, "The terms of the account deserve emphasis – not because the account is necessarily accurate, but because it discloses how Mark Twain was dramatizing the act of writing at this juncture of his career" (Cox 1966: 227). Cox continues: "[T]he novel is curiously and strikingly figured not as the child of the farce but as the *mother* from whom the child – the farce – is forcibly extracted" (p. 227). Cox is, as usual, perceptive, but if we carry Twain's metaphor to its logical conclusion, we can see that, rather than a "literary Caesarean operation," the operation he conducted is actually a "literary abortion." The writer is not delivering a story, but disposing of one – then, in compensation, tacking it on at the end of what most readers have in fact taken to be the primary text.

But this is to dismiss too easily the result of his operation. Most readers, as I say, ignore the cast-off story. It exists metaphorically half-alive, with an elaborate (and funny) introduction and with Twain's interspersed comments along the way. In these comments Twain represents himself, misleadingly, as a "jack-leg" writer (Twain 1894: 311), a judgment too many readers and critics have taken seriously. "I took those twins apart and made two separate men of them," he says. "They had no occasion to have foreign names now, but it was too much trouble to remove them all through, so I left them christened as they were and made no explanation" (p. 315). So, instead of making a clean break between the two stories, he leaves puzzling residues of the

Siamese twins in *Pudd'nhead Wilson*. They sit down to play a four-handed piece at the piano, and the villagers are "astonished" (p. 85). They say they were their parents' "only child" (p. 78), and that their "parents could have made themselves comfortable by exhibiting us as a show" (p. 79). What is more, after their parents' death, "We were seized for the debts occasioned by their illness and their funerals, and placed among the attractions of a cheap museum in Berlin to earn the liquidation money" (p. 79). None of this makes any sense if the brothers are merely twins and, as easy as it would have been to erase these comments, Twain leaves them in, even though he extensively revised the rest of the novel. Most curious is Tom's comment at a crucial moment in the plot, when he refers to the twins as a "human philopena" – two nuts in one shell – after which the narrator says, "The descriptive aptness of the phrase caught the house, and a mighty burst of laughter followed" (p. 151). The phrase, of course, is not nearly so apt if the twins are not conjoined.

Robert A. Wiggins says that "it is surprising to find Twain remiss in matters of detail," and I agree. He goes on, however, to call Twain here "a butcher rather than a surgeon in performing his 'literary Caesarean operation'" (Wiggins 1964: 108). "Twain," he says, "was simply careless in reworking his manuscript to remove these traces of his surgery" (p. 109). Whether a butcher or merely careless, neither act seems characteristic of the author, no matter how much he hated revision in general. And the fact that he also went to the trouble of revising *Those Extraordinary Twins*, before including it with *Pudd'nhead Wilson*, serves to call deliberate attention to his actions. I would suggest that, rather than being a careless or shoddy craftsman, Twain intentionally left these few vestiges of the Siamese twin story embedded in *Pudd'nhead Wilson* as a sign to his readers of their true linkage. He cuts the twins apart, but leaves enough evidence to point us to the story in which they are still joined. Only by reading *Those Extraordinary Twins* do these passages in *Pudd'nhead Wilson* make sense. And even more importantly, only by reading both stories do we fully get Mark Twain's point. One story remains at least partly embedded in the other because they cannot really be separated – again, you cannot kill half a novel.

If one influential critic is right, however, the troubling compositional history of the final text killed the *whole* production. In *Flawed Texts and Verbal Icons*, Hershel Parker devotes a long chapter to *Pudd'nhead Wilson*, painstakingly unraveling the compositional process that Mark Twain followed in writing the original longer book, then revising that manuscript into what we know as *Pudd'nhead Wilson*. His explanation of this process is valuable, but his conclusion is contestable. Because Twain inserted certain passages after he had written later ones, and after he had decided to focus on the slave twins switched in the cradle, Parker argues that "the published *Pudd'nhead Wilson* is . . . patently unreadable" (Parker 1984: 136), a viewpoint at odds with the experience of many thousands of readers. Parker then continues, and with some sarcasm, to excoriate and satirize critics who have made judgments based on the novel as published in 1894. Any passage Mark Twain revised or inserted after completing his original manuscript is invalid, for Parker, because it does not have the same authorial intention as at the time of Twain's original act of composition. Parker makes valid arguments against New Critical attempts to find unity in a fractured text, but his conclusion that *Pudd'nhead Wilson* is "unreadable" strikes me as excessive. Peter Messent, reading *Pudd'nhead Wilson* alongside *Those Extraordinary Twins*, reaches what I find to be a more satisfactory conclusion:

> The peculiar quality of the narratives lies in the lack of formal unity, the sense of incompletion and deferral, that results from their twinning. To suggest this is to see Twain on the verge of the type of artistic understanding which would only become commonplace in later, post-structuralist, times: that our representation of reality can only end in deferral and incompletion. (Messent 1997: 155–6)

In the case of *The Tragedy of Pudd'nhead Wilson and The Comedy of Those Extraordinary Twins*, having *both* texts presented to us heightens the reading pleasure. It seems to me that in presenting both texts as one, Mark Twain actually makes stronger art. But, as I say, only if we read them both, as twinned units.

What, then, does *Those Extraordinary Twins* reveal to us about *Pudd'nhead Wilson?* Much critical comment – perhaps too much – has been devoted to the "killing half a dog" comment in *Pudd'nhead Wilson* that seals the title character's fate and earns him his nickname. Some parallel scenes in *Those Extraordinary Twins* underscore the comment and help us further to understand Twain's point. When the Siamese twins are put on trial for kicking Tom Driscoll, Pudd'nhead Wilson carries out an absurd cross-examination that centers on which twin kicked Tom:

> "Mr. Rogers, you say you saw these accused gentlemen kick the plaintiff."
> "Yes, sir."
> "Which of them kicked him first?"
> "Why – they – they both kicked him at the same time."
> "Are you perfectly sure of that?"
> "Yes, sir."
> "What makes you sure of it?"
> "Why, I stood right behind them, and *saw* them do it."
> "How many kicks were delivered?"
> "Only one."
> "If two men kick, the result should be two kicks, shouldn't it?"
> "Why – why – yes, as a rule."
> "Then what do you think went with the other kick?"
> "I – well – the fact is, I wasn't thinking of two being necessary, this time."
> "What do you think now?"
> "Well, I – I'm sure I don't quite know what to think, but I reckon that one of them did half of the kick and the other one did the other half."
> Somebody in the crowd sung out:
> "It's the first sane thing that any of them has said." (Twain 1894: 375–6)

This statement clearly matches the "half a dog" comment, when, early in the narrative of *Pudd'nhead Wilson*, the title character says of a barking dog that he wished he owned half the dog, so he could kill his half.

Curiously, here the crowd quickly recognizes the absurdity and irony of the "half a kick" remark, while in *Pudd'nhead Wilson*, they take the "half a dog" comment and subject it to what amounts to a public cross-examination:

> "Said he wished he owned *half* of the dog, the idiot," said a third [speaker]. "What did he reckon would become of the other half if he killed his half? Do you reckon he thought it would live?"
>
> "Why, he must have thought it, unless he *is* the downrightest fool in the world; because if he hadn't thought that, he would have wanted to own the whole dog, knowing that if he had killed his half and the other half died, he would be responsible for that half, just the same as if he had killed that half instead of his own. Don't it look that way to you, gents?"
>
> "Yes, it does. If he owned one half of the general dog, it would be so; if he owned one end of the dog and another person owned the other end, it would be so, just the same; particularly in the first case, because if you kill one half of a general dog, there ain't any man that can tell whose half it was, but if he owned one end of the dog, maybe he could kill his end of it . . ." (Twain 1894: 24–5)

At the end of *Those Extraordinary Twins*, the twins run against each other for the board of aldermen, with Luigi winning over Angelo in a bitter election. But Luigi cannot be sworn in, because Angelo is not allowed to attend the meetings, and Luigi cannot attend without him. The government is consequently at a standstill – until the authorities come up with the idea of lynching Luigi. When some villagers protest that Angelo is innocent and should not be hanged, the answer comes: "Who said anything about hanging him? We are only going to hang the other one," with the reply: "Then that is all right – there is no objection to that." The narrator then concludes: "So they hanged Luigi. And so ends the history of "Those Extraordinary Twins" (Twain 1894: 431). The text ends with another killing of half a whole being. Twain's central motif (twinned identity) can thus be seen even more clearly if both narratives, including the half that Twain has pretended to kill, are read together. "Irony was not for those people," the narrator tells us early in *Pudd'nhead Wilson* (p. 71). Twain's own irony, on display for the consumption of his readers, becomes more intense if we read the two texts as one twinned story.

As many critics have pointed out, the "half a dog" scene in *Pudd'nhead Wilson* is a metaphoric comment on the situation of Tom and Chambers. By reading *Those Extraordinary Twins* alongside that first-placed novel, we can see that situation even more clearly.[2] In *Pudd'nhead Wilson* the twins function as relatively weak foils to Tom and Chambers, but as Siamese twins in *Those Extraordinary Twins* they suggestively reinforce the moves between conjoined identity (in the form of black and white dependency) and the fiction of difference (in a racially divided world) of the earlier text. Absurd and ludicrous as the second story is, it makes telling comments about twinship. Luigi and Angelo are supposedly identical Siamese twins, two heads and bodies joined with a single pair of legs, but one is light and one is dark. This absurdity points to the absurdity of racial identity in *Pudd'nhead Wilson*, where white and black (supposedly absolutely different) become intertwined and interchangeable terms – where

Roxy is one-sixteenth black, and that one-sixteenth does not show; and where a white baby and a black baby, born on the same day to a slave woman and her white mistress, look identical enough to be switched in the cradle. The identity confusion that rules *Pudd'nhead Wilson* is heightened when we read its companion text. For the whole of *Those Extraordinary Twins* plays on identity difference – one body containing completely divergent halves. Angelo is a teetotaler, but Luigi likes to drink; Angelo is prone to illness, but Luigi is the picture of health; Angelo is very religious and a Whig, but Luigi is a freethinking Democrat. The twins take turns being in control of the body, one week at a time, and as Luigi says:

> "So exactly to the instant does the change come, that during our stay in many of the great cities of the world, the public clocks were regulated by it; and as hundreds of thousands of private clocks and watches were set and corrected in accordance with the public clocks, we really furnished the standard time for the entire city." (Twain 1894: 357)

The two men are one twinned being, but they are as different from each other as they can be, and in the end turn out to be adversaries.

In *Pudd'nhead Wilson*, "Tom" is really "Chambers," and "Chambers" really "Tom." The switch of identity means that the narrator has to call them by the "wrong" names to prevent the story from lapsing into utter confusion. Their two separate beings are interchangeable: white becomes black, and black becomes white. The social world represented in *Pudd'nhead Wilson* judges race the biggest difference between individuals, but Tom and Chambers – one "black," the other "white" – are so nearly identical that their society cannot tell them apart. In *Those Extraordinary Twins*, on the other hand, the identical twins are so different that, even before they appear on the scene, Rowena wonders which one is the taller, which one the better-looking (Twain 1894: 319). Twain represents a world so topsy-turvy that Luigi actually convinces Patsy Cooper and Aunt Betsy that he is six months older than his own Siamese twin. His cracked logic takes in these two old women (women who also swallow the equally distorted reasoning of a slave-holding society):

> "It is very simple, and I assure you it is true. I was born with a full crop of hair, [Angelo] was as bald as an egg for six months. I could walk six months before he could make a step. I finished teething six months ahead of him. I began to take solids six months before he left the breast. I began to talk six months before he could say a word. Last, and absolutely unassailable proof, *the sutures in my skull closed six months ahead of his*. Always just six months difference to a day. Was that accident? Nobody is going to claim that, I'm sure. It was ordained – it was law – it had its meaning, and we know what that meaning was. Now what does this overwhelming body of evidence establish? It establishes just one thing, and that thing it establishes beyond any peradventure whatever. Friends, we would not have it known for the world, and I must beg you to keep it strictly to yourselves, but the truth is, we are no more twins than you are." (pp. 361–2)

Even though Luigi is putting these women on, his words cut two ways and point to a deeper truth that lies at the heart of *Pudd'nhead Wilson* too. If Siamese twins are no more twins than we are, then either *they* are not twins, or *we* are (in the logic of *Pudd'nhead*, black and white, twinned despite all claims of difference). This unsureness about the relation between separate and twinned individuals permeates both texts. Tom and Chambers are twins, yet they are not. Tom himself is internally divided in a way that brings him, no matter how despicable he is, great agony. In appearance, Roxy is white, but by social definition she is black.[3] Pudd'nhead Wilson is the biggest fool in town and its wisest man. The jury's finding in the twins' trial is that Luigi's "identity is so merged in his brother's that we have not been able to tell which was him" (Twain 1894: 392). This is the fundamental lesson of both novels, with all their characters, all their ironies, all their lessons about race and duality: that identity (both racial and individual) is a confused and problematic thing. The same finding can be extended to the case of Twain's own divided and problematic identity. Perhaps it is even the case with us. What Pudd'nhead can produce fingerprints to unravel the confusion of all such split identities? Who is brave or foolish enough to try to kill half a dog?

A description near the beginning of *Those Extraordinary Twins* highlights the absurdity but also the audacity of what Mark Twain's imagination has concocted here, as the twins undress to reveal the monstrous assault on the senses that they (and their narrative) contains. Metaphorically, too, I think that this passage tells us something about the struggles Mark Twain went through with his own creation, as well as the risk he took in telling his twinned stories:

> The Twins were wet and tired, and they proceeded to undress without any preliminary remarks. The abundance of sleeves made the partnership coat hard to get off, for it was like skinning a tarantula, but it came at last, after much tugging and perspiring. The mutual vest followed. Then the brothers stood up before the glass, and each took off his own cravat and collar. The collars were of the standing kind, and came up high under the ears, like the sides of a wheelbarrow, as required by the fashion of the day. The cravats were as broad as a bank bill, with fringed ends which stood far out to right and left like the wings of a dragon-fly, and this also was strictly in accordance with the fashion of the time. Each cravat, as to color, was in perfect taste, so far as its owner's complexion was concerned – a delicate pink, in the case of the blonde brother, a violent scarlet in the case of the brunette – but as a combination they broke all the laws of taste known to civilization. Nothing more fiendish and irreconcilable than those shrieking and blaspheming colors could have been contrived. (Twain 1894: 327–8)

The extraordinary book Leslie Fiedler imagines and pines for would indeed have been "a combination [that] broke all the laws of taste known to civilization." Twain's contemporary audience, and probably even many in a present-day one, would not have been able to swallow it. "[F]iendish and irreconcilable" – but also irreversibly connected – as the two stories are, Mark Twain found a way to present them both to us; if we would only read them both, as he clearly intended. You cannot kill half a dog, and you cannot kill half a novel. Unless, that is, you do not read the whole thing.

Mark Twain could have cleared up or hidden much of this trouble if he had chosen not to publish *Those Extraordinary Twins*, to throw it into the discard pile as he did so many other late manuscripts. But he chose instead to publish it and allow his readers access to it, and even though that decision may have seemed to *add* to the trouble, he actually succeeded in making these conjoined texts even more interesting as a result. And maybe trouble was his goal all along.

Notes

1   Some critics do call for the twinned reading of both texts. Thus Susan Gillman writes: "These twin novels must . . . be read together, despite the fact that the farce makes a mockery of the Siamese twins' grotesque attachment, whereas the tragedy, obsessed with genealogy, race, and miscegenation, offers a critique of an American historical actuality" (Gillman 1989: 55). Peter Messent devotes a chapter of his book *Mark Twain* to the twinned novels, arguing persuasively for their connections to one another, for reading both texts as one: "A symbiotic bond . . . continues to exist between the two parts of the original body of the work. The stories may have been pulled apart, but they remain, none the less, connected" (Messent 1997: 135). Rather than espousing Gillman's political argument, Messent emphasizes reader-response: "The quest for meaning in

Pudd'nhead Wilson and *Those Extraordinary Twins* becomes a form of collaborative project, as the reader puts the two together to find one broken whole" (p. 138).

2   For a good overview and argument, see Marvin Fischer and Michael Elliott (1972, in Twain 1980).

3   Tracing Roxy's one-sixteenth "black blood" reveals the full horror of miscegenation. Her great-great-grandmother would have been fully "black" (I assume inverted commas round these terms from this point) and her child from (one assumes) her white owner, must also have been a girl – half-black – Roxy's great-grandmother. The pattern would have been repeated with each generation. Roxy, then, would have been the product of four generations of (forced) miscegenation, a fact Twain presents to the reader obliquely.

References and Further Reading

Cox, James M. (1966). *Mark Twain: The Fate of Humor*. Princeton: Princeton University Press.

Fiedler, Leslie (1980). "As free as any cretur . . . ." (first publ. 1955). In Mark Twain, *Pudd'nhead Wilson and Those Extraordinary Twins*, 220–9. New York: Norton.

Gerber, John C. (1988). *Mark Twain*. Boston: Twayne.

Gillman, Susan (1989). *Dark Twins: Imposture and Identity in Mark Twain's America*. Chicago: University of Chicago Press.

Gillman, Susan, and Robinson, Forrest G., eds. (1990). *Mark Twain's Pudd'nhead Wilson: Race, Conflict, and Culture*. Durham, NC: Duke University Press.

Leavis, F. R. (1980). "Mark Twain's Neglected Classic: The Moral Astringency of *Pudd'nhead Wilson*" (first publ. 1956). In Mark Twain, *Pudd'nhead Wilson and Those Extraordinary Twins*, 229–42. New York: Norton.

Messent, Peter (1997). *Mark Twain*. New York: St. Martin's. (Modern Novelists.)

Parker, Hershel (1984). *Flawed Texts and Verbal Icons: Literary Authority in American Fiction*. Evanston, Ill.: Northwestern University Press.

Twain Mark (1980). *Pudd'nhead Wilson and Those Extraordinary Twins*. New York: Norton. (Norton Critical Edition.)

Wiggins, Robert A. (1964). *Mark Twain: Jackleg Novelist*. Seattle: University of Washington Press.

30

Dreaming Better Dreams:
The Late Writing of Mark Twain

Forrest G. Robinson

Mark Twain's later life was crossed by extremes of adversity and emotional upheaval. The worst of the trouble began in 1894 when, after years of imprudent financial speculation, the humorist suffered a humiliating plunge into bankruptcy. He partially righted himself by undertaking an around-the-world lecture tour, but that brief triumph was bitterly overturned when his favorite daughter, Susy, succumbed to spinal meningitis in August 1896. The shock was so great that Twain wavered between feelings of hatred for life and blank indifference. Death, he decided, was a blessing, and he looked forward to his own, Andrew Hoffman observes, "as a release from the dreadful responsibility he accepted for his daughter's demise" (Hoffman 1997: 415). Similar feelings overtook him when his beloved wife, Olivia, died in 1904. "I looked for the last time upon that dear face," he confided to his notebook, "and I was full of remorse for things done and said in the 34 years of married life that hurt Livy's heart" (Twain 1935: 387). His youngest daughter Jean, an epileptic, was equally distraught, and suffered her first seizure in more than a year, while her elder sister, Clara, collapsed in shock. Twain himself endured a variety of ailments, most ominously a heart condition diagnosed late in 1909. Toward the end of that year, on Christmas Eve, Jean suffered her last seizure and drowned in the bathtub. "In her loss," her father wrote, "I am almost bankrupt, and my life is a bitterness, but I am content: for she has been enriched with the most precious of all gifts – that gift which makes all other gifts mean and poor – death" (Twain 1959: 375). Twain was similarly enriched just four months later.

Though they disagreed rather famously about many things, Van Wyck Brooks and Bernard DeVoto were at one in recognizing the pervasive weight of guilt in Twain's long career. "There was something gravely amiss with his inner life," Brooks observes. "That conscience of his – what was it? . . . That morbid feeling of having lived in sin, which made him think of literature as primarily, perhaps, the confession of sins" (Brooks 1920: 24–5). DeVoto is more narrowly attentive to the late phase of Twain's life, when the writer felt "an imperative obligation, a psychological necessity, to deal with the catastrophes that had shattered him" (see Twain 1940: xx). The writing of the period, he argues, bears witness to "the terrible force of an inner cry: Do not blame me, for it was not my fault" (p. 116). Hamlin Hill has more recently confirmed and more fully elaborated the portrait of a vain, angry, self-indulgent, and deeply remorseful old man. Unlike DeVoto, who concludes that Twain finally triumphed over personal and artistic adversity, Hill believes that the weaknesses in the writer's character were exacerbated by the tribulations of his late years, and were increasingly erosive of his happiness and creativity. "Much of the last decade of his life," Hill somberly observes, "he lived in hell" (Hill 1973: xvii).

I am inclined to accept the main thrust of Hill's analysis; and I agree with Brooks and DeVoto that Twain's chronic guilt became more sharply acute toward the end of his life. I hasten to add, however, that these are not uncontroversial positions. Several recent scholars – William R. Macnaughton, Bruce Michelson, and Karen Lystra among them – have objected that Hill gives too little attention to Twain's resilient relish for life and to the energy and exuberance of his late writing. These are important, often well-argued perspectives. But while I readily concede that Hill is at points too relentlessly dark and unforgiving in his judgments, and that he tends to undervalue the late writing, his portrait of a man engulfed by volatile, often destructive emotions is thoroughly plausible and well grounded. To deny these realities is to turn a blind eye to a virtual mountain of direct testimony to the aging writer's contempt for human nature, hatred of God, anguished self-loathing, and impatient longing for the oblivion of the grave. True, Twain was resilient; true as well, he was baffled by his gravitation to the light. "Shall I ever be cheerful again, happy again?" he asked, just after Jean's death. "Yes. And soon. For I know my temperament. And I know that the temperament is *master of the man*, and that he is its fettered and helpless slave" (Paine 1912: 1552). It is altogether telling that Twain viewed his emotional levitations as an embarrassment, a constitutional perversity for which he took no responsibility, and whose evanescence he surely recognized. "He could wave aside care and grief and remorse," Paine observed at first hand, "but in the end he had only driven them ahead a little way and they waited by his path" (pp. 1073–4). Intervals of relief notwithstanding, varieties of grief and rage and remorse were the dire but durable burden of Twain's later life. Much of the rest of it – the banquets and speeches and fat-cat pleasure cruises, the late-night booze and billiards, and the flirtations with little girls – was distraction, often rather frantic, from what deeply ailed him.

Twain's late works – the writing undertaken between 1896 and 1910 – are centrally preoccupied with forming and articulating judgments of God, human nature, national and global politics, and – most urgently and compulsively – himself. Now more than ever before in his long career, he was disposed to find a depressing sameness in the spread of human folly over all time and space. "Really," remarked his friend Joseph Twichell in 1901, "you are getting quite orthodox on the doctrine of Total Human Depravity."[1] Granting as we must the broad sweep of Twain's late-life quarrel with the world, it cannot be too much emphasized that his anger was anchored in a profound and consuming quarrel with himself. He was tyrannized by conscience.

"Remorse was always [his] surest punishment," observes Albert Bigelow Paine. "To his last days on earth he never outgrew its pangs" (1912: 65). According to his daughter Clara:

> If on any occasion he could manage to trace the cause of some one's mishap to something he himself had done or said, no one could persuade him that he was mistaken. Self-condemnation was the natural turn for his mind to take, yet he often accused himself of having inflicted pain or trouble when the true cause was far removed from himself. (Clemens 1931: 6–7)

I hasten to add that this darkly self-scrutinizing figure is much more present to view in the unpublished late writings than in those more familiar books and essays that saw their way into print during Twain's last years. Much of this published work was occasional, ephemeral, and written hastily for profit, and has fallen from view. Much else continues to receive popular and scholarly attention. I am thinking here of "The Man That Corrupted Hadleyburg" (1899), "The $30,000 Bequest" (1904), *Christian Science* (1907), "Extract from Captain Stormfield's Visit to Heaven" (1907–8), and a large handful of incisive political and social essays, notably including "Stirring Times in Austria" (1898), "Concerning the Jews" (1899), "My First Lie and How I Got Out of It" (1899), "To the Person Sitting in Darkness" (1901), "To My Missionary Critics" (1901), "A Defence of General Funston" (1902), "The Czar's Soliloquy" (1905), "King Leopold's Soliloquy" (1905), and "Eve's Diary" (1905). A number of other important short works – "Corn-Pone Opinions," "The Stupendous Procession," "The United States of Lyncherdom," "The War Prayer," and "Letters from the Earth" – are similarly focused on social issues, but were withheld from publication, most often for fear of giving offense. In virtually all of these "public" writings, Twain makes strong, reasoned, eloquent arguments against racism, lynching, anti-semitism, American and European colonialism, and the predatory greed of expanding global capitalism. The tone throughout is sharply satirical, so much so at times that the prospects for reform seem to evaporate under the heat of anger at "the damned human race." For the most part, these works really are "public" in their subject matter, and in the outward trajectory of their moral energy: it is the world that the angry satirist finds wanting, not himself.

The importance of the late, published works is well established. They have been thoroughly and plausibly assessed in a small but expanding library of sophisticated, socially engaged criticism.[2] But while Twain wrote constantly and even compulsively during his late life, much (in addition to the social writings mentioned above) remained unpublished, either because it was unfinished, or because it revealed more about his interior life than he cared to share, or both. Of course, his writing is almost invariably autobiographical, but never more so than in this substantial corpus of "private" work. At one level, he felt compelled to tell the unvarnished truth about his own life: in a word, to confess. The result was nearly 250 autobiographical dictations that he completed with a stenographer between 1906 and 1909. In order to encourage complete veracity, he decided from the outset that the dictations would be set aside for posthumous publication. Despite such good intentions, however, the results were singularly tame and unrevealing, most especially about Twain's secret life. "I have been dictating this autobiography of mine daily for nine months," he observed; "I have thought of fifteen hundred or two thousand incidents of my life which I am ashamed of, but I have not gotten one of them to consent to go on paper yet" (Twain 1924: vol. 2, 331). "As to veracity," he wrote to William Dean Howells, the autobiography "was a failure" (Howells 1968: 316).

Thus Twain found in practice that the conscious commitment to personal candor worked paradoxically to produce its exact opposite. It is a kindred paradox that he came closest to revealing the truth about himself in his fiction, and to a lesser degree in the travel writing, where the pressure to tell the truth was much reduced. Along with "My First Lie" and "The Turning Point of My Life," *Following the Equator*, which was written just after Susy's death, stands out among the "public" works for the brief glimpses it offers into the writer's inner life, and most especially into his sense of guilty complicity in the world's degradation. Composition was understandably difficult, though Twain acknowledged in several letters that the project afforded him a welcome, and often very satisfying, distraction from his grief.[3] At the same time, however, he was confident that the writing successfully concealed his true feelings of anguish and fatigue. "The book has not exposed me," he wrote to Henry Huttleston Rogers. "I would rather be hanged, drawn and quartered than write it again. All the heart I had was in Susy's grave and the Webster debts. And so, behold a miracle! – a book which does not give its writer away" (Twain 1969a: 309). Quite to the contrary, however, *Following the Equator* is a troubled, often angry report on the misery wrought by Western imperialism along the equatorial black belt. The book is heavily laden with dozens of brief, sharply ironic observations on human suffering, greed, cruelty, and self-delusion: "Each person is born to one possession which outvalues all his others – his last breath" (Twain 1897: 386); "Man is the Only Animal that Blushes. Or needs to" (p. 256); and most tellingly of all: "Everything human is pathetic. The secret source of Humor itself is not joy but sorrow" (p. 119). These are not the sentiments of a happy man!

The deeper autobiographical drift of *Following the Equator* is well illustrated in Twain's shifting response to Bombay, where he is at first enchanted by the brilliant "color, bewitching color, enchanting color" (1897: 347) that everywhere meets his eye. The scene is abruptly transformed when a burly German employer, irritated at some minor offense, suddenly strikes his Indian servant. "I had not seen the like of this for fifty years," a startled Twain observes. "It carried me back to my boyhood, and flashed upon me the forgotten fact that this was the *usual* way of explaining one's desires to a slave." Running darkly through his memories, which descend in a rush, is a burden of guilt that he strains to dispel. Striking slaves "seemed right and natural" when he was a boy, "I being born to it and unaware that elsewhere there were other methods; but I was also able to remember that those unresented cuffings made me sorry for the victim and ashamed for the punisher" (p. 351). Nor can he forget the memory of the brutal murder of a slave "for merely doing something awkwardly – as if it were a crime . . . Nobody in the village approved of that murder, but of course no one said much about it" (p. 352). This furtive, troubled train of thought comes partially to rest in a reflexive turn inward on itself, as Twain reflects on the mystery of his own mental processes. "It is curious," he remarks rather coolly:

> the space-annihilating power of thought. For just one second, all that goes to make the *me* in me was in a Missourian village, on the other side of the globe, vividly seeing again those forgotten pictures of fifty years ago, and wholly unconscious of all things but just those; and in the next second I was back in Bombay, and that kneeling native's smitten cheek was not done tingling yet! (p. 352)

Twain's reflections on his own mental behavior are quite arresting, to be sure; so much so that they serve to distract attention from the more primary but largely submerged impulse driving his ruminations – to achieve cognitive distance, and a measure of relief, from the foregoing, conscience-laden memories of slavery. The abrupt epistemological swerve manifests a straining for moral "consolation" equally on display in a model of consciousness so rapid and far-flung in its movements as to have no fixed place or center. In such a construction of subjectivity there is indeed no "*me* in me," and thus no place for guilt to settle and fester. Twain doesn't draw this inference, yet its weight is felt in the dramatically reduced moral temperature of the passage that immediately follows. The German employer and the suffering native are forgotten; memories of slave murders in Missouri recede from consciousness; a cacophony of sounds rises to Twain's hotel bedroom from the street below, but the noise, while abrasive to the ear, offers no challenge to the spirit. And so, thanks to timely philosophical interventions, an awakened sense of moral anguish is laid at least temporarily to rest. "Then," Twain sighs, "came peace – stillness deep and solemn – and lasted till five" (1897: 353).

But of course the self does have a center of sorts, and so the silence is brief. The center is to be found along the line of association connecting Bombay to Missouri, the British Empire to the antebellum American South, and the suffering Indian servant to the murdered slave. These connections have their nexus in Twain's mind, where they intersect and form a center to consciousness, "the *me* in me." The story that emerges is one not so much of innocence lost as of an illusory innocence never possessed in the first place. A version of the same story links the boy in frontier Missouri to the aging sojourner in India. In both settings, separated by half a world, half a century, and only "two seconds by the watch" (1897: 352), he is witness to an uncanny repetition of events from which he draws back in horror. In both, stung by the hint of his own complicity, he retreats to the imagined moral shelter of youth, ignorance, and solipsism, only to find that in none of these is he truly, safely free from blame. The "shame" of the thing is obvious to him in Bombay, where he remembers that events in Missouri made him feel the same way. From the reader's perspective, it is clear that he always already knew what was wrong, that the shame at the center of his consciousness defines him, anchors him in history, and denies him the moral repose he so desires. But Twain is himself proof against a full, conscious reckoning with that hard knowledge. The deeper significance of the episode is deferred as the narrative rushes along, though the repressed is, of course, not forgotten. Twain will pass this way many times in the years ahead.

In this extraordinary passage, and in a few others like it, *Following the Equator* exhibits many of the characteristics – the collapse of familiar contrasts between people, places, and historical periods; the division and fragmentation of identity; and the drift into contradiction and incoherence – that turn up more frequently and in bolder relief in the "private" texts of the period, most notably in "Tom Sawyer's Conspiracy," "The Secret History of Eddypus," "My Platonic Sweetheart," "Refuge of the Derelicts," *What Is Man?*, the several so-called "dream writings," and the cognate narratives edited by William M. Gibson as *The Mysterious Stranger*. With the exception of *What Is Man?*, all of these works are unfinished, and all were unpublished in Twain's life-time. At their most fascinating, they are wildly imaginative, formally anarchic, often bizarre, sometimes obscure; but almost invariably they open a window on Twain's desperate attempt to find relief from the intolerable moral burden of being himself. The effort was continuous, because permanent relief was unfailingly elusive. In the course of things, Twain ranged widely into metaphysics, ontology, epistemology, and moral philosophy. He obsessed about God and the devil, time and space, the origins and status of knowledge, free will, determinism, and what he took to be the inherent perversity of human nature. He approached these topics, I emphasize, not with philosophical detachment, but as a man driven to find a justifying explanation for the terrible thing he inwardly knew he was. Though a professed atheist, he seldom missed a chance to denounce God as a cruel and immoral hypocrite who "created man without invitation, then tries to shuffle the responsibility for man's acts upon man, instead of honorably placing it where it belongs, upon himself" (Twain 1969c: 405). The moral correlative to this construction of the Christian deity is of course crystal clear. "Why do you reproach yourself?" Satan inquires of his human admirers, "You did not make yourself; how then are you to blame?" (p. 250).

Theological explanations for mortal degradation hardly diminished the humorist's contempt for human nature, which grew sharper in his later years, as he became more than ever convinced of its unchanging influence at all times and places in history. As he bitterly complains in "Man's Place in the Animal World," "Hypocrisy, envy, malice, cruelty, vengefulness, seduction, rape, robbery, swindling, arson, bigamy, adultery, and the oppression and humiliation of the poor and helpless in all ways, have been and still are more or less common among both the civilized and uncivilized peoples of the earth" (Twain 1973: 80). Roger B. Salomon is surely correct that such grave universalizing spelled the end of Twain's always uncertain faith in progress (Salomon 1961: 126). The same blanket skepticism informs his belief that humans everywhere recoil from the knowledge of their essential depravity into all varieties of evasion and denial. As Satan puts it in *The Mysterious Stranger*, "our race lived a life of continuous and uninterrupted self-deception" (Twain 1969c: 164).

Even as he inveighed tirelessly against universal moral hypocrisy, Twain continued to elaborate philosophical arguments on the side of ultimate human freedom from responsibility for sin. Yet the authority of guilt was always much greater with him than the authority of innocence, as his "gospel," *What Is Man?*, well illustrates. Written and revised over a period of several years, the little treatise, which its author regarded as potently subversive, was published in a small, anonymous edition in 1906. Twain insists centrally that virtue is a fond illusion concealing the invariable selfishness of human behavior, and, more narrowly, that the unyielding need for moral self-assurance is at the root of all motivation. Though "we ignore and never mention" it, he observes, "the Sole Impulse which dictates and compels a man's every act" is "the imperious necessity of securing his own approval, in every emergency and at all costs. To it we owe all that we are. It is our breath, our heart, our blood" (Twain 1973: 147). Humans are thus perforce as hopelessly selfish as they are hopelessly self-deceived about their true degradation. Behavior will vary as temperament, circumstances, and training dictate, but the compulsive need to deny pervasive guilt, and thus to maintain the illusion of perfect moral rectitude, is the engine driving it all.

Twain acknowledges that *What Is Man?* espouses "a desolating doctrine" that "takes the glory out of man" (1973: 207–8), and wonders how a person committed to such ideas could ever "be cheerful again, [as] his life would not be worth the living." As an answer to this perfectly reasonable question, he settles rather lamely for an appeal to temperament: "If a man is born with an unhappy temperament, nothing can make him happy; if he is born with a happy temperament, nothing can make him unhappy" (p. 211). Yet the more philosophically consistent response, surely, is that humans retreat in horror from "desolating" knowledge into the consoling illusion of their own innocence. Such, indeed, is the reflex response of *What Is Man?* itself, which commences in, and constantly reiterates, the argument that humans are machines "moved, directed, COMMANDED, by *exterior* influences – *solely*. [Man] *originates* nothing, himself – not even an opinion, not even a thought" (p. 128). It is the emphatic implication of this "law" that humans are exempt, as machines are, from moral responsibility. In one variant of this determinist position, God is the outside force governing human behavior: "He is unquestionably responsible for every foreknown and unforeknown crime committed by man, his creature" (pp. 481–2). Of course, logical consistency requires that we reject this argument as yet another evasion of guilt in the service of obligatory self-approval. Yet it is something more urgent than logic that restores us to a sense of the affective primacy of guilt in Twain's moral universe. "We very well know what Man is," he declares, in a section of the treatise that he shrank from publishing, doubtless because it reveals so clearly the anguish in his heart:

> Man hides himself from himself during most hours of the day, and in books and sermons and speeches calls himself by fine names; but there is one hour in the twenty-four when he does not do that . . . It is when he wakes out of sleep, deep in the night. You know the bitterness of that hour; we all know it. The black thoughts come flocking through our brain, they show us our naked soul, our true soul, and we perceive and confess that we are despicable. (pp. 486–7)

What Is Man? is quite evidently one among the many daytime "books and sermons and speeches" that Twain wrote in order to hide "himself from himself" in fine-sounding self-approval. Just as clearly, the effort failed to vanquish guilt, and would require repeating, though it provided no little distraction along the way. So viewed, the treatise is testimony to a process of auto-therapy to which Twain resorted frequently in his late writing. Jennifer L. Zaccara has usefully linked Twain's autobiographical dictations to the Freudian "talking cure." "Working with stream of consciousness, free association, memories, and dreams, Twain aimed to tell stories that would enable him to cope with loss: financial bankruptcy followed by the deaths of his daughter Susy and wife, Livy" (Zaccara 2001: 101). Writing – and most especially the fiction writing to which we will turn in a moment – afforded him even greater therapeutic benefits, for it freed him entirely from the demands of realism and historical accuracy – freed him, that is, from the painful thoughts, memories, and reflections that so weighed on his mind. On May 9, 1904, Twain dwelt guiltily on the fact that he had been denied his daily, two-minute visit to Livy's sick-room because his presence was judged a strain on her fragile health. "So I will give up waiting for the call," he wrote to a friend, "& get me to the work which sweeps the world away & puts me in one which no one has visited but me – nor will, for this book [*The Mysterious Stranger*] is not being written for print, & is not going to be published" (MTP). Seven years earlier, during the painful August anniversary of Susy's death, he confided to Wayne MacVeigh: "I have mapped out four books this morning, & will begin an emancipated life this afternoon & shift back and forth between them & make them furnish me recreation and entertainment for three or four years to come, if I last so long" (MTP). "The Secret History of Eddypus," Paine observes, "was not publishable matter, and really never intended as such. It was just one of the things which Mark Twain wrote to relieve mental pressure" (Paine 1912: 1188). Supplementary evidence surfaces in a series of letters to Howells. "I don't mean that I am miserable," Twain wrote in February 1897; "no – worse than that, indifferent. Indifferent to nearly everything but work. I like that; I enjoy it, & stick to it. I do it without purpose & without ambition; merely for the love of it" (Twain and Howells 1960: vol. 2, 664). From Vienna a year later: "I couldn't get along without work now. I bury myself in it up to the ears. Long hours – 8 & 9 on a stretch, sometimes. And all the days, Sundays included. It isn't all for print, by any means, for much of it fails to suit me; 50,000 words of it in the past year. It was because of the deadness which invaded me when Susy died" (vol. 2, 670). And again in April 1899: "Man is not to me the respect-worthy person he was before; & so I have lost my pride in him & can't write gaily nor praisefully about him any more. And I don't intend to try. I mean to go on writing, for that is my best amusement, but I shan't print much" (vol. 2, 689).[4]

The therapy worked, up to a point, because all of the "private" texts, with the exception of *What Is Man?*, were conceived as fictions. Fiction beckoned because it seemed to promise daytime relief from night-time demons. And yet, in a paradox that I have already drawn, that very release brought with it a relaxing of the censors, and thus produced openings for the return of the repressed. That return just as inevitably brought an end to the cure, and with it to the writing itself. This was, as Peter Messent has, for other reasons, quite rightly observed, work that could not be finished (Messent 1997: 159). Mark Twain hardly recognized this pattern; yet once glimpsed, it is unmistakable.

Consider "Tom Sawyer's Conspiracy," an unfinished short novel initially undertaken in 1897, soon dropped about midway, and then resumed at intervals until 1902, when it was abandoned. The story took imaginative rise from an extended notebook entry in which Twain's childhood reminiscences pitch headlong into horrific memories of sex, cruelty, and violence, akin in tone to the contemporary "Villagers of 1840–43," but focused exclusively on the monstrous injustice of slavery (see Twain 1969b: 153–4, 375–7; Pettit 1974: 166). Here the famous Hannibal idyll gives way to deeply troubling intimations of moral complicity reminiscent of the Bombay section in *Following the Equator*, and more generally of Twain's well-documented guilt over the Southern mistreatment of slaves. From the midst of the horror, the plot that he finally settled on seemed relatively benign. Huck and Jim are to steal Tom, who is disguised as a slave, from the local slave-trader, Pat Bradish, and then to enjoy the chase and climactic torchlight parade that, they assume, will follow. But the plot takes a number of improbable turns, among them the discovery that Bradish is already holding a white man disguised as a slave; Jim's incarceration for Bradish's subsequent murder; and the last-minute revelation that the king and the duke are the real villains. As the result, what begins as a vintage Tom Sawyer prank is transformed into a narrative of greed, exploitation, and bloody racial violence. The seeming idyll thus collapses back into the guilty memories from which it was extracted, and which it strains quite unsuccessfully to displace.

The story relentlessly foregrounds the influence of Providence in mortal experience, a topic that first arises when Jim, sensibly suspicious of Tom's scheming, protests: "If you's gwyne to try to plan out sump'n dat Prov'dence ain't gwyne to 'prove of, den ole Jim got to pull out." Tom shrewdly persuades Jim that it is morally acceptable to "keep on planning out things till I find out which is the one he wants done" (Twain 1969b: 164) – arguing in effect that whatever happens will flow irresistibly from the divine will. This is of course Tom's way of declaring his intention to do exactly as he pleases, though he recurs regularly to the "wiser wisdom" governing his plans, and to what he describes as "the inscrutable ways that [the] conspiracy was watched over and took care of" (pp. 191, 184).

Twain's tireless attention to Providence in a tale of proliferating mischance serves to underscore the mysterious origins of recurrent scourges like slavery. Why, Twain seems to be asking, do such terrible things happen? In one mood, as we have seen, he did not hesitate to assign blame for all the world's woes to a malign creator. In another, however, he rejected such theological arguments as contemptible moral evasions. As he put it in his notebook, "There are many scape-goats for our sins, but the most popular is Providence" (MTP). He fell into this latter mood as he composed "Tom Sawyer's Conspiracy," with the result that the story unfolds as a sharply satirical retelling of the famous "evasion" at the end of *Huckleberry Finn*. The plot similarities are numerous and striking: Jim, now a legally free man, is once again in bondage, and once again offers only feeble resistance to Tom's grandiose – and very dangerous – schemes for his liberation; Huck is also skeptical, but – characteristically – goes along; the king and the duke figure prominently as villains; and a "happy ending," though unwritten, appears imminent. But Tom is much changed in this version of the story. Not content merely to exploit the adventurous potential of Jim's predicament, he is now delighted to learn that the black man has been falsely accused of murder, and takes active steps to confirm the charges and to have the captive sent downriver for sale into slavery. Through it all, he is callously indifferent to Jim's suffering, and rapturous over the happy alignment of providential designs with his own.

The effect of Tom's transformation is to obliterate entirely the impression proffered by *Huckleberry Finn* that his scheming is only so much boyish good fun. For now, unmistakably, Tom's "design" is uncannily of a piece with the worst of the inhumanity spawned by the callous, brutal, self-serving culture of race-slavery. Providence has nothing to do with it. This reality is brought home most emphatically in the discovery that Tom's conspiracy is precisely duplicated in the fraud perpetrated at Pat Bradish's cabin by the king and the duke. "Ain't it curious?" Tom reflects; "They got in ahead of us on our scheme all around" (Twain 1969b: 211). There is a similarly mordant irony at play in a detective's surmise that Tom's schemes are the creations of "a gigantic intelleck . . . prob'ly the worst man alive," the dread Murrell himself (p. 230). True, toward the very end of the unfinished narrative, Tom is brought to a reckoning at Jim's courtroom conviction for murder. In the nick of time, however, the king and the duke are shuffled on stage to take the blame. Jim is freed, Tom is a hero once more – but then, just as the happy ending rounds toward a climax, Huck falls silent, leaving the story unfinished. This time around, Twain knew better.

Conceived as a therapeutic distraction from troubled memories, "Tom Sawyer's Conspiracy" rapidly, improbably, almost perversely transforms itself into a meditation on the twisted social logic of American slavery. In suggesting that the narrative somehow does this to itself, I am echoing Twain's acknowledgement – in *Pudd'nhead Wilson* – that his stories were prone to such independence, and that in telling themselves they invariably progressed from humor to tragedy (Twain 1894: 309–10). This mysterious process is at intervals obliquely glimpsed in the text of "Tom Sawyer's Conspiracy," most notably when Huck compares "Tom's idea to plan out something to do" with his own "much easier and more comfortable" inclination to "let [things] happen their own way" (Twain 1969b: 164). Here as elsewhere, Twain was evidently of Huck's persuasion, though with predictably grave results, both for the boy in the story, and for the author in its telling. Such denials of agency obviously recapitulate the evasive arguments from providential design scattered through the narrative, and to which Twain was often drawn. Those arguments fail, of course, just as the evasive impulse that gave rise to the story fails to contain Twain's restive intimations of complicity in the tragic realities his narrative seems bound to disclose. But real and permanent relief is thwarted because the uncanny resurfacing of elements repressed in *Huckleberry Finn* yields no cathartic recognition. To be sure, the story's concluding evasion is notably indecisive, but it is also where Twain decided to let it end.

At least: temporarily. The guilty knowledge imperfectly evaded in "Tom Sawyer's Conspiracy" would rise again and again to the troubled surface of Twain's late fiction. Conceived and written during a period of extreme adversity in the mid-1890s, "Which Was the Dream?" is one of several unfinished narratives in which he sought relief from his own nightmarish reality by construing it fictionally as a terrible dream from which he would eventually awaken. Invariably, however, such therapeutic flights foundered under the weight of guilt-laden intrusions from the personal past. In "Which Was the Dream?" Twain attempts to submerge his own life in a fictionalized portrait of his friend and great moral hero, Ulysses S. Grant, and thereby to earn a kind of absolution for his own failures in war and business. But once the nightmare of personal ruin has commenced, there is no return; instead, the narrative is left unfinished, as if to suggest that the moral acquittal of an awakening into Grant's reality is imaginatively beyond reach. The fictional fragment "Indiantown" is similarly drawn off course into an autobiographical self-portrait of a moral hypocrite. And the unfinished "Three Thousand Years Among the Microbes," written in 1905, according to Paine, as a mental diversion from guilty memories of Livy's death (Paine 1912: 1238–9), affords its narrator an interlude of moral "comfort . . . and an easy conscience" (Twain 1966: 527) soon dissipated in a fantasy of all-consuming greed reminiscent of Twain's years on the mining frontier.

But the longest and perhaps the most revealing of the unfinished dream narratives is "Which Was It?" Written at intervals between 1899 and 1903, and drawn from the same mold as "Which Was the Dream?," the story centers on the life of George Harrison, who is blessed by fortune with wealth, reputation, and a happy home, all of which are lost when he falls into a guilt-ridden nightmare of debt and family disgrace. Once again, the narrative is drawn ineluctably deeper and deeper into darkness, where it ends quite inconclusively, and without restoring Harrison, as originally planned, to his happy "waking" reality. Once again, then, we are impressed with the compelling authority of moral catastrophe in Mark Twain's creative imagination. While there is no gainsaying his persistent therapeutic impulse to contrast waking prosperity with a passing dream of personal degradation, we cannot fail to recognize the equal persistence with which his characteristically subversive narratives find their own, independent way from comedy to tragedy. Twain's commitment to his benign, therapeutic story of descent and recovery was evidently quite superficial; the deeper, sub-intentional motive driving his seemingly errant narrative was guilt, from which, just as evidently, there was no permanent relief.

I am arguing, of course, that "Which Was It?" is clearly and substantially autobiographical. George Harrison's waking world is closely modeled on the novelist's life with his family in their famous Hartford mansion in earlier, much happier times. Unlike Twain, Harrison has not yet fallen from paradise; he "has never had any troubles or sorrows or calamities to rouse up the literary fires that are slumbering in him and make them burst their bonds and find expression" (Twain 1966: 179). Soon enough, though, in his terrible dream, he will learn from bitter personal experience that there is "something fearfully disintegrating to character in the loss of money" (p. 195). Guilty self-loathing and hatred of life will overtake him, and with them the impulse to take pen in hand – "for the easement it may give me," he reflects, "to look myself in the face and confess whither I have lately drifted, and what I am become!" (p. 183). Twain's writing cure, his remorseful sense of financial failure, and his need to confess, are strikingly manifest here. But nothing quite prepares us for the uncanny self-revelation that immediately follows. "But I cannot do it in the first person," Harrison continues, echoing Twain's frustration with autobiography:

> I must spare myself that shame; *must* is the right word; for I could not say in the first person the things I ought to say, even if I tried. I could not say "*I* did such and such things;" it would revolt me, and the pen would refuse. No, I will write as if it were a literary tale, a history, a romance – a tale I am telling about another man, a man who is nothing to me, and whose weak and capricious character I may freely turn inside out and expose, without the sense of being personally under the knife. I will make of myself a stranger, and say "George Harrison did so and so." (p. 183)

Twain perfectly understood Harrison's need to confess, but he knew just as well that the truth would elude him so long as he attempted to tell it directly, as if he were "personally under the knife." Did Twain recognize himself in this most self-revealing portrait of Harrison? There is no certainty in such matters, though I am strongly inclined to think that he did not. The play of unconscious processes in his writing is pervasive and well documented.[5] Nor is Harrison's tale of personal failure even remotely similar in its specific circumstances to the confession that Twain felt reluctantly compelled to make. Yet despite the fact that he was probably blind to it – and indeed, quite probably because of that blindness – an intimate kinship between the writer and his fictional alter ego is clearly discernible in Harrison's tormented moral reflections, the correlative in fiction to Twain's real-life moral anguish. Harrison's shrewdly evasive literary strategy is thus uncanny because it exactly mirrors the one that Twain has repressed; the story that follows is uncanny in precisely the same way. It is yet another instance of the pleasurably evasive "writing cure" inadvertently opening opportunities for the return of the submerged impulse to confess. The result is yet another narrative with a mind of its own, that veers so irresistibly toward dark self-revelation as to be unfinishable.

Harrison's memories unfold in a series of movements comprising personally compromising plot complications accompanied by compensating moral reflections. More simply, he is ever morally on the defensive against what events reveal. The first movement finds Harrison entangled in a dizzyingly complex web of murder and deception that ensnares leading members of the entire community, and illustrates that human beings, no matter how principled and compassionate, are in thrall to the perversities of circumstance and temperament. "It's a rotten world!" Harrison concludes, and "we're all rotten together, and most of us don't suspect it" (Twain 1966: 223). The majority live in ignorance of their degradation, and of the guilt it spawns, because they take shelter in plausible evasions. One especially greedy character, for example, uses what she regards as justified revenge, "as a pretext-salve for her conscience's protesting dignity" (p. 223). Harrison takes refuge in kindred moral evasions, but they are no proof against the inward gnawing of guilt, which brings him to the brink of despair and suicide. "Ah, Moral Law," he complains, as his own guilt grows heavier and heavier, "you are a hard trader" (p. 236). Here, quite clearly, we are in company at one remove with the Mark Twain who had suffered terrible personal losses, and even more terrible guilt as the result. At the end of the first movement, which was the point at which Twain set his manuscript aside late in 1899, Harrison is bitterly resigned to a life of ceaseless moral anguish. Because he is too much a coward either to come clean with the world or to commit suicide, there is no hope for him. "Just for that one departure from rectitude," he complains, "I am to swim chin-deep in shames and sorrows for the rest of my days" (p. 260).

It is not unlikely that this first phase of composition ended as it did because Harrison's straining after relief from remorse had reached such an emphatic dead end. Variations on the same pattern recur in subsequent movements of the narrative. When Twain resumed composition, he turned, through Harrison, to the question whether there can be "worse luck than *death*?" (Twain 1966: 262). The question is of special significance for Harrison, who finds that he cannot clear his mind of guilty memories. "They flocked to the front as fast as they were banished, and with every return they seemed to come refreshed and reinforced for their bitter work upon his conscience" (p. 267). So painful is his suffering that he longs for the imagined relief of the grave, and reflects bitterly, when his wish is denied: "that charity is not for me" (p. 273). Twain was of course overtaken periodically by similar, guilt-laden longings for death. "Pity is for the living," he observes in *Following the Equator*, "envy is for the dead" (Twain 1897: 184). A notebook entry for March 19, 1903 accords praise to "Adam, man's benefactor – he gave him all he has ever received that was worth having – Death" (Twain 1935: 381).

Renewed prospects for relief from guilt alternate with dashed hopes in a pattern running through several subsequent movements of the narrative. Harrison is buoyed up at intervals by the crank philosophizing of a local eccentric, by surges of salutary anger, by humor, and by the prospect of vast inherited wealth. As the narrative advances, new characters are introduced and the plot grows increasingly complex, though the strong, organizing emphasis on strategies of moral evasion persists. At one point Harrison, who remains central to the narrative's enduring thematic concerns, arrives at an especially blissful state of denial. "If only I could feel like this, all the time!" he exclaims:

And why shouldn't I? Troubles are only mental; it is the mind that manufactures them, and the mind can forget them, banish them, abolish them. Mine shall do it. Nothing is needed but resolution, firmness, determination. I will exert it. It is the only wisdom.

I will put all these goblins, these unrealities behind me, I have been their slave long
enough; if I have done wrong I have atoned for it, I have paid the cost and more, I have
sweated blood, I have earned my freedom, I have earned peace and a redeemed and contented spirit, and why should I not have them? (Twain 1966: 406–7)

In Harrison's accelerating, finally rather desperate straining after moral redemption we cannot fail to be reminded of Twain's own equally urgent but frustrated
longings. The passage faithfully captures the spirit of one whose resolute skepticism did nothing to dampen his enthusiasm for contemporary mind cure – he "had
great faith in mind over matter," Paine observes (Paine 1912: 1022); who praised
Mary Baker Eddy, a woman he otherwise despised as a charlatan, for liberating
her followers from "the black hours" that "put a curse on the life of every human
being" (Twain 1973: 268); who viewed his dream writing as a species of therapy;
and who wrote (in "Three Thousand Years Among the Microbes") that "there was no
such thing as substance – substance was a fiction of Mortal Mind, an illusion" (Twain
1966: 492). The *locus classicus* among many kindred utterances is Satan's declaration,
toward the end of *The Mysterious Stranger*, that *"Nothing exists*; all is a dream . . . And
You are but a *Thought* – a vagrant Thought, a useless Thought, a homeless Thought,
wandering forlorn among the empty eternities!" This is saving news, Satan insists, for
it releases humans from the tragedy of history, and frees them to create realities of
their own choosing. "Dream other dreams," he counsels, "and better!" (Twain 1969c:
404).

We know for a certainty that Satan's liberating solipsism had its origins in the desperate need for relief from guilt that overtook Twain at moments of family tragedy.
His consciousness at such times was so heavily laden with remorse that he recoiled
into alternative realities. On the first anniversary of Susy's death he took refuge in the
thought that the "calamity [was] not a reality, but a dream, which will pass, – *must*
pass."[6] Livy's death prompted the retreat to variations on the same consoling illusion,
most movingly expressed in a letter to Joseph Twichell in which he explains that
during substantial periods of each day he regards the world "as being NON-
EXISTENT. That is, that there is *nothing*. That there is no God and no universe; that
there is only empty space, and in it a lost and homeless and wandering and compan-
ionless and indestructible *Thought*. And that I am that thought." He goes on to add
that during a "part of each day Livy is a dream" as well, "and has never existed."[7]
Here, then, is the ultimate cure for insupportable remorse: self-removal to eternal solitude in infinite space, and the deliverance of the deceased to the safety (from himself!)
of non-existence. Translated almost verbatim to the conclusion of *The Mysterious
Stranger*, this famous passage is the surest evidence of Twain's profound personal
investment in the evasive moral thematics of his unpublished late writing.

But there is a final turn to Harrison's harried narrative. For into the very midst of
his resolution to clear his mind of all discord, and to dream better dreams, steps Jasper,
a twice enslaved, twice self-liberated free black who surfaces abruptly, as if out of
nowhere, into the narrative. Jasper's advent is sudden and shocking because he is the

possessor of carefully guarded, profoundly damaging knowledge. As it happens, he is the sole possessor of the evidence that Harrison is guilty of murder. This is his leverage on the white man. Even more significantly, Jasper is a stubborn reminder of the guilt for the crime of slavery deeply repressed in the white psyche. His principal motive is to seek a just reprisal for the generations of brutal mistreatment and injustice endured by his people. "Dey's a long bill agin de lowdown ornery white race," he lectures his hostage, "en you's a-gwyneter to settle it" (Twain 1966: 415). Harrison's penalty is to change places with a lowly slave, and thus to experience at first hand the pain and humiliation that he once imposed, with unruffled moral complacency, on other human beings. When Jasper forces Harrison to change places, he gives outward expression to yet another subversive secret, the much deeper interchangeability of their identities. As the son of a slave woman and her master, Harrison's uncle, Jasper is blood kin; and as a party to Harrison's most guardedly guilty secrets, he is the white man's psychological double. So much, then, for the fictions of law and custom enforcing racial difference.

Mark Twain could not finish "Which Was It?" because the morally evasive impulse driving his narrative reaches an absolute impasse in the discovery, quite imperfectly grasped, that the personal guilt haunting his protagonist is inextricably bound up with the guilt of the entire nation. Just as Jasper is the final, insurmountable obstacle to Harrison's achievement of moral repose (it now makes perfect sense that it was Jasper who, much earlier in the narrative, asked whether there can be "worse luck than *death*?"), so slavery is the irreducible contradiction in America's redemptive errand into the wilderness. Beneath all the other personal and collective calamities there persists the memory, at once unbearable and irrepressible, of the terrible crimes against humanity gathered up and given voice by the former slave. This is a nightmare so real that Harrison cannot awaken from it. Nor could Mark Twain, as its persistent resurfacing in his work, and most especially in the late writing, demonstrates. The "why" of the great humorist's gravitation to this most tragic chapter in America's national history is a complex topic, best reserved for another day. Suffice it here to acknowledge his major role in restoring the moral challenge of race-slavery to the foreground of the national consciousness. This said, I hasten to add that it was a moral challenge he was himself able to address only intermittently, and often when it arose unsummoned and quite disruptively into his consciousness. We are witness to just such startled, reluctant, and decidedly incomplete moral encounters in the Bombay section of *Following the Equator*, in the subversive racial thematics of "Tom Sawyer's Conspiracy," and in the standstill produced by Jasper's abrupt appearance in "Which Was It?" These unfinished narratives dramatize in their action, their telling, and even in their reception, the great difficulty that Americans have had in addressing the morally unfinished business of slavery. Now, a century after Mark Twain labored with such brilliant confusion to come to terms with his conscience on this vexed issue, we understand better perhaps the dynamics of guilt in the national psyche, though we have yet to answer fully the redemptive impulse which he helped us to recognize as uniquely our own.

NOTES

1 Joseph Twichell to Mark Twain, December 9, 1901, Mark Twain Papers, Bancroft Library, University of California, Berkeley. Hereafter references to materials in the Mark Twain Papers (MTP) will be given parenthetically in the text.
2 See especially the work of Dolmetsch (1992), Gillman (1989), Harris (1982), Macnaughton (1979), Marotti (1990), Messent (1997), Michelson (1995), and Weinstein (1995).
3 Macnaughton (1979: 19–20) advances ample evidence on this score.
4 See also Twain and Howells (1960: vol. 2, 698); Hill (1973: 48, 50).
5 See Robinson (1995).
6 Mark Twain to Wayne MacVeagh, August 22, 1897 (MTP).
7 Mark Twain to Joseph Twichell, July 28, 1904, in William M. Gibson's introduction to Twain 1969c (p. 30).

REFERENCES AND FURTHER READING

Brooks, Van Wyck (1920). *The Ordeal of Mark Twain*. New York: Dutton.

Clemens, Clara (1931). *My Father, Mark Twain*. New York: Harper & Bros.

DeVoto, Bernard (1942). *Mark Twain at Work*. Cambridge, Mass.: Harvard University Press.

Dolmetsch, Carl (1992). *Our Famous Guest: Mark Twain in Vienna*. Athens: University of Georgia Press.

Gillman, Susan (1989). *Dark Twins: Imposture and Identity in Mark Twain's America*. Chicago: University of Chicago Press.

Harris, Susan K. (1982). *Mark Twain's Escape from Time: A Study of Patterns and Images*. Columbia: University of Missouri Press.

Hill, Hamlin (1973). *Mark Twain: God's Fool*. New York: Harper & Row.

Hoffman, Andrew (1997). *Inventing Mark Twain: The Lives of Samuel Langhorne Clemens*. New York: Morrow.

Howells, William Dean (1968). *My Mark Twain*. In *Literary Friends and Acquaintance*, ed. David F. Hiatt and Edwin H. Cady, 256–322. Bloomington: Indiana University Press.

Lystra, Karen (2004). *Dangerous Intimacy: The Untold Story of Mark Twain's Final Years*. Berkeley: University of California Press.

Macnaughton, William R. (1979). *Mark Twain's Last Years as a Writer*. Columbia: University of Missouri Press.

Marotti, Maria Ornella (1990). *The Duplicating Imagination: Twain and the Twain Papers*. University Park: Pennsylvania State University Press.

Messent, Peter (1997). *Mark Twain*. Basingstoke: Macmillan.

Michelson, Bruce (1995). *Mark Twain on the Loose: A Comic Writer and the American Self*. Amherst: University of Massachusetts Press.

Paine, Albert Bigelow (1912). *Mark Twain: A Biography. The Personal and Literary Life of Samuel Langhorne Clemens*, 3 vols. New York and London: Harper & Bros.

Pettit, Arthur G. (1974). *Mark Twain and the South*. Lexington: University Press of Kentucky.

Robinson, Forrest G. (1995). "An 'Unconscious and Profitable Cerebration'": Mark Twain and Literary Intentionality," *Nineteenth-Century Literature* 50, 357–80.

Salomon, Roger Blaine (1961). *Twain and the Image of History*. New Haven: Yale University Press.

Twain, Mark (1924). *Mark Twain's Autobiography*, 2 vols., ed. Albert Bigelow Paine. New York: Harper & Bros.

Twain, Mark (1935). *Mark Twain's Notebook*, ed. Albert Bigelow Paine. New York: Harper & Bros.

Twain, Mark (1940). *Mark Twain in Eruption*, ed. Bernard DeVoto. New York: Harper & Bros.

Twain, Mark (1959). *The Autobiography of Mark Twain*, ed. Charles Neider. New York: Harper & Bros.

Twain, Mark (1966). *Mark Twain's Which Was the Dream: and Other Symbolic Writings of the Later Years*, ed. John S. Tuckey. Berkeley: University of California Press.

Twain, Mark (1969a). *Mark Twain's Correspondence with Henry Huttleston Rogers 1893–1909*, ed. Lewis Leary. Berkeley: University of California Press.

Twain, Mark (1969b). *Mark Twain's Hannibal, Huck and Tom*, ed. Walter Blair. Berkeley: University of California Press.

Twain, Mark (1969c). *Mark Twain's Mysterious Stranger Manuscripts*, ed. William M. Gibson. Berkeley: University of California Press.

Twain, Mark (1973). *What Is Man? and Other Philosophical Writings*, ed. Paul Baender. Berkeley: University of California Press.

Twain, Mark, and Howells, William Dean (1960). *Mark Twain–Howells Letters: The Correspondence of Samuel L. Clemens and William Dean Howells, 1872–1910*, 2 vols., ed. Henry Nash Smith and William M. Gibson. Cambridge, Mass.: Belknap.

Weinstein, Cindy (1995). *The Literature of Labor and the Labors of Literature: Allegory in Nineteenth-Century American Fiction*. New York: Cambridge University Press.

Zaccara, Jennifer L. (2001). "Mark Twain, Isabel Lyon, and the 'Talking Cure'." In Laura E. Skandera Trombley and Michael J. Kiskis (eds.), *Constructing Mark Twain: New Directions in Scholarship*, 101–21. Columbia: University of Missouri Press.

PART VI
Mark Twain's Humor

31

Mark Twain's Visual Humor

Louis J. Budd

The minds that study *belles lettres* – literature, in relaxed discourse – have self-selected for appreciating the written language, humankind's exchange by inscribed words rather than visual statements such as gestures and facial signals. So scholarly–critical approaches to Mark Twain, focusing on his written humor, analyze even his speeches as stable texts, essentially all there as printed. They mostly ignore his continual, insistent use of visual jokes. Critics who do acknowledge this aspect of his work feel embarrassed for him, or at least apologize for it as mercenary and in any case so negligible that a few examples can mercifully close the subject. For the most deplorable instances they go to his drawings, which he started on the *Hannibal Daily Journal* in 1853 and which he sometimes tried to work into his books once *The Innocents Abroad* had earned him the clout of a bestselling author. Yet, proving the strength of his drive toward the visual, he still struggled at drawing comically after his fame and income as a humorist had accelerated into a self-feeding cycle that needed no extra fuel. So, without claiming to recover a national treasure, looking sympathetically at Twain's visual humor will better explain his popularity during his lifetime and his lasting power since then, will deepen our image of Twain both as a humorist and as a personality, and will even sensitize us further to his major texts – ultimately, of course, the enduring Mark Twain.

Before I set out upon demonstrating the extent of Twain's visual humor, six disclaimers will sharpen the issue, though they may concede more than they should.

First, that house in the Nook Farm enclave of Hartford amuses hit-and-run journalists, who like to describe it as gaudy in shape as well as spirit, looping back to his swagger as a pilot on the Mississippi. But Twain and his sedate wife had picked a fashionable architect who would have disdained involving his firm with a – literally – standing joke. Feeling and acting proud of their taste after they moved in, they kept adding upscale features and furniture even after they retreated to Europe in 1891. When, after ten years abroad, they considered moving back in (without daughter Susy), they decided not to ruffle their memories of an imposingly upper-middle-class idyll. When they eventually accepted that they should sell the house, they fretted more about finding an appreciative buyer than about getting top dollar. People eager to condescend to Twain's tastes have to ride a sounder high-horse.

Second, the bush of white hair and the muscular mustaches that he flaunted in old age did not aim primarily to amuse. He came to treat his hair so solicitously that psychoanalysts should dig deeper into its roots. After 1900 cartoonists competitively made it a prop more prominent even than his cigars or corn-cob pipe. But many studio portraits show his hair meticulously coiffed, and the official photograph from the banquet for his seventieth birthday shows a groomed head anticipating the posters for the first movie stars. Within swings of mood and a liking for bohemian ways, Twain, once he could afford it – as a steamboat pilot, to begin with – wanted to dress strikingly but impressively. Admittedly, by 1906 cartoonists focused so obviously on his hair that he probably cultivated (that is, sometimes left untrimmed) the flowing effect, with shaggy eyebrows, under the caps, derbies, and other headgear he enjoyed trying out. Still, if young Sam had felt defensive about his reddish top, the elderly Clemens, exacting about the daily washing of his white halo, wore it more proudly than slyly.

Third, still more seriously, Twain committed himself to that white suit not to amuse the public but above all to satisfy his psychic needs. Of course, readings of those needs clash loudly, amplified recently by fresh inferences about how gender is inflected through dress. But any theories about that suit should recognize that the crux was the wearing of it during the northern winter in cities heated and powered from coal and therefore grimy to the touch, sooty to the eye. More often than most upper-status men, yet raising no ripple of comments, Twain had sported white summer "ducks" or linen suits since the early 1870s. Actually, his most southern days as a steamboat pilot had already lured him into white ducks. By venturing a white suit in winter – though less regularly than legend now claims – Twain materialized a double helix of motives.

Once he settled down to family life, a concern for cleanliness edged toward a mild phobia – within a cultural web where a preoccupation with questions of sanitation and personal hygiene had seen humor dwindle away except for middle-class jokes about the unwashed poor. Dark clothing, notoriously, harbors – that is, hides – dirt. More positively, Clemens/Twain had always preferred bright colors, partly because of recurring ambitions to rate as a dandy in the contemporary lingo of fashion (and to compete with Bret Harte), and also because of still stronger tendencies to enjoy the public's stare. In demotic rather than clinical terms he was born a show-off, comfortable with Tom Sawyer as exhibitionist. William Dean Howells remembered trailing a deliberately visible Twain along Fifth Avenue in Manhattan; Albert Bigelow Paine had to take him through Peacock Alley at the Willard Hotel in Washington DC. But Twain, alert beneath his vanity, knew that both plebeians and tribunes of proper behavior sneered at men parading bright colors. So wearing that white suit in winter still took prolonged self-encouragement once wife Olivia's restraining influence ended in June 1904. A year and a half later, at the gala banquet for his birthday, he declared the right of a seventy-year-old to do as he pleases. Yet not until December 1906 did that white suit strut into the headlines – at a hearing in the capital on copyright. Most immediately, therefore, it made a political (or public relations) rather than a humorous statement. Conflicted feelings must have pulsed through Twain at the unveiling, and popular reaction – never fully determinable – surely included amusement. Daughter Clara would recall him enjoying his "doangivadam" suit. Today it does set off smiles first of all, I think. Nevertheless, whatever its instinctive meanings for his friends and publics, approaching it as visual humor shrinks its significance for Twain himself.

Fourth, heavily illustrated books about Twain will include that frontal photograph of him bare down to the waist – trimly built and hairy-chested. It dependably raises a smile at his openness, and I've heard hearty joking about it. But most probably Twain never meant for the public to peer at that photograph. The safest guess ties it to the dignified bust that his protégé Karl Gerhardt was making for the frontispiece used in *Adventures of Huckleberry Finn*. Visual as well as cultural sensitivities will give rise to different conclusions about whether it is humorous, either as clowning or as eccentric self-assurance. So far, there has been surprisingly little analysis of attitudes toward nudity in the later nineteenth century. Though the earliest photograph yet recovered – of young Sam as a typesetter – may have intended visual humor, up until the 1890s Twain faced the camera as a tool for making images of him worthy to give to family and admirers and to leave for posterity. Napoleon Sarony, specializing in celebrities, gave Oscar Wilde garish, almost sensational effects in 1882. But Twain's sittings for him in 1884 and 1895 produced solemn, almost grim portraits.

Fifth, keeping my own focus sharp calls for passing over the sight-gags in Twain's texts: that is, in the sequence of words that the reader follows. Like every attractive writer (and talker), Twain – from his personal letters to novels and especially travel books – evokes persons and events that raise a smile or chuckle when visualized mentally. Occasionally he downright insisted, as with the nose-thumbing by the petrified man. Happy to go along with the tastes of his public, he took increasing interest in choosing the illustrators for his works and then the scenes they would treat, sometimes urging them to soften his gritty realism with comedy. Readers are again learning to want editions with the original drawings, which bring them closer to Twain's intentions as well as his genius. Prime exhibits pop up from *The Adventures of Tom Sawyer*, *Huckleberry Finn*, and *A Connecticut Yankee in King Arthur's Court* (the knights touring as billboards or playing baseball in armor). In 1877 Twain proposed to cartoonist Thomas Nast that they tour as a team, with him commenting on the drawings Nast would create in what, given Nast's assertive graphics, would be essentially a program of sight-gags.

But Twain energizes imaginings without any help from drawings. Instancing scenes of "anachronistic incongruity" from *A Connecticut Yankee*, M. Thomas Inge, an expert on the comic strip, judges that "the reader can easily visualize them for his own amusement, suggesting that Twain himself had a talent for creating visual humor with words" (Inge 1994: 169–70). Since Twain's favorite modes – narrative, anecdote, reportage – function through concrete details, they keep transmuting into persons or scenes in the reader's mind; since his texts so continually suggest comic tableaux, Twain evidently thought to himself in such ways, apprehending people more kinetically than psychologically. Autobiographical by instinct, he created vivid, comic walk-ons of himself too. His illustrators, with not just his approval but his encouragement, exploited those episodes, particularly for his travel books. He praised to his fiancée as *"good"* the drawing ("Return in War-Paint", *The Innocents Abroad*, ch. 13) that made him a Western trapper brandishing head-feathers, bow and arrow, and a tomahawk; his publisher, therefore, used it for further advertising. Cumulatively, Twain cooperated in so many comic illustrations of himself that they amount perhaps to a major aspect of his visual humor after all.

Finally, sixth, Twain supplied so many head-on attempts at visual humor that we can dodge the questionable instances. Apparently he did think up "The Trouble Will Begin at 8" poster to hype one of his earliest lectures; probably he at least helped with later variations on his punchline. As late as 1906, for a pro bono lecture, he sketched a come-on poster suited to his iconic status. Perhaps he suggested rather than merely approved the crude graphics in the promos for his self-pasting scrapbooks. Evidently the caption "Twins of Genius" for the tour with George Washington Cable came from him as entrepreneur. When the box office dipped below his greedy hopes he proposed more hype, such as sending out sandwich-board men. That idea typifies another questionable mode, which experts in neuro-cognitive interplay will have to dissect for the originary force of any visual humor that resulted. They can go on to decide who gets what kind of credit for the visual–verbal objects – coffee mugs, T-shirts, bookmarks, tote bags – costing more because they carry an admired saying (or merely an image) of Twain. Twain himself, before belatedly trying to collect licencing fees, would have grinned on seeing them. However, he deserves little direct credit for the caricatures of him that started running in 1870 and increased steadily along with his fame and the technology for displaying them in newspapers and magazines.

Still, after all my disclaimers, a spread of materials deserves closer tabulating and analysis that cannot help verging into speculation.

"The Openly Dramatized Personality"

While the day-to-day aura of Sam Clemens's boyhood has faded beyond sound conjecture, scattered clues indicate a look-at- and listen-to-me stance. By early maturity his body language had a self-conscious verve that elicited smiles. Long before the white suit he made himself stand out, more amusingly or even intriguingly than imposingly. As a steamboat pilot he evidently struck landsmen as jaunty, trailing laughter. During his Nevada and California years, contemporary references – cued by the tones of his writing as well as by his persona Mark Twain – usually aimed for a jovial effect implying that it complemented rather than satirized its target. His matured walk struck people as loose-limbed – rolling or shambling or "undulating" (from appreciative W. D. Howells). At some level of mind, and only at times but recurringly so, Twain's manner must have alerted amusement. He compounded his effect with clothing – a sealskin coat that impressed in divergent ways Howells and Lilian Aldrich, various caps and hats and even a beret, and the scarlet Oxford gown for non-academic outings. He caught Matthew Arnold's eye across the room at a reception. People noticed him quickly – with differing feelings, to be sure. Most common though uncommonly well stated was another passenger's feeling on a transatlantic steamer in 1878. "Every feature of the face, indeed, backs up the twist in his speech. There is no incongruity between the man and his work. Everything about him becomes droll, his humor being a part of the body as well as of the spirit within" (Budd 1983: 73).

As early as January 1863, Twain admitted in print – actually, bragged about – "a sort of talent for posturing" (Twain 1979: 185). Especially out West, that meant behaving in the style of Davy Crockett or P. T. Barnum or George Train, who paraded alone in public with a sly smile that said you and I know this is a put-on but it entertains both you and me. While several factors dampened Twain's volume and pitch as he settled into New England, just before his death Henry Mills Alden, having long negotiated with him for the House of Harper, candidly named the "evident compulsion, however genially complied with, of the openly dramatized personality" (Alden 1910: 579.) In the parlor Twain could transform himself into the star character of his anecdote; on shipboard he joined and often led the games to kill time. For New Year's Eve in 1906 he acted out dour sobriety while his conjoined twin got drunk. Such private capers, he knew, would prove semi-public because of his celebrity. But having a larger audience encouraged him. In 1881, on a train from Hartford to West Point, he put on General W. T. Sherman's coat and hat to deliver "an incomprehensible speech at stops along the way" (Leon 1996: 53). When attending a masked ball in Paris as Uncle Remus he doubtless made his walk and gestures conform as much as his speech. When, at age seventy-two, he weighed himself at the train station in Baltimore, he expected the reporters to transmit that tableau to their clientele as another burst of the amusing spontaneity they were always hoping for.

The school of Erving Goffman would hold up Twain as a consummate exhibit of self-framing. Still, however disciplined, however protective the maneuvers we all deploy to promulgate our social image, his comic impulses kept bursting through. His rarefied self-consciousness had early made him a connoisseur of visual presentation and therefore of acting and actors. In family life he put gusto into parlor theatricals and charades, happy to dress outrageously as needed. Predictably, he had started as early as the mid-1860s to try writing drama.[1] But all such activities precessed into comedy, as much physical or visual as verbal. On stage, Mulberry Sellers postures for laughs as he enthuses about there being "millions in it!" For *Ah Sin*, which hoped for synergy from blending Twain's humor with Bret Harte's, he enjoyed coaching the cast. Writing "Cap'n Simon Wheeler, The Amateur Detective" (1877) and "Colonel Sellers as a Scientist" (1883), he wasted much time on farce too thick for even late nineteenth-century impresarios. Such pell-mell plots, with geysers of dialogue, may seem more aural than visual, but they work much better seen than read. Though in his Vienna months Twain tried both to translate and to write tragedies, he finished "Is He Dead?" – puffed by the University of California Press in 2004 as his humor "operating at its most energetic" – with "gleeful antics." Practitioners of the might-have-been guess that Twain could have succeeded as an actor instead of a playwright. If so, broad comedy would have been his forte.

Twain's humor outed itself no matter where he was or how he was supposed to behave. His "Advice to Youth" for Boston's Saturday Morning Club soared away into irreverent, almost anarchic burlesque. Meditating the death of daughter Jean led to wondering: "Shall I ever be cheerful again, happy again?" His honest self conceded: "Yes. And soon . . . My temperament has never allowed my spirits to remain depressed long at a time" (Paine 1912: 1552). Richard Lowry shrewdly decides that "what most fundamentally distinguishes" Twain "from his contemporaries is the degree to which he employed narrative to sustain his humor rather than . . . employing humor to sustain narrative" (Lowry 1996: 11). So he launched into visual humor whenever, however he could; or rather, his visual humor constantly pressed for venting.

My point could quit here if the consensus of Twain criticism had allowed it more prominence. But too few analyses of his texts acknowledge that he could seldom talk or write without somehow spending his comic urge. To bring the books to a sounder balance, I will detail his three clearest uses of visual humor.

Comic Drawings

The simplest line (no pun) of Twain's visual humor points to his drawings, known to his devotees but rarely considered and inadequately totaled up. Using crude materials, he produced three yet cruder woodcuts for brother Orion's *Hannibal Daily Journal* in 1853 that were little noticed by the immediate world, much less remembered. But he scored big with his childishly drawn, obtusely misinformed "Map of the Fortifications of Paris" in September 1870, keyed to the Franco-Prussian War (Twain 1992a: 474–5). It ran twice in his *Buffalo Express*, which also boosted it as a broadside; then the *Galaxy*, a popular monthly, presented it with embellishments; soon after, several pamphlets pirated it. Naturally, Twain strained for a follow-up with a portrait of "William III. King of Prussia," embedded in commentary even more heavy-handed. He probably felt he had added another ring to his circus as humorist. Though a professional artist perfected the sketch of Sellers's map for a railroad in *The Gilded Age*, Twain could consider himself the creator. Nobody in 1876 or now could bother about the credit for "Tom as an Artist" in *Tom Sawyer* (ch. 6). But for *A Tramp Abroad* Twain enthused to crony Joseph Twichell: "I shall make from 10 to 20 illustrations . . . with my own (almighty rude and crude) pencil, and shall say in the title page that some of the pictures in the book are from original drawings by the author" (Twain 1967: 110–11).[2] Thanks to Beverly David, who has led the overdue study of the illustrations in Twain's books, we know now that *A Tramp Abroad* worked in about 11 (depending on how we count) of his drawings, which squarely hits the level heralded in his letter to Twichell. Since *Life on the Mississippi* aimed higher both in format and in historical significance, Twain did not wheel out his full comic repertoire. Fortunately, where it could have served again, he did not care to supplement E. W. Kemble for *Huckleberry Finn* or Dan Beard for the few books after that. However, he critiqued both of them closely, as he had done with the artists for his previous books. And he insisted that they supply humor for the eyes. Unfortunately, he had no chance to object, if he wanted, to the racist drawings in *Pudd'nhead Wilson* that fitted the rawest years of Jim Crow debasement. The drawings he himself supplied, instructing that they serve as "chaptertops," got shelved, to the good of aesthetic standards at least (see McKeithan 1961: 16–17).

By the time of *Following the Equator* (1897), the technology could print either photographs or drawings so attractively that Twain wisely did not distract buyers from the first-rate artists pointing up his content. Nevertheless, in spite of his increasingly dignified celebrity, he itched to draw amusingly. "How To Make History Dates Stick" (1899; 1914), ostensibly leveled at children, invented pretexts for needing 26 of his fumbling illustrations.[3] During his wife's prolonged illness in 1902 he "sent in many illustrated notes. Usually they were would-be caricature-portraits of friends" (Clemens 1932: 236). Very private, of course. But his "Amended Obituaries" soon went ostentatiously public, appearing in the mass-circulation *Harper's Weekly* and the *New York World* and then in another magazine. Announcing a pseudo-contest for the most fitting obituary of himself, it offered and displayed a misshapen self-portrait as the prize (Twain 1902: 1704).[4] In 1903 that display was dimmed by his two-part "Instructions in Art (With Illustrations by the Author)" in which the commentary, supposedly inflated by unearned pomposity, fell flatter than the nine drawings that aimed – in the spirit of latter-day camp – at being so bad as to be good.[5] Only a mind that could compose several worthless manuscripts in between stints on *Huckleberry Finn* could bother with this lead balloon when financially airborne.

Twain strained so often to draw humorously that fantasies of success in this mode must have pulled him on while second looks tugged him back. Perhaps his deliberate clumsiness aimed to blur the fact that he couldn't do better. Perhaps he convinced himself that this ineptitude was a fresh way of satirizing the high-art tradition and especially the criticism perpetuating it, which irritated as much as it intimidated him. Whatever his motives, "Instructions in Art" could, 23 years after *A Tramp Abroad*, revert to the level on which he had chortled to Twichell that his drawings gave him "the belly-ache to look at them" or had postured to his publisher that "I've had a good deal of trouble with these things and thrown a world of mighty poor talent into them" (Twain 1967: 111, 115).[6] So, fundamentally, Twain's sense of humor had to keep testing every outlet, even one blocked by his mostly enviable genes.

Deadpan Frills

The most effective line of Twain's visual humor runs through his techniques as a raconteur, public speaker, and lecturer – that is, as a performer who mastered the deadpan

style. Of course, that is the most telling way to put across a joke: it holds off the listener's anticipatory smile, relaxing the psychic–physical tensions that the punchline
should release suddenly. But in Twain's ordinary behavior – an oxymoron? – spontaneity kept erupting. Typically, his irreverence started spurting through the prayer-
book piety of his letters courting Olivia Langdon. Though his psychic agenda did
encourage his drawl, the deadpan took practiced discipline. During his palmiest years
as a performer he refined it continually. By the time of his world tour it had to inter-
face with his emergent prestige as a belletrist, but he kept using an amusingly low-
key entrance and kept fine-tuning his perplexed pauses. Studying his texts as verbal
constructs underestimates that visual dimension reporters usually tried to describe.
For Twain's Western lectures they already competed to revisualize "the anxious and
perturbed expression of his visage, the apparently painful effort with which he framed
his sentences, and, above all, the surprise that spread over his face when the audience
roared with delight" (Brooks 1898: 98). A more succinct journalist, focusing on the
effect that the other expressions played against, would register "a man who is about
to preach his own funeral sermon."

While conjoined with a rounded presence (we have to imagine Huck Finn physically before we can hear his style fully) the deadpan appeals inward to cultural attitudes so deep that analysis can only intuit them. At the working level for Twain it
had to convey more than simple impassivity, adding at least mental awkwardness or
diffidence. Fundamentally, it aimed to convince audiences that he didn't realize he
was coming across as comical. Actually, it convinced even reviewers that he was
sincere, that he was trying to express . . . something not quite identifiable, perhaps
some instructive, positive purpose that excused the laughter and the spending of time
and money. But reaching a vague objective depended on precise craft. Twain boasted
that his platform style distilled many years of tracking the developing responses of
each audience, many pangs of self-criticism to make tested craft look natural. His patterned flexibility, when matured, adjusted degrees of the deadpan to the particular
audience scrutinizing him, often close up.

Twain achieved such a dazzling degree of craft that it blurs two perspectives. First,
he didn't always exert the deadpan, especially when shaping his career; later, when an
acknowledged master at it, he could and would drop into other styles that better
matched up with an audience. Once he was an established celebrity as Mark Twain,
humorist, many of his banquet speeches, bantering about his status, included gestural
interplay with the audience. But isolating a visual track or computing a ratio violates
the fact of his integrated – almost multimedia – performances. The pitch and timbre
of his voice helped, too. Few reviewers described it as lively or even pleasant; not incidentally, a drawl intensifies an audience's attention to the face of the speaker. Second,
during the first 20 years of his lecturing he tried other ways of clowning visually
besides an almost standard routine of bracketing his performances with amusing
entrances and exits – that is, with a more active visual humor.

Many observers have documented Twain's version of deadpan, famously explained
by himself in "How To Tell a Story" (1895). As early as December 1870 he encour-

aged a recruit with the exhortation: "you were born for the platform – you were intended to stand before an audience, & not smile or make a gesture"; a few months later he reminded his lecture agent that "I rely for my effects chiefly on a simulated unconsciousness & intense absurdities" (Twain 1995: 261, 408). Reviewers with differing tastes who saw him on different nights confirmed his self-analysis, at least generally. Some exited simply acclaiming what they had expected. Others strained to come up with appropriately absurd similes. The *Belfast* (Ireland) *Northern Whig* aimed at calmly vivid reporting of Twain's "steady deliberative gravity," his ability at "remaining stonily impassive" while "hardly changing his position, never moving the muscles of his face" (January 2, 1874: [3]). Some people who met him after watching a performance were startled by his lively mannerisms. The *Chicago Tribune*, competing with Twain for humor, made him onstage "as grave and solemn as the visage of an undertaker screwing down a coffin lid" (December 19, 1871). In fact, supplementing the deadpan, he could lean lazily, even fumblingly, on the lectern, perhaps recalling the hard drinker of his persona as bachelor. Still, scenes in his sketches and books, epitomized by the "Is he dead?" put-on of *The Innocents Abroad*, reinforced his dominantly impassive image as performer. As it became well known, audiences watched for it, all the more delighting in any breakdowns of self-control.

Fully enacting the deadpan had come slowly, however. For his first lecture in New York City the *Tribune*, contrasting him with Artemus Ward, noted his "most original gesticulation" and his establishing "a comfortable understanding with his audience" by pretending "to enjoy the joke quite as much as they do" (May 13, 1867: 4). By then Twain had at least given up applauding his winningest lines, which he had done (along with clenching his hands over his head like the winning boxer) in St. Louis as late as March 1867. For his first lecture in San Francisco he had appeared, complained one reviewer, in a "singular disguise," explaining he was "dressed for a masquerade" (Lauber 1985: 227). But as he settled in the East and thought nationally, his basic technique grew more cerebral; a reviewer in Detroit saw a "leisurely, easy manner" while Twain "sauntered about . . . and, when occasion demanded, gestured quietly and fitly" (quoted in Denney 1993: 22). The sober *Hartford Courant* recorded a "rather nonchalant manner" while "walking about the stage" for "a conversational performance." Yet, in summing up, its reviewer (probably Charles Dudley Warner) felt entertained enough to add that "the whole was leavened by a manner that would make the fortune of a comedian" (Twain 1992c: 407–8). As Twain's technique developed nuances, it used far more art than met the ear, but also more than met the rational eye.

Committing to the deadpan entailed working harder to warm up the audience. "No man knows better than I," he assured his fiancée, "the enormous value of a wholehearted welcome achieved without a spoken word – and no man will dare more than I to get it" (Twain 1995: 28). By 1872, according to the *Baltimore Sun*, his "comical appearance as he entered alone, at once excited laughter." He had been discussing "starters" with his two closest peers on the platform, Josh Billings (Henry W. Shaw) and Petroleum V. Nasby (David R. Locke). Usually he shambled out of the wings, seemingly disoriented and unaware of the audience. On noticing it, he could act out surprise or diffidence or just perplexity, sometimes keeping silent until it began reacting, also perplexed but amused. In 1887 a reporter memorialized this tactic at a recent performance:

> [H]e stood before the house as still and silent as an unopened oyster. The audience was as still as he. After a long pause, during which everyone was painfully wondering what ailed him, he said, "H'm!" and immediately relapsed into silence. A full minute went by during which he remained perfectly quiet with his eyes staring straight before him. Then he said "H'm!" again. At last, someone started a little ripple of applause. Mark looked up, radiant with smiles. "Thank you," he said, " I was waiting for you to begin!"[7]

Whether out of his own mood or his sense of the particular audience, he could shuffle onstage awkwardly – "like a ready made cripple" – and then act scared or bewildered – "like a small boy who has forgotten his piece" (Fatout 1960: 134–5). Comparing the reviewers' efforts at wit can distract us from the flexibility underlying the basic strategy of enlivening a restlessly passive group enough to appreciate the subtleties of deadpan. With British audiences he would feel, for several reasons, much less need for starters. But even when judging that he could and should show starchier dignity, he liked to wield the long pause. Analytic philosophers may debate whether Twain was working a visual effect or an aural one by negation.

Twain's successful tour with George Washington Cable in 1884–5 evokes both surprises and puzzlement today. Though the widespread greetings for his fiftieth birthday would confirm his arrival at respectworthy status, he again used clownish starters – and closers too (which perhaps support the idea that the "evasion" sequence of *Huckleberry Finn* aimed at a comic exit). Though biographers can debate why he did not assert firmer dignity, his routines perfected in the 1870s had carried over, with the deadpan still basic. Hamlin Garland, as a youngish student of "dramatic expression," noted for himself: "Never the ghost of a smile" (quoted in Stronks 1963: 85–6). Still, an Iowa newspaper recorded: "He starts on in a funny little jog trot half sideways . . . with a comical look of inquiry and half-appeal" (Lorch 1929: 532–3). Much later Cable recalled how Twain entered with "the one side of him dragging, one foot limping after the other"; the "house burst into such a storm of laughter" that Twain himself broke up. As for closers, he often "hippity-hopped" off the stage or else pretended trouble finding an exit. By the time of the world tour, his physical comedy had finally eased, but the deliberate tempo may even have slowed further. A South African journalist appreciatively noted that "when the audience did not at once catch the point of his joke, he considerately waited with a leer in his eye, which had the desired effect."[8] Overall, the accounts of Twain's world tour will read very familiarly for anybody who has tracked him until then.

Before lecturing, Twain had already entered on his career as a speech-maker, and this continued after he retired from performing for pay. For practical reasons – the much wider variety in kinds of audience and special demands of an occasion – his

speeches spread into a much looser mode, usually high-spirited or unabashedly eloquent, though seldom lacking some level of irony and emotional hoaxing. He bragged
several times about how well he faked the fumblings of an impromptu effort, and he
added theatrical effects whenever they helped. For "Post Prandial Oratory" (1887) he
simulated copious tears. On any rostrum Twain could be a sight to see, not just to
hear.

Embedded Photographs

The third line of Twain's visual humor, a sleeper, took little overt energy. Photographs
of him start surprisingly early, considering the history of the camera. By the 1870s
Twain was posing regularly for studio portraits, intimidated seemingly by an apparatus deaf to his charm but more likely by the fixity of the image preserved. He
restrained any impulse to smile, aware that current film and shutter speed could
distort it toward a grimace. Then the handy Kodak and roll film of the later 1880s
liberated photography from the professionals and their studios, and snapshots encouraged informality and even clowning. The American leg of Twain's world tour set up
the pictures of him riding on a baggage cart. Intriguingly, for his formal program he
considered an "illustrated lecture, showing a number of pictures of himself and each
time giving the photograph a different name" (Fatout 1960: 243). Yet *Following the
Equator* (1897) used photographs for documenting exotic scenes more than for
humor. In old age, however, surely he expected smiles over the snapshot of him in a
swimming suit and chuckles at his posturing with a handgun after a burglary at
Stormfield.

One photograph, which grew into a series, founds a major exhibit for study of
Twain's visual humor. While devotees may contemplate it solemnly and New Agers
may treasure it as laid-back, most people grin on seeing it. Compacted, like all lasting
humor, it works on several levels, rational as well as psychic. Most obviously that photograph – of Twain in bed wearing pajamas or, more often, a nightshirt – fit his sporadic pose as a drawling, lazy Southerner, a grown-up and domesticated Huck Finn
loafing on a mattress rather than a raft. However much that pose pleased contemporaries as stubborn escape, it now amuses biographers because it inverts the reality of
an outstandingly energetic and productive Clemens/Twain, who strikes us children of
a lesser god as hyperactive. For historians – including Twain as a reader – the irony
also works far beyond Huck's ambit: only royalty received anyone outside the family
while in bed. Between these poles of a celebrity embedded in the Sunday supplements
and a literary king in the pageant of Western monarchy, Twain was half-knowingly
reacting to changes roiling the current culture.

Knowing the origins of that in-bed photograph will help sort out its levels. By
1884, if not sooner, Twain, himself once a working journalist, had got so relaxed about
interviews as to sometimes oblige reporters while in bed. By the time of his world
tour he did so more often, even allowing the snapshots now feasible, though his wife

objected to his straining propriety again. After her death, at the banquet for his seventieth birthday he announced feeling entitled to terminal self-indulgence. Starting
in January 1906 he let at least five professional photographers – along with Albert
Bigelow Paine and probably some amateurs – get poses of him in bed. Since they were
working indoors he cooperated while they adjusted extra lighting. Supposedly reading
or writing, he usually betrayed his consent by leaving off his glasses. Anybody alert
could infer that he had approved both the taking and the publishing of those
photographs.

Patient research can establish their lineage. At the Library of Congress, handwritten ledgers list those submitted for copyright. Besides personal letters, the dates of
any newspapers and magazines visible, or the kind of blankets or the objects on the
bedside table, can help group the prints scattered among various libraries and collectors. The pose most reprinted today came late in the series. By W. M. Van der
Weyde – an art photographer who advertised also as Vander Weyde – it projects a
starkly brooding Twain in half-shadow, thus achieving a fresh angle, literally, for an
already well-known pose. Ironically, as Van der Weyde would recall, Twain acted especially playful during their session.[9] Most of the gloomy effect comes from tricks of
developing and printing. Tracking the popularity of Van der Weyde's photograph (the
one he chose to publish, that is) tells us why our generation has preferred it. The joke
here is on those who take it so portentously.

In Twain's time the first in-bed photographs – full view and prosaic – burst into
instant popularity. Several Manhattan newspapers printed a version, followed by the big
magazines; then a stereograph was published.[10] As the splash kept spreading, popular
magazines in England and France ran a version. In 1909 *Collier's Weekly*
featured a "fakeograph" that made Twain's bedchamber more ornate than any at
Versailles. Before then, cartoonists had exploited their chance, humorously of course. On
his death several major dailies used an in-bed print out of the hundreds of photographs
attractively available. Already on the market, postcards, sold or at least printed in
England and Germany besides the United States, improved their attempts at color.

The popularity of this basic shot, whatever the variants, overruns analysis, which
is unconstrained by any commentary from Twain. Most obviously, he personified for
restive American males the defiance of stiff manners; by loafing in bed, presumably
in daytime, he also flouted the work ethic. As a celebrity, furthermore, he was letting
the public feel they were observing his private life. But the term "private" opens
broader perspectives. For Twain's contemporaries, that basic photograph challenged
the long-thickening sanctity of the home as the inviolable refuge: culminating the
movement away from sleep as a communal activity, the bedroom now claimed the
very highest degree of privacy.[11] So teasing middle-class habits of inwardness gave liberating lift to that in-bed image.

Lately, the value of privacy had grown pricier as well. Cutting across the grass-
roots insistence on American informality that British travelers had ridiculed during
the nineteenth century, in the 1890s a new doctrine of privacy – defined primarily as

the right to avoid public notice – sprang up. In our own time that doctrine or right has branched out into a thicket; dozens of books by keen legal minds argue from analogy as much as from explicit statutes. Awards by juries flow more and more merrily when the argument segues into the right to publicity – crucially, the right to charge a fee for any perceptible use of another person's name or image. Potential oil-gushers attract the priciest if most humorless lawyers who ignore humanist qualms. However, the basic problem had already turned complicated before 1906. The *New York Times* had deprecated at length the "savage and horrible practices" of the "kodakers" hunting salable images (August 23, 1902, p. 8). Circulation wars and the halftone process making the printing of photographs both attractive and economical drove some personages to file civil complaints and also to push legislation for the right to control one's likeness being printed anywhere or used by advertisers.

At a still choosier level, the century-old resistance of some among the intelligentsia to "pictorialism" was waging its last stand, warning that enthusiasm for the illustrated media was destroying the appeal and efficacy of the written word, a keystone of loftier civilization.[12] Twain, whose books were lavishly illustrated whenever feasible, picked his side easily – to his profit, of course. Those in-bed photos lined up with the drive of mass taste; they also undercut any campaign to control the use of one's image. But where or how did humor come in? People laugh (or don't) for differing, even conflicting reasons. And a mute photograph is worth thousands of contradictory words. Yet those prints of Twain – supposedly reading or writing, sometimes smoking but never drinking, though a few unpublished prints show a seltzer bottle on the floor – support two broad conclusions. Better than anybody else at least, Twain may have appreciated both sides of the visual joke being played.

It played a fairly direct joke for the nobodies. It was not they, but the middle and upper classes, who claimed to dislike journalism centered on personalities and skewed toward entertainment. Not so incidentally, the would-be-somebodies could afford, if angry, to hire a lawyer to protect their privacy. To the delight of the defenseless, Twain, his accruing dignity certified by that banquet for his seventieth birthday, had defected to them, and they could grin as much triumphantly as derisively. The barely literate, who bought newspapers rather than magazines, would have liked seeing themselves in the rotogravure section. Furthermore, since their homes allowed little privacy, they resented as well as envied those who could insist on secluded domestic space, whether for sleeping or loafing, and who stood high enough on the job ladder to reach some privacy of workspace. Those photographs, despite showing an upscale bed, aligned Twain with the masses, who could enjoy a counterpoint of schadenfreude to their chuckles of self-affirmation.

Along the opposite vector of the joke, genteelists buying magazines like *Current Literature*, which flashed an in-bed photo for them, could also have their laugh, if guiltily. Twain, throughout his career, had fascinated some of the upward-striving by spoofing the proprieties they suffered to honor. That photograph dangled forbidden fruit that the consciously proper, releasing their inhibitions with a smile, could not

resist. While humor arcs through the circuit-board of the subconscious too intricately
to be captured in any diagram, at least the middlebrows, however wary of frowns from
above, enjoyed those in-bed photographs. Ironically for highbrows, Twain had just
solidified into a standard author encased in a collected edition, an author who inhabited the realm of literature rather than entertainment and so should behave accordingly; who, for instance, should no longer encourage the mass-pictorial mode. At best
they smiled wryly.

Twain's finest flights of humor have lasted. By that measure the in-bed pose ranks
high. In 1919 a respected portraitist did a striking version in charcoal that sold well
as a lithograph. For a kind of apotheosis in 1985, after a sculptor ingeniously made
a bust of it – about half life-size – the White House acquired a casting. But while
the pose holds its appeal, has the joke stayed the same? The deepest humor is inerad-
icably contextual. Besides other changes in American culture, the right to privacy,
while consolidating its base, is dimming under the glitter of marketing celebrities.
Today, it is acceptable, actually enviable, to generate and then flaunt visibility in the
jet-powered galaxy of financiers, rappers, actresses, and high-contract athletes. "Old"
society as well as incumbent Presidents have blended into their display, continually
photographed or scintillating in TV studios. At the tawdriest edge of the arena,
celebrities auction their privacy, politicians barter it, and would-be visibles compete
to sell their dignity. How does that in-bed pose look now?

Our commercializing society exploits every eye-catching image. Moreover, the
caterers to trends regularly sense a resurgence of nostalgia, and that pose can call up
a quieter lifestyle with time for reading or even longhand writing in bed. Deeper cir-
cuits may also engage. Neo-Freudians may smile knowingly because the chief prop is
a bed. Less darkly, that pose embodies the ideal of informality, ever more strongly
supported since Twain's death. Acting "natural" (or supposedly so) is a requirement
in most situations. Don't be a stuffed shirt, we say; show your rumpled nightshirt,
the photograph says. In fact, acting natural has aggressed into "letting it all hang
out." While Twain's allowing that series of photographs stops short of self-exposure,
it is bold for a somebody included by high-school anthologies. For me it says: do what
suits (literally, unsuits?) you and what you find easeful, even if welcoming the public
into your bedroom compromises your privacy, the most crucial right of all.

Risking tedium, researchers could compile a convincing list of Twain's other visual
jokes. Privately, he enjoyed making cancellations in his letters while dropping broad
clues or slyly inking out passages so as to leave them recoverable. His posted notice
to burglars still sells in facsimile. In 1907 his crossing a busy London street in his
bathrobe set off a flurry of stories with cartoons, as he must have expected. Letting a
reporter watch him, in his bedclothes, while shaving, he surely expected an illustrated
news story. Whether he expected the tableau of him playing billiards to be issued as
a stereograph, nobody has established; nor whether he intended it to amuse the public.
During his final trips to Bermuda he tolerated, probably cooperated with, various
Kodakers. His academic admirers tend to skim over such images as frivolous, as mean-
ingless for him or posterity. But Twain has lasted so vividly while competitors come

and go partly because his urge for humor sought so many outlets, in turn not just because of his energy and ambition but because of his innermost nature. If Twain's genome had a master gene, humor was its code.

NOTES

1 Thomas Schirer (1984) details Twain's many attempts to write for the stage and decides that often Twain's creative impulses first tried a dramatic format.

2 The final title-page of *A Tramp Abroad* noted "three or four pictures made by the author of this book, without outside help."

3 Written in 1899; published as the lead article in *Harper's Monthly* for December 1914.

4 Twain gave a copper etching of the self-portrait to each guest at the banquet for his sixty-seventh birthday.

5 *Metropolitan Magazine*, April and June 1903. I have seen this item only as a clipping.

6 Twain emitted drawings with such varying purposes that I do not pretend to cover them all. Those in "As Concerns Interpreting the Deity" (1905; 1917) teeter between burlesque and seriousness; those for "A Simplified Alphabet" seem businesslike – Twain supported simplified spelling until he realized that newspaper wits had overwhelmed serious debate.

7 *St. Louis Post-Dispatch*, December 11, 1887, reprinted in McWilliams (1997: 224).

8 Reprinted in "Twain in the South African Press," *Mark Twain Journal* 40 (Spring 2002), 47.

9 See Van der Weyde (1921: 830). On September 21, 1906 Twain inscribed a maxim in a copy of *Huckleberry Finn* for him. For an obituary of Van der Weyde see *New York Times*, July 18, 1929, p. 21.

10 For 30 years I have been tracking appearances of the in-bed pose and could compete for longest-footnote-of-the-year. Twain studies needs a finding list of photographs, portraits, and cartoons of him.

11 See especially Elias (1939: vol. 1, 165–8. Elias also comments on the development of the nightshirt, which Twain preferred to the pajamas that cartoonists often used for him; see chapter 49 of *Following the Equator*.

12 Neil Harris (1990: ch. 16, "Pictorial Perils: The Rise of American Illustration") analyzes the larger issue.

REFERENCES AND FURTHER READING

Alden, Henry Mills (1910). "Mark Twain: Personal Impressions." *Book News Monthly*, 28 (April).

Brooks, Noah (1898). "Twain in California." *Century*, 57 (Nov.).

Budd, Louis J. (1983). *Our Mark Twain: The Making of his Public Personality*. Philadelphia: University of Pennsylvania Press.

Clemens, Clara (1931). *My Father Mark Twain*. New York: Harper & Bros.

David, Beverly R. (1986). *Mark Twain and his Illustrators*, vol. 1: *1869–1875*. Troy, NY: Whitston.

Denney, Lynn (1993). "Next Stop Detroit: A City's View of Mark Twain's Evolution as a Literary Hero 1868–1895." *Mark Twain Journal* 31 (Spring), 22.

Elias, Norbert (1978). *The History of Manners: The Civilizing Process*. New York: Urizen. (First publ. 1939.)

Fatout, Paul (1960). *Mark Twain on the Lecture Circuit*. Bloomington: Indiana University Press.

Harris, Neil (1990). *Cultural Excursions*. Chicago: University of Chicago Press.

Inge, M. Thomas (1994). "Mark Twain and Dan Beard's Collaborative *Connecticut Yankee*." In James S. Leonard, Christine E. Wharton, Robert Murray Davis, and Jeanette Harris (eds.), *Author-ity and Textuality*, 169–227. West Cornwall, Conn.: Locust Hill.

Knoper, Randall (1995). *Acting Naturally: Mark Twain in the Culture of Performance*. Berkeley: University of California Press.

Lauber, John (1985). *The Making of Mark Twain*. Boston: Houghton Mifflin.

Leon, Philip W. (1996). *Mark Twain and West Point*. Toronto: ECW Press.

Lorch, Fred W. (1929). "Lecture Trips and Visits of Mark Twain in Iowa." *Iowa Journal of History and Politics* 27, 507–47.

Lorch, Fred W. (1968). *The Trouble Begins at Eight: Mark Twain's Lecture Tours*. Ames: Iowa State University Press.

Lowry, Richard S. (1996). *"Littery Man": Mark Twain and Modern Authorship*. New York: Oxford University Press.

McKeithan, D. M. (1961). *The Morgan Manuscripts of Mark Twain's "Pudd'nhead Wilson."* Cambridge, Mass.: Harvard University Press.

McWilliams, Jim (1997). *Mark Twain in the St. Louis Post-Dispatch, 1874–1891*. Troy, NY: Whitston.

Michelson, Bruce (1995). *Mark Twain on the Loose: A Comic Writer and the American Self*. Amherst: University of Massachusetts Press.

Paine, Albert Bigelow (1912). *Mark Twain: A Biography. The Personal and Literary Life of Samuel Langhorne Clemens*, 3 vols. New York and London: Harper & Bros.

Schirer, Thomas (1984). *Mark Twain and the Theatre*. Nürnberg: Verlag Hans Carl.

Stronks, James B. (1963). "Mark Twain's Stage Debut." *New England Quarterly* 36 (March), 85–6.

Twain, Mark (1902). "Amended Obituaries." *Harper's Weekly*, 15 Nov.

Twain, Mark (1967). *Mark Twain's Letters to his Publishers 1867–1894*, ed. Hamlin Hill. Berkeley: University of California Press.

Twain, Mark (1979). *Early Tales and Sketches*, vol. 1: *1851–1864*, ed. Edgar M. Branch and Robert H. Hirst. Berkeley: University of California Press.

Twain, Mark (1992c). *Mark Twain's Letters*, vol. 3: *1869*, ed. Victor Fischer and Michael B. Frank. Berkeley: University of California Press.

Twain, Mark (1995). *Mark Twain's Letters*, vol. 4: *1870–1871*, ed. Victor Fischer and Michael B. Frank. Berkeley: University of California Press.

Van der Weyde, W. M. (1921). "Photographing Mark Twain." *The Truth Seeker* 48 (24 Dec).

Wonham, Henry B. (1993). *Mark Twain and the Art of the Tall Tale*. New York: Oxford University Press.

32

Mark Twain and Post-Civil War Humor

Cameron C. Nickels

"Mark Twain's story in the [New York] *Saturday Press* called 'Jim Smiley and his Jumping Frog,' has set all New York in a roar," Richard Ogden wrote in his column "Pogers' Letter From New York" in the San Francisco *Alta California* (January 10, 1866). "I have been asked fifty times about it and its author, and the papers are copying it far and wide. It is voted the best thing of its day." Ogden concluded archly by asking, "Cannot the *Californian* [a rival San Francisco paper for which Twain wrote], afford to keep Mark all to itself?" This type of sally was characteristic of California journalism at that time, but it would prove prophetic. Mark Twain had enjoyed his four months as a correspondent in Hawaii in 1866, but, weary of the West, at the end of the year he gave his farewell lectures and partied his goodbyes in California and Nevada, leaving San Francisco by steamer and landing in New York on January 12, 1867.

For practical reasons, Twain was at this point a roving reporter for the San Francisco daily *Alta California*, hired to say funny things about the East. But he had also come to New York to take advantage of his burgeoning career as a lecturer and, above all, the celebrity brought on by the frog story. To that end, *The Celebrated Jumping Frog of Calaveras County and Other Sketches* appeared in April, published and co-edited by Charles Webb, a writer, publisher, and old friend from California days. It did not sell the 50,000 copies Twain had hoped for, but the reviews were kind, for the most part, and getting "between covers" was a major step toward becoming a bona fide writer. (A London pirated edition sold better and prepared the way for his popularity there, but it rendered no lucre.)

In retrospect, in fact, 1867 represents a major turning point, an *annus mirabilis* even, a truly wondrous year filled with events that would have profound consequences for Mark Twain's personal life and his place in American literature. In June he left New York on the *Quaker City* for a five-month voyage to Europe and the Holy Land with a commission to write travel letters about the experience, and by the end of the year he had a lucrative contract to publish those letters as a book. Appearing in 1869,

The Innocents Abroad would be his lifetime bestseller. However, what would, perhaps, ultimately prove most wondrous about that year – an event with the most meaningful implications both personally and professionally – took place with no fanfare as the year ended. On December 27, Twain joined a boon companion on that voyage, Charles Langdon, and his family, for dinner at the St. Nicholas Hotel in New York. Here he met his young friend's sister, Olivia Louise. On the last day of 1867 he accompanied them to a reading by Charles Dickens. He would marry Olivia (Livy) on February 2, 1870.

A Year of Changes: 1867, Mark Twain, and American Humor

For American humor generally, the year 1867, if not "wondrous" in quite the same way, is nonetheless memorable in retrospect, with something of a sea-change taking place, significant in itself, but all the more so given Mark Twain's life and career at the time. As early as 1835, a reviewer in the *Quarterly Review* had praised the "Jack Downing" letters of Charles Augustus Davis as an example of a "native American humour," a phrase that Leslie Stephen defined more clearly in the *Cornhill Magazine* (January 1866) as a humor that "has a flavour peculiar to itself. It smells of the soil, it is an indigenous growth." Two publications in 1867 suggest that American humor in that sense had come to a kind of culmination. One was George Washington Harris's *Sut Lovingood: Yarns Spun by a "Nat'ral Born Durn'd Fool,"* a collection of humorous stories and sketches that went back to 1845. Its publication symbolically closed an older, "frontier" tradition of native American humor. The other was James Russell Lowell's *Biglow Papers, Second Series*, signifying the culmination of another major strain of "indigenous" American humor, the New England tradition. Collections of the works of earlier humorists writing in both traditions – Frances Whitcher's "Widow Bedott," Thomas Chandler Haliburton's "Sam Slick," Benjamin Shillaber's "Mrs. Partington," Johnson Jones Hooper's "Simon Suggs," and George Washington Harris himself – would be republished and anthologized to the end of the century and even beyond, but the humorists of the new generation that Twain represented in 1867 were of a different type.

A tragic event, and a significant one in both the history of American humor and Mark Twain's place in it, was the death in March 1867 of "Artemus Ward" (Charles Farrar Browne). Only a year older than Twain, Ward was the most popular American humorist at the time, at home and abroad, and the active mentor to many – "Bill Arp" (Charles Henry Smith), "Josh Billings" (Henry Wheeler Shaw), and "Petroleum V. Nasby" (David Ross Locke), to mention only the names that are still recognized today. Mark Twain met and caroused with Ward in Nevada in 1863, and learned much from his humorous lecture there. Ward also encouraged him to write the "frog" story for a collection he was editing; arriving too late for inclusion, it was published instead in the *Saturday Press* in November 1865 (producing the "roar" that Ogden describes). Twain, though, was not unknown as a humorist in the East. The preface to the frog story in the *Saturday Press* put it this way: "We give up the principal portion of our editorial space, to-day, to an exquisitely humorous sketch . . . by Mark Twain . . . who has long a been a favorite contributor to the San Francisco press, from which his articles have been so extensively copied as to make him nearly as well known as Artemus Ward." High praise indeed, and the popularity of "The Jumping Frog" created a market for more (and original) Twain stories. Within the year, at least a dozen items appeared and were reprinted in Eastern journals, almost certainly more than by any other "Western" humorist, including Dan De Quille, another popular Nevada humorist of the time, remembered today as Twain's room-mate, mentor, and boon companion.

Twain and Webb wisely featured the frog story in the title of *The Celebrated Jumping Frog* and a handsome gilt-stamped frog on the cover. With 27 sketches, many of them edited for a supposedly refined Eastern sensibility, the collection provided readers and reviewers with a good sense of Twain's œuvre at that time. Despite the book's poor sales, the reviews portray a writer who had truly "arrived" in 1867. "Of the great army of humorists," the *New York Dispatch* (May 5, 1867) wrote, "we have always placed Mark Twain at its head."[1] Not everyone liked the book. The *New York Evening Post* (May 8, 1867) enjoyed the frog story, but with "one or two exceptions" found the rest of the collection too parochial, "not suited to this longitude." And the *San Francisco Evening Bulletin* (June 1, 1867) damned Twain with faint praise by saying "we regard him as by far the best of our second-rate-humorists," yet went on to compare him favorably to Ward, Billings, and Nasby, giving no clue as to who actually was first-rate. The *Nation* (May 9, 1867) was more forthright, deeming the book "not unworthy of a place beside the works of John Phoenix, A. Ward's books, and the two volumes of the Rev. Mr. Nasby." Many reviewers picked up on the preface by "John Paul" (Charles Webb) and distinguished Twain from the current generation of popular humorists who relied too much upon "tricks of spelling," orthographic contortions, and other literary "buffoonery" (some naming the obvious culprits: Ward, Nasby, and Billings). Twain would have agreed, but would have valued most the references to his work as "genuine" and "authentic."

When he landed in New York in January 1867, then, Mark Twain already had a firm place in the ranks of American humorists; and by the end of the year, with the publication of *The Celebrated Jumping Frog* in April and the *Quaker City* letters under book contract, he was at their head. A reviewer in the *Round Table* (May 25, 1867) said it all for the time: "In the double capacity of lecturer and humorist, Mark Twain has succeeded to the vacant chair of the lamented Artemus Ward."

Mark Twain and his Contemporaries

Reviews of Twain's books over the next two decades invoked some of the same points raised in 1867, citing the genius of the jumping frog story, for example, and its crucial role in his reputation as a humorist. They brought up as well his superiority to those who wrote in the "school of bad spelling." But some reviewers went further. As early as 1869 (September 14) the *Albany Journal* was no "longer willing to assign him to the school of caricature in which 'Nasby' and 'Artemus Ward' are bright and shining lights. His genius belongs rather to the refined and scholarly class of which Charles Lamb and Theodore Hook were the brightest specimens." If this seems hyperbolic to the contemporary reader, the *Philadelphia Press* (October 11, 1870) would include him as "one of the three great living American prose humorists," along with Oliver Wendell Holmes and Bret Harte.

A more fruitful, even intriguing, way of getting some sense of Mark Twain and his contemporaries is to look closely at *Mark Twain's Library of Humor*, published in 1888: an anthology of works by 47 writers, including Twain, together with several examples of anonymous newspaper humor.[2] The concept for such a book – initially for a multivolume series on world humor – was proposed in 1880 and, typically anticipating a cash cow, Mark Twain quickly embraced it. As usual too, he wearied of it. Given the number of projects of many kinds he always juggled, and his impatience with the tedious details of each of them after the initial enthusiasm, he cajoled others to help. In this case, he called on the always dependable William Dean Howells, and Charles H. Clark, a Hartford journalist and friend.

Given what I want to say here about *Mark Twain's Library* as an intriguing entry point to an understanding both of facets of Twain himself, and of post-Civil War humor generally, the crucial question is what role he played in the making of the book. In his introduction to the 1969 facsimile edition, Clarence Gohdes writes ambiguously that "There can be no question that Mark Twain did far less work on the anthology than either Clark or Howells, but he remained in command throughout" (Twain 1969: ix). Letters and notebook entries show that Twain not only had a hand in choosing texts, but also commissioned E. W. Kemble to do the nearly two hundred illustrations. (Kemble had been illustrator for the *Adventures of Huckleberry Finn* three years earlier). More relevant to the issue at hand, though, is a point that Peter Messent makes more than once in his study of the major collections of Mark Twain's short fiction: that Twain was often more responsible for their editorial direction than we are led to believe (usually by Twain himself).

We should consider, too, that while Mark Twain always had an eye to the bottom line represented by sales, he cared deeply about his reputation as a writer, and pursued both – at times conflicting – imperatives. Thus, while his name in the title was essentially a marketing ploy to improve sales (although in fact the book did poorly), that title made a statement about his place in American humor – and, with the possessive case, claims a sense of "ownership" of it. Significantly too, in that respect, the anthology opens with "The Notorious Jumping Frog of Calaveras County," which had consolidated his position as first among American humorists, and he has more selections in the book than anyone else. The "Compiler's Apology" by Mark Twain makes a joke of this, saying that his pieces were chosen "by my two assistant compilers, not by me. This is why there are not more" (Twain 1969: xi). Reproduced in the book as a handwritten, signed letter, the "apology" itself sends a message that renders its own kind of ultimate authority.

As we will see, though, what makes *Mark Twain's Library* particularly intriguing as a window onto Twain and American humor at the time is that he alone was responsible for the idiosyncratic order of texts – arranged neither chronologically, nor by topic or author. This confounded Howells, but he talked about it later with typical good humor: "I helped him with a Library of Humor, which he once edited," he wrote in *My Mark Twain*, "and when I had done my work according to tradition, with authors, times, and topics carefully studied in due sequence, he tore it all apart, and 'chucked' the pieces in wherever the fancy for them took him at the moment." (Howells 1910: 17–18).

Canonicity Then and Now

Any literary anthology represents what we would today call a "canon," representing the tastes and interests of the people who chose the contents as well as those of the readers of the time. Academic scholarship on American humor (and on American literature generally) began in the 1920s, identified a canon that seemed to evoke a "usable past," and emphasized the significance of region (particularly the frontier), of folk ways and talk, and (for several decades) of masculinity. Mark Twain studies began at the same time and saw him in terms of this canon (see Nickels 1993: 245–6). The word "library" in Twain's title appears more benign than the legalistic "canon," but the contents are nonetheless revealing in their own way. It is tempting to think that being a friend, or neighbor, of the principal editor played a major part in *Mark Twain's Library*, given the inclusion of Howells, Warner, Aldrich, and Stowe. And yet, while Twain enjoyed the company of David Ross Locke, nothing by "Petroleum V. Nasby" appears there. Also, although by this time Twain had come to despise Bret Harte with the creative passion that only he could wreak, he reread Harte's work in order to have some say in the choice of the four pieces by him that appear.

Three observations seem appropriate regarding the texts chosen for the collection. Most of the writers are from the northeast – the Philadelphia–New York–Boston axis. Also, although the contents reach back to the familiar likes of Washington Irving, Seba Smith, James Russell Lowell, George Washington Harris, Johnson Jones Hooper, and William Tappan Thompson, the great majority of the authors included, like Twain, began their career after midcentury. The most striking thing here, though, is the broad definition of "humor" in the title, given the inclusion of such familiar writers as William Dean Howells, Ambrose Bierce, Oliver Wendell Holmes, George Washington Cable, Joel Chandler Harris, Bill Nye, Artemus Ward, and Josh Billings. A later literary taxonomy would parse these figures out in terms of "local color," "humor," and "realism." The work of other writers represented here, however, does not figure at all in anybody's later notion of an American literary canon: William

Allen Butler, John T. Trowbridge, John Hay, Edward Harold Mott, and Frederic W. Shelton, among others. "Humor" in this library did include writing by women, but with none of our latter-day sense of political awareness. Harriet Beecher Stowe, and certainly Marietta Holley, "work" in this last respect, but Lucretia Hale, Mary Mapes Dodge, and Katherine Kent Child Walker have not been given much of a place, to put it kindly, in subsequent considerations of American humor or of nineteenth-century women writers generally. Dodge's "Miss Malony on the Chinese Question" speaks to the "servant problem" of the time, but most modern readers would surely read it, and with some discomfort, in terms of the Irish and Chinese caricatures it features. These entertained Twain and his contemporaries, though, as did the "Dutch" dialect poems of "Hans Breitmann" (Charles Godfrey Leland) also included in the book.

Literary Humor

To the extent that most of the writers featured in *Mark Twain's Library* represent a definable "school" of humor, they are "literary comedians," a catch-all term used to describe generally the humorists in the second half of the century.[3] More recent scholarship by David E. E. Sloane, David B. Kesterson, and others, however, has shown their significance to, and links with, Twain's work. Because so many writers included are not "comedians" in any sense of the word – Howells, Warner, Holmes, and Stowe, for instance – a more accurate term to describe much of what appears in this book would be "literary humor." The introduction by "The Associate Editors" (Howells) does speak of American humor as "racy of the soil" (Twain 1969: xiii) but, truth to tell, nearly all of the writers (or their personae) are urbane, and what they write about inherently urban. The aesthetic at work here can be seen in the brief biographies of Frederic Shelton, who wrote "humor of a quiet and refined sort" (Twain 1969: 362), and of Holmes, "the first of our more literary humorists" (p. 406). Torn throughout his life between seeing himself on one hand as a respectable writer and on the other as a "mere humorist," and thus between two very different audiences, Twain, in the 1888 library, appears as a genuine man-of-letters, his work comfortable in the company of men and women who wrote "good" literature, and not just humor.

Angles of Vision

The literature that appeared in *Mark Twain's Library* had everything to do with post-Civil War concerns: technology, urbanization, and capitalism, and the culture and society they created – or rather were creating, because the issues were dynamic, the processes current – and the selections reflect this.[4] In this new order of things, nothing is fixed. That itself is a problem, but not one so much to be solved as to be held up in this anthology for examination from several angles of vision – a realistic mode of looking at life represented in Twain's own unique ordering of selections. Putting the frog story at the beginning does make its own kind of statement, but there seems little by way of clear rationale about the organization of the remainder. There is no apparent, overall, unifying "vision": to the contrary, the selections from longer works are made and edited in ways that encourage imaginative, spontaneous associations among them, so creating a kaleidoscopic context for a variety of contemporary subjects. Thus, for example, there is an implied connection between the fence whitewashing episode from *Tom Sawyer*, edited and titled "A Day's Work" in *Mark Twain's Library*, and both the P. T. Barnum-like figure in Mortimer M. Thompson's ("Q. K. Philander Doestick's") "A New Patent Medicine Operation" and the humbug featured as the title character in Thomas Bailey Aldrich's "The Friend of My Youth." (James M. Bailey's "What He Wanted It For" includes the showman, Barnum, himself, but he plays second banana.) In this context, too, "Col. Sellers at Home," from *The Gilded Age*, takes on new meaning. George H. Derby's ("John Phoenix's") "Tushmaker's Toothpuller" both represents another Barnum-like character and sends up technology in the story of a "mechanical genius" with no medical training whose invention sucked an old lady's skeleton "completely and entirely from her body, leaving her a mass of quivering jelly in her chair!" – after which she lived on for seven years as the "India-Rubber Woman," and never suffered again from rheumatism (Twain 1969: 33). Another look at technology is Phoenix's "Sewing-Machine – Feline Attachment," which, complete with drawings, anticipates both the form and substance of Rube Goldberg's humor. J. T. Trowbridge's "Darius Green and His Flying-Machine" is a more conventional cautionary tale of the time.

Edward Harold Mott's "His Reasons for Thinking There is Natural Gas in Deep Rock Gully" makes for a particularly interesting understanding not just of taste but of the cultural relativity of canonicity. Obscure since its own time (as is its author), Mott's story looks back to the earlier frontier tradition of humor and shares much with what is now canonized as a true classic, Thomas Bangs Thorpe's "The Big Bear of Arkansas." The latter is regularly included in college-level anthologies of American literature, figuring largely in studies of what are seen as the meaningful tensions between nature and technology in nineteenth-century America. Both stories are written in rustic dialect, and Mott's protagonist, "the Old Settler," is a bear hunter much like the Jim Doggett who narrates Thorpe's tale. Speaking with the "Squire" about the current craze for finding petroleum leads the Settler to recall a "b'ar hunt" of ten years ago. He, like Doggett, is skilled at hunting bear, and after some preliminary "rassels" with his own bear-of-all-bears, he gets to the ultimate showdown. In Thorpe's classic story, the death of the bear represents the end of the frontier, a way of life that defines Jim Doggett and, implicitly, America. Telling his story of the past to a bunch of city slickers on the steamboat *The Invincible*, Jim, another metaphoric "big bear of Arkansas," is as anachronistic as the real bear he describes.

Mott's story, however, gives a very different reading of this hunter's shooting of his bear. "Poppin' mad" to "see my meat a layin' at the bottom" of an inaccessible gulley (Twain 1969: 488), the Old Settler watches dumbfounded as the bear (equally astonished) begins to float up and out of the fissure. Just as the critter is on the verge of sailing out of sight, the hunter comes to his senses, loads up his gun and shoots the bear – which catches fire and zooms out of sight "like a shootin' star" (Twain 1969: 489). What causes this? The bear had inhaled natural gas leaking from the floor of the gully, thus proving that the Old Settler knew what he was (previously) talking about regarding the presence of petroleum out in the hills. In other words, he knows as much about such modern things as he does about the bear. Charles Dudley Warner's "How I Killed a Bear," the account of a city dweller's frightened and accidental shooting of a bear, although different in most respects, is in its own way just as anti-heroic.

Many of the selections in *Mark Twain's Library* question received wisdom of different kinds, using a variety of forms to do so. Robert Burdette's "The Simple Story of G. Washington" shows the younger generation pig-headedly obtuse to the noble history of the founding father. "The Total Depravity of Inanimate Things," by Katherine Kent Child Walker, appeared in the *Atlantic* in 1864, and although forgotten today, was a sensation in its own time and originated the catch-phrase that its title became. Assuming an unrelentingly serious tone and using detailed but trivial examples, Walker pokes devastating fun at the fundamental Calvinistic principle of human depravity. Oliver Wendell Holmes's better-known "The Deacon's Masterpiece" echoes the satiric thrust of Walker's piece. And, while not about Calvinism, Twain's "The Tomb of Adam," extracted from a chapter in *The Innocents Abroad*, becomes (in the context created in this collection) a comic questioning of the roots of Christianity itself.

The 14 animal fables by Ambrose Bierce and George Lanigan also challenge conventional wisdom, but in a sense that reflects more profound uncertainties about the kinds of "maps" needed to negotiate the new "territory" represented by post-Civil War America. The classic fable provided a concise form ending with the "moral" to be taught, but for these writers the genre becomes, rather, an unyielding, unrelentingly sardonic take on life. Samuel Cox's versions of the fables of the Hodja (a thirteenth-century Turkish trickster) work this way, as do two or three pieces by Burdette. Josh Billings's aphorisms (some from his own popular *Allminax* series) go even further, distilling the moral to its trenchant essence. While he echoes the pithy sayings attributed to Benjamin Franklin (who admitted to borrowing nearly all of them from British sources), Billings's are more original – cynical sentiments very much of their own time that anticipate those of Pudd'nhead Wilson's calendar. Consider "Man waz kreated a little lower than the angells, and he haz been a gitting a little lower ever since" (Twain 1969: 492); and "Thare iz nothing that yu and I make so menny blunders about, and the world so few, az the aktual amount ov our importance" (Twain 1969: 473). Mark Twain wrote animal fables, of course, and "The Cayote" [*sic*] and "Dick Baker's Cat" (from *Roughing It*) are more clearly signaled as such in this context; but, like "Blue-Jays" (from *A Tramp Abroad*) they are more akin in literary terms to the two "Brer Rabbit" stories by Joel Chandler Harris in the collection than to the caustic moral musings of Bierce, Lanigan, and the others. (In this context, too, Harris's stories do not have quite the racial significance that they do today.)

Domestic Humor

While there is no one unifying and topical focus to the texts in *Mark Twain's Library*, domestic humor plays a significant part in the collection, taking up – in many different ways – courtship, marriage, and family life, and the male–female identities that lie at the heart of this realm. This form of humor prevails too in the sense that "domestic" has connotations we would not now readily recognize.[5] John Phoenix's piece on the sewing machine anticipates the twentieth-century humor of Rube Goldberg, but in its own time would have been seen as part of the multilayered discourse on the gender implications of one of the first home appliances. Warner's "Plumbers" and the anonymous "Butterwick's Little Gas Bill" have something to say about technology as well, but portray it in the context of the bedeviled husband and father of the day striving to maintain a cozy home life.

Taken as a group, the examples of domestic humor represented in this anthology also take up, in one way or another, the nascent feminist movement and the kinds of changes it engendered for women and particularly for men. As his title would suggest, Artemus Ward's "Women's Rights" takes on the new domestic order forthrightly, and in a traditional, anti-feminist way: "You air a angle when you behave yourself; . . . [but] when you desert your firesides, & with you heds full of wimin's rites noshuns go round like roarin lions . . . – in short when you undertake to play the man, you play the devil and air an emphatic noosance" (Twain 1969: 167). Ward's homespun way of speaking here in no way undercuts what he says but rather, as with certain of Josh Billings's aphorisms on this subject, is intended to give a common-sense authority to it. Other forthrightly anti-feminist satires are Burdette's "Woman's Suffrage" and James M. Bailey's "A Female Base-Ball Nine," which portrays women as "ninnies" for even presuming to become part of a sphere so emphatically male. Facile shots at "feminism," in other words, are troubled by no historical constraints.

For the most part, though, *Mark Twain's Library* takes domestic humor more seriously. Marriage, of course, begins with courtship, and comic rustic courtship had a long history in popular culture, including the classic example which appears here: James Russell Lowell's "The Courtin'" (1864).[6] "Sicily Burns's Wedding," the selection reprinted from George Washington Harris's "Sut Lovingood" stories, represents the very different frontier tradition of domestic humor, but is edited to better fit the context created in this anthology. Omitting the original ending shifts the focus away from the reason for Sut's revenge (Sicily Burns's jilting him) to the act of revenge itself. There is no moral center here: we are not asked to laugh at, or examine in any way, the conventions of courtship and marriage, but are rather asked to enjoy Sut's creation of frontier anarchy in turning a bee-maddened bull loose on Sicily's wedding dinner party.

Although earlier even than Harris's story, Joseph Neal's " 'Tis Only My Husband" (1838) more clearly anticipates post-Civil War domestic humor by addressing the crucial transition from courtship to marriage. In using the term "latents" – by which he means the fundamental gender make-up according to "nature," the male dominant and the female supine – Neal makes an early probe into the psychology of gender. Perhaps, he suggests, such "natural" roles are played out in courtship, but marriage seems to change the equation. As this story says emphatically, marriage can make a man more feminine – "born to be controlled" – and a wife more masculine – bearing "within her breast the fiery resolution" of a man (Twain 1969: 106, 107). Implicitly, in other words, these "latents" do not work according to nature at all.

In Neal's story, the violence of newly married Seraphina Serena Pumpilion, *neé* Dolce (Twain would have loved the way she swings a cat around the room by the tail when her husband says he is going fishing with the boys) has domestic significance that does not register in Sut's Lovingood's essentially masculine, frontier pandemonium. Her violent responses to her husband's plans to go with the boys, like her refusal to fix him breakfast or tea, are gender ploys that irrevocably define his role in the new terms of upper-middle-class marriage. At the end of the story, Neal writes that any "symptoms of insubordination" on the husband's part are "soon quelled – for Mrs. Pumpilion, with a significant glance, inquired, 'Are you going a-fishing again, my dear?'" (Twain 1969: 116).

Neal's style is decidedly Dickensian, but in not moralizing, in letting the drama play itself out, and in consciously addressing the psychology of gender, he anticipates the realistic point of view and the substance of the more contemporary examples of domestic humor in *Mark Twain's Library*. Robert Burdette's "Not in Like, but Like in Difference" gives a succinct example of the new order of things. The husband takes an oh-so-reasonable male exception to his wife's "destroying" her beautiful face with paint and powder as she readies herself to go to the theater and, ironically, proposes to make up his face too as a sign of their love and closeness. She demurely agrees – then asks him to wait so she can go to "Dutch Jake's and spice my up breath with a dish of beer and a Chinese cigarette." The brief episode ends with his thinking it over and then telling her "to go put on all the feminine fol-de-rols and crinkles she could find in the illustrated advertisements" (Twain 1969: 510). No feminist caricature, she makes a salient point regarding supercilious male behavior, to which he can only capitulate. His parting reference to "feminine fol-de-rols" is a weak shot but the best he can do in return. (And his reference to "the illustrated advertisements" speaks volumes to modern readers interested in the cultural context of such humor.)

The couple in Burdette's "She Had to Take Her Things Along" never makes it to the altar. The set-up is deceptively conventional: Erasmus falls in love with the daughter of the prosperous farmer he works for, who opposes the marriage. In the truest romantic tradition love must prevail, and thus "the night was set. So was the ladder" (Twain 1969: 479). Positioned at the bottom of it, the eager husband-to-be suggests that his beloved should first let her "things" drop, and promises to catch them. What happens next abruptly shifts everything from conventional romance to detailed, comic realism, as the four-by-four-by-eight-foot trunk (128 cubic feet and weighing 2,700 pounds), containing "a few 'things' that no woman could be expected to travel without," hammers Erasmus into the ground (p. 479). The story could end here with a satisfied, conventional chuckle at how materialistic women are, but there is more. Married twice, and the father of four daughters and two sons, the farmer had allowed the elopement to proceed, knowing the results: "if I don't know what baggage a woman carries when she travels, by this time," he says, "I'm too old to learn" (p. 480). But the story does not end even with this bizarre bit of smugness, but with an incongruous conclusion that Mark Twain would have savored. For "the jury brought in a verdict that he [Erasmus] came to his death by habitual drunkenness, and the temperance papers didn't talk about anything else for the next six weeks" (p. 480).

William Allen Butler's long poem "Nothing to Wear" (1857) was far more popular in Twain's own time, and perhaps included primarily for that reason, but it works too, intertextually, in the larger exploration of gender that the collection prompts. "Miss Flora M'Flimsey, of Madison Square," plays no pre-nuptial games with her fiancé, but lays down the law about what she expects: "So don't prose to me about duty and stuff, / If we don't break this off, there will be time enough / For that sort of thing . . ." (Twain 1969: 171). Writing as the husband-to-be, Butler seems good-natured for the most part and enjoys cataloging in comic detail the excesses of a female love of fashion. The poem ends, though, with his sarcastic admonishment that women such as his wife-to-be should visit the poor and wretched of the city: "Then home to your wardrobes, and say, if you dare – / Spoiled children of fashion, – you've nothing to wear!" (p. 177). The superior tone he adopts, though, is all he is finally left with, because (even more clearly than with Neal's protagonist) the patronizing condescension proffered up as masculine common sense simply does not change his partner's behavior: she, not he, prevails.

George William Curtis's "Rev. Creamcheese and the New Livery," from his *The Potiphar Papers* (1853), digs more thoughtfully into a wife's materialistic pretensions, but with a more complex, ambiguous approach to the questions of gender and marriage in post-Civil War America. Aided and abetted by the effeminate Reverend Creamcheese, Mrs. Potiphar yearns for all of the European, aristocratic trappings of a livery (a footman who must be corpulent, named "James," and wear red plush knee-britches) to prove the superiority of the Potiphars to her otherwise social equals. Her husband objects not to the expense but to the principle: "livery is a remnant of a feudal state, of which we abolish every trace as fast as we can. That which is represented by livery is not consonant with our [republican] principles" (Twain 1969: 42). His reasoning here is so clearly right that the reader is encouraged to identify accordingly. In the other six pieces in the original *Potiphar Papers* the husband's righteously masculine point of view dominates. But *Mark Twain's Library* reprints the only "paper" in that collection written by the wife, a letter to another woman who implicitly agrees with her point of view. The result is that the wife's voice and argument are given authority over her husband's and ultimately prevail. At the end of the story, "James" the footman (in fact "Henry") is decked out with plush purple knee britches, and Mrs. Potiphar's, "Now, Carrie, isn't that nice?" (p. 48) closes the letter. This is the "modern" version of Joseph Neal's fait accompli.

When the man of the family has such aspirations for material self-improvement, it is a different story. F. W. Cozzens's "A Family Horse," taken from his *Sparrowgrass* series, is linked to Twain's "A Genuine Mexican Plug," which follows it. Cozzens's story begins with the narrator being comically and conventionally duped in a horse deal. He, though (unlike Twain's similarly duped protagonist), is no cowboy wannabe, nor does he appear (like Mrs. Potiphar) to be materialistically motivated. Rather, he is portrayed, like husbands in other stories, as a conscientious family man who wants, as the title says, a "family horse" to pull a carriage for outings in the country with his family. As in other stories in the collection featuring husbands who take responsibility for domestic tranquility, however, the consequence is domestic chaos.

The most interesting examples of domestic humor in *Mark Twain's Library* are those by William Dean Howells – interesting if for no other reason than that in no other place, then or since, is he featured so clearly as a humorist. The book contains six selections taken from chapters of two novels by Howells – four from *Their Wedding Journey* (not in their original order) and two from *A Chance Acquaintance*. What makes Howells's work so interesting in this context is that with no other writer do the unique arrangement and editing of his work seem so clearly appropriate. A small part of chapter 6 from *Their Wedding Journey* gets printed under the mildly misogynistic title (thus akin to the more traditional humor by other writers) of "Trying to Understand a Woman." As with the other extracts from the novel, however, the editing brings a subtle, realistic insight into the nature of marriage, focusing not on the larger wedding journey of the novel's title but on a man who must reassess his preconceived notions about gender and wedlock. At the end of this excerpt, Basil March looks at his wife "with the gravity a man must feel when he begins to perceive that he has married the whole mystifying world of womankind in the woman of his choice" (Twain 1969: 126). Howells's perception of the problems of gender dynamics in marriage goes even deeper with what follows: "I supposed I had the pleasure of my wife's acquaintance. It seems I have been flattering myself" (p. 126). Although not "humorous" in the obvious ways of other pieces – and perhaps for that reason – Howells makes clear the most important message raised by the domestic humor here: that marriage does not change women, or their "nature," and men must come to terms with that fact.

The two Howells selections from *A Chance Acquaintance* feature Kitty Ellison's dialogues with her aunt and highlight the younger woman's effort to articulate her thinking about the courtship and marriage proposal of the very Bostonian Miles Arbuton. Here too, the main theme of the novel (Kitty is a Midwestern embodiment of the American democratic spirit, in contrast to the Old World pretensions of the proper Bostonian) is sidelined in order to focus upon her rejection of the engagement. As a result, the piece more clearly fits within the collection's domestic humor context. When she admits here that the things Arbuton says once amused her, but now "I can't bear up against them. They frighten me, and seem to deny me the right to be what I believe I am" (Twain 1969: 292), she speaks only as a woman, not as an Ohioan.

Although Mark Twain has the largest number of pieces in this collection, they do not dominate, because of the unique way that he arranged the contents. As the original introduction put it, "This has the effect of bewildering the reader, who thought it was going to be all Mark Twain, and perhaps of convincing him that there are other humorists besides his favorite author" (Twain 1969: xiii). Indeed, an arrangement, in turn, that diminishes the significance of the individual humorists (including Twain) and heightens the substance of what they wrote, encourages, even forces, the reader to make connections among the represented texts, and to create a variety of "contexts" from them all. We have seen how the whitewashing episode from *Tom Sawyer* connects with references to the world of conning fraud embodied in P. T. Barnum. But, like "A Dose of Pain Killer" (from the same Twain book), it connects as well with the "bad boy" humor of Thomas Bailey Aldrich's "How We Astonished the River-mouthians." So, similarly, the McWilliams story reprinted ("Experience of the McWilliamses with Membraneous Croup") connects with other examples of domestic humor in the book (a comparison that also confirms the general consensus that this kind of humor is not Twain's *métier*).

Mark Twain and 1888

The year 1888 was not wondrous in the same way that 1867 had been, but Mark Twain had again "arrived," in a sense. As Louis Budd writes in *Our Mark Twain*, the 1880s were good for Mark Twain in so many ways (he turned 50 in 1885; Budd titles the chapter in which he discusses that anniversary "The Year of Jubilee"). The fateful implications of the Paige typesetter were still a dark cloud on the horizon of an otherwise blue sky. Family life was good, finances apparently so, and not only had his public image broadened and improved, but he had gained the respect of the literary establishment, symbolically represented by his receiving an honorary Master of Arts degree from Yale in June 1888. The publication of *Mark Twain's Library* in December represented much the same thing, a comfortable and gratifying place to be. If his own humor in the book seems to engage contemporary issues less trenchantly than the work of other writers, we can see in retrospect that he had by no means lost his incisive and socially critical voice. Indeed, in the eight years that the collection took to evolve, Mark Twain was digging more deeply into the issues of postwar America than any other writer in the anthology. In retrospect, we can place 1880, the year in which the concept for *Mark Twain's Library of Humor* was initiated, as the time, too, when Twain had the germinal idea for what would become *A Connecticut Yankee in King Arthur's Court*. That novel was published the year after the humor collection. And "The Siamese Twins," a Twain squib that does appear in the collection, would evolve into one of his most socially troubling texts, *Pudd'nhead Wilson*, published just six years after the *Library* itself.

NOTES

1 Virtually all of the reviews of Mark Twain's works referred to at the start of this essay appear in Budd (1999).

2 All references are to the 1969 edition of *Mark Twain's Library of Humor* (referenced as Twain

1969), with foreword by Clarence Gohdes. This is a "photographic reprint" of the 1888 edition, except for the title-page: this is misleading because it includes Howells, Clark, and Clemens as editors, where the original identified none. For the true bibliophile, this is a curious volume because, for one thing, a large number of pieces are not included in either the author or title index. Most of these are very brief (aphorisms by Josh Billings and many more anonymous items from newspapers), but six fairly substantial works by Robert Burdette and two by Samuel Cox do not appear in the table of contents with their other works. Also, the Burdette piece in the table of contents is attributed to "anonymous" in the book itself. More significantly, "Warm Hair" does not appear in the table of contents, but is attributed to Twain in the first state of the first printing (Gohdes's edition), but not in subsequent ones. And in the detailed acknowledgments of publishing permissions at the end, Twain's "Blue-Jays" is attributed to *Roughing It*, not *A Tramp Abroad*, where it first appeared as "Jim Baker's Blue-Jay Yarn."

Not a facsimile, but based on the same text, is the Modern Library edition of *Mark Twain's Library of Humor* (referenced as Twain 2000), introduced by Roy Blount, Jr. Blount's opinions of some of the more obscure texts show his real knowledge of the book, and are worth reading – and, without rancor, he notes the dearth of Southern writers. However, while his admission that, to his taste, "the one truly terrible piece of writing in the book" is Katherine Kent Child Walker's "The Total Depravity of Inanimate Things" is acceptable, his notion that it first appeared in the *Atlantic* and again in *Mark Twain's Library* because William Dean Howells was "sweet on her or something" (Twain 2000: xvii) is not. Unless he can prove it, of course.

In 1906, Harper's published an expanded, three-volume work also titled *Mark Twain's*

Library of Humor, edited by Burges Johnson. Twain had nothing to do with the publication of this book and, in fact, tried to prevent it.

3   The term first appears in a significant way in "American Literary Comedians" (Lukens 1890). Lukens uses it in a survey of American humor from the seventeenth century to his own period, and although he ignores important women writers, Lukens does identify many humorists of his own time, now forgotten. See, too, "Literary Comedians (1868–1900)" in Blair (1960) and "Lost Characters" in Blair (1942).

4   Although underrepresented in *Mark Twain's Library*, Southern humor flourished after the Civil War and engaged many similar issues, albeit with a more regional agenda (such as the "Lost Cause" and all that it embodied, particularly race). See Hall (1965), and especially his valuable reading of Richard M. Johnston's "The Expensive Treat of Col. Moses Grice" (another of those now-obscure texts included in *Mark Twain's Library*).

5   Although his approach is very different from mine, see Gregg Camfield's important work on this subject (Camfield 1997). Camfield also provides sound analysis of some of the works of now-forgotten humorists included in *Mark Twain's Library of Humor*, including George William Curtis, William Allen Butler, Robert Burdette, and Katherine Kent Child Walker.

6   See my discussion of this type of humor in Nickels (1993: 101–6). Two later versions of the genre, but with a different "take" on gender, and included in *Mark Twain's Library*, are Francis Lee Pratt's "Captain Ben's Choice" and Robert Burdette's "The Romance of the Carpet."

REFERENCES AND FURTHER READING

Bier, Jesse (1968). *The Rise and Fall of American Humor*. New York: Holt, Rinehart, Winston.
Blair, Walter (1942). *Horse Sense in American Humor*. Chicago: University of Chicago Press.
Blair, Walter (1960). *Native American Humor*. San Francisco: Chandler. (First publ. 1937.)
Budd, Louis J. (1983). *Our Mark Twain: The*

Making of his Public Personality. Philadelphia: University of Pennsylvania Press.
Budd, Louis J., ed. (1999). *Mark Twain: The Contemporary Reviews*. New York: Cambridge University Press.
Camfield, Gregg (1997). *Necessary Madness: The Humor of Domesticity in Nineteenth-Century*

American Literature. New York: Oxford University Press.

Hall, Wade (1965). *The Smiling Phoenix: Southern Humor from 1865 to 1914*. Gainesville: University of Florida Press.

Howells, William Dean (1910). *My Mark Twain: Reminiscences and Criticism*. New York: Harper & Bros.

Kesterson, David B. (1982a). "The Literary Comedians and the Language of Humor." *Studies in American Humor* 1, 44–51.

Kesterson, David B. (1982b). "Mark Twain and the Humorist Tradition." In Hans Borchers and Daniel E. Williams (eds.), *Samuel Clemens: A Mysterious Stranger*, 55–69. New York: Peter Lang.

Kesterson, David B. (1984). "Those Literary Comedians." In William Bedford Clark and W. Craig Turner (eds.), *Critical Essays on American Humor*, 167–83. Boston: G. K. Hall.

Lukens, Henry Clay (1890). "American Literary Comedians." *Harper's New Monthly Magazine* 80, 483–99.

Messent, Peter (2001). *The Short Works of Mark Twain: A Critical Study*. Philadelphia: University of Pennsylvania Press.

Nickels, Cameron C. (1993). *New England Humor, from the Revolutionary War to the Civil War*. Knoxville: University of Tennessee Press.

Sloane, David E. E. (1979). *Mark Twain as a Literary Comedian*. Baton Rouge: Louisiana State University Press.

Twain, Mark, ed. (1969). *Mark Twain's Library of Humor*, with foreword by Clarence Gohdes. New York: Bonanza. (First publ. 1888.)

Twain, Mark (1981). *Early Tales and Sketches*, vol. 2, ed. Edgar Marquess Branch and Robert H. Hirst. Berkeley: University of California Press.

Twain, Mark, ed. (2000). *Mark Twain's Library of Humor*. Intr. Roy Blount. New York: Modern Library. (First publ. 1888.)

33

Mark Twain and Amiable Humor

Gregg Camfield

On the eve of his thirtieth birthday, having tried and discarded several different careers –typesetter, river-boat pilot, miner and newspaper reporter – Mark Twain wrote to his brother that he had at last found his true profession:

> I *have* had a "call" to literature, of a low order, *i.e.* humorous. It is nothing to be proud of, but it is my strongest suit, & if I were to listen to that maxim of stern *duty* which says that to do right you **must** multiply the one or the two or the three talents which the Almighty entrusts to your keeping, I would long ago have ceased to meddle with things for which I was by nature unfitted & turned my attention to seriously scribbling to excite the **laughter** of God's creatures. Poor, pitiful business! Though the Almighty did His part by me – for the talent is a mighty engine when supplied with the steam of **education** – which I have not got, & so its pistons & cylinders & shafts move feebly & for a holiday show & are useless for any good purpose. (Twain 1988b: 322–3, October 19 and 20, 1865)

The terminology of calling, here, is essentially religious, bearing the marks of Twain's Presbyterian upbringing. The conflict he feels, in seeing humorous writing as a pitiful business, stems from the contempt in which orthodox, fundamentalist Christians held humor. They cited biblical texts such as Luke, chapter 6, verses 21 and 25: "Blessed are ye that weep now: for ye shall laugh [in heaven]" and "woe unto you that laugh now! for ye shall mourn and weep" to suggest that taking joy in the things of this world was fundamentally sinful. Paul's Epistle to the Ephesians even lumps "foolish talking" and "jesting" with "fornication, and all uncleanness" as damning vices. No wonder that Twain considered his talent poor and pitiful.

Given that the nineteenth-century United States contained an overwhelmingly Christian population, it is perhaps difficult to believe that comedy was one of the nation's most important cultural products. The paradox can be explained, in part, by the multiple derivations of American culture. As much a by-product of the Enlightenment as of pietism, American culture could draw on rich traditions of comedy, some as old as Western civilization, some as new as the late eighteenth century. As his career unfolded and Twain found the education he earlier lamented lacking, he was able to articulate two very different justifications of humor, neither of which had the apologetic tone of his early creed:

> [The human] race, in its poverty, has unquestionably one really effective weapon – laughter. Power, Money, Persuasion, Supplication, Persecution – these can lift at a colossal humbug, – push it a little – crowd it a little – weaken it a little, century by century: but only Laughter can blow it to rags and atoms at a blast. Against the assault of Laughter nothing can stand. (Twain 1969 [1900]: 165–6)

> An absolutely essential part of any real humorist's native equipment is a deep seriousness and a rather unusually profound sympathy with the sorrows and sufferings of mankind. (Twain n.d., 22 May 1908)

The first of these defines humor essentially as satire, a mode of humor that arose at the latest in classical Greece and has been practiced in every period since. Satire is based in, and assumes a common understanding of, a sense of correctness. Laughter at those who transgress norms is designed to reinforce the status quo; it is, in short, a corrective. While classical thinkers usually saw such correctives as useful to a degree, all cautioned the well-bred from straining too much at wit or falling into the very errors of extremism or imbalance they were deriding. As Cicero put it:

> The seat and province of the laughable . . . lies in a kind of offensiveness and deformity . . . But very careful consideration must be given to how far the orator should carry laughter . . . [F]or neither great vice, such as that of crime, nor great misery is a subject for ridicule and laughter. People want criminals attacked with more forceful weapons than ridicule, and do not like the miserable to be derided, unless, perhaps, when they are insolent. (Cicero 1987: *On the Orator*, bk. II, ch. 58)

Of course, the great classical satirists, such as Horace and Juvenal, did not take such advice, and by the time of the Enlightenment, satirists such as Swift refused to stay within the bounds of manners in their ridicule.

Certainly Twain practiced satire energetically throughout his career of serious scribbling to excite the laughter of God's creatures. He often justified his work in this ancient tradition, one that was well practiced in the United States, primarily in political contexts. Twain himself certainly used it in politics, as in his sketches "Goldsmith's Friend Abroad Again," "The Curious Republic of Gondour," and "A Candidate for President." And he even expanded its common definition when in his autobiography he said that a humorist must preach if he wished to endure and that he had always preached. But as much as he enjoyed the sense of Olympian detachment and power that satire gave to him, he often rejected satire precisely for the detachment it required. As he put it in a dictation for his autobiography, talking of a recent "stupendous fancy" of his:

I must get [it] out of my head. At first it was vague, dim, sardonic, wonderful; but night after night, of late, it is growing too definite – quite too clear and definite, and haunting, and persistent. It is the Deity's mouth – His open mouth – laughing at the human race! The horizon is the lower lip; the cavernous vast arch of the sky is the open mouth and throat; the soaring bend of the Milky Way constitutes the upper teeth. It is a mighty laugh, and deeply impressive – even when it is silent; I can endure it then, but when it bursts out in crashing thunders of delight, and the breath gushes forth in a glare of white lightnings, it makes me shudder.

Every night he laughs, and every morning I eagerly search the paper to see what it is He has been laughing at. It is always recorded there in the big headlines; often one doesn't have to read what follows the headlines, the headlines themselves tell the story sufficiently; as a rule, I am not able to see what there is to laugh at; very frequently the occurrences seem to merely undignify the human race and make its acts pitiful and pathetic, rather than matter for ridicule. This morning's paper contains the following instances:

No, 1.
SPECIAL TRAIN TO SAVE HER DOG'S LIFE.
Rich, Childless Woman Spent
Thousands in Vain Efforts
for Her Pet.

It is matter for pity, not mirth. No matter what the source of a sorrow may be, the sorrow itself is respectworthy. (Mark Twain Papers, October 10, 1907)

It almost seems here as if Twain is rejecting his entire professional career. This, however, would be true only if one were to restrict the source of laughter to satire alone.

Amiable humor, as it came to be known in the eighteenth century, especially under the graces of the Scottish philosopher Francis Hutcheson, is a quite different approach to the risible. It grew out of a burgeoning democratic philosophy, one predicated not on human folly, but on human dignity, the capacity for self-government, and the belief that our common humanity holds us in sympathetic bonds that can, with proper cultivation, overcome selfishness. In this view humor has very distinct and important roles to play: it serves individual health and happiness; it provides a social lubricant; it gives insight into the human condition in all of its facets; and it serves as a sign, in the face of painful circumstances, of humans' capacities to ameliorate their common condition, at the very least through sympathetic understanding.

The first and simplest of these functions has a root much older than the Enlightenment, in the biblical proverb "Laughter doeth good like a medicine." But the real blossoming of this idea came with the gradual demise of the medical theory of the humors. According to this model, attributed to Galen and still vital as late as the Renaissance, the human body was governed by four humors in balance: melancholy, phlegm, blood, and choler. These were said to correspond with the four elements: earth, water, air, and fire. This correspondence was part of the medieval world-view, in which all matter is connected in a clearly organized, hierarchical cosmos. A person who was dominated by any one of the humors would have a corresponding temperament: melancholic, phlegmatic, sanguine, or choleric – terms still used, but no longer as representations of medical conditions. The ideal was balance among all four, and to be unbalanced was to be in a bad humor, that is to say, ill. A person in ill humor was laughable, but the derision to which he or she was subject was meant as a social corrective, ideally complemented by medical correctives also.

By the seventeenth century Galen's theory of the humors, along with the rest of his medicine, was under attack by such physicians as William Harvey and Thomas Sydenham, and the Ptolemaic world in which bodily humors corresponded to elements, seasons, winds, etc., was collapsing under the assault of Enlightenment thinkers. Not surprisingly, a new idea of "humor" arose in this period. According to the new usage, a humorist was someone departing from the norm; not ill, but merely eccentric. In this context, the older biblical idea of laughter as good medicine gained currency among rationalists and the devout alike. In laughing at a humorist one was not aiming to laugh him into social conformity, but to maintain one's own health. This idea was widely circulated by the time Samuel Clemens began to write, and he certainly heard it expressed, for example, by his friend the Reverend Whitney Bellows, who saw humor as requisite for the health of "mind and heart" (see Twain 1988b: 308). In the words, too, of another prominent American moralist, Catherine Beecher: "All Medical men unite in declaring that nothing is more beneficial to health than hearty laughter, and surely our benevolent Creator would not have provided risibles, and made it a source of health and enjoyment to use them, and then have made it a sin so to do" (Beecher 1977: 261). Thus the person who plays the clown serves as a kind of physician. As Twain put it in a sketch praising comic actor Dan Setchell: "I have experienced more real pleasure, and more physical benefit, from laughing naturally and unconfinedly at his funny personations and extempore speeches than I have from all the operas and tragedies I have endured, and all the blue mass pills I have swallowed in six months" (Twain 1981: 172).

Not surprisingly, then, the possibility of making a profession out of being a humorist, not just on the stage, but also in journals and books, began in the late eighteenth century. Comic writers adopted pen names and humorous personae in order to present themselves as literary versions of stage clowns. Washington Irving's "Geoffrey Crayon," Benjamin Franklin's "Poor Richard," and Charles Dickens's "Boz" are just a few examples Twain would have known. It comes as no surprise, then, that Twain developed various roles for the persona that carried his pen name. In 1863, in his first incarnation in the Virginia City *Territorial Enterprise*, "Mark Twain" was a drunken reprobate engaged in a recurring comic game of one-upmanship with "the Unreliable" (Clement T. Rice, a friend and a reporter for the Virginia City *Union*). Three years later, when working as a traveling correspondent for the Sacramento *Union*, Mister Mark Twain changed shape to become a prig, in the company of the rambunctious Mr. Brown. The role changed many times over the rest of his career, but no matter which way it played out, it took similar form. That is, Mark Twain played the fool rather than the wit; he played his role as if he were unconscious of his own absurdity while, all the time, the real person (Samuel Clemens) behind the role took the applause, and maintained a "normal" identity beyond his *nom de plume*.

Perhaps this technique is best described by Twain himself in his 1895 essay, "How to Tell a Story." Here he explains that the humorous story, as distinct from what he calls the comic or the witty story, depends entirely on the manner of the telling. In his explanation, the manner is a function of the character of the teller:

> The humorous story is told gravely; the teller does his best to conceal the fact that he even dimly suspects that there is anything funny about it; but the teller of the comic story tells you beforehand that it is one of the funniest things he has ever heard, then tells it with eager delight, and is the first person to laugh when he gets through. And sometimes, if he has had good success, he is so glad and happy that he will repeat the "nub" of it and glance around from face to face, collecting applause, and then repeat it again. It is a pathetic thing to see.
>
> Very often, of course, the rambling and disjointed humorous story finishes with a nub, point, snapper, or whatever you like to call it. Then the listener must be alert, for in many cases the teller will divert attention from that nub by dropping it in a carefully casual and indifferent way, with the pretense that he does not know it is a nub. (Twain 1992b: 201–2)

That Samuel Clemens could become internationally and enduringly successful as Mark Twain was entirely owing to such a humorous approach. Indeed, he catapulted to national fame when he first published his jumping frog story, an epitome of what Twain describes as the American humorous tale.

That so much of the humor filtered through the Mark Twain persona is self-deprecating is also in this same comic tradition. Indeed, once beyond his journalistic apprenticeship, Clemens adopted this posture as his primary literary and stage stance. The structure of *Roughing It*, for example, appears to follow the pattern of an initiation, in this particular case into the social and physical mysteries of the West. But if Mark Twain were truly an initiate, he would learn from his mistakes. As a literary clown, however, he repeatedly makes the same errors, the errors of a sanguine personality dealing with a reality more complex and less generous than his imagination conceives. In other words, this is the comedy of character rather than of plot (or, for that matter, of wit), and it served as the first and most important role in Clemens's humorous repertoire. In this, he knew he was serving not an intrinsically serious purpose, but instead one of comic relief. He explained this function well in a letter to one of his early mentors, Mary Mason Fairbanks. Fairbanks constantly encouraged him to write beyond humor, to live up to his talents by giving serious lectures and writing seriously, too. His reply was to say that "What the societies *ask* of me is to *relieve* the heaviness of their didactic courses – & in accepting the contract I am just the same as *giving my word* that I will do as they ask" (Twain 1990: 264).

But amiable humor, according to its apologists and practitioners, was more than healthy comic relief in a serious world. It was meant in nature's – or God's – plan to serve much nobler purposes. The first of these was as a social lubricant. As Francis Hutcheson put it in 1750: "Laughter, like other associations, is very contagious: our whole frame is so sociable, that one merry countenance may diffuse cheerfulness to many; nor are they all fools who are apt to laugh before they know the jest . . . Laughter is [one] of the . . . bonds to common friendships" (Hutcheson 1987: 36).

In coupling this definition with a vigorous attack on Thomas Hobbes's notion that we laugh when we feel superior to others, Hutcheson argued that humor serves not only to bind friendships, but to highlight the fundamental equality of all human beings. Indeed, as the eighteenth century rolled out and the nineteenth rolled in, humor became a conventional way of bridging gaps between social classes. Earlier humorous sketches had made the lower social orders the butts of jokes – one need look no further than the comic characters in most of Shakespeare's plays for evidence of this. Many eighteenth- and nineteenth-century humorous writers expanded such an approach, making all social classes the subject of laughter, and making it inclusive rather than scornful. In so doing, such sketches often elevate lower-class characters through humor alone.

Again, it is important to see how this different comic practice was derived from a changed world-view. In a hierarchical and static society, anyone out of humor, or anyone whose behavior challenged the status quo, needed to be corrected. Minor infractions were deserving of laughter. But in a society in which freedom of movement and class fluidity were coming to be the norm, class distinctions had to be eased and diminished, not solidified. Thus the Third Earl of Shaftesbury, for instance, postulated that human beings are bound, despite all differences, by moral sensibilities, among which (according to many other eighteenth-century commentators too) was the sense of humor. Thus, rather than the humorist being seen as an eccentric, ill because unbalanced, the person with a sense of humor could now be defined as one who could identify the peculiarities making for individuality, and delight in them. Laughter in this philosophy was a hearty way of congratulating a person on his or her individuality, of making community from a collection of individuals. The moral philosophers – particularly Shaftesbury, Hutcheson, and their many popularizers – who spread these ideas about humor also spread the ideas of human moral equality that would indirectly lead to the great revolutions of the late eighteenth and early nineteenth centuries in Europe and America.

Thus, in participating in a form of humor that challenged rigid class hierarchies, Mark Twain took his place in a century-old tradition, and one that can be seen as patriotic (in the sense that the United States is predicated on equality). Yet the fact that the argument about the form and function of humor was still there to be made suggests more than a slight ambivalence about class leveling. Clemens shared that ambivalence, and his satires, naturally, often are based on class distinctions. His amiable humor, however, usually works to collapse such distinctions even while acknowledging that they exist. Consider, for example, the sketch of Scotty Briggs and the Parson from chapter 47 in *Roughing It*. The narrative thrust of the piece contrasts the language and values of the refined minister and the rough. Pre-Enlightenment laughter would have validated the refined voice at the expense of the ignorant, but Twain levels the two languages, showing that each is powerful in its own context, and that over-refinement is as grotesque as boorishness. He shows, too, that both characters share good-heartedness, and capacities for growth and change. Their initial meeting is comic in the depicted failure of communication, but the sketch is, finally, profoundly optimistic about human community, for the two men do communicate the essentials despite their lapses, and also come to be allies in their quest to spread humane values in a frontier community.

Most significantly, much of *Adventures of Huckleberry Finn* depends on this kind of humor. As readers, we cannot identify with the protagonist without taking delight in his ignorance. Thus, Huck could easily be a target of contempt. He begins his life, after all, as a vagrant, wearing rags, living in hogsheads, the son of an Irish drunkard and rowdy. In *The Adventures of Tom Sawyer*, where Huck makes his debut, the respectable folks in town shun him and force their children, on pain of punishment, to shun him, too. He is, as Twain calls him, a "pariah." By that novel's end, he is raised to respectability through wealth and through the sponsorship of the Widow Douglas – but as his own novel begins this elevation is proving to be a struggle. His ignorance remains profound and his acceptance of bourgeois values is no more than a seed planted in his psyche. When his adventures rip him out of the respectable Douglas household and throw him back down the ladder of social respectability, he essentially checks out of society entirely.

It would be easy to scorn the boy and, indeed, some contemporary reviewers did just that. They refused him sympathy for fear that it would in fact encourage anti-social values such as lying and stealing. But if Twain had intended us to scorn Huck, his novel would merely have been brutal, and what laughter there was would have been contemptuous. Twain, instead, made the boy a powerfully sympathetic character. The reader's laughter tends toward amiability; it allows the embrace of Huck's ignorance as loveable. And once readers cross the divide from contempt to love, they can come, too, to accept the possibility of a good heart in an abused, lower-class child. Having embraced Huck's moral universe as valuable, readers are then further challenged to extend that sympathy to Jim, the runaway slave (whom Twain also intended to represent the *de jure* freed, but still *de facto* oppressed, blacks in post-Reconstruction America). The multiple ironies have the corrective power of satire, but they work as such only insofar as readers first embrace, through sympathetic humor, characters low on the social class scale.

When giving public readings from the novel in 1895, Twain himself used the sentimental language of amiable humor when describing the novel's moral process: "In a crucial moral emergency a sound heart is a safer guide than an ill-trained conscience. I sh'd support this doctrine with a chapter from a book of mine where a sound heart & a deformed conscience come into collision & conscience suffers defeat" (see Twain 1988a: 805). If this is so, then the thrust of the humor in the book is in turn to have the readers' sound hearts triumph over their deformed consciences through the amiable power of the sense of humor. Class barriers fall in a book that says, in agreement with the Enlightenment moralists' proposition, that all human beings are created morally equal.

In using amiable humor to present an argument for equality, the rhetorical theory of humor suggested that it sweetened a bitter pill, that it served as an effective window dressing for ideas that would ameliorate the human condition but at the cost of the social status quo. This could be taken further, for humor could be seen not merely as a way to persuade people to accept truths, but also as a way to reveal them in the first place. Relatively few commentators in the period stressed this aspect of humor and, when they did mention it, they often mixed it in with other attributes. For example, in his essay on the comic Ralph Waldo Emerson wrote:

> A perception of the Comic seems to be a balance-wheel in our metaphysical structure. It appears to be an essential element in a fine character. Wherever the intellect is constructive, it will be found. We feel the absence of it as a defect in the noblest and most oracular soul. The perception of the Comic is a tie of sympathy with other men, a pledge of sanity, and a protection from those perverse tendencies and gloomy insanities in which fine intellects sometimes lose themselves. (Emerson 1903: 161–2)

Emerson's claims that the comic sensibility ties humanity together in a sympathetic bond, and that it is a counterbalance to a seriousness that, by itself, would be damaging to health, fit two of the common justifications of humor already discussed. But the idea that humor is necessary to a constructive mind pushes the justification of humor further. To some degree, the capacity to understand the world, and to see it fully, requires a sense of the absurd. As Twain more succinctly put it: "The function of humor is that of the screw in the opera glass – it adjusts one's focus" (see Camfield 2003: 280).

Views on exactly what that focus was, of course, have varied among critical commentators, but the pattern of humor Twain himself commonly followed was articulated most influentially, perhaps, by Arthur Schopenhauer, who wrote, "laughter always signifies the sudden apprehension of an incongruity between . . . a conception and the real object thought under it" (Schopenhauer 1987: 54–5). This is the formula for a large portion of Mark Twain's humor, and it is the theory of the comic that underlies not merely his practice of an amiable humor, but often his use of satire, parody, burlesque, hoaxing, and other forms of comedy. This is important. *All* humorous practices, amiable and otherwise, can be explained under the umbrella theory of incongruity. Those critics who endorse the conception of humor as amiable and generous, as fostering sympathetic understanding, tend usually to combine this notion with its capacity to reveal the truth through incongruity, but the two things need not be so connected. Incongruity lies at the heart of satire, too, especially in the modified satire of many Enlightenment and post-Enlightenment writers whose satire attacks (rather than supports) the status quo.

Whether using humor to condemn, or to extend sympathy, Twain uses this formula for humor as revelation through incongruity frequently in his travel writings. From *Innocents Abroad* (1869) to *Following the Equator* (1897), his humor sets expectation against reality. In *Innocents Abroad*, for instance, he suggests that the beauty of European shop girls (a veiled allusion is made here to Sterne's *Sentimental Journey*) is overstated; that the aesthetic value of paintings by the "Old Masters" is held too high; that French barbers do not deliver one into the lap of luxury, and that neither do French hotels; that Lake Como in Italy and the Sea of Galilee in Palestine do not live up to their advance billing; and that the delights of Turkey are merely the idiotic "puffs" of previous tourists. The leitmotif of the book, here directed toward one particular region, is stated baldly in chapter 34: "When I think how I have been swindled by books of Oriental travel, I want a tourist for breakfast" (Twain 1869: 376). Clearly, Twain here is not an amiable humorist; he is using the humor of incongruity not only to discover, but also to condemn. In *Roughing It* (1872), Twain turns his attention not to the fabled East but to romances of the American West. In theory, the hardships and privations of a strange new world are more interesting than they turn out to be in fact. Preconceptions about Indians, scenery, animals, mining, gunfights, and even moral reform, are collapsed in the humorous contrast between them and the reality portrayed. Perhaps Twain puts it best in chapter 18, when he talks of crossing

> one of that species of deserts whose concentrated hideousness shames the diffused and limited horrors of Sahara – an *"alkali"* desert . . . [W]e were to cross a desert in *daylight*. This was fine – novel – romantic – dramatically adventurous – *this*, indeed, was worth living for, worth traveling for! We would write home all about it. This enthusiasm, this stern thirst for adventure, wilted under the sultry August sun and did not last above one hour. One poor little hour – and then we were ashamed we had "gushed" so. The poetry was all in the anticipation – there is none in the reality.

Twain judges less harshly in this second travel book, turning much of the humor onto himself rather than scorning the culture he is exploring, but the humor is still not overly amiable. In fact, this pattern of a deflating incongruity, established so powerfully in Twain's first two travel books, stands as the basis for three major studies of American Humor: Constance Rourke's *American Humor, a Study of the National Character* (1931), Walter Blair's *Native American Humor* (1937), and Henry Nash Smith's *Mark Twain: The Development of a Writer* (1962). All three suggest that the thrust of American humor was to contrast European norms of civilization, politics, and beauty with American experiences in order to help carve out an exceptional American identity. In other words, incongruity forms the basis for a progressive and nationalistic, rather than a conservative, satire. The humor itself lies, they suggest, in the incongruity between expectations and reality. Twain's second European travel book, *A Tramp Abroad* (1880), is once more explicit in its challenge to European norms and expectations. Of all his travel narratives it is, perhaps, the one that leans furthest from amiable humor in its use of laughter as a tool to gain insight.

But Twain did not stop with such aggressive use of incongruity as a mode of exploration. While he believed that humor clarified our vision, he would also, at times, question the degree to which incongruity revealed disappointment rather than truth.

In some cases, the pattern of measuring expectation against reality causes not a genuine assessment of reality but an excessive counter-reaction to the initial sense of promise. In chapter 59 of *Following the Equator*, for example, his discussion of the Taj Mahal and of Niagara Falls alerts us to the possibility that humorous over-reaction may in fact obscure truth:

> We saw forts, mosques, and tombs, which were built in the great days of the Mohammedan emperors, and which are marvels of cost, magnitude, and richness of material and ornamentation, creations of surpassing grandeur, wonders which do indeed make the like things in the rest of the world seem tame and inconsequential by comparison. I am not proposing to describe them. By good fortune I had not read too much about them, and therefore was able to get a natural and rational focus upon them, with the result that they thrilled, blessed, and exalted me. But if I had previously overheated my imagination by drinking too much pestilential literary hot Scotch, I should have suffered disappointment and sorrow. I mean to speak of only one of those many world-renowned buildings, the Taj Mahal, the most celebrated construction in the earth. I had read a great deal too much about it. I saw it . . . and I knew all the time, that of its kind it was *the* wonder of the world, with no competition now and no possible future competitor, and yet, it was not *my* Taj. My Taj had been built by excitable literary people; it was solidly lodged in my head, and I could not blast it out . . . I had to visit Niagara fifteen times before I succeeded in getting my imaginary Falls gauged to the actuality and could begin to sanely and wholesomely wonder at them for what they were, not what I had expected them to be. When I first approached them it was with my face lifted toward the sky, for I thought I was going to see an Atlantic ocean pouring down thence over cloud-vexed Himalayan heights, a sea-green wall of water sixty miles front and six miles high, and so, when the toy reality came suddenly into view – that beruffled little wet apron hanging out to dry – the shock was too much for me, and I fell with a dull thud. Yet slowly, surely, steadily, in the course of my fifteen visits, the proportions adjusted themselves to the facts, and I came at last to realize that a waterfall a hundred and sixty-five feet high and a quarter of a mile wide was an impressive thing. It was not a dipperful to my vanished great vision, but it would answer. I know that I ought to do with the Taj as I was obliged to do with Niagara – see it fifteen times, and let my mind gradually get rid of the Taj built in it by its describers, by help of my imagination, and substitute for it the Taj of fact. It would be noble and fine, then, and a marvel; not the marvel which it replaced, but still a marvel, and fine enough. (Twain 1897: 570–7)

The dialectic, facilitated by humor, between expectation and reality is an essential process in calibrating emotional, as well as intellectual, judgment. The crucial difference between Twain's use of it in this more mature travel narrative and in the earlier ones is that here, in using humor to discover reality, Twain is not egotistical. The humor comes not from a brash American iconoclast whacking Europe; it comes, rather, from a self-reflective dreamer, whose humor, in an amiable way, is self-directed and thus self-correcting. In that, it moves much closer to an ideal of amiable humor and away from the comedy of satire. In other words, Twain struggles to replace judgment with sympathy, and thus to ameliorate the pain of disappointment in a more balanced, more humane understanding.

The final type of humor to include under the umbrella of amiable humor is some-thing of a culmination of all the others. To see humor as consolation, as an anodyne to sorrow or to the pains of the human condition is to see it as combining sympathy for humanity, deep understanding of the reality of the human condition, and a restora-tive in the face of any loss or pain such understanding entails. This view of humor is perhaps best articulated by Søren Kierkegaard:

> The tragic and the comic are the same, in so far as both are based on contradiction; but *the tragic is the suffering contradiction, the comical, the painless contradiction* . . . The differ-ence between the tragic and the comic lies in the relationship between the contradic-tion and the controlling idea. The comic apprehension evokes the contradiction or makes it manifest by having in mind the way out, which is why the contradiction is painless. The tragic apprehension sees the contradiction and despairs of a way out . . . Humor has its justification precisely in its tragic side, in the fact that it reconciles itself to . . . pain. (Kierkegaard 1968: 459–64, emphasis in original)

Undoubtedly, Twain's humor often looks directly at the woes of the world and finds a way out of them, suggesting that humor comes when there is a sense of consolation to be found in that world. But for Twain, the practicing, professional humorist, humor itself often *was* the consolation.

In perhaps no other work does this emerge so clearly as in the masterpiece of comic writing "Jim Baker's Blue-Jay Yarn," originally from *A Tramp Abroad* and often anthol-ogized since. The history of its composition is relevant to its meaning. When Twain was writing *A Tramp Abroad* he was, in fact, not in the best of humor. He was feeling tremendous financial pressure, as a long economic depression beginning in 1873 cramped his income from book sales and his wife's income from her interests in coal mining and railroads. Traveling in Europe both to "economize" and to gain material for a new book, Twain found himself wanting to write satire and struggling to live up to the standards of gentle humor, and unable even to find the evenness of temper to do the former. As he put it in a letter of January 30, 1879 to William Dean Howells:

> I wish I *could* give those sharp satires on European life which you mention, but of course a man can't write successful satire except he be in a calm judicial good-humor – whereas I *hate* travel, & I *hate* hotels, & I *hate* the opera, & I *hate* the Old Masters – in truth I don't ever seem to be in a good enough humor with ANYthing to *satirize* it; no I want to stand up before it & *curse* it, & foam at the mouth, – or take a club & pound it to rags & pulp. I have got in two or three chapters about Wagner's Operas, & managed to do it without showing temper – but the strain of another such effort would burst me. (Twain and Howells 1960: 248–9)

The strain he felt, in fact, was the strain of a breadwinner having to be funny to win his family's bread. In a slightly later letter to Howells, he described writing the book as "a life-&-death battle" (Twain and Howells 1960: 286). This is no surprise considering that he was jaded before he began the book, exhausted from working on several major manuscripts (including *Adventures of Huckleberry Finn*), consumed by business affairs, and pestered incessantly by demands to answer fan mail. Europe was to provide an escape from much of this, but the journey there came with the duty to flesh out a large book, already under contract. No wonder, then, that after writing and discarding a number of disjointed chapters, he wrote this tale of a man destroyed by an impossible task.

The piece is a framed narrative in which Jim Baker, a profoundly unreliable narrator, tells the tale to Mark Twain. What looks at first glance to be a conventional animal fable proves to be something far deeper. Baker reveals that he has failed to strike it rich as a miner and, rather than return home in disgrace, has chosen a life of solitude and misanthropy in the Sierra foothills. He projects his hatred of himself and his own humanity onto the animals around him, calling the blue-jay the model human, carrying all negative human attributes and but two positive ones – volubility and sense of humor. Ironically, Baker himself lacks the latter, and in showing how a single jay, in parallel to his own circumstances, tried to provide for his family by tackling an impossible task, Baker reveals not only his own sorrow, but that of Samuel Clemens, too. When the jay can alleviate his pain first by sharing it with other jays and then, when "the absurdity of the contract came home to him," by laughing cathartically, we are given a truth Baker cannot fathom. Laughter teaches us about our reality in a way that allows us to let go of the egotism and seriousness that trap us in pain. The alternative is the beauty of the jest itself. The final character, an owl who cannot get the jest, also cannot see the beauty of one of the world's most spectacular places, Yosemite. Clearly, Twain suggests that the capacity for joys of almost all kinds are connected to the leveling insights of deep humor. In that sense, Twain argues for the most profound integration of the functions promoted by Enlightenment moralists with their praise of an amiable humor.

Twain himself was writing at the end of this tradition. Advocates of amiable humor tended to diminish the role of aggression in comedy, and as social Darwinism and depth psychology pushed ideas of human competition and aggression to the fore, amiable humor came to seem naïve. Moreover, as a professional humorist, Twain used the entire range of comic options open to him. Yet Twain was of his time as often as he was ahead of it. Without an understanding of both the theory and practice of amiable humor, one cannot fully understand the richness of the ways in which Mark Twain excited the laughter of God's creatures.

REFERENCES AND FURTHER READING

Academic studies of amiable humor are fundamentally shaped by Stuart Tave's excellent *Amiable Humor: A Study in the Comic Theory and Criticism of the Eighteenth and Early Nineteenth Centuries* (Chicago: University of Chicago Press, 1960). This study was published in a period in which many important studies of Twain's humor came out, but as Tave concerned himself with the British tradition, few of his insights found their way quickly into critical works on Twain. Most of the latter concentrated on other aspects of Twain's humor, though there were significant overlaps and, in some cases, arguments that Twain's humor challenges the sentimental tradition to which amiable humor belonged. The studies of Twain's humor with the broadest sweep are James M. Cox's *Mark Twain: The Fate of Humor* (Princeton: Princeton University Press, 1966); Henry Nash Smith, *Mark Twain: The Development of a Writer* (Cambridge, Mass.: Harvard University Press, 1962); Kenneth S. Lynn, *Mark Twain and Southwestern Humor* (Boston: Little, Brown, 1959), and (later) Bruce Michelson, *Mark Twain on the Loose* (Amherst: University of Massachusetts Press, 1995). Useful, too, are narrower studies, such as Franklin Rogers, *Mark Twain's Burlesque Patterns* (Dallas: Southern Methodist University Press, 1960), and Henry B. Wonham, *Mark Twain and the Art of the Tall Tale* (New York: Oxford University Press, 1993). Most specifically dealing with the tradition of Amiable Humor are Gregg Camfield, *Necessary Madness: The Humor of Domesticity in Nineteenth-Century American Literature* (New York: Oxford University Press, 1997) and *Sentimental Twain: Samuel Clements in the Maze of Moral Philosophy* (Philadelphia: University of Pennsylvania Press, 1994). Other essays in this volume guide readers to books that discuss different aspects of Twain's comic art.

Additional References

Beecher, Catherine (1977). *A Treatise on Domestic Economy*. New York: Schocken. (First publ. 1841.)

Blair, Walter (1937). *Native American Humor*. New York: American Book Company.

Camfield, Gregg (2003). *The Oxford Companion to Mark Twain*. New York: Oxford University Press.

Cicero (1987). *On the Orator* (1st cent. BC). In John Morreall, ed., *The Philosophy of Laughter and Humor*. Albany: State University of New York Press.

Emerson, Ralph Waldo (1903). "The Comic." In *Letters and Social Aims*. Boston: Riverside. (First publ. 1876.)

Hutcheson, Francis (1987). "Reflection upon Laughter" (first publ. 1750). In John Morreall, ed., *The Philosophy of Laughter and Humor*. Albany: State University of New York Press.

Kierkegaard, Søren (1968). *Concluding Unscientific Postscript*, trans. David F. Swenson and Walter Lowrie. Princeton: Princeton University Press. (First publ. 1846.)

Rourke, Constance (1931). *American Humor, A Study in National Character*. New York: Harcourt, Brace.

Schopenhauer, Arthur (1987). *The World as Will and Idea*. In John Morreall, ed., *The Philosophy of Laughter and Humor*. Albany: State University of New York Press. (First publ. 1819.)

Smith, Henry Nash (1962). *Mark Twain: The Development of a Writer*. Cambridge, Mass.: Belknap/Harvard University Press.

Twain, Mark (n.d.). "Autobiographical Dictations." Unpublished. Mark Twain Papers, Bancroft Library, University of California, Berkeley.

Twain, Mark (1969). *Mark Twain's Mysterious Stranger Manuscripts*, ed. William M. Gibson. Berkeley: University of California Press.

Twain, Mark (1981). "A Voice for Setchell" (first publ. 1865). In *Early Tales and Sketches*, vol. 2: *1864–1865*, ed. Edgar Marquess Branch and Robert H. Hirst. Berkeley: University of California Press.

Twain, Mark (1988a). *Adventures of Huckleberry Finn*, ed. Walter Blair and Victor Fischer. Berkeley: University of California Press.

Twain, Mark (1988b). *Mark Twain's Letters*, vol. 1: *1853–1866*, ed. Edgar Marquess Branch, Michael B. Frank, and Kenneth M. Sanderson. Berkeley: University of California Press.

Twain, Mark (1990). *Mark Twain's Letters*, vol. 2: *1867–1868*, ed. Harriet Elinor Smith and Richard Bucci. Berkeley: University of California Press.

Twain, Mark, and Howells, William Dean (1960). *Mark Twain–Howells Letters: The Correspondence of Samuel L. Clemens and William Dean Howells*, 2 vols., ed. Henry Nash Smith and William M. Gibson. Cambridge, Mass.: Belknap.

34

Mark Twain and the Enigmas of Wit

Bruce Michelson

In thinking about wit and humor, we have reached a moment when we may have to start over, almost from scratch. This possibility runs counter to common sense, because literature that makes us laugh is generalized about so freely now, by people with plausible credentials. Thus Daniel Mendelsohn, for example, a regular headliner in the *New York Review of Books*, can write:

> If a work like [Aristophanes'] *Frogs* is more fun for audiences, it's probably because the play, with its ruthless send-ups of the well-known weaknesses of each of the two contestants, satisfies a primitive pleasure that lies at the heart of all comedy: the *Schadenfreude*-laden enjoyment of the spectacle of someone else's humiliation and, ultimately, defeat. (Mendelsohn 2004: 43)

Holding a day job with Princeton's Classics department, Mendelsohn has academic license to ignore a few hundred years of artistic experiment and critical ferment, and pontificate on "all comedy" from Aristotelian heights. In a credentials face-off on the subjects of comedy and "the Greeks" between Mendelsohn and a plucky amateur (the American essayist Richard Rodriguez), Rodriguez would be outclassed – except that his amateur's insights are more relevant to our own cultural and interpretive predicaments. Rodriguez, in *Days of Obligation*, muses on the tragic or comic demeanor of modern nation-states:

> I use the word "comedy" here as the Greeks used it, with utmost seriousness, to suggest a world where youth is not a fruitless metaphor; where it is possible to start anew; where it is possible to escape the rivalries of the Capulets and the McCoys; where young women can disprove the adages of grandmothers. (Rodriguez 1992: xvi)

Search for passages in "the Greeks" to bolster Rodriguez's hunch and you will lose the afternoon, unless you consider pleasures and shock-waves in Aristophanes that Aristotle does not address. Rodriguez is alluding to the inconvenient power of comic literature to "disprove the adages" even of theorists and working critics, people like Aristotle and Mendelsohn and us, who come along later to lay down rules and argue the chaos into shape. As his paragraph goes haywire and moves from description to demonstration, it demonstrates how comic writers (like the mercurial Rodriguez himself) can thwart a reader's expectations in ways that both gratify and convince. He is suggesting that you will not catch the essence of wit or humor or comedy, as ancient or modern practices, by sticking to logic and making sense all the way down.

If Mendelsohn understands that paradox, he declines to stray from Aristotle's protective shadow. Praising *Poetics* as "the first full-scale and intellectually sophisticated attempt to *analyze the nature of aesthetic pleasure and to systematize the mechanisms* by which literary texts produce that pleasure," he concedes only that:

> [I]t would be hard to find a less humorous explanation of humor than "Comedy is (as we have said) an imitation of inferior people – not however with respect to every kind of defect: the laughable is a species of what is disgraceful. The laughable is an error or disgrace that does not involve pain or destruction," etc., etc.,). (Mendelsohn 2004: 44, emphasis added)

Mendelsohn's target in this article is a polemicist named Dale Peck. Rodriguez, for his part, is musing intemperately about the temperament of the modern United States. If invoking "the Greeks" in either case does not seem weird as an intellectual strategy, this is because the comic dimensions of our own cultures remain exempt from expectations that prevail elsewhere in the game of critique. Established reviewers and run-of-the-mill academics are usually expected to write from an understanding that Western cultures, and theoretical approaches to them, may have evolved somewhat in the past hundred years. The discussion of the comic is a major exception. Wit, humor, comedy, laughter (in the current slough, the categories are capriciously lumped together): these can supposedly be handled with wooden apparatus from the crypt. In many circles Freud has gone sour, viewed askance for (among other things) dubious research, narrow cultural interests, and peculiar ideas about women, but his *Jokes and their Relation to the Unconscious*, too short for the purpose and a century old, is still deployed, even by his detractors, to quell the significance of laughter in literary texts that humanists might want to exploit for other qualities or themes. What matter that, in *Le Rire* (*Laughter*; also a century old), Bergson's speculations on literary comedy and wit are grounded in courtly works of Molière? Or that another favored resource in the discussion of the comic, Bakhtin's *Rabelais and his World* (most of it written in the midnight of Stalinism), says nothing about modern humor or wit, or that its assumptions about carnival in the Middle Ages have been upended by historians with better archives to work with? In literary and cultural studies, discussion of the comic is torpid – and for anyone seeking to understand Mark Twain's genius, this inertia has consequences.

The heart of the problem is not laziness in keeping up with intellectual fashion. One underlying misconception, hanging on strongly in the dominant varieties of "humor studies" and turning up also in Mendelsohn's review, is the premise that the best way to open up a text that amuses is, as he says, to "systematize the mechanisms." To accept that proposition is to short-circuit possibilities for seeing that modern versions of the comic might target assumptions that everything around us, and within us, including the creative mind itself, is a "mechanism." Because Aristotle was more interested in logic and form than in aesthetics, aesthetic experience became for him another manifestation of logic and form. His experience with comic sketches, one-liners, barbarous wood-cut illustrations in back-country newspapers, or anything else that might trigger hilarity without the assistance of masked actors on a rounded stage, was probably sparse. And it might not have occurred to Aristotle – as it does not occur to many humanist scholars who continue to organize their thinking about wit and humor around a narrow set of deceased Great Men – that a comic outbreak might have complex and dynamic relationships to the medium in which it appears, and also to a special historical moment; or that there might be additional, anomalous connections among cultural predicaments in which that eruption was first and successively encountered, and how it is encountered now. Though an epigram, a joke, or a comic narrative can draw energy and prodigious possibilities from a given context, it may also be "about" the transience and volatility of context, creative and interpretive rituals specific to the medium, and culturally conditioned motions of the mind – motions that might seem synonymous with intense and original thinking, but actually are not.

Obviously, wit and humor come at us now from all sectors of the public sphere. Without stirring from the work-chair we can call up screen-windows of jokes about "breaking news," endure morning merriment from a gross of hacks on the radio, flip through 50 years of rerun sitcoms dumping day and night from low-earth orbit into the backyard dish. In such an assault on the human capacity for amusement, how can *The Acharnians* and *Lysistrata* be for us the same texts as they were for Athenian audiences in the dark of the Peloponnesian Wars? Systematize the mechanisms? As Thucydides so coldly made clear, it was systems and mechanisms, political logic and rational deliberation, that had brought this unending violence on. And in their comedic, supremely irrational turn away from militarism and city-state patriotism – and towards profligate sex and a mad separate peace – these plays refused those pathological habits of reason that had pushed everyone into this jam. Systematic analysis of Aristophanes, or any species of outrageous comedy, invariably reaffirms, as collateral damage, the psychological and cultural oppression that these texts are at least partly about. "Tragedy is clean," declares the Chorus in Jean Anouilh's twentieth-century rewrite of the Antigone story, repacking an ancient myth and its own academic critique into one clean modernist package. In the presence of tragedy, we witnesses think we know where we are, imagining we comprehend the cold equations of life and the penalties of transgression. In tragedy, structures can be analyzed with structure, suggesting, or gratifying, whatever in human consciousness is gratified by recognizing structures. But ancient and modern wit and humor and comedy are *not* clean, and if Aristophanes does not convince on that point, we can think about Alfred Jarry, who actually had studied with Bergson and subsequently came up with species of laughter and comedy that Bergson had never imagined, or chose not to find under his nose.

Figuratively or physically, comic discourse can also violate the etiquette of genre and mode, the segregation of audience from actor and reader from text – which means that "structure" of a basic sort, the private and supposedly autonomous mental organization of worldly experience, can also be a prime target. In Mark Twain's time, humor and comedy could be plotless, pointless, brief, wild insurrections against a world organized into plots and points. Wit can strike fast and refuse to explain its intention. And in its anarchy or multiplicity, the comic outbreak may celebrate the primordial mind itself – perhaps as it truly is, but in any case as a capability more agile and complex than any operative description now valorized in the humanistic disciplines will allow.

Since the beginning of the 1990s, and especially since the advent of magnetic resonance imaging in the study of neural activity, numerous discoveries and informed hypotheses have pulled the rug from under the kind of linear-algebra theorizing that underlies so much literary, sociological, and linguistic discussion of wit and humor, theorizing that had already proved unsatisfactory long before "creativity" and "understanding" and "laughter" became so much more interesting as concepts. Research at Stanford and Dartmouth has suggested that the brain responds to comic experience in different cortical regions simultaneously, implying that the human mind may in some dimension "get" the joke in several ways at once, and prior to any systematic decoding (Mobbs et al. 2003: 1041–8; Moran et al. 2004: 1055–60). In the *Journal of Research in Personality*, a team of researchers recently sought to supplant the restrictive Freudian discourse of repression and sublimation, the classical-physics paradigm of steam-engines and hydraulic presses, with a four-dimensional model of "Humor Styles"(Martin et al. 2003: 47–85). Though high-profile theorists in these rapidly evolving sciences quarrel about optimal new ways of describing and modeling "the mind," no one of importance in that controversy still holds that dyads, dualisms, ironies, and the rest of our cherished either/or and yes/no incongruities can suffice as descriptions of creative thought or processes of understanding, especially when the mind is moving at the velocities of wit.[1] Practitioners in the humanities can no longer privilege, without question, interpretive strategies which assume that the brain of the artist and the brain of the reader operate as simply, and clumsily, as a Babbage computer, a nineteenth-century stamping mill, or some vaguely Hegelian device that bumps along on dialectical propulsion.

Though it takes time for fresh ways of thinking about anything to make their way from the laboratories to the literary reading-rooms, in the case of the study of the comic the transit is impeded by the bifurcation in contemporary "humor studies." Customarily, that phrase refers to two ongoing conversations, which now seem as oblivious to one another as they both are to recent work in the cognitive neurosciences. Aristotle, Freud, Bergson, and Bakhtin, whose works share the virtue of clarity, still inform and represent the kind of "humor studies" that prevail in literary circles. Analysis of this sort might be spiced with Hobbes, Addison, Kant, Schopenhauer,

Kierkegaard, Herbert Spencer, Arthur Koestler, and other folk raised up as pundits on wit and humor because they were wise about other and unrelated subjects. But the general pattern of the argument will not surprise. The comic text is customarily unpacked, formalized, historicized, and in one way or another shown to be a vehicle or container for a solemn and profound theme. Literary "humor studies" prefers rituals of the "really about": *The Comedy of Errors* is "really about" the contingency of individual identity in a cosmopolitan early modern Europe; *Tristram Shandy* is really about the intractability of autobiography as a narrative form; and so on – following interpretive dance-steps that, with a new theoretical hip-shimmy here and there, have stayed largely the same for generations.

Also situated within the humanities, more or less, a different group gathers around a set of authorities associated with semantics and sociology. What goes on in that corner of the hall will be glanced at later. For both communities, however, the abiding problem is inattention to the evolving understanding of how human beings actually generate and respond to sequences of spoken and printed words. In the practice of literary and cultural criticism, as well as semantic analysis, systems borrowed from another age implicitly presume human creativity and response to be systematic, in the manner of nineteenth-century industrial and intellectual systems. Verbal and textual analysis rings truer, however, when a reading community apprehends that the analytic process emulates in some dimension the essential dynamics of thought, of artistic genius, and also the dynamics of intelligent, non-scholastic interpretation – varieties of response associated with lucid "common readers" in immediate encounters with text. This observation is neither original nor profound, though it is inconvenient. When literary theory wars were hotter than they are now, Norman Holland observed that the basic praxis of most working "theorists" was still only a variety of "simple introspection. They [these critics] apply to higher-level processes the control they feel with lower-level processes, basing the reading on what they take for granted as psychological truth" (Holland 1989: 434). In the course of that essay, Holland also warned that *psychological* theory was heading off in directions that humanist critics were not noticing, very much to our disadvantage – but in the humanist enterprises, no one took heed of Holland either.

To engage with Mark Twain's comic genius in a fresh way, we can embark instead from a handful of eccentric plain-language perceptions, as we wait, on the edges of the fray, for conflicting models in neuroscience and the cognitive sciences to stabilize and sort themselves out. In a recent book (Michelson 2000) I tried to describe *literary* wit as a discourse and cultural practice different from the creation and reception of wit and humor in other contexts. Even after the theoretical maelstrom of the past quarter-century, literary situations still seem recognizable and special to most thoughtful readers and critics – and with that in mind I offered the following perceptions:

• The literary context transforms intention, implication, and inference. We are conditioned to engage "literature" with a set of literary expectations, in a frame of mind more receptive to the possible significations of this kind of discourse. The modern literary context is sustained by an understanding that the literary is still a valorized process of giving and receiving. In such a context wit can take on a heightened intensity.

• Literary wit can be a center of thematic consequence, a source of textual and psychological intensity. It need not be the opposite of seriousness, "relief" from seriousness, or violation of whatever it is that the literary text is supposedly and "seriously" about.

• Nineteenth-century dismissive descriptions of *wit* as merely "intellectual" or cerebral, as opposed to *humor* as "heartfelt" or "humane" or anything of that sort, have lost credibility because they too are founded on models of consciousness which have become obsolete in the behavioral and cognitive sciences, though they persist in humanist disciplines.

• Literary wit can challenge paradigms and modes of analysis which condition the creation and reception of the text itself.

• Literary wit plays an essential role in the formulation and transmission of cultural wisdom. In many complex discourses, moments of wit are what readers remember – and not as "relief," but as insight. If there is any wit in this essay, you will probably recall that from reading it, rather than a plethora of "points" from which a few useful perceptions might emerge. Witty texts have promulgated revolutions in aesthetic taste and intellectual practice, which is perhaps why wit is seen as a nuisance to agenda-driven forms of analysis. Literary wit is playing a role in an intellectual revolution currently underway, helping us evolve paradigms that are better matched to a vastly expanding store of knowledge.

These are notes, then, toward an alternative description of *literary* wit. A more disheveled subject, a modernized description of wit extending beyond the literary, lies beyond, on a trail strewn with bones. The accumulated commentary on "wit" is centuries deep, contradictory, vague, and largely worthless, because of collective and sustained inattention to the importance and volatility of context. Nonetheless, in considering the comic achievement of Mark Twain in the cultures of the West we cannot stay entirely within the literary, for "Mark Twain" spoke, and acted, and charmed, and outraged in many notorious predicaments beyond the dominion of the printed page.

It is in order, then, to venture on a few additional surmises in pursuit of a modernized description of *wit*, at least as an Anglo-American practice. The basic need is to move at least a little distance beyond Romantic formulations about the conflict of head and heart, distinctions which for too long have valorized "feeling" and regarded succinct, cool, intelligent, funny discourse as inherently superficial and morally retrograde.

• *Humor foreshadows itself; wit does not.* In the English-speaking world we have rituals for signaling an onset of humor. As few as two words can do the job, as in the

American colloquial opening, "There's this . . ." for water-cooler recitations opening with, "There's this priest and this minister," or "There's this guy walks into a bar . . ." The fanfare and slapsticky jump-cuts which begin American television sitcoms perform similar functions, like perky overtures in musical comedies. With humor, we know in a broad sense where we are going before we go there, entering a realm where solemnity, if not seriousness, is momentarily to be left behind. In contrast, wit is figured to take by surprise, and part of the exhilaration is the experience of *not* quite knowing, intellectually or temperamentally, how to react, how to place this discourse, this moment when basic assumptions – about the subject supposedly under discussion, the underlying mood, the reliability of verbal communication – are jolted, and have to be stabilized or reconstructed quickly, after the instant of intellectual and psychological liberation. This is why wit can be cherished even in American eulogies, where "humor" rarely finds a welcome. And in one Anglo-American ritual more solemn even than funeral rites – scholastic literary and cultural theory – wit has an entrée that humor cannot achieve.

• *As utterance, wit is much more complex than conventional modes of linguistic, psychological, and literary analysis have comprehended.* For example, if puns are a variety of wit (which is not a question to be settled here), they are so because they draw attention to the slippage and inherent absurdities of the forms of language on which we necessarily rely, and of trying to organize worldly experience, value systems, or anything else out of words. This celebration of the limitations of discourse is a reason why wit is so often resisted as a dimension of discourse, literary or otherwise. If we are to construct, with language, a precise interpretation of a verbal text, language has to keep still and behave, in both the text under scrutiny and the analytic process. With wit, language can escape from such restriction, and text can escape from the confines of logical analysis.

• *Wit is essentially different from satire and ridicule.* Satire and ridicule may exploit wit, but the thematic potentiality of these other discourses is comparatively limited. Ridicule holds blameless the ideology of the attacker, affirms "us," and what "we" believe, against those others and whatever they are wrongly thinking. In that kind of conflict, however, wit is an unpredictable aggressive weapon whose effects can drift back into your own trenches. Wit, in other words, can disrupt *all* collectivity – except perhaps the collective wish to evade the collective. Because wit can affirm the sovereignty of individual consciousness over everything, within or without – even over the normative (which is to say, culturally inflected) patterns of consciousness – ideologues distrust it, or have no touch of it.

So to Mark Twain for an example – and to an epigram which first appeared in *Following the Equator*, and which suggests that inescapable uncertainties about the provenance and the implications of the text can be part of the "meaning" of that text, and part of its pleasure. In *not* knowing what is signified here, or who is speaking, or where to situate the utterance textually or historically, we can have a better time with it, richer both psychologically and intellectually.

"Man will do many things to get himself loved, he will do all things to get himself
envied." – *Pudd'nhead Wilson's New Calendar* (Twain 1897: 206)

These lines occur at the head of chapter 21 in a book about Mark Twain's travels
around the world in 1895–6. The chapter itself tells about the landscape of Australia,
the British conquest, and the displacement of the aborigines. Very little in this chapter
can be connected to securing either love or envy; nothing here connects with David
"Pudd'nhead" Wilson, whom Clemens had invented some years before as a diffuse
protagonist for a short, meandering mystery novel bearing that name. In *The Tragedy
of Pudd'nhead Wilson*, race and the identity problems of other characters prove to be
considerably more interesting than Wilson himself, who catches the reader's attention only now and then, usually as the imagined author of the calendar entries gracing
or bothering the top of each chapter, as they also do in the travel book. In both cases,
however, Wilson's epigrams usually have little or no thematic relationship to the
chapter at whose head they appear.

An eager, informed reader of *Following the Equator* might nonetheless resort to *Pud-
d'nhead Wilson* and construct, with a little interpretive violence, reveries about the title
character's predicament after the end of that novel. Suddenly (perhaps) Wilson is
respected as a local genius, envied (perhaps) in this small town, if not actually loved
by anyone there; and (again, perhaps) he accordingly ponders fame and glory as gifts
or burdens that he now understands first-hand. Such flights of readerly fantasy will
hit air pockets. Accepting many years of scorn and professional failure for a misunderstood wisecrack, Wilson has flagrantly not done "all things to get himself envied."
Personal ambition played no role in his solitary collecting of local fingerprints, and
he did not involve himself professionally in the lurid murder case in order to show
off. As a recourse, we might attribute Wilson's wisdom to his study of the behavior
of others, just as he has studied their fingerprints – but whatever our route, we would
still be spinning away on subjective ruminations and leaving textual evidence behind.
The Pudd'nhead Wilson epigrams in *Following the Equator* float loose from the novel
of a few years before, and from the title character who floated loose within that novel.
This textual attribution of epigrams to a fictional somebody-else, who even as a fiction
is nearly nobody, even in the book named after him, implicitly subverts the cultural
practice of epigram ascription, the sanctioned pretense of understanding better, or
understanding at all, any short, compelling, disconnected utterance merely because
we are told the name of the person who supposedly said it.

We should tread with care now, for this last delusion supports the innocent trade
of compiling books of quotable quotes. *Emerson, Macaulay, Shaw, Cicero, Shakespeare,
St. Paul, Mark Twain*: as headings for thick sections in such books, or as the italicized
by-line for the individual quip, ascription tells us almost nothing about the actual
moment, in a varied life and writing career, when these memorable words were
unleashed, or in what frame of mind, or about what subject. Arranged in enigmatic
sequences, catchy phrases from Shakespeare's buffoons and villains are inflated into
secular proverbs, verbal dances escaping the dancers. *Pudd'nhead Wilson's Calendar* is

a non-existent book by a non-existent author, and what radiates from it, as from every epigram in *Following the Equator*, is the enigma of the epigram, the inherent mystery of the discrete maxim, and perhaps of any other kind of free-range wisdom encountered on the printed page. Nothing can tell us whether such words are true except ourselves: their interpretation is inherently and inextricably personal, and finally free of prior grounding. And whether the name affixed is Pudd'nhead Wilson or Mark Twain, both authors, who might otherwise bulk in the imagination, cease to matter, at least for an instant, as we take up (in our own way) the meanings of their words.

However – and when the subject is Mark Twain's wit, there is predictably one "however" after another – in another instant (perhaps before, perhaps after, perhaps simultaneously), there are indeed an author and a context – both, perhaps, in the plural and to excess. In this case we have *two* authors (one real, in some ways; one entirely imaginary) and two texts, or three, or possibly a slough of them, all the Mark Twain-works and Wilson-works we might care to muster into mind, to help us dream up an escape from the interpretive predicament. For in a sense we know too much about Mark Twain; and the more we know, the more complex, or downright impossible, is the decision we face about what we are reading. Again, it is uncertainty that provides the intellectual and psychological gratification – and until some theory of wit or humor can countenance and describe adequately this condition of not knowing, this awkward and pleasurable predicament before the lumbering apparatus of logic can close in again, Mark Twain's wit will continue to evade our capacity to name its delights and complications.

When bright younger critics recognize this dilemma and try accordingly to expand and modernize the discussion of American literary wit or comedy or humor, they may cite contemporary authorities on other subjects, sometimes including all-weather intellectuals who confer dignity on almost any project. What you will not find in these recent books, however, are raids into the other variety of "humor studies." With a provocative thesis that the comic celebrates "the persistence of what is animal" (p. 8) in human nature, Howard Jacobson's *Seriously Funny: From the Ridiculous to the Sublime* (1997) cites Bakhtin and Bergson each at half a dozen places, and Freud thrice, adding doses of Baudelaire, Hazlitt, Aristophanes, Koestler, Christopher Bollas, and A. C. Zijderveld – yet not a single article from *Humor: International Journal of Humor Research* (the official publication of the International Society for Humor Studies) or from any scholar on its editorial board. In *Necessary Madness* (1997), Gregg Camfield discusses Bergson in three places and Bakhtin in about eight, and vigorously rebuts Freud with recourse to recent findings in psychology and the cognitive sciences. But once again, there is no mention of anything from *Humor*. Linda Hutcheon's well-known *Irony's Edge* (1994) follows a similar pattern.

Meanwhile, in the pages of *Humor* you will find very sparse engagement with the work of literary scholars, even when the subject under scrutiny is a literary text. Instead, for about 15 years, the ISHS has been publishing articles replete with statistics, neologisms, and other signifiers that research is taking place, penetrating to the core of humor as a cultural practice, linguistic anomaly, rhetorical strategy, or psychopathological behavior. Simply for their ambitious titles, some articles in *Humor* should pack the house: "Being Funny: A Selectionist Account of Humor Production" (Dewitte and Verguts 2001); "The Concepts and Language of Comic Art" (Pollio and Talley 1991); "Aspects of the Unsaid in Humor" (Dolitsky 1992); "A Theory of Humor" (Veatch 1998).

If the two communities of scholarship on wit and humor mean to continue ignoring each other, it would be well if we had reasonable cause, on the literary side at least, for paying so little attention to work coming from the ISHS. They have modern methodology, or so it seems – and we do not. Their essays cite portentous studies from others in the Society; our side favors theoretical formulations which took shape several generations ago. Even so, much of the content in *Humor* turns out to be irrelevant to reading literary texts or naïve as scholarship of any sort. With regard to literary discourse, and also to the cultural and contextual volatility of the comic, modes of analysis favored in *Humor* suffer from omissions which would not be tolerated in *Studies in American Humor*, or *Thalia*, or other journals which publish work on Mark Twain or other writers in the British and North American comic tradition. Several leaders of the ISHS are semanticists, proponents of "script theory" as a system for processing humorous texts, and some of the trouble results from how their work is exploited by lesser folk in the Society. A "script" in this context is a unit of information "which is prototypical of the entity being described, such as well-established routines and common ways to do things and go about activities. At the simplest level, a script is equivalent to the lexical meaning of a word" (Attardo 2001: 3). This means that the more implications, inferences, nuances, and contexts a single utterance has, the more scripts are required to complete the analysis – an exhaustive semantic, cultural, historical, and psychological map of one discrete joke among the ever-accumulating billions. The grander objective, however, is apparently to arrive, with supreme laboriousness, at the point where literary study of the comic usually begins:

> [A] formal theory of humor must describe how one can generate a funny text by manipulating objects that are not funny taken separately. From the point of view of recognition, the theory must provide the necessary and sufficient conditions that a text must meet for the text to be funny and an algorithm for checking whether a given text is funny or not. (p. 2)

The goal of the theory is to formulate the necessary and sufficient conditions, in purely semantic terms, for a text to be funny. Like any modern linguistic theory, this semantic theory of humor attempts to match a natural intuitive ability which the native speaker has: in this particular case, the ability to perceive a text as funny, that is, to distinguish a joke from a non-joke (p. xiii).[2]

What we can supposedly acquire from all this is a systematized mechanism for figuring out where and how Mark Twain is being humorous. How many scripts might be required to zero in on one witty line embedded in a novel as complex as *Huckleberry Finn*? It's easy to show how script-theory analysis can collapse under contingencies and complications. Moreover, the strategy in its current form fails to countenance the turbulent cultural history of wit and humor in America, a history in which the discrete joke, as Daniel Wickberg observes in *The Senses of Humor* (1998), may not have become the fundamental element of humor until the rise of vaudeville. Previously, says Wickberg, comic discourse was considerably less easy to distinguish within the total fabric of the verbal text, for "humor" was more commonly an intention or mood (pp. 121–8). What could we say is "the joke" in Mark Twain's "Encounter with an Interviewer," a sketch which, as Louis Budd has established, was an international favorite in Mark Twain's lifetime (Budd 2000: 226–9)? What lines in that sketch can be removed from their context for this kind of scrutiny? Could we possibly read "The Celebrated Jumping Frog of Calaveras County" as a linear sequence of modular jokes, rather than as a text which amuses and entertains in a unified way, establishing a realm of absurdity which is at once social, psychological, historical, and intertextual? In an analysis which puts such emphasis on semantics, the pressures and volatility of context are a nuisance.

In literary analysis, however, these last can count for everything. Once we "get" Mark Twain's "Journalism in Tennessee" and discern (perhaps without accumulating scripts) that it is funny, the adventure begins. How might the sketch be read as a reminiscence, about how far Sam Clemens had come from his own origins in a county-paper print shop, and what had been gained and lost on that journey? What might it suggest about some intractable rawness in the American profession of journalism, no matter what big-city airs and technologies it might acquire? What might this sketch imply about the impact of printed words on human relationships, reputations, even on survival?

Prowl through *Humor* for additional guidance on such problems and you will collide instead with the unconvincing sociological and linguistic argumentation I mentioned earlier, marshaled in unintentionally hilarious studies which somehow passed muster with the editorial board. Pollio and Talley, for example, lay out their purpose and methodology in "The Concepts and Language of Comic Art":

> Using oppositional pairs of adjectives . . . two different factor analytic studies were performed on results provided by subjects rating a number of contemporary comedians. Results of both analyses were consistent in revealing a sacred/angel factor, a spontaneous/flexible factor, a fat/oaf factor, a superiority factor, and in one analysis a wise/adult factor. (Pollio and Talley 1991: 1)

The "subjects" turn out to be college students: a tour through *Humor* will reveal that undergraduate classes are often hijacked for this kind of labor. Here they watched videos and reviewed 20 comedians, rating them under each of the prescribed word-pairs, the overall purpose being "to provide some empirical order to the language and concepts used in the major theories of humor . . . [and] to determine the feasibility of predicting a comedian's overall rating of funniness on the basis of his or her ratings on other theoretically relevant scales" (pp. 2–3).

We might wonder, for starters, whether students who sign up for a class like this constitute a valid demographic sample for evaluating the "art" of an American comedian. Moreover, the video clips they were required to watch were a historical and cultural bouillabaisse of night-club performers, random TV sitcom leads, stars in Hollywood films, and the living and the dead from Lucille Ball to Eddie Murphy (Pollio and Talley 1991: 13). Consider, furthermore, the circumstances of the exercise itself: the VHS in a bland classroom, the time of day, the pressures of the semester, the sullen breaks for marking the questionnaire, all of which (and much more besides) might have considerable impact on how a comic performance is received. Meanwhile, Dewitte and Verguts, in "Being Funny: A Selectionist Account of Humor Production" (2001) conclude that humorists tell a lot of jokes and pay attention to how they go over (p. 37); and Veatch, in "A Theory of Humor" (1998), with the lower-the-boom title of this set, takes 50 pages to reach the thunderous insight that jokes involve some species of incongruity, proving the point with morsels of script theory from Attardo and Raskin.

Perhaps it is an awkward moment for humor theories of any stripe, with the neurosciences so busy subverting our complacency about the dynamics of creativity and interpretation. If the mind does "compute" in non-linear ways, if intelligent human beings (assuming we can still call them so) can perform an indefinite array of calculations simultaneously, while negotiating efficiently among them, then modernized descriptions of wit and humor, literary and otherwise, will soon need to reckon with such changes, and contrive a more agile vocabulary than is in common use now. We may have to retire some of the old favorite terminology – "ambiguity," "repression," "sublimation," "aggression," "cognitive dissonance," "ambivalence," "irony," and many other terms which circumscribe consciousness in dyadic structures and mechanical motions. In the meantime, however, we can try to discuss wit and humor in ways that affirm and liberate their potentialities – including the power to liberate the individual mind from its own culturally acquired habits of analysis.

In literary circles, discussions of Mark Twain as a humorist regularly propose that his humor be understood as a means in the pursuit of some purpose of high seriousness. Much has been said about Mark Twain's concern with the dignity and destiny of the American folk, the value of untutored common sense, the resolution or expression of stubborn paradox or pain within the self, the construction of a public identity, and the quest for love, fame, and a place in history. Mark Twain was indeed a humorist and a wit. He began his writing and speaking career as a practitioner of "humor," a comic discourse which announced its own arrival, keeping readers and listeners in a zone of relative separation from "seriousness," and sometimes gravitating to consequential values that critics have been finding in his work for generations. Actually, however, Mark Twain opened his adult writing career, in Hannibal in his teens, with the enigmatic discourse that I was trying to describe earlier: a discourse of wit, sudden, brief, and obscure or opaque in its intention. In his professional life thereafter, a life in which he won international recognition as a "humorist," there are many marvelous outbreaks of wit – moments where surprise, psychological richness, and thematic and psychological complexity take these texts to a new level and intensify their continuing literary and cultural importance. To put it another way, Mark Twain's reputation for "humor" sold books to the American public and situated him on the correct side of the head–heart discrimination which his culture favored; however, vortices of wit within those books have helped keep them vital in our own time, and sometimes high on the lists of American classics. After 1880, Mark Twain's comic writings often escaped the doctrinal and formal constraints which had confined him earlier. If this move upward or outward, from humor to wit, causes structural and thematic trouble in the longer narratives, subverting continuity and readerly expectations so as to ruin them as novels or stories in any conventional sense, they bring on his golden age as a disrupter of conventions of thought and value, and made possible the lines which made him memorable, as a sage and a wit, to a global public.

To understand Mark Twain better as a master of the American art of wit, we can look patiently at one important moment, and at its strange return later within the same crucial text. This moment occurs in *Huckleberry Finn*, and it concerns the first thing that Huck says that he said to anyone else. In the opening pages Huck seems to adjust passively to life as a boy of means in a comparatively genteel household in St. Petersburg, Missouri. Though he talks (or writes) to us directly, he presents himself as staying silent in the company of those who step in to run his affairs, following the events which close *The Adventures of Tom Sawyer*. Judge Thatcher has arranged his finances, and the Widow has decided to civilize him. And when Huck flees to his sugar hogshead and his ragged free life of old, Tom shows up to persuade him to return to the Douglas house. All of this transpires without any utterance from Huck himself that he thinks worth relating. When Huck reports his own words for the first time, however, he says this:

> Miss Watson would say, "Don't put your feet up there, Huckleberry;" and "don't scrunch up like that, Huckleberry – set up straight;" and pretty soon she would say "Don't gap and stretch like that, Huckleberry – why don't you try to behave?" Then she told me all about the bad place, and I said I wished I was there. She got mad, then, but I didn't mean no harm. All I wanted was to go somewheres; all I wanted was a change, I warn't particular. (Twain 1885: 1)

This may be the funniest moment in the first three pages of Mark Twain's best novel, and at the same time the most mysterious. We need to open up its meanings without locking it into the kind of signification which will also diminish it. Huck's remark to Miss Watson is neither innocent nor outrageous, neither idiotic nor darkly clever. It is possibly all of these at once, and as readers we are *not* required to choose among such either/or interpretive options to evolve an idea of Huck, of his intelligence, his candor, his ethics, or his personality, or even of the essential meaning of the remark as we laugh at it. Given Huck's mildness and passivity in the paragraphs which precede this, his wisecrack (if indeed it is a wisecrack) may take everyone by surprise: Miss Watson, the reader, possibly Huck himself. For his explanation or excuse – if it *isn't* to be taken exclusively as a wry remark – suggests that his wish to get out of the Douglas house by going straight to hell is some variety of yelp, a spontaneous expression of pain and innocent candor.

As a joke, the line breaks out in innumerable directions. We can never be sure of its "real" intention, and at least one of its possible implications has to do with quick and perhaps ungovernable responses of the mind – in other words, with intention itself, with wit as something sometimes beyond one's own control. There is a swipe here too at nineteenth-century back-country theology, at mentalities which divide the world and enforce barriers between good and bad rather than letting "things get mixed up" (as Huck, a moment before, has said he prefers in the making of dinner, and as invariably does happen in ordinary life). There are implications, perhaps, about how we are conditioned to imagine pleasure and pain, about the loneliness of piety and the good-fellowship of depravity, about using faith and etiquette as weapons for abusing children, about cultural repression of boyish exuberance, about a parallel repression of narrative history or fiction into a form that has to "set up straight" and not fidget the way *this* book does, and so on. It doesn't really matter how, or how extensively, we might chart these possible meanings, for this remark of Huck's has many "points" and no point. It disrupts not only Miss Watson's dreary sequence of admonitions and lessons, but also our sense of Huck as some single-dimensional variety of human being, a character who can be construed to say exactly what he means, and to mean one thing and one thing only when he writes or opens his mouth.

What makes this a moment of literary wit, and a signal that the narrative that follows may leap in unexpected directions with regard to intention and interpretation, is that the remark is certainly "wit" from Mark Twain the author, and less certainly wit from Huck. He may or may not be making a wisecrack to Miss Watson, and may or may not be joking with his readers about what he meant by it. After all, Huck is supposedly telling his own story. In his splendid 1996 edition of *Adventures of Huckleberry Finn*, Victor Doyno includes a facsimile of the recently recovered opening page of the holograph manuscript, with what seems to be an early working title:

> *Huckleberry Finn*
> *As Reported by Mark Twain.* (Twain 1996: 389)

That ascription is gone from the front-matter of the Webster and Co. editions. "Mister Mark Twain" is credited with *Tom Sawyer*, but Huck is "reporting" to nobody but us, and he "makes" the book by himself. That, at least, is what we are encouraged to believe – or rather, we are encouraged to suspend our disbelief in Huck as the writer of the book. Indeed, the novel closes with his famous remark about "what a trouble it was to make a book," nudging us again to assume that we have been reading the words of a semi-literate boy who at least sporadically imagines and presents himself as an *author*.

What bearing might this have on Huck's opening wish about being in hell and out of Miss Watson's company, or his periodic leaps thereafter into a kind of discourse which for a hundred years has been construed as witty? Possibly much. Wit is a variety of performance, a discourse to amuse others and subvert conventions, including conventions of psychological and intellectual process – but it can also be self-gratification, in which the self achieves momentary liberation from its own crises and moods. If wit can be a moment of discovery, of insight, it can also be a moment of recognition: acknowledgment of the concealed strangeness of the other, or the self. Wit can be recovered surprise, at possibilities without and within.

Can we sense, then, that we know Huck a little better at this moment? If the answer is yes, then it is so because suddenly we know him a little less well. How are these words to be construed? As clever, subversive, obtuse, complaisant, naïve and compliant? As indicative of an identity as yet unformed? Or is Huck already too smart or self-possessed for his world and his readers? Or none or all of the above? This is a flicker, then, of what wit and humor can accomplish in narrative fiction. They can liberate a character from the conventions within which literary "character" is constructed, imagined, and discussed.

The trouble does not stop there, for this early moment resonates also in the supposedly supreme crisis of the book: Huck's decision to side with Jim against all the legal and moral authorities in the world he knows. "All right, I'll go to hell," he says, and he tears up the note he has written to Miss Watson: a wonderful moment, if *Huckleberry Finn* is to be read as moral fiction. But is this "hell" that Huck apparently imagines here, as the consequence of what he assumes to be a civil and mortal sin, really the same "hell" he wishes for in the novel's opening – the "bad place" where the companionship and amusements are better than the place "salvation," better even than this world between? Is Huck's opening off-hand wish transmuted now into something like heroic resignation or a vow? Or might it be the same variety of utterance as before, a variant of the same possibly dizzy wish to be somewhere else, anywhere else – and is that yearning naïve, or frivolous, or deadly earnest, or a hopeless mix of these, and more? Huck's first "hell," in other words, makes the later and more famous invocation of "hell" more complex than a self-dramatizing posture, more interesting and more human than a Romantic flash of moral inspiration, a transcendence into Virtue. Huck's affirmation, so important to generations of readers who admire the novel's moral core, still strikes home in part because it remains unstable, unsure, deepened and complicated by the wit that first breathes life into Huck's character, and sets his narrative in motion. This is and *is not* a serious moment – and the possible facetiousness within it, its hint of *refusal* of seriousness at this moment of crisis, makes the moment dramatically stronger, because it distinguishes it from conventions and rituals of moral Aristotelian drama, and situates it instead within a psychological and moral condition we can recognize as real, rather than generically dramatic. In the midst of intensity, there can be detachment. In the midst of a dilemma when everything seems to be on the line, there can be something within the self that is held back. In the crisis there can be realms in consciousness that refuse to accept crisis abjectly, or that refuse the organization of human experience into crises. Huck means what he says, and yet what he says also subverts an idea that people are essentially what they say – either as they address themselves alone, or others, including those who read a supposedly candid personal narrative. What Huck says, however, may also subvert the idea that words and concepts like "hell" and "good" and "evil" are adequate to help us express who and where we are. This is one way that an outbreak of wit in a Mark Twain narrative can burn like an acid that no laboratory crucible can contain. And when we encounter a moment of wit in Mark Twain's work, we need to respect its reach and its potentialities, and recognize that limits to its implications may lie only within ourselves.

NOTES

1 As a starting point, see Edelman (1992), Kosslyn and Koenig (1995), and Penrose (1990). As an astrophysicist rather than a neuroscientist, Penrose is the odd man out in this set, and his book has attracted hostile criticism for its presumptions. It makes, however, a strong case that the mind is not an algorithmic computer, and that the Turing Test no longer has credibility as an evaluation of cognitive processes.

2 As one of the founders and senior editors of *Humor*, Victor Raskin states the following objective: "The goal of the theory is to formulate the necessary and sufficient conditions, in purely semantic terms, for a text to be funny. In other words, if a formal semantic analysis of a text yields a certain set of semantic properties which the text possesses, then the text is recognized as a joke. As any modern linguistic theory, this semantic theory of humor attempts to match a natural intuitive ability which the native speaker has, in this particular case, the ability to perceive a text as funny, i.e., to distinguish a joke from a non-joke" (Raskin 1985: xiii). Attardo is Raskin's former student and sometime collaborator. It will be observed that Raskin's book, frequently cited in the pages of *Humor*, predates the scientific revolution described in this essay, with regard to the understanding of humor and the mind. To date, however, Raskin has published no subsequent book on this or any other subject related to humor.

REFERENCES AND FURTHER READING

Anouilh, Jean (1952). *Antigone*, trans. Lewis Gulantière, and *Eurydice*, trans. Lothian Small. London: Methuen.

Attardo, Salvatore (2001). *Humorous Texts: A Semantic and Pragmatic Analysis*. Berlin: Mouton de Gruyter.

Bakhtin, Mikhail (1984). *Rabelais and his World*, trans. Helen Iswolsky. Bloomington: Indiana University Press.

Bergson, Henri (1911). *Laughter: An Essay on the Meaning of the Comic*, trans. Cloudesley Bereton and Fred Rothwell. New York: Macmillan.

Budd, Louis J. (2000). "Mark Twain's 'An Encounter with an Interviewer': The Height (or Depth) of Nonsense." *Nineteenth Century Literature* 55: 2, 226–43.

Camfield, Gregg (1997). *Necessary Madness: The Humor of Domesticity in Nineteenth-Century American Literature*. New York: Oxford University Press.

Dewitte, S., and Verguts, T. (2001). "Being Funny: A Selectionist Account of Humor Production." *Humor: International Journal of Humor Research* 14: 1, 37–54.

Dolitsky, M. (1992). "Aspects of the Unsaid in Humor." *Humor: International Journal of Humor Research* 5: 1–2, 33–43.

Edelman, Gerald (1992). *Bright Air, Brilliant Fire: On the Matter of the Mind*. New York: Basic/HarperCollins.

Freud, Sigmund (1963). *Jokes and their Relation to the Unconscious*, trans. James Strachey. New York: Norton. (First publ. 1905.)

Holland, Norman M. (1989)."Film Response Eye to I: The Kuleshov Experiment." *South Atlantic Quarterly* 88: 2, 415–42.

Hutcheon, Linda (1994). *Irony's Edge: The Theory and Politics of Irony*. New York: Routledge.

Jacobson, Howard (1997). *Seriously Funny: From the Ridiculous to the Sublime*. New York: Viking.

Kosslyn, Stephen, and Koenig, Olivier (1995). *Wet Mind: The New Cognitive Neuroscience*. New York: Free Press.

Martin, R. A.; Puhlik-Doris, P.; Larsen, G.; Gray, J.; and Weir, K (2003). "Individual Differences in Uses of Humor and their Relation to Psychological Well-being: Development of the Humor Styles Questionnaire." *Journal of Research in Personality* 37, 48–75.

Mendelsohn, Daniel (2004). "Nailed!" (Review of *Hatchet Jobs: Writings on Contemporary Fiction* by Dale Peck.) *New York Review of Books* 51: 12 (July 15), 43–6.

Michelson, Bruce (1995). *Mark Twain on the Loose: A Comic Writer and the American Self*. Amherst: University of Massachusetts Press.

Michelson, Bruce (2000). *Literary Wit*. Amherst: University of Massachusetts Press.

Mobbs, Dean; Greicius, Michael D.; Eiman, Abdel-Azim; Menon, Vinod; and Reiss, Allan L.

(2003). "Humor Modulates the Mesolimbic Reward Centers." *Neuron* 40: 5, 1041–8.

Moran, Joseph M.; Wig, Gagan S.; Adams, Reginald B.; Janata, Petr; and Kelley, William M. (2004). "Neural Correlates of Humor Detection and Appreciation." *NeuroImage* 21: 3, 1055–60.

Penrose, Roger (1990). *The Emperor's New Mind*. New York: Oxford University Press.

Pollio, Howard R., and Talley, Judith Theg (1991). "The Concepts and Language of Comic Art." *Humor: International Journal of Humor Research* 4: 1, 1–21.

Raskin, Victor (1985). *Semantic Mechanisms of Humor*. Dordrecht and Boston: Reidel.

Rodriguez, Richard (1992). *Days of Obligation: An Argument with my Mexican Father*. New York: Penguin.

Twain, Mark (1996). *Adventures of Huckleberry Finn*, with foreword and addendum by Victor Doyno. New York: Random House.

Veatch, Thomas (1998). "A Theory of Humor." *Humor: International Journal of Humor Research* 11: 2, 161–216.

Wickberg, Daniel (1998). *The Senses of Humor: Self and Laughter in Modern America*. Ithaca, NY: Cornell University Press.

PART VII
A Retrospective

35

The State of Mark Twain Studies

Alan Gribben

Scholarly treatments of Mark Twain and his works commenced a dozen years after his death in 1910, and within half a century these commentaries were increasing exponentially. Books devoted entirely or partly to Twain now number in the many hundreds, and journal articles about him have become legion. Among these multitudinous publications certain paths of inquiry and patterns of approach can be discerned.

Biographies of Mark Twain, for instance, have evolved in perceptible stages. Twain himself launched the initial phase during his final years by appointing his own Boswell to prepare a flattering and dignified "author's life" such as was customary at the turn of the century. Albert Bigelow Paine's *Mark Twain: A Biography. The Personal and Literary Life of Samuel Langhorne Clemens* (New York: Harper & Bros., 1912) had the advantage of drawing on interviews with the subject that could never be repeated, as well as access to documents that have since disappeared. Paine's prose and the insights about his subject were vastly better than anything he ever attempted before or after this work; clearly he felt inspired by Twain's confidence in him and by the privilege of sharing Twain's final years in Redding, Connecticut. Those who turn to *Mark Twain: A Biography* expecting mere trivialities will be surprised; nearly every one of its 1,719 pages is filled with facts and judgments that endure.

Paine, however, understandably emphasized the last portion of Twain's life – when, after all, he virtually lived in the household of his subject. Moreover, he glossed over certain incidents, and his book predictably set out to make Twain look good in most respects. Nonetheless, all subsequent studies, no matter what their viewpoints, have essentially been either filling in the details or taking issue with Paine's redoubtable biography. Hamlin Hill reviewed some of the tendencies in "The Biographical Equation: Mark Twain," *American Humor* 3: 1 (1976), 1–5.

For at least three decades from the 1960s onward the standard biography was considered to be Justin Kaplan's *Mr. Clemens and Mark Twain* (New York: Simon & Schuster, 1966), which reached psychological conclusions about a deeply divided man whose artistry sometimes suffered but often benefited from his internal conflicts. Recently (and quite coincidentally) another Kaplan, Fred Kaplan, has stepped forward with *The Singular Mark Twain* (New York: Doubleday, 2003) to characterize the earlier Kaplan's thesis as merely "a useful way to dramatize some of Twain's inconsistencies," while objecting that "they do not add up to a split personality" and that "his pseudonym does not embody . . . a fundamental internal division" (p. 2). Nonetheless, *Mr. Clemens and Mark Twain* will always be the better "read." Justin Kaplan had a deft touch in shaping the story of Twain's life, and each page resonates with tension and vitality. Its chief disadvantage is that Justin Kaplan does not pick up his subject until Twain is on his way to the East Coast, having already made a name for himself in Nevada and California, but from there until the well-attended funeral of the lionized author, Kaplan's narrative – though it often skimps on details and skips over minor events – carries the reader along pell-mell through a hectic life.

One thing is certain. In the last three decades of the twentieth century Mark Twain scholars showed an increasingly bold willingness to probe the innermost, previously private regions of Twain's psyche and experiences. Hamlin Hill led off with an assault on the image Twain left behind of the genial, never-flustered, white-haired gentleman philosopher; behind this façade Hill discerned anguish over family disappointments and tragedies that left Twain soul-ravaged and cranky. Hill's *Mark Twain: God's Fool* (New York: Harper & Row, 1973) influenced dozens of subsequent books, films, and articles that have depicted the aging Twain as a nearly pathetic, Lear-like figure. Hill even hinted at Twain's overindulgence in alcohol and refused to wink at his elaborate flirtations with pubescent girls, which he saw as more suitor-like than grandfatherly. In part *Mark Twain: God's Fool* and its "discomforting facts" (p. x) constituted an attempt to dislodge "Mark Twain" from behind the protective shield held up by Albert Bigelow Paine, Clara Clemens Samossoud, and others who had shaped or deflected responses to Twain's life and works for half a century. A round-table discussion ruminated about the book's influence: "*Mark Twain: God's Fool* Redux," *Biography* 10 (1996), 417–27.

Other iconoclastic studies followed in Hill's wake. Guy A. Cardwell's *The Man Who Was Mark Twain: Images and Ideologies* (New Haven: Yale University Press, 1991) was severe in its indictments of Twain and his status in American culture. Making an especially controversial claim, Andrew Hoffman detected lifelong latent and occasional practicing homosexual inclinations in Samuel Clemens's behavior. Hoffman's assertions were made in an *American Literature* article, and then (in somewhat muted form) became part of his comprehensive biography, *Inventing Mark Twain: The Lives of Samuel Langhorne Clemens* (New York: William Morrow, 1997). No one has yet stepped forward to support Hoffman's theory with additional evidence.

Other biographers have either treated only a portion of Twain's life or else narrowed their focus. Dixon Wecter's *Sam Clemens of Hannibal* (Boston: Houghton Mifflin, 1952), of course, only chronicled Clemens's circumstances and family environment until 1853, when the young man audaciously set out for a larger world. Still, as Wecter observes, "No major artist ever made more of his boyhood . . . Mark Twain never said good-bye to Hannibal" (p. 264). Author and journalist Ron Powers deepened and darkened Wecter's portrait in *Dangerous Waters: A Biography of the Boy Who Became Mark Twain* (New York: Basic Books, 1999), which conjured up Twain's formative years and left off at Henry Clemens's death in 1858. John Lauber's straightforward *The Making of Mark Twain: A Biography* (New York: American Heritage Press, 1985) carried the author from boyhood to his marriage in 1870, as did Margaret Sanborn's *Mark Twain: The Bachelor Years, A Biography* (New York: Doubleday, 1990). Jeffrey Steinbrink's *Getting to Be Mark Twain* (Berkeley: University of California Press, 1991) filled in a large gap by highlighting Twain's Buffalo years in an interpretive "story" of the key period between 1868 and 1871.

Olivia ("Livy") Clemens's personal and intellectual capacities have undergone a remarkable reappraisal: once dismissed as ill-matched with her talented husband, she is now regarded as widely read and progressive in her attitudes. Credit for this overdue adjustment – and for the acknowledgment of Elmira, New York as a stimulating civic milieu for Livy's education and courtship – can go especially to Laura E. Skandera-Trombley's *Mark Twain in the Company of Women* (Philadelphia: University of Pennsylvania Press, 1994) and Susan K. Harris's *The Courtship of Olivia Langdon and Mark Twain* (New York: Cambridge University Press, 1996). Robert Keith Miller's highly compressed *Mark Twain* (New York: Frederick Ungar, 1983) primarily described Twain's adulthood. Dennis Welland's *Mark Twain in England* (Atlantic Highlands, NJ: Humanities Press, 1978) gave Chatto & Windus and other British publishers their due. Enduring loyalty was stressed in Kenneth E. Eble's *Old Clemens and W.D.H.: The Story of a Remarkable Friendship* (Baton Rouge: Louisiana State University Press, 1985). Carl Dolmetsch documented a little-understood chapter in *Our Famous Guest: Mark Twain in Vienna* (Athens: University of Georgia Press, 1992). In *Mark Twain and West Point* (Toronto: ECW Press, 1996), Philip W. Leon held up for scrutiny Twain's affectionate attachment to the officers and cadets of the United States Military Academy. John Lauber's *The Inventions of Mark Twain: A Biography* (New York: Hill & Wang, 1990) commemorated Twain's numerous personal and literary innovations. Arthur L. Scott's *Mark Twain at Large* (Chicago: Henry Regnery, 1969), pointing out that Twain "passed more than one-third of his life outside the United States," tracked his nomadic activities as "an Ambassador-at-Large" (p. vii). Miriam Jones Shillingsburg's *At Home Abroad: Mark Twain in Australasia* (Jackson: University Press of Mississippi, 1988) concentrated on one segment of these journeys. William R. Macnaughton's *Mark Twain's Last Years as a Writer* (Columbia: University of Missouri Press, 1979) praised the resilience and originality discoverable in Twain's less-venerated compositions. Karen Lystra's startling biography, *Dangerous Intimacy: The Untold Story of Mark Twain's Final Years* (Berkeley: University of California Press, 2004), re-examined the household of contentious personalities that clashed at Stormfield, and disagreed with Hamlin Hill about the Ashcroft–Lyon manuscript in which Twain attacked his former employees. (Laura E. Skandera-Trombley had interpreted this same document differently in "Mark Twain's Last Work of Realism: The Ashcroft-

Lyon Manuscript," *Essays in Arts and Sciences* 23 [1994], 39–48, as did Jennifer L. Rafferty in "'The Lyon of Saint Mark': A Reconsideration of Isabel Lyon's Relationship to Mark Twain," *Mark Twain Journal* 34: 2 [1996], 43–55.)

Important in their day but later swept aside by biographies benefiting from greater access to primary materials, Minnie M. Brashear's *Mark Twain: Son of Missouri* (Chapel Hill: University of North Carolina Press, 1934), DeLancey Ferguson's *Mark Twain, Man and Legend* (Indianapolis: Bobbs-Merrill Co., 1943), and Gladys Bellamy's *Mark Twain as a Literary Artist* (Norman: University of Oklahoma Press, 1950) kept alive the momentum of Twain studies and still offer nuggets of insight.

The commercial, capitalist side of Twain's psyche, first explored by Samuel Charles Webster in *Mark Twain, Business Man* (Boston: Little, Brown, 1946) and by Hamlin Hill in *Mark Twain and Elisha Bliss* (Columbia: University of Missouri Press, 1964) and *Mark Twain's Letters to his Publishers, 1867–1894* (Berkeley: University of California Press, 1967), came into clearer focus with *Mark Twain's Correspondence with Henry Huttleston Rogers, 1893–1909*, ed. Lewis Leary (Berkeley: University of California Press, 1969) and Alan Gribben's "Mark Twain, Business Man: The Margins of Profit," *Studies in American Humor*, n.s. 1 (June 1982), 24–43. Charles H. Gold, in *"Hatching Ruin," or Mark Twain's Road to Bankruptcy* (Columbia: University of Missouri Press, 2003), has written the latest but certainly not the last word on this largely regrettable yet inescapable element of Twain's personal makeup. With fortunes being made all around him, he always longed to cash in on a really big strike.

Taking a specific angle, Everett Emerson's *Mark Twain: A Literary Life* (Philadelphia: University of Pennsylvania Press, 2000) has become indispensable as the only examination of Twain's purely literary labors from adolescence until his last written words in 1910. Emerson even dared to tackle a near-sacred feature of Mark Twain's affable persona – his incessant puffing on cigars and pipes. Emerson's "Smoking and Health: The Case of Samuel L. Clemens," *New England Quarterly* 70 (1997), 548–66, suggested that Clemens's lifelong tobacco addiction (routinely adding up to 300 cigars a month, he bragged) conceivably explained certain of his recurrent health problems; moreover, Emerson went so far as to suggest that the second-hand smoke factor – particularly given Clemens's habit of smoking in bed at all hours – precipitated Livy Clemens's heart disease that so greatly grieved her husband. Assuredly nothing about Clemens's life seems sacrosanct after this foray against a trademark of his beloved public persona.

Biographies and all other studies are heavily dependent on the availability of the writer's works in reliable texts. Here is the real foundation of Mark Twain studies, and the proliferating editions have been a godsend to harried scholars. These texts, filling shelves upon shelves, are far too ample and repetitious to list in full, but their progress can be briefly acknowledged. The most extensive collection of Mark Twain manuscripts, letters, and notebooks – eventually known as the Mark Twain Papers – was bequeathed to the Bancroft Library at the University of California at Berkeley. In 1967 it spawned the Mark Twain Project, publishing his unpublished and previously published writings through the University of California Press. (John C. Gerber's candid "The Iowa Years of *The Works of Mark Twain*: A Reminiscence," *Studies in American Humor* 3: 4 [1997], 68–87, sheds light on why and how the editorial responsibilities formerly held at the University of Iowa were shifted in 1976 to the Mark Twain Project at Berkeley.) A series of nearly 30 carefully annotated volumes, vetted by the Center for Scholarly Editions and capped in 2003 by a magisterial edition of *Adventures of Huckleberry Finn* (ed. Victor Fischer and Lin Salamo [Berkeley: University of California Press, 2003]) joining both halves of Twain's manuscript, has issued from an editorial team headed by Frederick Anderson, who died in 1979, Henry Nash Smith, and then Robert H. Hirst. Hirst and his team of editors have assiduously ferreted out and obtained photocopies of thousands of Twain items in libraries and private collections around the world, in the process becoming the central clearinghouse for all research related to the author. Several of their volumes have been re-edited in scaled-down versions for trade and textbook markets. Some of the textual detective work has produced exciting results. John S. Tuckey revealed in *Mark Twain and Little Satan: The Writing of the Mysterious Stranger* (West Lafayette, IN: Purdue University Studies, 1963) the incredible extent of posthumous textual conflation and revision of which Albert Bigelow Paine and Frederick A. Duneka were guilty in releasing a book titled *The Mysterious Stranger, A Romance* in 1916. The three versions of this fantasy as Twain actually left them finally appeared as *Mark Twain's Mysterious Stranger Manuscripts*, ed. William M. Gibson (Berkeley: University of California Press, 1969), yet the Paine–Duneka pastiche had gained such a foothold in academe that some critics, editors, and publishers prefer it to this day.

Certain other works not yet edited by the Mark Twain Project have nonetheless reached print in improved versions: for example, L. Terry Oggel's "Speaking Out about Race: 'The United States of Lyncherdom' Clemens Really Wrote" (*Prospects* 25 [2000], 115–38), which corrects Albert Bigelow Paine's textual tampering with Twain's acidic 1901 essay. More of Paine's meddling – this time through excisions made in "To the Person Sitting in Darkness" – is documented by William L. Andrews in "The Politics of Publishing: A Note on the Bowdlerization of Mark Twain" (*Markham Review* 7 [1977], 17–20). With *more* fanfare, Roy Blount, Jr. provided an introduction and an afterword to Twain's unpublished and long-forgotten short story "A Murder, a Mystery, and a Marriage" (*Atlantic Monthly* 288: 1 [2001], 49–81). *Mark Twain at the Buffalo Express: Articles and Sketches by America's Favorite Humorist*, ed. Joseph B. McCullough and Janice McIntire-Strasburg (DeKalb: Northern Illinois University Press, 2000) rescued a year and a half of Twain's contributions (1869–71) to a daily newspaper of which he became part-owner. *The Bible According to Mark Twain: Writings on Heaven, Eden, and the Flood*, ed. Howard G. Baetzhold and Joseph B. McCullough (Athens: University of Georgia Press, 1995) helpfully collected Twain's stories and sketches with religious themes.

Commercial presses have published dozens upon dozens of competing editions of Twain's better-known works – many of them in paperback – to offer inexpensive options for general readers and classroom use. For the sake of convenience when citing sources, many students of Twain have turned to the 29-volume set of Mark Twain's writings edited by Shelley Fisher Fishkin and issued with much publicity by Oxford University Press in 1996. Facsimile reproductions of first editions serve as the texts, eminent modern-day authors supply introductions, and Twain scholars and critics provide brief afterwords. The wide sale of this set has made it more accessible than either the original first editions or the 25-volume "Author's National Edition" published in various years by Harper & Bros.; the Oxford set also has the original illustrations that Twain approved, contains far more works than the nicely packaged but unillustrated "Library of America" volumes have collected, and fulfills a need until the Mark Twain Project makes further progress in its publication schedules.

Mark Twain scholarship can be said to have come of age half a century after Twain's earthly existence ended. Four landmark studies of Mark Twain's writings that appeared in the early 1960s in effect charted the future directions of Twain scholarship. Walter Blair's *Mark Twain and Huck Finn* (Berkeley: University of California Press, 1960) demonstrated the value of genetic studies of textual composition, investigations into historical contexts, and examinations of literary sources available to the author. In a direct line of descent from Blair's detailed book is Victor Doyno's impressive *Writing "Huck Finn": Mark Twain's Creative Process* (Philadelphia: University of Pennsylvania Press, 1991) and its CD-ROM successor, *Beginning to Write Huck Finn: Essays in Genetic Criticism*, included in *Huck Finn: The Complete Buffalo and Erie County Public Library Manuscript – Teaching and Research Digital Edition* (Buffalo and Erie Public Library, 2002). Dozens of similar studies – meriting the rubric of "scholarship" in the truest sense – have looked at Twain's other fictional works.

A second book, Henry Nash Smith's *Mark Twain: The Development of a Writer* (Cambridge: Belknap/Harvard University Press, 1962), dominated Twain studies for three decades after its publication, and still today echoes in many endnotes (and a number of attempted rebuttals). During the 1960s, 1970s, and 1980s it was widely believed that no one should be writing about Mark Twain without having absorbed this book. Only in recent years have some critics become impatient with Smith's tracing of how Mark Twain's themes and narrative techniques evolved. The many honors accorded Smith before his death in 1986 suggested the near-reverence in which he and his book were held by Twainians.

Louis J. Budd's *Mark Twain: Social Philosopher* (Bloomington: Indiana University Press, 1962) proved prophetic of the scores of subsequent studies that would emphasize Twain's abrasive social and political commentary, such as Hunt Hawkins's "Mark Twain's Anti-Imperialism," *American Literary Realism* 25: 2 (1993), 31–45, and Jim Zwick's investigations of Twain's stance against the Philippine–American War and involvement with the Anti-Imperialist League. Taking the author seriously as a critic of his age and its controversies elevated Twain into a different sphere from most other writers of fictional literature, who had been content to let their works speak for them. Budd was the first to show the currents of Twain's social views and political thought, and books and articles since then have regularly paid homage to Budd's discernment.

Equally important as the foregoing three monumental studies was James M. Cox's *Mark Twain: The Fate of Humor* (Princeton: Princeton University Press, 1966), which

single-handedly freed Twain studies from being strictly tied to historical considerations. Cox's shrewd insights have been cited by nearly every theoretical critic ever
since, and he proved to be a transition figure and a model for those practicing more
abstract and social types of criticism, including Forrest G. Robinson (*In Bad Faith:
The Dynamics of Deception in Mark Twain's America* [Cambridge: Harvard University
Press, 1986]) and Susan Gillman (*Dark Twins: Imposture and Identity in Mark Twain's
America* [Chicago: University of Chicago Press, 1989]).

These four books by Blair, Smith, Budd, and Cox can be viewed as the intellectual
platform from which most subsequent studies were launched. Several other excellent
studies in that same decade had a supplementary measure of influence but lacked their
overall impact: Albert E. Stone, Jr.'s *The Innocent Eye: Childhood in Mark Twain's Imagination* (New Haven: Yale University Press, 1961), Roger B. Salomon's *Twain and the
Image of History* (New Haven: Yale University Press, 1961), Pascal Covici, Jr.'s *Mark
Twain's Humor: The Image of a World* (Dallas: Southern Methodist University Press,
1962), Robert A. Wiggins's *Mark Twain: Jackleg Novelist* (Seattle: University of
Washington Press, 1964), and William C. Spengemann's *Mark Twain and the
Backwoods Angel: The Matter of Innocence in the Works of Samuel L. Clemens* (Kent, Ohio:
Kent State University Press, 1966).

The decades leading up to the year 2000 built a sturdy staircase of reference works
focused on Mark Twain, offering even the beginning student access to information
that only the most erudite scholars had possessed in the 1960s and 1970s. Robert L.
Gale's *Plots and Characters in the Works of Mark Twain*, 2 vols. (Hamden, Conn.: Archon
Books, 1973), helpful though it was, eventually was eclipsed by J. R. LeMaster and
James D. Wilson's authoritative *The Mark Twain Encyclopedia* (New York: Garland,
1993) as well as R. Kent Rasmussen's almost unstumpable *Mark Twain: A to Z. The
Essential Reference Guide to his Life and Writings* (New York: Facts on File, 1995) and
its revised edition. The often-unconventional entry topics in Gregg Camfield's *The
Oxford Companion to Mark Twain* (New York: Oxford University Press, 2003) provided
pegs for leisurely essays by Camfield and eight others. E. Hudson Long and J. R.
LeMaster's *The New Mark Twain Handbook* (New York: Garland, 1985) and John C.
Gerber's *Mark Twain* (Boston: Twayne, 1988) gave everyone two reliable introductory
primers. But what scholar could possibly have imagined, in 1960 or 1970 or 1980,
possessing at his or her fingertips the wealth of information in James D. Wilson's *A
Reader's Guide to the Short Stories of Mark Twain* (Boston: G. K. Hall & Co., 1987)?
Jason Gary Horn's *Mark Twain: A Descriptive Guide to Biographical Sources* (Lanham,
Md.: Scarecrow Press, 1999) popped up as another bonus.

A clutch of dictionaries made Twain's clever quips and maxims far less elusive:
Everyone's Mark Twain, ed. Caroline Thomas Harnsberger (Cranbury, NJ: A. S. Barnes
and Co., 1972); *When in Doubt, Tell the Truth and Other Quotations from Mark Twain*,
ed. Brian Collins (New York: Columbia University Press, 1996); *Mark My Words:
Mark Twain on Writing*, ed. Mark Dawidziak (New York: St. Martin's Press, 1996);
and *The Quotable Mark Twain: His Essential Aphorisms, Witticisms, and Concise Opinions*,
ed. R. Kent Rasmussen (Chicago: Contemporary Books, 1997) – each compilation

good in its own way, though Rasmussen's is the most comprehensive. Various volumes in the distinctive blue bindings of the gargantuan Dictionary of Literary Biography series have devoted ample pages to Mark Twain's achievements as journalist, short-story writer, novelist, humorist, realist, and naturalist, among other categories. Louis J. Budd's inestimably valuable "A Listing of and Selection from Newspaper and Magazine Interviews with Samuel L. Clemens" (*American Literary Realism* 10 [1977], 1–100) summarized 278 items, reprinting many of them; augmentations followed, including "Listing and Selections from Newspaper and Magazine Interviews with Samuel L. Clemens: A Supplement" (*American Literary Realism* 28 [1996], 63–90). Twain's quick thinking and instinctive rapport with reporters shines forth on every page. In *Mark Twain: The Contemporary Reviews* (New York: Cambridge University Press, 1999), Budd brought together 656 pages of reviews that noticed and judged Twain's books between 1867 and 1917, surpassing Frederick Anderson's *Mark Twain: The Critical Heritage* (1977, repr. New York: Routledge, 1997), which contained 88 notices published between 1869 and 1913. Two huge tomes quietly compiled by Paul Machlis – *A Union Catalog of Clemens Letters* (Berkeley: University of California Press, 1986) and *Union Catalog of Letters to Clemens* (Berkeley: University of California Press, 1992) – function as a documentary log of where Twain was, and who was writing to him, each day of his life (though hundreds of additional letters still surface in every passing decade). Thomas A. Tenney commenced a lifetime of listing books and articles about Mark Twain with *Mark Twain: A Reference Guide* (Boston: G. K. Hall, 1977), a task that he continued subsequently in a succession of journals. Even with Tenney's yeoman labors, the sheer volume of Twain studies can become nearly overwhelming. *American Literary Scholarship, An Annual* (Durham: Duke University Press, 1963–) has assisted the curious scholar in keeping up with the surging tide, inasmuch as Mark Twain has been accorded his own separate chapter since the inception of that yearly critical assessment. Even so, the massive quantity of the scholarship buries good articles and causes impatient writers to reinvent various Twainian wheels.

Mark Twain, when contemplating the decidedly mixed blessings of his own times, often pondered the possibility that human history might operate in cyclical patterns rather than following a continuous line of progress. Similarly, commentators have periodically noted that the world of Mark Twain scholarship sometimes seems cursed (or blessed) to follow the dichotomy of two of the earliest critics, Van Wyck Brooks and Bernard DeVoto, in either faulting Mark Twain's environment, courage, and divided personality or applauding his artistry, authenticity of sources and experiences, and resilience of the will to write. The clashes between Brooks's *The Ordeal of Mark Twain* (1920, rev. edn. 1933) and Bernard DeVoto's *Mark Twain's America* (Boston: Little, Brown, 1932) and *Mark Twain at Work* (Cambridge, Mass.: Harvard University Press, 1942) have echoed through the years. Guy A. Cardwell's "The Metaphoric Hero as Battleground," *ESQ* 23 (1977), 52–66, makes a good starting point for grasping the ironies of this argument.

A momentous variant on this tug-of-war is the mounting evidence that Twain grew up in a society that practiced, and himself fully subscribed to the tenets of, dehumanizing forms of slavery. This current generation of scholars has been the first to confront unsavory aspects of Hannibal's history and its racial implications in Twain's writings. Shelley Fisher Fishkin, though a defender of Twain's intentions in composing *Adventures of Huckleberry Finn* (1885), nonetheless opened this line of inquiry in *Lighting Out for the Territory: Reflections on Mark Twain and American Culture* (New York: Oxford University Press, 1997) with a series of charges against antebellum as well as latter-day Hannibal, Missouri. In Fishkin's view the town of Hannibal has done an inadequate job of confronting its racist heritage and celebrating Mark Twain's emergence from that distorted environment. Hannibal attorney Terrell Dempsey followed up on Fishkin's charges with a more detailed historical account of the slave hell that was early-day Hannibal in *Searching for Jim: Slavery in Sam Clemens's World* (Columbia: University of Missouri Press, 2003). Dempsey describes in detail John Marshall Clemens's enthusiastic punishment of abolitionists and errant slaves, and traces the derogatory racial remarks that young Sam Clemens scattered through his sketches and letters before the Civil War. Especially valuable is Dempsey's compilation of newspaper editorials and historical documents testifying to the pervasiveness of anti-black, anti-abolitionist sentiments in the Hannibal region. Robert Sattelmeyer even turned up proof (cited by Dempsey) that Samuel Clemens went so far as to trick a Boston anti-slavery society into paying for his imagined trip to the East Coast in 1854. Concomitantly, a growing list of critics have re-examined the imagery and occasional contradictions of Twain's treatment of race, particularly in *Huckleberry Finn* but also in his other writings. One might mention, among many examples, Harold Beaver's "Run, Nigger, Run: *Adventures of Huckleberry Finn* as a Fugitive Slave Narrative," *Journal of American Studies* 9 (1974), 339–361; the excellent *Satire or Evasion? Black Perspectives on Huckleberry Finn*, ed. James S. Leonard, Thomas A. Tenney, and Thadious M. Davis (Durham: Duke University Press, 1992); Eric Lott's "Mr. Clemens and Jim Crow: Twain, Race, and Blackface," in *The Cambridge Companion to Mark Twain*, ed. Forrest G. Robinson (Cambridge: Cambridge University Press, 1995), pp. 129–52; and Peter Schmidt's "The 'Raftsmen's Passage,' Huck's Crisis of Whiteness, and *Huckleberry Finn* in U.S. Literary History," *Arizona Quarterly* 59: 2 (Summer 2003), 35–58.

Clemens's family relationships have come under closer and less sympathetic examination, as well. Philip Fanning makes a compelling case that Twain held a lifelong grudge against his elder brother Orion and took many opportunities unfairly to malign and ridicule his sibling. Fanning discerns the basis of this tragic rivalry in a combination of John Marshall Clemens's early death, Orion's decision to take Sam out of school and put him to work in print shops, the brothers' competition for Jane Lampton Clemens's admiration, Orion's insightful opposition to slavery, and Orion's early successes. Fanning's points have been received without enthusiasm by those inclined to idolize Mark Twain, but *Mark Twain and Orion Clemens: Brothers, Partners, Strangers* (Tuscaloosa: University of Alabama Press, 2003) complicates the familial picture in irrefutable ways.

Although Mark Twain was equally well known as a platform artist and a writer in his own day, most notably in the 1870s and 1880s, far less scholarly attention has been paid to the performative side of his talents. Fred W. Lorch left a useful study on this topic – *The Trouble Begins at Eight: Mark Twain's Lecture Tours* (Ames: Iowa State University Press, 1968) – building on the work of Paul Fatout's pioneering *Mark Twain on the Lecture Circuit* (Bloomington: Indiana University Press, 1960). The main problem for those interested in Twain's oral performances is the unreliability of available texts, many of them deriving from newspaper reports. Because of his acclaimed prowess as a public speaker, Twain was often called upon for after-dinner toasts, opening-day remarks, graduation and benefit speeches, talks at reunions, and other oral entertainments. Albert Bigelow Paine published collections of selected (and corrupt) texts, both entitled *Mark Twain's Speeches*, in 1910 and 1923. A vastly preferable collection is Paul Fatout's *Mark Twain Speaking* (Iowa City: University of Iowa Press, 1976), which at least cites the source of the text for each speech and provides an index. Fatout includes Twain's lectures as well as his speeches, but neither category is remotely complete.

Twain's frequently quoted *Autobiography* represents another dilemma for would-be editors and scholars. The author left behind so many dictated drafts – and so many revisions of these drafts – that it will take a modern-day cryptographer, a true unraveler of mysteries, to pick a way through the maze that will satisfy the standards of the Center for Scholarly Editions or other textual critics. What we have instead of a complete edition is a series of partial editions that are certainly better than nothing, since this animated and often entertainingly opinionate autobiography is potentially one of the great works in its genre. What a pity that Twain never could bring himself to sort out his drafts for publication. Again Albert Bigelow Paine led the way with an edition, *Mark Twain's Autobiography*, 2 vols. (New York: Harper & Bros., 1924), but it is considered highly unreliable. Bernard DeVoto (*Mark Twain in Eruption* [New York: Harper & Bros., 1940]), Charles Neider (*The Autobiography of Mark Twain* [New York: Harper & Bros., 1959]), and Michael Kiskis (*Mark Twain's Own Autobiography: The Chapters from the "North American Review"* [Madison: University of Wisconsin Press, 1990]) have prepared editions of extracted portions.

Mark Twain was one of the earliest authors to expend considerable thought and effort in crafting his image as a public figure; and so successful was he at this endeavor that his name, face, and inclinations became as familiar in his own day as they have remained to the present date. The best-known study of this phenomenon is Louis J. Budd's *Our Mark Twain: The Making of his Public Personality* (Philadelphia: University of Pennsylvania Press, 1983). Twain's extreme possessiveness about his life-events is documented in Alan Gribben's "Autobiography as Property: Mark Twain and his Legend," in *The Mythologizing of Mark Twain*, ed. Sara deSaussure Davis and Philip D. Beidler (Tuscaloosa: University of Alabama Press, 1984), 39–55.

Dominating the scholarly discussions of Mark Twain's achievements, rather predictably, are the burgeoning dissections of his acclaimed novel *Adventures of Huckleberry Finn* (1885). Four questions about this book have preoccupied scholarly critics. Initially, they probed the influences and literary sources that went through the author's mind as he worked on the novel at Quarry Farm and elsewhere over a period of more than eight years. Then they asked whether the book genuinely merited its status as a literary masterpiece. Related to that issue has been a question of how grossly the "boy-book" ending mars Huck Finn's narrative. Recently, however, commentators have turned to a far more serious matter: whether this novel, with its racial stereo-typing and problematic language, is still teachable at the dawning of an era in which the feelings of a multiracial readership are increasingly taken into account.

The so-called "debate" over the ending of *Adventures of Huckleberry Finn* – which has shifted ground in recent decades from an earlier acceptance of the "evasion" episode to a general condemnation of Twain's decision to reintroduce Tom Sawyer and return to his "bad-boy book" antics – has become both complex and repetitive. Interested kibitzers should especially look up (skipping over T. S. Eliot, Lionel Trilling, Leo Marx, and the initial generations of critics) Judith Fetterley, "Disenchantment: Tom Sawyer in *Huckleberry Finn*," *PMLA* 87 (January 1972), 69–74; George C. Carrington, Jr., *The Dramatic Unity of "Huckleberry Finn"* (Columbus: Ohio State University Press, 1976), pp. 153–187; Gary Henrickson, "Biographers' Twain, Critics' Twain, Which of the Twain Wrote the 'Evasion?,'" *Southern Literary Journal* 26: 1 (1993), 14–29, a clever appraisal of the entire issue; Jeffrey Steinbrink, "Who Shot Tom Sawyer?," *American Literary Realism* 35: 1 (Fall 2002), 29–38; and Gene Jarrett, "'This Expression Shall Not Be Changed': Irrelevant Episodes, Jim's Humanity Revisited, and Retracing Mark Twain's Evasion in *Adventures of Huckleberry Finn*," *American Literary Realism* 35: 1 (2003), 1–28. For a few dissenters, see William C. French, "Character and Cruelty in *Huckleberry Finn*: Why the Ending Works," *Soundings* 81, nos. 1–2 (1998), 157–79; Richard Hill, "Overreaching: Critical Agenda and the Ending of *Adventures of Huckleberry Finn*," in *Mark Twain among the Scholars: Reconsidering Contemporary Twain Criticism*, ed. Richard Hill and Jim McWilliams (Albany, NY: Whitston Publishing Co., 2002), pp. 67–90; and Laurel Bollinger, "Say It, Jim: The Morality of Connection in *Adventures of Huckleberry Finn*," *College Literature* 29: 1 (2002), 32–52.

The artistry of Twain's *Adventures of Huckleberry Finn* has inspired some of the most sophisticated and impressive critical responses to Twain's work. Among the literally hundreds of worthwhile studies should be mentioned, in recent decades, James L. Colwell, "Huckleberries and Humans: On the Naming of Huckleberry Finn," *PMLA* 86 (January 1971), 70–6; Neil Schmitz, "The Paradox of Liberation in *Huckleberry Finn*," *Texas Studies in Literature and Language* 13 (Spring 1971), 125–36, and "*Huckleberry Finn* and the Reconstruction," *American Studies* 12 (Spring 1971), 59–67; Allen F. Stein, "Return to Phelps Farm: *Huckleberry Finn* and the Old Southwestern Framing Device," *Mississippi Quarterly* 24 (Spring 1971), 111–16; Michael Egan, *Mark Twain's Huckleberry Finn: Race, Class and Society* (London: Chatto & Windus/Sussex University Press, 1977); Tom H. Towers, "Love and Power in *Huckleberry Finn*," *Tulane Studies in English* 23 (1978), 17–37; David Carkeet, "The Dialects in *Huckleberry Finn*," *American Literature* 51 (1979), 315–32; Harold H. Kolb, "Mark Twain, Huck Finn, and Jacob Blivens: Gilt-Edged, Tree-Calf Morality in *The Adventures of Huckleberry Finn*," *Virginia Quarterly Review* 55 (1979), 653–69; John Seelye, "The Craft of Laughter:

Abominable Showmanship and *Huckleberry Finn*," *Thalia* 4: 1 (1981), 19–25; Laurence B. Holland, "A 'Raft of Trouble' – Word and Deed in *Huckleberry Finn*," in *American Realism: New Essays*, ed. Eric J. Sundquist (Baltimore, Md.: Johns Hopkins University Press, 1982), pp. 66–81; Beverly R. David, "Mark Twain and the Legends for *Huckleberry Finn*," *American Literary Realism* 15 (1982), 155–65; *New Essays on Adventures of Huckleberry Finn*, ed. Louis J. Budd (Cambridge: Cambridge University Press, 1985); Kenneth S. Lynn's "Welcome Back from the Raft, Huck, Honey!," in *The Air-Line to Seattle: Studies in Literary and Historical Writing about America* (Chicago: University Chicago Press, 1983), pp. 40–9 – in part a response to Leslie A. Fiedler, "Come Back to the Raft Ag'in, Huck Honey," in *An End to Innocence: Essays on Culture and Politics* (Boston: Beacon, 1955), pp. 142–51; Victor Fischer, "Huck Finn Reviewed: The Reception of *Huckleberry Finn* in the United States, 1885–1897," *American Literary Realism* 16 (Spring 1983), 1–57; *One Hundred Years of Huckleberry Finn: The Boy, his Book, and American Culture*, ed. Robert Sattelmeyer and J. Donald Crowley (Columbia: University of Missouri Press, 1985); Everett Carter, "The Modernist Ordeal of Huckleberry Finn," *Studies in American Fiction* 13: 2 (1985), 169–83; Harold Beaver, *Huckleberry Finn* (London: Unwin, 1987), highly respected, especially given its brevity; Louis J. Budd, "The Recomposition of *Adventures of Huckleberry Finn*," *Missouri Review* 10 (1987), 113–29, droll and penetrating; David E. E. Sloane, *Adventures of Huckleberry Finn: An American Comic Vision* (Boston: G. K. Hall & Co., 1988), aware of Twain's contemporaries; Forrest G. Robinson, "The Characterization of Jim in *Huckleberry Finn*," *Nineteenth-Century Literature* 43 (1988), 361–91; Jerome Loving, "Twain's Cigar-Store Indians," in *Lost in the Customhouse: Authorship in the American Renaissance* (Iowa City: University of Iowa Press, 1993), 125–40; Gary P. Henrickson, "How Many Children Had Huckleberry Finn?," *North Dakota Quarterly* 61: 4 (1993), 72–80, questioning the premises of many critics; Hugh J. Dawson, "The Ethnicity of Huck Finn – and the Difference It Makes," *American Literary Realism* 30: 2 (1998), 1–16, proposing that Huck's Irish American surname had definite connotations; Carl F. Wieck, *Refiguring Huckleberry Finn* (Athens: University of Georgia Press, 2000), difficult to categorize but illuminating; Robert Jackson, "The Emergence of Mark Twain's Missouri: Regional Theory and *Adventures of Huckleberry Finn*," *Southern Literary Journal* 35: 1 (Fall 2002), 47–69; and Victor A. Doyno, "Huck's and Jim's Dynamic Interactions: Dialogues, Ethics, Empathy, Respect," *Mark Twain Annual* 1 (2003), 19–29.

Two deliberately provocative books have roiled the waters in recent years. Shelley Fisher Fishkin's *Was Huck Black? Mark Twain and African-American Voices* (New York: Oxford University Press, 1993) has drawn the support of notable Twain authorities in her insistence that a short sketch Twain published in 1874, "Sociable Jimmy," illustrates how Twain appropriated a black dialect in creating Huckleberry Finn's speech patterns. Others, however, point out additional sources for Huck's folkspeech and question her linguistic techniques. Some of Fishkin's supporters seem relieved by this theory that Huck's character might be a racial composite of sorts, thus perhaps mitigating current controversies over racial slurs casually uttered in the novel.

On that score an ominous note has been sounded by Jonathan Arac in a hard-hitting book, *"Huckleberry Finn" as Idol and Target: The Functions of Criticism in our Time* (Madison: University of Wisconsin Press, 1997), and in his series of articles, such as "Why Does No One Care about the Aesthetic Value of *Huckleberry Finn?*," *New Literary History* 30 (1999), 769–84, which question at a fundamental level the ranking and appropriateness of Twain's novel in the American literary canon. Arac is not the only critic concerned about the unblinking adulation paid to this literary work. The novelist Jane Smiley ("Say It Ain't So, Huck: Second Thoughts on Mark Twain's 'Masterpiece,'" *Harper's Magazine* 292, Jan. 1996) launched a frontal assault on the revered status of *Huckleberry Finn*. In "The Struggle for Tolerance: Race and Censorship in *Huckleberry Finn*" (*Satire or Evasion*, 25–48), Peaches Henry wondered about the proper age for exposing students to a novel requiring them to possess a conception of irony. James S. Leonard has related his own change of heart about "real problems" he eventually perceived about assigning the book ("Racial Objections to *Huckleberry Finn*," *Essays in Arts and Sciences* 20 [2001], 77–82). Only time will tell whether these concerns will make major inroads into the classroom and the opinions of readers. This is the strongest challenge that Twain's novel has faced since the initial uproar over its unconventionality, and guilt over its depiction of black characters may conceivably prove compelling for high-school teachers and university academics. The most sustained and vigorous defense of Twain's classic has been Jocelyn Chadwick-Joshua's *The Jim Dilemma: Reading Race in Huckleberry Finn* (Jackson: University of Mississippi Press, 1998).

Noteworthy critical studies of Twain's works in general, according to most experts, would definitely include Robert Regan's *Unpromising Heroes: Mark Twain and his Characters* (Berkeley: University of California Press, 1966); Leslie A. Fiedler's *Love and Death in the American Novel* (New York: Stein & Day, 1960; rev. edn. 1966), 270–96; Edward Wagenknecht's *Mark Twain: The Man and his Work* (Norman: University of Oklahoma Press, rev. edn. 1967); William M. Gibson's *The Art of Mark Twain* (New York: Oxford University Press, 1976), especially good on Twain's shorter writings; David E. E. Sloane's *Mark Twain as a Literary Comedian* (Baton Rouge: Louisiana State University Press, 1979); Leslie A. Fiedler's *What Was Literature? Class Culture and Mass Society* (New York: Simon & Schuster, 1982), 232–245; Neil Schmitz's *Of Huck and Alice: Humorous Writing in American Literature* (Minneapolis: University of Minnesota Press, 1983), 65–125; Thomas Schirer's *Mark Twain and the Theatre* (Nürnberg: Verlag Hans Carl, 1984); Beverly R. David's *Mark Twain and his Illustrators, Volume 1 (1869–1875)* (Troy, NY: Whitston Publishing Co., 1986) and *Mark Twain and his Illustrators*, vol. 2 *(1875–1883)* (Albany, NY: Whitston Publishing Co., 2001), expanded upon by a dozen related articles by various commentators; David R. Sewell's *Mark Twain's Languages: Discourse, Dialogue, and Linguistic Variety* (Berkeley: University of California Press, 1987); Richard Bridgman's endlessly suggestive *Traveling in Mark Twain* (Berkeley: University of California Press, 1987); Sherwood Cummings's insightful *Mark Twain and Science: Adventures of a Mind* (Baton Rouge: Louisiana State University Press, 1988); Maria Ornella Marotti's intriguing *The Duplicating Imagination:*

Twain and the Twain Papers (University Park: Pennsylvania State Press, 1990); Peter Stoneley's unconventional *Mark Twain and the Feminine Aesthetic* (New York: Cambridge University Press, 1992); the eclectic collection *Mark Twain's Humor: Critical Essays*, ed. David E. E. Sloane (New York: Garland Publishing Co., 1993); Tom Quirk's *Coming to Grips with Huckleberry Finn: Essays on a Book, a Boy, and a Man* (Columbia: University of Missouri Press, 1993), a brief for contextual and genetic studies; Randall Knoper's *Acting Naturally: Mark Twain in the Culture of Performance* (Berkeley: University of California Press, 1995); Peter Messent's pithily astute assessment *Mark Twain*, in the Modern Novelists series (New York: St. Martin's Press, 1997); Tom Quirk's *Mark Twain: A Study of the Short Fiction* (New York: Twayne Publishers, 1997), which combined Quirk's 125-page treatment of Twain's short stories with essays by half a dozen other scholars; Peter Messent's *The Short Works of Mark Twain: A Critical Study* (Philadelphia: University of Pennsylvania Press, 2001), approaching Twain's stories within the thematic context of the collections in which they appeared; Susan K. Harris's unsparing "Mark Twain and Gender," in *A Historical Guide to Mark Twain*, ed. Shelley Fisher Fishkin (New York: Oxford University Press, 2002), 163–93; Jeffrey Alan Melton's *Mark Twain, Travel Books, and Tourism: The Tide of a Great Popular Movement* (Tuscaloosa: University of Alabama Press, 2002), which looked at his penchant for travel within the larger context of a vogue for tours and travelogues; Joseph L. Coulombe's *Mark Twain and the American West* (Columbia: University of Missouri Press, 2003), which studied "the Western aspect of Twain's public character"; and K. Patrick Ober's *Mark Twain and Medicine: "Any Mummery Will Cure"* (Columbia: University of Missouri Press, 2003), which amounted to an eye-opening survey of the multitudinous medical practices with which Twain was acquainted.

Occasionally individual journal articles have never grown into larger monographs, yet have wielded significant influence over the decades. One of these was Paul Baender's "Alias Macfarlane: A Revision of Mark Twain's Biography," *American Literature* 38 (May 1966), 187–97, pondering an alleged intellectual influence whom Clemens supposedly encountered in Cincinnati in 1856–7. Another was Howard G. Baetzhold's "Found: Mark Twain's 'Lost Sweetheart,'" *American Literature* 44 (November 1972), 414–29, which convincingly made a case for having identified a "dream" figure whom Twain often mentioned. Peter G. Beidler's "The Raft Episode in *Huckleberry Finn*," *Modern Fiction Studies* 14 (Spring 1968), 11–20, has echoed through many subsequent studies and editions of Twain's novel. Stanley Brodwin's "Mark Twain's Masks of Satan: The Final Phase," *American Literature* 45 (May 1973), 206–7, "The Theology of Mark Twain: Banished Adam and the Bible," *Mississippi Quarterly* 29 (1976), 167–89, and several other essays hinted at an extended study that never came into being. Taylor Roberts's "The Recovery of Mark Twain's Copy of *Morte Darthur*," *Resources for American Literary Study* 23 (1997), 166–80, announced the astounding news that the primary source for *A Connecticut Yankee* had miraculously surfaced. Guy A. Cardwell's "*Life on the Mississippi*: Vulgar Facts and Learned Errors," *ESQ* 19: 4 (1973), 283–93, corrected many impressions about Twain's river narrative. Larzer Ziff's

"Authorship and Craft: The Example of Mark Twain," *Southern Review* n.s. 12 (April 1976), 246–60, got at the heart of Twain's creative psyche. John E. Bassett's "Tom, Huck, and the Young Pilot: Twain's Quest for Authority," *Mississippi Quarterly* 39 (1986), 3–19, found connections among three of Twain's river narratives. Hamlin Hill's "Mark Twain: Audience and Artistry," *American Quarterly* 15 (Spring 1963), 25–40, was the first article to document and explain Twain's dependence on the subscription method of book publishing and marketing. (Keith Arbour followed this up with "Book Canvassers, Mark Twain, and Hamlet's Ghost," *Papers of the Bibliographical Society of America* 93 [1999], 5–37.) Lawrence I. Berkove's "Mark Twain: A Man for All Regions," in *A Companion to the Regional Literatures of America*, ed. Charles L. Crow (Blackwell, 2003), 496–512, offered an unusual and perspicacious overview of the reasons why "a variety of regions can lay legitimate claim to him" (p. 496). Henry Nash Smith's "'That Hideous Mistake of Poor Clemens's,'" *Harvard Library Bulletin* 9 (Spring 1955), 145–80 probed the implications of Twain's embarrassing 1877 speech in Boston, a topic taken up again in Harold K. Bush, Jr.'s "The Mythic Struggle Between East and West: Mark Twain's Speech at Whittier's 70th Birthday Celebration and W. D. Howells's *A Chance Acquaintance*," *American Literary Realism* 27: 2 (1995), 53–73. Harold H. Kolb, Jr.'s "Mere Humor and Moral Humor: The Example of Mark Twain," *American Literary Realism* 19 (1986), 52–64, set out to locate the perfect balance of Twain's comedic impulses. Harold K. Bush, Jr.'s "'Broken Idols': Mark Twain's Elegies for Susy and a Critique of Freudian Grief Theory," *Nineteenth-Century Fiction* 57 (2002), 237–68, powerfully took to task those commentators who have made light of the Clemenses' ritualistic displays of mourning over the loss of their daughter Susy. James D. Wilson's "'The Monumental Sarcasm of the Ages': Science and Pseudoscience in the Thought of Mark Twain," *South Atlantic Bulletin* 40 (1975), 72–82, ruminated on Twain's unfolding views of science and technology. Louis J. Budd's "Mark Twain Sounds Off on the Fourth of July," *American Literary Realism* 34: 3 (Spring 2002), 265–80, followed Twain's various speeches delivered on the Fourth of July over the years. Budd's "Mark Twain's Books Do Furnish a Room: But a Uniform Edition Does Still Better," *Nineteenth Century Prose* 25 (1998), 91–102, surveyed the collected editions of authors in Twain's day and suggested that Twain was still competing in his mind with Bret Harte when craving a uniform set of his works.

Collections of themed essays on Twain have raised and often answered lingering questions. *Making Mark Twain Work in the Classroom*, ed. James S. Leonard (Durham, NC: Duke University Press, 1999) is one such study that shares the experiences and advice of 20 academics. Along a different line, Thomas A. Tenney edited a special issue of the *Mark Twain Journal*, 40: 1 (Spring 2002), 1–51, devoted to "Mark Twain in South Africa"; its contents contain interviews and newspaper reports dating from his 1896 visit. A "Mark Twain in the 1870s" issue of *Studies in American Humor*, 2: 3 (1976), edited by Louis J. Budd, assembled an interesting potpourri of articles. Michael J. Kiskis and Laura E. Skandera-Trombley put together a special issue of the *Mark Twain Journal*, 34: 2 (1996), dedicated to "Mark Twain and Women," which clarified a puzzling picture.

Ever since the time of Van Wyck Brooks's barbed criticisms, Mark Twain's uneasy relationship with American and Victorian culture has been a matter of continuing interest. Two representative studies assess Twain's attitudes and reach drastically different conclusions. Bruce Michelson's *Mark Twain on the Loose: A Comic Writer and the American Self* (Amherst: University of Massachusetts Press, 1995) perceives that Twain's "war against convention widened toward the absolute" until he eventually opposed "whatever seemed rigid and regulating to mind and identity: any confining orthodoxy, whether political, religious, aesthetic, imaginative, or even biological" (p. 4). Leland Krauth's *Proper Mark Twain* (Athens: University of Georgia Press, 1999), seemingly argues to the contrary that "there is a bounded Twain – the proper Twain who honors conventions, upholds proprieties, believes in commonplaces, and even maintains the order-inducing moralities . . . Far from subverting, . . . the proper Twain upholds; instead of contesting, this Twain confirms; rather than questioning, this Twain answers" (pp. 3–4). Taking a somewhat different tack, Richard S. Lowry, in *"Littery Man": Mark Twain and Modern Authorship* (New York: Oxford University Press, 1996), seeks to deduce how Twain straddled the conflicts between commerce and culture, and between rehearsing burlesque and appealing to educated readers, in an endeavor to find and establish "his authority as an author" (p. 12).

The earliest years of Twain's life and writings were most thoroughly charted by Edgar M. Branch in a series of monographs and articles: *The Literary Apprenticeship of Mark Twain, with Selections from his Apprentice Writings* (Urbana: University of Illinois Press, 1950); *Clemens of the Call: Mark Twain in San Francisco* (Berkeley: University of California Press, 1969); "'My Voice Is Still for Setchell': A Background Study of 'Jim Smiley and His Jumping Frog'," *PMLA* 82 (December 1967), 591–601; "'The Babes in the Wood': Artemus Ward's 'Double Health' to Mark Twain," *PMLA* 93 (October 1978), 955–72; "Mark Twain: The Pilot and the Writer," *Mark Twain Journal* 23: 2 (Fall 1985), 28–43; "A Proposed Calendar of Samuel Clemens's Steamboats, 15 April 1857 to 8 May 1861, with Commentary," *Mark Twain Journal* 24 (Fall 1986), 2–27; and *Mark Twain and the Starchy Boys*, Quarry Farm Volume Series (Elmira: Center for Mark Twain Studies, Elmira College, 1992), a study of the Mississippi River pilots' associations. Others investigating the early period of Clemens's writing included Allan Bates, "Sam Clemens, Pilot Humorist of a Tramp Steamboat," *American Literature* 39 (March 1967), 102–9, and Paul Fatout, *Mark Twain in Virginia City* (Bloomington: Indiana University Press, 1964).

All of Mark Twain's full-length works have attracted monographs and articles analyzing his artistic decisions. For example, Robert Regan's "The Reprobate Elect in *The Innocents Abroad*," *American Literature* 54 (1982), 240–57, reviewed Twain's remarks about his fellow passengers on the *Quaker City*. Lawrence I. Berkove's "The Trickster God in *Roughing It*," *Thalia* 18, nos. 1–2 (1998), 21–30, makes a good starting-point for studying that narrative. Bryant Morey French's *Mark Twain and The Gilded Age* (Dallas: Southern Methodist University Press, 1965) defended the comic satire in Twain's jointly composed novel, and Hamlin Hill's "Toward a Critical Text of *The Gilded Age*," *Papers of the Bibliographical Society of America* 59 (1965), 142–9, adduced the incredible difficulties of ever establishing its proper copy-text. Walter Blair's "On the Structure of *Tom Sawyer*," *Modern Philology* 37 (August 1939), 75–88, inaugurated a series of astute articles that have included Hamlin Hill's "The Composition and Structure of *Tom Sawyer*," *American Literature* 32 (January 1961), 379–92; Judith Fetterley's "The Sanctioned Rebel," *Studies in the Novel* 3 (Fall 1971), 293–304; Virginia Wexnan's "The Role of Structure in *Tom Sawyer and Huckleberry Finn*," *American Literary Realism* 9 (1974), 1–11; Tom H. Towers's "'I Never Thought We Might Want to Come Back': Strategies of Transcendence in *Tom Sawyer*," *Modern Fiction Studies* 21 (Winter 1975–76), 509–20; John Seelye's "What's in a Name? Sounding the Depths of *Tom Sawyer*," *Sewanee Review* 90 (1982), 408–29; Fred G. See's "Tom Sawyer and Children's Literature," *Essays in Literature* (Western Illinois University) 12: 2 (1985), 251–71; Henry Wonham's "Undoing Romance: The Contest for Narrative Authority in *The Adventures of Tom Sawyer*," *Critical Essays on "The Adventures of Tom Sawyer,"* ed. Gary Scharnhorst (Boston: G. K. Hall & Co., 1993), 228–41; Harold Aspiz's "Tom Sawyer's Games of Death," *Studies in the Novel* 27 (1995), 141–53; and Peter Messent's "Discipline and Punishment in *The Adventures of Tom Sawyer*," *Journal of American Studies* 32 (1998), 219–35.

Horst H. Kruse's *Mark Twain and "Life on the Mississippi"* (Amherst: University of Massachusetts Press, 1981) has become the central point for appreciations of that narrative. James D. Williams contributed important information about Twain's romantic fantasy set in the Middle Ages in "Revision and Intention in Mark Twain's *A Connecticut Yankee*," *American Literature* 36 (1964), 288–97, and "The Use of History in Mark Twain's *A Connecticut Yankee*," *PMLA* 80 (March 1965), 102–10, but Howard G. Baetzhold's *Mark Twain and John Bull: The British Connection* (Bloomington: Indiana University Press, 1970) has long been the standard work on this novel, supplemented by Henry Nash Smith's *Mark Twain's Fable of Progress: Political and Economic Ideas in A Connecticut Yankee* (New Brunswick, NJ: Rutgers University Press, 1964); Everett Carter's "The Meaning of *A Connecticut Yankee*," *American Literature* 50 (1977), 418–40; Howard G. Baetzhold's update, "'Well, My Book Is Written – Let It Go . . .': The Making of *A Connecticut Yankee in King Arthur's Court*," in *Biographies of Books*, ed. James Barbour and Tom Quirk (Columbia: University of Missouri Press, 1996), pp. 41–77; and Betsy Bowden's "Gloom and Doom in Mark Twain's *Connecticut Yankee*, from Thomas Malory's *Morte Darthur*," *Studies in American Fiction* 28 (2000), 179–202.

The tangled racial perspectives of Twain's *The Tragedy of Pudd'nhead Wilson* (1894) have made it a modish hot spot of critical commentary, prompting a collection edited by Susan Gillman and Forrest G. Robinson, *Mark Twain's 'Pudd'nhead Wilson': Race, Conflict, and Culture* (Durham, NC: Duke University Press, 1990), and numerous articles such as Eric J. Sundquist's "Mark Twain and Homer Plessy," in his *To Wake the Nations: Race in the Making of American Literature* (Cambridge: Harvard University Press, 1993), 225–70; Henry B. Wonham's "Getting to the Bottom of *Pudd'nhead Wilson*; or, a Critical Vision Focused (Too Well?) for Irony," *Arizona Quarterly* 50: 3 (1994), 3–26; Louis J. Budd's wide-ranging "Mark Twain's Fingerprints in *Pudd'nhead Wilson*," in *New Directions in American Humor*, ed. David E. E. Sloane (Tuscaloosa:

University of Alabama Press, 1998), 171–85; Robert Moss's "Tracing Mark Twain's Intentions: The Retreat from Issues of Race in *Pudd'nhead Wilson*," *American Literary Realism* 30: 2 (1998), 43–55, remonstrating with critics who persist in a "predetermined approach"; and Stephen Railton's supremely intelligent "The Tragedy of Mark Twain, by Pudd'nhead Wilson," *Nineteenth-Century Literature* 56: 4 (2002), 518–44. All commentators should bear in mind, however, the sobering conclusion of Hershel Parker in *Flawed Texts and Verbal Icons: Literary Authority in American Fiction* (Evanston, Ill.: Northwestern University Press, 1984), pp. 115–45, that too many critics rush to judgment about this novel without taking into account its curious stages of composition. William Searle, *The Saint and the Skeptics: Joan of Arc in the Work of Mark Twain, Anatole France, and Bernard Shaw* (Detroit: Wayne State University Press, 1976), exalted Twain's often-denigrated historical novel. Twain's "dream" pieces – and the reasons behind them – received thoughtful analysis in Susanne Weil's "Reconstructing the 'Imagination-Mill': The Mystery of Mark Twain's Late Works," in *Mark Twain's Humor: Critical Essays*, ed. David E. E. Sloane, 505–39. Joseph Csicsila – building on Sholom J. Kahn's *Mark Twain's Mysterious Stranger: A Study of the Manuscript Texts* (Columbia: University of Missouri Press, 1978) – wrote two trenchant explications of that work: "Life's Rich Pageant: The Education of August Feldner in Mark Twain's *No. 44, The Mysterious Stranger*," *Studies in American Humor* 3: 4 (1997), 54–67, and "Religious Satire to Tragedy of Consciousness: The Evolution of Theme in Mark Twain's 'Mysterious Stranger' Manuscripts," *Essays in Arts and Sciences* 28 (1998), 53–70. Derek Parker Royal's "Terrible Dreams of Creative Power: The Question of No. 44," *Studies in the Novel* 31 (1999), 44–59, also bears reading.

Mark Twain's sporadic efforts to compose poetry gained recognition through Arthur L. Scott's *On the Poetry of Mark Twain with Selections from his Verse* (Urbana: University of Illinois Press, 1966). By Scott's estimate Twain wrote 120 poems, most of them comic but more than 30 in a serious vein. According to Scott, "there was scarcely a major theme of his prose which did not find voice in his poetry" (p. 38). Twain's tribute to his all-around favorite poet took the form of a rhyming burlesque about the effects of old age, published as *Mark Twain's Rubaiyat*, ed. Alan Gribben and Kevin B. MacDonnell (Austin: Jenkins Publishing Co., 1983).

Twain's relationships with, and struggles against, various authors were summarized in Sydney Krause, *Mark Twain as Critic* (Baltimore: Johns Hopkins University Press, 1967). Anthony J. Berret's *Mark Twain and Shakespeare: A Cultural Legacy* (Lanham, Md.: University Press of America, 1993) treated Twain's extensive use of the bard's plays. Numerous commentators have been intrigued by Twain's equivocal feelings about Charles Dickens, including Joseph H. Gardner, "Mark Twain and Dickens," *PMLA* 84 (January 1969), 90–101; Nicolaus Mills, "Charles Dickens and Mark Twain," *American and English Fiction in the Nineteenth Century* (Bloomington: Indiana University Press, 1973), 92–109; and Howard G. Baetzhold, "Mark Twain and Dickens: Why the Denial?," *Dickens Studies Annual* 16 (1987), 189–219. Charles Farrar Browne's impact on Twain's subsequent career has been summarized in Paul C. Rodgers, Jr., "Artemus Ward and Mark Twain's 'Jumping Frog,'" *Nineteenth-Century*

Fiction 29 (December 1973), 273–86; and Robert Rowlette, "'Mark Ward on Artemus Twain': Twain's Literary Debt to Ward," *American Literary Realism* 6 (Winter 1973), 13–25. Margaret Duckett's *Mark Twain and Bret Harte* (Norman: University of Oklahoma Press, 1964) painted an unflattering portrait of Twain's jealous nature, and Gary Scharnhorst added essential details about the doomed relationship in "The Bret Harte–Mark Twain Feud: An Inside Narrative," *Mark Twain Journal* 31: 1 (1993), 29–32; "Mark Twain, Bret Harte, and the Literary Construction of San Francisco," in *San Francisco in Fiction: Essays in a Regional Literature*, ed. David Fine and Paul Skenazy (Albuquerque: University of New Mexico Press, 1995), 21–34; *Bret Harte: Opening the American Literary West* (Norman: University of Oklahoma Press, 2000); and "A Coda to the Twain–Harte Feud," *Western American Literature* 36 (2001), 81–7. Leland Krauth, *Mark Twain & Company: Six Literary Relations* (University of Georgia Press, 2003), looked at Twain's links to Harte, Howells, Stowe, Arnold, Stevenson, and Kipling.

Alan Gribben's *Mark Twain's Library: A Reconstruction*, 2 vols. (Boston: G. K. Hall & Co., 1980) offered many leads about Twain's intellectual interests and background reading. Gribben's annotated catalog exposed Twain's habitual inclination to portray himself as only a sporadic, lazy, unsystematic reader – and thus, by implication, an entirely original talent. Several of Clemens's preferences in historians have elicited repeated studies. Joe B. Fulton, for example, paid extensive attention to W. E. H. Lecky, Thomas Carlyle, and Thomas Macaulay in *Mark Twain in the Margins: The Quarry Farm Marginalia and A Connecticut Yankee in King Arthur's Court* (Tuscaloosa: University of Alabama Press, 2000). Twain's fascination with Lecky also received treatments in Harold Aspiz, "Lecky's Influence on Mark Twain," *Science & Society* 26 (Winter 1962), 15–25, and Mary Boewe, "Twain on Lecky: Some Marginalia at Quarry Farm," *Mark Twain Society Bulletin* 8 (January 1985), 1–6.

Joseph Csicsila explored in a rewarding manner how the presentations of Mark Twain and his writings have evolved in American college classroom textbooks. His *Canons by Consensus: Critical Trends and American Literature Anthologies* (Tuscaloosa: University of Alabama Press, 2004) noted, for example, that "'Jim Smiley and His Jumping Frog' was reprinted in more college-level textbooks between 1919 and 1999 than any other short story by Mark Twain . . . When considering all of Mark Twain's writings, only the cub-pilot episode from *Life on the Mississippi* appeared in more collections." Many other surprising facts crop up in *Canons by Consensus* about the ways that college instructors have been encouraged to lecture about Mark Twain.

Great improvements have occurred in the areas of scholarly get-togethers and communication. For the better part of the twentieth century there were few venues for papers and articles on Mark Twain – but in the 1970s and 1980s the advent of individual "author" societies (and an initial refusal of the Modern Language Association to authorize a convention session devoted to Mark Twain) resulted in the creation of the Mark Twain Circle of America (1986). That organization publishes a newsletter (*The Mark Twain Circular*) and a journal of criticism and pedagogy (*The Mark Twain*

Annual), affiliates itself with *The Mark Twain Journal* (which features biographical and historical studies and the presentation of primary materials), and sponsors sessions at meetings of the American Literature Association, the Modern Language Association, and regional groups such as the South Atlantic Modern Language Association. Consequently, students of Mark Twain now have opportunities to present their findings at a wide range of meetings and can publish their work in several reputable journals besides *American Literature*, *American Literary Realism*, and other broader periodicals. the *Mark Twain Journal*, edited since 1983 by Thomas A. Tenney, has carried such groundbreaking articles as Max L. Loges's "Horace Ezra Bixby: The Life and Times of a Frontier River Pilot" (36: 1 [1999], 19–40), the definitive study of Clemens's river-pilot mentor; Edgar M. Branch's "Bixby vs. Carroll: New Light on Sam Clemens's Early River Career" (30: 2 [1992], 2–22), changing both the date and the steamboat on which Clemens commenced his cub piloting; Horst Kruse's "Mark Twain's *Nom de Plume*: Some Mysteries Resolved" (30: 1 [1992], 1–32), the best summary of the origins of Twain's pseudonym; Barbara Schmidt's "Paine in the Lost and Found" (31: 2 [1993], 32), establishing that Albert Bigelow Paine did indeed lose, in Grand Central Station, Orion Clemens's autobiography; Miriam J. Shillingsburg's "Down Under Day by Day with Mark Twain" (33: 2 [1995], 3–41), charting another leg of Twain's lecture tour; Paul Sorrentino's "Mark Twain's 1902 Trip to Missouri: A Reexamination, a Chronology, and an Annotated Bibliography" (38: 1 [2000], 12–45), emotion-packed; and periodic updates of Tenney's ongoing bibliography of Twain studies. Capping this scholarly momentum is a large quadrennial gathering of the Mark Twain clan, an international conference known as "The State of Mark Twain Studies" sponsored by the Center for Mark Twain Studies at Elmira College in Elmira, New York; started in 1989, this symposium often takes up some of the most provocative issues swirling within the world of Twain scholarship. This conference was also, for example, where the discovery of Twain's long-lost personal copy of Thomas Malory's *Morte Darthur* was announced (and the volume exhibited) in 1997.

   All in all, then, the future for Mark Twain studies seems to justify a highly optimistic forecast as a potentially golden age of textual, historical, and critical commentary. Scholarly critics who conduct research in the second century after Samuel L. Clemens's demise can build upon enormous advantages. Most of Twain's writings are available in accurate versions as never before. Biographies have charted far more than the main outlines of his accomplishments and his misadventures. To a large extent we know what books and articles Twain read and to what use he put this reading. Letters to and from him have gradually been cataloged and are becoming accessible in print and digitally. (Robert H. Hirst estimates that at least 11,000 letters written by Twain are known to exist.) There have arisen various venues where students of Mark Twain can attend conferences, read academic papers, correspond with scholars through the internet, subscribe to the lively Mark Twain Forum, and find outlets for their publications; gone are the days of inhibiting isolation for those interested in this author. Polished studies of Mark Twain are no longer restricted to the United States,

England, and France, either; articles and books from Japan, South Korea, India, and other countries regularly offer international perspectives on his works. *Mark Twain and Nineteenth Century American Literature*, ed. E. Nageswara Rao (Hyderabad, India: American Studies Research Centre, 1993), *Mark Twain: An Anthology of Recent Criticism*, ed. Prafulla C. Kar (Alexandria, Va.: Pencraft International, 1993), and Harsharan Singh Ahluwalia's "Mark Twain in India," *Mark Twain Journal* 34: 1 (1996), 1–48, are only three examples of this promising trend. Twain scholars also enjoy the benefits of studying a writer widely admired by the public at large, so that announced discoveries within the field – as Shelley Fisher Fishkin has proven – often receive wide publicity in the *New York Times* and elsewhere. Although Twain was a stern critic of his own culture, he has nevertheless been taken to the heart of his nation. Few other authors elicit this kind of name recognition and sustained connection, and it translates into cooperative assistance from librarians, collectors, publishers, university colleagues, and grant foundations.

The only sobering note for the days ahead – and this is a troubling outlook that should concern everyone – is Twain's tendency to employ frank and explicit language reflective of the shirtsleeve culture through which he passed in his travels as a pilot, prospector, and journalist. Lurking within half of his writings are pejorative terms certain to set off alarm bells for those preoccupied with political correctness and unable or unwilling to see that Twain as a realist author was obligated to report the words and phrases that his acute ear picked up as the coin of the realm in his own age. Whether he can and will be forgiven for this casualness about racial epithets and crude cultural characterizations (comparing, for example, in *Roughing It*, the "degraded" Goshoot tribe of Native American Indians to the anthropologically "inferior" bushmen of South Africa in an attempt to discredit James Fenimore Cooper's concept of the noble Red Man) remains dubious. If the current march of rigid condemnations of past historical epochs and their observers continues unabated, then many of Twain's writings are likely to be expurgated or purged, and scholarship must then treat him as an amusing but proscribed historical figure of an unenlightened era. This prospect is not a remote possibility; it encroaches upon the contents of nineteenth-century literature from every direction. Publishers, book reviewers, and readers will ultimately make the judgment that decides Twain's fate. On his side are his immense public popularity, his reputation (after he had gained the perspectives of travel) as a champion of racial equality and fair play, and the energy and penetration of his chronicles. Still, it remains to be seen whether he will become a victim of his own penchant for vivid, uncompromising expression in this age of sensitivity to the possibilities for giving offense to minorities, women, religions, and cultures.

What are the most promising avenues beckoning those wishing to pursue future studies of Twain and his works? David E. E. Sloane and Michael J. Kiskis proffered suggestions in *Prospects for the Study of American Literature: A Guide for Students and Scholars*, ed. Richard Kopley (New York: New York University Press, 1997), 155–76. Clearly a new age has arrived in Mark Twain studies, and questions that would have occupied and bedeviled scholars for months in 1960 now lie open and answerable at the touch of a computer key or the turning of a page. And while the nuances and entirety of Mark Twain's life and mind are unlikely ever to be completely inventoried (which is one sign of his genius), this in itself guarantees that Twain studies will be endless. As Laura E. Skandera-Trombley and Gary Scharnhorst implied in "'Who Killed Mark Twain? Long Live Samuel Clemens" (in *Constructing Mark Twain: New Directions in Scholarship*, ed. Laura E. Skandera-Trombley and Michael J. Kiskis [Columbia: University of Missouri Press, 2001]), what we should value from this point forward is discernment instead of cautious discretion, vision rather than mere pedantry. Already-well-tilled terrain now calls for scholars of comprehension, courage, and ingenuity who should, above all, relish rather than begrudge this author's supremely comic vision of humanity.

Index

Note: Alan Gribben's final essay in this volume consists of a bibliographical review, and the many names of authors, essays and books it contains are not indexed individually here. The chapter should be consulted in its own right as a listing of Twain criticism over the years.